METROPOLITAN COLLEGE OF NY
LIBRARY, 12TH FLOOR
431 CANAL STREET
NEW YORK, NY 10013

What Happened in and to Moral Philosophy in the Twentieth Century?

WHAT HAPPENED IN AND TO
MORAL PHILOSOPHY
IN THE TWENTIETH CENTURY?

Philosophical Essays in Honor of
ALASDAIR MACINTYRE

edited by
FRAN O'ROURKE

University of Notre Dame Press
Notre Dame, Indiana

Copyright © 2013 by University of Notre Dame
Notre Dame, Indiana 46556
www.undpress.nd.edu
All Rights Reserved

Manufactured in the United States of America

Library of Congress Cataloging-in-Publication Data

What happened in and to moral philosophy in the twentieth century? :
philosophical essays in honor of Alasdair MacIntyre / edited by Fran O'Rourke.
          pages   cm
          Includes index.
   ISBN 978-0-268-03737-6 (pbk. : alk. paper) —
     ISBN 0-268-03737-X (pbk. : alk. paper)
  1. Ethics, Modern — 20th century — Congresses.
       2. MacIntyre, Alasdair C. — Congresses.
   I. MacIntyre, Alasdair C.   II. O'Rourke, Fran.
           BJ319.W46   2013
             170.9'04 — dc23

                2013000508

∞ *The paper in this book meets the guidelines for permanence
and durability of the Committee on Production Guidelines
for Book Longevity of the Council on Library Resources.*

Contents

	Introduction *Fran O'Rourke*	1
ONE	On Having Survived the Academic Moral Philosophy of the Twentieth Century *Alasdair MacIntyre*	17

PART I. Reading Alasdair MacIntyre

TWO	Keeping Philosophy Relevant and Humanistic *John Haldane*	37
THREE	Ethics at the Limits: A Reading of *Dependent Rational Animals* *Joseph Dunne*	57
FOUR	Alasdair MacIntyre's Revisionary Aristotelianism: Pragmatism Opposed, Marxism Outmoded, Thomism Transformed *Kelvin Knight*	83

FIVE	Alasdair MacIntyre: Reflections on a Philosophical Identity, Suggestions for a Philosophical Project *Arthur Madigan, S.J.*	122
SIX	Against the Self-Images of the Age: MacIntyre and Løgstrup *Hans Fink*	145

PART II. Complementary and Competing Traditions

SEVEN	MacIntyre and the Emotivists *James Edwin Mahon*	165
EIGHT	Naturalism, Nihilism, and Perfectionism: Stevenson, Williams, and Nietzsche in Twentieth-Century Moral Philosophy *Stephen Mulhall*	200
NINE	Marxism and the *Ethos* of the Twentieth Century *Raymond Geuss*	221
TEN	Parallel Projects: Alasdair MacIntyre's Virtue Ethics, Thirteenth-Century Pastoral Theology (Leonard Boyle, O.P.), and Thomistic Moral Theology (Servais Pinckaers, O.P.) *James McEvoy*	244
ELEVEN	The Perfect Storm: On the Loss of Nature as a Normative Theonomic Principle in Moral Philosophy *Steven A. Long*	271
TWELVE	Forgiveness at the Limit: Impossible or Possible? *Richard Kearney*	304

PART III. Thematic Analyses

THIRTEEN	Evolutionary Ethics: A Metaphysical Evaluation *Fran O'Rourke*	323
FOURTEEN	The Social Epistemological Normalization of Contestable Narratives: Stories of Just Deserts *Owen Flanagan*	358
FIFTEEN	History, Fetishism, and Moral Change *Jonathan Rée*	376
SIXTEEN	Relativism, Coherence, and the Problems of Philosophy *Elijah Millgram*	392
SEVENTEEN	Ethics and the Evil of Being *William Desmond*	423
EIGHTEEN	The Inescapability of Ethics *Gerard Casey*	460
	Epilogue: What Next? *Alasdair MacIntyre*	474
	List of Contributors	487
	Index of Names	493

Introduction

In a celebrated phrase Dante praises Aristotle as "master of those who know." Aristotle would be happier, I believe, described as "master of those who *desire to know*." Aside from the fact that those who already know have no need of a master, Aristotle was convinced that as humans we can never master all there is to be known about ourselves and our place within the cosmos. As teacher and philosopher he was himself characterized by a perpetual spirit of investigation. In this, as in many other respects, Alasdair MacIntyre is a true follower of the Greek master: his philosophical work is imbued with the impetus for renewed exploration. There is no such thing as a MacIntyrean philosophy, only the MacIntyrean practice of seeking groundbreaking answers. Over decades he has struggled with real questions and, like Socrates, has relentlessly followed the questions wherever they have taken him.

MacIntyre's inquiry has led him to visit various schools of thought, framing different periods of his career: analytic, Marxist, Christian, atheist, Aristotelian, Augustinian, and Thomist. John Haldane, in a lecture honoring Alasdair MacIntyre at the Royal Irish Academy, remarked that these stages are unified by a perennial honesty and deep humanism: "His fundamental sensibility to what is central and profound in human affairs is expressed first, by fascination with the products of human thought and action, especially as these reveal the characteristics of particular cultures and traditions; second, by sympathy and admiration for human achievement, be it intellectual, moral or, in the broad sense spiritual; and third, by a desire to understand these achievements from the 'inside' as an engaged participant."

MacIntyre's interest has been first and foremost in moral philosophy, and his influence has been far-reaching. His most famous book, *After Virtue*, laid bare the inconsistencies inherent in the conflicting ethical systems that were born of the Enlightenment and that have for the most part shaped current social and political values. The common error, argued MacIntyre, was the failure to adequately ask the most basic of all questions: What is it to be a good human being? It is rare that a single work provokes such radical self-interrogation in equal measure across widely diverging theories of moral philosophy. For his own part, MacIntyre invited readers to rediscover with Aristotle the centrality of the virtues as concretely exemplifying the goals and practices of the good life.

As with Aristotle, MacIntyre's interests and influence extend to the entire range of human activity. Without sacrificing the autonomy of philosophy, he can accommodate the truth implicit in Marx's challenge that the point of philosophy is not only to variously interpret the world but also to change it. Philosophy must be true to itself—to its inquiring spirit—and never become subservient to a practical agenda; but it must also inspire human agents to be true to themselves in the search for concrete personal goods. MacIntyre has thus been concerned with questions fundamental to all human agents and the customs that form societies and communities. His influence has extended beyond academic philosophy to political theory, economics, business, and management. University College Dublin's professor of banking has prescribed *After Virtue* as mandatory reading; he recommended attendance at a public lecture to his students with the words: "MacIntyre is one of the Greats—you will not see his like again."

The contribution of Alasdair MacIntyre to contemporary philosophy is enormous. His academic scholarship has spanned more specializations and numbered more books and articles—over 250 in all—than many scholars could hope to match in eight lifetimes, let alone in eighty years. One thinks of the eleventh-century poem "Colmcille the Scribe," in Seamus Heaney's version: "Wisdom keeps welling in streams . . . / Through books through thick and thin / To enrich the scholar's holdings."

In his writings Alasdair MacIntyre has emphasized the importance of tradition. He himself grew up at the confluence of two traditions, inhabiting on the one hand the world of his Gaelic heritage and on the other the world of modern liberal rationalism. His imagination fed upon the Gaelic oral culture of farmers and fishermen, poets and storytellers, whose values were embedded in the narratives of kinship and place. These were challenged by the claims of universal rational humanity, which relied upon the liberal ideas of Kant and Mill. This tension between opposing systems and versions of morality would characterize MacIntyre's intellectual quest for a lifetime.

Visiting his relatives in Donegal, he saw no distinction between Irish and Scottish Gaelic. Ireland has always had a special place in Alasdair's heart. He has an intimate and extensive knowledge of Irish literature, both in English and in Irish. He has lectured and published on Yeats and Burke. Among his favorite writers are Máirtín Ó Cadhain and Máirtín Ó Direáin; he sends Christmas cards to his Irish friends *as Gaeilge*. It was thus a pleasure for his Irish friends, in March 2009, to celebrate with colleagues from all over the world the eighty years of Alasdair MacIntyre's life and philosophical achievement. Everyone experienced during those days his generosity, acuity of mind, humility, and great sense of humor. We remain deeply grateful for the way in which he enriched our philosophical endeavor.

The present volume contains most of the papers delivered at the conference held in honor of Alasdair MacIntyre at University College Dublin, March 6–8, 2009. For practical reasons it is not possible to include all papers delivered on that occasion. The volume also includes a number of contributions from friends and colleagues of Professor MacIntyre, which again for practical reasons could not be included in the original schedule. What marks the ensemble is the variety of approaches and perspectives—involving not only diverging but contradicting positions. This is symptomatic of the fact, already noted, that what characterizes MacIntyre's thought is an ever fresh approach to timeless and significant questions—an attitude that serious philosophers of every shade and nuance cannot but find motivating.

The theme of the Dublin conference, suggested by Alasdair MacIntyre in response to the organizers' invitation, was the question: "What happened in and to moral philosophy in the twentieth century?" Although he requested that his own work should not be the focus of proceedings, I am very pleased that many papers engaged with Professor MacIntyre's approach to moral philosophy, either directly or in its historical setting.

In the opening paper, "Keeping Philosophy Relevant and Humanistic," John Haldane develops themes from his lecture to the Royal Irish Academy on Alasdair MacIntyre's philosophical contribution. Haldane examines MacIntyre's conception of the character and purposes of philosophy in its application to understanding and guiding human action. In particular he assesses the implications of two aspects of moral philosophy's embeddedness within human practices and institutions: one relating to the phenomenology of the personal, the other to the practical concerns (or lack of such) of professionalized academic philosophy. In the former connection he discusses MacIntyre's exploration of the phenomenology of Edith Stein, and in the latter his treatment of "rival Aristotles" among Renaissance and modern Aristotelians and his reconsideration of some Enlightenment projects.

In "Ethics at the Limits: A Reading of *Dependent Rational Animals*," Joseph Dunne focuses on the philosophical anthropology that emerges from MacIntyre's analysis in that book of the primordial "facts" of human animality, vulnerability, and dependence, leading him to a striking reformulation of his key ethical and political claims. Having traced the main lines of that analysis, Dunne raises some critical questions about the emphasis on "local community" in MacIntyre's elaboration of the "networks of giving and receiving" that are central to his reconceived politics. He goes on to argue that the ethical demands articulated in this book, different from and strikingly more exacting than those that had earlier been met in *After Virtue*, may overdraw the resources available to MacIntyre in what he presents as his still basically Aristotelian position. In particular, Dunne questions whether the extremity of these demands allows the ethics in which they arise to be presented as in any sense *naturalistic*. And he buttresses this critical interrogation by reference to other, earlier and later, works of MacIntyre himself and of two other contemporary philosophers, Raimond Gaita and Charles Taylor, whose substantive ethical positions are, as he argues, very close to those of *Dependent Rational Animals*—though holding these positions drives them toward a philosophical anthropology strikingly different from what is found in this book.

In "Alasdair MacIntyre's Revisionary Aristotelianism: Pragmatism Opposed, Marxism Outmoded, Thomism Transformed," Kelvin Knight argues that MacIntyre has revised and reenergized the Aristotelian tradition, partly by informing it with a social theory. *After Virtue* proposes that social "practices," teleologically ordered to the pursuit of internal goods, are schools of the virtues. These practices MacIntyre juxtaposes to state and corporate "institutions." Whereas Thomistic Aristotelians traditionally looked to states to promote the common good, MacIntyre instead points to social practices. Institutions, though necessary, pose a constant threat of demoralization through their pursuit of external goods. This juxtaposition may be understood as an ethical revision of Marxism's opposition of labor to capital, but MacIntyre does not share Marxists' faith that history is on the side of the oppressed. What history tells us is that Aristotelianism confronts rival and powerful traditions of ethical and institutionalized reasoning. What MacIntyre tells Thomistic Aristotelians is that, if they wish to resist those rivals, they must learn to combine metaphysical biology with history and sociology.

In "Alasdair MacIntyre: Reflections on a Philosophical Identity, Suggestions for a Philosophical Project," Arthur Madigan, S.J., contrasts MacIntyre with those contemporary Aristotelians who seek a rapprochement with the dominant contemporary liberalism; those who sympathize with MacIntyre's antiliberal Aristotelianism need to revisit the claims of liberalism and to understand why so many contemporary Aristotelians find liberalism attractive. Madigan points out that MacIntyre's brand of Thomism is distinctive, which partly explains why he has not exercised greater influence within the Thomistic tradition. MacIntyre's Thomism might be more influential if MacIntyreans would take a more definite stance toward the debates of moral philosophers and theologians that currently divide the Thomistic tradition. Madigan argues that while MacIntyre no longer sees himself as a Marxist, he remains committed to a number of Marx's views; the coherence between MacIntyre's Aristotelian Thomism and his debts to Marx could be worked out more clearly and explicitly than has been done so far. Madigan also tries to extend and deepen MacIntyre's analysis of tradition and of the encounter between traditions.

Much more happened in and to moral philosophy in the twentieth century than has been recounted in standard histories of mainstream Anglo-American thought. Alasdair MacIntyre has always had a keen eye for figures and episodes that might be quite important in spite of, or maybe even because of, their initial marginality. Edith Stein is one such philosopher MacIntyre has helped rescue from oblivion. Another is the Danish phenomenologist and Lutheran theologian K. E. Løgstrup, who has remained central to Scandinavian moral discussion over the last fifty years. Hans Fink treats this important encounter in his paper "Against the Self-Images of the Age: MacIntyre and Løgstrup." Fink has worked together with MacIntyre on a new American edition of Løgstrup's main work *The Ethical Demand*, and in his paper he presents some of Løgstrup's main ideas in comparison with aspects of MacIntyre's better-known position. A central theme is the precise status of the singular ethical demand that according to Løgstrup can arise immediately in personal relationships prior to and independently of any demands arising from social or moral rules. Løgstrup's emphasis on the incommensurability between the ethical demand and all questions of rule following presents a challenge to most traditions of moral philosophy, a challenge MacIntyre has tried to meet in his Mark Sacks lecture for 2009: "Danish Ethical Demands and French Common Goods." According to Hans Fink, the challenge still stands.

An admirable quality of Alasdair MacIntyre the scholar is his intellectual openness: throughout his philosophical career he has sought to learn from those of differing standpoints, and he has repeatedly engaged with a variety of philosophical approaches to the fundamental questions of morality. One of his earliest engagements was with the moral theory of emotivism. An enduring influence has been the ethical and social critique of Karl Marx (reflecting MacIntyre's belief that ethics needs the insights of sociology). An early challenge was presented by various English Thomists MacIntyre encountered in the 1950s. Nor was he insular in his interests: he was critically receptive to the insights of continental ethical theorists—phenomenology, existentialism, and hermeneutics. This variety of divergent and competing influences is appropriately reflected in the second section of the present collection.

Two contributors assess the place of emotivism in twentieth-century ethics. In "MacIntyre and the Emotivists," James Edwin Mahon considers the critique of emotivism presented in *After Virtue*. This critique, which has its roots in MacIntyre's master's thesis on metaethics in 1951, "The Significance of Moral Judgments," is that emotivism fails both as an account of the meaning of moral judgment and as an account of the function of moral judgment. The importance of this critique, however, lies in what it reveals about the degeneration of moral judgment. The fact/value distinction on which emotivism is premised is not a timeless truth that was discovered by the emotivists but the inevitable result of the "Enlightenment project." It was this historical turn that led to moral judgment degenerating to the state in which it is found in the metaethical theory of emotivism.

Stephen Mulhall is partly concerned also with MacIntyre's assessment of emotivism. In his paper "Naturalism, Nihilism, and Perfectionism: Stevenson, Williams, and Nietzsche in Twentieth-Century Moral Philosophy," he examines the merits of three different varieties of naturalism in ethics—Stevenson's emotivism, Williams's realistic moral psychology, and Nietzsche's perfectionism. Williams reevaluates the force of MacIntyre's criticisms of both Stevenson and Nietzsche, and in particular MacIntyre's relatively recent attempt (in his Gifford Lectures) to subvert what he calls the genealogical tradition of moral inquiry by querying its ability to construct and maintain a sufficiently substantial notion of the author. The Nietzsche who might survive that critique turns out to be indebted to the American transcendentalist philosopher Emerson.

In "Marxism and the *Ethos* of the Twentieth Century," Raymond Geuss claims that social development in the twentieth century can best be seen relative to the conceptual pair "production/consumption." Western capitalism outproduced Soviet-style societies and thus constituted a refutation of the Soviet system on its own terms. He further suggests that if we are to overcome the economic, political, and moral difficulties in which we find ourselves at the start of the twenty-first century it will be through changing society so that it no longer seems at all plausible to us to divide our lives into a sphere of the merely instrumentally useful and a sphere of the inherently valuable. Only if we can really abolish the absolute distinction between means and ends will a human life worth living be possible.

In the opening essay of this volume Alasdair MacIntyre chronicles his own discovery of Thomist ethics. It is thus appropriate that two essays consider the contribution of Thomism to twentieth-century ethics. In his paper entitled "Parallel Projects," James McEvoy finds parallels for MacIntyre's project in the research of two contemporary Dominican scholars, Leonard Boyle (d. 1999) and Servais Pinckaers (d. 2008). Their work, he suggests, throws light on the wider intellectual relationships of MacIntyre's oeuvre. Boyle was the historian of medieval pastoralia, including treatises on the virtues and vices. His explorations of the relevant Dominican moral literature led Boyle to suggest that the aim of Thomas Aquinas was to bring order into the existing chaos in professional studies within the order by placing the theology of the virtues in the setting of the widest theological and philosophical perspectives available. Servais Pinckaers located the virtues (both theological and moral) at the very center of moral theology. He argued that the idea of virtue presupposes a conception of the human being as sociable (i.e., naturally inclined to live in society), including the intellectual and moral levels of social existence. Man is not morally undifferentiated but is moved by an aspiration toward the good. His aim was to identify solid foundations on which to build an ethics that would be Christian, theological, and modern all at once.

In a wide-ranging paper, "The Perfect Storm: On the Loss of Nature as a Normative Theonomic Principle in Moral Philosophy," Steven Long argues that during the latter part of the twentieth century three distinct tendencies toward the derogation of proportionate natural teleology in moral thought came to their cultural fruition, exerting maximal influence. Two of these tendencies he considers preponderantly secular while also found in Catholic circles, whereas the third he deems to exist principally within Catholic theology. These tendencies are (1) the transcendental turn to the subject in continental thought, (2) analytic logicism, and (3) the negation of the proportionate natural end by Henri de Lubac, who denied Thomas's teaching that man qua man receives his species from the proximate natural end (*ST* I, 75, 7), holding instead that the natural end for man is supernatural beatific vision. These three tendencies converged in the 1960s in particular and defined a significant period during which the essential requisites for Thomistic moral thought were widely denied: a denial with very clear implications in the theological, cultural, moral, and legal spheres. Yet the scope of this denial prompted profound response to these varied doctrinal influences. As a result, although the institutional presence of Thomist moral thought today is starkly limited by comparison to the period of the 1950s, this thought has been intensively revitalized in responding to these challenges. This revitalization began even in the time prior to the temporary eclipse of Thomistic moral thought in the 1960s and 1970s and only grew in intensity in the response catalyzed by this eclipse. Thus it joins names as disparate as those of Maritain, Garrigou-Lagrange, Gilson, and Pinckaers with those of MacIntyre, McInerny, Cessario, Hittinger, and others. In consequence, contemporary Thomistic moral thought can boast a coherent, and systematically and historically adequate, account of the travails of moral thought in the twentieth century.

Richard Kearney's paper "Forgiveness at the Limit: Impossible or Possible?" provides a continental perspective on the phenomenon of interpersonal morality as he discusses the widely diverging responses of Derrida and Ricoeur to the question of forgiveness at the limit. The challenge of radical forgiveness has been raised by many recent thinkers: Jankelevitch and Levi claim it is impossible to forgive those who do not ask for forgiveness, while Arendt maintains that radical evil cannot be forgiven. Derrida declares pure forgiveness to be simply impossible: we can only forgive the unforgivable, and that is precisely what cannot humanly be forgiven. If someone asks for forgiveness, that person has already atoned and so does not require forgiveness. Only radical evil and hatred are matters for forgiveness, a forgiveness that, he argues, is unconditional, undeserved, and hence impossible. In his alternative response Paul Ricoeur takes previous objections into account but proposes a move from "impossible" to "difficult." Acknowledging the extreme difficulty, he views pardon as a secret gift, which points to a superhuman origin of gift, and a capacity belonging to an order of spirit and love, surplus and superabundance. What is impossible to humans—conceded by Derrida—is not impossible for God: the divine capacity for renovation and forgiveness restores the miracle of origin in each human being.

A number of contributors to the present volume respond to the question: "What happened in and to moral philosophy in the twentieth century?" by focusing on a particular historical or thematic aspect; the variety of topics, matched by the divergence of perspectives, is presented in the third section of the collection. My own contribution, "Evolutionary Ethics: A Metaphysical Evaluation," assesses the project of E. O. Wilson, founder of sociobiology, to establish ethics exclusively upon the theory of evolution. The essay deals primarily with the metaphysical presuppositions of the theory. According to Wilson, human behavior is to be explained in terms of basic universal features of human nature laid down by evolution. Morality is based upon genetics; ethics should be removed from philosophers and biologicized. I argue that because of an excessive reductionism, Wilson fails to recognize the crucial differences between humans and other animals. Restricting the value of morality to the conditions from which it arose, sociobiology is guilty of the genetic fallacy. An early victim of sociobiological ethics is personal purpose, since all duty is toward the so-called epigenetic rules governing evolution. Wilson dismisses the question of self-existence: the moral question of suicide is a false one, to be overcome by the control centers of the hypothalamic-limbic complex. Such a view, I suggest, not only runs counter to experience but is the vitiation of morality and ultimately the abandonment of philosophy.

In his contribution, "The Social Epistemological Normalization of Contestable Narratives: Stories of Just Deserts," Owen Flanagan reflects upon a theme emphasized by Alasdair MacIntyre as fundamental for human self-understanding. According to MacIntyre, the human sciences explain how self- and other comprehension works through narratives, and how narratives that render action intelligible are structured, formally and contentfully, in different social ecologies. But the human sciences, especially in their purely descriptive pose, can contribute to concealment or, what is different, to legitimation of questionable self-understanding, and thus to the practices that such self- and other-understanding engenders, encourages, and endorses. One way this happens is when allegedly neutral but in fact deeply contestable philosophical or social scientific assumptions are rendered part of common sense and are incorporated into narratives that are normatively expected to apply to lives that are intelligible as good, or decent, or worthy of respect—self-respect and other-respect.

Flanagan provides a MacIntyrean reading of a common contemporary Western narrative about accomplishment and desert that might seem to be descriptively and normatively spare but in fact is freighted and contestable. The master-narrative trope is that hard work and effort pay, that they should pay, and that the direct and indirect payoffs for choosing to be educated and then to work conscientiously in a good profession are just desert for rationality, moral seriousness, and conscientious deliberation and choice. The target narrative expresses an understanding, perhaps even a theory, of luck, work, effort, and desert. The core, or master-narrative trope, is normatively endorsed by (and for) both the victims and the beneficiaries of the narrative and is thought to be based on facts or, if not facts, then on minimalist, commonsense assumptions about agency, accomplishment, and desert that in fact are neither factual nor philosophically innocuous. How exactly contestable narrative frameworks come to be favored and then become uncontested, taken for granted, seen as truistic, is a complicated question about how social epistemology works to confer its imprimatur on certain ways of conceiving of persons, their projects, and their worth. This can and does happen and can produce moral and political harm. According to Flanagan, the target narrative of accomplishment and desert is such a morally harmful master narrative and rests on philosophically and scientifically implausible claims about human psychology and agency.

In "History, Fetishism and Moral Change," Jonathan Rée illuminates the historical setting for one of the distinguishing novelties of MacIntyre's approach: his sustained interest in the history not only of moral philosophy but also of moral practice. Analyzing the widespread indifference to the phenomenon of moral change, Rée traces it in part to a reaction against certain progressive figures in Victorian philosophy—particularly J. S. Mill and Henry Sidgwick. He also connects it with what he calls "the fetishism of morality," meaning an attempt to sideline various other practical disciplines—notably politics—in order to elevate morality into a suprahistorical source of perfect standards for judging human conduct.

In his thematic paper "Relativism, Coherence, and the Problems of Philosophy," Elijah Millgram observes that disciplinary attitudes toward relativism are often to be explained by features of a discipline's subject matter. Philosophers have mixed attitudes toward relativism, and he suggests that this is best accounted for by two related structural features of what he calls the philosophical problem space. On the one hand, the list of the problems philosophy must address has remained remarkably stable over time, and this explains a good deal of philosophers' resistance to relativism. On the other hand, the dependency relations between philosophical problems form cycles, which explains much of philosophers' leanings toward relativism: cycles seem to leave the choice of a joint solution to the problems on the list up to the philosopher. The author argues, however, that drawing relativist conclusions from the presence of cycles in the dependency relations would be a mistake.

In "Ethics and the Evil of Being," William Desmond addresses an alternative not quite explicitly stated but certainly suggested by MacIntyre's work: Nietzsche or St. Benedict. The question that concerns him is not so much this or that ethical system but the grounds of ethical value as such. To the fore are the issues of nihilism and the sense of being as valueless in itself, a sense that is pervasive in modernity. Desmond explores different dimensions of this sense of valuelessness, and how it frequently mutates into something darker, namely, a sense of the evil of being. For many intellectuals the good is bland but evil arouses perplexities whose form,

Desmond suggests, is itself perplexing, if it is true that the good is bland. This sense of valuelessness is frequently coupled with a view which holds that human beings are the originators of value, as well as one that strongly stresses freedom as autonomy. Among other themes treated in this connection are the way given creation is reduced to purposeless process, while our values are said to determine and be determined by our "projects"; the manner in which Kantian autonomy is haunted by heteronomies it cannot assimilate; how with thinkers like Schopenhauer and Nietzsche the ontological attunement associated with the evil of being comes more explicitly to the fore; how this ontological attunement poses a radical question more or less acknowledged by thinkers like these in the nineteenth century but neither addressed adequately nor answered by twentieth-century ethics. Desmond himself offers an account of freedom as endowed, in which there is a receiving as well as an endeavoring. Without fidelity to the receiving, the ethical will can easily mutate into a tyrannical will to power. Freedom as autonomy does not exhaust the promise of ethical freedom. There is a being free beyond both autonomy and sovereignty, bound up with the agapeic release of willing. Likewise, the will to say "yes" that we find in Nietzsche makes no sense if our basic ontological orientation is still enmeshed in the darker vision of the evil of being. Desmond suggests we need to rethink the ground of the good in terms shaped by St. Benedict rather than Nietzsche and break the taboo, widely effective since Kant, that silences the ontological and ethical significance of the divine ground.

In his essay entitled "The Inescapability of Ethics," Gerard Casey argues that ethics cannot coherently be abandoned and thus, given that freedom and rationality are necessary conditions of ethics, that determinism and irrationalism are fundamentally incoherent. Taking his point of departure from Iris Murdoch's claim that "the phenomena of rationality and morality are involved in the very attempt to banish them," he goes on to make the case for what he calls "explanatory pluralism." Claiming that every inquiry has as an ineliminable element, the act of inquiry itself, he proceeds to outline a self-stultifying argument that rests on a maxim, M, that reads: "No theory can be seriously maintained such that, if it were to be true, its maintenance would become impossible, meaningless, contradictory, or self-refuting." Determinism falls foul of the maxim since, of necessity, the very attempt to argue for determinism is itself a free act by the arguer that commends itself to the rational judgment of its intended audience; irrationalism, on the other hand, while not quite as neatly self-destructive as determinism, is nonetheless obviously rationally unsustainable. Urging that philosophical argument must be serious, Casey claims that those who preach determinism, if they are to be taken seriously, must be prepared to live by that doctrine but that since determinism is practically impossible it cannot be a serious philosophical position. Likewise, irrationalism, though not impossible in quite the same way as determinism, cannot be rationally defended and so too cannot be seriously maintained.

I wish to express my sincere gratitude to everyone who contributed to the success of the Dublin conference and to all those who collaborated in the present publication. I express my gratitude to Dr. Hugh Brady, president of University College Dublin, for his support, and for officially welcoming the participants. His predecessor, emeritus professor of philosophy Dr. Patrick Masterson, graciously delivered a scintillating response to Alasdair MacIntyre's public lecture. The event would not have been possible without major support from the Seed Funding scheme of University College Dublin. The College of Human Sciences also supported the conference with a significant subvention; I express sincere gratitude to the principal, Professor Brigid Laffan. I am grateful to the UCD John Hume Institute for Global Irish Studies, and its director, Dr. Brian Jackson, for providing a venue for the conference, but most of all for providing scholarships for a large number of international postgraduate scholars. I am grateful to the Notre Dame Center for Ethics and Culture, and its director David Solomon, for a generous donation to the Conference Scholarship Fund. I am also grateful to the following who generously supported scholarships: Duckworth Press, Nuffield College, Oxford, University of Essex, David B. Wong (Duke University), Tad Schmaltz (Duke University), Jeffrey Tlumak (Vanderbilt), and Larry Russell (Elon).

Professor Brian O'Connor, head of the School of Philosophy, supported the conference with characteristic enthusiasm from the outset, as did all of my colleagues. Margaret Brady, administrator in the School of Philosophy, took charge of many organizational and logistical matters with ease and expertise, and Helen Kenny, manager of the School, supervised finances and provided invaluable advice at crucial moments of preparation; to both I record my personal indebtedness for their indispensable support. Patrick McKay designed an excellent website for the conference, giving patiently and cheerfully of his time and expertise. No words can convey my gratitude to a number of postgraduates of the School of Philosophy who gave physical and moral support, ensuring that the program ran efficiently: Heleana Theixos, Fionn Dempsey, Angelo Bottone, Stephen Caldwell, and Tziovanis Georgakis. For the webcam recording of Alasdair MacIntyre's public lecture, I want to thank Dominic Martella and Dominic Fogarty of UCD's University Relations. I am most grateful also to Sean O'Connor, whose skillful photography has preserved a permanent record of the weekend (www.ucd.ie/philosophy/archive). In a special way I am grateful to members of the International Society for MacIntyrean Enquiry, who greatly enlivened the conference by attendance in great numbers and by their enthusiastic participation; I am especially grateful to Sean MacGiollarnaith, Kelvin Knight, and Christopher Lutz for their wise counsel. I express special gratitude to John Haldane, who delivered a lecture to the Royal Irish Academy at a separate event honoring Professor MacIntyre.

I express my thanks to all who attended and participated either as speakers or members of the audience.[1] In the final place, because ultimately in the first, I am honored on behalf of all to express our collective gratitude to Alasdair MacIntyre, not only for allowing us to join him in a celebratory conference, but for his philosophical oeuvre, which has been personally enriching for so many. We wish him many more years of creative and fruitful reflection: *Go mara tú an céad!*

Notes

1. With sadness but with affection I wish to honor the memory of five members of the Irish philosophical community who died since participating in the conference. John Cleary was a friend of mine since 1962 and a treasured friend of Alasdair MacIntyre for over thirty years. John participated fully in the conference and was in splendid form, proudly preserving intact his record of always asking the first question of the speaker. Few were aware that he was at every moment on the alert for a call from a nearby liver transplant unit. When the message came on Holy Thursday John texted his friends: "Halleluiah, rejoice with me." Tragically he died in the operating room in the early hours of Easter Sunday. Everyone will recall the hilarity of his speech at the conference banquet in which

he regaled us with anecdotes from his days as Alasdair's assistant. His loss to the philosophical community, and to his many friends, is immeasurable. Mgr. Michael Nolan, emeritus professor of psychology at UCD, was unique in every way: having once met him, one could never forget him. He lectured in philosophical psychology, wrote a number of perceptive philosophical articles, and frequently attended events of the Irish philosophical community. He died on December 14, 2009. Cardinal Cahal Daly lectured for many years at Queen's University Belfast; he was a renowned philosopher and author of many important works. At ninety-two he traveled to the conference with the intention of attending a few sessions: he did not miss a single one. He died on New Year's Eve 2009, having lived a full and rewarding life. James McEvoy, who contributed a major paper at the conference, was one of the leading international medievalists of his generation; he held full chairs in Louvain, Maynooth, and Queen's University Belfast. He died on October 2, 2010. Ernan McMullin was one of the leading international experts in philosophy of science; he was a long-term friend and colleague of Alasdair MacIntyre at Notre Dame. He died February 8, 2011, in his native County Donegal. We retain cherished memories of these five unique individuals.

CHAPTER ONE

On Having Survived the Academic Moral Philosophy of the Twentieth Century

ALASDAIR MacINTYRE

How I Discovered That, by the Standards of Contemporary Academic Philosophy, Thomist Claims *Must Be* Problematic

I was already fifty-five years old when I discovered that I had become a Thomistic Aristotelian. But I had first encountered Thomism thirty-eight years earlier, as an undergraduate, not in the form of moral philosophy, but in that of a critique of English culture developed by members of the Dominican order. Yet, although impressed by that critique, I hesitated, for those Dominicans made me aware of the philosophical presuppositions of their critique, of a set of Thomistic judgments about the relationships between body, mind, and soul, about passions, will, and intellect, about virtues and reason-informed human actions. And those theses I found problematic. Why so?

From 1945 to 1949 I was an undergraduate student in classics at what was then Queen Mary College in the University of London, reading Greek texts of Plato and Aristotle with my teachers, while also, from 1947 onwards, occasionally attending lectures given by A. J. Ayer or Karl Popper, or by visiting speakers to Ayer's seminar at University College, such as John Wisdom. Early on I had read *Language, Truth and Logic,* and Ayer's student James Thomson introduced me to the *Tractatus* and to Tarski's work on truth. Ayer and his students were exemplary in their clarity and rigor and in the philosophical excitement that their debates generated. And I became convinced that the test of any set of philosophical theses, including those defended by Thomists, was whether it could be vindicated in and through such debates. Yet I also had to learn—and this took a little longer—that in the debates of academic philosophy in the twentieth century no set of theses is ever decisively vindicated.

To excel as a contemporary academic philosopher is a matter of the quality of one's analytic and argumentative skills, especially in their negative use to expose failures in the distinction making of others or gaps in their arguments, together with an ability to summon up telling counterexamples. Conceptual inventiveness is also valued. Excellence in the exercise of these qualities is compatible with holding different and incompatible sets of beliefs about which of the various philosophical positions in contention in one's own specialized area is to be regarded as true and rationally justified, including those positions in contention over how truth and rational justification are to be understood. Disagreement on fundamental issues is in practice taken to be the permanent condition of philosophy. The range of continuing disagreements is impressive: realists versus antirealists in respect of mathematical, moral, perceptual, and historical judgments; dualists versus materialists in the philosophy of mind; utilitarians versus Kantians versus virtue theorists in ethics; Fregeans versus direct reference theorists in the philosophy of language; and a great many more. Add to these a range of disagreements in religion and politics that, themselves nonphilosophical, are closely related to philosophical disagreements: theists versus atheists, conservatives versus liberals versus libertarians versus Marxists.

It is not that there is no progress in philosophical inquiry so conceived. Arguments are further elaborated, concepts refined, and creative new ideas advanced by the genius of a Quine or a Kripke or a Lewis. But this makes it the more striking that there is *never* a decisive resolution of any central disputed issue. So how should we think about this and respond to it? David Lewis wrote that "whether or not it would be nice to knock disagreeing philosophers down by sheer force of argument, it cannot be done" and that "once the menu of well-worked-out theories is before us, philosophy is a matter of opinion."[1] Each philosopher, that is, considers the costs of accepting this body of philosophical theses and arguments or rejecting that, tries to bring her or his judgments, philosophical and nonphilosophical, into equilibrium, and in so doing take sides in one of these irresolvable disputes. My own immediate response to my recognition of the conditions of academy philosophy was more modest. It was that, however strong the case for Thomism, there was bound to be a strong case against it.

How I Discovered from Sartre and Ayer That Thomist Claims Are Problematic

Very soon I was impressed by the force of one such case. In 1947, while visiting Paris, I had been introduced to Sartre's 1945 lecture "L'existentialisme est un humanisme," in which Sartre argues that although we may have reasons for making our choices as we do, those reasons have only such weight as each of us chooses to give to them. What makes a particular reason a good or a sufficient reason for me to act depends on my decision to treat that reason as good or sufficient. The practical reasoning of any individual derives its conclusions from premises that that individual has chosen to make the premises of her or his practical reasoning. And on this Ayer concurred, even though he and Sartre disagreed about much else. "It is one of Sartre's merits," Ayer wrote, "that he sees that no system of values can be binding on someone unless he chooses to make it so."[2]

What Ayer and Sartre had combined to put in question was a set of theses central to Thomism according to which what makes a reason a good reason for action is independent of the agent's choices. It is, on the Thomist view, a good reason for acting in this way rather than in that, that by so acting one will achieve some good or avoid some bad and whether that at which one aims is good or bad is a matter of fact, a matter of whether the object aimed at contributes to or is constitutive of some aspect of one's flourishing as a human being. For Ayer and Sartre, by contrast, there are acts of choice, implicit or explicit, that are prior to and determinative of one's judgments of good and evil. For Thomists acts of choice are themselves to be evaluated by logically prior judgments concerning the good to be achieved or the evil to be avoided by those acts. How, I asked, was I to decide between these rival claims?

It was not that I could not find a number of reasons for favoring something closer to a Thomist view than to Ayer's or Sartre's. But I was well aware that none of these reasons were conclusive, were such that they could not be rationally resisted. So it seemed that the only reasonable conclusion about this particular disagreement was to agree with what David Lewis was to say: that this, like other disputed issues, "is a matter of opinion." But so to conclude was to conclude against Thomism. For it is crucial to the Thomistic view that such disagreements are not, in the sense that Lewis gives to that expression, matters of opinion, but rather matters on which reason renders a decisive verdict, even if highly intelligent people continue to disagree.

How Marxism Made It Possible for Me to Recognize the Nature of the Dominant Contemporary Morality

Thomism had also become problematic for me for another reason. The Communist Party at Queen Mary College had introduced me to the texts of the Marxist canon, and I had become and to this day remain convinced of the truth and political relevance of Marx's critique of capitalism and of his historical insights as presented in the narrative of the *Eighteenth Brumaire of Louis Bonaparte*. To how much else of Marxism I was thereby committed I was unclear, although I greatly admired both the work of George Thomson, author of *Aeschylus and Athens* and translator of Plato into Irish, and the writings of Lucien Goldmann. Since one thing on which Marxists and Thomists seemed to agree was that Marxism and Thomism were incompatible, I found myself confronting yet another set of question marks. Nonetheless it was on the basis of Marxist insights into the nature both of morality and of moral philosophy that I began to formulate another, more constructive kind of question.

Marx and Engels had argued that every morality is the morality of some particular social and economic order and that every moral philosophy articulates and makes explicit the judgments, arguments, and presuppositions of some particular morality, either in such a way as to defend both that morality and the social and economic order of which it is the expression, or in such a way as to undermine them. And my acknowledgment of the truth of this thesis was reinforced by my encounters with social anthropology, especially first with the work of Franz Steiner and later with that of Rodney Needham. I therefore asked: What is the distinctive morality of this social and economic order that I inhabit, and how does contemporary moral philosophy stand to that morality? And in pursuing an answer to this question I was guided not only by Marx and Engels but also by John Anderson, who had urged that, if we were to understand social institutions and relationships, we should ask not what function or purpose they serve but to what conflicts they give expression. This suggested that both the morality and the moral philosophy of the present age are best understood as milieus of conflict, sites of disagreement. But those disagreements find significantly different expression in the arenas of philosophical debate on the one hand and in those of everyday moral and political practice on the other.

In philosophical debate utilitarianism and Kantianism are presented, with some rare and sophisticated exceptions, as incompatible and rival standpoints. To adhere to some version of one is to be at odds with every version of the other. But in many areas of the everyday life of modernity what we find instead is an oscillation between those two standpoints and a moral rhetoric designed to disguise that oscillation. So there are moments in which principles are laid down without qualification and moments in which exceptions to those principles are justified in the name of either the maximization of prosperity or the maintenance of public security. And it is in negotiating their way between such moments, both in private and in public life, that the characteristic skills of those who are socially and politically successful are exhibited. What we have then is a morality whose oscillations and contradictions show it to be in a state of disorder, but a kind of disorder that enables it to function well as the ideology of our present social, political, and economic order.

Yet although I had come to recognize this as a result of reflecting on the Marxist critique of morality, I had also had to acknowledge that within the communist movement there was to be found much the same oscillation between quasi-Kantian attitudes and a consequentialism that parodied utilitarianism, and this not only in the brutal and corrupting ethics of Stalinism but also in the ethics of Stalinism's Marxist critics. Marxism as a form of practice too often suffered from the same lack of moral resources as the social order that it aspired to replace, and this unsurprisingly, since it had been generated from within that social order. It was with the rise of the New Left in Britain, after the suppression of the Hungarian Rising of 1956, that the question of whether and how this defect in Marxist theory and practice could be remedied became urgent. But what were the resources needed to remedy it? I was able to answer this question only by considering further not only the issues posed by Kantianism and utilitarianism but also those raised by the disagreements between Thomists on the one hand and Ayer and Sartre on the other, concerning the nature and status of reasons for action. And to make progress with either of these sets of issues I had to look in a different direction, and my narrative has to move backwards in time.

Two Lines of Thought about the Meaning and Use of Good

Two opposed lines of thought about the meaning of the word *good* and its cognates had been developed in English-speaking philosophy since the 1930s. One of these finds its first formulation in Ayer's *Language, Truth and Logic* in 1936. To call something good or bad is to express one's feelings for or against it. To evaluate is to approve or disapprove. By the late 1940s Ayer was recommending C. L. Stevenson's better-developed version of this view, according to which uses of *good* have both an expressive and an imperative component. To say of something that it is good is both to commend it and to urge those whom one is addressing to do so as well. Stevenson recognized that the conventions governing many uses of *good* are such that it also commonly has a descriptive component. But insofar as this is so, the descriptive component on the one hand and the expressive and imperative elements on the other are distinguishable and disparate. The step beyond this was to be taken by R. M. Hare, who provided both a sketch of the logic of imperatives and an account of moral judgments that was in some respects Kantian, in others utilitarian.

I had found Ayer and Stevenson more persuasive than Hare, and from them I acquired both an insight and a problem. The insight was a corollary to their successful undermining of the intuitionism of Moore, Prichard, and Ross. Viewed in the light cast by Ayer and Stevenson, intuitionist moral philosophers turn out to be under the illusion that they are asserting moral truths when they are in fact doing no more than expressing their own individual feelings and attitudes. They suffer from a lack of self-knowledge. The problem was that this mistake by some English moral philosophers seemed to have its roots in the general moral culture of their time and place. For while, so far as I could judge, Ayer, Stevenson, and other expressivists had provided a compelling account of the characteristic *uses* to which moral judgments were now put in a particular culture, they had taken themselves to have provided an adequate account of the *meaning* of moral and evaluative sentences as such, whatever the culture. Yet the meaning of those sentences was such that they at least appeared to give expression to some impersonal standard of judgment to which appeal was being made. Meaning and use had, so it seemed, come apart, something on which the current philosophy of language shed no light. How might this have happened?

In asking this question, I had of course understood the significance of Ayer's and Stevenson's work very differently from the way in which they themselves understood it. The question that I therefore faced was: If moral judgments here and now are used, at least in large part, as Ayer and Stevenson say that they are, what else, in other social and cultural circumstances, might moral judgments and evaluative judgments be? Might there be or have been a condition from which they had degenerated to their present state? And what would that condition be? An answer to this question was suggested by quite another and deeply incompatible line of thought about the meaning and use of *good*.

This second line of thought began by taking seriously J. L. Austin's injunction to begin with lexicography, to accumulate a wide range of different types of examples of the relevant expressions. Those who do so find themselves also following Aristotle—and this is no accident. Austin's habits of thought were in several ways Aristotelian and certainly so in recognizing the multiplicity and the heterogeneity of our uses of *good, better, bad, worse,* and their cognates. We speak of bad kings and good jam, of a good day at the races and a bad holiday in Casablanca, of a good time to go on a spree and a bad way to do it, of someone's being good at tennis or good for nothing. And these are only a few examples of the variety that we need to catalogue. Austin himself took there to be an irreducible and inescapable heterogeneity here.[3] But Aristotle had identified a unity underlying that heterogeneity, and the clue to that unity was supplied by Peter Geach. In 1956 Geach had pointed out that *good* and *bad* are noun-dependent or noun-phrase-dependent adjectives and that *well* and badly are correspondingly verb-dependent adverbs.[4] What it is for an X to be good depends upon what an X is, so the criteria of goodness in a king are very different from those of goodness in jam. And what it is to X well depends upon what X-ing is, so the criteria by which someone who plays tennis is judged to have played well or badly are not the same as those by which someone who shoes horses is judged to do so well or badly. And so we take a first step toward answering the question: What makes these various uses of *good* more than puns?

Here we need to bear in mind the distinction between attributive and predicative uses of *good,* as W. D. Ross originally formulated it, together with Geach's thesis that *good* is essentially attributive, that to be good is always to be a good someone or something, and that predicative uses of *good* can be translated into attributive uses. We speak of "good parents" but also of "good burglars," of "the best athlete in the games" but also of "the best forger still at work." It matters therefore that we can always ask, "Is it good for someone to be a good parent?" and "Is it good for someone to be a good burglar?" and what we learned from Geach is that to ask these questions is to ask, "Is a good parent a good human being?" and "Is a good burglar a good human being?," questions that can be answered only by first answering the question "What is it to be a good human being?"

It is at this point that this line of thought has sometimes been thought to encounter insuperable difficulties. That there are criteria independent of our choices, feelings, and attitudes governing our applications of "good parent," "good burglar," or for that matter "good boxer" or "good violinist," is difficult to deny. For in each area, drawing on Aristotle's thesis that to be a good X is to excel in the activities characteristic of an X, we can say what it is to exhibit such excellence as parent, as burglar, as boxer, as violinist. But, many have urged, any analogy between goodness as attributed to these and goodness as attributed to human beings breaks down. There is, they argue, no set of activities characteristic of a human being, as there are activities characteristic of parents, burglars, boxers, and violinists. Hence it was to be argued by Hampshire and by Berlin, following Austin, that there is no such thing as *the* good life for human beings, no such thing as *the* human good.

To this it can be replied that there are indeed many different ways of leading a good human life, but that there are at least four sets of goods that are characteristically needed by every human individual if she or he is to flourish. First, without adequate nutrition, clothing, shelter, physical exercise, education, and opportunity to work no one is likely to be able to develop his or her powers—physical, intellectual, moral, aesthetic—adequately. Second, everyone benefits from affectionate support by, well-designed instruction from, and critical interaction with family, friends, and colleagues. Third, without an institutional framework that provides stability and security over time a variety of forms of association, exchange, and long-term planning are impossible. And fourth, if an individual is to become and sustain her- or himself as an independent rational agent, she or he needs powers of practical rationality, of self-knowledge, of communication, and of inquiry and understanding. Lives that are significantly defective in any one of these respects are judged worse, that is, less choiceworthy, than lives that are not. These goods are goods without which excellence in activity is often impossible, and so the key to our various uses of *good* with regard to them is a shared conception of excellence in activity, of what it is to live virtuously.

Thus on any version of this line of thought—and there are different versions of it, for example, Philippa Foot's naturalism and Iris Murdoch's Platonism—there are standards independent of our feelings, attitudes, and choices by which we may judge whether this or that is choiceworthy, whether this or that is good to choose, to do, to be, to have, to feel. And every version is in conflict with the view that our evaluative uses of *good*, unless in a linguistically degenerated culture, are no more than expressions of or determined by our feelings, attitudes, and choices.

This radical disagreement concerning how our uses of *good* are to be construed is of course closely related to the disagreement that I identified earlier concerning the nature of reasons for actions, one in which Thomists were at odds with Ayer and Sartre. What it means to say that, in giving a reason for doing this rather than that, we are identifying some good that will be achieved by doing this rather than that depends on whether we understand *good* in expressivist or in other terms. Only if our uses of *good* are governed by standards independent of our feelings, attitudes, and choices can something like the Thomistic account of reasons for action be justified. So how are the issues between these two incompatible and antagonistic lines of thought to be resolved?

How at the Level of Theory the Debate between the Protagonists of These Two Lines of Thought Is Interminable and Inconclusive

Someone disposed to find credible the account of the condition of academic philosophy that I advanced earlier would, without knowing any of the facts about the subsequent debates concerning the use of *good,* predict that neither side would be able to provide conclusive arguments for its own view and against the other, except by its own standards. And so it turned out. For this disagreement was integrated into the longer and continuing quarrel between self-styled moral realists and self-styled moral antirealists, a disagreement in which the contending parties have enriched the statements of their rival positions by drawing on discussions of realism and antirealism in other areas. And, just as in those other areas, the debates between moral realists and moral antirealists have had no decisive outcome. Consider one theme of those debates.

On the expressivist view, when I assert that "doing such and such is bad," the meaning of the asserted sentence is such that it gives expression to the speaker's sentiments of disapproval. But suppose that someone says tentatively, "If doing such and such is bad, then so and so." Then, since no sentiments of disapproval are expressed, "Doing such and such is bad" as a constituent of this conditional must have a quite different meaning from that which it has when asserted. But if this is so, then inferences of the form "If doing such and such is bad, then so and so, but doing such and such is bad, therefore so and so" must be invalid, which is absurd. So the expressivist account of the meaning of such sentences must fail. It was Peter Geach who argued this thesis powerfully, thereafter referring to it as "the Frege point."[5]

To this Simon Blackburn replied by giving an admirably ingenious account of the relevant class of inferences,[6] a reply that was followed by a series of replies to the reply and replies to the replies to the reply by, among others, G. F. Schueler, Bob Hale, Mark van Roojen, Nicholas Unwin, Alan Thomas, and Mark Schroeder. At each stage in this still ongoing debate Blackburn and his allies reformulated their view in response to the most recent objections, and their success in so doing has made it clear that here we have one more example of an interminable controversy. The philosophical interest resides in the detail of the arguments. But what emerges from that often instructive detail is the large fact that, given the shared understanding of moral thought and practice presupposed by the two contending parties, and given their philosophical methods, neither party has the resources to defeat the other.

This is true more generally. Expressivists, whether followers of Alan Gibbard or Simon Blackburn or the earlier emotivist writers, have been able without notable difficulty to accommodate somehow or other every objection advanced against them. And a variety of antiexpressivists have been able equally easily to fend off the objections advanced against them. Each remains deeply convinced of the errors of the other. Both would regard it as intolerably frivolous to suggest that one should choose one's side by flipping a coin. But how then is one to decide?

How It Is Only at the Level of Practice That We Can Become Aristotelians

We need to begin again and to do so by returning to the social context in which we learned the use of *good* and its cognates. What we first had to learn was how to make the distinctions between what we desire and the choiceworthy, and between what pleases those others whom we desire to please and the choiceworthy. We characteristically and generally learn—or fail to learn—to make these distinctions, as we emerge through and from the family into the life of a variety of practices: such practices as those of housework and farmwork, of learning Latin and geometry, of building houses and making furniture, of playing soccer and playing in string quartets. What we can learn only in and through such practices is what the standards of excellence are in each type of activity and how our desires and feelings must be disciplined and transformed and our choices guided by the standards of excellence in each type of activity if we are to achieve such excellence and through it the goods internal to each type of practice.

So long as our desires have not been disciplined and transformed in the relevant ways, our uses of *good* and of cognate expressions will tend to be what expressivist moral philosophers have taken them to be, and our choices will give expression to our feelings and attitudes. Insofar as our desires have been disciplined and transformed in the relevant ways, our uses of *good* and of cognate expressions will be what Geach and others have argued them to be. So everything turns upon what we have been able to learn from the kind of practices in which we have engaged and on the nature of the particular moral culture or cultures in which we have participated. Understood in this light the philosophical quarrel between the two lines of thought that I sketched rests on a misunderstanding. It is not that we have two rival philosophical representations of one and the same subject matter but that we have two different subject matters, two different types of moral culture, an older one whose objectivist idioms and judgments are grossly misrepresented by expressivism, and one whose moral vocabulary exhibits just that blending of nonexpressivist meanings and expressivist uses that had forced itself on my attention a good deal earlier, a blending characteristic of the dominant moral culture of advanced modernity.

Consider now some further aspects of a practice-based understanding of goods, virtues, and rules. The identification of a variety of types of goods poses the question: What place should *we* give to each type of good in *our* lives? And it is no accident that this question is framed in terms of "we" and "our," rather than "I" and "mine." For this is a question that I can only hope to ask and answer with good reason if I ask and answer it in the company of trusted but critical others, others to whom I recognize that I am bound by certain unconditional commitments—commitments not to harm the innocent, to be truthful, to keep our promises, commitments that allow us to reason together without the distortions that arise from fears of force and fraud—and this for at least two reasons. First, it is only in and through such interaction with trusted but critical others that our practical reasoning is tested, so that our evaluations become less one-sided and partial and less liable to distortion by our not always conscious hopes and fears. Second, it is only insofar as we direct ourselves toward common goods, the common goods of family, neighborhood, school, clinic, workplace, and political community, that we are able to achieve our individual goods.

We learn what place in our individual and common lives to give to each of a variety of goods, that is, only through a discipline of learning, during which we discover what we have hitherto cared for too much and what too little and, as we correct our inclinations, discover also that our judgments are informed by an at first inchoate but gradually more and more determinate conception of a final good, of an end, one in the light of which every other good finds its due place, an end indeed final but not remote, one to which here and now our actions turn out to be increasingly directed as we learn to give no more and no less than their due to other goods.

This discovery of a directedness in ourselves toward a final end is initially a discovery of what is presupposed by our practice, as it issues in a transformation of ourselves through the development of habits of feeling, thought, choice, and action that are the virtues, habits without which—even if in partial and imperfect forms—we are unable to move toward being fully rational agents. Only secondarily, as we articulate at the level of theory the concepts and arguments presupposed by and informing our practice, are we able to recognize that we have had to become some sort of Aristotelian. I am not suggesting that in order to become an Aristotelian one first has to become virtuous—even a slender acquaintance with Aristotelians would be enough to dispose of that claim. I am saying that it is only through recognition at the level of practice of our need for the virtues, and through practical experience of how the exercise of the virtues stands to the achievement of goods, that a number of Aristotle's philosophical arguments become compelling.

To have become such an Aristotelian is to have found good reasons for rejecting both utilitarianism and Kantianism. What renders any form of consequentialism unacceptable is the discovery of the place that relationships structured by unconditional commitments must have in any life directed toward the achievement of common goods, commitments, it turns out, to the exceptionless, if sometimes complex, precepts of the natural law. What makes Kantian ethics unacceptable is not only that our regard for those precepts depends upon their enabling us to achieve our common goods but also that the Kantian conception of practical rationality is inadequate in just those respects in which it differs from Aristotelian *phronēsis* or Thomistic *prudentia*. Note, however, that these grounds for asserting that there are conclusive reasons for rejecting both utilitarian and Kantian ethics are Aristotelian grounds. Take away the Aristotelian premises from which this assertion is derived and it will cease to convince. Unsurprisingly, therefore, it lacks force precisely for those against whom it is directed, utilitarians and Kantians.

It is therefore of some importance that in arriving at a certain kind of Aristotelian standpoint I was not taking up one more theoretical position within the ongoing debates of contemporary moral philosophy. It is because I have been thought to have done just this that I have been unjustly accused of being one of the protagonists of so-called virtue ethics, something that the genuine protagonists of virtue ethics are happy to join me in denying. But what then is it to adopt this kind of Aristotelian standpoint? There are at least three aspects to such a change of view.

First, it enables one from a standpoint outside academic moral philosophy, that of an older tradition of moral practice, to understand why such moral philosophy was condemned to become what it has become, a scene of theoretical disputes between fruitlessly contending rival parties. The widespread loss of a shared practical grasp of the teleological structure of human nature and activity at the threshold of the modern world not only led to the theoretical fragmentation that I described in *After Virtue* but was itself the result of a prior loss of a shared mode of practical life. And there is no way to make the relevant concepts and arguments once more compelling except within some restored and contemporary version of just such a mode of practical life. Detach those concepts and arguments from the contexts of social practice from which and within which they draw their intelligibility and they too become mere debatable theoretical constructions.

Second, it is to adopt a standpoint that enables individuals, by situating themselves within such a mode of social practice, to make intelligible features of the narratives of their own lives and of the lives of others that will otherwise remain opaque, confused, disguised, or trivialized. A basic Aristotelian thesis is that only insofar as we understand our individual and common lives as potentially directed toward the achievement of goods and of *the* good through the exercise of the virtues are we able to identify the various types of frustration, misunderstanding, and failure by which our lives are marked.

Third, just as Aristotelian moral and political theory provides us with resources for interpreting and redirecting our practical lives, so too our practical experience provides us with reasons for criticizing and sometimes rejecting some of Aristotle's own concepts, theses, and arguments. We learn to identify that in Aristotle which derives from the limitations and prejudices of Athenian and Macedonian elites. So we develop Aristotle beyond Aristotle and in so doing may find—as I found—that our Aristotelianism has had to become that of Aquinas.

How from the Standpoint of Aristotelian Practice Contemporary Academic Moral Philosophy Appears Defective as a Mode of Inquiry

The conception of moral philosophy at which I had thus arrived put me at odds not only with the standpoint dominant in contemporary moral philosophy but also with the established analytic understanding of how philosophical inquiry should proceed. For on the view that I have found myself compelled to take, contemporary academic moral philosophy turns out to be seriously defective as a form of rational inquiry. How so?

First, the study of moral philosophy has become divorced from the study of morality or rather of moralities and by so doing has distanced itself from practice. We do not expect serious work in the philosophy of physics from students who have never studied physics or on the philosophy of law from students who have never studied law. But there is not even a hint of a suggestion that courses in social and cultural anthropology and in certain areas of sociology and psychology should be a prerequisite for graduate work in moral philosophy. (It was my great good fortune as a student at Manchester that I was required to take a course in anthropology with Max Gluckman and was driven by my resistance to Gluckman's views to an engagement with the work of very different anthropologists, such as Franz Steiner, and of such sociologists as Tom and Elizabeth Burns.) Yet without such courses no adequate sense of the varieties of moral possibility can be acquired. One remains imprisoned by one's upbringing. And the particular form that that imprisonment now takes is that of an inability to recognize, first, that the contemporary morality of advanced capitalist modernity is only one morality among many and second, that it is, as a morality of everyday life, in a state of disorder, a state of fragmentation, oscillation, and contradiction. So we should not be surprised when academic moral philosophers misconstrue their own subject matter.

It would not of course be sufficient to remedy this for students of moral philosophy to take courses in anthropology and sociology. A second necessary condition is a prior and continuing engagement with a variety of practices and a reflective grasp of what is involved in such engagement. Lacking such practical engagement and such reflection, there can be no adequate knowledge of the range and application of evaluative and prescriptive concepts. So we ought to require on the CVs of those who aspire to teaching or research appointments in moral philosophy accounts of their relevant experiences on farms and construction sites, in laboratories and studios, in soccer teams and string quartets, in political struggles and military engagements. And we do not.

A third respect in which academic moral philosophy fails as a discipline of inquiry is a result of the extraordinary pressure exerted to sustain the status quo. What is the penalty that threatens academics who do not conform to the established norms? It is that their writing will go unpublished and disregarded. And this threat is the more telling because of the intensive pressure to write, a pressure initially generated by two successive apprenticeships. The first is that of producing a PhD dissertation intended to be publishable in either article or book form by those at an age at which almost no one has as yet anything genuinely of interest to say, something easily confirmed by reading large numbers of recent dissertations in moral philosophy.

A second apprenticeship is devoted to the achievement of tenure or its equivalent. Once again the pressure to publish is intense, since the future career of a philosophy teacher will be determined almost exclusively by how much, on what, and where she or he publishes. The result is unsurprisingly a large quantity of publications, as well as an even larger quantity of unpublished writing. So far as moral philosophy is concerned, it is instructive to look at the proportion of articles submitted to articles published in one especially prestigious journal, *Ethics*. In 2006, the number of submissions was 321, and the number of articles accepted, all of them after revision, was 16. In 2007, the corresponding numbers were 334 and 16.

A high proportion of those rejected articles will later have been submitted to other journals, which either are devoted entirely to moral philosophy or contain articles on moral philosophy appearing alongside articles on epistemology, metaphysics, and other philosophical subdisciplines. The former class includes not only *Ethica, Ethical Perspectives, Ethics and Behavior, Ethics Today, Journal of Ethical Studies, Journal of Ethics, Journal of Value Enquiry,* and *Journal of Moral Philosophy* but also over thirty journals dedicated to business ethics, medical ethics, bioethics, and the like. The latter class includes journals published in Australia, Canada, Ireland, Norway, the United Kingdom, and the United States. (I am considering only the English-speaking world.) An inescapable conclusion emerges. In moral philosophy, as in other areas of philosophy, much of what is written must go unpublished and much of what is published must go unread. What function then is served by this cruel academic treadmill?

Its function is to inculcate the currently established conception of the tasks of moral philosophy and of its past history. It is to ensure that habits of mind are transmitted, so that students by and large follow their teachers in their assumptions about which few books and articles must or may be read and which may be safely ignored. It is to make certain that the young recognize whose arguments are to be taken seriously and whose disdained, when and about what to make jokes, and at whom and with whom it is permissible to sneer or condescend. It is to shape minds so that they are open to some ideas and closed to others. Academic moral philosophy is a conformist discipline, and habituation in writing what is well designed to secure the approval of those with established academic power is one principal means of producing and reinforcing that conformism.

Epilogue

Two salient thoughts emerge from this narrative. The first concerns the importance for the moral philosopher of living on the margins, intellectually as well as politically, a necessary condition for being able to see things as they are. The two standpoints without which I would have been unable to understand either modern morality or twentieth-century moral philosophy are those of Thomism and of Marxism, and I therefore owe a large and unpayable debt of gratitude to those who sustained and enriched those marginal movements of thought in the inhospitable intellectual climate of capitalist modernity, including Thomists as various as Maritain, Garrigou-Lagrange, De Koninck, and McInerny, and Marxists as various as Lukacs, Goldmann, James, and Kidron. One way to make it highly improbable that you will enjoy outstanding academic success is to enter contemporary debates in moral philosophy as either a Thomist or a Marxist.

A second thought, perhaps in tension with the first, concerns the importance for the moral philosopher of nonetheless learning as much as she or he can from those at the academic center, those who have made definitive contributions to the ongoing debates of academic moral philosophy. For interestingly it is often they who supply the resources that one needs if one is to free oneself from the limitations of their standpoint. If one is to evaluate both the achievements and the defects of twentieth-century academic moral philosophy, it needs to be understood both from within and from a standpoint that is at once external and radically critical. It is such a standpoint that I have tried to define.

Notes

1. David Lewis, *Philosophical Papers*, vol. 1 (Oxford: Oxford University Press, 1983), x, xi.

2. A. J. Ayer, "Jean-Paul Sartre's Doctrine of Commitment," *Listener*, November 30, 1950, 633–34.

3. J. L. Austin, *Philosophical Papers* (Oxford: Clarendon Press, 1961), 1510.

4. See Peter Geach "'Good' and 'Evil,'" *Analysis* 17 (1956): 32–42, repr. in *Theories of Ethics*, ed. Philippa Foot (Oxford: Oxford University Press, 1967), 64–73.

5. Peter Geach, "Assertion," *Philosophical Review* 74, no. 4 (1965): 449–65.

6. Simon Blackburn, *Spreading the Word* (Oxford: Oxford University Press, 1985), ch. 6.

PART I
———————

Reading Alasdair MacIntyre

CHAPTER TWO

Keeping Philosophy Relevant and Humanistic

JOHN HALDANE

I

It is a privilege to participate in honoring one of our great living philosophers, but it is also somewhat daunting, the more so when the thinker has ranged as widely and proceeded as deeply as has Alasdair MacIntyre. One response to the challenge of discussing his ideas at this stage of his long and highly productive career is to survey his writings: identifying their themes; charting courses of development; noting critical reactions and his responses to these; taking stock, and taking breath, before continuing the retrospective toward a summary conclusion. I have not chosen to do this, however, in part because that task is so large and would require, as the record shows, the space of many chapters;[1] also, it would have limited appeal to a readership likely to be already familiar with his writings and would test the patience of those interested in engaging issues addressed or posed by that work.

It is perhaps ironic, though not at all paradoxical, that Alasdair MacIntyre has attracted the interest of intellectual chroniclers, for although his own work is sensitive to the personal, social, and historical contexts in which ideas are formed and embraced or rejected, he is not himself a chronicler at heart, or so I have concluded. Rather, he is an investigator keen to pursue the truth about a matter, or the practical good that is to be discovered by philosophical inquiry. In that respect his interest in the historical development of certain concepts, schemes of thought, and arguments is not that of the historian of ideas but that of one who sees value in making explicit, and gaining insights from, the fact that all philosophy is done historically.

With that in mind, rather than offer an intellectual biography, I wish to try to characterize something of the spirit of MacIntyre's approach to philosophy as I see it, and to say something about three sets of issues within recent and contemporary philosophy with which he has been concerned. These are first, the nature of *ethics,* second, the nature of *thought and action,* and third, the nature and practice of *philosophy.* The last of these, since it includes reflection on the first two but is more general, may also seem the most abstract and thereby the least ethically and politically relevant; but it is a striking feature of the way in which MacIntyre reflects on this issue that it focuses attention directly and somewhat uncomfortably on contemporary professional academic practice, particularly in the area of moral philosophy. In that way it becomes a form of social criticism, for what his analysis suggests is that much of what moral philosophers now do is characterized by a lack of cultural depth and of anthropological insight and may often exhibit *mala fides.*

Before turning to these matters, however, I shall say something about the general character of MacIntyre's thought as it is expressed in his writings. A prominent mode of his thinking appears to be a distinctive form of immanent critique, prompted by reflecting on what various figures and traditions have written about good and bad in action and in the social structures through which we are brought to action. That is, of course, an observation about the particularities of the man; but as it happens it happily corresponds to an idea he favors, namely that thinking is not primarily a matter of detached speculative reflection on the part of a purely intellectual and unencumbered self. Rather, it is an encultured social activity, reflecting its time and circumstances, and aiming at solutions to problems generated by experience and practice.

II

Since the publication in 1981 of *After Virtue,* MacIntyre has come to be regarded as one of the most significant critics of the morality and moral philosophy of modernity. Long prior to its publication, however, he had argued, in a manner then unusual in Anglo-American philosophy, that any attempt to understand moral concepts and moral reasoning without locating them in their social and historical contexts was bound to fail and, what is worse, was likely to lead to skepticism about the very possibility of moral justification, for as he claimed: "Moral concepts are embodied in and are partially constitutive of forms of social life."[2] If this thesis is now more familiar, that is largely due to MacIntyre's influence.

At that stage his insistence upon the contextual character of moral thought was offered primarily as a methodological corrective to the style of ethics then dominant within English-language philosophy. By the time of *After Virtue* and in the works published since then, however, the claim that moral concepts are interwoven with cultural traditions and social institutions had become part of his general critique of modern moral and political philosophy, and it has served in the development and defense of his own quite distinctive version of "Thomistic Aristotelianism." I feel some hesitation in using this expression, since I am sure that MacIntyre long ago grew weary of being labeled, even by friendly labelers—particularly when that might be to co-opt him for their own purposes. Rather than try to summarize his ideas in doctrines constitutive of a philosophical creed, it is much better in talking about MacIntyre as a particular kind of philosopher to try to characterize his sensibility and outlook. In this context I do not mean by *sensibility* either sentiment, or emotion, or subjectivity, in the sense of these that might be associated with ethical emotivism. Instead, I use the term more in the manner associated with the characterization of an artist's ways of perceiving, reflecting, and responding—ways that may serve to disclose the existence and significance of features of the situation that may otherwise go unobserved.

MacIntyre's writings are marked by a broad and deep humanism, expressed first by fascination with the products of human thought and action, particularly as these reveal the characteristics of particular cultures and traditions; second, by sympathy and admiration for human achievement, be it intellectual, moral, or, in a broad sense, spiritual; and third, by a desire to understand these achievements from the "inside" as an engaged participant. These interests, talents, and sensibilities combine in an approach to understanding the defining aspects of human nature that is itself *humanistic* in the sense that it identifies the subject matter of inquiry as being personal life: that is to say, *human life* as it consists in the exercise of various sensitive, affective, volitional, and intellectual powers, developed and modified through social practices.

In keeping with this view of the subject, MacIntyre has seen the task of philosophical study as being one of understanding the aspects of personal life at various levels of constitution and expression, in their interrelatedness, and in their orientation toward various goods and away from various evils. Philosophy in this way of conceiving it is very largely moral philosophy, in the broad sense of this term that encompasses the several aspects of action directed toward the "living goods" of virtue, be they aesthetic, economic, political, or religious. Moral philosophy in this expansive sense was most self-consciously and arguably in modern times best developed in Scottish universities and associated literary and scientific societies during the eighteenth and nineteenth centuries. This development began with Gerschom Carmichael and Francis Hutcheson and continued with Adam Smith and Thomas Reid, with Adam Fergusson and Dugald Stewart, on through into the period of James Frederick Ferrier and the Scottish idealists, surviving into the twentieth century in the work of personalist thinkers now little known, let alone honored in their native land. And today it is all but gone—for reasons to which I shall return later.

III

I said that philosophy in this way of conceiving it is largely moral philosophy, and I might now add that moral philosophy so conceived is an aspect of philosophical anthropology, the study of human nature. But it is not a form of external study as might be the chemistry of the human body, for it aims to arrive at general descriptions and interpretations of human life, as well as particular evaluations and prescriptions not only from the point of view of the observer-theorist but from that of an engaged participant.

Allowing for the fact that philosophical illumination is achieved at a level of abstraction from ordinary modes of description, what is understood in this view of the discipline is what was already given in experience and in reflection. Comprehending the human in this sense is a matter not of fashioning a theory of subpersonal causal processes and mechanisms but of discerning the meanings and purposes that shape and direct human action. This has long been a theme of MacIntyre's writings, but I think that it has been best expressed when put to work in his exploration of Edith Stein's philosophy of the person, an approach that focuses on what is given to us in conscious perception.

In his book on Stein and the phenomenological movement, MacIntyre shows how her main contribution to phenomenology was to identify the need to provide an account of knowledge of self and of other.[3] This was first conceived by Stein as a complement to the recovery by her teacher Edmund Husserl of knowledge of the objective world. I say "recovery" because it had previously been judged as lost to the snares of Humean skepticism and the obscuring mists of Kantian idealism. MacIntyre explores Stein's subtle analysis (anticipatory of ideas to be found in Wittgenstein but given prominence by John McDowell) of the way in which the mindedness of others is given *in,* not inferred *from,* their perceivable actions, and the way also in which our sense and knowledge of self is derived from observing others observing us.[4] He also develops the theme of the interplay between philosophical reflection and everyday practice by considering the impact on Stein's thoughts (about empathy) of her work as a nurse dealing with men whose sexuality, condition, experiences, and habits of mind were quite unlike her own.

At around the same time as MacIntyre was beginning to shape his own thinking about the nature of moral philosophy, Peter Strawson introduced into general philosophy a distinction between "descriptive" and "revisionary" metaphysics in order to mark a contrast between approaches to understanding the structure of our thought about the world.[5] It is a somewhat indeterminate distinction, and, as Strawson allowed, few great philosophers have confined themselves narrowly to one or the other. Nonetheless, the terms capture a difference that has relevance beyond the sphere with which Strawson himself was principally concerned. As he viewed it, *descriptive metaphysics* takes as givens the structure and categories of everyday thought as these are expressed in language. So, for example, the implicit distinctions between subject and attribute, event and process, space and time, particular and general, and so on, are taken into philosophical reflection. This may then proceed either by using them to clarify some issue or by embedding them within a yet more abstract conceptual scheme that is intended to show their wider and most fundamental relationships.

Revisionary metaphysics, by contrast, stands prepared to reject the forms of everyday thought in favor of schemes that enjoy some explanatory or a priori advantage.

It is, of course, a real question what makes a conceptual feature advantageous, and how any such merit stands in comparison to the advantage of reproducing an existing working scheme. To illustrate the point, however, consider the "reism" of the Polish philosopher Tadeusz Kotarbinski.[6] I mentioned that ordinarily we recognize events and processes as well as individual things that may participate in or be the sites of such occurrents. We also recognize the attributes or characteristics of substances, events, and processes, and various relations that may hold between instances of these several categories. According to Kotarbinski, however, it is necessary to practice the method of *Sprachkritik:* analyzing expressions with a view to showing that they can be reformulated so as to avoid reference to more extensive categories. Kotarbinski coined the term *onomatoids* to signify "pseudo-names" and aimed to show that the only credible semantic category is that of genuine names. Apparent reference to events, processes, relations, and attributes might then be eliminated—either reformulated to refer to some more basic category or rejected as vacuous. The ontological aspect of this view is that every referent is a *thing* (hence *reism*) and that every thing is a *body* (thus *somatism*). Whatever the merits of semantic economy and ontological modesty, it should be clear enough that Kotarbinski's somatic metaphysics is revisionary, both of the broad Aristotelianism that has characterized most Western metaphysics and of the familiar understanding of things of which that same Aristotelianism is a descriptive representation.

Revisionism has generally been more exotic and spiritualistically inclined. Consider, for example, Plotinian emanationism, or Leibniz's monadism, or Berkleyean idealism, or Whitehead's panpsychism. The fact that these metaphysical schemes have tended away from materialism may easily lead someone to suppose that what is now termed "naturalism" is not also revisionary, but the case of Kotarbinski's reism shows that this may not be so. This point is important because today the main source of revisionary metaphysics does not lie in the direction of ontological idealism; indeed, it lies outside philosophy as that would ordinarily be thought of, in areas defined or at any rate occupied by other kinds of study. There is, on the one hand, the sort of thing that appeals to those who hope, in the spirit of cultural revolutionaries, to overturn familiar understandings of nature, society, and culture and who see resources for doing so in psychoanalysis, or post-Marxism, or gender theory, and so on. I put it this way because I do not think that the revolutionary motive derives from the anthropological theory; rather, the revolutionary intent is in search of a theoretical justification. Applied to the subject matter of traditional philosophy, these theories encourage a hermeneutic of suspicion that queries such categories as "substance" and "accident" as artifacts of various kinds of social power struggles. If this seems to describe only certain modern trends, however, it is worth recalling that elements within the Judaic and Christian traditions have proposed analogous deconstructions of social categories.

It is still the case, however, that these sources of challenge remain broadly humanistic and normative, retaining a notion both of the subject of lived experience and of the correctness of evaluating actions and policies as just or unjust, compassionate or cruel, and so on, as they bear upon the well-being of such subjects. More threatening, I believe, and less widely seen as such, in part because it derides the foregoing as irrational ideology, is the challenge posed by *scientism* to ordinary human self-understanding, the understanding held implicitly and often explicitly by what MacIntyre might term "the plain person."

Analytical philosophers are accustomed to dismissing postphenomenological movements in continental thought as unrigorous and obscurantist, but this oft-warranted dismissal of the quality of argument (admittedly sometimes no more than rhetorical rhapsody) leaves unaddressed the importance of the subject, which is, after all, the ancient one of determining what constitutes a good human life and how society might be arranged to provide for that. On account of their abandonment of logical analysis and argumentation, the wilder forms of postdeconstruction inflict the same harm as did the Sophists of antiquity, giving a bad name to a valuable practice, namely moral philosophy. That, however, is not the substance of the contemporary analytical attack; rather, it focuses on the existential character of continental thought and opposes to this something real: *science*, or at least scientifically respectable inquiry.

MacIntyre has suggested that it is disingenuous to represent analytical philosophy as neutral with regard to such fundamentals as the nature of human beings. One might counter that there need be no necessary connection between a method and the results it delivers. Yet the fact of the matter is that not only philosophical psychology, and the philosophies of thought, language, and action, but even moral philosophy are all in the process of being reconfigured in ways that correspond to assumptions imported from scientific theorizing, principal among which is the belief that human beings are physical objects no different in fundamental nature from other material objects. This leaves the question of what to make of talk of mind and mental activities, and increasingly the answer has been "Not that much," or certainly nothing more than can be accommodated within a scientific theory of behavior and its neurological foundation.

It may seem odd that specialists in ethical theory or normative philosophy will pursue debates about moral justification without considering whether there could be such a thing if the prevailing orthodoxies in metaphysics are true; but this is evidence of the extent to which specialization has fragmented philosophical thought and thereby established the conditions for pervasive bad faith. Sometimes, scientifically minded philosophers will allow that ordinary talk of thought, feeling, and intention cannot be reduced to neuroscience but will then assign moral psychology to evolved biological strategies, thereby presuming to disarm it of any power to unsettle a physicalist worldview. We may go on talking about persons and their purposes, but all that really exists are physical causes and physical effects. MacIntyre objects to this way of proceeding that it confuses matter and substance, or, put another way, it fails in considering the substantial nature of human beings to take account of their form, and especially the fact that at the level at which we may speak of moral subjects, that is, as responsive and responsible agents, this form is essentially social. He writes:

> Human bodies [in the sense in which these may be referred to using possessive pronouns] are intelligible only as potentially and actually in relationship with others, others who are recognized as possessing the same kinds of powers. . . . It follows that any attempt to give an account of the body exclusively in terms of the particulars of which it is composed [muscles, nerves, etc., and these in terms of fibers and so on, and these in terms of particles] is bound to fail, for all those features of the body that belong to it in virtue of its social character will have been omitted.[7]

It looks, moreover, as if a general argument can be constructed to refute the idea that personal psychology could simply be an interpretative imposition. For the interests of those who might construct and apply such a scheme, as well as the processes of construction and application, must themselves be exercises of cognition and intentional action of an interpersonal kind. Mindedness on the part of the interpreter is a precondition of the possibility of psychological description. As MacIntyre once put it, "The concept of an intelligible action is a more fundamental concept than that of an action as such."[8] Insofar as we are concerned with characteristic human behavior, and science itself is a form of such behavior, then we are dealing with the intelligible, with what makes sense in terms of reasons and purposes and values. MacIntyre is not the only philosopher to have made this point, but there is no one who made it more often, more variably, and more illuminatingly or connected it more extensively with moral philosophy than he.

IV

In her famous essay "Modern Moral Philosophy," published around the same time as Strawson's and MacIntyre's own early work, Elizabeth Anscombe argued that the basic moral vocabulary of requirement and prohibition—"ought," "ought not," "must," "must not," and so on—is a remainder from earlier religious ways of thinking.[9] This vocabulary, she argued, derives from a conception of ethics in which certain actions are prescribed by a divine legislator, whether personal, as in the Judeo-Christian scheme, or "cosmic," as in the style of the Stoics. With the subsequent detachment in Western culture of morality from religion, this vocabulary lost its source of authentic meaning but retained its commandatory force, this latter then seeming to be unwarranted, and at best explicable in subjectivist or emotivist terms as descriptive or expressive of certain commitments or attitudes of approval and disapproval.

In *After Virtue* MacIntyre adopted this analysis as part of his own diagnosis of the irresolubility of moral disputes in contemporary life; but he also enlarged and complicated the "lost meaning" account, according to which ethical language has become an incoherent assemblage of disordered fragments from earlier moral systems. One significant complication is that whereas Anscombe proposed the abandonment of the ethics of quasi-legal requirement in favor of an Aristotelian approach built around concepts of virtue and natural norms, MacIntyre discerned the vocabulary of virtue itself as echoing through the babble of competing moral claims. On this account he argued that, as things stand, modern, secular liberal consciousness is no better placed to make sense of Aristotelian virtue ethics than it is of the strongly prescriptive vocabulary of the Judeo-Christian moral law. In both cases what we lack are the historical and cultural contexts that give meaning to these ways of evaluating and commending character and conduct.

In keeping with the Aristotelian moral psychology that Anscombe recommended, MacIntyre has argued that the value and indeed the moral meaning of actions derive not from their efficacy in maximizing the satisfaction of desires or from their conforming to some abstract principle of pure practical reason but instead from habits of action and avoidance whose standing as virtues derives from their orientation toward ends that constitute good human lives. Like Anscombe, Philippa Foot, and other neo-Aristotelians, therefore, MacIntyre hopes to restore coherence to morality by relating it to an account of life as ordered toward naturally fulfilling ends. In part, however, because of conclusions drawn from his earlier studies of thought and action, MacIntyre has seen that ordering very largely in terms of social practices rather than in terms of culturally invariant natural functions. He allowed in *Dependent Rational Animals* that the attempt to deal only in terms of (diverse) social natures fails to allow for the possibility that these are themselves expressions of common humanity and are implicitly seen as such. Even so, it may be fanciful to suppose that every intelligible form of human activity can be redescribed in a common vocabulary of basic aims and purposes while still retaining the intelligibility assigned it by more specific interpretations.

To see this, consider an area of activity he discusses in the essay "Colours, Cultures and Practices,"[10] where he is concerned with the question of the conditions that allow us to treat color judgments as objective. One (broadly Wittgensteinian) answer refers to social practices that deliver rules and concepts that both establish consensus and render it normative for judgment. The issue, however, is that divergent practices sustaining incommensurable judgments are imaginable, and both are empirically demonstrable. These, of course, are the familiar conditions appealed to in arguments for relativism. MacIntyre argues, however, that this would follow only if it were also impossible to appeal to any standards of right judgment other than those embodied in the language and practices of particular groups. To see how it is otherwise, he considers the history of European painting. He argues that the practices constitutive of this in its various aspects and phases both ground judgments of value applicable to the products internal to these aspects and phases and also give rise to standards that can be applied more generally, both self-critically and in relation to the painting traditions of other cultures. Anyone familiar with the practice of an art or skill who has also taken an interest in comparable practices of other times or cultures will recognize the truth in this; but there remains a question of how far this may carry truth-apt judgment from relativism to universalism.

The analysis of the "Colours" essay recapitulates a mode of argument developed by MacIntyre in *Three Rival Versions of Moral Enquiry* and in response to criticisms of it;[11] but while it has persuasive power against crude relativism it falls short of establishing a tight connection between diverse human practices and common human nature. Indeed, it is hard to see how a fully common human nature could be identified and described beyond a very basic subsocietal kind of type that, in writing about the human body, MacIntyre wished to reject as failing to capture the interpersonal nature of human beings fully considered. It has long been a recurrent theme in MacIntyre's philosophy that in asking "What ought I to do?" or "What ought I to think?" one is, in effect, asking via some practice(s) about the kind of life one should lead. The unit of moral assessment is not, strictly, individual actions but the life from which they issue and to which they contribute. Furthermore, moral character is formed and developed in a social context, out of participation—originally unchosen and not reflected upon—in practices whose meaning is given by their traditional goals. The problem for philosophy is in seeing how this is compatible with the rejection of relativism, or perhaps less provocatively of how it can be fitted into a common humanism. The consequence for contemporary life, however, is that there is no single unifying culture and hence no shared set of values and virtues by reference to which actions may be interpreted and judged. As MacIntyre observes: "The rhetoric of shared values is of great ideological importance, but it disguises the truth about how action is guided and directed. For what we genuinely share in the way of moral maxims, precepts and principles is insufficiently determinate to guide action and what is sufficiently determinate to guide action is not shared."[12] For example, and superficial appearances to the contrary, modern societies lack substantial agreement on such basic questions as whether or why lying is bad. In traditional societies, by contrast, actions are subject to sets of norms appropriate to various roles (though these norms are not always codified or codifiable); and these prescribe what is honorable and dishonorable, vicious and virtuous.

The interest of MacIntyre's explorations of these issues is testified to by the attention his work has attracted. As I have indicated, however, it raises problematic philosophical and practical questions, and although he has addressed these repeatedly I remain uncertain as to the extent to which he has resolved, within the diverse terms and moments of his own philosophy, the question of moral objectivity (as contrasted with intersubjectivity). Evidently this issue, or issues close to it, continue to challenge him, as is evidenced by the ways in which it, or they, keep breaking through, often setting the very theme of a discussion. A further example is the interesting essay "Aquinas and the Extent of Moral Disagreement," where the challenge is addressed precisely from the universalist side of the debate, there represented by St. Thomas's version of natural law.[13] The general subject can also be regarded as posing a question for practical philosophy: that of how in general we might rationally resolve moral disputes. The structuring of the problems is familiar. The contending parties are viewed as presenting rival accounts of an issue, and rival verdicts regarding it, each from broad ethical standpoints; and they invoke various foundational principles typically connected with diverse accounts of human nature and the goods that constitute its well-being. Aquinas is then taken to hold that while there may genuinely be a multitude of goods, nonetheless their status as goods derives from their relation to a single final end that is an end for all human agents. How is this assertion of a common human good to be reconciled with the fact of apparently intractable disagreement? The answer is again given in terms of the structure of shared rational inquiry. If the contending parties are to move beyond flat opposition to serious engagement, then each has to subscribe to certain common norms of discourse. In doing that and in probing the question of why *these* norms, they then open the way to recognizing a set of common precepts, which, as it happens, are those identified by Aquinas in his account of the content of the natural law. Slightly more expansively:

When confronted by some immediate disagreement as to what you or I or we should do here and now, reason requires us to ask who is in the right, and . . . if we are to enquire effectively who is in the right, we must do so in the company of others and more especially of those others with whom we are in disagreement. . . . What such deliberative enquiry sometimes discloses is that practical disagreement about what to do here and now derives from underlying disagreement about the nature of the final end for human beings. So in order to answer questions posed by practice enquiry has to become theoretical and systematic. But . . . it is a condition of the rationality of shared enquiry that the social relationships of those engaged in it should be structured by certain norms, norms that find their expression in the primary precepts of the natural law.[14]

There are several questions that might be pressed here about the content and status of these norms, such as the extent to which they are formal and/or hypothetical or substantive and/or categorical. There is also the issue of their relation to an account of human nature: that is, whether there is any such relation, and if there is, whether the relationship may not be one of constitution rather than derivation, in which case the original disagreement is immediately fundamental and seemingly irresoluble. I mention these questions not to suggest a general fault in MacIntyre's approach but because I am persuaded by its analysis of the roots of moral reason as lying in shared forms of good-seeking, yet also take very seriously his earlier claims as to the deeply conflicted nature of modern Western cultures.

V

MacIntyre began by challenging those who suppose there is no such thing as moral truth; but in arguing that there is moral truth he also shows that the conditions of coming to discern and to act in accord with it involve a prior orientation to goods of human life—an orientation that is frequently obscured, distorted, or denied in contemporary culture. One aspect of the latter problem is revealed in the desire for politics to provide moral direction while conceiving of the political in terms of the state. As MacIntyre observes: "The modern nation-state, in whatever guise, is a dangerous and unmanageable institution.... To empower it as a bearer of values always imperils those values."[15] In conclusion, however, I want to return to the matter of philosophy itself, in its contemporary professional form as that is to be found in universities, in academic books and journals, and in scholarly and research associations. The character of professional English-language philosophy has interested MacIntyre for more than half a century, but it has become a renewed focus of criticism in essays gathered in *Ethics and Politics* (2006), in *Edith Stein: A Philosophical Prologue* (2006), and subsequently in *God, Philosophy, Universities* (2009). His ideas and arguments about the nature of philosophy as it is and as it ought to be are important if correct, and they are liable to ring true to those who inhabit research-intensive environments but also share MacIntyre's humanistic orientation. In using the expression "research-intensive environments" I am also deploying it ironically, for what it signifies is symptomatic of how advanced academic philosophy now conceives itself, namely as a form of positive science.

Two recent examples of the "scientization" of philosophy, not only of the general style of its self-conception but of its method and substance, are "neurethics" and "experimental philosophy," particularly as the latter is being applied in moral theory and metaethics. Paul Churchland illustrates the first in a 1995 discussion of the capacity for moral judgment: "[It consists of] a hierarchy of learned prototypes for both moral perception and moral behavior, prototypes embodied in the well-tuned configuration of a neural network's synaptic weights. We may find here a more fruitful path to understanding the nature of *moral learning, moral insight, moral disagreements, moral failings, moral pathologies,* and *moral growth* at the level of entire societies."[16] Patricia Churchland similarly writes a decade later, "As we understand more about the details of the regulatory systems in the brain and how decisions emerge in neural networks, it is increasingly evident that moral standards, practices, and policies reside in our neurobiology.... Recognition of these various determinants means that the traditional field of ethics must itself undergo recalibration. Philosophers and others are now struggling to understand the significance of seeing morality not as a product of supernatural processes, 'pure reason' or so-called 'natural law,' but of brains."[17]

No one is denying the role of the brain in sustaining mental life, but in the language of an earlier style of humanistic philosophy it is a "category mistake" to locate a capacity for judgment in the synaptic weights of neural networks, and an even worse one to regard moral standards, practices, and policies as residing in neurobiology; it also fails precisely to understand the point that moral judgment is rooted in experience shaped by shared conceptions formed and "located" in the working of social institutions, cultural modes, and so on—that is, in ineliminably personal realities.

A more recent celebration of the possibility of assimilating philosophical inquiry to empirical research is provided by the development of "experimental philosophy." This looks for validation to the science of psychology, but given the associated physicalist impulse of contemporary scientific naturalism, that domain might in turn be thought amenable to a neurophilosophical reduction. For the experimentalists, the favored form of a philosophical question is a transformation from the traditional "What is the nature of F" to "What is the preponderance of beliefs about Fs among a statistically adequate sample population?," and along with this the question "What is the nature of the cognitive processes that guide everyday attributions of F-ness among such a population?" It has always been germane to philosophical inquiry to gather opinions on the subject at hand, but that is quite different from handing over philosophy to psychology and sociology. It is as if the elementary distinction between what people think and what they ought to think (because it is true, or otherwise correct) had been lost sight of.

A reflexive example of the experimental school at work is provided by an article published in *Mind* in 2009 entitled "The Moral Behaviour of Ethicists: Peer Opinion," in which the authors report on an experiment in which attendees at the Pacific Division Meeting of the American Philosophical Association were invited to complete questionnaires in which they were asked to compare the moral behavior of ethicists to that of philosophers not specializing in ethics and to nonacademics of similar social background. To the expressed disappointment of the experimenters, it transpired that participants did not judge that ethicists were more likely to behave in morally better ways. There is much that might be commented upon as regards the simplicity of the questions, the unreflective use of such portmanteau terms as *moral behavior,* and the naïveté of the assumptions that shape their conclusions such as the following: "If empirical inquiry eventually reveals, instead [of the favored belief that moral reflection and philosophical ethics, done well, can positively affect one's own behavior, and can be valuable for their tendency to point the person who reflects toward the good], that philosophical moral reflection is personally inert or even harmful, many of us will have to rethink our assumptions about moral psychology, moral education, and the role of reflection in the morally good life."[18]

The thing to notice here are the factors that are not mentioned as providing a possible explanation, such as whether the general culture of which the respondents and their colleagues form a part is a generally degraded one, and more particularly whether academic moral philosophy has become detached from moral practice because of the material and social conditions under which it operates. Here the scientific and technological and commercial imperatives of the general culture are relevant, as is the very conception of philosophy as empirical observation-cum-scientific theorizing. Absent a moral commitment or an existential immersion in the life of values, why would one expect that moral philosophers conceived of as scientific specialists would be any more identified with the life of moral virtue than logicians?

By way of marked contrast, consider the life of one of the subjects of MacIntyre's case studies. He begins his account of the philosophy of Edith Stein (subsequently Saint Teresa Benedicta of the Cross) acknowledging the skepticism liable to arise in the mind of a contemporary Anglo-American analytical philosopher presented with the story of a life defined by religious conversion, a vocation to religious life, and elevation through canonization and declaration as "Co-Patroness of Europe." He titles the first chapter "Why Take an Interest in Edith Stein as a Philosopher?" and soon identifies a degree of prejudice. It is, however, less that of the secularist per se than that of the professional academic philosopher who regards his subject as a professional discipline with no more of an intrinsic relationship to the practice of life than that of physics or botany.

In response MacIntyre argues that most academic philosophy is involved in a kind of bad faith: on the one hand separating private and professional life; on the other insisting upon the importance of the subject as providing a critique of ordinary thought, while also failing fully to accept that everyday life and language bear the imprint of former, and often persisting philosophical theories. To acknowledge and be faithful to its special status, philosophers have to allow that "private" practice is permeated by theories and values and thus is a proper object of inquiry, and that the outcome of this may require revision of existing beliefs, practices, and commitments.

In connection with the particular oppressive circumstances of Stein's life and work, MacIntyre considers how the ideology of strict separation of life and theory has served the interest of tyrannies by allowing academics to compartmentalize their activities and excuse one another on that account. A historically and geographically immediately proximate example is that of Martin Heidegger, a contemporary and onetime colleague of Stein's and to some degree both a Nazi apologist and appointee. It would be easy to represent Heidegger's case as an aspect of the particular time and place in which he lived, and also perhaps as a malignancy in the tradition of politicized romantic thought. Yet while MacIntyre's example is a special one, it is certainly not unique, and the general relevance of his claims about the effects of the modern professionalization of philosophy should not be lost sight of by pointing to the extremity of the case. His argument is otherwise put in discussions of rival interpretations of Aristotle's account of moral philosophy and of its relation to moral practice that appear as the first two chapters of *Ethics and Politics*. There he follows Aristotle in maintaining an internal connection between practicing moral philosophy and living virtuously. In exposition of that view he writes: "Only the good are in a position to make justified true theoretical judgements about the nature of moral practice. The construction and evaluation of sound moral theories, unlike the construction and evaluation of sound theories in the physical sciences, require more than intellectual virtues."[19]

What moral philosophers need are sound understandings of human life as ordered to particular goods as those are brought into view and pursued through specific forms of community life. Moral philosophy thus requires that its practitioners be decent human beings, helped to be and to remain such by living within and contributing to decent communities. And *communities* in this sense means families and social groups in which ranges of human goods are pursued in a spirit of mutual concern. The contrast between this conception of the philosopher as tending toward a teacher-sage and that dominant in elite philosophy departments, which has him or her tending toward the scientific specialist, is evident, and it is quite unclear how the widening gulf may be closed.

One suggestion, however, may lie in the identification of a second gap, and for this I return to the Scottish moral philosophy tradition that I described earlier and with which MacIntyre is well acquainted. I said that it had survived into the twentieth century but now is all but gone. Let me quote from one writer whose life spanned parts of the nineteenth and twentieth centuries and who was still alive when MacIntyre was born. Nearly fifty years earlier, in 1885, Andrew Seth Pringle-Pattison published a work entitled *Scottish Philosophy: A Comparison of the Scottish and German Answers to Hume*. There he writes as follows (and since the work is now little known and not generally accessible I quote at some length):

> The thread of national tradition, it is tolerably well known, has been but loosely held of late by many of our best Scottish students of philosophy. It will hardly be denied that the philosophical productions of the younger generation of our University men are more strongly impressed with a German stamp than with a native stamp. . . .
>
> The *Fachmann*, or specialist, has hitherto not flourished among us, and the disadvantages of his absence are obvious. But it is possible that what Scottish philosophy lost in scientific precision may have been compensated for, in part, by the greater influence which it has exerted upon the body of the people—an influence which has made it a factor, so to speak, in the national life. It is a matter of history, on the other hand, that the great idealistic movement in Germany in the beginning of this [nineteenth] century passed to a great extent over the heads of the German people. . . . It spoke in an unknown tongue, and the people were not edified; it may be said to have died of its technical defect.[20]

Like the contemporary academic analytical school, Scottish philosophy had professionalized, specialized, and gone "technical," devising new vocabularies and multiplying theories through narrowed expertise; but in the process of becoming scientific it also ceased to speak meaningfully to the wider society and in the terms of MacIntyre's analysis thereby also become less properly philosophical in spirit and orientation. No one doubts the merits of David Hume, Adam Smith, and Thomas Reid as moral philosophers, yet they are read today as they *never* were in their own time, as if they were specialist investigators in some abstruse theoretical field. Instead they aspired to and generally achieved wide readership among an educated public, in no small part because they directed their writings to it and thereby helped to maintain it in existence. If philosophers insist that their subject is a scientific specialism, not only will they move further apart from those of their number who cleave to the Aristotelian view, but they will also drift away from the general society out of which they have emerged. In recent years the patterns of research funding have sustained that development, but things are now changing and universities face real challenges. Being more familiar than most moral philosophers with ideas about the material basis of culture, MacIntyre would be among the first to appreciate the irony if the restoration of an older tradition were to be assisted by a collapse of the economic structure of research-led higher education. But I think that before then he would want to remind us that human liberty means that we do not have to wait for economic forces to change our ways: we can choose what kind of philosophy we want to practice and to engage with. In considering how to pursue a route back to the living sources of moral philosophy, again in the broadest sense, we could hardly do better than consider the example presented by Alasdair MacIntyre and engage with his work in the spirit and to the end that it has been presented: in pursuit of the truth about human nature, action, and value, and with a view also to realizing the practical goods immanent within that pursuit.

Notes

The present text derives from that of an address given at the Royal Irish Academy, Dublin, on March 9, 2009.

    1. See, for example, Peter McMylor, *Alasdair MacIntyre: Critic of Modernity* (London: Routledge, 1993); Susan Mendus and John Horton, eds., *After MacIntyre: Critical Perspectives on the Work of Alasdair MacIntyre* (Oxford: Polity Press, 1994); Mark C. Murphy, ed., *Alasdair MacIntyre* (Cambridge: Cambridge University Press, 2003); Thomas D. D'Andrea, *Tradition, Rationality and Virtue: The Thought of Alasdair MacIntyre* (Aldershot: Ashgate, 2006); Christopher Lutz, *Tradition in the Ethics of Alasdair MacIntyre: Relativism, Thomism, and Philosophy* (Lanham, MD: Rowman and Littlefield, 2009); and Paul Blackledge and Kelvin Knight, eds., *Virtue and Politics: Alasdair MacIntyre's Revolutionary Aristotelianism* (South Bend, IN: University of Notre Dame Press, 2011).

2. Alasdair MacIntyre, *A Short History of Ethics* (London: Routledge, 1967), 1.

3. Alasdair MacIntyre, *Edith Stein: A Philosophical Prologue* (London: Continuum, 2006).

4. See, for example, J. McDowell, "Criteria, Defeasibility, and Knowledge," *Proceedings of the British Academy* 68 (1982): 455–79.

5. P. F. Strawson, *Individuals: An Essay in Descriptive Metaphysics* (London: Methuen, 1959).

6. See Tadeusz Kotarbinski, "Le réalisme radical," in *Proceedings of the 7th International Congress of Philosophy* (London: Milford, 1931), 488–500; and Tadeusz Kotarbinski, "Reism: Issues and Prospects," *Logique et Analyse* 11 (1968): 441–58.

7. Alasdair MacIntyre, "What Is a Human Body?," in *The Tasks of Philosophy*, vol. 1 of *Selected Essays* (Cambridge: Cambridge University Press, 2006), 101.

8. Alasdair MacIntyre, *After Virtue: A Study in Moral Theory* (London: Duckworth, 1981), 195.

9. Elizabeth Anscombe, "Modern Moral Philosophy," *Philosophy* 33 (January 1958): 1–19.

10. Alasdair MacIntyre, "Colours, Cultures and Practices," in *Tasks of Philosophy*, ch. 2.

11. See John Haldane, "MacIntyre's Thomist Revival: What Next?," in Mendus and Horton, *After MacIntyre*, 91–107; and Alasdair MacIntyre's reply in "A Partial Response to My Critics," in Mendus and Horton, *After MacIntyre*, 283–304.

12. Alasdair MacIntyre, "The Privatization of Good," *Review of Politics* 52, no. 3 (1990): 349.

13. Alasdair MacIntyre, "Aquinas and the Extent of Moral Disagreement," in *Ethics and Politics*, vol. 2 of *Selected Essays* (Cambridge: Cambridge University Press, 2006), ch. 4.

14. Ibid., 80.

15. MacIntyre, "Partial Response," 303.

16. Paul Churchland, *The Engine of Reason, the Seat of the Soul* (Cambridge, MA: MIT Press, 1995), 144.

17. Patricia Churchland, "Moral Decision-Making and the Brain," in *Neuroethics: Defining the Issues in Theory, Practice and Policy*, ed. Judy Illes (Oxford: Oxford University Press, 2005), 3–16.

18. Eric Schwitzgebel and Joshua Rust, "The Moral Behaviour of Ethicists: Peer Opinion," *Mind* 118, no. 472 (2009): 1043–59.

19. Alasdair MacIntyre, "Rival Aristotles: Aristotle against some Renaissance Aristotelians," in *Ethics and Politics*, 4.

20. A. Seth Pringle-Pattison, *Scottish Philosophy: A Comparison of the Scottish and German Answers to Hume* (Edinburgh: Blackwood, 1885), 1–2, 129–30.

CHAPTER THREE

Ethics at the Limits
A Reading of *Dependent Rational Animals*

JOSEPH DUNNE

Some of the different reasons for one's indebtedness to philosophers whom one has read may be gleaned from Iris Murdoch's dictum that "to do philosophy is to explore one's own temperament while at the same time attempting to discover the truth."[1] In some philosophical writings one finds intuitions, and a way of articulating and defending them, with which one has an unforced, if not connatural, affinity: it seems as if truth and temperament tally so that to read is at the same time to recognize and be confirmed. But the texts that support such reading are hardly those from which one has most to learn. The latter may rather be those that, by offering greater resistance, put one's thinking more on its mettle: they not only expose one to conflict between temperament and truth but ensure that in such conflict it is the claims of truth that are more strongly pressed. For me, Alasdair MacIntyre's works belong in this latter category—though saying so does too little to disclose the scale of the debt I owe to him. Since the first irruptive impact of *After Virtue* nearly thirty years ago, his writings have become familiar features in my philosophical landscape: to think about almost any topic central to ethics and politics—or to education, the area of my special concern—is to think with (which may include against) him. In this essay I shall focus on one of his main works,

Dependent Rational Animals. If I seek not only to emphasize the sympathetic and inspiring quality of this book but also to press a line of critical questioning against it, I have what I take to be good MacIntyrean reasons for doing so. For it is MacIntyre who has urged that "education . . . should be a preparation for constructive engagement in conflict"[2]—with no implication that one should exclude from the range of such conflict those few thinkers whom one gratefully acknowledges as one's indispensible teachers. And, as will become apparent toward the end of the essay, not least among those whom I enlist as allies in the present conflict with MacIntyre is MacIntyre himself.

I

Before indicating the purpose of my focus on *Dependent Rational Animals* (1999), and the direction of the discussion into which it will lead, I shall first situate this book within MacIntyre's oeuvre by offering a construal of its relationship to its three immediate predecessors, *After Virtue* (1981), *Whose Justice? Which Rationality?* (1988), and *Three Rival Versions of Moral Enquiry* (1990). For all the many ways in which *After Virtue* might be characterized—as, for example, an essay in philosophical history (in which the history of ideas is conceived as inseparable from the history of practices and institutions), a vindication of a reconstructed Aristotelianism, an anti-Enlightenment polemic, a confrontation with Nietzsche and with the postmodernist thought of which he is the ur-prophet, or a diagnosis of contemporary malaises—it was most essentially concerned with ethical-political analysis, and especially of virtue as the crucial constituent of human flourishing. In its two sequels, *Whose Justice? Which Rationality?* and *Three Rival Versions of Moral Enquiry*, however, this substantive engagement was largely to give way to analysis of the epistemological presuppositions of moral inquiry (with the historical dimension, to be sure, still to the fore). What motivated this turn was MacIntyre's acute awareness that the prosecution of his argument in *After Virtue* could do little to attain wider acceptance of his case—that, to the contrary, it was likely, given the positions occupied in contemporary philosophical debate, to leave him "step by step deprived . . . of very nearly all possible argumentative allies."[3] But from this awareness he concluded that the settlement of disputes in moral philosophy must be deferred not indefinitely but only until one of the contending parties has "stood back from their dispute and asked in a systematic way what the appropriate rational procedures are for settling this kind of dispute" (242). It was such systematic meta-investigation of "rational procedures"—a now "imperative . . . task" if progress was to be made in ethics, as he suggested at the end of *After Virtue*—that he went on to undertake in the two later books.

Whatever the gains of this kind of proceduralist turn, it is striking that in *Dependent Rational Animals* MacIntyre returns to more substantive ethical inquiry. Whereas epistemological concerns in *Whose Justice? Which Rationality?* had led him to inveigh against those who would begin in moral inquiry not "from any theory . . . but rather . . . from *the facts themselves*"—and later in the same work to write that "facts, like telescopes and wigs for gentlemen, were a seventeenth century invention"—in the preface to *Dependent Rational Animals* he invites rival philosophers to show how, "from each of their standpoints, due place can be given to the facts," and later in that book he writes: "When philosophers have said: 'it must be so' and those with the relevant kind of experience say 'it is not so,' the philosophers have not always been in the right."[4] The facts here, which the book is designed to draw attention to, are those of human *animality, vulnerability,* and *dependence;* and people with the "relevant kind of experience" include ethologists, animal trainers, child psychologists, and women—though in principle they can hardly exclude any human being (one of the book's intended lessons, indeed, being to make clear the respects in which "men need to become more like women" [164]).

A focus on these facts, and attention to the kinds of experiences that bring them to the fore, returns MacIntyre to the central Aristotelian question of *After Virtue*: What is human flourishing? And he still gives the Aristotelian answer: a virtuous life. What is new, however, is the enlarged understanding he goes on to offer of the human being about whom the question is asked—and who also of course asks it—leading to a quite different emphasis in the account of virtuous living that provides the answer. True to his oft-repeated claim that a tradition lives only by self-correction and renewal, he engages in a self-conscious revision both of Aristotle and of his own previous work on Aristotle. The first of the book's main themes—the fact of human animality—involves a correction of his earlier attempt to correct Aristotle in *After Virtue*. There he had offered a core conception of the virtues that, while still recognizably Aristotelian, discarded Aristotle's "metaphysical biology," whereas in *Dependent Rational Animals* he writes: "I now judge that I was in error in supposing an ethics independent of biology to be possible" (x). Much of the originality of *After Virtue* lay in its arguing for the coincidence of the rise to prominence of three main characters in the dramatic script of modernity—the aesthete, the therapist, and the manager—with the decline of a cultural milieu hospitable to virtue, *and* in its then supplementing this critique with a conceptual elaboration of "practices," "the narrative unity of a life," and "tradition" as together forming the necessary matrix for a reconstruction of "virtue." With this reconstruction MacIntyre took himself to be replacing a "biologically teleological" account of virtue by a "socially teleological" account, that is to say, one that "does not require the identification of any teleology in *nature*" (183, emphasis added). The view that he was thus rejecting was that "human beings, like the members of all other species, have a specific nature; and that nature is such that they have certain aims and goals, such that they move by nature towards a specific *telos*" (139).

It is just this polarization between "biological," "natural," and "animal" on one hand, and "social" and "human" on the other, and the supposition that the latter can somehow be conceived as independent of the former, that MacIntyre goes on to put in question in *Dependent Rational Animals* as he adroitly unpicks arguments presented in its defense by both analytical philosophers such as Davidson, Kenny, and McDowell and hermeneuticists such as Heidegger and Gadamer. The outcome of this unpicking is a master concept of "flourishing," underpinning the "focal use" and the "underlying unity" in all our multifarious ascriptions of "good," applying in the same sense—and not merely analogously—to humans and to other animals (and indeed plants), whether as species or as individuals-of-a-species, and thus committing him, as he sees it, to "in some sense a naturalistic account . . . of 'good'" (78).

I shall not adumbrate here MacIntyre's compelling arguments for the considerable cognitive capacities displayed by some nonhuman animals (especially dolphins), arguments that not only permit a strong comparison rather than contrast between these animals and humans but also serve to

> undermine the cultural influence of a picture of human nature according to which we are animals and in addition something else. We have, on this

view, a first animal nature and *in addition* a second distinctively human nature. The force of the "and" is to suggest that this second nature can, at least in the most important respects, only be accounted for on its own terms. Its relation to our given biological nature is thought of as external and contingent in a way and to a degree that permits a single sharp line to be drawn between human beings and members of all non-human species. (49–50)

Nor shall I attempt here what MacIntyre himself does not undertake: to contend with the indeterminacy in his phrase "in some sense a naturalistic account," and so to tackle the "notorious and difficult philosophical problems . . . aris[ing] in this area," which he acknowledges while at the same time "put[ting] them on one side" (78). What I do want to consider is his analysis of the other two primary anthropological facts, related to though distinct from animality, that he analyzes: our *vulnerability,* or proneness to many different kinds of disability and affliction, and our consequent *dependence* on others for our flourishing. With respect to these two features of human living, it is Aristotle himself, rather than his own earlier debiologized reconstruction of Aristotle, that he seeks to correct. More precisely, he repudiates a characteristic element in Aristotle's catalogue of virtues, "greatness of soul" *(megalopsychia).* For in the conception of the great-souled man, who is masterful and strong, comfortable in giving but not in receiving, the facts of human vulnerability and dependence are disguised and disallowed.

In what follows I shall set out the main lines of the account (at once psychological, ethical, and political) that emerges in the course of MacIntyre's analysis of these two primordial "facts" (§ II). I shall then turn from this chiefly exegetical and interpretative concern to the more critical task of this chapter. I shall first register dissatisfaction with the role accorded to "local community" in MacIntyre's elaboration of the "networks of giving and receiving" through which he sees the obligations foregrounded in his reconceived ethico-political viewpoint being discharged (§ III). And I shall then go on to argue—and this will be my main purpose in the chapter—that meeting these obligations or demands, which are different from and strikingly more exacting than those that had earlier been met in *After Virtue,* may overdraw the resources available to MacIntyre in what he presents as his still basically Aristotelian (and now avowedly naturalistic) position (§ IV). I shall then buttress this argument by advertence to the work of two other contemporary philosophers, Raimond Gaita and Charles Taylor, whose substantive ethical claims are, as I shall try to show, very close to those of *Dependent Rational Animals*—though they are bound up with a philosophical anthropology that is quite different from what we find in the latter book. Moreover, I shall contend that this anthropology is very close to what MacIntyre had himself espoused, as an Augustinian, in writings between *After Virtue* and *Dependent Rational Animals*, especially *Whose Justice? Which Rationality?* (§ V).[5] I shall conclude, then, with a claim, or rather a brief acknowledgment, that the line of reasoning that I shall have pressed in the two previous sections accords also with MacIntyre's own argumentation in some of his more recent writing (§ VI).

II

In Dependent Rational Animals, as in many of MacIntyre's other works, human flourishing is understood as consisting most fully in the exercise of independent practical reasoning. But what he here brings out much more emphatically is the depth of our dependence on others for this very exercise—for its character as independent no less than as rational. Our dependence is most apparent in infancy and childhood, and a great merit of the book is the way it foregrounds the care and education we receive at these early stages as intrinsic to the quality of our moral lives—whereas in most moral philosophy they are made to disappear behind the facade of a putative moral competence, already unproblematically established. Here MacIntyre draws on psychoanalytical work that had long been of interest to him,[6] especially Donald Winnicott's illumination of the crucial role of the "ordinary good" (or "good enough") mother in providing the kind of responsive, trustworthy, and nonretaliatory recognition required for relaxed, exploratory, and sometimes aggressive play—and with it the formation of a secure sense of selfhood and the beginnings of properly rational activity. MacIntyre is alive to the full intimacy and particularity of the parental bond: the fact that care must be for *this* unique child, must actively convey a sense of unconditionality (even if in most cases, happily, this is never fully tested by the actual occurrence of, for example, severe disability or disfiguring injury), and must give resolutely without expectation of proportionate receiving.

For MacIntyre, the purpose of this care, and hence its essential ethical import, is to open the child to "the good and the best." And this entails enabling it to make the transition from having immediate reasons for action (which it already has, in common with many kinds of nonhuman animals) to (a) *evaluating* its reasons, and—as a condition both for engaging in this evaluation and for being disposed to redirect its actions accordingly—(b) *separating* itself from and transforming its desires, and (c) *expanding* the range of alternative future action scenarios it can imaginatively and at the same time realistically entertain. To make this transition successfully—and success here is always a matter of more or less—one must release oneself both from the tyranny of "clamorous felt need" *and* from the distortions of one's attachments with, and inevitable ambivalences and antagonisms toward, those primary figures on whom one's need fulfillment first concentrates. In doing this, one makes oneself educable into a range of practices, with the goods and standards internal to them; at the same time one begins to become an independent practical reasoner and, as MacIntyre well shows, to acquire the ethical virtues. What he is more particularly concerned to show in this book, however, is that such becoming and acquisition on my part are dependent on the prior possession by others of those same virtues and of some other virtues specific to the offices of caring and teaching. Nor is it only that I depend on others if I am first to acquire and then to be sustained in the exercise of independent reasoning and of virtue. Rather, this very exercise is in itself shot through with otherness. I cannot, for example, claim to be the sole authority on my good as I can on my wants or desires; to evaluate my reasons for actions is at the same time to make myself accountable to others; my self-knowledge is importantly mediated and confirmed by others' knowledge of me; and against my unavoidable proneness to intellectual error and moral failing there is no better antidote than the responses of friends and colleagues (not excluding, as MacIntyre is concerned to show, those who may be severely disabled).

Much of MacIntyre's point here might be claimed to have been already present in his thought, albeit with less explicit emphasis. There is a striking departure, however, in the way in which he goes on to translate the inescapable fact of dependence into the ethical/moral currency of *indebtedness* and *obligation*. Indebtedness resides in the fact that one has received. And one's corresponding obligation is to give. In specifying the norms proper to this pattern of giving and receiving he gives substance to his revised understanding of flourishing and of the virtues that, as constitutive of it, must be at the center of moral and political life. This specification strongly excludes any calculus of reciprocity, any attempt to measure what a person has received so that a proportionate degree of giving can be exacted in return. What carries enormous weight in his sense of things here is not only the profoundly asymmetrical nature of the relationships out of which we all first emerge (if we have had "ordinary good" parenting) but also the depth of affliction and disability to which we remain exposed as an ever present possibility. The weight of this actual past and always possible future shatters the basis on which we might have supposed, in "the illusion of self-sufficiency," that bargaining in the present on costs and benefits with other robust preference maximizers is a well-supported endeavor. What this weight enforces, rather, as a realistic obligation, is attentive care to the needs of "those whom contingency and chance put into our care," so that "we can set no limit to those possible needs" but must exercise an "unconditional care for the human being as such, whatever the outcome" (100).

In writing these words, MacIntyre takes himself to be still within a recognizably Aristotelian orbit: he later suggests that how to understand ourselves and others within the kind of patterns of giving and receiving he depicts "is perhaps best captured" in Aristotle's discussion of friendship in *Nicomachean Ethics* IX (160). But the very different ethical viewpoint that, as it seems to me, he approaches here is that of Emmanuel Levinas (and this despite the admittedly huge contrast in philosophical styles between these two philosophers): the magnitude of what MacIntyre recognizes as a properly ethical demand, and the incommensurability of this demand with what the normalized ego takes as rational expectations—the peremptoriness with which it imposes the claims of the other on the self—seems to be much the same as what we find in Levinas.[7]

MacIntyre, however, does not take himself to be canvassing an ethic of extreme supererogation (or, in Levinas's more supercharged rhetoric, of "traumatic command"). To the contrary, it is an ethic implicit in "networks of giving and receiving" that he sees as the substance of ordinary political community. Ethics and politics meet in the coincidence he posits between my individual good and the common good. Undercut in this coincidence is the dichotomy between egoistic and altruistic motives and actions—between, on the one hand, pursuit of self-interest regulated by rules that restrain me no more than they restrain those who might otherwise take unfair advantage of me and, on the other hand, solicitude for others as simply a given of sentiment or a matter of individual discretion *outside* the ambit of reason. The common good is common in that it is neither "mine rather than others'" nor "others' rather than mine"; and it is underwritten by reason insofar as it is based on a recognition of our human lot as one in which any heavy misfortune that befalls another should incline me truthfully to say, "This could have been me."[8] Just as the other cannot calculate when or how such misfortune may occur, so I must not calculate when or how I may be called on to respond to it.

What disposes toward uncalculated giving is "just generosity," a key virtue not found in MacIntyre's earlier work and for which he finds precedent, among elaborated catalogues of the virtues, only in Aquinas's treatment of *misericordia*. Giving is *just* insofar as it honors a debt I have incurred by the attentive and affectionate regard I have already enjoyed from others (though not necessarily from *this* person—here is part of the uncalculated nonreciprocity MacIntyre insists on) and may at any time greatly need again. And it is *generous* insofar as it partakes of charity and compassion—it responds to the real need of another human being and is moved by her distress as if it were my own (for MacIntyre, one's sympathies and affections are always subject to norms of appropriateness, and one has acquired a virtue only when they have been made harmonious with these norms). If just generosity is the virtue most strongly profiled in this book, its counterpart and perhaps its necessary condition is that abiding sense of one's own indebtedness that grounds *gratitude* as another of what MacIntyre calls the "virtues of acknowledged dependence."

III

One can hope to flourish only by finding one's place within a network of giving and receiving in which one's own good is aligned (though not identical) with a common good; and the most important such network is that of "local community." MacIntyre anticipates and disarms some possible criticisms of his position here—or shows more clearly why he has resisted being tagged as a "communitarian"—by the extent of his qualifications in relation to local communities.[9] Such communities, he acknowledges, "are always open to corruption, by narrowness, by complacency, by prejudice against outsiders and by a whole range of other deformities, including those that arise from a cult of local community" (142). Moreover, he grants that a person may simultaneously belong to several communities and move consecutively in and out of different ones. And *every* community, he seems to insist, is limited by two different shadow figures: the stranger, who evokes from it the virtue of hospitality, which, if it is to prove itself a decent community, it must show itself capable of offering; and the deeply indigent, who might indeed be taken to show that any community worthy of the name can exclude no human being (and thus, in a sense, to shatter the very idea of "local community") since just generosity must extend to *anyone* in "urgent and extreme need."

But despite these qualifications, the politics that MacIntyre espouses in *Dependent Rational Animals* is that of local community, which he sees as the primary locus of the "common good," prior to the family and, more emphatically, to the nation-state. His hostility to the nation-state is well known, and his charges against it (e.g., its being in thrall to large moneyed interests, its inability to engage the great bulk of its citizens in meaningful political participation, its incapacity to be a genuine moral community—and the even direr consequences should it attempt nonetheless to masquerade as one) are indeed hard to rebut. Still, the nature and contours of what he means by "local community" remain indistinct. In some places—as when he mentions schools, workplaces, clinics, clubs, or churches, he admits that one may belong to more than one community, and sees the nation-state as "an ineliminable feature of the contemporary landscape" (133) to which people should relate strategically—one takes "local community" to refer to those multifarious clusterings of people bound by some common purpose that exist throughout "civil society" (a term he does not use). But in other places—as when he speaks of "the whole political society," or refers to decisions about the priority to be accorded through the allocation of resources to the place of dramatic art in "the life of our community," or recommends a quite systematic subordination of economic considerations to social and moral ones (so that disparities in income are kept small, there are "self-imposed limits to labour mobility," and there is "some significant degree of insulation from and protection from the forces generated by outside markets" [145])—he seems to intend by "local community" a much more formally organized political unit, albeit one on a smaller scale than the nation-state. If by "local community" MacIntyre means only the former, then it is hard to see how it could have the cohesiveness needed to constitute, and bind people into, a pattern of giving and receiving of the kind he envisages. But if, on the other hand, "local community" does indeed mean something like the latter, then I do not see how it can escape the difficulty that he himself raises against the family: the fact that it lacks "self-sufficiency" and can flourish only if its wider social environment also flourishes.

As one who has always been to the fore among philosophers in deploring the abstraction of a great deal of philosophical argumentation from relevant contexts, MacIntyre characteristically regards a consideration of local community as "one point at which the discussions of moral and political philosophers benefit from becoming historical and sociological" (142–43). It is striking, however, that the examples of local community that he then invites us to consider are of "fishing communities in New England over the past hundred and fifty years . . . Welsh mining communities . . . farming cooperatives in Donegal, Mayan towns in Guatemala and Mexico, some city-states from a more distant past" (143). He has sometimes been accused of nostalgia for his attachment to examples such as these. The charge of "nostalgia" of course—to echo his own remarks about utopianism in *Three Rival Versions of Moral Enquiry*—may often say less about an unrealistic hankering by those against whom it is leveled than about the inadequate appreciation of values realized in earlier periods and places on the part of those leveling it. Still, one would like MacIntyre not only to direct us to exemplary cases in the past but to show us—as he does not attempt—how the genuine goods they embodied might be carried over the threshold of hypermodernity so as to be exemplary *for us*. He might of course retort that crossing this threshold is precisely what we must *not* do—or rather, since we have already done so, what renders us incapable of realizing the kind of flourishing he so inspiringly evokes.

It is not clear that he would in fact make this retort. But even if the kind of networks of giving and receiving that he envisages can indeed be sustained only through a quite radical redirection, or even reversal, of the thrust of industrial and postindustrial societies, how is this to be achieved? I do not believe that the kind of local protectionism he suggests can supply an answer. It is disappointing that his commitment to sociological analysis leaves issues concerning technological transformations and globalization so unaddressed. To be sure, the nation-state is increasingly exposed as a political entity incapable of regulating economic forces, let alone of promoting cultural or moral well-being. And one appropriate response to this is indeed a devolutionary one, encouraging the reanimation of local communities. But the subsidiarist insight that supports this move calls for a move *also* in the opposite direction: for the creation of political structures well beyond the limits of any nation-state. MacIntyre is surely right to see unrestrained market forces as inimical to the kind of politics he espouses. But these forces are no respecter of borders, national *or* local, and it is hard to see how they can ever be properly checked without political institutions whose scope is coterminous with themselves.

IV

The difficulties I have just raised, concerning as they do the nature of a world dominated by advanced capitalism, are ones that confront all contemporary moral and political thought and for which perhaps no theorist now has a satisfactory response. I want to go on here to press a different question with a more particular bearing on MacIntyre's project in *Dependent Rational Animals* and a more significant import for my purpose in this chapter. There are very good reasons for persisting, as he does, with the classical insight that flourishing is possible neither for myself nor for others outside reliable patterns of giving and receiving that, while irreducible to rules of contract or of the market, are inextinguishably political. Still, the relationship between the ethical and the political is perhaps more problematic than he allows. Or, rather, the depth of human solidarity for which he argues not only severely strains the normal recourses of politics but tests to the limit—and perhaps, as I shall try to show, beyond the limit—what we can draw on in "ethics."

On the one hand MacIntyre lessens the burden on an individual by placing as much weight as he does on the "institutional forms" of the political. This weight is evident in what I have already said about the intrication of an individual's good with a common good, and the consequent need for a "common mind," to be achieved through shared deliberative procedures, "as to how responsibilities for and to dependent others are allocated and what standards of success or failure in discharging these responsibilities are appropriate" (133). And it comes out too in his seeing these "dependent others," however deep or permanent their disability, as no mere recipients of beneficence but as "in one way or another" contributing to "our shared education in becoming rational givers and receivers"—so that we must "accord them political recognition . . . [and] treat them as someone whom it would be wrong to ignore or to exclude from political deliberation" (141). Politics, thus understood, benefits not only those who are dependent but also those on whom they must depend, by ensuring that the caring that falls to the latter is a shared and not merely an individual burden. Within the economy of this sharing, however, the burden on some can be relieved only by increasing the burden on others. It is MacIntyre's thesis of course that this kind of calculus of benefits and costs is undercut precisely by individuals' reconciling their own good with the common good. But a politics founded on the reliable expectation of such reconciliation, as he readily grants, is committed to "Utopian standards, not often realized outside Utopia, and only then . . . in flawed ways" (145).

The reference to Utopia is itself an acknowledgment of how strained politics becomes here. But on the other hand it also shifts the burden back from politics to ethics; for what such a politics requires above all is citizens endowed with virtue—most especially perhaps the virtue of just generosity. It is in relation to this virtue that my question arises. For there may be good reason to believe not only that it translates awkwardly into the idiom of politics but also (and relatedly) that it is a good deal more demanding as an ethical virtue than one might gather from this book. With respect to the first of these points it has to be borne in mind that the common good, while common, is itself always plural, constituted by an ensemble of richly varied good*s*. And, this being the case, an individual, even when well disposed to serve it, "as an independent practical reasoner has to answer the question of what place it is best that each of those goods should have in her or his life" (109). The issue here is "the diversity of goods,"[10] and I'm not sure that MacIntyre takes sufficient account of the potential for conflict it imports into a person's judgment about the *good for her or him* and how the goods and needs of others are to find a place within it (at one point he notes but makes no judgment on the conflict for Gauguin between his good qua painter and his goods qua father and qua human being). Because of this potential for conflict there may be an element of indeterminacy in many of the judgments we have to make about conduct. To be sure, this indeterminacy can be reckoned with insofar as we can call upon the virtue of good judgment *(phronesis)* to deal with it in each case; still, it may be greatly increased by the second point mentioned above, the peculiar demandingness of just generosity.

Consider what MacIntyre writes: "What I am called on to give has no predetermined limits and may greatly exceed what I have received"; "The care that I give to others has to be in an important respect unconditional, since the measure of what is required of me is determined in key part, even if not only, by their needs"; "I must know that . . . you will not blench when some task for which you have taken responsibility turns out to be much more unpleasant—coping with vomiting or persistent bleeding or screaming, for example—or much more burdensome than expected" (126, 108, 110). It is not difficult immediately to embrace these words when they refer to parents' relationship with their children, or perhaps some other relationship within the family or among close friends. But what do they require if their denotation is extended, as it is by MacIntyre, so that we are enjoined by them in our relations not just with our children, other family members, or intimate friends but perhaps with any member of our wider community or indeed with *anyone* "whom contingency and chance put in our care"? What do they require, and from where can we draw the moral resources to meet this requirement?

MacIntyre's answer to this question, notwithstanding his removal of *megalopsychia* from the catalogue of virtues, is deeply Aristotelian. It relies on a moral education that is able to "transform and integrate" our divided impulses and desires "as infants, as children, and even as adolescents," so that, when morally mature, our "passions and inclinations are directed to what is both our good and the good of others." Our character, then, when this education has succeeded, is such that "self-sacrifice is as much of a vice, as much of a sign of inadequate moral development, as selfishness" (160). There is something very admirable about this ideal of the harmonious ethical agent and about the whole middle register of "virtue" and "flourishing" through which it is articulated. But the question—already intimated in my earlier reference to Levinas—is whether it can meet, or motivate a response to, the brokenness and depth of human need evoked by MacIntyre's words in the previous paragraph. And the point of this question can be sharpened by reference to some other recent work, closer in philosophical idiom than Levinas's to MacIntyre's, which has pressed ethical claims very similar to those of *Dependent Rational Animals,* while understanding them as having a quite different kind of import.

V

In "Goodness beyond Virtue," Raimond Gaita considers the work of "love, justice and pity" (all of which are combined in MacIntyre's "just generosity") in responding to those suffering "affliction so severe that they have irrecoverably lost everything that gives sense to our lives."[11] Like MacIntyre, Gaita attends to unconditionality as a standard internal to the practice of parental love. But this standard, he suggests, can come to have wider ethical salience—of the kind it has for MacIntyre—only if parental love is understood in intimate dialectic with another form of love, the impartial love of saints. This suggestion is related to Gaita's belief that "an ethics centred on the concept of human flourishing does not have the conceptual resources to keep fully among us . . . people who are severely and ineradicably afflicted" (19). Foreclosure on the possibility of flourishing on the part of such people tends to hide their common humanity; and so the peculiar quality of a saint's love is its "power to reveal the full humanity of those whose affliction had made their humanity invisible" (20). The important question then becomes: How is this love possible, and where does it find its source? Gaita's own answer to this question brings parental love back into the picture. "Children come to love their brothers and sisters," he writes, "because they see them in the light of their parents' love. Often we learn that something is precious only when we see it in the light of someone's love." Universalizing this sense of preciousness, so that even the direst disability (or indeed, for Gaita, great wickedness) does not place a person outside it, would depend then on the claim, embodied in the practices of a saint, that "God loves us, his children" (24).

Gaita is both impressed by the "simple power" of this religious way of speaking, "unashamedly anthropomorphic" though it may be, and mindful of its large role in the genealogy of Western moral sensibility. Perhaps unsurprisingly, however—given not only the deeply secularist turn of our scientific culture and liberal-democratic politics but also the terrible excesses of "religion" and what may seem its endemic divisiveness—he wants to affirm that the ethical reality it gestures to "can stand independently of explicit religious commitment and independently of speculation about supernatural entities. What grew and was nourished in one place . . . might take root and flourish elsewhere." But he is diffident about what is involved in—and perhaps even doubts the very possibility of—the transposition through which this independence is secured. He believes that it is "on credit from" a "language of love" "transformed [and] deepened" by the "love of saints" that we have built the "tractable structure of rights and obligations" characteristic of modern secular morality. The sublimation of this morality to the point where it can embrace those who are most disabled, afflicted, and marginalized depends then on a language that "goes dead on us" unless it is "nourished" by the living witness of saintly love. It is a crucial question, then, whether this love could survive "in the prolonged absence of the kind of practices that were part of [a] religious vocation"—whether, that is to say, "with the demise of religion, we can find objects of attention that can sustain that love, or whether they will always fail us." Gaita admits: "I don't know the answer."

A question very similar to Gaita's is raised by Charles Taylor in "Iris Murdoch and Moral Philosophy."[12] (Gaita's own formulation of the question, and the force that he gives to it, is heavily indebted to Murdoch's exploration of a region puzzlingly intermediate between ethics and religion, where "secular sanctity" or a "religion without theology" is made possible by the "sovereignty of the Good"—the capital "G" here not canceling the double "o.") Taylor suggests that Murdoch's work helped to release philosophical thought from the "corral of morality," leading out "to the broad fields of ethics," *and* "beyond that again to the almost untracked forests of the unconditional" (5). This is a movement beyond "the question of what we ought to do [corral] to that of what it is good to be [field], and then beyond that again, to what can command our fullest love [forest]." The field is the place of virtue and flourishing, and most modern moral philosophy, if not blind to it (when confined to the corral of duties, rights, and rules), understands it through the lens of a prior commitment to the primacy of life. Entry to the forest, on the other hand, involves "full-hearted love of some good beyond life," and Taylor well understands the secularist attitude (akin, he suggest to postrevolutionary vigilance) that opposes it as a threat to this hard-won primacy and to the "flourishing" it exclusively defines. "Forest-dwelling" involves a kind of "renunciation" that is a "radical decentering of the self" and that seems to be at loggerheads with flourishing just to the extent that "most conceptions of a flourishing life assume a stable identity, the self for whom flourishing can be defined" (21). Taylor contends, however, that there are religious traditions and spiritual practices in which renunciation leads away from flourishing only to lead back to a fuller and more powerful affirmation of it (these include ways of understanding the Buddhist teaching to which Murdoch was drawn and the Christian faith in which he himself shares, as well as the "very different paths" to which "people of great spiritual depth and dedication and, beyond this, people of holy lives, are drawn" [19]).

Taylor goes beyond this contention to argue, in the essay on Murdoch and in another somewhat later piece, "A Catholic Modernity?" (both of which develop a perspective already tentatively opened up in the final chapter of *Sources of the Self*), and most fully in his epic *A Secular Age,* that commitment to the "practical primacy" of life, so impressively manifested in humanitarian concern, is in fact jeopardized by the "metaphysical primacy" of life affirmed in exclusivist (i.e., forest-denying) articulations of the corral and of the field. Like Gaita—and, I am suggesting, MacIntyre in *Dependent Rational Animals*—Taylor calls attention to ethics at its limits, to what he sees as the "colossal extension of a Gospel ethic to a universal solidarity," in which people are asked "to stretch out so far . . . to the stranger outside the gates."[13] Like Gaita, too—though unlike MacIntyre in my reading of *Dependent Rational Animals*—he points to the demandingness and the cost of this concern, as well as its shadow side. It has to deal with "the immense disappointment of actual human performance, with the myriad ways in which real, concrete human beings fall short of, ignore, parody and betray . . . [their] potential" (32); and in the face of "all this stupid recalcitrance" and the "reality of human shortcomings," what can sustain it? All too easily, and in its religiously inspired as well as in its secular variants, it can be "invested with contempt, hatred, aggression," as in "a host of 'helping' institutions . . . from orphanages to boarding schools for aboriginals" (of major concern in Gaita's book). This is the "tragic turn, brilliantly foreseen by Dostoevsky"; but it is also, as Taylor recognizes, the "Janus face" ruthlessly unmasked by Nietzsche in his exposure of the *ressentiment* at the rotten core of much philanthropy. For Taylor it is a standing threat in the pursuit of all our highest ethical aspirations; and it can be averted only if our concern for others is ultimately an expression of a love whose unconditionality is sustained by a divine love in us.

I have been suggesting that while we meet with the same scale of ethical demand in these three writers, the anthropological backgrounds of this demand in Gaita and Taylor are quite different from what we find in *Dependent Rational Animals*. And there is a puzzle here. For in his two immediately preceding books, *Whose Justice? Which Rationality?* and *Three Rival Versions of Moral Enquiry*, MacIntyre had embraced the Thomist perspective that integrated Aristotelian insights into an Augustinian framework. That perspective is, I believe, more congruent with Gaita's and Taylor's approaches than with MacIntyre's own in *Dependent Rational Animals*— and this *despite* MacIntyre's indication in his preface to this book that reading a prayer of Aquinas had led him "to reflect upon how Aquinas's account of the virtues not only supplements, but also corrects Aristotle's to a significantly greater extent than I had realized" (xi). It seems to me that, on the contrary, Aquinas's "correction" of Aristotle is *more* evident in MacIntyre's two earlier works than in *Dependent Rational Animals*. In *Whose Justice? Which Rationality?* he had already written that "Aquinas does not merely supplement Aristotle but shows Aristotle's account . . . to be radically defective"—though this, as he put it, is not "so much a radical defectiveness in Aristotle's account as a radical defectiveness in that natural human order of which Aristotle gave his account" (205). It is Augustine of course, mainly through his novel conception of the will as a motivating agency distinct both from intellect and from the appetites of the nonrational part of the soul, who had brought this defectiveness to the fore both for Aquinas and for MacIntyre himself in *Whose Justice? Which Rationality?* and *Three Rival Versions of Moral Enquiry*. And perhaps the most remarkable feature of *Dependent Rational Animals* is precisely *Augustine's absence from it* (in contrast with his unmistakable, if implicit, presence in Taylor's words cited above).

I have already shown how MacIntyre construes "just generosity" in this book as the product of a moral education that redirects the passions and desires. In *Whose Justice? Which Rationality?*, however, the "direction and ordering of human desires is the work of the will" (154); and the will is itself "systematically . . . misdirected in such a way that it is not within its own power to redirect itself" (156). Its condition of misdirectedness, then, remains "ineradicable by even the best moral education in accordance with reason" (181); and so it "is only divine grace which can rescue . . . [it] from that condition" (which is one of being misdirected "to the love of self rather than of God" [156–57]). This Augustinian position was also Aquinas's in *Whose Justice? Which Rationality?* But a quite different position seems to be attributed to him in *Dependent Rational Animals* when it is claimed that his notion of *"misericordia"* (which, as we saw, MacIntyre invokes in developing his own account of "just generosity") "has its place in the catalogue of virtues, independently of its theological grounding" (124). MacIntyre makes this claim because *misericordia* "is recognisably at work in the secular world and the authorities whom Aquinas cites on its nature, and whose disagreements he aspires to resolve, include Sallust and Cicero as well as Augustine" (124). But the fact of its being "at work in the secular world" is hardly the issue; the question, rather, is from what source it is empowered to perform its works of charity in that world.

Moreover, that Cicero and Augustine take very different views of the depth and range of such charity—and that Aquinas follows Augustine and not Cicero on this—is very clear from MacIntyre's own reading of all three of them in *Whose Justice? Which Rationality?* Although the characteristically Stoic universalizing of the range of *caritas* is indeed to be found in Cicero, MacIntyre goes to some lengths in that book to show how nugatory is our debt to "someone to whom we owe whatever we owe merely as a fellow member of the human race"—so that the "word 'caritas' may . . . mislead us if . . . we project into its Ciceronian use a Christian meaning" (148). The kind of community presupposed by Augustine's concept of justice, then, "is very different indeed from that presupposed by Cicero," and its "universality requires far more than had Stoic universality, particularly in relation to the poor and oppressed, so much more indeed that its requirements have from time to time been discovered to have yet further and more radical application throughout the subsequent history of the church" (153).

It is, I believe, a quite "radical application" and transposition of these "requirements" that we meet in *Dependent Rational Animals*. But the puzzling feature of this book, to which I have been trying to draw attention by reference to Gaita, Taylor, and MacIntyre's own two books between *After Virtue* and *Dependent Rational Animals* (and indeed to Levinas), is the fact of its not taking the full measure of the ethical requirements it proposes—or, more particularly, of the kind of capability we would need to really meet them. Perhaps my final statement of this difficulty can be put in MacIntyre's own words. In *Whose Justice? Which Rationality?* he wrote: "The highest type of human being, according to Aristotle, is the magnanimous man. The highest type of human being on any Christian view, including Augustine's, is the saint." The puzzle about *Dependent Rational Animals* is that, in raising the ethical stakes so high, it discards the magnanimous man while at the same time finding no need to introduce the saint.[14]

VI

The conditions of human life leave us vulnerable; and ethics as construed in *Dependent Rational Animals* takes shape as an essential component of any attempt to remedy this vulnerability.[15] The vulnerability is rooted in our nature as animals but also in our unavoidable dependence on other human beings who, by oppression or neglect, may inflict damage on us or withhold what is necessary for our flourishing. The remedy that ethics provides, then, seeks to ensure that those on whom we depend are dependable, that they are disposed to respond caringly and resourcefully to our neediness, as we are to theirs. I have been reading Gaita and Taylor, however, and MacIntyre himself in other writing, as arguing for a depth of human vulnerability that affects our very capability for ethical responsiveness; there is as it were an ethical vulnerability that leaves us devoid of the full resources we would need for the kind of response to human suffering and affliction evinced in *Dependent Rational Animals*. If there is any further remedy, then, for *this* vulnerability, it consists, the argument would proceed to claim, in opening ourselves to a different and deeper dependence—on an Other who can empower us beyond our own natural resources. Such opening (in which prayer would have an irreplaceable role) would allow for the possibility of a radical self-transformation[16]—more radical than that envisaged in Aristotle's moral psychology just to the extent that the passions and impulses, and above all the *desire,* that must somehow find expression in our way of living are a great deal more complex and fraught than they appear in that psychology. (To borrow a Taylorian locution with strong resonance both in *A Secular Age* and in this present discussion, they are "metabiological.")[17]

We are faced here, of course, with large and contestable issues about the nature of secularization, as well as with complex issues about the relation between "grace" and "nature" within the specifically Christian tradition that Aquinas brought to such a high point of articulation (and it must always be remembered—this being the point of his Aristotelianism—that for him nature "requires to be corrected in order to be completed but not displaced").[18] We are faced, too, with issues about the boundary between the proper jurisdictions of philosophy and theology or, more particularly, about how this boundary may be understood with different degrees of strictness by different thinkers who, while open to a horizon of faith, ply their trade as philosophers. And in the judgment of many readers, a particular merit of *Dependent Rational Animals* may be precisely the fact that it is *not* embroiled in issues such as these—not least, perhaps, because, for these readers, they raise no genuine or relevant questions.

I cannot conclude, however, without the acknowledgment—which must seem ironic in the context of this whole chapter—that the viewpoint from which this judgment is delivered, and which manifestly is not Gaita's or Taylor's or indeed my own, is not Alasdair MacIntyre's either. And that this is no less the case of his writing *after* than before *Dependent Rational Animals* is perhaps sufficiently clear from what he writes at the end of his most recent book: "Augustine is always there to remind us how finitude and sinfulness issue in the fragility of all our projects."[19] It is altogether congruent with the generous and inspiring claims of *Dependent Rational Animals,* however, that the note which he immediately strikes after this allusion to Augustine's postlapsarian vision is one not of pessimism but of hope. Moreover, this is an insistent note in much of his recent writing. "Any account of how human life is to be lived or of how crises in human life are to be confronted," he writes in a very recent paper, is "incomplete unless and until [its] author [has] reckoned with the place of hope in our lives." Hope, as he avows, is a theological virtue, one that "allows us to be fully aware of what we would be rationally justified in expecting and yet to hope for far more than that." Education being my chief concern philosophically, I end with and embrace words of his from another very recent paper that bring together hope and our capacity to learn: "St. Paul and St. Thomas Aquinas tell us how there is always more to be hoped for in any and every situation than the empirical facts seem to show. It is insofar as we are able to find through the virtues a mode of social life in which practical rationality is informed by shared hope that we will know that we have begun to learn what we need to learn."[20]

Notes

This chapter draws on my review essay on *Dependent Rational Animals*, "Ethics Revised: Flourishing as Vulnerable and Dependent," *International Journal of Philosophical Studies* 10, no. 3 (2002): 339–63, and I am indebted to the editor for permission to use material from it here.

    1. Iris Murdoch, "On 'God' and 'Good,'" in *Revisions: Changing Perspectives in Moral Philosophy*, ed. Stanley Hauerwas and Alasdair MacIntyre (Notre Dame: University of Notre Dame Press, 1983), 63.

    2. Alasdair MacIntyre, "Aquinas's Critique of Education: Against His Own Age, against Ours," in *Philosophers on Education: New Historical Perspectives,* ed. Amelie Oksenberg Rorty (London: Routledge, 1998), 107.

    3. Alasdair MacIntyre, *After Virtue: A Study in Moral Theory* (Notre Dame: University of Notre Dame Press, 1981), 4. Subsequent page citations to this work are given parenthetically in the text.

    4. Alasdair MacIntyre, *Whose Justice? Which Rationality?* (London: Duckworth, 1988), 332, 357; Alasdair MacIntyre, *Dependent Rational Animals: Why Human Beings Need the Virtues* (Chicago: Open Court, 1999), xii, 18. Subsequent page citations to both these works are given parenthetically in the text.

    5. Here I shall be dealing with an aspect of this book that involves considerations quite different from the epistemological ones to which I have adverted above.

    6. See especially Alasdair MacIntyre, *The Unconscious: A Conceptual Analysis* (London: Routledge and Kegan Paul, 1958; rev. ed., Routledge, 2004).

    7. MacIntyre has not, to my knowledge, written about Levinas. But he briefly adverts to the striking affinities between Levinas's thought and that of the Danish philosopher-theologian Knud Ejler Løgstrup in his very sympathetic introduction, coauthored with Hans Fink, to an English translation of Løgsrup's *The Ethical Demand* (Notre Dame: University of Notre Dame Press, 1997). Although Løgsrup is nowhere mentioned in *Dependent Rational Animals*, one may wonder whether his influence is not present in it.

    8. Reason is stretched here in dealing with what is precisely beyond reason in that it either happens to me contingently (as in an accident at birth) or is imposed by a necessity of nature (as in the growing infirmity of old age); MacIntyre explicitly excludes from the circle of what obligates to responsive giving misfor-

tunes that result from a person's own deliberate wrongdoing (128, though for possible qualification here, see 124). It would be interesting to clarify, as I cannot do here, why there are deep differences, in determining an acceptable basis for justice, between a MacIntyrean saying "This could have been me" and a Rawlsian surveying (from behind the veil of ignorance) all the possible positions she might occupy as a result of the "natural lottery." (Apparent convergence here might seem to be reinforced by the fact that whereas in his chapter on justice in *After Virtue* MacIntyre sharply distinguishes his own "desert"-based conception from Rawls's "needs"-based conception of justice, in *Dependent Rational Animals* need seems to have superseded—though not indeed replaced—desert as the decisive consideration for a just sociopolitical order.)

9. Some qualification, it should be said, was already present in *After Virtue*. For he had acknowledged there that the particularity of one's historical identity (as "someone's son or daughter, someone else's cousin or uncle . . . a citizen of this or that city, a member of this or that guild or profession") does not imply that "the self has to accept the moral limitations" of this identity, and he had insisted that "it is in moving forward from such particularity that the search for the good, the universal, consists" (204–5).

10. The phrase is Charles Taylor's; see his essay with this title in *Utilitarianism and Beyond,* ed. Amartya Sen and Bernard Williams (Cambridge: Cambridge University Press, 1982), 129–44.

11. Raimond Gaita, *A Common Humanity: Thinking about Love and Truth and Justice* (London: Routledge, 2000), xix. Subsequent page citations to this work are given parenthetically in the text.

12. Charles Taylor, "Iris Murdoch and Moral Philosophy," in *Iris Murdoch and the Search for Human Goodness,* ed. Maria Antonaccio and William Schweiker (Chicago: University of Chicago Press, 1996), 3–28, repr. in Charles Taylor, *Dilemmas and Connections: Selected Essays* (Cambridge MA: Harvard University Press, 2011), 3–23. Subsequent page citations to this work are to the 1996 edition and are given parenthetically in the text.

13. Charles Taylor, "A Catholic Modernity?," in *A Catholic Modernity? Charles Taylor's Marianist Award Lecture,* ed. James L. Heft (Oxford: Oxford University Press, 1999), 30. Subsequent page citations to this work are given parenthetically in the text.

14. MacIntyre has rejected the elitism, inherited from Plato, that Aristotle explicitly espouses in the *Nicomachean Ethics* (e.g., at X, 9, 1179b7 ff.): "Aristotle's rough and ready equation of the distinction between 'the good' and the others with the distinction between 'the few' and 'the many' can and should be excised from any Aristotelianism with a claim to our rational allegiance" ("Preface to the Revised Edition," in *The Unconscious: A Conceptual Analysis* [London: Routledge, 2004], 36). This rejection may seem to be in marked contrast with Taylor's recent, decidedly Augustinian, articulation of a "spiritual register" in which, as he writes, "the 'normal,' everyday, beginning situation of the soul is to be partly

in the grip of evil. Something heroic or exceptional is required to get beyond this; most of us are in the middle range, where we're struggling.... If we see our impotences, incapacities, divisions, as the fruit of sin, evil, moral inadequacy [as, in Taylor's view, we should], we will expect to find them in virtually all human beings; we will expect them to be overcome in rare cases only at the ultimate pinnacle of sanctity" (Charles Taylor, *A Secular Age* [Cambridge, MA: Harvard University Press, 2007], 619, 623). However, the impression created by *Dependent Rational Animals* apart, there seems no good reason to suppose that MacIntyre would disagree with Taylor here.

15. While *Dependent Rational Animals* offers penetrating discussion of the capabilities and required conditions for flourishing of dolphins and other animals, it does so only to clarify issues of *human* animality. Curiously, it is a book on ethics that gives an important place to animals—while giving no attention to ethical issues concerning humans' treatment of nonhuman animals (or indeed of the "environment"). Such "anthropocentrism" has of course been heavily criticized in much recent moral philosophy.

16. Whether prayer is a genuine possibility for us is a key concern in Gaita's discussion already alluded to. And in a complexly nuanced critique of the "therapeutic turn" in recent culture, Taylor refers to prayer as a medium for "working through" our deeply ambiguous embroilment in evil—ambiguous because it implies a dignity that is absent from a sin-blind psychotherapy aimed simply at restoring a conflict-free normalcy. Prayer then can open one to a transformation radical enough to count as "conversion"; for a Christian—and there are strong affinities in Buddhism—this entails coming to terms with the fact that "God has given a new transformative meaning to suffering" and that "following him will dislocate and transform beyond recognition the forms which have made life tolerable for us" (see Taylor, *Secular Age*, 618 ff.; quotations from 656 and 655). In a more sympathetic discussion of psychoanalysis, MacIntyre links Freud's insights into "the transformation of desire" and "the complex connections between desire and knowledge" with those of Augustine. (See "Preface to the Revised Edition," in MacIntyre, *Unconscious*, 1–38). And, worked from the other side, this link recurs in a later discussion of Augustine (published a decade *after Dependent Rational Animals*). Having pointed out that for Augustine "[it] is only insofar as we make God the object of our desire, acknowledging that to desire otherwise is to desire against our nature, that our desires in general become rightly ordered and that we are rescued from the self-protection informed by pride," he immediately adds: "The present-day reader cannot but be reminded of Freud." He goes on to draw an intriguing parallel between the practices of prayer and of psychoanalysis: "For both [Augustine and Freud] there is someone before whom and to whom one talks, so that in the end one's prevarications and concealments and self-justifications are heard as what they are and the truth about oneself, including the truth about one's resistance to acknowledging that truth, is acknowledged. In both cases the talking involves a discipline, in the one case that of prayer, in the other that of psycho-

analysis" ("Augustine," ch. 5 of *God, Philosophy, Universities: A Selective History of the Catholic Philosophical Tradition* [Lanham, MD: Rowman and Littlefield, 2009], 28, 29). I should add here that, characteristically for MacIntyre, prayer is not only a matter of interior dialogue with God; for "productive work" can be "thought of as a kind of prayer and performed as an act of prayer"—though this is a truth all too likely to be obscured in a fragmented culture that consigns prayer to "'religion,' religion conceived of as no more than one more compartmentalised area of activity" (Alasdair MacIntyre, "Where We Were, Where We Are, Where We Need to Be," in *Virtue and Politics: Alasdair MacIntyre's Revolutionary Aristotelianism*, ed. Paul Blackledge and Kelvin Knight [Notre Dame: University of Notre Dame Press, 2011], 323).

17. Calling these passions and impulses "metabiological" arises in the context of Taylor's argument that they are not just determined by body chemistry or "set in the biological concrete of our DNA" (*Secular Age*, 674) but rather are always imbued with meaning and hence embedded in the specific cultural matrices within which meaning arises. Inextricably, then, they are caught up in our being and vision as well as our desire (though "as well as" misleads here); and it is the passions themselves and not only our attempts to control or sublimate them that are to be thus characterized. This is especially the case of the aggressive and sexual impulses, which are potentially the most disruptive and destructive. As Taylor notes, these not only were invested with numinosity in preaxial religions (e.g., in temple prostitution or ritualized warfare) but are still affirmatively charged in the philosophy of what he calls the "immanent counter-Enlightenment" (e.g., in Schopenhauer, Nietzsche, Jünger, Bataille, and Foucault) and the various kinds of "transgression" that it licenses and celebrates. While Taylor does not endorse this positive valuation, he sees it as acknowledging a truth often denied in the civilizing morality of modern liberal humanism: the truth, that is to say, of how deeply these impulses define our specifically human mode of being, how refractory they are to "normalization"—whether through coercion, therapy, or reductive programs of reeducation—and how threatening they are to this humanism's commitments to very high standards of justice and benevolence (commitments that Taylor himself fully shares). What I am pointing out here in the text is that they are no less threatening to the worthy conception of ethical formation and virtuous living bequeathed by Aristotle—and that they may therefore require the kind of radical, spiritual/religious transformation that Taylor sketches in *A Secular Age* (especially in ch. 17, "Dilemmas 1"). Such transformation may also be required, I may add, if credence is given to other "metabiological" accounts that see human desire chained within cycles of futility—such as Jacques Lacan's psychoanalytical postulation of the "real" as that which is most yearned for while at the same time being most unavailable, or in Rene Girard's "mimetic theory," which construes all desire as mediated by the desire of the "other" (who is one's "model"). As mimetic, desire is also "metaphysical" in the sense that it seeks not the putative object but rather, beyond (*meta*) that, the recognition, prestige, or "identity" that comes through relationship

with the other—even while this relationship locks one into rivalry with and potential violence toward the other *and* renders illusory one's sense of oneself as a substantial source of desire and initiative. Girard's theory would, among other effects, undercut any basis for distinguishing, as MacIntyre does in *After Virtue*, internal and external goods of a practice (all goods being reduced to the rewards of social status); but perhaps the importance of maintaining just such a distinction constitutes one of the strongest reasons for resisting or at least modifying Girard's undeniably powerful theory—which, incidentally, Taylor frequently invokes in attempting to explain the roots of violence.

18. Alasdair MacIntyre, *Three Rival Versions of Moral Enquiry* (Notre Dame: University of Notre Dame Press, 1990), 140.

19. MacIntyre, *God, Philosophy, Universities*, 180.

20. These quotations on hope are from MacInytre, "Where We Were," 334, 333, and "How Aristotelianism Can Become Revolutionary," 19, in Blackledge and Knight, *Virtue and Politics*.

CHAPTER FOUR

Alasdair MacIntyre's Revisionary Aristotelianism
Pragmatism Opposed, Marxism Outmoded, Thomism Transformed

KELVIN KNIGHT

This essay argues for the significance of Alasdair MacIntyre's revisions to the tradition of Thomistic Aristotelianism. After contextualizing MacIntyre's philosophical development within Aristotelianism's recent history, it summarizes his account of the moral importance of a teleological conception of goods, identifying a problem for past Aristotelian accounts of extant social order. It then looks more closely at teleology, and especially at Hegel's identification of good with a singular rationality and actuality of historical progress and social order. MacIntyre's pluralist account of practices and institutions is explored in the fourth section of the essay, where it is contrasted with Robert Brandom's recasting of Hegelian claims in linguistic and pragmatist form. I argue that the teleology involved in MacIntyre's account of practices is free from the errors of any such Hegelian holism. The next section argues that MacIntyre's account of institutionalized causes of demoralization transforms Thomistic Aristotelianism into a radical mode of social critique, challenging theoretical justifications of the ethical life of contemporary capitalism. This critique is normatively teleological, not in the modern sense that attributes a goal to history and a functionality to society that is independent of actors' purposes but rather in an Aristotelian sense, making explicit the goal directedness of actors' practical reasoning and allowing that virtuous action constitutes the human good. The error from which MacIntyre thereby saves Aristotelianism is that of identifying the common good with the dominant institutions of contemporary social order.

Aristotelianisms

From *After Virtue* onward, Alasdair MacIntyre's work has advanced a new and compelling account of what Aristotelianism is and ought to be. Previously, Aristotelianism was spoken of in at least four different ways. First, the term was used in the sense given to it by Coleridge and Goethe, to signify an empiricism opposed to Platonic metaphysics. Contrastingly, it referred to Aristotle's *development* of Platonic metaphysics and ethics, and to the profound and pervasive influence of this comprehensive philosophy upon people's way of thinking, both past and present. This second usage was that of both J. L. Stocks and Martin Heidegger. Stocks thought that Aristotelianism might be superseded, but only on the basis of the intellectual progress of which it constitutes an ineliminable part. Much more radically, Heidegger regarded what had come to be understood as Aristotelianism as a metaphysical system that could be rethought and, thereby, replaced. Whereas Stocks sought only to identify "the limits of purpose," Heidegger wished to deconstruct traditional ways of thinking of human existence and action as means to a final end.

Whereas Heidegger and Stocks identified Aristotelianism with *the* Western tradition, a third usage juxtaposed Aristotelianism to other currents in Western thought. In this sense, Aristotelianism provided a warrant for resisting alike liberal empiricism, Marxist materialism, and Nietzschean perspectivism. Such an understanding of Aristotelianism was developed by Luigi Taparelli d'Azeglio and Vincenzo Gioacchino Pecci (Pope Leo XIII), by Étienne Gilson and Jacques Maritain, by Vincent McNabb and Herbert McCabe, and by many other Catholic philosophers. For them, Aristotle's greatest follower was St. Thomas Aquinas. The metaphysics of substances and attributes, actuality and potentiality, questioned by Stocks and rejected by Heidegger, was presented by these Thomistic Aristotelians as the basis of the one perennially true philosophy, according to which human action is ultimately directed to the goodness of God.

Finally, *Aristotelianism*—or *neo-Aristotelianism*—was used by a number of post-Heideggerian thinkers from the 1960s onward to denote a specifically "practical" kind of philosophy. Their common project was, in the famous phrase of Manfred Riedel, "the rehabilitation of practical philosophy." Joachim Ritter and others took from Aristotle's *Ethics* their understanding of *praxis* or action in terms of *ethos* and understood *ethos* as both personal habituation and cultural tradition. Accordingly, ethics was grounded in human temporality and sociality, and therefore in obvious (even if occasionally contested) contrast with the "pure practical reason" of Kantian "critical" philosophy. Indeed, in the texts of its most famous expositor, Hans-Georg Gadamer, this neo-Aristotelian practical philosophy is divorced entirely even from Aristotle's own theoretical philosophy. Whereas the earlier understandings of Aristotelianism took Aristotle's corpus as a whole, these interpreters neglected or dismissed his metaphysical naturalism and realism in conceptualizing *praxis* as entirely distinct from both abstract theorization and material production.

MacIntyre's own understanding of Aristotelianism has been influenced by all but the first of these usages. Biographically, his earliest encounters with Aristotle were as a part of classical Greek culture. He soon learned, from followers of McNabb, that a special significance was attached to Aristotelianism by Thomists, but he could not yet accept the philosophical force of their claims for Aquinas's reconciliation of Aristotelianism with Augustine's Christian and neo-Platonic theology. His own understanding of Aristotle was therefore closest to that of Heidegger, whose stance toward Aristotelianism he understood to be informed by Thomist claims for the singularity of "*the* tradition." Despite this skepticism, MacIntyre was, after thinking through philosophical alternatives, persuaded by Gadamer that there remained something uniquely valuable in Aristotle's ethics. Initially, he concurred with Gadamer's disavowal of Aristotelianism's traditionally foundationalist "metaphysical biology." Subsequently, in thinking through the logic of final ends in Aristotelian practical philosophy, he dug down through hermeneutics to metaphysical first principles.

Although MacIntyre's understanding of Aristotelianism has been influenced by three different accounts of it, he now describes his position as a specifically *Thomistic* Aristotelianism. That a philosopher who has engaged so intimately, incisively, and famously with many of Thomism's philosophical rivals should finally turn to it has delighted most of those theorists who have been brought up in it as if it were a philosophical faith, while repelling the Heideggerians, Marxists, and others who were so attracted to those earlier works in which he had written in their terms. From each of these perspectives, he is normally portrayed as having simply shifted between preexisting philosophical positions without effecting any important philosophical advance. In contrast, this essay is premised upon an acknowledgment that he developed his philosophy by thinking through what he has since identified as rival paradigms.

Traditional Truths and Aristotelian Absences

MacIntyre's identification with Aristotelianism in *After Virtue: A Study in Moral Theory* shared Gadamer's focus upon and his eschewal of the traditional metaphysics and naturalism of Aristotelianism but differed in its embrace of the tradition's morality of the virtues. His achievement in leading the revival of virtue ethics arose from his lifelong concern with moral psychology, the philosophy of action, and the mutual intelligibility of moral actors. His book's argument advanced in two stages. First, it deconstructed "the Enlightenment project" in moral theory, alleging that the historical fragmentation of Aristotelianism's conceptual scheme had rendered morality incoherent. Second, it reconstructed the "teleological" form of "the core concept of virtue," according to which virtues are motivated and justified as the "constitutive means" by which to actualize the human good.

After Virtue's bipartite structure of deconstruction and reconstruction approximates to the sequence of moves in which Heidegger was followed by Gadamer.[1] However, whereas they sought to uncover a primordially Greek understanding of such ideas as "the good" *(agathon)* from beneath historical strata of metaphysical and naturalistic theory, and whereas MacIntyre had been similarly concerned with "the prephilosophical history of 'good' and the transition to philosophy" in his earlier *A Short History of Ethics,* in *After Virtue* he simply declares ethical motivation to be "teleological."[2] As an argument in the history of ethics, its message is (in the words of the title of its fifth chapter) that, in rejecting teleology, "the Enlightenment project of justifying morality had to fail."

The teleology that MacIntyre reconstructs in *After Virtue* is a teleology of the human good. It conceptualizes how humans can move over time from their initial condition to become how they ought, naturally, to be.[3] The vital importance of the virtues, as excellences of character, is that they are *the* constitutive means in actualizing this good life for a human being. Much of what was most innovative in the book appeared to derive from its positing of a need for a conception of a human *telos* without stipulating any definitive content of that end or completed good. This position appeared perplexing, as Aristotle had accorded priority to being over becoming and had identified the good life for human beings with—as MacIntyre had put it in *A Short History*—the life of an "Athenian gentleman." Perplexity was deepened by the book's avoidance of normative moral theorizing; instead, it contrasted Aristotle's account of the virtues with the accounts of disparate others—Homer, Hume, Austen, Aquinas, Franklin, the New Testament—and with other cultures. Against this diversity, he proposed what he specified (in chapters 14 and 15) as the three elements of "the core concept of virtue": "tradition," lives narratively unified as "quests," and, most basically, "practices."

The structure of *each* of the three ideas that constitute MacIntyre's core concept of virtue is, he proposes, teleological, and his rejection of "modern moral philosophy" is therefore intended as a rejection of *its* rejection of Aristotelian teleology. Deontology and consequentialism each express a necessary aspect of an adequate morality, but they are each insufficient and incompatible with the other unless and until they are reintegrated into a conceptual scheme with a teleological scheme. MacIntyre's task was to establish morality's need of such a scheme.

The logical relation between the three elements of *After Virtue*'s "core concept" is itself intended to be teleological. Human beings are educated into the virtues though participation in social practices, each of which is structured in pursuit of what MacIntyre calls "goods internal to a practice." As we will see later in this essay, this first-order idea of "practices" entails that the good life for human beings is a life that can be actualized in many different ways. Nonetheless, pursuit of the good internal to any one practice is necessarily insufficient for the good life. Therefore, to actualize the human good, individuals must integrate their understanding of various such goods into a unified narrative of their quest for their personal good, as a human being. Finally, reflection on such ordered pursuit of their own good should lead, philosophically, to an appreciation of how their and others' personal practice is made fully intelligible by what MacIntyre calls the "classical" or Aristotelian "tradition of the virtues." This, MacIntyre says, was his own experience in discovering that he "had been—without knowing it—an Aristotelian," and he has often claimed that this should be the experience of almost anyone who asks "what it is to which we are already committed by our everyday life and our everyday judgements."[4]

MacIntyre's core claim about Aristotelianism in *After Virtue* was that it is the philosophical tradition that articulates humans' practical reasoning about goods and about the human good, wherein to identify something as a good is to give a reason for action. Aristotelian teleology is therefore the philosophical expression of ordinary, purposive reason and action. To this, he has since added three further crucial claims about Aristotelianism as a tradition.

The first of these supplemental claims was first made in *Whose Justice? Which Rationality?* It repeats the conventional Thomist claim that Aquinas effected a genuine philosophical synthesis of Aristotelian metaphysics with Augustinian monotheism, although MacIntyre focuses on the rational justification of action and on the account of practical reasoning that Aquinas drew from that synthesis. This account is, he proposes, rationally superior to the accounts of each of those two prior traditions, and its rational superiority is philosophical, not theological, so that, "if the requirements of practical reason are rightly understood, then practical rationality provides everything that is required for the moral life, independently of any theological ethics."[5]

The second claim is that this theoretical tradition is "the best theory so far about what makes a particular theory the best one,"[6] because it rationally justifies itself by reference to truth as the *telos* of its inquiries. On this account, Thomistic Aristotelianism is no *philosophia perennis* passing on already known and indubitable truths but only, so far as we can know, the best theory of reality so far. To understand Thomism as a tradition of *inquiry* is to understand it in terms of questions—as exemplified by Aquinas's own method of *quaestio*—rather than of any apodictic answers. To understand Thomism as a *tradition* of inquiry is to understand it as a quest. So long as it remains "in good order"—which means that it remains oriented toward truth, and therefore open to the possible falsification or improvability of its claims—Thomism may be understood as progressing toward a more adequate identification with the objects of its inquiry, by critically scrutinizing past arguments and by building upon them insofar as they continue to be sustainable. Any view of reality is a view from somewhere, but a view that is self-consciously informed by an ongoing tradition of previous views, inquiries, and arguments—as in Aristotle's references to *endoxa,* and in Aquinas's confrontation of Aristotle with other authorities— is a view from a vantage point that has already been defined, extended, and successfully defended. "Philosophy is a form of enquiry that is directed toward the discovery and formulation of timeless truths . . . but such discovery always provokes new questions, so that philosophy perennially has to renew itself, in part by revisiting its history."[7] This, on MacIntyre's account, is what is required for Thomistic Aristotelianism to be what it ought to be: a reflexively self-conscious tradition of inquiry, as concerned with questioning its own heritage as was Aquinas himself. Here he concurs with a genealogical critique of Thomism's flight from Aquinas's own appreciation that "the truth is not a possession but a task."[8] This is one way in which MacIntyre's Thomism is revisionary.

That these first two supplemental claims are interrelated is indicated by Heidegger, as it is by Richard Rorty's complaint that the idea of truth as "the goal of scientific inquiry" is a part of "the common sense of [our] community, a common sense much influenced by Greek metaphysics and by monotheism."[9] The "kind of respect for truth" that MacIntyre commends to Thomists and attributes to their tradition is the same kind "that natural scientists endorse," and philosophical traditions are therefore similar to traditions and practices of scientific inquiry. Dogmatism is no model, as is demonstrated in the history of science by the sorry story of early modern impetus theory.[10] Here Enlightenment theory was right and Aristotelianism wrong. Nonetheless, what we now know to be an error about projectiles entails no error in Aristotelian accounts of ethics, or of metaphysics, or of tradition.

The third major way in which MacIntyre has added to *After Virtue*'s account of Aristotelianism as *a* tradition is in clarifying that it is not *the* tradition but *one* version of moral inquiry, in confrontation with rival traditions. In *Whose Justice? Which Rationality?* he discusses how Athens was "put to the question" after "the division of the post-Homeric inheritance" between two rival traditions. One tradition continued to equate personal excellence with causal effectiveness in achieving one's ends, whatever those ends might be (in a way symbolized for some by Homer's Odysseus). Politically, it promotes the "cooperative effectiveness" of individuals under the rule of law. This tradition, MacIntyre suggests, continues in contemporary liberalism. The rival tradition, begun by Socrates, went further in asking for the rational justification of ends and in postulating the human good as a final end, and this as the standard of moral excellence.

In identifying rival philosophical traditions, MacIntyre's conception of tradition broke decisively from that of Heidegger and Gadamer. For them, tradition is identical with culture and language. On MacIntyre's account, traditions of inquiry and practice may be "embedded in . . . social tradition," but "the criteria for the identity of practices are in important respects transcultural," so that practices may "acquire a certain real, if limited, independence of their own social and cultural order."[11] This is, indeed, the case with the practice of philosophy, and "the emergence of moral philosophy in a culture . . . is a mark of that culture having reached a point at which it can become self-critical."[12]

The emergence of moral philosophy in Athens demonstrated that its culture had become self-critical, as is evident from the way in which Socrates' practice of *philosophia* brought him into conflict with the *polis*. To measure temporal actions and institutions against ideals of atemporal perfection is to find them lacking, and Aristotelianism has traditionally judged what exists by reference to timeless standards. This is the case with Aquinas's accounts of both natural law and evil. Evil "has no independent existence" but "is the absence of a good that ought to be present," "a failure to be."[13] From Socrates onward, the ideal or completed good is the standard of what ought to be.

Aristotle attributed a specific good to each kind of living being and, therefore, to each individual of that natural kind. If over time an individual actualizes that good, then it has completed its specific nature and form. This specific *telos* is postulated as the internal cause of that being's activity. Plants cannot flourish in the way that animals flourish because they lack the motive and perceptual capacities that animals possess, and nonhuman animals cannot excel as humans can because they lack human *nous* and *logos*. Its actualization of its specific good requires any individual being to possess all the internal capacities of its kind. Additionally, such actualization requires that individual to have a sufficiency of external goods, such as food. Therefore, an individual's failure to actualize its specific good could be explained by reference to a lack either of internal capacities or of external conditions.

The coming-to-be of artifacts provided the analogical paradigm for Aristotle's ideas of completion, potentiality, and actualization. Artifacts lack any animating dynamic or *telos*. When engaged in *praxis,* human beings actualize their potential, whereas in production they function not for their own sake but for the sake of the product. The excellence of excellent production inheres in the product and not in its human producer, in contrast with both intellectual and ethical excellence, which are qualities internal to human beings. Indeed, for Aristotle productive activity cultivates not habits of personal excellence but habits of servility. Production does not actualize human potentialities; to the contrary, it alienates humans from their characteristically human powers.

Aristotle's famous conjecture in the *Politics* (1253b33–1254a1) that, were machines able to automatically weave clothes or play music, then "master-craftsmen would have no need of assistants nor masters of slaves" has been interpreted as an acknowledgment that slavery is explicable by reference to factors external to the slave. However, Aristotle had no theory of social causality by which to elaborate such an explanation. Instead, he explained the subordinate position of those he called "natural slaves" by reference to their individual incapacity to lead any more fulfilling life. An individual's enslavement might be attributable to chance, but wholesale subordination must be due to nature. As with akratics, who lack rational self-control, the failure of most slaves—and of women, workers, and barbarians—to actualize human excellence is attributed to a lack of intellectual capacity. Aristotle himself lacked any other way of explaining such failure. This has been a failing of Aristotelianism.

Aristotle's theory of action was political, not social, in that it posited a single good at which human community should aim. Politics was the "architectonic" practice of ordering other, lesser activities to that highest human good, and a community of citizens *(politai)* was a human community that was rationally ordered to such a good. The citizens of Greek *poleis* (and, also, of Carthage) supposedly lived in such communities. For Aristotle this fact was of fundamental importance, and its importance was not diminished by the fact that the status of *politēs* was enjoyed by neither the members of tribal communities nor the subjects of civilized empires, nor yet Greek women, slaves, or workers. None could be participants in politics; all were excluded from political community.

The postulate of a final, "political" good provided the premise for Aristotle's *Politics,* for his analyses of the constitution of many individual *poleis,* and, indeed, for his *Nicomachean Ethics.* The content of that final end remained vague, primarily because it was to be determined by the reasoning and activity of those who constituted the community. This rational action was institutionalized in the structure—the *eunomia* or good order—of the *polis.* Later, Aristotle's political hypothesis was applied to their own societies by his medieval and modern followers. Such application was often justified by analogy with a biological organism, whereby a monarch was described as the "head" that directed different functional parts for their common good. Disdainful of merely human reason, philosophers imputed good order to society by reference to divine providence. In this way, "politics" could be attributed to an order in which power was institutionalized quite apart from its putative members' potentialities, purposes, reasoning, or actions.

Such an uncritical extension of "teleology" to institutionalized orders has led many philosophers, including many Thomists, to identify sovereign states with a common good. On this view, it is the task of philosophers to illuminate the rational purposiveness supposedly actualized in modern institutions.[14] If such rationality is hidden from those in whose actions it is supposedly expressed, this may be cited as proof of the specifically philosophical nature of the task. If this claim has been true of Thomists, it has, as we shall see, been articulated still more elaborately by others.

Teleology, Society, Ideology

Teleology is a modern amalgam, compounded by Christian Wolff from *telos* and *logos.* In a sense, far from having been rejected by the Enlightenment, teleology is an Enlightenment invention. What does this entail for MacIntyre's critique of the Enlightenment? Although it shows that the conceptual history recounted in *After Virtue* (as in the earlier *A Short History of Ethics* and the later *Whose Justice? Which Rationality?*) was less genealogical and philological than were Heidegger's excavations, it does not invalidate what I have called the book's first, deconstructive argument.

This argument is that the Enlightenment project in moral theory discarded the idea of a human *telos*—that is, of a good specific to persons qua human beings—as the justification of moral precepts, and this remains true of the logic of contractarian, Kantian, and utilitarian justifications alike. In this sense, it is entirely valid to describe Aristotelian virtue ethics as teleological in a way that the main Enlightenment theories were not (and to describe the latter as expressing fragmentary truths rendered incoherent by dismissal of the former teleological scheme). Matters are not so straightforward with *After Virtue*'s second, *re*constructive argument, but before this can be assessed it is necessary to elaborate that argument. That will be done in the next section; I will first summarize the logic of post-Wolffian accounts of human society, and of social history, by reference to a *telos*.

In neologizing *teleology,* Wolff denoted a providential and harmoniously functioning order that, he proposed, informs both nature and action with purpose. The very possibility of knowledge of such a causal and perfectionist order was subsequently denied by Kant in his "critical" philosophy. For Kant, teleology is a "*regulative* ideal" and "*reflective* principle of the understanding," as distinct from any constitutive ideal or determinant principle of causality. Teleology is his "idea" of the way in which human subjects intuitively "judge" apparently ordered temporal change in objects *as if* that change were purposive. All humans desire to know, and this desire induces them to systematize, even where knowledge is impossible, and, since Kant is human, he systematizes.[15] Even though he judges that he cannot know, he can at least try to understand. In the second half of his *Critique of Judgement* he applies his reflective principle of teleology to organisms as natural orders, but only after he has already applied it to human history as if that, too, were an ordered object or "a *system.*"[16] It turns out that Kant's enthusiasm for teleology is scarcely less than that of Wolff. For Kant, we might say, teleology is the idea with which a logical space of practical *reasons* transcends the space of empirical *causes,* in that he attributes to a historical teleology the achievement of a kingdom of moral and cosmopolitan ends in a way that exceeds the limits of our possible knowledge.

The idea that the Enlightenment's "civil (*bürgerliche,* or 'bourgeois') society" was a historically progressive order that extended beyond the locale of any one city and subsisted apart from any sovereign state developed independently of Wolff's teleology.[17] Most especially, it was developed theoretically in Scotland, alongside empiricism, after Scotland's disempowering entry into England's empire. Kant's attempt, in his *Idea for a Universal History with a Cosmopolitan Aim*, to explain progress as the beneficial effects of "unsociable sociability" therefore elaborated upon a common Enlightenment theme, which had been expressed still more famously in Adam Smith's proposition that the human good is promoted as if "by an invisible hand."

The ideas of a systemic teleology, of action's unintentional causality, and of social order were sublimated by Hegel into "the Idea" of the historical actualization of human self-consciousness and freedom (and, incidentally, welfare) as a single process, independent of subjective purposiveness. What is actualized in history is the final cause of rational human being and action, even if not of individual human beings. Whereas for Aristotle a specific *telos* is temporal in relation to individuals but not in relation to their unchanging natural kind, for Hegel the human *telos* is irreducibly historical.

Hegel's "philosophy of right" elaborated a systematic account of the particular institutions constituting modern ethical life as a concrete universal, juxtaposed to the abstractions of individual morality. This non-contractarian legitimation of society as a rational order differentiates three modern institutions: the family, civil society—which revolves around a Smithian "system of needs"—and, finally, the sovereign and bureaucratic state, which progressively imparts purposive intentionality to the whole. The state is credited with institutionalizing the rational freedom of individuals under the impersonal rule of its law and educatively directing those individuals (through the administration of justice, and through particularistic corporations) toward that fully rational freedom that is the end of history.

The philosophical importance of Hegel's celebration of "history and system [as] jointly articulat[ing] the form of reason itself" has been asserted by an erstwhile student of Rorty, Robert Brandom, for whom Hegel's greatest insight was that the normative "commitments" of Kantian theory are socially "instituted."[18] Those "young Hegelians" who wished to politically radicalize philosophy's project of "critique" into a crusade for "the free state" would have agreed to this. Against it, though, stands Karl Marx. For the young Marx, that state's historical bifurcation from civil society precludes the rational ordering of goods for the sake of meeting human needs. In being "freed" from civil society, citizenship is alienated from real social relations, and therefore its championing by Hegelians is the paradigmatic case of a falsely justificatory "ideology." On Marx's rival account, the "right" actualized by the state is the private right to own alienable individual or joint-stock property and to appropriate the labor of others, thus to alienate them from their activity and its material products, and thereby to accumulate further capital. In enforcing this right, the state pursues the end of capital accumulation and the interests of individuals qua capitalists, while workers' goals and reasons for action are entirely separated from the reasons for which they are employed. This indeed constitutes a rationally apprehendable system, but one in which truly human needs and powers are institutionally subordinated to the particular needs and interests of capital.

Turning to political economy in elaborating a newly "materialist interpretation of history," Marx reconceptualized civil society as a capitalist mode of production and abandoned the language of teleology for that of causal "laws." It is, he argued, not the state but the capitalist mode of production—and the process of commodification that such production causes—that systematically structures society as a whole. Under this system, reason is the slave of capital. As under all previous modes of production, human action is heteronomously determined by material necessity.

Even though he turned away from philosophy in writing *Capital,* Marx there claimed a similarity to Aristotle. In the first chapter of the first volume, he called Aristotle "the great investigator who was the first to analyse the value-form . . . by his discovery of a relation of equality in the value-expression of commodities." Where Marx claimed to go beyond Aristotle was in discovering what had eluded him: "the homogeneous element, i.e. the common substance," that renders material products as commensurable and equalizable monetary "exchange-values," as distinct from their particular and incommensurable "use-values." This "common substance . . . is—human labour."[19] Marx argues that under capitalism labor should be characterized in terms not only of the "specific kind[s]" of "concrete labour" that form different objects for use but also of an "abstract labour" that "produces" "value" as an abstract "form." Capitalism's commodification of labor is separated analytically from concrete and "useful labour [as] . . . an eternal natural necessity."[20] It was, Marx proposed, "only the historical limitation inherent in the society in which he lived" that prevented "Aristotle's genius" from identifying the "twofold nature of the labour contained in commodities" that, therefore, Marx himself "was the first to point out."[21] Had Aristotle lived with the capitalist mode of production, Aristotelianism would have become Marxism.

Certainly, Marx's critique of exchange-value and "commodity fetishism" shares much with Aristotle's denigration of commerce and *pleonexia*, while his account of the concrete labor contained in commodities resembles Aristotle's account of production as such. Although Marx wrote of the "*social* relations of production" within precapitalist modes of production, his discussion of "the commodity" at the start of *Capital* echoes Aristotle in describing precapitalist production as a "private" relation between producer and product. Where he departs decisively from Aristotle is in identifying productive labor as the "power" and potentiality that is most distinctively and essentially human. Through labor "man . . . confronts the materials of nature as a force of nature," thereby "simultaneously . . . develop[ing] the potentialities slumbering within [external] nature" and "chang[ing] his own nature."[22] Material conditions may determine human consciousness, but it is intentional human labor that progressively determines those material conditions. It is the exercise of labor-power that causally enables the actualization of the broader potentialities within what Marx early identified as humanity's "species-essence." Even capitalism's abstraction of labor is historically progressive because it renders production fully public and social. However, the full actualization of human potentiality cannot occur within the capitalist "social formation."[23] On the contrary, capitalism's systemic processes of alienating and exploiting workers through its commodification of "free wage labour" causally prevent their actualization of their human potential. Without ownership of capital, individuals have to sell their own labor, and if one cannot direct one's own actions one is incapable of actualizing one's potential. This is inscribed in the historically necessary structure of capitalism, enforced by the state, and legitimated by liberalism. It is also, Marx thought, explained by the science of political economy. To explain it is to move beyond Aristotle's denigration of labor and beyond the critique of Bruno Bauer or even of Moses Hess. It is to understand and know the causes of the negation of human potential and, Marx thought, to know that this negation must, in time, be negated. Therefore, Marx concluded, the goal of the *historical* process must be a different, "socialist" mode of production.

What differentiates Marx from Kant and Hegel is not any real eschewal of historical teleology. Rather, what makes his "historical materialism" more than a grim version of the Enlightenment's metanarrative of progress is the way in which he isolates the *telos* of history (socialism) from the process of its actualization (class society's succession of modes). His "prehistory" is a tale not of the unintentional actualization of the human good but merely of the unintentional actualization of the necessary conditions for a fully intentional act of revolution. Only once this point has been finally reached can those who have been oppressed by history finally act for themselves rather than for the sake of capital.

MacIntyre has never accepted Marx's totalizing historical narrative, which he interpreted in his first book, *Marxism: An Interpretation,* as a secularized retelling of Christian eschatology. There he described Marx in largely Hegelian terms, and long before Brandom's leading of a Hegelian revival he attempted to "recover the Hegel of fact from the Hegel of fiction."[24] Even more, though, he tried to rebut Herbert Marcuse's "Hegelianizing of Marx,"[25] after praising Marcuse's account "of the connection between Hegel's logic and his social theory."[26] Now, rejecting both that logic and that social theory, MacIntyre tries to identify what Aristotelians should learn from Marxism, while discarding those fatal "mistakes inherited" by Marx from Hegel.[27] He therefore declares himself "irremediably anti-Hegelian in rejecting the notion of an absolute standpoint,"[28] the standpoint of a universalizing historical teleology that has forgotten even Kant's strictures. He, too, analyzed practice apart from power.

Practices

MacIntyre claims a kind of impersonal objectivity for Aristotelianism, but not the objectivity of Hegel's absolute standpoint. Hegelian objectivity and rationality are embodied in the actuality and ethical life of the institutions of family, civil society, and, above all, the state. In contrast, an Aristotelian objectivity is that of "standards of goodness, rightness and virtue" that an individual must acknowledge in order to achieve excellence by those standards. This "objectivity" can "be understood only from within the context . . . and in terms of the structure of certain types of historically developed practice, in which the initial interests of those engaged in such practices are transformed through their activities into an interest in conforming to the standards of excellence required by those practices, so that the goods internal to them may be achieved."[29] This ethical thought shares something with that of Hegel's "objective activity," and MacIntyre allows its expression in overtly Hegelian terms: "Objective activity is activity in which the end or aim of the activity is such that by making that end their own *individuals* are able to achieve something of *universal* worth embodied in some *particular* form of practice through cooperation with other such individuals."[30] On MacIntyre's account, practices that "can be thus characterized stand in sharp contrast" to what he calls the individualist "standpoint of civil society." The same, he thinks, is true of the young Marx's account of objective activity, but he recasts Marx's account because the "contrast . . . is best expressed in Aristotelian rather than in Hegelian terms."[31]

We have noted the post-Heideggerian rehabilitation of the concept of *praxis*, but a still more important source of *After Virtue*'s core concept of the virtues was the Wittgensteinian idea of "practices." Like Heidegger, Wittgenstein took philosophy away from metaphysical abstractions and toward lived experience, so that theory was not separated from practice. However, whereas Heidegger dealt ontically with *Dasein* and its equipment, Wittgenstein dealt in language and communication. If actors are rational language users, and if actors are socialized into language use and rationality, then we should understand ourselves as sharing reasons for action with others. Taking a game, such as chess, as paradigmatic, Wittgenstein's own usage of *practices* referred to rule-governed kinds of linguistic usage and behavior. At the same time, a few analytic philosophers developed expressly "teleological" theories of goal-directed individual action. MacIntyre combines these ideas. If actors are socialized into shared practices and reasons for action, and if—as Aristotle said—their actions are rationally directed to the achievement of *goods*, then social practices should also be understood as rationally directed to the actualization of goods.

MacIntyre's account of practices broke new ground in social theory. It differs from both Marxist and functionalist sociologies in that it is pluralistic, in the sense that it does not treat society as—like Aristotle's *polis*—a single order. Where it differs from Wittgensteinian social theory (such as that of Peter Winch, David Bloor, or Raimo Tuomela, or John Searle's Austinian variant) is in being teleological rather than nomological. MacIntyre's practices are constituted not only by sets of rules that are followed but also, and more crucially, by goals or goods that are pursued and that are, if the practice is in good order, progressively actualized. For a practice to be in good order requires, therefore, less that its rules be followed than that its participants act with a common end in mind, giving point and purpose to their rule following and to their initial learning of those rules. This requires from practitioners not merely conventional behavior, replicating the practice over time, but the exercise of purposive and critical rationality, causally driving their practice progressively through time.

One of the two types of good internal to a practice—that is, internal to any one of a plurality of practices—that MacIntyre specified in *After Virtue* sounds remarkably Wittgensteinian. It "is the good of a certain kind of life" (190). This pluralistic good revises Aristotelianism in obviating its traditional presumption that there must be some single best form of life for human beings to lead. It overcomes the aporia of Aristotle's dual prioritization of the exclusively philosophical life and the more inclusive life of politics.[32] For MacIntyre's newly egalitarian Aristotelianism, the good human life is that of actualizing good human potentialities (i.e., potentialities that are identified by the tradition as good) in community with others, which can be done in many ways.

For Aristotle, the philosophical life is paradigmatic of the human good because philosophizing, in its purest form as a human activity, is the activity of contemplating God, and Aristotle's God is the paradigm of self-sufficiency, of thought simply reflecting upon itself, so that philosophy is the activity of thinking about thought thinking of itself. When philosophizing, a human being comes as close to divine self-sufficiency as it is possible for such a being to become. Therefore, the human good can be achieved only through activities that have no ends apart from their actors. As we have seen, one who functions servilely for the sake of others is herself incapable of actualizing human excellence apart from the excellence of her products and of her products' consumers. One who rules others is more self-sufficient than those who supposedly require his commands, so that the head of a household is more self-sufficient than those he requires to fulfill his needs. To be philosophical is, for Aristotle, to be supremely unproductive.

MacIntyre disagrees. An elemental revision of Aristotle is entailed by the other type of good internal to a practice that he specifies in *After Virtue*: "the excellence of the products" (189). Like Marx, MacIntyre considers the power to produce to be a fully human potentiality. Going well beyond Marx, he proposes that personal pursuit of excellence in productive work cultivates the excellences of character that are constitutive of the specifically human good, "that there is a close connection between being a good human being and doing good work."[33] Whereas Aristotle attempted (with never more than partial success) to differentiate *praxeis* from *technai*, actions from productive crafts, MacIntyre's concept of practices obliterates that distinction. Indeed, in implying that practices necessarily have products, his concept of practices is more redolent of *technai* than of *praxeis*. This is especially evident in *Three Rival Versions of Moral Enquiry*, where he writes of practices as "crafts." Rather, as the first kind of good internal to practices—that of certain kinds of lives—overcomes the Aristotelian aporia of political versus philosophical lives, so this second kind of good overcomes the aporia of Aristotle's attempted distinction between action and production. "Products" can, of course (and here Aristotle and MacIntyre avoid what may be considered an aporia in Marx), be performances as well as material things. That MacIntyre clearly intends the term to include scientific and philosophical truths (even when these truths are *discovered* facts) entails that the concept of practices obliterates, also, Aristotle's conceptual isolation of *theoria*.

Scientific progress is to be explained as the progress of practices of inquiry, in which truth is treated in the way to which Rorty objects: as the goal in pursuit of which inquiries are directed. Where MacIntyre would agree with Rorty, and with "Bacon, Dewey, and Kuhn," is in "see[ing] artisans and natural scientists as doing the same kind of thing."[34] And, MacIntyre would add, philosophers, too, are doing that same kind of thing. All are engaged in specific practices, and all are pursuing goods internal to their practices. All are—to borrow words from Brandom—"giving and asking for *reasons*," and this because—on Brandom's account—all "are seekers and speakers of *truth*."[35] It follows—even though this is denied

by Brandom—that truth is "a concept that has an important *explanatory* role to play in philosophy," as it does in the sciences.[36]

MacIntyre has defended the importance of truth against Brandom.[37] Besides warranting assertion, truth is what crucially motivates practices (indeed, "disciplines") of philosophical and scientific inquiry. If philosophers qua philosophers are seekers of truth, then truth, as their motivating goal, explains their common social practice. Truth is both the first principle and the final end, the presupposition and the goal, of any inquiry. Brandom, in contrast, radicalizes Rorty's antirepresentationalism into an "inferentialist" account of normative language use as *the* practice of giving and asking for reasons. This aligns Wittgenstein (especially the later, "pragmatist" Wittgenstein, but also the earlier, Fregean and functionalist one) with Kant and Hegel in a "tradition" that is at once "idealist" and "pragmatist"; Kant because he rationalizes morality in terms of deontic *commitments,* and Hegel because he adds that commitments can only be *inferred* through language, semantically *instituted* in society, and juridically enforced by states. It is from this social language game, and not from Kant's Platonic "intuition," that we derive our power of representational judgment. Brandom here radically restates the standpoint of civil society in the terms of linguistic philosophy.

Against this standpoint, MacIntyre maintains that people engage in a plurality of practices in which their desires are tutored. His example in *After Virtue* is of a candy-desiring child who is tempted to play chess and thereby learns to desire excellence in something more intellectually rewarding. MacIntyre's moral claim is that, in transforming desires, practices serve as the schools of the virtues. So, in pursuing truth as a *telos* one learns (again borrowing Brandom's words) "that *truthfulness* is . . . an important virtue."[38]

MacIntyre's revision of Aristotelianism in establishing the plurality and productivity of excellent practices was made when he entered the Aristotelian tradition, but he has quietly continued to revise the tradition ever since, even while digging down deeper into it. His most explicit revision to Aristotle has been in *Dependent Rational Animals: Why Human Beings Need the Virtues* and is at its most vivid in his critique of Aristotle's praise of the magnanimous *megalopsychos*—a being neither beast nor God, but nonetheless purportedly godlike in pretending to a nonphilosophical self-sufficiency. This figure, though Aristotelian, anticipates Nietzsche's antisocial Overman and seemingly disregards the need for the virtue of "truthfulness about ourselves, both to ourselves and . . . in accountability to . . . others."[39] In denying his need of others, and instead demanding their recognition of his superiority, the *megalopsychos* denies his own true good as a human, and therefore necessarily social, being. Against him, MacIntyre argues, throughout the book, for the moral importance of the facts of our embodied animality, and therefore of our dependence upon others within social relations of "giving and receiving."

MacIntyre exculpates Aristotle from the "mistake" of intending "that rationality . . . [is] a property that separates humans from their animality" (5), even though the tradition has, with justification, made much of Aristotle's specification of human being in terms of those intellectual virtues that separate "men" from "beasts" and therefore bring them closer to God. Whereas *logos* and *nous* (or intelligence) have been traditionally understood as potentialities entirely lacking in all nonhuman animals, MacIntyre attributes a degree of prelinguistic practical reasoning to such species as bottlenose dolphins.[40] As with humans, their natural capacity for practical reasoning is cultivated, naturally, within what might be called social and even (because variable) *cultural* practices. He "ascribe[s] reasons for action to non-language-using species" and, further, describes as "a question of fact" whether an animal is "flourishing *qua* member" of its species, "even though the question of what it is to flourish has to be answered in part through evaluative and conceptual enquiry. As a question of fact it receives answers in a variety of scientific contexts" (64). He has recently set out questions about practice that "other animal species lack the rational powers" to address, while insisting that if we are not to "misunderstand ourselves" we need to address such questions of practical rationality in the context of prior questions about our nature.[41] Accordingly, there is no absolute divide separating a space of reasons from one of natural causes. Reasons *are* causes. Further, "Reasons not only can be causes, they have causes,"[42] including untutored passions and fully natural needs. If our reason does not address our natural needs and potentialities, then it is likely to remain enslaved to our passions.

In this way, MacIntyre dug down into the bedrock of human nature in analyzing rational justifications for action. To say of something that it is a good is to say that it contributes to the flourishing of some member of a species, qua member of that species. This is one way in which he has left behind such "modern Aristotelians" as Brandom's Sellarsian and Pittsburgh colleague John McDowell.[43] For McDowell, as for Gadamer, Aristotelian practical reasoning should be independent of naturalistic explanation, and Kant's antinomy of freedom and determination should be evaded. By contrast, MacIntyre now renders ethical justification susceptible to scientific fact and to all of the discoveries of modern scientific inquiries. In rerelating Aristotelian practical philosophy to both empirical and "metaphysical" biology, MacIntyre is both returning to and revising traditional, Thomistic Aristotelianism.

In all of this, MacIntyre is fundamentally opposed to Brandom's standpoint. Brandom separates "us," as "sapient" beings, from other, merely "sentient" species. We are, on Brandom's account, *uniquely* "*rational* animals, *discursive, concept-using, sapient*," as well as "social, normative . . . free, self-consciously historical animals," and "expressive, self-interpreting, self-constituting historical" ones.[44] Such "essentially self-conscious beings don't have *natures,* they have *histories.*"[45] As we have seen, MacIntyre regards this as a false opposition. If we are to excel in practical reasoning, we must be mindful of our nature in recounting our narrative. If we are to flourish, we need to give and receive not only reasons but also, as a matter of fact, physical help and psychological care.

Brandom's concern is with giving and asking for reasons as a single "practice" and "space," within which inferences build systemically upon inferences and individuals make explicit commitments for which they hold one another accountable. In contrast, MacIntyre considers different traditions as *rival* spaces of reasons and different practices as *separate* spaces of reasons. Within those separate spaces "we are educated . . . so that certain kinds of reason become the cause of certain kinds of action by ourselves and so that we learn how to cause certain kinds of action on the part of others by affording them reasons."[46] These spaces of practical reasoning are the basic constituents of society and culture. He writes in *Dependent Rational Animals* that "our second culturally formed language-using nature is a set of partial, but only partial, transformations of our first animal nature" (49) and that our "use of a language is always embedded in forms of social practice" (30), as is "successful communication of beliefs and intentions" among nonhuman animals (31). Practice precedes language, language is learned through use, and its use is motivated by pursuit of perceived goods. Through participation in practices one is socialized into pursuit of *common* goods, to be actualized by emulating shared standards of excellence that are internal to the practice in that only participants can be competent judges of what constitutes excellence. To become an excellent philosopher or chess player, or farmer or builder, one must therefore learn "as an apprentice learns."[47] One must learn to revise and order one's desires, to acknowledge the excellence and authority of others, and to accept their judgment when one's own reasoning fails according to shared standards. To become an excellent practitioner oneself requires that one cultivate such virtues of character as truthfulness, courage, temperance, and justice, because these excellent characteristics enable one to rationally direct one's own actions in cooperation with others.

To flourish as a human being is, MacIntyre says, to become an "independent practical reasoner": that is, a rationally independent *actor*. Here we have a substantive, but inclusive, conception of the human *telos*. That this independence of practical judgment and action is tantamount to neither self-sufficiency nor self-legislation MacIntyre makes clear in his accounts of what it is to initially *become* independent, to excellently exercise independence within shared practices, and, as in old age, to again become dependent upon others. Its socially critical character is clear in his account of the external obstacles to our actualization of independence.

MacIntyre as Modern Critic

MacIntyre has been called a "critic of modernity."[48] That said, it is a distinctively modern idea that philosophy should be concerned with social criticism. To make a critical theory out of Aristotelianism is, therefore, to revise the Aristotelian tradition.

MacIntyre has seldom called himself a social "critic," and never a "critical theorist." As he reminds us, the young Marx mockingly undertook a "Critique of Critical Critique,"[49] and it was in reaction to "the German ideology" by which Left Hegelians sought to politicize philosophy that Marx abandoned philosophy and instead turned to political economy. "Criticism" is a "pre-Marxist" idea "that Marx criticized," MacIntyre noted long ago in his own searing *Polemic* written against Marcuse's latter-day "critical theory."[50] Marcuse was only one of many twentieth-century Germans who wished to rescue the rational patrimony of Kant, Hegel, and Marx alike from the barbarism of their contemporary compatriots. Pivotal was Max Horkheimer, who declared that "critical theory is the heir not only of German idealism but of philosophy as such."[51] Believing that "reason exists in the whole system of ideas," his Frankfurt School of critical theory was to realize "the good" by "bring[ing] reason into the world."[52] Such a hypertheoretical standpoint is obviously far from the standpoint of practice that MacIntyre wants specifically Aristotelian philosophy to make explicit.

Moral philosophy, MacIntyre has said, provides a culture with the capacity for self-criticism. Socrates and Plato were certainly critical of Athens, and, MacIntyre concedes, "the theorists of European Enlightenment were brilliantly successful . . . in identifying certain types of social institution which could not but frustrate" their "pursuit of the goods of reason."[53] Nonetheless, both of these types of criticism were more theoretical than practical.

Horkheimer was right to claim that Aristotelianism's "defect lies in its making truth and goodness identical with reality," so that "neo-Thomists' use of categories such as cause, purpose, force, soul, entity, is necessarily uncritical."[54] Aristotle and Aquinas affirmed what *is*, whether actual or potential. It has been contended above that such a metaphysics of presence (to borrow a Heideggerian phrase) can explain a person's failure to actualize the human good only by reference to an absence. This lack can be of either internal capacities or external conditions, but a lack of external conditions is explicable only as a matter of chance and not by reference to any further, necessary cause. Conversely, Marxism explains the failure of whole classes of people to actualize their potential by reference to a structural denial of necessary external conditions. On this account, alienation, exploitation, and oppression are not accidental or occasional events but systematic and continuous processes obstructing, opposing, and, indeed, causally negating the satisfaction of human needs and the actualization of human potential.

MacIntyre now wants to join "theoretical resources . . . from Aristotle, Aquinas, and Marx . . . in negative critique," in order to elaborate a newly "negative and critical stance to the dominant norms, values, and institutions of the contemporary social order."[55] Marx is necessary to *supplement* Aristotle and Aquinas because neither of them shows us how to treat society as an object of critique.

The value of Marxism to Thomistic Aristotelianism must not be misunderstood. Marxism is, for MacIntyre, a failed tradition. Therefore, his own achievement is other and less than the kind of synthesis between two previously rival traditions that was effected by Aquinas. In failing to break adequately from Hegel, Marxism failed to break from the Enlightenment. Its failure is a failure of practical or moral philosophy. Dismissing ethics as ideology—as a reflection of real, material interests, and not an expression of objective reasons for action—Marxists never recombined the deontological and consequentialist fragments of a properly teleological morality. Nonetheless, Marx articulated ideas that can and should be appropriated by a moral critique of capitalism. We have seen Marx claim that Aristotle would have agreed with his labor theory of value, and we may also note that MacIntyre opened his first book with the epigram "The true descendant of the doctrines of Aquinas is the labour theory of value. The last of the Schoolmen was Karl Marx."[56] This he has now echoed in claiming, in turn, that "the moral dimension of the appropriation of surplus value was a Christian truth quite some time before it become a Marxist truth."[57]

Speaking from "the standpoint of . . . a Marx-informed Aristotelianism," MacIntyre enumerates other "Marxist truths" that provide "a permanently valuable identification of the most important economic and political obstacles to the achievment of common goods in . . . modernity." Here we have what Aristotelianism has previously lacked: a systemically causal explanation of the denial of human potential. Three of these "truths" are that "a class war is waged against those who have only their labor to sell," in which "surplus value has to be appropriated" because of "the nature of capitalism as an immensely productive exploitative system"; that "the nature of work within that same system" is such that "workers are . . . valued only for their producing and consuming functions"; and that "capital flows in whatever direction will secure it the highest rate of return," rather than where it would best "meet human need." All of these truths "can be derived from Marx's overall theory of capitalist development and of capitalism as a self-sustaining system." The final Marxist truths are that the state has become increasingly integrated with the market and that the resistance that "capitalism inevitably elicits . . . issues in institutions designed to protect workers and the needy from the exploitation and deprivation inflicted on them" but that these unions, cooperatives, and parties are readily "coopt[ed] and domesticate[d]" by the state, which must therefore be treated "with the greatest suspicion."[58] MacIntyre has often referred to corporate capital and the state, which taxes it and gives it legal form, as constituting a single system, in which each is utterly dependent on the other. If this were not already obvious to both "Right" and "Left" in liberal democratic politics, it must be so after states have rescued the banks from capitalism's latest crisis. As he says, "Exploitation through debt is now our most urgent political problem."[59]

MacIntyre learned early how to speak Marxist, and it is now one of what he calls the "second first languages" that he retains from his pre-Thomist past. He has been keen to empty that language of its Hegelian vocabulary. Parts of that vocabulary were inherited by Hegel from Aristotle,[60] although we have seen that in using *telos* and *logos* to name a reflective principle applicable to history as a whole concepts were wrenched from Aristotelianism's scheme. However, the question must be raised as to what can remain of Marxist critique from "the standpoint of . . . a Marx-informed Aristotelianism" that has abandoned Marxism's idea of a socialist mode of production as *the* historical *telos*.

Here comparison with the Frankfurt School of critical theory can again be drawn. Jürgen Habermas long ago proposed that the tradition of Aristotelian practical philosophy had been finally ended in the nineteenth century "by the critique of Historicism,"[61] but his own subsequent trajectory appears to be a performative confirmation of the proposition that "without a *theory* of history there could be no immanent critique that . . . distinguished what things and human beings could be from what they actually are."[62] What critical theory has become in his work is an attempt to sublate previous sociologies within a new theoretical system that describes reason's immanence in present society. Both he and Brandom recognize that the one's theory of communicative action has converged with the other's linguistic pragmatism. Brandom's inferentialist "understanding of normativity . . . requires a social functionalism, in which the functional system in question is a linguistic community and its practices,"[63] and he presents the subject of his idealist-cum-pragmatist tradition to be "the whole system of social practices of the most inclusive possible community."[64] Following Hegel, this holistic functionalism becomes "*historically* extended."[65] Its extension into the philosophy of mind is more elemental, and Brandom makes the classic sociological move of modeling the postulated system "on the relations between" such organic or artificial objects as "valves," fluids, pumps, and filters.⁶⁶ Where Brandom's understanding of normativity departs from that of Habermas is in the latter's claim that the point of discourse is recognitive understanding, to which Brandom responds that, although linguistic practice fulfills "many functions," "it does not, as a whole, have an aim or a goal."⁶⁷

As against the linguistic communitarianism of both Brandom and Habermas, MacIntyre is fundamentally anticommunitarian. Nonetheless, there is some agreement between him and Habermas. Habermas draws a divide, as Brandom does not, between "lifeworld" and "system," and therefore retains a normative standpoint that cannot be simply assimilated into the "whole" of Brandom's systemic and legitimatory space of reasons. This is the lightest of shadows still cast by Marxism's opposition of labor to capital, but it is a way in which a discourse ethic can continue critical theory's traditional opposition to "instrumental reason."

We might say of Habermas, in heavily Aristotelian terms, that his fundamental difficulty is to differentiate the being and attributes of the socially constitutive lifeworld from those of the system (or vice versa). Brandom may be attracted to Habermas's project, but from his pragmatist premises it can make no sense to differentiate an instrumental kind of reason from a communicative kind. Brandom's system is communicative, all the way down. Pragmatically, language has many functions, many uses, and it is these myriad uses with which meanings and intentionality must be identified. To isolate and privilege one aim or goal is to try to retain an essentialism that is incompatible with linguistic philosophy, rightly understood. Habermas's project of theoretical sublation therefore fails.

Perhaps MacIntyre can succeed where Habermas fails. As MacIntyre says, rival rationalities both inform and are informed by rival social structures.⁶⁸ The principal tradition against which he ranges Aristotelianism is that which expresses and legitimizes the prioritization of instrumental "goods of effectiveness" over "goods of excellence" or virtues. In *After Virtue* MacIntyre cited Kant in opposing "manipulation" and cited manipulation in opposing "bureaucratic management,"⁶⁹ but if this seems redolent of "the heirs of the Frankfurt School" it must also be noted that he accused those heirs of unwitting collaboration with "neo-Weberian organization theorists" (31). He has since acknowledged "incidental resemblances to the thought of the Frankfurt School, although this was a matter of common influences rather than of direct indebtedness."⁷⁰ Both took from the work of Marx and Lukács the thought that social structures can embody contradictions, even if MacIntyre and Habermas abandoned the logic of Hegelian social theory that holds that such contradictions necessarily can and will be resolved.

What most divides MacIntyre, and divides him fundamentally, from the work of Habermas is his desire to make explicit what he regards as the goal directedness of ordinary actors insofar as they can exist *apart from* the system. His conception of that system is Marx's, suitably updated and de-Hegelianized. This is certainly not an all-encompassing system like that of Hegel or Brandom, even if it could be described as a system of domination or hegemony. What he prizes most in Marxism is that which its tradition has often called "praxis," and he accordingly asserts that an "alternative" to the standpoint of civil society "cannot begin from any kind of philosophical or theoretical statement" but "only in the struggles, conflicts, and work of practice."[71] These include the struggles of those specific kinds of Marx's "concrete labour" that may be called productive practices. Where Habermas writes affirmatively of communicative reason and action, MacIntyre writes of a plurality of practices and their internal goods, and also of goods of personal excellence that are cultivated within those various practices. Where Habermas writes of instrumental reason and action, MacIntyre writes of goods of personal effectiveness that may be exercised instrumentally to any end, of goods external to practices, and also of a plurality of "institutions" that deal in those external goods.

After Virtue juxtaposes practices to institutions. "Practices must not be confused with institutions," MacIntyre warns. "Chess, physics and medicine are practices; chess clubs, laboratories, universities and hospitals are institutions" (194). Institutions are organizations. Here we can see that MacIntyre has taken a different line from those medieval Aristotelians who first legitimated the feudal order of their time by analogy with a biological organism, so that serfs could be told that they participated in a common good along with their lords. As MacIntyre implies (and as he states outright in the later book *Whose Justice? Which Rationality?*), the work of the most influential of these systematizing writers, John of Salisbury, was itself "unsystematic."[72] Their organic analogy is another example of what Marx called ideology. The modern concept of an organization is a descendant of that organic analogy, and a chief executive officer or a president may be unreflectively referred to as an organization's "head." MacIntyre does not use these analogical terms, but his institutions are nonetheless the "organizations" of ordinary language. What makes the familiar organic metaphor invalid but the concept of organization valid is that the former is holist whereas the latter is pluralist. The one is, at best, a reflective principle of theoretical reason: that is, of the reasoning of the sociological observer. The other is—also, and primarily—a principle of the practical reasoning of fully intentional actors. It expresses an aspect of the self-understanding of veritable participants in an order within which they have concrete and particular rights, duties, and commitments, as well as being an intentional object for any others who have, in some way, to deal with that ordered structure. This organization is likely also to have some express purpose, perhaps in the form of a mission statement, that serves to justify individuals' rights, duties, and commitments. Such is the case with chess clubs, laboratories, universities, and hospitals.

Institutions, MacIntyre continues, "are characteristically and necessarily concerned with what I have called external goods." Such goods are "external" in the sense in which Aristotle used the term, to mean that they are not constituents of the being or character of a person, but MacIntyre also importantly intends by "external" that such goods are only "contingently attached" to any practice and that "there are always alternative ways" in which individuals can acquire them besides participation in some particular practice (194). Such goods include the candy desired by the child who is thereby tempted to practice chess, as well as "prestige, status and money" (188). Like the households described in Aristotle's *Politics,* institutions "are involved in acquiring money and other material goods; they are structured in terms of power and status, and they distribute money, power and status as rewards." This is no complaint, as practices cannot "survive for any length of time unsustained by institutions." Chess can be played apart from chess clubs, but chess could not have progressed as it has—indeed, could not exist or be played as it is—if it had no agreed rules and no organized "bearers" (194). Practices can no more be self-sufficient than can their individual participants.

Although practices require the external goods—the money, power, and status—that are the currency of institutions, these instrumental goods can cause difficulties. Characteristically, "the more someone has of them, the less there is for other people," so that they are normally "objects of competition in which there must be losers as well as winners" (190). If competition encourages emulation, and therefore causes excellence, it is good for both the individual practitioner and the entire practice. Where the flourishing of grand masters promotes both the standards of excellence internal to chess and the cultivation of club players, all is fine.

"Institutions and practices characteristically form a single causal order" (194). This is the case, for example, with hospitals and medicine, about which MacIntyre wrote much in the years leading up to *After Virtue*. As he states in *After Virtue,* the kind of sociology to which he aspires is one that lays "bare the empirical, causal connection between virtues, practices and institutions" (196), and such a sociology could hardly use the category of cause "uncritically," as Horkheimer proposed of Thomism. MacIntyre concludes *After Virtue*'s discussion of the necessity and cultivation of virtues in such "a common project" as "founding and carrying forward . . . a hospital" (151) by proposing "that it is through conflict . . . that we learn what our ends and purposes are." This may have been "a Sophoclean insight" (164) of the kind that *Whose Justice? Which Rationality?* allocated to Athens' anti-Aristotelian tradition, but he has since retained and elaborated the more Marxist insight that conflict is necessary and systemically caused. As some contradictions are irresolvable, some conflicts are permanent. Often he refers to "goods of conflict." Conflict is another of his categories; harmonious functionality is not.

Virtues have a function within MacIntyre's causal orders, which is to promote the goods internal to the practice and, indeed, to defend them. "The integrity of a practice causally requires the exercise of the virtues" by its participants (195). Within the context of a single causal order of a practice and its organizing institution, "the *essential* function of the virtues is clear. Without them, without justice, courage and truthfulness, practices could not resist the corrupting power of institutions" (194; emphasis added).

This is the crux of MacIntyre's critical theory of social practice. Shared practices require institutions, but those institutions are necessarily concerned with goods external to the practice and typically use their power over practices to prioritize external over internal goods and to further subordinate practices to their managerial control. Insofar as they succeed, the practice is corrupted. If they succeed fully, the practice is destroyed.

MacIntyre's indictment of modernity is, primarily, that most people expend most of their energy—their *energeia,* work, or characteristic functioning—in alienated labor that cannot meet *After Virtue*'s criteria of "a practice." He has since illustrated the process of destruction historically, with the classic Marxist example of Lancashire weavers driven by capitalist competition into Manchester's mills.[73] Once there, they became the proletarians in whom Marx and Engels placed the hopes of history. For MacIntyre, however, it was *before* their expropriation that the weavers were willing and, for a while, able to resist capitalism's systemic pressures, because it was only before their proletarianization that they were not alienated from their own activity and work. Then they were engaged in a veritable practice; afterward, they were not. The first situation suggests a causally virtuous circle in which practices function to habituate practitioners into the intellectual and moral virtues necessary to defend those practices; the second, a vicious circle in which people are too demoralized to resist managerial manipulation and therefore never cultivate a capacity for independent practical reasoning. In *Dependent Rational Animals,* MacIntyre asserts that one way in which theory might reinforce practice is by promoting "an awareness of how power is distributed and of the corruptions to which its use is liable," as it is only when informed by such awareness that "genuine virtues" can "function" (102).

MacIntyre's claim about the structure of ethical life is that organization and external goods are properly regarded as means to ends that are internal to practices. Only when rules and external goods function for the sake of goods internal to the practice can practices function as schools of the virtues. When institutions stand apart from practices and in domination over them, then practitioners are denied the rational power over their own actions that is necessary to moral education and agency. Institutional domination now causally obstructs the actualization of ethical life, as most social activity is dominated by managerial and governmental institutions of unprecedented size and complexity. Here we can see that even the single causal orders constituted by particular institutions and practices are not independent of the kind of systemic pressures described by Marx. This, though, is only a part of MacIntyre's critique.

I have stressed what I have called MacIntyre's pluralism of practices and of causal, organizational orders. He now stresses "the importance of empirical studies of past and present relationships between institutions and practices."⁷⁴ Such studies would have to be undertaken apart from the methodological individualism of the rational choice theory that developed within neoclassical economics, which puts humans' goals beyond the reach of reason and which had, by the time of *After Virtue,* already colonized other "social sciences." Nor can such studies be premised in the functionalist methodological holism that developed within a Western sociology separated from socialism and that rivaled Marxism's claim to a privileged position of observational objectivity. MacIntyre denies the possibility of any such neutral, transcendental, or theoretically architectonic standpoint. Rather, social relations and their ethical effects have to be studied in their plurality and particularity.

The plurality of practices is a lived reality. Practices in good order may be ethically educative, but one thing that they should therefore teach is that to live a good life is to have integrity. Here the second stage of MacIntyre's core concept of virtue becomes critically important. To live a fulfilled life is to be able to tell a coherent story about one's life as a whole, and this requires that one be able to integrate and order the goods one pursues for the sake of one's overall good as a person. That is elemental to what Aristotelians regard as practical rationality. Such a virtue is often precluded precisely because of the plurality of different practices in which one engages, or, alternatively, because one is compelled to prioritize one activity—typically, one's paid employment—at the cost of others. Moreover, different activities, especially those dominated by different institutions, impose different codes of behavior, so that one is compelled to display certain characteristics in one sphere and to adopt others in another. Integrity is impossible. This pluralism is the stuff of classical, pre-Brandomian pragmatism. MacIntyre condemns it as "compartmentalization."

Compartmentalization is incompatible with the kind of purposively rational ordering of goods in terms of which Aristotle defined "political community." The task of an Aristotelian politics is to make explicit what is for the sake of what, and to combine previously compartmentalized spaces of reasoning within a single communal space of giving and asking for reasons. In this way, activities can become expressly rational and ordered to what is agreed to be the common good. Politics, in this sense, is incompatible with the structures and scale of the modern state. A politically functional society must be a participative society, and truly participative institutions cannot be of indefinite size.

In *Dependent Rational Animals* MacIntyre proposes that "one cannot generally become an effective practical reasoner without becoming in some measure a political reasoner" because, just as practical reasoning necessarily involves ordering various goods in one's own life, so it involves ordering the various goods that one pursues in cooperation with others. In this sense, at least, political reasoning is "one aspect of the everyday activity of every adult." Political reasoning therefore benefits from reflection on one's relations with others, but MacIntyre also recommends that we look further for examples of political community. In *Dependent Rational Animals* he points to "fishing communities in New England . . . the history of Welsh mining communities . . . farming cooperatives in Donegal, Mayan towns in Guatemala and Mexico, some city-states from a more distant past" as "social forms within which networks of giving and receiving can be institutionalized and the variety of ways in which such networks can be sustained and strengthened or weakened and destroyed" (143). Looking at such examples may help us to see "what relationships of the relevant kinds of giving and receiving already exist in our own local community" (144). This, then, is another way in which Aristotelianism should make explicit "what it is to which we are already committed by our everyday life and our everyday judgements."[75]

It is to everyday social practice that MacIntyre looks for real ethical "resources," and especially to what he perceives as a plurality of morally educative practices. His Aristotelian quest is "to find through the virtues a mode of social life in which practical rationality is informed by shared hope."[76] What afford grounds for hope are those shared practices that are already basic to ethical life, because they inform kinds of practical reasoning that give point to goods of effectiveness and resist any systemic prioritization of institutionalized power and capital accumulation.

MacIntyre stands in the tradition of Thomistic Aristotelianism, but it is a tradition whose arguments he has transformed. In so doing, he has demonstrated how this tradition can respond to challenges issued by rivals. Having previously adopted and thought his way through the arguments of some of those rival traditions, he has learned what is valid in the challenges they pose.

One kind of challenge has come from arguments and discoveries about history. MacIntyre has revised Thomistic Aristotelianism's understanding of philosophical tradition and of itself as such a tradition. A tradition that is in good order is a tradition of inquiry and argument, in which claims to rational justification presuppose truth as the goal toward which its participants try to progress. Philosophy, on his account, is inseparable from its history, and that history is one of error as well as truth. It is a Hegelian error to identify truth with history, and a Nietzschean error to deny that there can be any progress toward truth. Aristotelians must avoid the error of assuming that they already possess a truth that is apodictic, unfalsifiable, and beyond challenge.

A related challenge identifies rational justification and truth with science and opposes science to philosophy. In response, MacIntyre observes that, in being paradigmatic of ideas of genuine progress, practices of scientific inquiry are inseparable from *their* histories and that scientific claims, too, are susceptible to falsification as well as verification. Traditionally, Aristotelians have claimed that human being is a unique and unchanging kind, but scientific progress has told us how much we continue to share with other animals, and why. Sciences that (unlike phrenology, for example) have histories of progress are paradigmatic for our understanding of activity in pursuit of common goods, and of truth as a good.[77]

The challenge with which this essay has been concerned is the sociological one that characterizes claims to truth as legitimations of power and self-interest. MacIntyre rejects this challenge in its Nietzschean form but accepts something of it from Marxism. Aristotelianism has erred in failing to explain either illegitimate power or theoretical justifications of such power. Lacking such explanation, it has often been an ideology of legitimation. On MacIntyre's account, however, Aristotelian teleology, rightly understood, makes explicit the goal-oriented logic of ordinary actors' shared practices. Therefore, Aristotelians should understand their distinctive tradition as the philosophical expression and justification of shared practices ordered in pursuit of internal goods. This sociological recasting of Thomistic Aristotelianism renders its scope pervasive but its position particularist. Its rivals have their own traditions and express rival interests. One strength of rivals that prioritize goods of effectiveness is that they require no educative reorientation of individuals' desires, and another is that they can make fine sense (whether in terms of a will to power or in the academically refined terms of rational choice theory) of institutional power and of individual competition for its possession. Bureaucratic and capitalist institutions, and traditions of their philosophical legitimation, are identifiable and causal obstacles to the achievement of the human good. It is a strength of MacIntyre's Thomistic Aristotelianism that it can identify and understand these obstacles and also that it can identify and articulate resources for hope. In this, the arguments of Thomistic Aristotelianism now exceed those of Heidegger and Gadamer, and of Hegel and Brandom, as well as those of Marx and Marcuse.

What remains is for MacIntyre to propose how political reasoning about shared goods should be conducted within a polity that is, on his account, structurally incapable of combining the pursuit of diverse goods into a single order for the sake of the common good. Perhaps Thomistic Aristotelians need to learn, as a second first language, the rival practical rationality that informs that nonteleological structure, in order to operate within that polity for the sake of goods internal to practices and local communities, while maintaining the integrity of their separate pursuit. MacIntyre insists that such rational pursuit of shared goods is always at least potentially political and that in some places it succeeds in ordering goods for the sake of a veritably political good. What is revisionary is his insistence that such an order should never be dogmatically assumed and that the rationality institutionalized in modern state and corporate structures is not a merely deficient practical rationality but a different and rival tradition. In arguing this, he makes of Thomistic Aristotelianism a newly critical theory of ethical and political action.

Notes

I thank Tom Angier, Caleb Bernacchio, Ruth Groff, Francisco Mota, S.J., Mustafa Ongun, and Fran O'Rourke for comments on drafts of this paper.

1. Martin Heidegger, *Basic Concepts of Aristotelian Philosophy*, trans. Robert D. Metcalf and Mark B. Tanzer (Bloomington: Indiana University Press, 2009), 44–70; Hans-Georg Gadamer, *The Idea of the Good in Platonic-Aristotelian Philosophy*, trans. P. Christopher Smith (New Haven: Yale University Press, 1986).

2. "The Prephilosophical History of 'Good' and the Transition to Philosophy" is the title of ch. 2 of Alasdair MacIntyre, *A Short History of Ethics: A History of Moral Philosophy from the Homeric Age to the Twentieth Century*, 2nd ed. (London: Routledge, 1998).

3. Alasdair MacIntyre, *After Virtue: A Study in Moral Theory* (Notre Dame: University of Notre Dame Press, 2007), 52–53. Subsequent page citations to this work are given parenthetically in the text.

4. Alasdair MacIntyre, "The Illusion of Self-Sufficiency," in *Conversations on Ethics*, ed. Alex Voorhoeve (Oxford: Oxford University Press, 2009), 117. He elaborates this argument most fully in "Plain Persons and Moral Philosophy: Rules, Virtues and Goods," in *The MacIntyre Reader,* ed. Kelvin Knight (Notre Dame: University of Notre Dame Press, 1998), 136–54.

5. Alasdair MacIntyre, "From Answers to Questions: A Response to the Responses," in *Intractable Disputes about the Natural Law: Alasdair MacIntyre and Critics*, ed. Lawrence S. Cunningham (Notre Dame: University of Notre Dame Press, 2009), 315.

6. Alasdair MacIntyre, "An Interview with Giovanna Borradori," in Knight, *MacIntyre Reader*, 264.

7. Alasdair MacIntyre, *God, Philosophy, Universities: A Selective History of the Catholic Philosophical Tradition* (Lanham, MD: Rowman and Littlefield, 2009), 166.

8. Philipp W. Rosemann, *Understanding Scholastic Thought with Foucault* (New York: St. Martin's Press, 1999), 93 and passim.

9. Richard Rorty, "Is Truth a Goal of Inquiry? Donald Davidson versus Crispin Wright," in *Truth and Progress,* vol. 3 of *Philosophical Papers* (Cambridge: Cambridge University Press, 1998), 40–41.

10. Alasdair MacIntyre, "Intractable Moral Disagreements," in Cunningham, *Intractable Disputes,* 21, 36–37.

11. Alasdair MacIntyre, "What More Needs to Be Said? A Beginning, Although Only a Beginning, at Saying It," in *Revolutionary Aristotelianism: Ethics, Resistance and Utopia*, ed. Kelvin Knight and Paul Blackledge (Stuttgart: Lucius and Lucius, 2008), 278; Alasdair MacIntyre, "Colors, Cultures, and Practices," in *The Tasks of Philosophy,* vol. 1 of *Selected Essays* (Cambridge: Cambridge University Press, 2006), 47–48.

12. MacIntyre, "Illusion of Self-Sufficiency," 117.

13. Brian Davies, introduction to *The De Malo of Thomas Aquinas*, ed. Brian Davies (Oxford: Oxford University Press, 2001), 21, 20, 52.

14. Such a legitimatory account of actuality—made by John Finnis, Robert P. George, and, in *Aquinas, Aristotle, and the Promise of the Common Good* (Cambridge: Cambridge University Press, 2006), Mary M. Keys—is further extended by Michael Novak to encompass the institutions of corporate capital. Mark C. Murphy, who is more mindful of MacIntyre's concerns, concludes

Natural Law in Jurisprudence and Politics (Cambridge: Cambridge University Press, 2006) with "doubts."

15. See Immanuel Kant, "The Canon of Pure Reason" and "The Architectonic of Pure Reason" in *Critique of Pure Reason*.

16. Immanuel Kant, "Idea for a Universal History with a Cosmopolitan Aim," 8.29, trans. Allen Wood, in *Kant's "Idea for a Universal History with a Cosmopolitan Aim": A Critical Guide*, ed. Amélie Oksenberg Rorty and James Schmidt (Cambridge: Cambridge University Press, 2009), 21; Kant's emphasis. Within this fine collection, Karl Ameriks, in "The Purposive Development of Human Capacities," 46–67, emphasizes the importance and problems of "the big Idea" of a teleological imperative. For critical commentary from the perspective of critical theory, see Thomas McCarthy, *Race, Empire, and the Idea of Human Development* (Cambridge: Cambridge University Press, 2009).

17. Civil society was widely praised as "polite" (as, increasingly, distinct from "political") and "cultured" or "cultivated," implying that it is conducive to human flourishing. Kant addressed an aspect of this idea in the *first* half of *Critique of the Power of Judgement*.

18. Robert B. Brandom, *Tales of the Mighty Dead: Historical Essays in the Metaphysics of Intentionality* (Cambridge, MA: Harvard University Press, 2002), 1.

19. Karl Marx, *Capital: A Critique of Political Economy*, trans. Ben Fowkes, vol. 1 (New York: Penguin Books, 1976), 151–52. To the first major critic of Marx's economics, his belief in the "'equivalence' in the commodities to be exchanged" is both "untenable" and consistent with "the old scholastic-theological theory"; Eugen von Böhm-Bawerk, *Karl Marx and the Close of His System*, trans. Alice M. Macdonald (New York: Augustus M. Kelley, 1949), 69.

20. Marx, *Capital*, 132–33.

21. Ibid., 152, 132. MacIntyre expresses appreciation for Marx's "labour theory of value" and a desire "to say considerably more on . . . the theory of value"; Alasdair MacIntyre, *Marxism and Christianity*, 2nd ed. (London: Duckworth, 1995), xx.

22. Marx, *Capital*, 283.

23. For an Aristotelian elaboration of this idea, see Ruth Groff, "Aristotelian Marxism/Marxist Aristotelianism: MacIntyre, Marx and the Analysis of Abstraction," *Philosophy and Social Criticism*, forthcoming.

24. Alasdair MacIntyre, introduction to *Hegel: A Collection of Critical Essays*, ed. Alasdair MacIntyre (New York: Doubleday, 1972), viii.

25. Alasdair MacIntyre, *Marcuse: An Exposition and a Polemic* (New York: Viking, 1970), 35. MacIntyre here objects to Marcuse's use of the term *negation* for "merging the logical and the evaluative."

26. Alasdair MacIntyre, "Herbert Marcuse: From Marxism to Pessimism," in *Alasdair MacIntyre's Engagement with Marxism: Selected Writings, 1953–1974*, ed. Paul Blackledge and Neil Davidson (Leiden: Brill, 2008), 340.

27. Alasdair MacIntyre, "The *Theses on Feuerbach*: A Road Not Taken," in Knight, *MacIntyre Reader*, 224.

28. Alasdair MacIntyre, "A Partial Response to My Critics," in *After MacIntyre: Critical Perspectives on the Work of Alasdair MacIntyre*, ed. John Horton and Susan Mendus (Cambridge: Polity Press, 1994), 295.

29. MacIntyre, "*Theses on Feuerbach*," 233.

30. Ibid., 225; emphases added. On Hegel's relevant usage of *objective*, see Michael Quante, *Hegel's Concept of Action*, trans. Dean Moyar (Cambridge: Cambridge University Press, 2004), esp. 52–55. For elaboration of MacIntyre's meaning, see his *The Objectivity of Good* (Canton, NY: St. Lawrence University, 1993).

31. MacIntyre, "*Theses on Feuerbach*," 225.

32. Brandom, although no Aristotelian, tellingly repeats this dual prioritization of the "two sorts of paradigmatically sapient forms of life"; Robert B. Brandom, *Reason in Philosophy: Animating Ideas* (Cambridge, MA: Harvard University Press, 2009), 150.

33. Alasdair MacIntyre, "Where We Were, Where We Are, Where We Need to Be," in *Virtue and Politics: Alasdair MacIntyre's Revolutionary Aristotelianism*, ed. Paul Blackledge and Kelvin Knight (Notre Dame: University of Notre Dame Press, 2011), 323.

34. Rorty, "Is Truth a Goal," 40.

35. Brandom, *Reason in Philosophy*, 175–76; Brandom's emphases.

36. Ibid., 158; Brandom's emphasis.

37. Alasdair MacIntyre, "Moral Relativism, Truth and Justification," in Knight, *MacIntyre Reader,* 202–22. Jeffrey Stout, one of MacIntyre's best-informed and most long-standing critics, now expresses his critique in Brandomian terms; see *Democracy and Tradition* (Princeton: Princeton University Press, 2004).

38. Brandom, *Reason in Philosophy*, 156; Brandom's emphasis.

39. On the anticipation of Nietzsche's Overman, see Alasdair MacIntyre, *Dependent Rational Animals: Why Human Beings Need the Virtues* (London: Duckworth, 1999), 127, cf. 162–66, and *After Virtue*, 257–59. For contrasting defenses of Aristotle's account of magnanimity, see Thomas Aquinas, *Commentary on Aristotle's "Nicomachean Ethics"* (South Bend, IN: Dumb Ox Books, 1993), 244–49, and Kristján Kristjánsson, *Justifying Emotions: Pride and Jealousy* (London: Routledge, 2002). The quote is from MacIntyre, *Dependent Rational Animals,* 95 (subsequent page citations are given parenthetically in the text). Elaboration of this point at 148–53 leads to a critique of Rorty's ironism.

40. Or "intelligence." Ch. 3 of *Dependent Rational Animals* is entitled "The Intelligence of Dolphins."

41. MacIntyre, "Where We Were," 308.

42. MacIntyre, "What More Needs to Be Said?," 274. MacIntyre here also differs from Marx in his way of drawing the divide between bees and architects (*Capital*, 283–84), in observing that "rabbits impose new and distinctively rabbity forms upon material nature, wolves new and distinctively wolverine forms."

43. Alasdair MacIntyre, "Rival Aristotles: Against Some Modern Aristotelians," in MacIntyre, *Ethics and Politics,* vol. 2 of *Selected Essays* (Cambridge: Cambridge University Press, 2006).

44. Brandom, *Reason in Philosophy*, 12, 17, 149; Brandom's emphases.

45. Ibid., 146; Brandom's emphases.

46. Alasdair MacIntyre, "Positivism, Sociology and Practical Reasoning: Notes on Durkheim's *Suicide*," in *Human Nature and Natural Knowledge: Essays Presented to Marjorie Grene on the Occasion of Her Seventy-Fifth Birthday*, ed. Alan Donagan, Anthony N. Perovich Jr., and Michael V. Wedin (Dordrecht: Kluwer, 1986), 99.

47. MacIntyre, *After Virtue*, 258; cf. Alasdair MacIntyre, *Three Rival Versions of Moral Enquiry: Encyclopaedia, Genealogy, and Tradition* (Notre Dame: University of Notre Dame Press, 1990), 61–66.

48. Peter McMylor, *Alasdair MacIntyre: Critic of Modernity* (London: Routledge, 1994).

49. MacIntyre, "*Theses on Feuerbach*," 224.

50. MacIntyre, *Marcuse*, 22.

51. Max Horkheimer, "Postscript" to "Traditional and Critical Theory," in *Critical Theory: Selected Essays*, trans. Matthew J. O'Connell (New York: Herder and Herder, 1972), 245–46.

52. Max Horkheimer, "The Social Function of Philosophy," in *Critical Theory*, 262–67.

53. Alasdair MacIntyre, "Some Enlightenment Projects Reconsidered," in *Ethics and Politics*, 180.

54. Max Horkheimer, *Eclipse of Reason* (Oxford: Oxford University Press, 1947), 90, 63.

55. Alasdair MacIntyre, preface to *Ethics and Politics*, xi.

56. Alasdair MacIntyre, *Marxism: An Interpretation* (London: SCM Press, 1953), 3, quoting R. H. Tawney's *Religion and the Rise of Capitalism*.

57. MacIntyre, "Where We Were," 325. This argument is elaborated in Alasdair MacIntyre, "The Irrelevance of Ethics," in *Virtue and Economy*, ed. Andrius Bielskis and Kelvin Knight, forthcoming.

58. MacIntyre, "Where We Were," 316.

59. Ibid., 332.

60. See Alfredo Ferrarin, *Hegel and Aristotle* (Cambridge: Cambridge University Press, 2001).

61. Jürgen Habermas, *Theory and Practice*, trans. John Viertel (London: Heinemann, 1974), 41. He goes on to describe Aquinas's reception of Aristotle's politics as "a social philosophy."

62. Jürgen Habermas, *Lifeworld and System: A Critique of Functionalist Reason,* vol. 2 of *The Theory of Communicative Action,* trans. Thomas McCarthy (Cambridge: Polity Press, 1987), 382; Habermas's emphasis.

63. Brandom, *Reason in Philosophy,* 12–13. The taproot of Brandom's functionalism is presumably Sellars's "central claim" that "the function of a linguistic expression depends on its role in the rules for the language to which it belongs." Kevin Sharp and Robert B. Brandom, "Editors' Introduction," in *In the Space of Reasons: Selected Essays of Wilfrid Sellars,* ed. Kevin Sharp and Robert B. Brandom (Cambridge, MA: Harvard University Press, 2007), xiii.

64. Brandom, *Tales of the Mighty Dead,* 227. Brandom is more Kantian than Hegelian in indicating elsewhere that his community is cosmopolitan.

65. Ibid., 47; Brandom's emphasis.

66. Robert B. Brandom, *Between Saying and Doing: Toward an Analytic Pragmatism* (Oxford: Oxford University Press, 2008), 71–72.

67. Robert Brandom, "Facts, Norms, and Normative Facts: A Reply to Habermas," *European Journal of Philosophy* 8, no. 3 (2000): 363. Habermas's concern with recognition of "the other" has a parallel in MacIntyre's call for Thomism to learn from Knud Ejler Løgstrup, but that revision of Thomism is beyond this essay's scope.

68. Alasdair MacIntyre, "Practical Rationalities as Forms of Social Structure," in Knight, *MacIntyre Reader,* 120–35.

69. See especially MacIntyre, *After Virtue,* ch. 3 and the closing pages of chs. 7 and 8.

70. MacIntyre, "Where We Were," 314.

71. Alasdair MacIntyre, preface to MacIntyre, *Ethics and Politics,* xi.

72. Alasdair MacIntyre, *Whose Justice? Which Rationality?* (Notre Dame: University of Notre Dame Press, 1988), 167.

73. MacIntyre, "*Theses on Feuerbach,*" 231–32.

74. Alasdair MacIntyre, "How Aristotelianism Can Become Revolutionary: Ethics, Resistance, and Utopia," in Blackledge and Knight, *Virtue and Politics,* 17.

75. MacIntyre, "Illusion of Self-Sufficiency," 117.

76. MacIntyre, "How Aristotelianism Can Become Revolutionary," 19.

77. Alasdair MacIntyre, "Hegel on Faces and Skulls," in *Tasks of Philosophy*.

CHAPTER FIVE

Alasdair MacIntyre
Reflections on a Philosophical Identity,
Suggestions for a Philosophical Project

ARTHUR MADIGAN, S.J.

While drafting this paper I went through a phase of illusion in which I thought I might tell you how Alasdair MacIntyre's philosophical achievements had changed the climate of English-speaking academic moral philosophy and were beginning to transform the surrounding culture. My eyes were opened, however, as I read his 1992 essay "What Has *Not* Happened in Moral Philosophy." There he faults a certain conference program for assuming that

> "abstract principles are [now] thought to be an inadequate and unreliable guide to action," that appeal is instead being made to "the concrete experiences that constitute the norms and social understanding of a particular community at a particular time," and that recognition has been accorded to "the importance of tradition for all questions of judgment and value." The question which has then been posed to us is: What are the implications of this development for contemporary culture? My problem in answering it is that I do not believe that anything like this change in moral philosophy has in fact occurred.[1]

MacIntyre's diagnosis remains as accurate today as it was then. More work is being done on the history of moral philosophy. There is more talk about virtues and virtue ethics. But on the whole, moral philosophy is being practiced pretty much as it was practiced before *After Virtue* appeared on the scene. Yet if I cannot tell you the story of Alasdair MacIntyre's triumphs, I can at least reflect upon his place within the contemporary Aristotelian and Thomistic traditions and offer some suggestions as to how his philosophical project might be extended.

Among the many achievements for which we owe MacIntyre our gratitude are his analyses of the concept of a philosophical tradition, of the rationality of traditions, and of the ways in which traditions may confront one another. In a number of places, such as chapter 18 of *Whose Justice? Which Rationality?* and the essay "Moral Relativism, Truth and Justification," he has formulated his view of how one tradition can in certain circumstances show itself to be clearly superior to a rival tradition.[2] Here is his formulation in the 2007 prologue to the third edition of *After Virtue*.

> How then, if at all, might the protagonists of one of these traditions hope to defeat the claims of any of its rivals? A necessary first step would be for them to come to understand what it is to think in the terms prescribed by that particular rival tradition, to learn how to think as if one were a convinced adherent of that rival tradition. To do this requires the exercise of a capacity for philosophical imagination that is often lacking. A second step is to identify, from the standpoint of the adherents of that rival tradition, its crucially important unresolved issues and unsolved problems—unresolved and unsolved by the standards of that tradition—which now confront those adherents and to enquire how progress might be made in moving towards their resolution and solution. It is when, in spite of systematic enquiry, issues and problems that are of crucial importance to some tradition remain unresolved and unsolved that a question arises about it, namely, just why it is that progress in this area is no longer being made. Is it perhaps because that tradition lacks the resources to address those issues and solve those problems and is unable to acquire them so long as it remains faithful to its own standard[s] and presuppositions? Is it perhaps that constraints imposed by those standards and deriving from those presuppositions themselves prevent the formulation or reformulation of those issues and problems

so that they can be adequately addressed and solved? And, if the answer to those two questions is "Yes," is it perhaps the case that it is only from the standpoint of some rival tradition that this predicament can be understood and from the resources of that same rival tradition that the means of overcoming this predicament can be found?

When the adherents of a tradition are able through such acts of imagination and questioning to interrogate some particular rival tradition, it is always possible that they may be able to conclude, indeed that they may be compelled to conclude, that it is only from the standpoint of their own tradition that the difficulties of that rival tradition can be adequately understood and overcome. It is only if the central theses of their own tradition are true and its arguments sound, that this rival tradition can be expected to encounter just those difficulties that it has encountered and that its lack of conceptual, normative, and other resources to deal with these difficulties can be explained. So it is possible for one such tradition to defeat another in respect of the adequacy of its claims to truth and to rational justification, even though there are no neutral standards available by appeal to which *any* rational agent whatsoever could determine which tradition is superior to which.[3]

With this passage as my guide, let me now speak about Alasdair MacIntyre the Aristotelian.

MacIntyre the Aristotelian

Before MacIntyre was a Thomist, he was an Aristotelian. As a Thomist, he necessarily remains in some sense an Aristotelian. It was from an Aristotelian standpoint that he was finally able, after many years of research, to understand and diagnose what had gone wrong in the early modern period, and what had led to the Enlightenment project of justifying morality with its trail of unfortunate sequels. *After Virtue,* still in so many ways fundamental to MacIntyre's present position, is an Aristotelian book. I propose, then, to reflect on the nature of Alasdair MacIntyre's Aristotelianism and his place in the contemporary Aristotelian tradition. Here I leave aside the purely exegetical and historical debates that divide Aristotle scholars into various camps and give rise to numerous publications every year.

I focus instead on those Aristotelians of the present and the recent past who have presented Aristotelian moral philosophy as a live philosophical option.

MacIntyre is something of an exception among Aristotelians, and this in two respects. First, the great majority of contemporary Aristotelians present Aristotelianism as a form of ethics that individuals can and should adopt for the conduct of their personal or even private lives. Not only is this kind of Aristotelian ethics largely divorced (usually with embarrassment!) from the political, social, and economic thinking of the historical Aristotle; it is largely divorced from any kind of political, social, or economic thinking. This would be true of, for instance, Henry Veatch's popular *Rational Man: A Modern Interpretation of Aristotelian Ethics*.[4] MacIntyre, by contrast, has long insisted that an Aristotelian ethics of the virtues can be lived only in a certain kind of social context, a context in which practices can flourish, the goods internal to these practices can be discussed, and the virtues required for the practices can be cultivated—a social context available to certain kinds of relatively small communities but by no means readily available in the nation-states of advanced modernity. Much present-day Aristotelian moral philosophy represents what from MacIntyre's perspective is not to be had: a form of ethical life without a corresponding social or political embodiment.

Second, the great majority of contemporary Aristotelians have worked out some sort of truce with the dominant contemporary liberalism; and some have even concluded alliances with it. In *The Time of Our Lives: The Ethics of Common Sense*,[5] Mortimer Adler, one of the twentieth century's most successful popularizers of a kind of Aristotelian ethics, saw what he thought was practically a perfect fit between Aristotelian ethics and the then-current American political and economic systems. His response to the protests of the late 1960s was to admit that the American educational system indeed stood in need of a revolution but to insist that the American political and economic systems were essentially in good order. Alasdair MacIntyre, by contrast, has long insisted that the politics and economics of advanced liberal modernity are definitely not in good order.

More recent Aristotelians have taken this demarche with liberalism further. Consider, for instance, the majority of the contributors to the collection *Aristotle and Modern Politics: The Persistence of Political Philosophy*.[6] While they argue for modifications or corrections of contemporary liberalism, these Aristotelians assume that contemporary liberalism is fundamentally sound and needs only modifications or corrections of detail. But far and away the best-known proponent of a synthesis of Aristotelianism and liberalism is Martha C. Nussbaum of the University of Chicago, who has attempted to carry out this project in a series of articles and books.[7] It is no accident, then, that Martha Nussbaum has at times sharply criticized MacIntyre's Aristotelianism.[8] Her widespread recognition as a public intellectual has given some currency to the view that hers is the direction in which Aristotelianism is going and ought to go. What are those of us who sympathize with MacIntyre's reading of the Aristotelian tradition to respond to this situation? I see three main possibilities.

The first would be to insist that Nussbaum, the contributors to *Aristotle and Modern Politics,* and people of similar mind are not authentic Aristotelians but rather liberals who fancy themselves to be Aristotelians. We could, as it were, try to expel them from the Aristotelian party. For this it would not be enough to point to places where they might have gotten this or that point of Aristotelian exegesis wrong, important as that might be. To be effective, our criticism would have to show that the liberal Aristotelians had gotten Aristotle wrong on points of such importance that they no longer deserved to be called Aristotelians. But even if this were the right move, it would mean dissociating ourselves from the Aristotelian tradition as it has in fact developed and concretely embodied itself.

An alternative, then, would be to admit that Nussbaum and company are genuine Aristotelians but to maintain that all this shows is that the Aristotelian tradition is not in good order. The disorder would not lie in the fact that Aristotelians were differing with one another. MacIntyre has argued persuasively that a tradition in good order is typically marked by an ongoing argument among its adherents about the goods of the tradition. And so the bare fact that Aristotelians are differing with one another should neither surprise nor disconcert us. When have Aristotelians not disagreed? The problem would be rather that a great number of contemporary Aristotelians had failed to recognize that an Aristotelian moral philosophy requires a distinctive kind of social embodiment and that many of them were also committed, inconsistently, to the claims and practices of contemporary liberalism. But if this is the case, then we need to ask why people who think of themselves as Aristotelians have neglected or misconstrued important elements in their own tradition. Could it be that in our days the Aristotelian tradition is not in good order? Could it be that, to borrow MacIntyre's terms, contemporary Aristotelians have found themselves in an epistemological crisis, facing problems that they cannot solve, and so have turned to the liberal tradition for help? I thought it was supposed to be the other way around, that liberalism was in crisis and that it was liberals who needed to turn to the Aristotelian tradition for help.

And so I would suggest, as a third response to the current situation, that those of us who follow Alasdair MacIntyre's brand of Aristotelianism may need to study liberalism once again, in the hope of understanding why so many of our fellow Aristotelians find it attractive or even compelling. This is not the place to attempt a detailed study of Martha Nussbaum or of the contributors to *Aristotle and Modern Politics*. But their attempts to reconcile Aristotelianism and liberalism deserve more searching study from the MacIntyrean wing of Aristotelianism than they have (so far as I know) received. MacIntyre's essays "Rival Aristotles: Aristotle against Some Renaissance Aristotelians" and "Rival Aristotles: Aristotle against Some Modern Aristotelians" are models of the kind of work that needs to be done.[9]

MacIntyre the Thomist

Alasdair MacIntyre is now not only an Aristotelian who follows or draws on St. Thomas's interpretation of Aristotle but an actual Thomist as well. I now propose to explore his identity as a Thomist, with a view both to understanding him better and to identifying certain agenda that might advance his project. Here I have to begin by acknowledging what I find to be the painful fact that MacIntyre's Thomism has not been nearly as influential among his fellow Thomists as I would have hoped and expected.

Consider, for example, *Wisdom, Law, and Virtue: Essays in Thomistic Ethics,* a collection of twenty-seven of Father Lawrence Dewan's essays, most of them first published after 1981, and many from the 1990s and early 2000s.[10] There is no entry for Alasdair MacIntyre in the sixteen small-print pages of bibliography or in the twenty-two pages of index. My aim in pointing this out is not to sow tares among brethren but to draw attention to a phenomenon that calls for explanation. For the neglect, or the comparative lack of influence, of MacIntyre's work among Thomists is no accident. On the contrary, it has at least three explanations.

The first is that MacIntyre's Thomism is in very many ways distinctive. Most Thomists come to their Thomism in early adulthood, and for the rest of their lives the encounter with Thomas controls their philosophical vocabulary, not to mention their prose style. I cannot say when MacIntyre first read St. Thomas, but his embrace of Thomism came in middle life, in the years after *After Virtue;* and his philosophical idiom is still in many ways that of twentieth-century Anglo-American analytic philosophy. Few Thomists have had anything like the depth of his encounters with Hume and the Scottish Enlightenment, with Hegel, with Marx and the Marxists, with Freud, with Wittgenstein and Collingwood, and with contemporary social science and philosophy of science. While many Thomists have been conspicuous for their knowledge of the history of philosophy, few, I think, have been so historically conscious as MacIntyre. Few, that is, have taken so seriously the historical situatedness that characterizes, and on his view must characterize, philosophical views and systems. And so MacIntyre has been able to write about the history of moral philosophy in a way that is, so far as I know, unparalleled in the annals of Thomism. A comparison with Jacques Maritain's *Moral Philosophy: An Historical and Critical Survey of the Great Systems* or with Vernon J. Bourke's *History of Ethics* would make this point clear.[11]

A second explanation for the comparative lack of influence of MacIntyre's Thomism within the Thomistic tradition arises, paradoxically, from a signal contribution that he has made to that tradition. I am thinking of his view that Aquinas's claims represent not definitive, unsurpassable, and irreformable achievements but rather the best accounts available to Aquinas in his time—a view that opens up the possibility that an evolving Thomistic tradition might in one or another respect improve on St. Thomas himself.

Consider the implications of this advance. One of the bedeviling problems of the Thomistic tradition, at least to the eye of this observer, has been the presumption that many, perhaps most, philosophical problems can be settled at the level of Thomistic exegesis—the presupposition that nine times out of ten the answer is already on the page, waiting to be found in Thomas's text, provided that that text is rightly understood. This presumption has been a formula for failed encounters with the modern world, and MacIntyre's view that Aquinas's positions represent the best accounts available to him in his time has in principle done away with it.

I wish that he had also been able to do away with it in practice. But to the extent that I can judge, this part of MacIntyre's work has so far had little impact on his colleagues within the Thomistic tradition. He has solved a serious problem in that tradition, but he has received precious little credit for it, because, I think, few Thomists had even noticed that their tradition was suffering from that problem, while some, I suspect, might even deny that there was a problem to begin with.

I sometimes worry that MacIntyre may have had—contrary, I am sure, to his intention—a bad influence on some of his fellow Thomists. While I cannot point to anything in print, I think I have spoken with Thomists who sincerely welcomed Alasdair MacIntyre's criticism of modernity and modern moral philosophy but welcomed it precisely as legitimating their own neglect of modernity and modern moral philosophy, their declining to come to any kind of intellectual terms with these phenomena. "MacIntyre has refuted them, so we don't have to read them." I fear that MacIntyre's criticism of modernity may have soothed the intellectual consciences of some of his fellow Thomists in a way that he never intended.

My aim, however, is not to console Alasdair MacIntyre on the insufficient appreciation of what he has done for the Thomistic tradition. I am sure he is familiar with the axiom that no good deed goes unpunished. My aim is to suggest ways in which his philosophical project can be extended. For this I must turn to a third explanation of why his work has not yet had the influence that it should have had.

This third explanation is that Thomists (and here I use the term somewhat elastically, to include moral philosophers and theologians brought up in the Thomistic tradition or acknowledging some debt thereto) have been preoccupied with a set of arguments internal to their tradition, and that the relevance of MacIntyre's Thomism to these arguments has not been as clear as it might have been. I refer, of course, to the serious and often heated debates in the areas of Catholic moral philosophy and moral theology. Of course not all the participants in these debates are Thomists. But many, perhaps even most, of them were brought up on some form of Thomistic philosophy and even theology; and from what I have read and heard, a majority would like to think of themselves as faithful to the insights of St. Thomas.

One of our many debts to MacIntyre is for his recognition that there is a kind of disagreement in which the parties not only differ about some issue or issues but differ about how their differences are to be characterized. The current debates in moral philosophy and moral theology are of this kind, and so my characterization here is preliminary and tentative. I see the following differences. There are philosophers and moral theologians who understand themselves as continuing the Aristotelian-Thomistic tradition that was in place before the Second Vatican Council (1962–65) and the discussions that led up to and followed the encyclical *Humanae Vitae* (1968). Their opponents tend to label them the old-line natural law theorists. These opponents are also philosophers and especially moral theologians, most of whom were brought up as Thomists, many of whom would still identify themselves as Thomists, but who found themselves dissenting from the controverted teaching of *Humanae Vitae* and who have in the ensuing four decades developed a brand of moral philosophy or moral theology that is significantly different from that defended by the first group. Their opponents tend to label them the proportionalists.

To complicate the picture, a third group of philosophers and theologians known as the new natural lawyers have insisted, against the first group, that the philosophical underpinnings of their traditional moral theology were grossly inadequate and that their traditional moral theology itself was seriously marred by legalism; and they have trenchantly criticized the second group for capitulating to utilitarianism or consequentialism. Needless to say, their proposed replacement for the old-line natural law theory, the new natural law theory, has come in for serious criticism. To complicate the picture further, thinkers taking inspiration from the late Pope John Paul II argue that what is needed in moral philosophy and theology is a kind of Christian personalism, an ethics with roots in St. Thomas but also in a certain kind of phenomenology, or at least expressed in a kind of phenomenological language, and framed as a philosophy or theology of the human body and of interpersonal relations.

If you will allow me to voice a disquieting suggestion: the situation within Catholic moral theology bears more than a passing resemblance to the landscape of incommensurable claims and unsettlable disagreements that MacIntyre painted for us in the second chapter of *After Virtue*. But at this point I need to face an objection: "Aren't you trying to turn MacIntyre's moral philosophy into a theology? His Thomistic Aristotelianism is professedly a philosophy, not a theology. Leave well enough alone."

Here I recall that Giovanna Borradori once asked Alasdair MacIntyre the following question: "Some critics suspect that your more recent philosophical positions conceal a reassertion of Christianity, that they are a new version of Catholic theology. Is there a basis of truth in all this?" To which he replied: "It is false, both biographically and with respect to the structure of my beliefs. What I now believe philosophically I came to believe very largely before I reacknowledged the truth of Catholic Christianity. And I was only able to respond to the teachings of the Church because I had already learned from Aristotelianism both the nature of the mistakes involved in my earlier rejection of Christianity, and how to understand aright the relation of philosophical argument to theological inquiry. My philosophy, like that of many other Aristotelians, is theistic; but it is as secular in its content as any other."[12]

I have no wish to dispute, and no reason to dispute, anything that MacIntyre said in this reply. His Thomistic Aristotelianism is a philosophy. It does not claim to be a theology. It is not intended to function as a crypto-theology or a stealth theology. But my proposal is not that MacIntyre, or anyone else, should transform his Thomistic Aristotelian philosophy into a theology. All that I am calling for, and I admit it is considerable, is that MacIntyrean Thomist moral philosophers bring to bear on the debates of moral theology the resources of the renewed Aristotelian-Thomistic tradition, augmented by Alasdair MacIntyre's contributions of historical consciousness and rigorous standards of argumentation. It would not be a bad thing if a certain number of those who function as professional moral theologians were to have a training in the MacIntyrean style of moral philosophy. And this would not compromise the secular character of MacIntyre's moral philosophy in the least.

The relations between moral philosophy and moral theology are close and complex, in such a way that each has things to contribute to the other. MacIntyre has explored some of these relations in his 1998 John Coffin Memorial Lecture, "What Has Christianity to Say to the Moral Philosopher?"[13] In recent years he has also paid considerable attention to the work of the Danish philosopher-theologian Knud Ejler Løgstrup.[14] Løgstrup's argument is, to be sure, primarily philosophical rather than theological.

But I wonder if there is not something in the inner dynamics of Thomism that sooner or later pushes Thomists to engage with theological issues.

I have now, however, opened myself up to a second objection: "You have suggested that MacIntyre's moral philosophy has not had the influence it should have had because it has not been recognized as relevant to the debates carried on by contemporary Roman Catholic moral theologians. Guilty as charged! MacIntyre's moral philosophy does not address the issues as formulated by contemporary Catholic moral theologians, and so be it! The deficiency lies not with MacIntyre's moral philosophy but with the ways in which the moral theologians have framed their issues. To have intervened in such badly conducted debates would have been a waste of time and intelligence."

I find a hint that Alasdair MacIntyre himself may possibly view the situation in this way in the preface that he wrote to the book *Morality: The Catholic View,* by the Dominican Servais Pinckaers.[15] There, referring to Pinckaers's *Les sources de la morale chrétienne* (1985), he writes:

> What Father Pinckaers made clear to us was the irrelevance of those preceding debates of recent years, debates that had been informed by false choices between inadequately characterized alternatives: Is the moral life about rules or consequences? Which has priority, authority or autonomy? Is our language to be scholastic or patristic? Should we make use neither of the scholastics nor of the Fathers, but return to the New Testament? Are we to look to the Second Vatican Council or to its predecessors? What Father Pinckaers provided was a historical perspective in which later Christian writers, whether patristic or scholastic or modern, are understood as contributing to and enriching our reading of scripture. The culmination of his argument is a wonderfully illuminating enquiry into the relationship of human freedom to the natural law.[16]

I am just beginning to study the work of Servais Pinckaers, and it may well be that his work will show some or all of the debates to which I have referred to be nothing more than false choices between inadequately characterized alternatives. And perhaps it will turn out that a MacIntyrean moral theology will be pretty much the same as a Pinckaersian moral theology. At this point I just do not know, and so I need to leave open the questions of whether and on what terms a MacIntyrean moral philosophy should contribute to the debates of Catholic moral theology.

A question that I cannot leave open, however, is whether MacIntyreans should be involved in the contemporary Catholic discussion about the proper stance toward the dominant liberal modernity. For from MacIntyre's point of view, it would seem that Thomists, and those Catholics who think of themselves as Thomists, should refuse any sort of alliance with a modernity whose thinking and institutions are so seriously flawed. To conclude a permanent alliance with modernity would be to betray important elements in the Thomistic tradition. It would be a good thing, then, for MacIntyreans, or for Thomists of the MacIntyrean variety, to take a more vigorous and critical part in the discussion of politics within the Catholic community. To the extent that the assumptions and rhetoric of liberal modernity go unchallenged in the Catholic milieu, Catholics will be less and less capable of recognizing and challenging the limitations of liberal modernity. In "Politics, Philosophy and the Common Good," MacIntyre spoke of the parish community as one possible setting in which practices and their associated virtues could flourish. How is that to happen if the presentation of Catholic social thought in the parishes largely reinforces the presuppositions of the dominant liberal modernity? But this practical reference brings us to the next section.

MacIntyre the Revolutionary

At one point I thought of entitling this section "MacIntyre the Marxist." But such a parallelism with the titles of the first and second sections would suggest that Alasdair MacIntyre still identified himself as a Marxist. And that, I take it, is false. Let me instead use this section to address the revolutionary aspect of MacIntyre's identity and of his project. Here of course I owe a great debt to Kelvin Knight's "Revolutionary Aristotelianism."[17] And I have to recognize that the contributors to *Revolutionary Aristotelianism: Ethics, Resistance and Utopia* have covered this aspect of MacIntyre's work far more thoroughly than I could ever do.[18]

Alasdair MacIntyre has long been committed, and remains committed, to certain theses and basic insights of Marxism, while acknowledging difficulties in the way that Marxism developed, and no longer identifying himself as a Marxist. As the essays "The *Theses on Feuerbach*: A Road Not Taken" and "Three Perspectives on Marxism: 1953, 1968, 1995" make clear, he holds that the early Marx's criticism of liberalism and capitalism was and remains essentially correct.[19] But MacIntyre's Marxism is residual in the sense that it has been shorn of the materialism, the atheism, and the historical determinism that were thought for so long to be essential, even foundational, to Marxism. (In particular I note that MacIntyre follows George L. Kline in rejecting the view that the historical Karl Marx was a philosophical materialist.) MacIntyre's residual Marxism is the kind of Marxism that a Thomist can endorse without compromising any of the logical, metaphysical, or ethical commitments that are essential to a Thomistic moral philosophy, and without compromising those religious commitments that are fundamental to the Thomistic *sacra doctrina*.

About this I am glad. But it would still be a useful exercise to settle accounts between Marxism and Thomistic Aristotelianism more explicitly, that is, for someone working in a MacIntyrean context to write an essay (and here I borrow from Croce) setting out clearly and concisely what exactly is living and what is dead in the philosophy of Marx, and then to set alongside this reckoning the central theses and the metaphysical requirements of a Thomistic Aristotelian moral philosophy. Such a comparison would be a modest but real contribution to MacIntyre's project and to the MacIntyrean movement. I am not suggesting that there is any contradiction between MacIntyre's debts to Marx and his Aristotelian-Thomistic commitments. If I recall, he himself has characterized Marx as the most Aristotelian of the moderns. But he himself has taught us that when concepts and claims that have developed within the framework of one tradition are lifted from that tradition and placed in the context of another tradition, the results can sometimes be problematic.

Whose Justice? Which Rationality? is a very long book. The following paragraph from chapter 20 was for me at least a great reward:

> Liberalism, as I have understood it in this book, does of course appear in contemporary debates in a number of guises and in so doing is often successful in preempting the debate by reformulating quarrels and conflicts with liberalism, so that they appear to have become debates within liberalism, putting in question this or that particular set of attitudes or policies,

but not the fundamental tenets of liberalism with respect to individuals and the expression of their preferences. So so-called conservatism and so-called radicalism in these contemporary guises are in general mere stalking-horses for liberalism: the contemporary debates within modern political systems are almost exclusively between conservative liberals, liberal liberals, and radical liberals. There is little place in such political systems for the criticism of the system itself, that is, for putting liberalism in question.[20]

The 2007 Prologue to the third edition of *After Virtue* reads as follows:

> This critique of liberalism should not be interpreted as a sign of any sympathy on my part for contemporary conservatism. That conservatism is in too many ways a mirror image of the liberalism that it professedly opposes. Its commitment to a way of life structured by a free market economy is a commitment to an individualism as corrosive as that of liberalism. And, where liberalism by permissive legal enactments has tried to use the power of the modern state to transform social relationships, conservatism by prohibitive legal enactments now tries to use that same power for its own coercive purposes. Such conservatism is as alien to the projects of *After Virtue* as liberalism is.[21]

So not only is contemporary liberalism to be rejected, but contemporary conservatism and communitarianism as well. Within an overall context of agreement, I would like to draw attention to two groups of thinkers, both as possible exceptions to the norm that contemporary conservatives are fundamentally liberals and as thinkers who, even if they are liberals, may still have things to teach us about how to go about embodying a revolutionary Aristotelian tradition.

First the disciples of Leo Strauss. The Straussian phenomenon is complex and not easy to understand. But for all that one may criticize their readings of classic texts and their appropriation of the term *classical political philosophy,* they have succeeded in setting up a subculture that is at least slightly subversive of modernity. At a practical level, of course, Straussians accommodate themselves to the conditions of contemporary liberal modernity, especially academic liberal modernity. They are not revolutionaries. But arguably they are subversives, constantly reminding their disciples of the antithesis between the classical outlook and the modern outlook. And I use the term *disciples* advisedly, for the Straussians manage to attract the attention and shape the identity of a significant number of intelligent students and to form them into groups or cadres, thus creating small intellectual communities with a certain relative autonomy from the state and the university. They certainly network! And even if we conclude that the differences between the Straussian form of the classical tradition and the MacIntyrean form of the Aristotelian-Thomistic tradition are serious, even radical, I suspect that these will not be quite the same differences as those that separate both these movements from contemporary liberalism.

Whatever one makes of the Straussians in general, the Catholic Straussians deserve particular attention. Here I am thinking of the late Ernest Fortin, a formidably learned man and a formidable critic of at least certain trends in contemporary liberalism and of allied trends in contemporary Catholicism.[22] Whatever one ultimately thinks of Father Fortin's work, it would not be adequate simply to categorize him as a conservative liberal. I would suggest the same of the French political theorist Pierre Manent. Manent admits that he is a liberal—in his own words, a "sad liberal"—but his liberalism is surely conscious of its own inner tensions and difficulties.[23] Manent would seem to be the kind of thinker who would be open to the claims of a rival tradition to explain and resolve the difficulties of liberalism, if such a rival tradition should appear.

A second group to which we should attend is a group of intellectual conservatives or would-be conservatives, followers, at least in a general way, of the late Russell Kirk. We may see Kirk and his followers as attempting to criticize and amend the errors of twentieth-century liberalism by recourse to the earlier liberalism of the seventeenth, eighteenth, and nineteenth centuries.[24] We may even judge that Kirk's *The Conservative Mind from Burke to Eliot* is largely a study of a certain form of liberal mind.[25] But fairness requires the admission that Kirk and his followers are at least sensitive to some of the issues that MacIntyre raised in the early chapters of *After Virtue*—certainly to the issues of the objectivity of judgments of value and judgments of obligation—even if their diagnoses are less radical and their remedies less apt to cure. But apart from this, I mention them because they have had at least moderate success in embodying their movement institutionally. Here I am thinking of organizations like the Intercollegiate Studies Institute, the Witherspoon Institute, the Russell Kirk Center, and the Fund for American Studies. My sense is that all these organizations are trying to criticize liberalism while still embracing capitalism. But if they are not revolutionary in the way that a Thomistic Aristotelian might desire, they are at least to some extent subversive of the paradigm or paradigms that dominate contemporary American higher education.

Even if the followers of Leo Strauss and the followers of Russell Kirk turn out in the last analysis to be liberals, they may yet be the kind of liberals who are most likely to recognize, or most capable of recognizing, that the liberal position stands in an epistemological crisis. And so we have things to teach these two groups of people. But to do so—and here I echo the passage from the prologue to the third edition of *After Virtue* quoted at the outset of this paper—we will need to learn how to speak their language and to think as they think; and we should be open to the possibility that they may have things to teach us, especially about how to give our tradition institutional embodiment.

In his interview with Giovanna Borradori and elsewhere Alasdair MacIntyre has maintained that the politics of the contemporary nation-state are barren, so barren that the reasonable course is to abstain from taking part in those politics. But what is not barren is "the politics involved in constructing and sustaining small-scale local communities, at the level of the family, the neighborhood, the workplace, the parish, the school, or clinic, communities within which the needs of the hungry and the homeless can be met."[26] I think this is right, and I do not have anything special to add to it, except to note that in the United States at least it is very difficult for small-scale local communities to develop and maintain enough insulation from the surrounding society and the state to be even relatively autonomous. Perhaps we need to supplement the Catholic teaching on subsidiarity—the prescription to higher authority not to overreach its proper function by interfering unnecessarily in the activities of lower or more limited communities—with a "subsidiarity from below," a rationale and a set of strategies that small-scale local communities might use to safeguard and even enhance their relative autonomy.

As MacIntyre sees it, contemporary universities and contemporary academic disciplines are organized and function in ways that reinforce many of the objectionable features of liberal modernity. It is appropriate, indeed urgent, to develop alternative institutional forms for education and for the intellectual life. This is particularly important for colleges and universities of Catholic foundation. This point comes across very clearly in the essay "Catholic Universities: Dangers, Hopes, Choices," and in greater detail in *God, Philosophy, Universities*.²⁷

Once again I agree. I have learned from MacIntyre that the issue is not simply the maintenance of Catholic identity in an institution that is otherwise indistinguishable from its secular peers but a readiness to reconsider the whole way in which education is organized and in particular the relations between philosophy and theology and the other disciplines. But after four decades of involvement with North American academe, most of it in the Catholic and Jesuit variant of same, I am impressed, or depressed, by the difficulty of making any progress along these lines. We need to learn more about some of the more experimental or marginal or both educational institutions: St. John's of Annapolis and Santa Fe, Thomas Aquinas College in California, the Franciscan University in Steubenville, Ohio, and the new Ave Maria University in Florida. In this context, we need to reflect on how to destabilize what some take to be the natural alliance between theologically traditional Catholicism and conservative free-market capitalism. Another phenomenon that we need to study is the movement toward home-schooling. While this movement tends to be associated in the public mind with Christian fundamentalism and political conservatism, it does at least represent both a form of resistance to the dominant educational establishment and a form of community among those who practice it. In all this I am mindful of the advice of the business guru Peter Drucker, that it is generally easier to do new things through new units and organizations than to persuade an existing unit or institution to do things in new ways.

I am, then, in general sympathy with Alasdair MacIntyre's revolutionary project, at least to the extent that I have understood it. I regret that I am not in a position to spell out the practical steps that would best promote this revolutionary project. I would be interested to learn more from MacIntyre about how he thinks plain persons should proceed in the practical order. Would he, for instance, favor some version of the style of community organization practiced by the late Saul Alinsky?²⁸ I do, however, believe that two pieces of historical and theoretical work would help to advance the revolutionary project of Thomistic Aristotelianism.

One such task would be a careful reexamination of the legacy of thinkers such as the influential Thomist Jacques Maritain and the Jesuit

John Courtney Murray. Both men wrote before MacIntyre advanced his criticism of liberal modernity, and it is at least worth examining the possibility that they may have conceded more to liberal modernity than they should have — to see, for example, to what extent such works of Jacques Maritain as *Man and the State* represent a coming to terms with liberal modernity. John Courtney Murray, S. J., was certainly raised in the Thomistic tradition and continued to maintain a Catholic natural law position in his *We Hold These Truths: Catholic Reflections on the American Proposition*.[29] But this book, and Murray's work generally, have been taken as heralding the reconciliation of the natural law tradition with the American tradition of political liberalism. Murray died in 1967, even before Maritain, but he, or at least this reading of his work, has influenced a whole generation of American Catholic intellectuals and educators. Murray's position could stand a critical reexamination from a MacIntyrean perspective.

For essentially the same reasons I think it would be good for some of us to reread, or to read for the first time, some works of Catholic Aristotelian-Thomistic social philosophy and political theory by early- and mid-twentieth-century neoscholastics, such as Johannes Messner's *Social Ethics: Natural Law in the Modern World* and Heinrich Rommen's *The State in Catholic Thought: A Treatise in Political Philosophy*,[30] not to mention the voluminous works of Oswald von Nell-Breuning, S. J. These authors were trying to understand and to prescribe for modern families, communities, and nation-states. As they were working within the Aristotelian and Thomistic traditions, even their failures, if they failed, should be instructive. And if we think that some contemporary exponents of the Aristotelian and Thomistic traditions are too comfortable with the presuppositions of liberal modernity, then it would make sense to step back a generation or two and to learn what was going on.

Let me round out this consideration of Alasdair MacIntyre's revolutionary project by expressing a concern. It would be unfortunate if those of us attracted by MacIntyre's Aristotelian-Thomistic moral philosophy, along with his metaphysics, his theism, and his Catholicism, and those of us attracted by his revolutionary project were to walk in separate paths, the metaphysically and religiously oriented MacIntyreans in one path and the more secular and activist MacIntyreans in another, somewhat like the Right Hegelians and the Left Hegelians. I do not wish to cause a problem where none exists; but it will be important for us who stand in such debt to MacIntyre to work out in greater detail how his Aristotelian, Thomistic, and Catholic identity and his revolutionary project can support and reinforce one another.

Let me now try to sum up what I have tried to do in this paper. I have suggested that insofar as MacIntyre's philosophical identity is Aristotelian, and insofar as a significant number of contemporary Aristotelians are exploring the compatibility of Aristotelianism with liberalism, or even promoting a synthesis of Aristotelianism and liberalism, those of us who sympathize with MacIntyre's antiliberal Aristotelianism should revisit the claims of liberalism in this new context.

I have suggested that while MacIntyre's philosophical identity is Thomistic, his Thomism is unusual and even distinctive—a fact that goes some way toward explaining why such an articulate exponent of the claims of Thomism has not exercised a greater influence within that tradition. I have also suggested that it would be appropriate for MacIntyre and for those of similar mind to intervene more vigorously in the debates of moral philosophers and theologians that currently divide, not to say confuse, the Thomistic tradition—not that MacIntyre's philosophy should give up its integrity and persuasive power as a secular philosophy and turn itself into a theology, but that this very philosophy should be leading us to pose philosophical questions to our brothers and sisters the theologians.

I have suggested that, while MacIntyre no longer sees himself as a Marxist, he remains committed to a number of Marx's views. While not suggesting that these Marxist views are inconsistent with MacIntyre's identity as a Thomistic Aristotelian, I have suggested that the coherence between them and the core theses of Thomistic Aristotelian moral philosophy could be worked out more clearly and explicitly than (so far as I know) has been done so far.

I am in deep sympathy with the main lines of MacIntyre's revolutionary project, though I admit to dismay at the size of the obstacles that stand in the way of realizing the project in even a small way. I have offered a few suggestions for the project, suggestions that will have to be tested by the discipline of practice.

In all this commentary on MacIntyre's identity and project I was also trying to extend and deepen the analysis of tradition that has been one of his most important contributions. And so the first part on MacIntyre's

Aristotelian identity posed the question: How should Aristotelians who see Aristotelianism as clearly superior to modern liberalism understand and respond to the fact that people who also think of themselves as Aristotelians make concessions to, or even try to fashion a synthesis with, modern liberalism? The second part on MacIntyre's Thomistic identity posed the question: How should those of us who regard ourselves as Thomists and who find MacIntyre's reading of Aquinas persuasive understand and respond to the fact that his moral philosophy has not had the influence within the Thomistic tradition that we might have hoped and expected? And the third part, on MacIntyre's revolutionary project and his debts to Marxism, posed the question: What happens when someone who is thoroughly committed to a certain tradition, in this case Thomistic Aristotelianism, also brings to that tradition questions and insights that were originally at home in what was, or at least was thought to be, a radically discordant tradition?

Alasdair MacIntyre has acknowledged that he stands in debt to John Henry Newman's analysis of tradition. To conclude this paper, I am struck by three ways in which MacIntyre's career resembles Newman's. They both went through long years exploring various positions, adhering to them for a while, then becoming conscious of their problems, and eventually abandoning them in favor of other positions. After these long itineraries, once they came to rest, Newman in Roman Catholicism and MacIntyre in Aristotelian Thomism and Catholicism, they became notable exponents of those traditions. But despite their commitment to and exposition of these traditions, they did not at the time have the level of influence within their traditions that one might have hoped or expected.

In his Biglietto Speech of May 12, 1879, Newman admits that he has made many mistakes, but then says, "To one great mischief I have from the first opposed myself. For thirty, forty, fifty years I have resisted to the best of my powers the spirit of Liberalism in religion."[31] I think Alasdair MacIntyre could make these words his own. True, religion would seem to be one thing, philosophy and politics other things; and so the parallel between Newman's campaign against liberal religion and MacIntyre's campaign against liberalism might seem to be purely verbal. But listen to how Newman defines liberalism in religion: "the doctrine that there is no positive truth in religion, but that one creed is as good as another . . . . It is inconsistent with any recognition of any religion, as *true*" (emphasis

Newman's). In this paper I have not spoken about MacIntyre's insistence that a realistic conception of truth is indispensable to any rational inquiry, but on this great point, as on so much else, he and John Henry Newman are at one.

Notes

I wish to express my gratitude to Fran O'Rourke and to all those involved in the organization of the Dublin conference in celebration of Alasdair MacIntyre's eightieth birthday. I am also much indebted to Alasdair MacIntyre for his generous help in correspondence and conversation. Any errors and inadequacies in the interpretation of his philosophical positions are solely and regrettably my responsibility.

1. Alasdair MacIntyre, "What Has *Not* Happened in Moral Philosophy," *Yale Journal of Criticism* 5 (1992): 193.

2. Alasdair MacIntyre, *Whose Justice? Which Rationality?* (Notre Dame: University of Notre Dame Press, 1988), and "Moral Relativism, Truth and Justification," in *The MacIntyre Reader*, ed. Kelvin Knight (Notre Dame: University of Notre Dame Press, 1998), 202–20.

3. Alasdair MacIntyre, *After Virtue: A Study in Moral Theory*, 3rd ed. (Notre Dame: University of Notre Dame Press, 2007), xiii.

4. Henry Veatch, *Rational Man: A Modern Interpretation of Aristotelian Ethics* (1962; repr., Indianapolis: Liberty Fund, 2003).

5. Mortimer Adler, *The Time of Our Lives: The Ethics of Common Sense* (1970; repr., New York: Fordham University Press, 1996).

6. Aristide Tessitore, ed., *Aristotle and Modern Politics: The Persistence of Political Philosophy* (Notre Dame: University of Notre Dame Press, 2002).

7. For example, Martha Nussbaum, "Aristotelian Social Democracy," in *Liberalism and the Good*, ed. R. Bruce Douglas, Gerald M. Mara, and Henry S. Richardson (New York: Routledge, 1990), 203–52, *Women and Human Development: The Capabilities Approach* (Cambridge: Cambridge University Press, 2000), and *Frontiers of Justice: Disability, Nationality, Species Membership* (Cambridge, MA: Harvard University Press, 2006).

8. For example, Martha Nussbaum, "Recoiling from Reason," review of *Whose Justice? Which Rationality?*, by Alasdair MacIntyre, *New York Review of Books,* December 7, 1989, 36–41.

9. Alasdair MacIntyre, "Rival Aristotles: Aristotle against Some Renaissance Aristotelians" and "Rival Aristotles: Aristotle against Some Modern Aristotelians," in *Ethics and Politics*, vol. 2 of *Selected Essays* (Cambridge: Cambridge University Press, 2006), 3–21 and 22–40 respectively.

10. Lawrence Dewan, O.P., *Wisdom, Law, and Virtue: Essays in Thomistic Ethics* (New York: Fordham University Press, 2008).

11. Jacques Maritain, *Moral Philosophy: An Historical and Critical Survey of the Great Systems* (London: Geoffrey Bles, 1964); Vernon J. Bourke, *History of Ethics* (Garden City, NY: Doubleday, 1968).

12. Alasdair MacIntyre, "An Interview with Giovanna Borradori," in Knight, *MacIntyre Reader,* 265–66.

13. Alasdair MacIntyre, "What Has Christianity to Say to the Moral Philosopher?," in *The Doctrine of God and Theological Ethics,* ed. Michael C. Banner and Alan J. Torrance (London: Continuum, 2006), 17–32.

14. See Alasdair MacIntyre, "Human Nature and Human Dependence: What Might a Thomist Learn from Reading Løgstrup?" in *Concern for the Other: Perspectives on the Ethics of K. E. Løgstrup,* ed. Svend Andersen and Kees van Kooten Niekerk (Notre Dame: University of Notre Dame Press, 2007), 147–66; also Hans Fink and Alasdair MacIntyre, introduction to *The Ethical Demand,* by K. E. Løgstrup (Notre Dame: University of Notre Dame Press, 1997), xv–xxxviii.

15. Alasdair MacIntyre, preface to *Morality: The Catholic View,* by Servais Pinckaers (South Bend, IN: St. Augustine's Press, 2001).

16. Ibid., vii–viii. Servais Pinckaers's *Les sources de la morale chrétienne: Sa méthode, son contenu, son histoire* (Fribourg: Éditions universitaires, 1985) is now available in English as *The Sources of Christian Ethics* (Washington, DC: Catholic University of America Press, 1995).

17. Kelvin Knight, "Revolutionary Aristotelianism," in *Contemporary Political Studies,* ed. Iain Hampsher-Monk and Jeffrey Stanyer (Belfast: Political Studies Association of the United Kingdom, 1996), 2:885–96.

18. *Revolutionary Aristotelianism: Ethics, Resistance and Utopia,* ed. Kelvin Knight and Paul Blackledge (Stuttgart: Lucius and Lucius, 2008).

19. Alasdair MacIntyre, "The *Theses on Feuerbach*: A Road Not Taken," in Knight, *MacIntyre Reader,* 223–34, and "Three Perspectives on Marxism: 1953, 1968, 1995," in *Ethics and Politics,* 145–58. A historical perspective on MacIntyre's Marxism is found in *Alasdair MacIntyre's Engagement with Marxism,* ed. Paul Blackledge and Neil Davidson (Leiden: Brill, 2008).

20. MacIntyre, *Whose Justice?,* 392.

21. MacIntyre, *After Virtue,* xv.

22. Fortin's essays have been collected in four volumes. The first three have been edited by J. Brian Benestad: *The Birth of Philosophic Christianity: Studies in Early Christian and Medieval Thought* (Lanham, MD: Rowman and Littlefield, 1996); *Classical Christianity and the Political Order: Reflections on the Theologico-Political Problem* (Lanham, MD: Rowman and Littlefield, 1996); and *Human Rights, Virtue, and the Common Good: Untimely Meditations on Religion and Politics,* ed. J. Brian Benestad (Lanham, MD: Rowman and Littlefield, 1996). The fourth volume has been edited by Michael P. Foley: *Ever Ancient, Ever New:*

Ruminations on the City, the Soul, and the Church (Lanham, MD: Rowman and Littlefield, 2007).

23. See, among many works, Pierre Manent's *An Intellectual History of Liberalism* (Princeton: Princeton University Press, 1995) and *The City of Man* (Princeton: Princeton University Press, 1998).

24. Kirk's estimate of Edmund Burke is as positive as MacIntyre's estimate of Burke is negative.

25. Russell Kirk, *The Conservative Mind from Burke to Eliot,* 7th rev. ed. (1985; repr., Washington, DC: Regnery, 1994).

26. MacIntyre, "Interview with Giovanna Borradori," 265.

27. Alasdair MacIntyre, "Catholic Universities: Dangers, Hopes, Choices," in *Higher Learning and Catholic Traditions*, ed. Robert E. Sullivan (Notre Dame: University of Notre Dame Press, 2001), 1–21; Alasdair MacIntyre, *God, Philosophy, Universities* (Lanham, MD: Rowman and Littlefield, 2009).

28. Alinsky was a close friend of the Thomist Jacques Maritain. Their surviving correspondence, most of it from Alinsky's side, may be found in Jacques Maritain, *The Philosopher and the Provocateur: The Correspondence of Jacques Maritain and Saul Alinsky*, ed. Bernard Doering (Notre Dame: University of Notre Dame Press, 1994).

29. John Courtney Murray, S.J., *We Hold These Truths: Catholic Reflections on the American Proposition* (1960; repr., Kansas City, MO: Sheed and Ward, 1988).

30. Johannes Messner, S.J., *Social Ethics: Natural Law in the Modern World* (St. Louis: B. Herder, 1949); Heinrich Rommen, *The State in Catholic Thought: A Treatise in Political Philosophy* (St. Louis: B. Herder, 1945).

31. In *A Newman Reader*, ed. Francis X. Connolly (Garden City, NY: Doubleday, 1964), 384.

CHAPTER SIX

Against the Self-Images of the Age
MacIntyre and Løgstrup

HANS FINK

Alasdair MacIntyre has always insisted on the social and historical situatedness of even the most abstract forms of thinking, while at the same time trying to avoid the pitfalls of relativistic historicism. His work has involved a serious engagement, not only with the standard figures of the history of philosophy, but also with marginal philosophers of earlier periods and with contemporary philosophers who are little known in the English-speaking world. Few other major anglophone philosophers of his generation would have done so much detailed work in order to learn from a philosopher like Edith Stein, and his account of her position within the early phenomenological movement seems to me masterly.[1] The Danish moral philosopher Knud Ejler Løgstrup is another thinker at the margins of the phenomenological movement whom MacIntyre has helped to make more widely accessible.[2] By demonstrating the continuing importance of philosophers who might otherwise be consigned to oblivion, he is, I suppose, trying to show that the philosophers who feel most certain that they occupy the center of things may be rather more parochial than they think.

In this paper I shall concentrate on MacIntyre's connections with Løgstrup. Both of them have been consistent and articulate critics of the self-images of the modern age, or of what they have seen as the complacent, narrow-minded, and self-congratulatory illusions accompanying much mainstream thinking especially on moral issues. Their points of departure are, however, somewhat different, and so are their accounts of what typically goes wrong in contemporary moral philosophy. Løgstrup was a Lutheran and a phenomenologist, and MacIntyre has worked his own way to a form of Thomism, but they both combine their religious commitments with a strong commitment to truth in all areas of philosophy, including ethics. I shall discuss what I regard as Løgstrup's distinctive contribution to the moral philosophy of the twentieth century—his account of the incommensurable but complementary relationship between, on the one hand, the various types of social and moral demands and, on the other, what is, for him, the one and only ethical demand. In his confrontations with this singular conception of the ethical, MacIntyre has tried to incorporate what he takes to be Løgstrup's insights within his own systematic and comprehensive Thomist position. It is of course too late for Løgstrup to reciprocate, and there are rather deep reasons why he would probably not have been willing to try. His way of developing the traditions he belonged to—both Lutheran and phenomenological—was not so much to confront other traditions as to open them as much as possible to facts that are so simple that philosophers tend to overlook them. On his view, it belongs to the essence of the ethical demand that it resists being philosophically "domesticated" within any unifying account of morality. I shall try to explain why Løgstrup's very narrow and admittedly somewhat idiosyncratic conception of the ethical should remain a challenge for MacIntyre and other contemporary moral philosophers.

I

K. E. Løgstrup (1905–81) worked as a pastor in the Danish state church before becoming a professor of ethics and philosophy of religion at the University of Aarhus in 1943. His theological education involved an unusually extensive and intensive study of philosophy both in Denmark and in Germany, France, and Austria. He wrote dissertations on Edmund Husserl and Max Scheler, attended lectures by Martin Heidegger, and was deeply influenced by seminars with Hans Lipps, who was an independent-minded student of Husserl. Løgstrup's main work, *The Ethical Demand*

(*Den etiske fordring*, 1956), continues to have an unusually broad and deep influence on both scholarly and public thinking about moral questions in Denmark and the other Scandinavian countries, but despite translations into German and English it has yet to make its mark among philosophers elsewhere. When he has been taken note of he tends to be subordinated to Emmanuel Levinas.[3]

Though always primarily a theologian, Løgstrup regarded strictly philosophical arguments as crucially important both in their own right and within theology. He also knew that the fact that he was a theologian meant that many readers would dismiss him as irrelevant. In 1978 he opened a volume of metaphysical and theological essays by saying: "In the eyes of the epoch—even when its glance is at its gentlest—this book will appear to represent the rearguard of a retreating army fighting a defensive battle before both army and rearguard disappear into the darkness of anachronicity. But—the eyes of the epoch—what eyes are they?" And the rest of the book supplies his answer: they are eyes that have been blinded to something that remains of the highest importance whether one sees it or not. They are eyes that see nothing but what they focus on, and that focus on nothing but what is in their own immediate interest. How are they to be opened to what is plainly to be seen? How is a change of focus to be achieved? This theme is, of course, not uncommon among conservatives or theologians in a secular culture, but Løgstrup has a quite distinctive philosophical approach to it that is very far from being conservative.

In a paper entitled "God and the Theologians," first published in 1963, MacIntyre writes about the situation of Protestant theology in the period after the Second World War:

> We can see the harsh dilemma of a would-be contemporary theology. The theologians begin from orthodoxy, but the orthodoxy which has learned from Kierkegaard and Barth becomes too easily a closed circle, in which believer speaks only to believer, in which all human content is concealed. Turning aside from this arid in-group theology, the most perceptive theologians wish to translate what they have to say to an atheistic world. But they are doomed to one of two failures. Either they succeed in their translation: in which case what they find themselves saying has been transformed into the atheism of their hearers. Or they fail in their translation: in which case no one hears what they have to say but themselves.[4]

Seven years earlier, in *The Ethical Demand*, Løgstrup had tried to find a way round this dilemma. He was a theologian who had turned aside from arid in-group theology, seeing it as an important theological task to address the largely atheistic modern world. His orthodoxy, however, represented an explicit break with both Søren Kierkegaard and Karl Barth. For him Christian orthodoxy had a human content that ought to be explicated in purely human terms, and not just for the sake of communicating with the atheistic world. For humans there is no other understanding than human understanding on strictly human terms, and "faith without understanding is not faith but coercion" (2). Further, no one can appreciate what orthodoxy says over and above what it discloses about human life, without articulating precisely what this disclosure consists in. A line should be drawn between what is universal and what is specific to Christianity, and Christians should welcome the fact that the human content of orthodoxy, or at least part of it, can be shown to be universally valid and thus equally true for believers and nonbelievers alike. Christians should not pretend to hold a patent on a secret truth about human life, but they do have a special duty to remind the world—especially the modern world—of certain universal truths that are in danger of being overlooked. This seems to me, as an outsider, an honest attempt to integrate a purely philosophical understanding into theology, while at the same time presenting this understanding as no more than philosophy to anyone who cares to listen and follow the argument. Of course, this leaves it open for atheists to accept what is universal in Christianity without accepting what is distinctive about it, but it avoids the dilemma of either bowing to atheism or remaining within the closed circle of believers.

II

The Ethical Demand is Løgstrup's attempt to explain philosophically that neighborly love is required of Christians not because they are Christians but because they are human and because it is required equally of all. This is not a matter of revelation. Regardless of what your faith is, Løgstrup argues, you cannot help being responsible for something in the life of every person you encounter, and you ought to live up to that responsibility unselfishly and for the sake of that other person. This, according to him, is the unique ethical demand, and it belongs to the universal part of Christianity. It is not true because it was proclaimed by Jesus; rather, Jesus proclaimed it because it is true. All of us, according to Løgstrup, are invited to understand the ethical demand as having a divine origin because that will make sense of its singular status as antecedent to and independent of all other principles and norms; but if we choose to decline the invitation, then we can understand the ethical demand as the expression of an elementary normativity arising directly from the inevitable interdependency of human beings—a fact that even an ardent atheist has no reason to explain away. The Good Samaritan was certainly neither a Christian nor a Jew and might for that matter even have been an atheist, but he acted in accordance with that normativity.

This elementary normativity tends to be disregarded by the kind of liberal individualism (or individualist liberalism) that underlies most modern moral philosophy. According to Løgstrup, the reason is that individualist liberalism takes it for granted that we basically live our lives in splendid isolation, so that it is entirely up to us whether and on what terms we enter into contact with others.

> Unconsciously, we . . . have the strange notion that the rest of us are not part of another person's world. We have the curious idea that a person constitutes his own world, and that the rest of us have no part in it but only touch upon it now and then. . . .
>
> This is really a curious idea, an idea that is no less curious because we take it for granted. The fact is, however, that it is completely wrong because we do indeed constitute one another's world and destiny. There are many reasons why we usually ignore this fact.
>
> It is a common observation that the most elementary phenomena of our existence are the ones we are least aware of. It should be added that the phenomenon we are discussing here is highly disquieting. For the sake of our own peace of mind it is perhaps fortunate that we are not more aware of the extent to which, by what we were or said or did in our relationship with them, we have actually determined other people's joy or pain in living, their sincerity or duplicity. (16)

Løgstrup reminds us that we are as a matter of fact mutually dependent through and through and that we do not understand real independence unless we recognize this. We live in a social and historical world not of our own making, and this world is not just abstractly constituted by norms and meanings, it is populated by quite particular others. The mutual dependency Løgstrup is pointing to here is related to what Heidegger calls *Mitsein*, being-with, and it goes much deeper than the kind of dependence MacIntyre describes in *Dependent Rational Animals*—namely our need for the assistance of others in childhood, illness, and old age. Even the most mature and healthy independent practical reasoners depend on others in everything they are and everything they do, and others similarly rely on them. Our lives are inextricably interwoven with the lives of others. It is entirely possible for someone to withdraw more or less from human company, but even then his or her mental life will have been and will remain being formed to an unfathomable extent by the influence of particular others.

Our mutual dependency is shown also by the fact that we generally meet others with trust unless we have been given reason to do the opposite. We may be rather reserved in our dealings with others, but still an attitude of trust is prior to an attitude of distrust. "We would simply not be able to live; our life would be impaired and wither away if we were in advance to distrust one another, if we were to suspect the other of thievery and falsehood from the very outset" (8–9). To trust, however, is to lay oneself open, to let something be up to the other. Our interdependency thus means that whenever we meet others they have some power over us and we cannot help having power over them. "A person never has something to do with another person without also having some degree of control over him or her. It may be a very small matter, involving only a passing mood, a dampening or quickening of spirit, a deepening or removal of some dislike. But it may also be a matter of tremendous scope, such as can determine if the life of the other flourishes or not" (15–16). But if you have power over others, you are responsible for them. You are responsible for anything in the life of another that has, so to speak, been placed in your hands. It takes a special effort to make yourself indifferent to the ways in which you affect the life of someone else, and even if you succeed in becoming cynical, you will still have left your mark, and it will not be up to you, or to anyone else, to decide whether what you did was good or bad for the person concerned. The factual, objective, and indisputable character of this evaluation implies that you always act under an implicit demand that you take care of that part of the life of the other that has become your responsibility. There will be something wrong with the way you acted if you did otherwise. It is not a demand that somehow miraculously forces you to take care of the other, and there is no guarantee that it will make you feel inclined to do so. You are quite likely not to act in accordance with what is implicitly demanded of you, but then that is precisely what it is for you to be ethically at fault, to have failed in your relations with others.

III

The ethical demand is implicit, or as Løgstrup puts it, silent, tacit, unspoken, and anonymous. It is the demand of the situation you are in—of the fact that others depend on you, and that the situation therefore presents a task to you whether you acknowledge it or not. There are of course many demands that your situation confronts you with; but the ethical demand is unique. It is, for example, not the demand of the other person—it is not fulfilled by doing what you are asked to do. What is ethically demanded is care, not indulgence. Nor is it the demand of a social authority—it is not fulfilled by doing what is socially expected of you. What is ethically demanded is care, not conformity to rules or norms. Nor is it a demand of reason—it is not fulfilled by acting on a principle that could be acceptable as a universal law. What is ethically demanded is care, not consistency. What *is* ethically demanded is simply that you do what, according to your best and most imaginative understanding, would be best for the other person in the given situation. This ethical demand is implicit even in the rather dramatic sense that what is demanded is that no demand should be necessary. Being there and caring for the other is demanded, not because there is a prior demand to that effect, but because anything else would be less than ethically good. According to Løgstrup, a sensitivity to this elementary ethical fact must be understood to be prior to and independent of all explicit prescriptions of personal, conventional, traditional, or universal morality. The Good Samaritan had this sensitivity. His action was exemplary precisely because he did not try to live up to an example or follow a rule.

In a paper called "What Morality Is Not," written in 1957, the year after the publication of *The Ethical Demand*, MacIntyre shows that he was well aware that explicit rules are not all there is to morality. In that paper he was attacking the view, propagated at the time by R. M. Hare, that it is the essence of moral evaluations to be prescriptive and universalizable. MacIntyre's counterexamples are drawn from Jean-Paul Sartre, but Løgstrup would be in agreement with his general case against seeing morality on the model of universal prescriptivism.

> When you leave the ground of conventional morality, you leave the guidance of maxims behind. Yet it is just here that one needs guidance. Where men pass from one set of maxims to another, or act morally without maxims, there is an area where the logician and the linguistic analyst are necessarily helpless. For they are not presented with the kind of material which they need for analysis. Only the phenomenologist can help us here and the kind of phenomenology we need is that supplied by the novelist. It is because the moral philosophers of existentialism have been primarily concerned with this kind of situation that they have so often resorted to the novel. For all that can be done is to exhibit the passage of the moral agent through perplexity. To offer us a maxim on which or according to which the moral agent finally acted is to tell us what the resolution of the perplexity was but not how the perplexity was resolved. In this clear-cut sense then the maxims of morality do not guide us, nor do they prescribe conduct to us. And to describe the function of moral valuation in general or of "ought" in particular as prescriptive is highly misleading unless this is made clear. The catalogue of possible uses of "ought" needs to be supplemented by a catalogue of those moral purposes for which "ought" and words like it and sometimes any words at all can be of little or no use.[5]

Løgstrup often made his point by way of examples from E. M. Forster, D. H. Lawrence, Joseph Conrad, and other authors, and in *The Ethical Demand* he could be said to be elucidating a moral purpose—and a crucially important one—for whose fulfillment an explicit "ought" will be of little or no use—namely that you should take care of anyone who depends on you. Sartre tells the student who comes to ask advice that he is free and that he has to work out for himself what to do. No moral system could make the decision for him. Similarly, the ethical demand is the demand that you yourself work out what to do. You yourself have to discover what is best for the other. The ethical demand does not excuse you from thinking for yourself; on the contrary, it consists in your being tied to a task that you might prefer to run away from. Here the parallel with Sartre breaks down, however. For Sartre conventional morality is of no help in situations of great urgency and seriousness because according to him human beings must choose their own values. Løgstrup, in contrast, does not regard all values as the outcome of human choices. You are indeed free to do whatever you like, but neglecting or suppressing another person is ethically wrong, even if you choose to do so and are ready to prescribe your choice universally. You are not free to choose whether what you do is ethically good or bad. The basic ethical demand is not of your own making, though it is up to you to find out exactly what it requires of you on each occasion. This is a matter of discovery, not invention. Løgstrup is neither a situationist nor a particularist on the basic ethical level.

In spite of some of Sartre's own formulations, one could say that he, too, takes some values to be given. For him, authenticity cannot fail to be good. Though our daily lives are lived largely in various forms of inauthenticity, we nevertheless live under an implicit demand to break through conventionality and invent ourselves anew in what we do. When we try to escape from our freedom we stand condemned, not by conventional standards, but by a deeper normativity. This existentialist demand for authenticity resembles the ethical demand in that it cannot be made explicit. You cannot achieve authenticity by striving for it: it will be perverted if it is turned into a conventional ideal.

The concept of authenticity is not prominent in Løgstrup's writing, and he is highly critical of what he sees as the egocentricity of the existentialist concern for individual freedom and independence, but one could perhaps say that for him the ethical demand is a demand for a certain kind of authenticity, an ethical authenticity, expressed when you are completely absorbed in the other person, thereby being true to yourself, but behind your own back, as it were. It is ethically demanded that there be more to your life with others than is required by explicit norms.

It might be illuminating to look at yet another contrast with Sartre—who was born the same year as Løgstrup and died just a year earlier. In his posthumously published notes from 1947–48, the *Cahiers pour une morale,* there is a phenomenological analysis of what is involved in helping another.⁶ Here Sartre goes beyond his earlier views in claiming that it is a fundamental and valuable human disposition to go out of our way to help others in need, but even here a contrast with Løgstrup stands out. What is important for Sartre is that we freely choose to help the other in his or her freely chosen projects. Freedom remains the fundamental source of all value. It could never be up to you to judge whether the other person's project is actually good or bad for him or her. For Løgstrup, however, this is precisely part of what is demanded of you in your life with and against the other. Our interdependency is a source of value no less than our freedom.

In his 1957 paper MacIntyre seemed ready to acknowledge that phenomenologists have a good point when they claim that there is an implicit demand in morally problematic situations that cannot be captured by reference to any explicit system of norms. I suspect that he would now regard Sartrean authenticity as a declaration of moral bankruptcy, while Løgstrup's account of an implicit ethical demand would be at best an isolated fragment that ultimately has no meaning outside an older tradition of social virtues guided by knowledge of natural laws.⁷ Løgstrup's own account of the ethical demand could indeed be taken as inviting that construal, in that he was presenting it as a humanly comprehensible account of the content of what was once a living Christian tradition. But according to Løgstrup, no matter how far you go back in time, there would always have been a morally important distinction between doing something for another just because he or she depends on you and doing it to conform to an explicit law or norm. The point is to help the other rather than to secure your own moral standing. Again the Good Samaritan provides us with an excellent example, and so does the general anti-Pharisaism of Jesus. The moral importance of meeting others directly, as opposed to responding to them through a filter of norms, seems to me to be a challenge not only to Thomism but to all moral traditions.

Løgstrup's attempt to elucidate an elementary and primordial form of normativity can of course be seen as the product of a very particular set of circumstances, in which a modern Danish Lutheran theologian with a training in phenomenology seeks to rescue something from a Christian tradition that could be seen as suffering decline or impoverishment. But it does not have to be seen that way. It could just as well be seen as the gradual freeing of an important truth from types of context that it does not need and that may indeed deform it.

IV

Throughout *The Ethical Demand* Løgstrup applies the terms *moral* and *morality* to explicit social demands, whereas *ethical* is reserved for the normativity implicit in interpersonal relations as such. Unlike moral norms, the ethical demand is unconditional and absolute rather than historically and culturally conditioned; it is implicit in human life and is not subject to change. But if the ethical demand stands on its own ground, it does not operate in a moral vacuum. It presupposes and is presupposed by an established order in human life—an order that depends on conventional or traditional norms.

> The conventional forms however have a twofold function. For one thing, regardless of how these forms originated, they facilitate our relationship with one another, making it smooth and effortless, not least because they protect us against psychic exposure. Without the protection of the conventional norms, association with other people would be unbearable. . . .
>
> In the second place, however, we employ the very same conventional forms for reducing trust and its demand. Instead of allowing convention to give needed form to our life, we use it as a means for keeping aloof from one another and for insulating ourselves. The one who trusts has in advance, by way of convention, guarded him or herself; he or she has rendered his or her trust conventionally reserved, and the one who is trusted is thus relieved of hearing the demand contained in the trust, the demand to take care of the trusting person's life. (19–20)

Without conventional norms and the social sanctions attached to them, the other would be completely at your mercy and vice versa. Such norms are important for deciding what is best for the other because they help determine what the other expects and because they can also allow you the comfort of feeling that you have done what can be reasonably expected of you.

There is thus a duality or complementarity between the ethical demand, which is singular and unique, and moral demands, which are many and various, or between the unconditional ethical order and the socially conditioned moral order. Thus the ethical demand must always be complemented by the demands inherent in forms of praxis, in traditions, or in rationality and other forms of normativity. On the other hand, it has a special place among the other demands that we are subject to. Something would be missing from our lives if all that was demanded of us was that we comply with explicit norms and strive to live up to ideals of rationality. And whereas elders, the police, moralists, or public opinion will normally be on hand to remind us of the various moral demands, it may take a phenomenological effort to become sensitized to the background normativity of the ethical demand that good people are immediately sensitive to.

In some ways the distinction between the ethical demand and moral demands resembles the classical distinction between natural law and positive laws. Neither the ethical demand nor natural law is of our own making. Their normativity does not depend on our acceptance of them. Like natural law, the ethical demand would remain in force even if all social institutions broke down. But whereas natural law is classically conceived as consisting of separate laws—it is a law with many chapters, so to speak—there is only one ethical demand, and it cannot be spelt out in terms of a system of subsidiary ethical demands. Hence there is no straightforward disagreement between Løgstrup and adherents of classical natural law regarding the wrongness of lying, breaking promises, or harming or killing the innocent, except that for him what is ethically wrong with such actions is that they disregard or directly take advantage of the other, not that they involve the breaking of certain rules.

Unlike natural law, the ethical demand cannot be used to legitimize or criticize positive moral or legal rules, and it does not lend itself to casuistry. It is silent. It does not, for example, endorse one pattern of family life or social organization rather than another. No political program could call upon the ethical demand. Large-scale social reform may be desirable for all kinds of good reasons, but there is no direct link between such reasons and the ethical demand. There is no way in which it could be institutionalized. It represents a form of normativity according to which your action or attitude toward another person may stand condemned even if you do not infringe any positive or explicitly formulated natural laws, and under some circumstances it might even be ethically demanded that you disobey a positive law or even, perhaps, what is regarded as a natural one. According to Løgstrup morality would risk descending into moralism if the only types of demands that our conduct was responsible to were those of positive or explicated natural law.

Løgstrup's distinction between the ethical demand and social rules could also be elucidated by comparison with Hume's distinction between natural and artificial virtues. Hume rejected the Hobbesian proposition that self-preservation provides the only natural normativity we are subject to, maintaining that we have a number of other-regarding natural virtues, such as "generosity, humanity, compassion, gratitude, friendship, fidelity, zeal, disinterestedness, liberality, and all those other qualities which form the character of good and benevolent."[8] These natural virtues, however, are not sufficient to ground an ordered social life: we also need the artificial virtues—especially justice, which, according to Hume, was developed historically through our gradual realization that it is in our long-term interests to regulate our short-term interests by establishing common rules. Yet it remains important for him that there is more to morality than the artificial virtues, just as it is essential for Løgstrup that we are under a demand that cannot be expressed by any social norms. A disposition to care for those who depend on you could be said to be a natural virtue that cannot be replaced by any number of artificial virtues.

The ethical demand requires you to do whatever is best for the other. This may go far beyond the call of social or moral duty. What is ethically demanded may be something that would be regarded as heroic or saintly by normal standards. But what is ethically demanded may also just be straightforward kindness or friendliness. And it is characteristic that someone who actually acts in accordance with the ethical demand will regard this as being the ordinary or the only possible thing to do under the circumstances, even though others may think it goes far beyond the call of duty.[9]

V

Apart from being implicit and unconditional, the ethical demand differs from social and moral norms in that it is concerned exclusively with responsibilities to those we encounter. The normativity involved in our relations with particular individuals is thus sharply distinguished from that involved in our relations with people in general or people of specific types or classes. There is here a certain similarity between Løgstrup's thought and the *I—Thou* philosophy of Martin Buber.[10] Moral normativity as Løgstrup understood it could be expressed in Tim Scanlon's phrase *what we owe to each other;*[11] ethical normativity, in contrast, consists in *what we owe to the other*. The ethical demand is one-sided; it requires you to be there for the other and live up to your responsibility, and it is not for you to demand or expect anything in return. Moral demands, on the other hand, are generally open to a contractual construal; you follow the rules in the expectation that others will do so too.

It is ethically demanded that you relate to the other, not just as a person, or as a person of a particular type, but as him- or herself. If you are a married man, what you owe to your wife is not just an instance of what you owe to others in general, or what husbands in general owe to their wives. If you are a parent what you owe each of your children is not just an instance of what parents in general owe their children. Even complete strangers are more than examples of a type. Any meeting between two people involves something over and above what is entailed by their social roles or their common humanity. Your individual responsibility is called upon in a singular way when you are involved with another, no matter in what capacity. You should be there as yourself for the other as him- or herself. There is an irreducibly individual dimension to all your relations with others to which words like *owe* and *moral* have little relevance. The ethical demand arises from your interdependency with others, but ethically speaking it isolates you and breaks whatever symbiosis there is between you and the other (45). In a sense the ethical demand requires that you should be truly independent and that you should treat the other as truly independent regardless of any actual dependency between you. Løgstrup was highly critical of Kantian moral philosophy as he understood it, but both according to the ethical demand and according to the categorical imperative you should always treat the other as an end, and never merely as a means to your own ends.

In his criticism of the individualism and egocentricity of much modern moral philosophy MacIntyre appeals mainly to the fact that our lives would be bereft of any common goods or binding standards of value if they were not lived within well-functioning forms of social praxis and tradition. Løgstrup might well agree, but what is especially powerful about his criticism of individualism and egocentricity is his appeal to what might be called altro-centricity. Common social goods are indeed crucial for individual flourishing, but so is one person's concern for the good of another for his or her own sake. Løgstrup would criticize the individualism and abstract universality of utilitarianism and Kantianism with reference not only to the normativity of shared goods and community but also to what could be called the micro-sociological normativity inherent in any meeting of two people regardless of the larger social context. For Løgstrup there is something wrong with any system of moral philosophy that tries to subsume the good of the other under some larger good, whether communal or universal. Of course, we are constantly forced to make decisions where the good of one person is weighed against that of another person or that of a whole group of persons, but whenever such a choice is made the ethical demand is compromised. For Løgstrup it is crucial that such dilemmas should be acknowledged rather than taken to be solved or dissolved with the help of some decision procedure. The harm you do to one person can never be justified by the good you do to someone else even if your choice was morally the best one possible under the circumstances. One might wish that Løgstrup had been more explicit about how one should act when such dilemmas arise, but according to him we should not expect moral philosophy to give us detailed instructions about how to solve problematic situations: the most it can do is offer us reminders of crucial factors that we are likely to overlook or systematically repress.

VI

MacIntyre has argued that modernity has continually eroded the forms of community that once provided the intellectual resources that might lead to genuine solutions to moral problems, and that few have any awareness of the problem. "The modern self which has too many half convictions and too few settled coherent convictions, too many partly formulated alternatives and too few opportunities to evaluate them systematically brings to its encounters with the claims of rival traditions a fundamental incoherence which is too disturbing to be admitted to self-conscious awareness except on the rarest of occasions."[12] But while Løgstrup shares MacIntyre's view that twentieth-century moral philosophy has been vitiated by its individualism, he is concerned less with inconsistencies in our thinking than with systematic neglect of the elementary goodness demanded of us.

For MacIntyre there is very little moral philosophers can do except bear witness to what is and is not possible under present circumstances. For Løgstrup, in contrast, the philosophical task is to prevent our habitual or philosophical ways of thinking from blunting our awareness of those moments of straightforward goodness that we can recognize when we meet them.

MacIntyre has acknowledged that there is something a Thomist could learn from Løgstrup both about the role of trust in social life and about the importance of immediate responsiveness to others in urgent need. Such integration might provide a way of overcoming the fragmentation that Løgstrup's sharp distinction between moral and ethical normativity represents for MacIntyre. At the very end of "Danish Ethical Demands and French Common Goods: Two Philosophies," MacIntyre says:

> We need to understand a good deal better than we do how under certain circumstances the moral life can be fragmented, so that different aspects of it—on the one hand, schemes of reasoning about goods and virtues which enable us to be practically reflective, on the other, capacities of feeling and judgment that enable us to be immediately responsive to urgent need—take on a life of their own. If we were to understand that fragmentation, we might also begin to understand how to reintegrate those two aspects. How we might become able to do that is the question that issues from the overall argument of this paper.[13]

For Løgstrup, however, acknowledging the difference between the ethical demand and moral norms belongs to a proper understanding of the moral life. It is not to be seen as a fragmentation of what was once integrated and could once again be made whole. The ethical demand has constantly figured in the background of the long historical development of social and moral norms, but it has never been captured by moral theory, and it never will be. The ethical demand will always remain a standard by which human behavior can be judged, a standard that has no common denominator with our traditional and explicitly endorsed norms. According to Løgstrup it is crucial that our moral life be informed not only by a number of more or less easily fulfillable and explicable demands but also by a demand that is unfulfillable in the sense that we cannot try to fulfill it without thereby failing. We will never be able to establish in advance what it would take to fulfill the ethical demand. Yet in a way nothing is easier than living in accordance with it. We have all experienced the difference between being met with consideration and neglect, support and destruction, unselfishness and selfishness.

For MacIntyre truth is the *telos* of practical reflection, whereas for Løgstrup reflection needs to recognize a truth to which no philosophical or religious tradition has privileged access. He was constantly engaged in philosophical dialogue, but rather than trying to develop his own tradition by confronting it with other traditions, he wanted to point us to certain truths that we cannot help taking for granted even though our self-images are more than liable to distract us from them. If truth is not the alpha of inquiry, it cannot be the omega either.

Notes

I would like to thank Jonathan Rée for many helpful comments to earlier versions of this paper.

1. Alasdair MacIntyre, *Edith Stein: A Philosophical Prologue* (London: Continuum Books, 2006).
2. See K. E. Løgstrup, *The Ethical Demand,* introd. Hans Fink and Alasdair MacIntyre (Notre Dame: University of Notre Dame Press, 1997); subsequent page citations to this work are given parenthetically in the text. For MacIntyre on Løgstrup, see Alasdair MacIntyre, "Human Nature and Human Dependence: What Might a Thomist Learn from Reading Løgstrup?," in *Concern for the Other: Perspectives in the Ethics of K. E. Løgstrup,* ed. Svend Andersen and Kees van Kooten Niekerk (Notre Dame: Notre Dame University Press, 2007); Alasdair MacIntyre, "Danish Ethical Demands and French Common Goods: Two Moral Philosophies," *European Journal of Philosophy* 18, no. 1 (2010): 1–16.
3. See Zygmunt Bauman, *Postmodern Ethics* (Oxford: Blackwells, 1984), and Simon Critchley, *Infinitely Demanding* (London: Verso, 2007).
4. Alasdair MacIntyre, "God and the Theologians," in *Against the Self-Images of the Age: Essays on Ideology and Philosophy* (London: Duckworth, 1971), 19–20.
5. MacIntyre, *Against the Self-Images,* 107.
6. Jean-Paul Sartre, *Cahiers pour une morale* (Paris: Gallimard, 1983), translated as *Notebooks for Ethics* (Chicago: University of Chicago Press, 1992).

7. This is the argument in MacIntyre, "Danish Ethical Demands."

8. David Hume, *A Treatise of Human Nature* 3.3.3.

9. This is a point that MacIntyre himself has emphasized; see his introduction to Løgstrup's *Ethical Demand*, xxxvi, and MacIntyre, "Danish Ethical Demands," at the end of § 1.

10. Martin Buber: *Ich und du* (Leipzig: Insel-Verlag, 1923), translated as *I and Thou* (London: Continuum, 2004).

11. T. M. Scanlon, *What We Owe to Each Other* (Cambridge, MA: Harvard University Press, 1999).

12. Alasdair MacIntyre, *Whose Justice? Which Rationality?* (Notre Dame: University of Notre Dame Press, 1988), 397.

13. MacIntyre, "Danish Ethical Demands," 16.

PART II

Complementary and Competing Traditions

CHAPTER SEVEN

MacIntyre and the Emotivists

JAMES EDWIN MAHON

"Do this, because it will bring you happiness"; "Do this because God enjoins it as the way to happiness"; "Do this because God enjoins it"; "Do this." These are the four stages in the development of autonomous morality.

—Alasdair MacIntyre, "Notes from the Moral Wilderness"

Emotivism looms large in Alasdair MacIntyre's *After Virtue: A Study in Moral Theory*.[1] Chapters 2 and 3 — the first two real chapters of the book, after the preliminary disquieting suggestion — are directly concerned with emotivism, as the chapter titles indicate: "The Nature of Moral Disagreement Today and the Claims of Emotivism" and "Emotivism: Social Content and Social Context." MacIntyre's declaration in the first of these two chapters that "it is indeed in terms of a confrontation with emotivism that my own thesis must be defined" has prompted at least one commentator to claim that "the core of Alasdair MacIntyre's *After Virtue* is an attack on emotivism."[2]

That MacIntyre is preoccupied with the metaethical theory of emotivism in *After Virtue* comes as no surprise to those who are familiar with his intellectual biography.[3] MacIntyre completed a bachelor's degree in classics at Queen Mary College in the University of London between 1945 and 1949. While he was there, "from 1947 onward, [he] occasionally attend[ed] lectures by A. J. Ayer or Karl Popper, or by visiting speakers to Ayer's seminar at University College [London], such as John Wisdom," after Ayer had become Grote Professor of the Philosophy of Mind and Logic at University College London in 1946 (see chapter 1). Indeed, as MacIntyre tell us, "Early on I had read *Language, Truth and Logic*, and Ayer's student James Thomson introduced me to the *Tractatus* and to Tarski's work on truth. Ayer and his students were exemplary in their clarity and rigor and in the philosophical excitement that their debates generated" (see chapter 1). After graduating from Queen Mary College, MacIntyre went to Manchester University, where he wrote a master's thesis on the subject of metaethics, entitled *The Significance of Moral Judgments*, in 1951.[4] MacIntyre's very first work in philosophy, therefore, was devoted to criticizing emotivism (and the intuitionism that inspired it). In the years that immediately followed, he published a number of articles on metaethics, including "What Morality Is Not" (1957), "Notes from the Moral Wilderness I" (1958), "Notes from the Moral Wilderness II" (1959), "Hume on 'Is' and 'Ought'" (1959), and "Imperatives, Reasons for Action, and Morals" (1965), in addition to his introduction to *Hume's Ethical Writings* (1965) and "Modern Moral Philosophy," the final chapter of *A Short History of Ethics* (1966).

In this essay I will provide an account of emotivism and its history and will examine MacIntyre's critique of it, according to which emotivism fails both as an account of the meaning of moral judgment and as an account of the function of moral judgment. In part, this will serve as a defense of MacIntyre's critique against the charge that he has provided "interpretations of Stevenson and emotivism that are plainly travesties."[5] However, my concern is not to defend his critique from those contemporary critics who would seek to argue in favor of some form of emotivism.[6] My concern is to show that what is important about MacIntyre's critique is what it reveals about the historical degeneration of moral judgment. On this account, the fact/value distinction on which emotivism is premised is not a timeless truth but the result of the "Enlightenment Project." It was this historical turn that led to the degeneration of moral judgment. Moral judgment reached its nadir in the metaethical theory that is emotivism.

Principia Ethica

As MacIntyre says in *After Virtue*, "It is only in [the twentieth] century that emotivism has flourished as a theory on its own. . . . It did so as a response to a set of theories which flourished, especially in England, between 1903 and 1939."[7] The year 1903 was when G. E. Moore's "quietly apocalyptic" first book on consequentialist axiological intuitionism, *Principia Ethica*, was published,[8] and 1939 was the year of the publication of W. D. Ross's last book on deontological intuitionism, *Foundations of Ethics*.[9] Emotivism, then, was a response to the two forms of intuitionism that flourished in England at this time, at Cambridge (Moore) and at Oxford (H. A. Prichard and Ross). It was, however, especially a response to Moore.[10]

Moore was a moral cognitivist.[11] He held that a moral judgment expresses a *belief*. Since beliefs are capable of being true, it follows that moral judgments are capable of being true. Moore was also a moral realist. He held that moral properties *exist* and that they *make* certain moral judgments *true*.[12] Finally, Moore was a moral nonnaturalist.[13] He held that moral properties are not natural properties or supernatural properties, and furthermore that they cannot be reduced to natural or supernatural properties.[14] As MacIntyre says in *A Short History of Ethics*, although Moore gave the name of the "naturalistic fallacy" to what he considered the error of believing that the moral properties (or qualities) that are denoted by moral expressions ("that quality which we assert to belong to a thing, when we say that the thing is good") either *are* natural or supernatural properties, or *can be reduced to* such properties, Moore could just as easily have called the supposed error the "supernaturalistic fallacy":[15]

> To the doctrine that good was the name of a natural property Moore gave the name "the naturalistic fallacy." For Moore this fallacy is committed in the course of any attempt to treat *good* as the name of a property identifiable under any other description. *Good* cannot mean "commanded by God," any more than it can mean *pleasant*, and for the same reasons the expression "the naturalistic fallacy" has since been adopted by the adherents of the view that one cannot logically derive an *ought* from an *is;* but although this latter doctrine is a consequence of Moore's, it is not identical with it.[16]

According to Moore, moral properties are non-natural, nonsupernatural properties that are not part of the causal order; they are *sui generis,* simple, and intrinsic, hence indefinable and unanalyzable.[17] These moral properties, it seems, supervene on natural properties, without being reducible to them.[18] These moral properties are apprehended by means of a nonsensible intuition. In particular, the moral property of goodness, it seems, supervenes on the natural properties that constitute "certain states of consciousness," such as "personal affection and the appreciation of what is beautiful"[19]—for example, as he suggests years later in his *Ethics,* "the state of mind . . . of a man who is fully realizing all that is exquisite in the tragedy of King Lear"[20]—and we apprehend this moral property of goodness nonsensibly. As MacIntyre has pointed out, "The values which Moore exalts belong to the realm of private rather than public life; and, supremely important as they all are, they exclude all the values connected with intellectual inquiry and with work. Moore's values are those of a protected leisure."[21]

In the *Short History,* MacIntyre makes two objections to Moore's intuitionism. The first is that Moore provides no account of how it is that we apprehend the moral property of goodness ("The only answer Moore offers is that we just do");[22] hence, his account stands in need of "an account of how the meaning of good is learned, and an account of the relation between learning it in connection with some cases, and knowing how to apply it in others."[23] The second objection, one very similar to that made by G. C. Field, and P. H. Nowell-Smith, is that Moore's account of the moral property of goodness fails to explain how it provides us with any "reason for action":[24] "Moore's account leaves it entirely unexplained and inexplicable why something's being good should ever furnish us with a reason for action. . . . Any account of good that is to be adequate must connect it intimately with action, and explain why to call something good is always to provide a reason for acting in respect of it in one way rather than another."[25] As William K. Frankena has pointed out, this kind of objection to Moore trades on an ambiguity in "reason for action," since this can be understood either motivationally or normatively.[26] It may be true that, on Moore's account, something's being good does not necessarily motivate us to act, in the sense of moving us (even only somewhat) to act. Crudely put, it may not satisfy any desire or interest we have. This is what makes Moore a true motivational externalist.[27] However, it may still be true that something's being good is an "intrinsically normative" fact about it,[28] and hence that it does provide us with a reason to act, in the sense that we ought to pursue or promote it, regardless of whether that would satisfy any desire or interest we have. Nevertheless, if this is the case, then Moore must provide an account of how anything can be reason-giving in a way that does not connect with desires or interests. To invoke Mackie's argument from (metaphysical) "queerness" on MacIntyre's behalf: "An objective good would be sought by anyone who was acquainted with it, not because of any contingent fact that this person, or every person, is so constituted that he desires this end, but just because the end has to-be-pursuedness somehow built into it. . . . If there were objective values, then they would be entities or qualities or relations of a very strange sort, utterly different from anything else in the universe."[29]

In *The Significance of Moral Judgments,* MacIntyre advances a third objection. If our nonsensible intuition of goodness is infallible, then this fails to explain why there exists moral disagreement, and if it is fallible, then our nonsensible intuition may be mistaken about goodness.[30] Since Moore cannot allow that our nonsensible intuition about goodness may be mistaken, he must argue that "moral disagreement" is not, in fact, disagreement about goodness. On Moore's account, there can be no genuine moral disagreement and no genuine moral argument. Instead, all putative moral disagreement is disagreement about the nonmoral natural facts. Hence, in the case of a putative moral disagreement, which is actually a case of natural factual disagreement, the task is to get the other person to fully appreciate the natural facts of the situation, real or imagined. Only then will he or she have the same moral intuition.[31] As MacIntyre says in *After Virtue,* however, after pointing out that Moore's account of goodness as a non-natural property is "*plainly* false" and that his arguments for his non-naturalism are "*obviously* defective," such attempts to get other people to have the same moral intuition as a result of fully appreciating the natural facts of a situation, real or imagined, appear to amount to manipulation by emotion.[32] This much is clear from the reports of Moore's Bloomsbury followers:

> But, of course, as [John Maynard] Keynes tells us, what was really happening was something quite other: "In practice, victory was with those who could speak with the greatest appearance of clear, undoubting conviction and could best use the accents of infallibility" and Keynes goes on to describe the effectiveness of Moore's gasps of incredulity and head-shaking,

of [Lytton] Strachey's grim silences and of Lowes Dickinson's shrugs. . . . Keynes himself retrospectively might well have put matters thus: these people take themselves to be identifying the presence of a non-natural property, which they call "good"; but there is in fact no such property and they are doing no more and no other than expressing their feelings and attitudes, disguising the expression of preference and whim by an interpretation of their own utterance and behavior which confers upon it an objectivity that it does not in fact possess.[33]

It was Moorean intuitionism that led to the emotivist theory of ethics. As MacIntyre says: "It is, I take it, no accident that the acutest of the modern founders of emotivism, philosophers such as F. P. Ramsey . . . Austin Duncan-Jones and C. L. Stevenson, were pupils of Moore."[34] There is even more support for this Cantabrigian sociological thesis than MacIntyre suspects. As will be shown, it was the Cambridge duo of C. K. Ogden and I. A. Richards who first advanced the emotivist thesis, the thesis that inspired Ramsey, Duncan-Jones, and Stevenson, as well as R. J. Braithwaite and A. J. Ayer.

The Meaning of Meaning

In *Principia Ethica* Moore argues that, "in fact, if it is not the case that 'good' denotes something simple and indefinable, only two alternatives are possible: either that it is a complex, a given whole, about the correct analysis of which there may be disagreement; or else it means nothing at all, and there is no such subject as Ethics."[35] One way of understanding the response to Moore by the emotivists is that they embraced the second alternative: *good* does mean nothing at all, and there is no such subject as ethics. As MacIntyre says in his *Short History*, one explanation of how emotivism originated is to think of the following response to Moore: "But if there is no such property as Moore supposes, then all they can be doing is to express their feelings."[36]

In *The Meaning of Meaning* in 1923, C. K. Ogden and I. A. Richards advance a distinction (which is not completely original) between the symbolic, or referential, use of language and the emotive, or nonreferential, use of language.[37] They argue that the use of *good* highlighted by Moore in *Principia Ethica*—the "indefinable 'good'"—is purely emotive and does not refer to any property whatsoever.[38] In what has been called their "historic sentence," they say that "this peculiar use of 'good' is, we suggest, a purely emotive use":[39]

> But another use of the word is often asserted to occur . . . where "good" is alleged to stand for a unique, unanalysable concept. This concept, it is said, is the subject-matter of Ethics [there is the footnote reference to Moore's *Principia Ethica*]. This peculiar use of "good" is, we suggest, a purely emotive use. When so used the word stands for nothing whatsoever, and has no symbolic function. Thus, when we so use it in the sentence, "*This* is good," we merely refer to *this*, and the addition of "is good" makes no difference whatsoever to our reference. When on the other hand, we say "*This* is red," the addition of "is red" to "this" does symbolize an extension of our reference, namely, to some other red thing. But "is good" has no comparable *symbolic* function; it serves only as an emotive sign expressing our attitude to *this*, and perhaps evoking similar attitudes in other persons, or inciting them to actions of one kind or another.[40]

Unlike other uses of *good*, which are not purely emotive (e.g., "This is a good sportscar"), the use of *good* in assertions such as "The appreciation of literature is good" is *purely* emotive. It *only* expresses a (positive) attitude and evokes a similar attitude in others or incites them to act in some way. Importantly, Ogden and Richards never spoke of purely emotive *meaning*, only of the purely emotive *use* of language.[41] Nor did they develop a distinct metaethics.[42]

Frank P. Ramsey reviewed *The Meaning of Meaning* when it was published and praised its account of the distinction between the symbolic and emotive functions of language.[43] Some time later he wrote: "Theology and Absolute Ethics are two famous subjects which we have realized to have no real objects."[44] Ogden and Richards's book led another Cambridge philosopher, R. B. Braithwaite, to argue in his paper at a meeting of the Aristotelian Society in 1928, "Verbal Ambiguity and Philosophical Analysis," that most apparent ethical judgments are not "genuine ethical judgments" (i.e., judgments that express propositions) but expressions of emotion:[45]

> A great number of the sentences in which the word "good" occurs are merely noises made either to "purge" an emotion in the speaker or to produce

directly a definite action or emotion in the hearer. They do not represent propositions at all: their object is not symbolic, but emotive.... These uses of language Messrs. Ogden and Richards call "emotive," and distinguish from the "symbolic" or "scientific" use in the direct expression of a judgment.... Now, of course, in any philosophical discussion, including "Prolegomena to any future Ethics that can possibly pretend to be scientific" (which Dr. Moore hoped *Principia Ethica* to be), we are concerned with the "symbolic" or "scientific" or "referential" meaning of sentences, and not at all with their uses as gestures or commands. But since it seems to me clear that our most frequent use of ethical words is only "emotive" so that the sentences in which they occur do not represent propositions at all, it is important in any ethical discussion to emphasize at the outset that the science of ethics has not to analyse all the things that are conveyed by ethical words, but only such as are propositions. Most apparent ethical judgments, on my view, are not judgments at all, but expressions of emotions or volitions.[46]

Moore's student Austin Duncan-Jones wrote a reply to Braithwaite's critique of Moore, entitled "Ethical Words and Ethical Facts," in which he offered, without advocating it, an "out and out naturalism" about ethical judgments, according to which all ethical judgments were "emotive": "It might be said that the only proper use of ethical expressions is to evoke feelings in the hearer or reader ... that is, they are meaningless.... This would I suppose be the most extreme kind of naturalistic theory which could be found.... I do not believe in the out and out naturalism which I have described, because I am sure that our ethical expressions are not all meaningless."[47]

Duncan-Jones's "extreme kind of naturalistic theory," according to which "ethical expressions" are all "meaningless," a theory that he himself was not advocating, was given a brilliant summary by another Cambridge philosopher, C. D. Broad, in a talk on Moore at a meeting of the Aristotelian Society in 1934, entitled "Is Goodness a Name of a Simple Non-Natural Quality?":

> We must remember that a sentence, which is grammatically in the indicative mood, may really be in part interjectional or rhetorical or imperative. It may be in part the expression of an emotion which the speaker is feeling. In that case to utter the sentence: "That is good" on a certain occasion might be equivalent to uttering a purely non-ethical sentence in the in-

dicative, followed by a certain interjection. It might, e.g., be equivalent to saying: "That's an act of self-sacrifice. Hurrah!" Similarly, to utter the sentence: "That is bad" on a certain occasion might be equivalent to saying: "That's a deliberately misleading statement. Blast!" Again, a sentence may be used partly to evoke a certain kind of emotion in the hearer. In that case to utter the sentence: "That is good" might be equivalent to uttering a purely non-ethical sentence in the indicative in a pleasant tone and with a smile. To utter the sentence: "That is bad," might be equivalent to shouting a purely non-ethical indicative sentence at the hearer with a frown. Here the use of the ethical words "good" and "bad" is merely a stimulus to produce certain emotions in the hearer, as smiling at him or shouting at him might do. In this case the sentence might be called "rhetorical." Lastly, such sentences may be used to command or to forbid certain actions in the hearer. To utter the sentence: "That is good" might be equivalent to uttering a purely non-ethical indicative sentence followed by a sentence in the imperative. It might, e.g., be equivalent on a certain occasion to: "That's an act of self-sacrifice. Imitate it!" To utter the sentence: "That is bad" on a certain occasion might be equivalent to saying: "That's a deliberately misleading statement. Don't do that again!" . . . It seems to me then that Mr. Duncan-Jones's theory is quite plausible enough to deserve very serious consideration. It would have to be refuted before we could be sure that the question: "Are the characteristics denoted by ethical names analysable or unanalysable?" is a sensible question. If this theory were correct the question would be like asking whether unicorns are or are not cloven-hoofed.[48]

This theory would find a true believer in A. J. Ayer.[49] Indeed, Ayer's emotivism would come to be known as the "'Boo-Hurrah Theory' of ethics," almost certainly not because of anything that Ayer wrote, but because of the summary of Duncan-Jones's alternative in this article by Broad (although it seems that it should have been called the "Blast-Hurrah Theory"). It was Ayer who was quite happy to consider Moore's non-natural moral properties as unreal as unicorns.[50]

Language, Truth and Logic

Ayer had accepted Moore's non-naturalistic moral realism in his youth. However, while still an undergraduate at Oxford he came to reject it,[51] and after embracing logical positivism in the 1930s he argued for the antirealist emotivist theory of ethics in the sixth chapter of his logical positivist tract *Language, Truth and Logic*.[52] Nevertheless in his book he borrows Moore's own arguments against naturalism in order to reject "the 'naturalistic' theories" (157) of ethics that attempt to translate or reduce "statements of ethical value . . . into statements of empirical fact" (152).

Ayer noted years later that his main concern in the infamous chapter 6, "Critique of Ethics and Theology," was simply to accommodate ethical judgments in his logical positivism. Emotivism is certainly not entailed by logical positivism. Some logical positivists—such as Moritz Schlick, Otto Neurath, and Karl Menger—embraced a naturalist metaethic. Ayer's emotivism was due to two Cambridge influences: Ogden and Richards's *The Meaning of Meaning*, and Austin Duncan-Jones. Ayer acknowledged the latter's influence years later in his autobiography: "Digressing next to ethics, I put forward the view which had been suggested to me by Duncan-Jones that moral pronouncements were expressions of emotion rather than statements of fact, and for good measure I added a short 'Critique of Theology,' in which I maintained that statements purporting to refer to a transcendent deity were literally nonsensical. This chapter, which was peripheral to the main tenor of the book, was the one that aroused the greatest animosity."[53] Later Ayer would acknowledge the influence of Ogden and Richards:[54]

> The emotive theory which I put in its place was not my own invention. I was reminded quite recently that it had been advocated by C. K. Ogden and I. A. Richards in their book *The Meaning of Meaning*, which was published as early as 1923. Since I made no acknowledgment to them, this is a fact that I must have forgotten when I espoused the theory, though I was aware that the use by myself and others of the word "emotive" to cover the aspects of meaning that were not "literal," in the sense of issuing in truth or falsehood, was due to them.[55]

Though it was only an accommodation, and though the idea was taken from Ogden and Richards and Duncan-Jones, Ayer can nevertheless be credited with advancing the first comprehensive emotivist theory of ethics. Furthermore, as early as the second edition of *Language, Truth and Logic* in 1946, Ayer insisted that the emotivist theory was independently valid: "I was concerned with maintaining the general consistency of my position; but it is not the only ethical theory that would have satisfied this requirement, nor does it actually entail any of the non-ethical statements which form the remainder of my argument. Consequently, even if it could be shown that these other statements were invalid, this would not in itself refute the emotive analysis of ethical judgments; and in fact I believe this analysis to be valid on its own account."[56]

The argument of *Language, Truth and Logic* is that there are only two kinds of propositions that are genuine propositions, that is, that are capable of being true or false: analytic propositions and synthetic propositions. Furthermore, only genuine propositions are literally meaningful. Hence, there are only two kinds of statements or judgments that are capable of being true or false, and that are literally meaningful: statements or judgments that express analytic propositions (i.e., tautologies) and statements or judgments that express synthetic empirical hypotheses (i.e., empirical hypotheses). This is Ayer's logical positivism. It rules out Moore's non-natural (and nonsupernatural) moral realism, since on Moore's account moral statements or judgments are "genuine synthetic propositions" (157) and yet are not empirical hypotheses:

> In admitting that normative ethical concepts are irreducible to empirical concepts, we seem to be leaving the way clear for the "absolutist" view of ethics—that is, the view that statements of value are not controlled by observation, as ordinary empirical propositions are, but only by a mysterious "intellectual intuition." A feature of this theory, which is seldom recognized by its advocates, is that it makes statements of value unverifiable. For it is notorious that what seems intuitively certain to one person may seem doubtful, or even false, to another. So that unless it is possible to provide some criterion by which one may decide between conflicting intuitions, a mere appeal to intuition is worthless as a test of a proposition's validity. . . . But with regard to ethical statements, there is, on the "absolutist" or "intuitionist" theory, no relevant empirical test. We are therefore justified in saying that on this ethical theory statements are held to be unverifiable . . . it is clear that the acceptance of an "absolutist" theory of ethics would undermine the whole of our main argument. (156–57)

Ayer's "radical naturalism" (157) must somehow accommodate ethics. The first part of his argument for emotivism is that moral statements or judgments are not tautologies and are not empirical hypotheses either.[57] In arguing that moral statements or judgments are not empirical hypotheses, Ayer agrees with Moore's critique of naturalism in ethics. Indeed, he uses Moore's "Open Question Argument." This was the argument that "whatever definition be offered" of goodness, "it may be always asked, with significance, of the complex so defined, whether it is itself good."[58] In the case of utilitarianism, Ayer argues that "to call an action right" is not the same as to say that "of all the actions possible in the circumstances it would cause, or be likely to cause, the greatest happiness," because "we find that it is not self-contradictory to say that it is sometimes wrong to perform the action which would actually or probably cause the greatest happiness" (153–54). By *wrong* here Ayer means "morally wrong"; hence, the argument is that saying that an action is morally right or wrong does not have the same meaning as saying that it has the natural property of actually or probably causing the greatest happiness. This is his argument against definitional naturalistic utilitarianism.[59] He uses similar Moorean arguments against two varieties of subjectivism.

Since moral statements or judgments are neither tautologies nor empirical hypotheses, it follows that they cannot be true or false. They are literally meaningless. For this reason, Ayer often places "judgments of value" and "statements of value," in scare quotes: "It will be said that 'statements of value' are genuine propositions" (149); "to give an account of 'judgements of value'" (149).

If that were all that Ayer had to say about moral statements or judgments, then they would be in the same category as metaphysical statements. Metaphysical statements cannot be true or false and are literally meaningless also. However, metaphysical statements differ from moral statements or judgments in an important way. A metaphysical statement, such as a theological statement—"that 'God exists'" (115) or "that 'there is no god'" (115)—is a statement that "purports to express a genuine proposition, but does, in fact, express neither a tautology nor an empirical hypothesis" (31) and hence "is neither true nor false but literally senseless" (12). A moral judgment or statement, by contrast, does not purport to express a genuine proposition. A moral judgment or statement does not purport to be truth-apt or literally meaningful. Hence moral judgments or statements are not like metaphysical statements. While metaphysical statements are failed attempts at meaningfulness (and so, there is not even an "error theory" of metaphysics, but rather a "meaningless theory" of metaphysics), moral statements or judgments are not even *attempts* at meaningfulness.[60]

Instead, moral judgments purport to be, and are, the expressions of emotions: "'Judgements of value' . . . are not in the literal sense significant, but are simply expressions of emotion which can be neither true nor false" (149–50). Importantly, moral judgments do not "express propositions about the speaker's feelings" (162), that is, they do not "assert the existence of certain feelings" (163), in the matter of a description of the person's emotional state. If they did, then "ethical judgements would clearly be capable of being true or false," since "they would be true if the speaker had the relevant feelings, and false if he did not" (162). Rather, when a person makes a moral judgment, such as "Tolerance is a virtue" (162), the person is evincing emotions, and not stating or judging that she has (certain) emotions: "In saying that tolerance was a virtue, I should not be making any statement about my own feelings or about anything else. I should simply be evincing my feelings, which is not at all the same thing as saying that I have them" (162).

Moral judgments purport to be, and are, the expressions of particular kinds of emotions, however. The emotions that moral judgments express are *moral* emotions:[61] "For in saying that a certain type of action is right or wrong, I am not making any factual statement, not even a statement about my own state of mind. I am merely expressing certain moral sentiments. And the man who is ostensibly contradicting me is merely expressing his moral sentiments" (159). Ayer uses the expression *moral sentiments* most often to capture the emotions involved, but he also uses the expressions *ethical feeling* (160, 165, 170) and *moral attitude* (166). (He never uses the expression *moral emotion* or *ethical emotion,* presumably because such an expression would be awkward.) Although such moral emotions are clearly to be distinguished from "aesthetic feeling" (170), which is the emotion expressed in aesthetic judgment, the only example of a moral emotion Ayer provides is "moral disapproval" (158, 159, 167) or moral approval. Ayer is not interested in saying anything more about these moral emotions, only commenting that "the further task of describing the different feelings that the different ethical terms are used to express, and the different reactions that they customarily provoke, is a task for the psychologist" (168). He must hold, however, that these moral emotions may be distinguished from nonmoral emotions using purely empirical methods in order for his claim to be consistent with his logical positivism.

Strictly speaking, Ayer holds that there are two kinds of moral judgments: particular moral judgments and general moral judgments. A particular moral judgment, such as "You acted wrongly in doing X," both expresses an empirical hypothesis ("You did X") and expresses a moral emotion—moral disapproval. The empirical hypothesis it expresses is either true or false, and is literally meaningful, whereas the moral emotion it expresses is neither true nor false, and is literally meaningless. A general moral judgment, such as "Doing X is wrong," does not express an empirical hypothesis; it merely expresses a moral emotion (moral disapproval) about a class of actions:

> If now I . . . say, "Stealing money is wrong," I produce a sentence which has no factual meaning—that is, expresses no proposition which can be either true or false. It is as if I had written "Stealing money!!"—where the shape and thickness of the exclamation marks show, by a suitable convention, that a special sort of moral disapproval is the feeling which is being expressed. It is clear that there is nothing said here which can be true or false. . . . For in saying that a certain type of action is right or wrong, I am not making any factual statement, not even a statement about my own state of mind. I am merely expressing certain moral sentiments. (158–59)

Even general moral judgments do not only *express* moral emotions, however. Moral judgments are "expressions and excitants of feeling" (163). Hence, moral judgments are "calculated to arouse feeling, and so to stimulate action" (160) in others. A general moral judgment such as "It is your duty to do X," for example, both expresses the emotion of moral approval of X, and expresses a command to do X: "the sentence 'It is your duty to tell the truth' may be regarded both as the expression of a certain sort of ethical feeling about truthfulness and as the expression of the command 'Tell the truth'" (160).

One important entailment of the emotivist theory is "the impossibility of purely ethical arguments" (167), due to the fact that "it is impossible to dispute about questions of value" (164), since moral judgments are the expressions of moral emotions rather than propositions. According to Ayer, there is no moral argument that "does not reduce itself to an argument about a question of logic or about an empirical matter of fact" (167). In all moral argument with another person, "we do not attempt to show by our arguments that he has the 'wrong' ethical feeling toward a situation whose nature he has correctly apprehended. What we attempt to show is that he is mistaken about the facts of the case" (165). This is because "argument is possible on moral questions only if some system of values is presupposed" (166–67). If it is the case that "our opponent concurs with us in expressing moral disapproval of all actions of a given type t, then we may get him to condemn a particular action A, by bringing forward arguments to show that A is of type t. For the question whether A does or does not belong to that type is a question of plain fact" (167). However, if the other person does not express the same moral disapproval of actions of a certain type as we do, then there can be no argument.

> But if our opponent happens to have undergone a different process of moral "conditioning" from ourselves, so that, even when he acknowledges all the facts, he still disagrees with us about the moral value of the actions under discussion, then we abandon the attempt to convince him by argument. We say that it is impossible to argue with him because he has a distorted or undeveloped moral sense; which signifies merely that he employs a different set of values from our own. We feel that our system of values is superior, and therefore speak in derogatory terms of his. But we cannot bring forward any arguments to show that our system is superior. For our judgement that it is so is itself a judgement of value, and accordingly outside the scope of argument. It is because argument fails us when we come to deal with pure questions of value, as distinct from questions of fact, that we finally resort to mere abuse. (166)

MacIntyre does not normally single Ayer out for criticism in his critique of emotivism (his target is normally Stevenson, and sometimes Hare). However, there are at least two arguments in his writings that directly concern Ayer's emotivism.[62] The first is what MacIntyre refers to as "the basic weakness of all psychological theories in ethics."[63] According to Ayer, when I make a moral statement or judgment, "I am merely expressing certain moral sentiments" (159). However, according to MacIntyre, what Ayer cannot do is provide an account of what makes this emotion *moral* as opposed to *nonmoral:* "To say that moral judgments express a sentiment or feeling is vacuous and unhelpful. Of course they do. But what sentiment or feeling? We can find no useful definition of moral sentiment, except as that sentiment which is bound up with moral judgment. What it is that makes moral judgment and sentiment distinctive, what entitles them to the appellation 'moral,' what their relation is to other kinds of judgment and sentiment—to none of these questions do such theories return an answer."[64] The objection, here, is that emotivism is "opaque" and that lying behind its opacity is circularity:

> One can justifiably complain of the emotive theory not only that it is mistaken, but also that it is opaque. For its proponents seek to elucidate moral expressions in terms of the notions of attitudes and feelings, and it is relevant to ask for further characterization of the attitudes and feelings in question. How, for example, are we to identify these attitudes and feelings so that we may distinguish them from other attitudes and feelings? Emotivist writers are, in fact, largely silent on this point; but the suspicion is strong that they would be compelled to characterize the attitudes and feelings under discussion as just those attitudes and feelings which are given their definitive expression in acts of moral judgment. Yet if this is so, the whole theory is imprisoned in uninformative circularity.[65]

This charge is repeated in *After Virtue*: "'Moral judgments express feelings or attitudes,' it is said. 'What kind of feelings or attitudes?' we ask. 'Feelings or attitudes of approval,' is the reply. 'What kinds of approval?' we ask, perhaps remarking that approval is of many kinds. It is in answer to this question that every version of emotivism either remains silent or, by identifying the relevant kind of approval as moral approval—that is, the type of approval expressed by a specifically moral judgment—becomes vacuously circular."[66] In Ayer's case, the task of providing an account of what makes moral emotions distinctively moral is especially difficult, given that this must be done in terms of the observable behavior of those who are expressing the moral, as opposed to the nonmoral, emotions. As another commentator has pointed out:

> But are there observable behavioural occurrences which would constitute the expression of this special sort of moral or ethical emotion? It is difficult to see how Ayer could answer this in the affirmative: we can perhaps imag-

ine patterns of observable behaviour which would express disapproval, but what observable behaviour could possibly manifest the presence of a distinctively *moral* or *ethical* sort of disapproval? This suggests that if we are to be consistent in our application of the generalized criterion of significance, ethical sentences actually get relegated to the category of nonsense and verbiage along with the sentences of metaphysics.[67]

The second argument that MacIntyre makes directly against Ayer's emotivism concerns the dismissal of both ethical judgments or statements and metaphysical statements—in particular theological statements—as literally meaningless:

> Ayer's critique of intuitionism has quite different roots [from Collingwood's]. In *Language, Truth and Logic* he revived some of Hume's positions, but did so in the context of a logical-positivist theory of knowledge. So moral judgments are understood in terms of a threefold classification of judgments: logical, factual, and emotive. In the first class come the truths of logic and mathematics, which are held to be analytic; in the second come the empirically verifiable or falsifiable truths of the sciences and of common-sense knowledge of fact. The third class necessarily appears as a residual category, a rag-bag to which whatever is not logic or science is consigned. Both ethics and theology find themselves in this category, a fact in itself sufficient to make us suspicious of the classification. For on the face of it, statements about the intentions and deeds of an omnipotent being and judgments about duty or about what is good do not obviously belong together.[68]

MacIntyre's objection that theological statements and moral judgments or statements do not appear to "belong together" is correct as far as it goes, since theological statements certainly appear to be more descriptive in nature than moral judgments or statements. However, what this suspicion reveals is a deeper problem with Ayer's analysis. Ayer's basis for distinguishing between the two different kinds of meaninglessness is that a theological statement "purports to express a genuine proposition," whereas a moral judgment or statement does not purport to express a genuine proposition. Surely, however, this is false. Moral judgments or statements *do* purport to express genuine propositions. They *do* purport to be objective. As such, it seems, Ayer must classify them with theological statements, by his own argument. He should have simply advanced the "meaningless theory" of ethics. As another commentator has said: "Since Ayer wants to deny that there are objective moral facts, and since our ethical concepts are inherently objectivist, the conclusion he should have reached is that these concepts are defective. In other words, instead of trying to salvage ethics by an emotivist analysis, he should have eliminated ethics altogether, in the way he eliminates metaphysics. He should have classified ethical sentences as assertoric nonsense rather than as expressions of feeling."[69] The failure of Ayer and other emotivists to recognize that moral concepts are inherently objectivist is pointed out by MacIntyre in a criticism aimed in the first instance at Stevenson:

> What [Stevenson] did not note however—precisely because he viewed emotivism as a theory of meaning—is that the prestige derives from the fact that the use of "That is bad!" implies an appeal to an objective and impersonal standard in a way in which "I disapprove of this; do so as well!" does not. That is, if and insofar as emotivism is true, moral language is seriously misleading and, if and insofar as emotivism is justifiably believed, presumably the use of traditional and inherited moral language ought to be abandoned. This conclusion none of the emotivists drew; and it is clear that, like Stevenson, they failed to draw it because they misconstrued their own theory as a theory of meaning.[70]

As I mentioned, however, MacIntyre does not normally single Ayer out for criticism in his critique of emotivism. That dubious honor is usually reserved for Stevenson.

"The Emotive Meaning of Ethical Terms"

J. O. Urmson has said about Charles L. Stevenson that he was "the first emotivist to take ethics seriously, for its own sake, in print."[71] After he finished a BA in English at Yale University in 1930, Stevenson went to Cambridge University "to continue his study of literature, only to be attracted to philosophy by G. E. Moore and Ludwig Wittgenstein. He earned a Cambridge B. A. in philosophy in 1933," before returning to the United

States to do his PhD in philosophy at Harvard University.[72] It has been said that "the theories of Ayer and Stevenson are independent,"[73] and this is true, although both were inspired by Ogden and Richards. As Stevenson says in 1935 in his doctoral dissertation, "The Emotive Meaning of Ethical Terms": "The suggestion came from Ogden and Richards, and from a discussion with Mr. R. B. Braithwaite, of King's College, Cambridge."[74] In his 1937 article, "The Emotive Meaning of Ethical Terms," which is adapted from a chapter of his dissertation, Stevenson says that when he refers to "'emotive' meaning" he is referring to it "in a sense roughly like that employed by Ogden and Richards," and he footnotes the passage from *The Meaning of Meaning* about the "purely emotive use" of "'good'" by Moore.[75] In his book *Ethics and Language,* in 1944, Stevenson quotes the entire passage from Ogden and Richards before the book's preface.[76] In his 1935 dissertation he also acknowledges Broad's "Is Goodness a Name of a Simple Non-Natural Quality?," which contains the summary of Austin Duncan-Jones's proposal, and W. H. F. Barnes's "A Suggestion about Value." About these authors he says, however, "I trust neither Mr. Broad nor Mr. Duncan-Jones are acquainted with the work of Ogden and Richards," and "I am indebted to Mr. Broad and Mr. Barnes not for suggestions, since I did not become acquainted with their articles until quite recently, but wish to express my gratification that others should have come to the same conclusions from apparently different sources."[77]

In "The Emotive Meaning of Ethical Terms," Stevenson's concern is to provide a "relevant definition of 'good'" (15).[78] He claims that to be an adequate definition it must meet at least three criteria. First, people must be "able sensibly to *disagree* about whether something is 'good'" (16). That is, an adequate definition of "good" must allow for sensible or "intelligent" (18) disagreement about something's being good. Second, "'goodness' must have, so to speak, a magnetism. A person who recognizes X to be 'good' must *ipso facto* acquire a stronger tendency to act in its favour than he otherwise would have" (16). That is, an adequate definition of *good* must allow for the necessary connection between something's being good and people being motivated to pursue it or promote it.[79] Third, "the 'goodness' of anything must not be verifiable solely by use of the scientific method" (16).[80] Here Stevenson simply invokes Moore's Open Question Argument against a scientific definition of *good:* "Mr. G. E. Moore's familiar objection about the open question is chiefly pertinent in this regard.

No matter what set of scientifically knowable properties a thing may have (says Moore, in effect), you will find, on careful introspection, that it is an open question to ask whether anything having these properties is *good*" (18). Stevenson's argument is that the adequate account of goodness must not be purely descriptive, since "ethical statements" (18) or "ethical judgments" are made, not to describe, but to influence others: "Doubtless there is always *some* element of description in ethical judgments, but this is by no means all. Their major use is not to indicate facts, but to *create an influence*. Instead of merely describing people's interests, they *change* or *intensify* them" (18). The question this raises, of course, is "How does an ethical sentence acquire its power of influencing people—why it is suited to suggestion?" (20). Stevenson thinks that this power that moral judgments have to influence others comes from the "dynamic" use of words, which have the ability "to give vent to our feelings (interjections), or to create moods (poetry), or to incite people to actions or attitudes (oratory)" (21). Stevenson here distinguishes between use and meaning: "One thing is clear—we must not define 'meaning' in a way that would make meaning vary with dynamic usage" (22).

For Stevenson, "meaning" is to be identified with those "psychological causes and effects" that a word's utterance "has a *tendency* (causal property, dispositional property) to be connected with" (22). The tendency must "exist for all who speak the language; it must be persistent; and must be realizable more or less independently of determinate circumstances attending the word's utterance" (22). He argues that there is one kind of meaning that has an "intimate relation to dynamic usage" (23) of language. This kind of meaning is emotive meaning:

> I refer to "emotive" meaning (in a sense roughly like that employed by Ogden and Richards). The emotive meaning of a word is a tendency of a word, arising through the history of its usage, to produce (result from) *affective* responses in people. It is the immediate aura of feeling which hovers about a word. Such tendencies to produce affective responses cling to words very tenaciously. It would be difficult, for instance, to express merriment by using the interjection "alas." Because of the persistence of such affective tendencies (among other reasons) it becomes feasible to classify them as "meanings." (23)

Emotive meaning "assists" (24) the dynamic purpose of a moral judgment. *Good* (in general) has "a pleasing emotive meaning which fits it especially for the dynamic use of suggesting favourable interest" (25). Hence "'This is good' has something like the meaning of 'I *do* like this; do so as well'" (25). In the case where *good* is being used morally, "the ethical sentence differs from an imperative in that it enables one to make changes in a much more subtle, less fully conscious way" (26). The ethical or moral emotive meaning of *good* is not the same as the nonmoral emotive meaning of *good:* "A word must be added about the moral use of 'good.' This differs from the above in that it is about a different kind of interest. Instead of being about what the hearer and speaker *like,* it is about a stronger sort of approval. When a person *likes* something, he is pleased when it prospers, and disappointed when it doesn't. When a person morally approves of something, he experiences a rich feeling of security when it prospers, and is indignant, or 'shocked' when it doesn't" (26). Thus the moral emotive meaning of *good,* for Stevenson, is approximately "I morally approve of this; do so as well."

With this account in mind, Stevenson proceeds to show how his definition of *good* in general—approximately, "I like this; do so as well"—and of moral *good* in particular—approximately, "I morally approve of this; do so as well"—satisfies the three criteria for defining *good*.[81]

With respect to the possibility of intelligent disagreement about what is good, Stevenson first distinguishes between "disagreement in belief" and "disagreement in interest" (27), where "interest" is understood broadly enough to include moral approval. In the case of ethics, the disagreement is always disagreement in interest: "It is disagreement in interest which takes place in ethics. When C says 'This is good,' and D says 'No, it's bad,' we have a case of suggestion and counter-suggestion. Each man is trying to redirect the other's interest. There obviously need be no domineering, since each may be willing to give ear to the other's influence; but each is trying to move the other none the less. It is in this sense that they disagree" (27).

With respect to how an adequate definition of *good* must allow for the necessary connection between something's being good and its being the case that people are motivated to pursue it or promote it, since the speaker's interest is included in both definitions, it follows that both definitions incorporate such a connection. In the moral case, when people judge something to be morally good, they are expressing moral approval of it, and hence they are in a state of morally approving of it. This entails that they have a stronger tendency to pursue it or promote it.

Finally, with respect to the scientific method, Stevenson asks: "When two people disagree over an ethical matter, can they completely resolve the disagreement through empirical considerations, assuming that each applies the empirical method exhaustively, consistently, and without error?" (27–28). His reply is that sometimes they cannot. Here he provides an example of an ethical disagreement that exists even though the two parties agree on all of the (scientific) facts:

> For instance: A is of a sympathetic nature, and B isn't. They are arguing about whether a public dole would be good. Suppose that they discovered all the consequences of the dole. Isn't it possible, even so, that A will say that it's good, and B that it's bad? The disagreement in interest may arise not from limited factual knowledge, but simply from A's sympathy or B's coldness. Or again, suppose, in the above argument, that A was poor and unemployed, and that B was rich. Here again the disagreement might not be due to different factual knowledge. It would be due to the different social positions of the men, together with their predominant self-interest. (29)

In this case, it can be said, *A* morally approves of the dole and is attempting to get *B* to morally approve of the dole, whereas *B* morally disapproves of the dole and is attempting to get *A* to disapprove of the dole. Both of them agree on the scientific facts, however. Hence, science cannot resolve this disagreement.

Importantly, Stevenson does not conclude that in the case of such moral disagreement there is no way to arrive at moral agreement, that is, agreement of moral approval. There is indeed a way. It is simply that this way is not a rational way—it is the way of nonrational persuasion:

> When ethical disagreement is not rooted in disagreement in belief, is there *any* method by which it may be settled? If one means by "method" a *rational* method, then there is no method. But in any case there is a "way." Let's consider the above example, again, where disagreement was due to A's sympathy and B's coldness. Must they end up by saying, "Well it's just a

matter of our having different temperaments"? Not necessarily. A, for instance, may try to change the temperament of his opponent. He may pour out his enthusiasms in such a moving way—present the sufferings of the poor with such appeal—that he will lead his opponent to see life through different eyes. He may build up, by the contagion of his feelings, an influence which will modify B's temperament, and create in him a sympathy for the poor which didn't previously exist. This is often the only way to obtain ethical agreement, if there is any way at all. It is persuasive, not empirical or rational; but that is no reason for neglecting it. (29)

In his *Short History,* MacIntyre states that "the most powerful exponent of emotivism has been C. L. Stevenson."[82] Here he contrasts Ayer and Stevenson: "Ayer, in his version of the emotive theory, concentrated upon my expression of my own feelings and attitudes; Stevenson, in his, concentrates on my attempt to influence your feelings and attitudes."[83] Nevertheless, he highlights what Stevenson has in common with Ayer, which is actually something both took from Moore: "Thus Stevenson agrees with Moore that *good* cannot function as the name of a natural (empirically descriptive) property. The facts are logically divorced from the evaluations for Stevenson as much as for Moore."[84] Stevenson and Ayer also have in common the view that "philosophical ethics is a morally neutral activity. The doctrines that we hold about the meaning of moral expressions cannot commit us to any particular moral view."[85]

According to MacIntyre, two things are important about the emotivist position on the complete divorce between natural facts on the one hand and moral judgments on the other. First, any set of natural facts is compatible with any moral judgment whatsoever. Second, since moral disagreement is not based on natural facts, moral disagreement is in principle interminable, and there is no way to rationally resolve such moral disagreement. It is an a-rational process:

> For, presumably, we can use emotive words to commend any class of actions whatsoever. Moreover, if Stevenson is right, evaluative disagreement may always be interminable. There is no limit to the possibilities of disagreement, and there is and can be no set of procedures for the resolution of disagreements.... The reasons which we cite to support our evaluative, and more specifically, our moral judgments cannot stand in any logical

relationship to the conclusions which we derive from them. They can only be psychological reinforcements. It follows that words like *because* and *therefore* do not function as they do in other parts of discourse.[86]

Indeed, as Ayer pointed out, such moral disagreement, which Stevenson characterizes as "persuasive," instead of "rational," can simply be abuse.

In addition to the circularity objection to the emotivist account of moral emotion, MacIntyre makes further objections to emotivism, especially in the form in which Stevenson advances it. One objection is that, quite simply, there is no such meaning as "emotive meaning":

> The notion of "emotive meaning" is itself not clear. What makes certain statements guides to, or directives of, action is not that they have any meaning over and above a factual or descriptive one. It is that their utterance on a specific occasion has import for, or relevance to, the speaker or hearer's interests, desires, or needs. "The White House is on fire" does not have any more or less meaning when uttered in a news broadcast in London than it does when uttered as a warning to the President in bed, but its function as a guide is quite different. Emotivism, that is, does not attend sufficiently to the distinction between the meaning of a statement which remains constant between different uses, and the variety of uses to which one and the same statement can be put.[87]

MacIntyre further illustrates this point with an example taken from Gilbert Ryle: "The angry schoolmaster, to use one of Gilbert Ryle's examples, may vent his feelings by shouting at the small boy who has just made an arithmetical mistake, 'Seven times seven equals forty-nine!' But the use of this sentence to express feelings or attitudes has nothing whatsoever to do with its meaning."[88] MacIntyre's own account of meaning, it seems, is Frege's: "meaning—understood as including all that Frege intended by 'sense' and 'reference.'"[89] MacIntyre accuses emotivism of confusing meaning with use: "The expression of feeling or attitude is characteristically a function not of the meaning of sentences, but of their use on particular occasions."[90]

MacIntyre argues, moreover, that emotivism fails to account for other uses of moral language, such as those that are necessary for the formation and expression of one's moral approval (and disapproval) of one's own actions:

Moreover, not only does Stevenson tend to conflate meaning and use, but the primary use which he assigns to moral expressions is not, and cannot be, their primary use. For the use to which he attends is the second-person use in which we try to move other people to adopt our own views. Stevenson's examples all picture a thoroughly unpleasant world in which everyone is always trying to get at everyone else. But in fact one is only in a position to try to convert others to one's own moral views when one has formed views of one's own; yet none of those uses of moral language which are necessary to the formation and expression of one's own views with an eye to one's own actions figure in Stevenson's initial account.[91]

MacIntyre elaborates on this criticism in *The Significance of Moral Judgments,* as has been pointed out: "To illustrate this with reference to an example, *Significance* notes that when one deliberates about whether one ought to defend democracy by enlisting in the army to fight in a war, or whether one ought to oppose war by conscientious objection, one's thoughts have a self-transcendent reference: they are governed in a certain sense by cognitive considerations about external states of affairs. Such deliberation seems not at all merely to involve the introspective weighing of one's inclinations as Stevenson has it."[92]

Against Bourgeois Formalism in Ethics

MacIntyre's criticism that emotivism confuses meaning with use allows him to make the claim that emotivism might be better understood as a sociological thesis about the use of moral language:

> Let us in the light of such considerations disregard emotivism's claim to universality of scope; and let us instead consider emotivism as a theory which has been advanced in historically specific conditions. . . . We ought therefore to ask whether emotivism as a theory may not have been both a response to, and in the very first instance, an account of *not*, as its protagonists indeed supposed, moral language as such, but moral language in England in the years after 1903 as and when that language was interpreted in accordance with that body of theory to the refutation of which emotivism was primarily dedicated. The theory in question borrowed from the early

nineteenth century the name of "intuitionism" and its immediate progenitor was G. E. Moore.[93]

The claim, then, is that the emotivists "did in fact confuse moral utterance at Cambridge (and in other places with a similar inheritance) after 1903 with moral utterance as such, and that they therefore presented what was in essentials a correct account of the former as though it were an account of the latter."[94] They had given a correct account of how moral language is used, but the "meaning of those sentences was such that they at least appeared to give expression to some impersonal standard of judgment to which appeal was being made," and thus "meaning and use had, so it seemed, come apart" (see page 23, this volume). MacIntyre has posed this problem in the form of a question: "I had of course understood the significance of Ayer's and Stevenson's work very differently from the way in which they themselves understood it. The question that I therefore faced was: If moral judgments here and now are used, at least in large part, as Ayer and Stevenson say that they are, what else, in other social and cultural circumstances, might moral judgments and evaluative judgments be? Might there be or have been a condition from which they had degenerated to their present state? And what would that condition be?" (ibid.).

On this interpretation, as it turns out, emotivism is the final stage in a metaethical history that begins with the Greeks and ends with the early twentieth century. For the Greeks, "The connection between the moral life and the pursuit of what men want is always preserved. . . . Desire is always kept in the picture."[95] "The Greek moral tradition asserted . . . an essential connection between 'good' and 'good for,' between virtue and desire. . . . Morality, to be intelligible, must be grounded in human nature."[96] In the Bible (and later in Thomism), "What God offers is something that will satisfy all our desires. . . . And desire remains at the heart of morality in the Middle Ages."[97] "So an Aristotelian moral psychology and a Christian view of the moral law are synthesized even if somewhat unsatisfactorily in Thomist ethics."[98] In the Protestant Reformation, "because human beings are totally corrupt their nature cannot be a function of true morality"; thus "We obey God's commandments not because they and He are good, but simply because they are his. The moral law becomes a connection of divine fiats, so far as we are concerned totally arbitrary."[99] Hence "The moral law is a collection of arbitrary fiats unconnected with anything we may want or desire."[100] The next stage is that of the Enlightenment, in which "two other considerations suggest themselves. The first is that if the moral rules have force, they surely do whether God commands them or not. The second is that perhaps there is no God."[101] In the Enlightenment, and in particular in Kant, there is a change from a "characterization of morality in terms of content . . . to the attempt . . . to characterize morality purely in terms of the form of moral judgments," and this is "the significant change in philosophical ethics."[102] For Kant's moral philosophy "is, from one point of view, the natural outcome of the Protestant position."[103] It heralds "the tradition which upholds the autonomy of ethics from Kant to Moore to Hare," according to which moral judgments "are logically independent of any assertions about human nature."[104] As MacIntyre has said:

> Neither Satan nor Kant can claim to be the first prescriptivist; but in their joint insistence on autonomy they helped to father the categorical "ought" of nineteenth-century invocations of Duty, an "ought" which furnished an ultimate ending for the chain of moral justifications and so is the immediate ancestor of the "ought" of prescriptivism. This "ought" is criterionless. . . . It has been insufficiently remarked that the use of "ought" statements to make categorical moral judgments not supported by further reasoning does not originate with philosophical theorizing, but is a feature of ordinary non-philosophical discourse in the last two hundred years; theories such as intuitionism, emotivism, and prescriptivism can all be viewed as attempts to provide a philosophical account of a use of language which is best explained as survival from a theistic age.[105]

While it is true that "morality, like the railway and the polka, is an innovation of the nineteenth century,"[106] nevertheless the tradition of the autonomy of morality reached its apogee in Moore, who, with the attack on all naturalistic ethics, ushered in the fact/value distinction, or is/ought divide, on which emotivism is premised. All emotivists are Mooreans, in that sense. However, this distinction need not be accepted. It is not a timeless truth but a historical consequence of rejecting human nature, desires, or interests as a basis for ethics. Its legacy is interminable moral disagreement without the possibility of rational resolution.

Notes

Research for this essay was conducted while I was at Princeton University in the summer of 2009. I would like to thank the Philosophy Department, as well as the staff of the Firestone Library, for their assistance. A Lenfest Summer Grant from Washington and Lee University funded my research, and I would like to thank the university for their continued generosity. Parts of the essay are adapted from chapter 4 of my PhD dissertation (Duke University, 2000), which was supervised by Alasdair MacIntyre and later published under the title *Motivational Internalism and the Authority of Morality* (Saarbrücken: VDM, 2011). I would like to take this opportunity to thank Professor MacIntyre a second time for his supervision.

1. Alasdair MacIntyre, *After Virtue: A Study in Moral Theory*, 3rd ed. (Notre Dame: University of Notre Dame Press, 2007).
2. Ibid., 22; Bruce N. Waller, "The Virtues of Contemporary Emotivism," *Erkenntnis* 25 (1986): 61.
3. My apologies to MacIntyre, who has said that "no one, including Frankena, has as yet made clear to me the meaning of that barbarous neologism 'metaethics.'" "A Rejoinder to a Rejoinder," in *Knowledge, Value and Belief: The Foundations of Ethics and Its Relationship to Science*, ed. H. Tristram Engelhardt and Daniel Callahan (Hastings-on-Hudson, NY: Hastings Center, 1977), 2:76.
4. Alasdair MacIntyre, "The Significance of Moral Judgments" (MA thesis, University of Manchester, 1951). He wrote this thesis under the supervision of Dorothy Emmet, who had defended metaphysics from the criticisms of the logical positivists in her book *The Nature of Metaphysical Thinking* (London: Macmillan, 1945). Emmet called him "the ablest student I had at that time, or probably at any time" (*Philosophers and Friends: Reminiscences of Seventy Years in Philosophy* [Basingstoke: Macmillan, 1996], 86). Thomas D. D'Andrea has commented that, "interestingly, nowhere in the thesis does MacIntyre advert to, or seem fully cognizant of, the distinction between meta-ethics and first-order ethical theory (i.e. normative ethics)" (*Tradition, Rationality and Virtue: The Thought of Alasdair MacIntyre* [Aldershot: Ashgate, 2006], 4). This interpretation, however, seems anachronistic. In his foreword to P. H. Nowell-Smith's *Ethics* (Harmondsworth: Penguin, 1954), A. J. Ayer writes: "There is a distinction, which is not always sufficiently marked, between the activity of a moralist, who sets out to elaborate a moral code, or to encourage its observance, and that of a moral philosopher, whose concern is not primarily to make moral judgments but to analyse their nature" (7). This was how the distinction was made at the time, and MacIntyre was clearly aware of the distinction (see also note 3 above).
5. Stephen Satris, *Ethical Emotivism* (Dordrecht: Martinus Nijhoff, 1987), viii.

6. For arguments defending emotivism from MacIntyre's critique, see Waller, "Virtues of Contemporary Emotivism," 64–81, and Nicholas Unwin, "Can Emotivism Sustain a Social Ethics?," *Ratio* 1 (1990): 61–75. For a response, see John Lemos, "The Problems with Emotivism: Reflections on Some MacIntyrean Arguments," *Journal of Philosophical Research* 25 (2000): 285–309.

7. MacIntyre, *After Virtue*, 14.

8. Alasdair MacIntyre, *A Short History of Ethics,* 2nd ed. (Notre Dame: Notre Dame University Press, 1998), 249; G. E. Moore, *Principia Ethica* (Cambridge: Cambridge University Press, 1903).

9. W. D. Ross, *Foundations of Ethics* (Oxford: Clarendon Press, 1939).

10. As Stephen R. L. Clark has said, "Moore has a special place in MacIntyre's demonology" ("Morals, Moore, and MacIntyre," *Inquiry* 26 [1984]: 433).

11. In this section I am indebted to Alexander Miller's *An Introduction to Contemporary Metaethics* (Cambridge: Polity Press, 2003).

12. Moral cognitivism does not entail moral realism. J. L. Mackie is a moral cognitivist, but he is also a moral antirealist, since he holds that *no* moral properties exist that would make any moral judgments true. He holds that all (positive) moral judgments are false. See J. L. Mackie, "A Refutation of Morals," *Australasian Journal of Psychology and Philosophy* 24 (1946): 77–90, and *Ethics: Inventing Right and Wrong* (Harmondsworth: Penguin, 1977), for his error theory of moral judgments.

13. Moral realism does not entail moral nonnaturalism. So-called Cornell realists hold that moral properties are natural properties, although they hold that these natural properties are not reducible to other natural properties. See, for example, Nicholas Sturgeon, "Moral Explanations," and Richard Boyd, "How to Be a Moral Realist," in *Essays in Moral Realism,* ed. Geoffrey Sayre-McCord (Ithaca: Cornell University Press, 1988), 229–55 and 181–28, respectively. Meanwhile, some moral realists who are naturalists hold that moral properties are reducible to other natural properties. For an example of a moral realist naturalist reductionist, see Peter Railton, "Moral Realism," *Philosophical Review* 95 (1986): 163–207.

14. Moore's definition of *natural* is "that which is the subject matter of the natural sciences and also of psychology" (*Principia Ethica,* 40). Miller improves upon this: "I will simply take natural properties to be those which are either causal or detectable by the senses. . . . Non-natural properties, on our characterization, are simply properties which are neither causal nor detectable by the senses" (*Introduction to Contemporary Metaethics*, 11). By *supernatural* Moore means "supersensible," and the position that moral properties are supernatural properties he calls "Metaphysical Ethics" (*Principia Ethica*, 110–11). Examples of this would be Plato's Theory of Forms, as well as various transcendent theological moral realisms.

15. Moore, *Principia Ethica*, 9.

16. MacIntyre, *Short History of Ethics*, 252.

17. Moore's moral non-naturalism is not the only version of moral non-naturalism available. John McDowell, for example, is also a moral non-naturalist. See his *Mind, Value, and Reality* (Cambridge, MA: Harvard University Press, 1998).

18. I follow Thomas Baldwin in availing myself of the concept of supervenience to refer to Moore's conception of the relationship between moral properties and natural properties. See his *G. E. Moore* (London: Routledge, 1990) and his editor's introduction to Moore's *Principia Ethica*, rev. ed. (Cambridge: Cambridge University Press, 1993), ix–xxxvii.

19. Moore, *Principia Ethica*, 188.

20. Moore, *Ethics* (1912; repr., Oxford University Press, 1965), 102. Importantly, Moore is contrasting this state of consciousness with that of "the state of mind of a drunkard, when he is intensely pleased with breaking crockery" (102). The point is that Moore is not a hedonist, as Jeremy Bentham is. For Bentham's position, see Elizabeth Anderson, "John Stuart Mill and Experiments in Living," *Ethics* 102 (1991): 4–26.

21. MacIntyre, *Short History of Ethics*, 256.

22. Ibid., 252.

23. Ibid.

24. "As we have just seen, Mr. Moore is compelled to say that the goodness of a thing must be thought of as a reason for aiming at it. But on his theory how can this be so? How can it be a motive for action? We are told that it is a simple quality which we perceive immediately. But our mere cognition of it cannot move us to action. . . . The mere fact of a thing being good can never by itself influence us to aim at it or move us to action. In fact, it is not necessarily of any interest to us at all." G. C. Field, *Moral Theory* (London: Methuen, 1921), 56–57. "[A] world of non-natural characteristics, is revealed to us by a . . . faculty called '*intuition.*' . . . A new world is revealed for our inspection . . . No doubt it is all very interesting. . . . But what if I am not interested? Why should I *do* anything about these newly-revealed objects?" (Nowell-Smith, *Ethics*, 36).

25. MacIntyre, *Short History of Ethics*, 252–53.

26. See William K. Frankena, "Obligation and Motivation in Recent Moral Philosophy," in *Essays in Moral Philosophy*, ed. A. I. Melden (Seattle: University of Washington Press, 1958), 40–81.

27. See James Edwin Mahon, "Internalism and Emotivism: Ayer and Stevenson," *Studies in the History of Ethics*, August 2005, www.historyofethics.org/082005/082005Mahon.shtml.

28. Christine Korsgaard, *The Sources of Normativity* (Cambridge: Cambridge University Press, 1996), 19.

29. Mackie, *Ethics*, 40, 38.

30. See D'Andrea, *Tradition, Rationality and Virtue*, 5.

31. Although he is talking about a person being in doubt about an obligation, as opposed two people disagreeing about an obligation, Prichard's remedy is essentially the same: "The only remedy lies in actual *[sic]* getting into a situation

which occasions the obligation, or—if our imagination be strong enough—in imagining ourselves in that situation, and then letting our moral capacities of thinking do their work." H. A. Prichard, "Does Moral Philosophy Rest on a Mistake?," *Mind* 21 (1912): 37.

32. MacIntyre, *After Virtue*, 16 (emphasis in the original).

33. Ibid., 17.

34. Ibid.

35. Moore, *Principia Ethica*, 15.

36. MacIntyre, *Short History of Ethics*, 257.

37. Ogden and Richards were influenced by Anton Marty, who in his *Untersuchungen zur Grundlegung der allgemeinen Grammatik und Sprachphilosophie* (Halle, 1908) divided sentences into "statements which express and evoke judgments, and emotives, which express and evoke desires, intentions, emotions and states of interest" (Satris, *Ethical Emotivism*, 18).

38. C. K. Ogden and I. A. Richards, *The Meaning of Meaning* (London: Kegan Paul, Trench, Trubner, 1923), 228 n. 1.

39. "Historic sentence" is from J. O. Urmson, *The Emotive Theory of Ethics* (Oxford: Oxford University Press, 1968), 16.

40. Ibid., 227–28.

41. Richards emphasized this point in a later article: "My distinction was between two different *uses* of language." I. A. Richards, "Emotive Meaning Again," *Philosophical Review* 57 (1948): 147 n. 4 (emphasis in original).

42. As Charles L. Stevenson said later: "In *The Meaning of Meaning* the emotive theory of value was stated with extraordinary brevity: it was outlined rather than developed." Charles L. Stevenson, "Richards on the Theory of Value," in *I. A. Richards: Essays In His Honor*, ed. Reuben Brower, Helen Vendler, and John Hollander (New York: Oxford University Press, 1973), 121.

43. In his review Ramsey says: "Our authors stress particularly the distinction between the symbolic and emotive functions of language, believing that many notorious controversies in the sciences can be shown to derive from confusion between these functions, the same words being used at once to make statements and to excite attitudes. This distinction seems to me to be of great importance, and in the emphasis laid on it lies the chief value of this book." Frank P. Ramsey, review of *The Meaning of Meaning*, by C. K. Ogden and I. A. Richards, *Mind* 23 (1924): 109.

44. Frank P. Ramsey, "Epilogue," in *The Foundations of Mathematics and Other Logical Essays*, ed. R. B. Braithwaite (London: Kegan Paul, 1931), 289. The other possible source of his ethical antirealism is Bertrand Russell's paper to the Apostles in 1922, "Is There an Absolute Good?," in which Russell argued for an error theory of ethics. See Bertrand Russell, *Russell on Ethics: Selections from the Writings of Bertrand Russell*, ed. Charles Pigden (London: Routledge, 1999), 122.

45. R. B. Braithwaite, "Verbal Ambiguity and Philosophical Analysis," *Proceedings of the Aristotelian Society* 28 (1928): 138.

46. Ibid., 137–38.

47. Austin Duncan-Jones, "Ethical Words and Ethical Facts," *Mind* 42 (1933): 498–99.

48. C. D. Broad, "Is Goodness a Name of a Simple Non-Natural Quality?," *Proceedings of the Aristotelian Society* 34 (1933–34): 250–54.

49. Not necessarily with Duncan-Jones's approval, however. In a review of Stevenson's *Ethics and Language*, Duncan-Jones commented, "At last an able writer [Stevenson] has thought it worth while to produce a detailed study of the expletive theory of morals, which was set adrift on the tides of philosophical discussion by writers who were not strongly interested in ethics." Austin Duncan-Jones, review of *Ethics and Language,* by Charles L. Stevenson, *Mind* 54 (1945): 363.

50. Perhaps the first advocate of this idea was W. H. F. Barnes, who, in his 1933 paper "A Suggestion about Value," argued that "value judgements in their origin are not strictly judgments at all" but rather are "exclamations expressive of approval, delight, and affection, which children utter when confronted with certain experiences." W. H. F. Barnes, "A Suggestion about Value," *Analysis* 1 (1933–34): 45. Barnes did not work his suggestion up into a theory, however. Ayer, in his argument against Mackie's error theory in later years, himself compared non-natural moral properties to unicorns: "What puzzles me, however, is his conclusion that the belief in there being objective values is merely false, as if the world might have contained such things, but happens not to, just as it happens not to contain centaurs or unicorns. Whereas I think that the conclusion to which his argument should have led him is that the champions of objective values have failed to make their belief intelligible." A. J. Ayer, "Are There Objective Values?," in *Freedom and Morality and Other Essays* (Oxford: Clarendon Press, 1984), 33.

51. In his autobiography Ayer says that while he was at Eton he read Clive Bell's *Art* and followed Bell's instruction to "run out this very minute and order a masterpiece" (*Art,* 2nd ed. [London: Chatto and Windus, 1948], 80), namely, Moore's *Principia Ethica*. He "became an equally ardent convert to Moore's ethical views. It was not until my second year at Oxford that I came to doubt whether 'good' was an indefinable non-natural quality." A. J. Ayer, *Part of My Life* (New York: Harcourt Brace Jovanovich, 1977), 54.

52. A. J. Ayer, *Language, Truth and Logic* (London: Victor Gollanz, 1936). Subsequent page citations to this work are, unless otherwise noted, to this edition and are given parenthetically in the text. Regarding Ayer's views in the thirties, MacIntyre has said that "in the Thirties in Oxford the young A. J. Ayer was seen by most of his philosophical elders as expounding an alien and distinctively Germanic doctrine in *Language, Truth and Logic*." Alasdair MacIntyre, "Ayer, Anscombe and Empiricism," *London Review of Books*, April 17, 1980, 9.

53. Ayer, *Part of My Life*, 155.

54. It was, however, noted by one of his early reviewers: "Of Mr. Ayer's distinction between 'emotive' and 'scientific' terminology (derived ultimately from I. A. Richards)." E. W. F. Tomlin, "Logical Negativism," *Scrutiny* 2 (1936): 216.

55. A. J. Ayer, "Reflections on *Language, Truth and Logic*," in *Essays on Language, Truth and Logic*, ed. Barry Gower (Totowa, NJ: Barnes and Noble, 1987), 26.

56. A. J. Ayer, introduction to *Language, Truth and Logic*, 2nd ed. (London: Gollanz, 1946), 20.

57. Ayer does not take seriously the possibility that moral statements or judgments are tautologies. However, as several early reviewers pointed out, Ayer's own example of a pure moral statement or judgment, "Stealing money is wrong" (158), would appear to be a tautology: "'Stealing money is wrong' is redundant, since 'stealing' means nothing less than 'wrongfully taking'" (Tomlin, "Logical Negativism," 215). See also Martin D'Arcy, "Philosophy Now," *Criterion* 15 (1936): 593; A. J. Milne, "Values and Ethics: The Emotive Theory," in Gower, *Essays*, 96–97; and Cahal Daly, *Moral Philosophy in Britain: From Bradley to Wittgenstein* (Dublin: Four Courts Press, 1966), 150. It seems that the only way for Ayer to argue that moral statements or judgments are not tautologies is to argue for some form of internalism.

58. Moore, *Principia Ethica*, 15.

59. Against the metaphysical naturalistic utilitarian, who holds that the property of moral rightness, upon investigation, is identical to the natural property of maximizing happiness, Ayer may argue that such an identification is an *a posteriori* necessary truth, and Ayer "denies that there are any *a posteriori* truths." Michael Smith, "Should We Believe in Emotivism?," in *Fact, Science and Morality: Essays on A. J. Ayer's "Language, Truth and Logic,"* ed. Graham Macdonald and Crispin Wright (Oxford: Basil Blackwell, 1986), 293.

60. Since Ayer holds that moral judgments do not purport to be truth-apt or meaningful, and hence are neither true nor false, Ayer rejects Mackie's error theory of ethics (see note 12), according to which moral judgments *do* purport to be truth-apt and meaningful, and *are* truth-apt and meaningful, but are *all false* (since there are no moral properties). For Ayer's argument against Mackie, see Ayer, "Are There Objective Values?"

61. The distinction is to be found in Moore's earlier argument against subjectivism, as opposed to emotivism, in ethics: "Others might say, more plausibly, that it is not mere liking and dislike that we express by these judgements, but a peculiar sort of liking and disliking, which might be called a feeling of *moral approval* and of *moral disapproval*" (*Ethics*, 37).

62. Here I will omit other arguments against emotivism, including the "Frege-Geach Problem" or "Embedding Problem," the objection made originally by Peter Geach in a series of articles in the 1960s, including "Assertion," *Philosophical Review* 74 (1965): 449–65, and by John Searle in "Meaning and Speech Acts," *Philosophical Review* 71 (1962): 423–32.

63. Alasdair MacIntyre, introduction to *Hume's Ethical Writings: Selections from David Hume* (London: Collier-Macmillan, 1965), 15.

64. Ibid., 15–16.

65. MacIntyre, *Short History of Ethics*, 260.

66. MacIntyre, *After Virtue*, 13.

67. Alexander Miller, "Emotivism and the Verification Principle," *Proceedings of the Aristotelian Society* 98 (1998): 111. Miller considers some possible defenses but ultimately concludes that "emotivism actually undermines the verification principle, and vice versa" (123).

68. MacIntyre, *Short History of Ethics*, 255.

69. John Foster, *Ayer* (London: Routledge and Kegan Paul, 1985), 83.

70. MacIntyre, *After Virtue*, 20.

71. Urmson, *Emotive Theory of Ethics*, 22.

72. Arthur W. Burks, preface to *Values and Morals: Essays in Honor of William Frankena, Charles Stevenson, and Richard Brandt*, ed. Alvin I. Goldman and Jaegwon Kim (Dordrecht: D. Reidel, 1978), xi.

73. Stephen A. Satris, "The Theory of Value and the Rise of Ethical Emotivism," *Journal of the History of Ideas* 43 (1982): 124.

74. Charles Leslie Stevenson, "The Emotive Meaning of Ethical Terms" (PhD diss., Harvard University, 1935), 196.

75. Charles Leslie Stevenson, "The Emotive Meaning of Ethical Terms," *Mind* 46 (1937): 23, 23 n. 1.

76. Charles L. Stevenson, *Ethics and Language* (New Haven: Yale University Press, 1944).

77. Ibid., 197.

78. Here and subsequently, page citations are to the 1937 article of that title rather than the dissertation.

79. Here Stevenson cites the criticism of Moore by G. C. Field (see note 24 above).

80. It should be noted that if certain commentators are correct, then Stevenson's second and third criteria are the same, since the Open Question Argument is simply the internalism requirement in disguise. See Stephen Darwall, Allan Gibbard, and Peter Railton, "Towards *Fin de Siècle* Ethics: Some Trends," *Philosophical Review* 101 (1992): 117; Charles Pigden, "Bertrand Russell: A Neglected Ethicist," in *Bertrand Russell and the Origins of Analytical Philosophy*, ed. Ray Monk (Bristol: Thoemmes Press, 1996), 349. (On this interpretation, Moore's own account of goodness fails the Open Question Argument.)

81. In *Ethics and Language*, the general definition of *good* advanced is "I approve of this; do so as well" (22).

82. MacIntyre, *Short History of Ethics*, 255.

83. Ibid., 258.

84. Ibid.

85. Ibid.

86. Ibid., 259.

87. Ibid.

88. MacIntyre, *After Virtue*, 13.

89. Ibid.

90. Ibid.
91. MacIntyre, *Short History of Ethics*, 259.
92. D'Andrea, *Tradition, Rationality and Virtue*, 7.
93. MacIntyre, *After Virtue*, 14.
94. Ibid., 17.
95. MacIntyre, "Notes from the Moral Wilderness," The MacIntyre Reader, ed. Kelvin Knight (Cambridge: Polity, 1998), 43.
96. Alasdair MacIntyre, "Hume on 'Is' and 'Ought'" [1959], in *Against the Self-Images of the Age: Essays on Ideology and Philosophy* (New York: Schocken Books, 1971), 123.
97. MacIntyre, "Notes from the Moral Wilderness," 43.
98. MacIntyre, "Hume on 'Is' and 'Ought,'" 123.
99. MacIntyre, "Notes from the Moral Wilderness," 43.
100. MacIntyre, "Hume on 'Is' and 'Ought,'" 124.
101. MacIntyre, "Notes from the Moral Wilderness," 43.
102. MacIntyre, "Hume on 'Is' and 'Ought,'" 116. MacIntyre follows this by saying: "Since I would agree with Marxists in thinking this change a change for the worse—for reasons which I shall indicate later in the argument—I have been tempted to retitle this essay 'Against Bourgeois Formalism in Ethics.'"
103. MacIntyre, "Hume on 'Is' and 'Ought,'" 124.
104. Ibid. Note that MacIntyre rejects the interpretation of Hume on the is/ought distinction provided by prescriptivists such as Hare, according to which Hume argues that "ought" is logically independent of "is": "Hume is not in this passage asserting the autonomy of morals—for he did not believe in it; and he is not making a point about entailment—for he does not mention it. He is asserting that the question of how the factual basis of morality is related to morality is a crucial logical issue, reflection on which will enable one to realize how there are ways in which this transition can be made and ways in which it cannot" (122). Hume was not always interpreted as an autonomist about ethics. For a non-autonomist interpretation of Hume, see C. D. Broad, *Five Types of Ethical Theory* (London: Kegan Paul, Trench, Trubner, 1930). Stevenson, no doubt inspired by Broad, does not read Hume as an autonomist about ethics either. See Stevenson, "Emotive Meaning," 16.
105. Alasdair MacIntyre, "Ought," in *Against the Self-Images*, 150.
106. Alasdair MacIntyre, "Some More about 'Ought,'" in *Against the Self-Images*, 165.

CHAPTER EIGHT

Naturalism, Nihilism, and Perfectionism
Stevenson, Williams, and Nietzsche in
Twentieth-Century Moral Philosophy

STEPHEN MULHALL

Naturalism as Pragmatism: Stevenson's Inheritance of Dewey

Can any moderately well-worked-out, general philosophical position ever be decisively refuted? Consider emotivism, for example, and more particularly that highly influential variant of it propounded in Charles L. Stevenson's *Ethics and Language*.[1] Perhaps only its equal and opposite partner in crime, G. E. Moore's intuitionism, is now so widely presumed to share the distinction of having been exhaustively and witheringly criticized to the point of retaining only historical interest (at least within the academy—the state of play beyond its walls is another matter entirely). And yet, when one examines the cogency of the most familiar of those lines of criticism, it can be hard to maintain one's conviction in their capacity to deprive Stevenson of any words of defense, of any way of redescribing the nature and significance of that criticism in terms that render it not merely argumentatively null but also actually confirmatory of the truth of the emotivist analysis of moral discourse.

Take, as an example, two of Stevenson's most notorious claims, as articulated in the following passages:

> *Any* statement about *any* matter of fact which *any* speaker considers likely to alter attitudes may be adduced as a reason for or against an ethical judgement. (*EL,* 114)

> When the terms are *completely* neutralized, one may say with tranquillity that all moralists are propagandists, or that all propagandists are moralists. Either statement can be made true by definition, without violence to the boundaries of conventional usage. (*EL,* 252)

These two claims are plainly related: indeed, the latter might be seen as a concrete instantiation of the former, insofar as our grasp of the difference between morality and propaganda is very likely to turn on our sense of a difference between two familiar ways in which one might attempt to alter the moral judgments and orientation of one's interlocutor. By the same token, however, our sense that the more general claim is obviously false ought therefore to be shaken insofar as we encounter difficulties in demonstrating the falsehood of its more specific counterpart.

Stanley Cavell takes particular exception to Stevenson's tranquil equation of the moralist and the propagandist. As he forcefully presents his counterview: "To propagandize under the name of morality is not immoral; it denies morality altogether. And in sentimentalizing propaganda, it denies to propaganda its practical urgency and extreme utility, which are all that can justify it, *when* it is justified."[2] The burden of Cavell's disgust is expressed here by his citation of Kate Croy in Henry James's *The Wings of the Dove:* her interpretation of her project to attract a legacy from Millie Theale in ways that muddle and blunt Merton Densher's perception of his guilt would make her (in Stevenson's neutralized terminology) a spokesman for morality; whereas (in Cavell's view) her willingness to use Densher's love for her to entice him into a course of action that, if he properly comprehended it, would appall him, is not merely immoral but an evil of a different order altogether.

Cavell regards Stevenson's legitimation of such a reinterpretation of Kate Croy as indicating his refusal to acknowledge that "when a moralist confronts us he is recognizing us as persons about whom he cares, and to whom he acknowledges a commitment, . . . that he accepts . . . responsibility for the act of confronting us . . . [which is not] something he can have decided upon quite privately, and with no particular knowledge of our other cares and commitments."³ For Cavell, to address oneself to one's interlocutor as one moral being to another is to do so in a way that acknowledges both parties as possessed of cares and commitments whose nature and reality condition both the considerations that can have a bearing on the matter at hand and the mode of our presentation of them. One might think of this as a specification of a nonmanipulative mode of intercourse with another human being; Kant would have regarded it as partly constitutive of treating that other as an end. By implicit contrast, the propagandist discounts any such constraints, speaking from a position that takes account of his hearers' position only to the extent necessary to manipulate their feelings and conduct; he treats others solely as means. Such a stance can be justified in circumstances in which matters of great moral moment are at stake and practical efficacy might trump certain forms of respect for persons; but that stance cannot be equated with the central stance of morality without annihilating the notion of a moral relationship altogether.

Suppose, however, that we now make the effort to imagine how these righteous words might sound in Stevenson's ears—the ears of an author who, by the time of his book's first publication in 1944, might well have felt deafened by propagandizing public discourse, first as his country argued with itself over the matter of entry into the fight against European fascism, and then as it became embroiled in the consequent global war of words as well as deeds. What he will hear is an attempt to distinguish morality from propaganda that is ineliminably indebted to morally charged concepts, and hence one that fails either to recognize or to accommodate the distinction around which *Ethics and Language* as a whole explicitly pivots—the "marked distinction between conclusions that are drawn *about* normative ethics and those that are drawn *within* it" (*EL*, preface). Call this the distinction between ethics and metaethics: what it means for Stevenson in this particular case is that if one cannot distinguish morality from propaganda without presupposing a substantial array of normative ethical resources, then that distinction cannot carry the impersonal authority of properly conducted logical or conceptual analysis—the distinguishing mark of the philosopher's contribution to human self-understanding—but must rather be seen as itself essentially emotive in character: that is, as no more than propaganda for one first-order ethical stance operating under the guise of an objective characterization of the nature of morality as such.

One need not feel that Cavell's way of distinguishing morality from propaganda is either unconvincing or unfruitful in order to acknowledge that something important about its underlying nature is brought to the surface by Stevenson's imaginary response to it. For it may well be that both Cavell and Stevenson are right about this matter—that on the one hand there *are* ways of distinguishing morality from propaganda and that an inability to grasp them is tantamount to an inability to delineate the subject matter of which Stevenson's emotivism is intended to be a conceptual analysis; and yet, on the other, that there is no ethically neutral way of specifying the domain of the ethical. If Stevenson's way of articulating that latter insight threatens the very concept of morality, one should at the very least acknowledge that his opponents' ways of attempting to neutralize that threat at least risk posing an equally grave (if rather different) threat to the health of morality—that of appearing to claim a kind of authority for their conception of ethics that it cannot conceivably possess. Unless Stevenson's opponents learn to be rather more honest in acknowledging that their characterizations of morality are as ineliminably personal as (hence essentially continuous, logically or grammatically speaking, with) their first-order moral judgments, they will continue to court the criticism that they are propagandizing for one conception of ethics while claiming merely to recount the essence of the ethical, and will thereby contribute one further layer of apparently sincere but actually manipulative discourse to the blooming, buzzing manifold of such discourse to which Stevenson himself was so painfully sensitive.

We might, accordingly, interpret Stevenson's more general unwillingness to distinguish legitimate from illegitimate modes of supporting one's ethical judgments as a further (undoubtedly excessive and ultimately self-subverting) expression of his unwillingness to contribute further to manipulative discourse about ethics by illegitimately invoking the authority of philosophy. But that unwillingness had a further source or purpose, which becomes explicit only in the concluding chapter of his book, and which embodies a further, positive insight (even if not one that his broader project actually helped to develop). For when he attempts to specify the practical implications of his metaethical account, Stevenson links his studied neutrality about supporting reasons to a desire to acknowledge "the *great variety* of knowledge that has a bearing on ethical issues" (*EL*, 329). To be sure, what most impresses Stevenson (in part, no doubt, because of his acknowledged debt to Dewey, and thereby to one strand of American pragmatism) is the wide variety of relevant *empirical* knowledge. Indeed, a key virtue of his recognition that any matter of fact that has a bearing on attitudes might be relevantly adduced in an ethical discussion is supposed to be that it prepares the ground for acknowledging to an unprecedented extent the ways in which a proper understanding of the full range of an extremely diversified array of empirical scientific findings (including not only psychology but economics, and even geography and meteorology—indeed, any body of knowledge that illuminates "human nature and its environment" [*EL*, 332]) is integral to a genuinely rational grasp of ethics.

In other words, part of what is driving his reluctance to set a priori conceptual limits on what matters might be of ethical significance is a desire that finds expression in the following rhetorical question: "What knowledge is there, indeed, that has *not* a potential bearing on evaluation?" (*EL*, 332). Stevenson's goal is here to acknowledge the embeddedness of moral thinking in the broader domain of human understanding of nature, including those inhabitants of nature who are distinctively capable of attempting to comprehend both themselves and their environment. He wants, in short, to acknowledge not only the internal relation between ethical understanding and all other forms of human understanding but also the open-ended, essentially unpredictable ways in which any and every other mode of human understanding might come to have a bearing on ethical understanding. Once again, Stevenson's way of avoiding what he sees as a fundamental philosophical error—that of excluding in advance on a wholly illegitimate, essentially ungrounded basis the relevance of other modes of knowledge to ethics—might itself amount to an equally serious error (as it threatens once more to dissolve the subject matter of his metaethical analysis before his very eyes); but if so, it has the considerable merit of bringing into focus another, vitally important way in which one's supposedly impersonal specifications of the boundaries of the ethical might in fact encode a set of substantive ethical views. For when Stevenson declares that "empirical inquiry must pervade the whole of an enlightened ethics; it cannot be confined to some distinctively terrestrial part" (*EL*, 330), then (*modulo* his emphasis on distinctively empirical modes of inquiry) he leaves metaethical room for a range of first-order ethical views that are often systematically occluded in philosophical discussions of ethics—those that view the ethical not as a distinct territory within the broader territory of human modes of understanding but rather as a distinctive dimension of human life as such.

What, after all, might seem less prejudicial than to pursue the philosophical business of characterizing the nature of the ethical (as opposed to that of the political, the aesthetic, the religious, the empirical, and so on) by attempting to characterize the distinctive subject matter of ethical judgments? Yet there are first-order ethical viewpoints that are partly constituted by a rejection of the idea that ethics is primarily or exclusively a domain of judgment, and hence that it can be identified by identifying that about which such judgments judge. In recent moral philosophy, the work of Cora Diamond and Alice Crary is in part devoted to an articulation and defense of such positions—positions that might, for example, be particularly sensitive to the ways in which a novel written from the perspective of a child might (even when the events it narrates are not obviously ones invoking ethical issues) reveal to us the ethical significance of children having a distinctive perspective on the world; or they might underline the extent to which our basic ability to project words into new contexts might itself draw upon ineliminably evaluative modes of response to those contexts.[4] And once again, the point is not so much to endorse such first-order views over other candidates as to indict philosophers who construct supposedly neutral characterizations of the ethical that nevertheless manage to suppress entirely the existence of such views. Stevenson might well view his own project as a precursor of exactly this inflection of the drive to uncover propagandizing in the guise of conceptual analysis.

Of course, historical distance might well make it easier to detect these rather more philosophically fruitful aspects of Stevenson's writing; it is not at all hard to see why they were passed over by those who read him in the immediate postwar period, when by far the most salient aspect of his project was likely to be that which resonated most deeply with the most morally salient aspect of the war that had so recently ended—a narrowly avoided threat to morality as such, an evil of a different order flourishing in the heart of European culture that revealed the inherent fragility of ethical life. And it might be worth emphasizing before we move on that, in some ways, even these scandalized responses to Stevenson if anything underestimate the range, if not the nature, of the threat his way of accounting for ethics posed for the coherence of our culture.

To accuse Stevenson of annihilating the concept of morality is, in effect, to accuse him of nihilism: his failing is to characterize moral evaluation as if it were purely a mode of manipulating others, a means of exercising power over others that functions by disguising itself as the invocation of impersonal, objective, and hence authoritative values that in truth lack any genuine substance or reality. So phrased, nihilism appears as a more contemporary mask of sophistry, as Plato understood it. For when, in the *Republic,* Thrasymachus confronts Socrates with the claim that justice is best understood as whatever is in the interest of the stronger party, he is not himself best understood as offering one among a variety of possible interpretations of our concept of justice (as if he were merely a dramatically compelling anticipation of the stance Adeimantus and Glaucon adopt in their subsequent discussions with Socrates). For Thrasymachus's claim amounts to doubting the reality of justice altogether. If what we talk of as "just" and "unjust" merely reflects the balance of power in a given social group, then there is in fact no substance or reality to that stretch of our discourse at all; all there is to talk about in this domain could be exhaustively expressed in terms of power, and hence language could suffer the loss of the concept of justice altogether without losing its ability to register the reality of things in our human social world.

The analogy between Thrasymachus and Stevenson here should be evident; but what may be less evident is a further reach of that analogy. For of course, it is part of the Sophists' position as Plato understands it that the view they hold about justice is the view they hold about human discourse in general. Their characteristic doctrine that mastery of discourse is a matter of understanding how to achieve rhetorical effectiveness—how to use words to achieve one's goals, to move others to align themselves with the speaker—reduces all speech to a matter of practical efficacy or power. For Thrasymachus the true nature of talk about justice is also the true nature of human speech as such: it has no reality to it, it embodies distinctions and values to which nothing corresponds in reality, and hence it lacks genuine substance. (This is why he is rightly wary even of engaging Socrates in philosophical dialogue; for he knows that in so doing he is merely entering another arena for the exercise of rhetorical power, of which Socrates is an acknowledged master.)

Stevenson's nihilism about evaluative meaning ramifies to a similar extent, and does so for a parallel reason. For in their concern to avert the risk of morality's annihilation by contesting Stevenson's account of evaluative discourse as a matter of manipulating others' attitudes, Stevenson's critics often fail to recognize that this essentially causal vision of evaluative intercourse is merely a specific application of Stevenson's more general vision of all linguistic meaning as essentially causal. Indeed, insofar as Stevenson's critics take his analysis of evaluative meaning in causal terms as a way of downgrading the cognitive status of such discourse, they fail to see that it might equally well be seen from his perspective as a way of giving evaluative discourse exactly the status he accords to descriptive discourse. For his account of descriptive meaning, and the bearing of descriptive utterances on belief formation, in the third chapter of his book, is couched in exactly the same causal-dispositional mold (one he inherits from Ogden and Richards, the only authorities he invokes alongside Dewey in the twin epigraphs to that volume).

From a Platonic perspective, however, this equality of treatment for evaluative and descriptive dimensions of linguistic meaning amounts to the universalization of nihilism. Despite Stevenson's quietly passionate desire to reconnect ethical discussion to the broader reaches of human understanding of the natural world, the theory of meaning by means of which he attempts to do it unmoors human discourse as such from even the aspiration to make contact with reality in any of its dimensions. For if the articulations of even empirical discourse are essentially efficacious modes of manipulating the psychology of one's interlocutors, then the distinction between making contact with reality and failing to do so is rendered utterly unreal or empty—call it merely persuasive—right across the board. And insofar as it is language that informs and articulates our forms of life, then to void human discourse of sense is to empty human life of meaning. Little wonder that Plato is prone to treat sophistry less as a very big philosophical mistake than as a form of human corruption or depravity.

In a strange way, however, fully appreciating the nature and extent of the threat Stevenson's account poses to human culture brings us back to the two more positive morals I initially tried to draw from his admittedly misbegotten project. For to see him as a nihilist about meaning is to acknowledge both the instability of the distinction between ethics and metaethics (if emotivism is sophistry, its vision of human life is depraved), and the unpredictable but ineliminable bearing of any branch of human culture upon any other (insofar as emotivism's vision of ethics takes its bearings from a conception of language, science, and reason and bears fatefully upon the claims to intelligibility made by any form of discourse that aspires to capture reality). As we shall see, all three of these interrelated points prepare the ground in a certain way for Anglo-American receptions of the most notorious philosopher of nihilism—Friedrich Nietzsche.

Naturalism as Realism: Bernard Williams's Inheritance of Nietzsche

In English moral philosophy of the 1960s and 1970s, Nietzsche's presence was not exactly widely felt: but felt it nevertheless was, and it will turn out to be a matter of more than merely historical interest to explore in more detail the nature of, and the reasons for, the particular kind of impression his writings made on one member of a rather small band of idiosyncratic but distinguished thinkers. I have in mind the work of a widely respected analytical moral philosopher who, in the course of a long and fruitful career, never produced more than a handful of short essays explicitly addressing Nietzsche's writing, and who explicitly claimed to be deploying a version of Nietzsche's genealogical method only in his last book, *Truth and Truthfulness*—Bernard Williams. What I want to suggest is that, in reality, the main aspects of Williams's engagement with moral matters carry an implicitly Nietzschean inflection, and more specifically that they constitute the beginnings of a way of reading Nietzsche that makes him someone both significantly different from, and a great deal more interesting than, the Nietzsche of popular philosophical imaginings.

Williams's lifelong goal, rather like that of Stevenson, was to contribute to the construction of a naturalistic moral psychology—understood as a view of our moral capacities that should be consistent with (even perhaps in the spirit of) our understanding of human beings as part of nature.[5] Unlike Stevenson, however, Williams clearly understood the difficulty of specifying exactly what such a naturalistic stance actually involves in a way that rules out neither too much nor too little. To expect a naturalistic moral psychology to characterize moral activity in a vocabulary that could be applied equally to every other part of nature would commit it to an utterly hopeless physical reductionism; but if we describe moral activity in whatever terms moral activity seems to invite, then we render ourselves impotent to criticize even the most dubious elements of its self-image.

Williams learns from Nietzsche to make progress in articulating a usable version of ethical naturalism by committing himself to two general principles: first, to aim at providing accounts of distinctively moral activity that add as little as possible to our accounts of other human activity (call this moral psychological minimalism); and second, to identify apparent excess of moral content in psychology by appealing to what an experienced, honest, subtle, and unoptimistic interpreter might make of human behavior elsewhere (call this the realistic dimension of naturalism). Taken together, these principles specify an unashamedly evaluative hermeneutics of suspicion. Williams's project aims, not to cast doubt on everything about morality, but rather to locate and substantiate particular points of doubt by showing how what seems to demand more moral material actually makes sense in terms of what demands less; and it aspires to no morally neutral metaethical standpoint but rather depends upon inviting its readers to make as much use as possible of such knowledge of human nature and the world as they have acquired through personal experience as well as acquaintance with broader reaches of human inquiry.

Consider, for example, Williams's famous interest in the phenomenon of moral luck.[6] Most immediately, his concern here is to isolate and criticize a particular, excessively contentful conception of moral responsibility that in his view renders the self essentially discontinuous with its environment. Williams primarily associates this view with Kant, who—he claims—to make room for a purified conception of blame, and more specifically to satisfy the apparently intuitive demand that a person be held responsible only for what was entirely within his control, envisions not only the movements of a person's body but also the full ramifying worldly consequences attendant upon those movements as essentially extrinsic to her domain of responsibility. That domain, coincident as it must be with that of the will and its orientations, becomes the essence of genuine human action, and contracts to an extensionless point; and the self who orients that will likewise retreats beyond the reach of empirical reality, so that its control over its will might float clear of causal determination, as if amounting to a species of creation ex nihilo.

Against this highly moralized interpretation of human action, Williams offers us a series of related reminders of ways in which we operate with conceptions of personal responsibility that cut across this interpretative grain. A truck driver who, through no fault of his own, knocks down and kills a child, would not be charged either with murder or manslaughter; but if he adopted a perspective on the child's death that was indistinguishable from that of someone who viewed the accident from the pavement (as if he simply had a closer view of the horrible event) and failed to acknowledge in any way in his future behavior that he was the one who killed the child, then we would suspect the presence of some kind of psychopathology. And in the much more morally specific cases of Gauguin and Anna Karenina, we are reminded of ways in which the embeddedness of our actions in the world and its vicissitudes render us vulnerable to essentially retrospective revelations of the justifiability of choices we might make to sacrifice one value for another. In these ways, Williams attempts to show not only that assignments of responsibility for actions do not require certain highly moralized interpretations of agency in order to hold good but also that the basic logical structure of agency is in fact threatened by that interpretation. For what presents itself as necessary if the self's moral responsibilities are to be justly calibrated turns out to occlude the creatureliness and finitude of distinctively human agency—the fact that individual human agents are embodied, and thereby embedded in a natural world, inhabited by others, whose reality and ordering are given independently of the agent's will.

Part of what threatens to muffle the impact of Williams's essay on this topic is his use of Gauguin as his central example. For the specific choice Gauguin makes is between supporting his wife and children and devoting himself wholeheartedly to becoming a painter; and Williams's concern to show that whether he might think himself justified in sacrificing his family will critically depend upon whether he turns out to have it in him to become a great painter is often deflected by those inclined to contest the assumption that anyone could ever be justified in sacrificing a moral duty for a matter of aesthetic achievement, even one that concerned individual self-expression. Matters might be clarified directly by changing the example, so that our protagonist is imagined to be choosing between family life and a life devoted to alleviating suffering in an isolated refugee camp (about which he cannot know—because there is no fact of the relevant kind to know concerning—whether he is up to it). But this aspect of Williams's original example is in fact far from accidentally related to his primary purpose.

For Williams, Gauguin represents a reminder of the extent to which our very natural assumption of the trumping power of moral over nonmoral considerations depends upon adherence to one particular interpretation of ethics—not just one interpretation of its importance but also one interpretation of its scope. For it is only if one understands ethics to be a matter of answering the question "What is my duty?" that it appears self-evident that if Gauguin chooses to go to Tahiti he thereby violates moral demands for the sake of essentially selfish concerns; whereas if, as Williams argues at length in *Ethics and the Limits of Philosophy,* one takes the central question of ethics to be "How should one live?" or "What is it to flourish or excel as a human being?," then Gauguin's choice will appear to be an intra-ethical one—a choice between two genuine forms or modes of human flourishing, ways of living well that have come into irreconcilable conflict in this individual's life.[7]

In other words, part of what Gauguin represents for Williams is an attempt to remind us that a more ancient, essentially un-Kantian and apparently un-Christian, understanding of the nature and hence the scope of ethics continues to live on in our post-Enlightenment ways of thinking and feeling. On this Socratic conception, what a Kantian might understand as a vital distinction between aesthetics and ethics, and an equally vital distinction between other-regarding moral duties and concerns about one's own well-being, are either nonexistent or intrinsically open to contestation. Once again, then, we are invited to acknowledge the unavailability of an ethically neutral characterization of the domain of ethics; and more specifically, we are invited to appreciate the attractions of one, currently recessive but hardly unprecedented, way of reinterpreting the limits of that domain. For if the pursuit of aesthetic excellence might plausibly be regarded as an ethical matter, then what other (in Kantian terms, non-moral) branch or dimension of human forms of life might not be interpretable as of ethical significance? In this respect, Williams's realistic ethical naturalism outdoes Stevenson in its openness to the sheer variety of human accomplishments that have a potential bearing on evaluation and is plainly oriented toward recovering a version of that interpretation of the ethical which regards it as a dimension of human life as such rather than a bounded terrain within it.

And it doesn't seem unduly speculative to regard Nietzsche's work as having a marked influence on Williams's thought at exactly this point.

After all, Nietzsche's genealogical critique of Christian morality and its secular descendants also invites us to appreciate the contingency of its dominance, and so the availability of alternative interpretations of the ethical, precisely by contrasting it with the understanding of ethics that he claims to find in ancient Greek culture (a culture in which, as his much earlier analysis of *The Birth of Tragedy* makes clear, the apparently immutable borders between the ethical and the aesthetic, the religious and the metaphysical, were both porous and provisional).[8]

Transcendentalism as Perfectionism: Nietzsche's Inheritance of Emerson

Might one, however, regard this aspect of Williams's Nietzscheanism as a ground for questioning one element of its attempted recuperation of Socratic interpretations of ethics? The potential problem here lies with Nietzsche's apparent willingness to endorse the claims of individual flourishing over those relating to the well-being of others. Is not Nietzsche's awestruck admiration for the blond beasts of master-morality repugnantly committed to demanding the sacrifice of the interests of the community in the name of promoting the flourishing of those happy few whose nature displays the glorious vitality of the will-to-power? And if so, is not Williams's willingness to value Gauguin's and Anna Karenina's self-concern above the needs of their respective families implicated in the same inherently elitist form of what is standardly labeled moral perfectionism? In the remainder of this essay, I would like to suggest that such a conclusion can be drawn only if one fails to appreciate that there is a way of reading Nietzsche's perfectionism (and so, perhaps, of reading Williams) otherwise.

This reading has been principally developed by Stanley Cavell and James Conant,[9] and just as understanding Stevenson depends on taking seriously his American inheritance of Deweyan pragmatism, so Cavell and Conant's reading of Nietzsche depends upon taking seriously the latter's lifelong admiration for Emerson (an admiration that pervades the early *Untimely Meditations* but is just as evident in the late *Twilight of the Idols*), and thereby for American transcendentalism. In particular, they see Nietzsche's critique of the Kantian conception of the self (as noumenal, self-creating, and capable of creation ex nihilo) not as being in service of some general and self-subverting skepticism about selfhood as such but rather as designed to clear the way for a less highly moralized (although no less ethically charged) Emersonian conception of the self as endlessly becoming, essentially transitional, and hence always evaluable in terms of its willingness or its refusal to leave itself open or undefined in relation to the future.

This Emersonian conception characterizes the self as split or divided, between its present, attained state and its next, unattained but attainable state. This is Emerson's way of recounting the canonical perfectionist vision of the self (first known to philosophy in Plato's Socratic vision of the soul) as on an upward or onward journey that begins when it finds itself lost to the world. Such lostness is a matter not of regret or remorse for some particular thought or decision (or series of them) but rather of disorientation—of finding that the basic terms in which one makes sense of one's existence ring hollow, as if one had lost the means to give genuine expression to one's sense of life's significance in terms to which others might be genuinely responsive. Such lostness is uncovered in Norah's realization (in *A Doll's House*) that Torvald does not mistreat her so much as treat her like a child, and in Tracy Lord's new perception of her glorious Philadelphian story as the tale of a woman who has turned herself (not unaided) to stone. It is the kind of crisis of meaning or intelligibility that we associate mythologically with both the onset of adult life and its middle ground—with the adolescent's confrontation with what his elders present to him as genuinely grown-up human existence, or with an adult's midlife crisis (to which Dante's dark wood more soberly adverts). Its articulation amounts to a redistribution of emphasis within what Williams (following Socrates) presents as the defining question of ethics: "What is it for your life to flourish?" For Nietzsche's Emersonian reformulation asks whether your apparently flourishing life is truly yours or whether it has in truth gone dead for you—whether its vitality is mere appearance, so that you find yourself haunting your own existence.

To recover from such disorientation, the self must accordingly refuse the terms in which it currently understands itself, reorient itself by reference to some conception of a currently unattained but more cultivated way to be, and commit itself to attaining that state or condition. But in Emerson's version of perfectionism, no such unattained but attainable state of the self is final or complete; for every such state, once attained, always projects or opens up another, unattained but attainable state, to the realization of which we might commit ourselves, or alternatively whose attractions might be eclipsed by the attractions of the state we currently inhabit. In that sense, every attained state is (that is, it can present itself as, and be inhabited as) perfect—in need of no further refinement; indeed, the primary internal threat to this species of perfectionism is that of regarding genuine human individuality as a realizable state of perfection (even if a different one for each individual—perhaps according to one's talents or dispositions or nature), rather than as a continuous process of self-perfecting (selfhood as self-improvement or self-overcoming), or as Nietzsche puts it, selfhood as Becoming rather than Being.

As a result, such perfectionism cannot be characterized as elitist. For to aspire to, and to maintain, oneself in the condition of self-overcoming is a possibility of any and every self and has precisely nothing to do with the aspects of human endowment (whether naturally acquired or the result of some particular culture's modes of cultivation) that are differentially distributed between persons. This vision of human flourishing is thus not intrinsically hostile to liberal democracy, even if it may ground hostility to various forms of the democratic impulse (particularly those that see perfectionist self-concern as essentially undemocratic). And neither is it a mode of ethical concern that stands in any simple opposition to the social dimension of morality. For Emerson conceives of the condition of those fixated on their attained states as both reinforced by and reinforcing the present state of the society they inhabit; constituted as it typically is by a multitude of individuals who each instantiate that state of conformity, the social state they thereby constitute is bound to encourage and reinforce that mode of self-relation. Accordingly, he conceives of the aspiration to realize one's unattained state as inseparable from a commitment to contribute to the task of achieving a higher or further (say a more cultivated) state of society—one in which others might more easily achieve the self-overcoming to which we ourselves aspire.

This broader vision of the internal relation between self and society has two more specific features that are of particular concern for our discussion. The first concerns the internality of such perfectionist concerns even to ethical matters particularly prized by defenders of morality. For Emerson regards an individual's capacity to prioritize her unattained over her attainable state as a precondition for the genuine fulfillment of other-regarding moral values. We might put the point in Kantian terms as follows: if fulfilling one's moral duties to others is a matter of each self's deriving the moral law from itself and applying it to itself, then being genuinely moral presupposes the existence of a self from whom that law can be derived and to whom it might be applied. In this respect, properly managing the relation between one's attained and attainable self is a condition for the possibility of regarding others as genuinely other to oneself (another self), because in its absence there is no genuinely individual or self-individuating self to which that other could be genuinely other.

The second specific feature of this internal relation concerns the manner in which any given individual might reorient herself from her attained to her unattained state. Since a typical indication of the eclipse of one's unattained by one's attained self is a loss of the sense that there might even be an unattained but attainable further state of oneself to which one might aspire, and hence the absence of any perception of oneself even as failing to have such an aspiration, we can typically come to an awareness of ourselves as lost, and hence of our present state as something to which there is an alternative, via the intervention of another — someone who exemplifies for us what it might mean to enact a process of self-overcoming, and thereby to recover responsibility for our own existence, relating to one's life as our own, ours to own rather than to disown. This exemplary other (Emerson thinks of him as a friend) cannot successfully facilitate our transition to a mode of self-overcoming by convincing us to adopt his own conception of the next or further state of his existence as if it were our own, for then we would have exchanged a form of self-enslavement for one of enslavement by another. What he must do is diagnose us as lost, attract us to the idea of recovery from that lostness, and return the responsibility for how exactly to manage that recovery in our own case to us — the individuals who can attain genuine individuality only if their modes of self-overcoming come from themselves rather than from elsewhere.

Within the confines of the present essay, I cannot hope to canvass the textual evidence on which this Emersonian reading of Nietzsche's perfectionism must stand or fall. But I hope to have provided enough of a sketch of the basic structure of that perfectionism to conclude my discussion by showing how such an interpretation might radically alter our sense of Nietzsche's vulnerability to criticism from those who inhabit other traditions of ethical thought. More specifically, I would like to indicate the bearing of his conception of the self as essentially transitional or self-overcoming upon Alasdair MacIntyre's respectfully tentative, intimately engaged, and undeniably powerful critique of the project of genealogical critique from the perspective of Thomism, as outlined in his 1988 Gifford Lectures, *Three Rival Versions of Moral Enquiry*.[10]

The core of MacIntyre's critique, about which Williams has admiring things to say in his *Truth and Truthfulness,* is that the genealogical critique of what are usually termed metaphysical conceptions of the self has an ineliminably self-subverting effect, insofar as it deprives the genealogist of the conceptual resources needed to make sense of the relation in which he stands to his readers by virtue of his writing those genealogical critiques.[11] As MacIntyre puts it:

> It is . . . necessarily presupposed by the act of writing for a particular reader or readers that the ego of writer and that of reader have enough fixity and continuity to enter into those relationships constitutive of the acts of reading-as-one-who-has been-written-for and of writing-as-one-who-is-to-be-read. . . .
>
> Some forms of writing and reading can . . . occur without this metaphysical dimension; but its absence makes of the encounter of writer and reader one in which each can be no more than and no other than the other's intentional object, cast for whatever role that particular intentional stance requires, victim to the other's victimizer.[12]

And if Nietzsche were to respond by acknowledging the constitutive nature of such constraints during the moments at which reader confronts writer in his writing but claiming that they were part of what is no more than a temporary stance, part of a process of putting on, displaying, and then discarding masks, MacIntyre is ready with the following riposte: "The problem then for the genealogist is how to combine the fixity of particular stances, exhibited in the use of standard genres of speech and writing, with the mobility of transition from stance to stance, how to assume the contours of a given mask and then to discard it for another, without ever assenting to the metaphysical fiction of a face which has its own finally true and undiscardable representation, whether by Rembrandt or in a shaving mirror. Can it be done?"[13] After carefully examining and criticizing Foucault's highly influential way of attempting to inherit and manage this internal tension in Nietzsche's genealogical project, MacIntyre cautiously concludes that the genealogical tradition has not yet succeeded in overcoming this difficulty. Suppose, however, that Foucault is not Nietzsche's best reader. What if the originator of genealogical critique rather conceived of both its writers and its readers along the Emersonian perfectionist lines I have just sketched?

From that perspective, I submit, MacIntyre's dramatic characterization of the genealogical author as committed simultaneously to fixity and to mobility would appear less as the structure of a problem about his selfhood than as a specification of the nature of selfhood as such. The idea of a single, finally true, and undiscardable representation of the self would indeed remain subject to critique as a metaphysical fiction unless one wished so to characterize the perfectionist representation of the human self as inherently double or divided, always already either fixated upon its present state or in transition to its next or further, currently unattained state—hence always either adopting a stance (and hence identifying itself with that which is not itself, necessarily not the whole truth about itself) or discarding it (but only in the name of adopting another, however provisionally). In short, if the self's fixity is understood as that to which and from which it can and does travel, and its mobility is understood as from one fixed state to another, then there seems no contradiction in the thought that it is both fixed and mobile—willing to be held accountable for any state it realizes until and unless it chooses to relinquish that state for another, whose realization will reconfigure its accountability without ever transcending accountability as such.

And if this is the perfectionist vision of selfhood, its vision of textual integrity—of what MacIntyre illuminatingly treats as an issue of genre—will match it. For according to the Emersonian reading, what unifies the variety of different textual forms Nietzsche invents and adapts across his writing lifetime—the fixity of purpose that persists across (rather than behind) each change from generic mask to another, and hence accounts for each transition between more specific modes of accountability—is his attempt to activate or realize the structure of genuine selfhood in his readers by the way in which he enacts that same structure in his text (perhaps under the guise of conjuring an opposition between Apollo and Dionysus, or between self-mastery and self-enslavement). In this sense, the perfectionist structure of selfhood is not simply one element in a general interpretation of reality that the texts present; it is in addition what accounts for the specific form of each text and thereby shapes the relation between author and reader that each text aspires to facilitate. To understand Nietzsche's reasons for adopting each generic mask would thus be a matter of understanding how each such textual mode aimed to disclose its reader as lost to herself and to invite her to recover herself by internalizing the example of the author she is perusing without simply imitating his particular, present response to the universal human requirement to manage the relation between one's attained and one's unattained self.

It will then appear to be no accident that each generic mask that Nietzsche provisionally adopts itself puts in question the absoluteness of the distinctions we typically draw between genres. For the perfectionist vision of individuals as capable of disowning their existence as a whole—of failing, not to meet certain specific claims made upon them, but to acknowledge themselves as accountable at all for the existence they lead—by its very nature discloses a dimension of ethical responsiveness that pervades human life as such rather than limiting itself to one clearly delineated part of it. As a consequence, its demands can as easily show up within what other ethical views might denominate as the aesthetic, religious, and metaphysical domains as within that of morality. Hence a central part of reorienting readers toward this dimension of ethical accountability will be making an issue of the business of distinguishing these various domains from one another—by, for example, making a case for the porousness and provisionality of these territorial borders. And insofar as such a case must be enacted rather than simply asserted—if only to preserve the authority of the perfectionist author as one who lives his accountability for and to himself—then the form of his texts should be expected to render their generic identity or integrity problematic. And so, of course, it proves in Nietzsche's case: his *Genealogy of Morality* undeniably renders itself accountable as a work of ethical inquiry no more and no less than it asks to be read as a work of etymology, of history, of sociology, of anthropology, and of mythology. And in this respect, it resembles (and at the same time differs from) such early works as *The Birth of Tragedy*, which is no more a work of classical studies than it is one of aesthetics, ethics, politics, metaphysics, mythology, or lyric drama (call it operatic).

One might well ask: Is there no mode of human textual articulation that may not prove to have a potential bearing on the perfectionist evaluation of human selfhood and culture? And in thus recalling Stevenson's suggestive but ultimately misbegotten commitment to avoiding the imposition of a priori limitations on the relevance of any domain of human knowledge to the business of moral philosophy, we are brought in conclusion to appreciate the vital importance of the subtle difference between the willingness to make an issue of such generic, disciplinary, and experiential boundaries and the inability to retain a grip on ethics as a distinctive subject matter for philosophical reflection—between an author who remains accountable for the ways in which he assembles his textual masks and moves between them, and one who refuses to commit himself to any specific mask at all. From Nietzsche's perspective, the ultimately sophistical or nihilistic position in which Stevenson finds himself—in which every moral word has lost its substance in his metaethical accounting of it, in part no doubt because he experienced his present society as one in which those words seemed to preserve only the appearance of first-order moral substance—is an exemplary instance of the lostness or disorientation to which perfectionism is a response. But at the same time, Stevenson maneuvers himself into a Thrasymachean corner precisely because of his desire not to abuse the authority of philosophy in order to repress aspects of the reality of human ethical experience to which perfectionists pay particular attention—the non-neutrality of any and all characterizations of ethics, and the openness of ethical understanding to the deliverances of any and all forms of human understanding of ourselves and our world. In moving on from Stevenson's version of emotivism, we should acknowledge the extent to which his work might—even if by determinate negation—open up the possibility for a further, unattained but attainable state of moral philosophy in the twenty-first century: one in which the relation between perfectionism and elitism is seen as deeply questionable, and in which so (accordingly) is the opposition between Nietzsche and Aristotle.

Notes

1. Charles L. Stevenson, *Ethics and Language* (New Haven: Yale University Press, 1944), subsequently cited parenthetically in the text as *EL*.

2. Stanley Cavell, *The Claim of Reason* (New York: Oxford University Press, 1979), 288.

3. Ibid., 287.

4. Cf. Cora Diamond, "Anything but Argument?," in *The Realistic Spirit* (Cambridge, MA: MIT Press, 1991); and Alice Crary, *Beyond Moral Judgement* (Cambridge, MA: Harvard University Press, 2007).

5. This and the following paragraphs summarize portions of Williams's essay "Nietzsche's Minimalist Moral Psychology," in *The Sense of the Past*, ed. M. Burnyeat (Princeton: Princeton University Press, 2006).

6. As outlined in the eponymous essay of his collection *Moral Luck* (Cambridge: Cambridge University Press, 1981).

7. Bernard Williams, *Ethics and the Limits of Philosophy* (London: Fontana, 1985).

8. Philippa Foot's early and valuable sensitivity to Nietzsche's way of reconceiving the relation between the aesthetic and the ethical thus can be said to have at least identified one important issue for him here, although she did not recognize the full extent of the reinterpretative project on which he thereby embarked.

9. Stanley Cavell, *Conditions Handsome and Unhandsome* (Chicago: University of Chicago Press, 1990); James Conant, "Nietzsche's Perfectionism," in *Nietzsche's Postmoralism: Essays on Nietzsche's Prelude to Philosophy's Future*, ed. Richard Schacht (Cambridge: Cambridge University Press, 2001).

10. Alasdair MacIntyre, *Three Rival Versions of Moral Enquiry* (London: Duckworth, 1990).

11. Bernard Williams, *Truth and Truthfulness* (Princeton: Princeton University Press, 2002) 18–19.

12. MacIntyre, *Three Rival Versions*, 46.

13. Ibid., 47.

CHAPTER NINE

Marxism and the *Ethos* of the Twentieth Century

RAYMOND GEUSS

One of the things I have always most admired about Alasdair MacIntyre's work is the particular kind of intellectual courage it exhibits. This virtue manifests itself in a number of ways, including a willingness to address large philosophical questions head on and to give straightforward answers to them. This is a form of courage, rather than merely of some other more etiolated cognitive excellence, because giving relatively bald and unvarnished answers to big questions makes it difficult to avoid facing up to the implications of what one says for action, and the action involved might be of a kind that requires exhausting, deeply disruptive, and potentially radical changes in the way one lives. In the spirit of an attempt to emulate, at least to some extent, this one of MacIntyre's intellectual virtues, let me try to give a simple answer to the simple question that is the topic of this conference, or rather let me try to give two simple answers to the two components of the double-barreled question that the participants in the conference are invited to consider: What happened *in* moral philosophy in the twentieth century, and what happened *to* moral philosophy in the twentieth century? My answer to this is that Nietzsche is what happened "*in*" moral philosophy,[1] that is, the very idea of a "universal" moral philosophy having any kind of trans-subjective authority came under attack. The notion of "trans-subjective authority" is both unclear and problematic, but that does not mean that it is not attempting, even if not with complete success, to designate something important. It certainly does not mean what philosophers call "validity," and in general it is not a mere epistemic notion. A practice with its associated concepts and forms of thought has what will be called "trans-subjective authority" if it is capable of effectively structuring the basic functions of society around itself, endowing them with meaning, telling us how we should understand them, and issuing commands, injunctions, and recommendations that "stick"—that are as a rule taken to have weight and standing—and finally if it is able to give some reasonable account of itself and stand up to criticism. So Christianity is a clear historical example of a form of life and thought that had trans-subjective authority for a long time in the West. Christianity adds to the mix the idea that its authority is "universal." So the claim is that in the twentieth century Christianity in particular and the very traditional idea of a "universalist" form of ethical life and thought were replaced by a consumerist array of views that was a reflection of a life devoted to more or less unreflective consumption, structured only by aesthetic predilections and the usual sociological imperatives of novelty, snobbism, and so on.[2] What happened "*to*" moral philosophy is that Marxism, which to some extent came from outside the stuffy *intérieur* of academic philosophy, presented the only genuine and potentially viable attempt at reconstituting some notion of objective moral authority, an authority that was to be based on attributing to production an absolute social and political priority. If this attempt had succeeded, it would have changed the world and with it our intellectual and moral universe, but it failed. It used to be said that Marxism was a pseudoreligion or a religion substitute, and this claim was presented as if it was *in itself* a criticism, as if Marxists had simply not fully grasped the implications of the death of God. My view is that the problem was not that this was Marxism's aspiration but rather that it failed to achieve its aspiration. Philosophically, then, the story of the twentieth century is the story of the failure of Marxism.

The main philosophical "problem" in the twentieth century, then, is the complex of anarchic beliefs and anomic modes of living for which the proper name "Nietzsche" stands as the designator. This phenomenon "Nietzscheanism" is not a mere historical aberration or an accidental philosopher's mistake. Rather, it is in some sense a veridical reflection of our social reality, and thus Nietzsche can be seen as giving a correct diagnosis of a set of ills with deep roots in modern Western societies. One of the ways in which Nietzsche uses the term *nihilism* is to designate the contemporary situation of disorientation in which "[all] the highest values lose their value" and all forms of authority lose their hold over individuals.[3] This disorientation is thought to be so intolerable that the most urgent task for contemporary philosophers is to try to help social actors replace practical and theoretical Nietzscheanism with something more salubrious. Philosophers should be looking for a stable way of living together that would be potentially universal, in some yet-to-be-specified sense of *universal*. This common life would need to be one that would allow us to cultivate certain individual and collective goods, many of which are highly context specific and dependent on historically fragile construction. In addition, it would ideally be one that would tolerate and support, or even foster, a correct reflective conceptualization of itself and thus would allow us to see it as having some kind of standing, validity, or authority.

This does not yet by itself imply that Marxism is the only viable attempt to provide a coherent moral philosophy that would respond adequately to Nietzsche's challenge, so that the story of the twentieth century can be told as essentially the story of the development and failure of Marxism. Surely, one might think, there must have been other possible contenders for solutions to the problem we were looking to solve. Why is the story not told as one of the failure of Christianity or liberalism? I wish to suggest that Christianity and liberalism did not, properly speaking, "fail" because they were never real contenders. The reason for this is that neither one is properly "universalist." What *universalist* means is, of course, itself a matter of controversy. This is in no way surprising. After all, it is an oft-noted property of the most interesting philosophical questions that they are reflexive. In asking "What form of life, what worldview, what philosophy, what authority is universalist?" one is at the same time asking "What exactly is, or could be, meant by *universalist*?" In a preliminary way one can say, first, that a "universalist" worldview would be one that was relevant to everyone—it was not from the very start intended to be the worldview *only* of aristocrats, football enthusiasts, medical practitioners, and so on[4]—and second, that it would have to be a worldview that gave people orientation toward *all* the important features of human life.[5] This preliminary account is not false, but it shares the same indeterminacy mentioned at the start.[6] We don't know what *relevant* means in the phrase "relevant to everyone," or what *important* means in the phrase "all the important features of human life." Part of what we have to do is conduct a unitary inquiry of some kind within which we both discover what is relevant and ought to be important to us and what *relevant* and *important* should be taken properly to mean.

Despite its original (Pauline) intentions to provide a mode of access to salvation to all irrespective of their ethnic affiliation, Christianity, like all the revealed monotheistic religions, is so mixed up with highly local forms of human customary imagination that it is unthinkable that it ever could become truly universal, in the sense of being shared by all humans, unless it were imposed by a form of sustained unchallenged military, cultural, and economic power that no Christian country had in the twentieth century and that certainly none seems now likely ever to acquire. This is, of course, a variant of a theme common in Hegel, who connects religion with the ability of the human spirit to produce specific images and concrete narratives,[7] what Hegel calls "myths, phantasms, and contentful narratives that are in fact mere stories."[8] There is, of course, a place, even an important place in human life, for historically specific forms of narrative that engage strong human emotions and for local forms of the imagination, but our image-making capacities seem to have a limited ability to give a kind of persuasive account of themselves and their products that would render them universally acceptable and binding. Unless the particular revelation at a specific time and place on which a given religion is founded can be detached from its context in local fact and fiction, it seems unlikely to be able to command the unrestricted assent it would require to constitute a proper response to Nietzsche, by exerting a visible and palpable universal moral authority.[9]

Under modern circumstances, then, religion is fated either to degenerate into folklore, a particular emotionally tinged set of provincial ways in which the genuinely universal pressures of global capitalism are inflected in particular localities, or to become an inherently sectarian matter, something relating to the specific choice a small group makes and through which that group isolates itself. Recall the origin of the term *heresy* in the Greek word αἱρέω ("to choose, or pick"): the heretical sect is a group that by choice cuts itself off from a wider "catholic"—that is, genuinely all-encompassing—community, thus becoming a "sect."[10] Its members choose some doctrines and practices rather than others. Members of a "catholic" community do not *choose* their way of life but are born into it, or "grow" into it. An intact "catholic community" would be one situation, but if it doesn't exist, no amount of wishing or engineering will in itself bring it back into existence. If no truly "catholic" community exists, then every religious grouping, even those into which the members are "born," must be seen as in a very important sense a "sect." So one slightly paradoxical way of describing the contemporary world is as one in which there is no (proper, universal, "catholic") religion but only (various) sects. A sect may have some healthy, admirable, and morally positive features, but it is not a framework for the reliable exercise of potentially overarching moral authority for the modern world as a whole.

That no revealed religion can be the solution of the Nietzschean predicament, then, does not imply that "clarified" and intellectualized successors of Christianity, like, precisely Marxism, might not aspire to being successful in this enterprise. MacIntyre himself occasionally emphasizes that Marxism can be seen as being something like a Christian heresy, although a "heresy" that might, even if in some sense finally a failure, potentially have been more universal than the original religious matrix out of which it emerged. Still it would be a "heresy," part of the essential point of which was that it had turned itself into a philosophy and a kind of political and social thought and had so deprived itself of precisely those attributes that made Christianity not a philosophy but a religion.

One might, of course, argue that "liberalism" is not a contender as a solution to the Nietzschean predicament because it is not really a full-scale philosophy at all. Rather, it is one or the other of two things. Either it is an attitude that is inherently adverbial, so that to be *a* liberal is to be "liberal," that is, to do *whatever* one does in a certain way or spirit of openhandedness, flexibility, and toleration with a minimal use of force. That is, to put it in an exceedingly tendentious way, a liberal is a person who accepts the first half of the slogan that is often associated with the Jesuits, "suaviter in modo," but who ignores or blanks out, and thus tacitly cancels, the second half ("fortiter in re"). Alternatively, liberalism is a highly specific political program, such as the demand that constitutional government be introduced in a particular country (such as Spain in the early nineteenth century). A psychological disposition or attitude, however, is not by itself an ethics at all because it is too indeterminate, referring exclusively to *how* we ought to act rather than what we should do. It might be thought to have some limited ethical value in that it would exclude certain forms of individual or collective action, such as certain crude inquisitorial practices, but that in itself will not give anyone a very useful orientation in life or answer perfectly reasonable questions such as: What courses of action should I (or we) pursue in a free-spirited and openhanded way, of which institutions should I approve, why exactly is toleration of error an overwhelming human good? When is discussion or negotiation possible and fruitful, and when is it useless or inappropriate? What alternatives do we have when discussion will not serve? Who counts as "one of us"? For which purposes and why? Similarly, a particular political program like constitutionalism might be compatible with any number of very different worldviews.

I don't doubt that *liberalism* was used originally in this adverbial way and then later as the designation of a specific political program, but I think it is equally clear that nowadays, in much academic and periacademic discourse, it is presented as a kind of worldview or philosophical position. During the course of his long career MacIntyre has diagnosed four problems with liberalism considered as a full-scale political and moral doctrine.[11]

First, much mainstream liberalism is characteristically and inherently duplicitous in a way that will eventually reveal itself, particularly when liberals are most in need of orientation and moral guidance, namely when they encounter intact and self-confident nonliberal societies. Doctrinal liberals generally pretend to be above the fray in substantive ideological and moral disagreements. They claim, that is, not to be advocating one particular substantively specified way of life over another, yet they clearly are. Thus the British state, accepting it for the moment as an institution committed to the lowest-common-denominator liberalism that unites the Conservative and the Labour Parties, now enforces a ban on forced marriages and intervenes, coercively if necessary, to prevent female circumcision, et cetera,[12] even against groups who take these customs to be an integral part of their way of life. To turn one of Isaiah Berlin's central contentions back against liberalism itself, one might say that even forcing people to acquire the preconditions for acting in an individually autonomous way is *forcing* them to do something (and not something else, e.g., "merely" liberating them or rendering them "more rational").[13]

Second, liberalism cannot easily be extracted from at least some kind of complicitous association with laissez-faire capitalism, and so it inherits whatever deficiencies might be associated with that specific form of economic organization. I might also add that if one central strand of twentieth-century Marxism is correct, this association with laissez-faire capitalism is a further reason to think that liberalism cannot be an ethical system that lays claim to any real universality. One reason for this is that laissez-faire capitalism seems to require an excluded underclass that is exploited (whether that be an internal proletariat or one externalized in quasi-colonial arrangements), and to which various liberal claims about voluntary contracting, transfer of ownership of property, free choice of occupation, and so on are effectively irrelevant. Another reason is that a laissez-faire economy depends on the continued existence of a series of social domains and institutions like the family, the legal system, the education system, and health system. These institutions must operate according to pre- or noncapitalist principles and cannot coherently be fully subjected to the imperatives of the "free market" (although they can be significantly distorted and damaged by attempts to do this).

Third, the substantive moral conception to which liberalism as a philosophy is committed, despite the protestations of neutrality made by many of its most vocal proponents, is one based in a pernicious way on a conception of the isolated individual as the locus of an absolute moral autonomy. This represents a serious cognitive limitation, because on this basis no adequate understanding of human society is possible, nor does it permit even individual human agents who are engaged in any serious forms of social behavior to attain any satisfactory form of self-understanding. It is in fact exceedingly difficult to see how liberalism's pet recommendation "Increase individual freedom" can constitute a contribution to solving any of the world's major problems.

An ethic based on this kind of hyperindividualist moral autonomy is, however, not merely cognitively mistaken; rather, and this I take to be MacIntyre's fourth point, any form of social action based on or guided by such a view will also be deeply and actively destructive, dissolving forms of collective life that have real value without replacing them with anything of equal value. For these reasons, then, liberalism is not the answer.

Initially it might look as if Marxism were simply orthogonal to the whole universe of discussion marked out by Nietzsche, Christianity, and liberalism. It does not seem to be focused on providing views about the universal validity of moral principles, the salvation of the soul, or the proper role of flexibility and toleration in human life. What it promised was three things. The first was something very concrete: an end to the boom-and-bust cycle of capitalist growth, and a regime of full employment, economic stability, and full social welfare and security for all. This first promise had particular importance in circumstances in which it called attention to the comparison with capitalist economies that were subject to recurrent, severe crisis, such as those of the 1920s and 1930s, and it retains its importance to the extent to which capitalist societies, despite Gordon Brown's foolish boast, still are subject to boom-and-bust. This first promise was concrete and empirical in the sense that it came about as close as one ever gets in the social sciences to being something the fulfillment of which could be determined by something like empirical scientific means.

Second, Marxism was committed to the view that the appropriately structured abolition of the private ownership of means of production would do away with what were historically superseded social fetters on the development of human powers and would unleash an unexpected and hitherto unprecedented increase in human productivity. This increase in human productivity would have as its natural effect an increase in material well-being, that is in the level of satisfaction of human needs and in levels of human consumption. This second promise, too, was something that, with the usual caveats and qualification, could be connected with at least some crude standards of empirical confirmation.

The third promise was altogether more problematic for historical and philosophical reasons. That was the promise to end alienation. It was historically problematic because it was most clearly formulated in unpublished writings by Marx that became widely available only after the First World War and therefore did not directly influence the formulation in the late nineteenth century of the basic Marxist canon. It has been thought to be philosophically problematic because it seemed to depend on a series of Hegelian views that might perfectly reasonably be thought to be questionable for any number of reasons (not least because they might be thought to remain implicated in basically idealistic ways of thinking about the world that were found to be objectionable). "Alienation" is best understood relative to a distinction between the (mere) exercise of human powers and the "appropriation," or "reappropriation" *(Aneignung/Wiederaneignung)*, of these powers.[14] The intuition behind this distinction is that an individual human agent (or a group of such agents) can be the real locus through which certain powers are applied to the physical world without it being the case that the human individual, or group, in question has "made the (relevant) powers its own." Making certain powers "our own" in turn means acquiring full control over the conditions of further development and the application of those powers and being able to affirm ourselves in the exercise of those powers. *Alienation* refers to the state of affairs in which we have not appropriated some of our most basic human powers, especially those closely connected with material production and reproduction of our form of life. Apart from concerns about the possible idealist overtones of this concept, one might worry that I have given an account of it that is circular and empty, just replacing one undefined and obscure counter or token with another: alienation is supposed to be the lack of appropriation of powers. That in turn is "defined" by reference to "making the power one's own." "Making a power my own," however, is said to have taken place when I can "affirm myself" in exercising it. Is "self-affirmation," however, a well-understood concept? The reference to "self-affirmation" means at the very least that a very significant interpretative activity is required to connect the conceptual structure described in any way with anything that empirical social science would recognize as part of itself, and this might be thought to be a further reason to be wary of "alienation." I do not wish in any way to minimize these genuine difficulties, but I do not think they finally matter for the question at issue.

The self-proclaimed Marxist regimes of Eastern Europe were remarkably successful in making good on the first of these promises. To the very end their populations enjoyed full employment and what was by Western European standards a very ample schedule of other benefits that provided more or less complete economic security. Nevertheless they collapsed, not just economically, but, as it were, also morally. They failed, that is, to find enough ideational and motivational support among their own populations to continue to reproduce themselves. This happened, I submit, not because they were oppressive, and certainly not because they failed to be "democratic" in the sense in which this term is used in Western liberal societies. It is also hard to think that they collapsed merely because they failed to end "alienation," although it is true that they did thus fail, or perhaps more exactly, as Sartre sometimes claimed, they did not so much fail to end capitalist alienation as replace it with a specific, slightly different kind of alienation. In one of his essays he cites a poster in a factory in Eastern Europe in which workers are enjoined to take care of their health in order not to damage national production.[15] In cases like this one's own health itself (and hence presumably one's own biological possibility of self-activity) is seen merely as a means to a fully external end. Still, politics is usually about differential, not categorical, forms of judgment and action, that is, we characteristically choose, not X "for itself alone," but X in preference to Y or Z. So the spectrum of envisaged realistic possibilities that is presupposed in political decision is usually an important variable. If the choice, then, was exclusively between Soviet forms of economic and political organization and Western capitalist ones, the failure of Soviet-style societies to end alienation would not be a very strong differential argument in favor of capitalist regimes, because the latter made no serious attempt at all to make labor (and life) unalienated and unalienating (whatever *alienation* might turn out to mean). Yet when offered the opportunity, in the last decade or so of the twentieth century, populations in Eastern Europe overwhelmingly chose to abandon the self-proclaimed Marxist form of economy and of society and to look toward Western European models of modern capitalism.

The lethal failure of twentieth-century European Marxism was its inability to produce consumer goods at the level of quality and quantity that was attained by Western Europe. So a failure in the second of the three promises. Those of us who have always lived in prosperous societies and have been materially comfortable may well be tempted to be somewhat condescending about this: Is mere failure to provide a steadily increasing stream of luxury consumer goods really good grounds for rejecting a social order, provided ample means for minimally decent living are available? Is even lack of "economic efficiency" a good grounds for criticism? I think this is a temptation to adopt a morally shameful attitude that we should staunchly resist.

The positive attraction of the West, then, was completely understandable. It was the attraction of greater productivity combined with a social and political framework that was perceived as permitting a greater distribution of consumer goods. The failure of the Soviet system consisted in the joint incapacity to provide their populations with capitalist levels of consumption, combined with an inability to elaborate any plausible alternative evaluative standard relative to which life in Soviet-style societies could be seen as distinctively good.

The difficulty was that a central strand of Marxism shared with capitalist ideologies a tacit or explicit productivist ethos. In a kind of parody of a motif taken from the High Enlightenment, a more economically and industrially productive society was expected to be a society that was "more advanced" in almost every way. Marx himself was well aware of this strand in his own thinking but did not think it in any way problematic: he expected socialist economies to out-produce capitalist ones, and also to be self-evidently more rewarding, satisfying, and choiceworthy to those who lived in them than capitalist societies were; finally, he also expected these two things naturally and easily to go together. Perhaps the clearest expression of the productivist view occurs in the *Grundrisse*:

> Among the ancients we never find an investigation of which form of landownership is most productive, creates the most wealth? Wealth does not appear as the end of production, although Cato is quite capable of investigating which form of cultivation of the field has the highest yield, and even Brutus knows how to lend out his money at the best rate of interest. The investigation is always which form of property creates the best citizens. Wealth appears as an end-in-itself only among some few trading nations— monopolists of the carrying trade—who live in the pores of the ancient world, like the Jews in medieval society. . . . The ancient conception according to which man in whatever narrow national, religious or political form appears as the end of production, seems to be very sublime compared with the modern world, where production appears as the end of man and wealth the end of production. In fact, however, when the narrow bourgeois form is stripped away, what is wealth other than the universality of the needs, abilities, forms of enjoyment, productive powers, etc. of the individuals generated in universal exchange? The full development of human domination over natural powers, both of so-called nature and of his own nature? The absolute elaboration of his creative capacities without any further presupposition that the previous historical development which makes this totality of development, that is the development of all human power as such, not measured by any *pre-given* yardstick, into an end in itself?[16]

On the positive side, this does seem to give one at least a possible kind of response to Nietzsche, that is, it can be seen as a description of a universal framework that could be construed as containing a potential kind of quasi-moral but nonsubjective authority, an authority derived from the requirements for maximally developing needs and human productive powers and capacities for their own sake. However, this response does require one to put a huge amount of weight on a particular anthropological conception that emphasizes the mutual dependence of human powers and human needs and the necessary and potentially mutually reinforcing relation between individual and collective development of powers. Nietzsche, of course, would have rejected this conjunction of individual and collective. This disagreement between Marx and Nietzsche about the interconnection of individual and social powers ought not, however, to obscure a further deep-seated similarity. Both Marx's productivism and Nietzschean conceptions of the exercise of the individual will-to-power contain a very strong substantive quasi-normative commitment to the development of power as an "end in itself."

Is the development of *every* human power and of *every* need really good, and, more than that, is it a kind of absolute good-in-itself, as Marx's construction seems to imply? Historians often point to Rousseau as systematically introducing the idea of a "false need" into Western social thought.[17] In human society we all develop forms of dependency on the good opinion of others, which give rise to any number of cognitively delusory but motivationally deeply seated "needs" that make no contribution to any real human good and that we would in principle be better off without. Notoriously Marx will have none of this line of thought. He has a theory of needs but no analysis of what it could be for a need to be false.[18] A "rich" person is a person "rich in needs," and this is a thoroughly positive and laudatory description (*MEW*, Erg. 1:544, 546). He thought any attempt to introduce a distinction between true and false needs would represent a return to what he took to be Rousseau's proto-Romantic primitivism and or to an inherently ascetic view of life that could be justified only by reference to discredited forms of religious belief.

Parallel to these difficulties about "needs" is a question about the idea of a "(natural, human) power," the development of which is here described as an end in itself. In some of Marx's early works one finds a very broad construal of this term. So even "forms of enjoyment" that might play a role in my relation to objects in the world (as mentioned in the above quotation), such as the cultivation of the senses and the ability to appreciate the beauty of nature (*MEW*, Erg. 1:539–42), are construed as "natural human powers" (actually as "menschliche Wesenskräfte").[19] Arguably this would not give rise to some of the worst features of productivism, because saying that a "form of enjoyment," or even a larger configuration in which a specific form of enjoyment is an essential constituent, is an "end in itself" does not seem to leave open certain classic forms of alienation. It really would seem strange to claim that I was being inappropriately forced to develop my own powers of enjoyment of some type of object, at any rate provided that the development of such powers was part of what Marx sometimes calls an "all-sided" exercise of human powers and capacities.[20] Unfortunately, sometimes Marx seems to give "human powers" a significantly narrower reading than the one just canvassed, as if the phrase was not equivalent to "all" the human powers included in one way or another in the cycle of production and consumption (including those of aesthetic appreciation, enjoyment, and discrimination) but was restricted to the power to produce goods or material objects that could be used or consumed. "Power" means, or at any rate is strictly modeled on, *industrial* production (*MEW*, Erg. 1:542: "The history of industry . . . is the opened book of essential human powers").[21] A "human power" is then tacitly understood essentially as a kind of instrument that is deployed to bring physical things into existence or to change their location or material properties.

MacIntyre, in his paper on the "Theses on Feuerbach," pointed to a "road not taken" by the early Marx that diverges from that trod by later Marxists.[22] In the "Theses" the early Marx does *not* construe production in either the narrower or the wider of the two senses distinguished above as the end-in-itself of human life. Rather, he appeals to a different kind of human action altogether that is not construed as in the first instance a form of relating to "objects" at all. This form of human action is apparently conceived as standing altogether outside the context of the instrumental transformation of nature in the production of goods or the cultivation of powers to appreciate those goods (and then also perhaps natural phenomena of all kinds, considered as potential "objects"). Marx calls this form of activity praxis. Whatever praxis is supposed to be, it is supposed to be a radically autotelic—that is, having its end in itself and not in some external product—and noninstrumental form of activity. Marx, however, does not really give a sufficiently detailed account of praxis for us to get a firm grasp on the concept and discover to what extent it is or is not genuinely enlightening. Appeal to praxis is a gesture at something not further analyzed rather than a satisfactory explanation.

One can see the work of some of the members of the so-called Frankfurt School as developing lines of argument that are parallel to the ones just discussed. Most of the members of this school agree on two points. First, Marx was either confusing or confused about the exact nature of human action. He tended to construe all human action on the model of instrumental action or under the aspect of its possible mean-ends rationality. He tended, that is, to identify praxis and production, and then to construe production in a narrow way as industrial production. This in effect meant both conceptually reducing noninstrumental forms of action (such as "praxis," whatever that finally meant) to forms of production and subordinating all human life to the imperatives of increased instrumental control over the environment (and over ourselves). Seen from this perspective, Marx's use of the phrase "the *domination* [italics mine] over the natural powers of our own nature" (Herrschaft über die Naturkräfte [unserer] eignen Natur) in the passage from the *Grundrisse* cited above can be read in a chilling way, as potentially the extension of a paradigm of coercive manipulation from our relations to nature to our relations to other humans, and from our relations to other humans to our relations to ourselves.[23]

Second, the members of the Frankfurt School thought it essential to rehabilitate the distinction between true and false needs by showing how one could speak of "false needs" without asceticism, without a return to an Aristotelian conception of a substantively fixed human nature that could be used as a criterion, and without commitment to a Romantic "return to nature" view. This attempt was not very successful, because it ended up either with the pessimistic aesthetic vision of Adorno, which had no obvious connection to any form of concrete politics, or with the debased liberalism of Habermas and his neo-Kantian ideal speech theory.

Up to now I have not mentioned what I call in my title "the *ethos*" of the twentieth century. To speak of "the" ethos is slightly misleading because it suggests that there is a single unitary such *ethos*. In one sense this is right, in that there seems agreement on a cycle of need-production-consumption pursued for its own sake. On the other hand, though, there are two slightly different ways of accentuating the components in this cycle. Marx emphasizes the priority of production and tries to find a way of seeing how that production can be a form of human freedom and self-activity. This view dominated Eastern Europe during much of the twentieth century. The various ideologies of the capitalist societies, on the other hand, focused on consumption. The first way of inflecting the need-production-consumption cycle, just to repeat, was, I have claimed, finally unable to maintain itself partly because it was unable to out-produce the group of countries that eventually became the European Union—also perhaps because it could give no plausible answer to the question why production for its own sake was an end-in-itself and because it had no genuinely *alternative* value system, or mode of self-congratulation, to propose. The second, consumption-oriented variety of this same basic worldview and form of society, as MacIntyre has shown, is the natural matrix for the various varieties of emotivism, existentialism, and moral anarchism that are characteristic of the philosophy and the life of our societies. Mainstream Marxism, then, was an attempt to answer the questions of the twentieth century in a way that was in some sense still commensurate with an important part of its *ethos*.

How might one break out of the cycle of needs-production-consumption? One way would certainly be to find a single overarching goal outside it, if any such goal existed. And so it is very tempting to follow Aristotle down the path that leads from this reflection to the views that he presents in his ethical and political writings. In a famous passage in the beginning of the *Nicomachean Ethics*, Aristotle writes: "If then there is some end of our practical undertakings which we wish for the sake of itself, whereas we wish for the other things [we wish for] for the sake of it, and if we do not choose everything for the sake of something else (for if *that* is the case, the sequence will go on without limit, so that our desire was empty and vain), it is clear that this [end] will be the good, i.e., the best."[24] This is my own *pons asinorum*, the bridge from ignorance into the Promised Land of Understanding that I have found myself always unable to cross. Why, I have always wondered, should my desire be considered "empty and pointless" just because it is part of a sequence of further desires that goes off into infinity (i.e., that continues indefinitely, has no definite stopping point)? I am thirsty today and want to drink. I know that even if I do now drink, I will be thirsty again tomorrow or the next day. Does that mean that my desire to drink now is "empty"? Even if my action on a specific desire is (doomed necessarily to be) frustrated and "pointless" (ματαιά), I do not see why that makes the desire or the course of action to which it gives rise empty. Such desires and such actions are an important, in fact constituent, part of human life.

To take a slightly more weighty example, I may desire (both for its inherent properties and for the other good things it leads to) world peace, greater European integration, the prosecution of Tony Blair in the Hague as a war criminal, and a more rigorous standard in education without having any idea how these different goals might be related to each other. Even if I were to agree that I need *some* central structure of desire unified under a single overarching end to give my life meaning, I do not see how it follows from that that *all* my desires need to be seen in reference to that central core. I don't, of course, mean to assert that *all* human desire is undifferentially or equally good or valid, or that it might not be perverted, inopportune, or otherwise unwise to act on some desires in some circumstances, but has human desire *no* weight and dignity in itself *at all*, apart from its integration into a single overarching end? Isn't human life in fact like this: a series of desires that at some indeterminate point, we know not when, eventually peters out?

One of the reasons I have always felt great resistance to this Aristotelian line of thought is that it seems to me to add fuel to a view of human life that I find repellent. This is the view that life is either like a race or an ἀγών with clear winners and losers or like the exercise of a craft with a determinate end, say like the production of shoes, so that univocal success or failure is always discernible. First of all, I have always thought there was much to be said, not exactly in favor of failure *tout court*, but in potential appreciation of some of the aspects of failure. One would think that this would be a line of thought that would recommend itself with particular force to Christians who took seriously Paul's preaching of "Christ crucified." Second, much of human life, and some of the most interesting and important parts of it, do not seem to me to lend themselves plausibly to analysis in terms of success or failure at all. Some aspects of life are not appropriately construed relative to the idea that life is a single continuous narrative about the desire for and pursuit of a single unified (conception of the) good. Furthermore, a human life "as a whole" does not seem to me at all like a single huge race or the deployment of a craft.[25] It seems to me highly questionable whether my whole life admits of treatment as a single narrative in any interesting sense, but even if I were to grant that it is or could be such a narrative, the kind of narrative in question would have to be one that would be only contingently related to the "story" of a single ἀγών, competition, or race.²⁶ Narrative should be seen as a way of distancing ourselves from Aristotle, not of rehabilitating him.²⁷ If we at any *particular* time give our desires some minimal order by reference to some conception of a single overarching good, we also know that those conceptions of a unitary good *change* during our lives. Any unity of desire is "necessarily" and unavoidably fleeting, transitory, fragile, and imposed on much more chaotic structures, which are, however, not just nothing or "empty."

Thus Aristotle's view has always seemed to me utterly implausible as a view about the nature of human desire, and thus also of human life as a whole. Human desire has at least *some* validity in itself, a validity that is not derived merely from some external higher end to which it is devoted. The passage cited from *Nicomachean Ethics* has also always seemed to me to indicate that, regardless of the rather sophisticated discussion one can find in his work of forms of human action that are autotelic, Aristotle is still fixated on a relatively rigid division of actions into those performed "for their own sake" (as end-in-themselves) and those performed "[*merely*] for the sake of something else." In fact if he were to be able to rid his thought of the centrality of this distinction and see it as of merely local or contextual relevance, the argument for the existence of a single overarching end, on which the rest of the work to some extent rests, would be seen to be implausible. Even interpretations of Aristotle that emphasize the extent to which the conception of εὐδαιμονία ("happiness" or "human flourishing") will be affected by reflection on the real conditions of human life and real human desires seem to me to hold fast to the "(mere) means" / "end (in itself)" distinction. It is one thing to say that in determining what the end-in-itself is one must reflect even on the means that will be necessary for its attainment, and quite another to do away with the distinction between means adopted for the sake of something other than themselves and ends in themselves altogether.²⁸

There is, at any rate, a whole traditional sequence of philosophers who think of themselves as turning their backs resolutely on the strict Aristotelian distinction between means and ends, actions under the dominance of instrumental rationality and some form of autotelic human activity. I would include in this tradition Hegel, Marx (in *some* of his moods), Dewey, Trotsky (sometimes), and Adorno (but not Habermas). Obviously the members of this group differ in any number of significant ways, but what seems to me characteristic of all of them is their conviction that one must try to break out of the cycle of need-production-consumption and in particular get away from the idea that some component of that cycle is a kind of end-in-itself. Rather, however, than thinking that there is some other single good that is the one overarching human goal, as Aristotle claims, but that that goal is not production, they hold that there is no pre-given overarching single goal. Human life is a matter of "*biens à construire*" rather than of a "*bien à trouver.*" Furthermore, they connect this thought, and see it as in some way inherently connected with, the idea of overcoming the very distinction between means and ends or instrumental and substantive rationality, or at any rate demoting any such distinction to the status of a mere contextual convenience with no final significance. Thus Trotsky speaks of the "dialectic of means and ends."[29] "Dialectical materialism does not know dualism between means and end. The end flows naturally from the historical movement. Organically the means are subordinated to the end. The immediate end becomes the means for a further end." Appeal to such a dialectic, however, is one way to try to save the deepest intuition behind Marxism, which is that humanity should be capable of collectively self-organizing activity, which instantiates appropriate self-control, self-direction, and even, when necessary, self-limitation without needing to appeal to any external principle.[30] The central idea that humanity is constituted by a self-activity in which the distinction between instrumental action and action performed for its own sake is not relevant is detachable from productivism. This specific conception of self-activity seems to me more perspicuously graspable in Hegelian than in Aristotelian categories.[31] I am sorry to say that I believe that I disagree with MacIntyre on this.

That leaves the issue of Nietzsche. Simply deciding in discussion to abandon Aristotle's distinction between instrumental action and action performed for its own sake will not by itself suffice to do away with Nietzscheanism, unless such a decision is part of a successful project of action to transform society. Marx thought it in some sense pointless to "refute" religion because it arose from human needs that were not satisfied by a certain social formation and would disappear only when those needs were more directly and palpably satisfied. Similarly Nietzscheanism will disappear only when it loses its plausibility as a mirror of and guide to and in our social life. That will happen only if our social life takes a different form. Nevertheless, the framework provided by some conception of collective self-activity gives us, it seems to me, the best chance we have of constructing a world in which Nietzsche would be an irrelevance. Even if such an institutionally embedded and socially realized framework effectively did exist, it would still be possible for individuals to make a decision to try to reject it, but this decision would have a completely different status from that which a "lifestyle decision" has now. It would be more like what Christians in the medieval period had in mind when they considered the possibility that the fool might say in his heart that there is no God. Taking seriously the attempt to abolish the distinction between instrumental and substantive reason, between actions performed merely for the sake of other things and actions performed for their own sake, and finally between means and ends by transforming society in a way that would make these distinctions really marginal and subordinate would, I think, move one beyond the ethos of the twentieth century. Not, of course, that there is politically the slightest chance of this happening at present.

Notes

In all my thinking about the subject matter of the above essay I have been deeply influenced by discussions with the members of the Cambridger Forschungskolloquium, especially Richard Raatzsch. I am also very grateful to the members of the audience at University College Dublin for their resistance to some of the glibber parts of the original version of this paper.

1. See Alasdair MacIntyre, *After Virtue* (London: Duckworth, 1981), esp. 103–13 and 238–45.

2. See Pierre Bourdieu, *La distinction* (Paris: Gallimard, 1979).

3. See Friedrich Nietzsche, *Nachgelassene Fragmente, 1885–1887,* vol. 12 of *Sämtliche Werke: Kritische Studienausgabe,* ed. Giorgio Colli and Mazzino Montinari (Berlin: de Gruyter, 1967–77), 350.

4. One of the central parts of Foucault's analysis of the difference between ancient and Christian forms of ethics is that the former are not necessarily proposed as having relevance to everyone: slaves are not even candidates for leading a good life. See Michel Foucault, *L'histoire de la sexualité: L'usage des plaisirs* (Paris: Gallimard, 1984).

5. Much of what we now call "ancient religion"—a usage that already to some extent represents an anachronistic, retrospective construction that forces a variety of phenomena into a fixed format derived from later monotheistic patterns of

thought—did not even aspire to be all-encompassing or tell any kind of truth about the whole world or all of human life. For an almost random selection of relevant works, see Jan Assman, *Moses the Egyptian* (Cambridge, MA: Harvard University Press, 1998); Clifford Ando, *The Matter of the Gods* (Berkeley: University of California Press, 2008); Polyumnia Athanassiadi and Michael Frede, eds., *Pagan Monotheism in Late Antiquity* (Oxford: Oxford University Press, 1999); and Moses Halbertal and Avishai Margalit, *Idolatry* (Cambridge, MA: Harvard University Press, 1992).

6. The meaning of *universalist* might not, of course, be limited to the two components cited, by way of example, in the text. It hardly requires stating, I hope, that discussion of "universalism" in this context does not imply any special privileging of Kantian or Habermasian perspectives.

7. Hegel's way of putting this point is usually that religion is a matter of "Vorstellung" (representation) rather than "Begriff" (concept), which is the realm of philosophy. Thus he writes, "In den Religionen haben die Völker allerdings niedergelegt, wie sie sich das Wesen der Welt, die Substanz der Natur und des Geistes vorstellten, und wie das Verhältnis des Menschen zu demselben." G. W. F. Hegel, *Vorlesungen über die Geschichte der Philosophie I,* vol. 18 of *Werke in zwanzig Bänden,* ed. Eva Moldenhauer and Karl Markus Michel (Frankfurt: Suhrkamp, 1969–79), 82. The contrast here is that philosophy does not "represent," for instance, the "essence of the world"; rather, it "grasps it in a concept" ("In der Philosophie wird das Wesen der Welt nicht vorgestellt, sondern begriffen"). Even when religion presents "deep, sublime, speculative thoughts," which are not mere images, it presents them as objects of external devotion ("Andacht") rather than as argumentatively structured processes that we grasp "from the inside" by enacting (see 83–92).

8. "Mythen, Phantasievorstellungen und positive, eigentliche Geschichten." Ibid., 94.

9. Christian theologians have long discussed this issue, and many of these discussions are highly enlightening, even when finally unsatisfactory. The three most important discussions since the eighteenth century seem to me to have been those of Lessing, Hegel, and Kierkegaard. Analogues to some of the problems that arise here have reemerged in Alain Badiou's recent work. See his *L'ethique: Essai sur la conscience du mal* (Paris: Hatier, 1998) and *Saint Paul: La fondation de l'universalisme* (Paris: PUF 1997). How can what Badiou calls an "event" that, like the French Revolution, occurred at a particular time and place have the appropriate kind of universality? Isn't "fidelity" to such an event like commitment to the content of a historically specific form of religious revelation? I can merely state here that for various reasons having to do with the detailed structure of his views I do not think this is as serious a difficulty for Badiou as the parallel problem is for advocates of revealed religion. A second possible strand of argument here, associated with Nietzsche rather than with Hegel, emphasizes not inherent limitation of the human image-making capacity but the claim that Christianity is committed

to specific substantive delusions that it also has a tendency, in the long run, to undermine. Nietzsche was of the opinion that this process of self-destruction was essentially complete by the end of the nineteenth century. For this view, see Friedrich Nietzsche, *Zur Genealogie der Moral,* in *Sämtliche Werke,* 5:247–412.

10. The most conceptually interesting and enlightening modern discussion of "sects" is that of Max Weber. See esp. *Wirtschaft und Gesellschaft* (Tübingen: Mohr, 1972), 721–26. I should mention, however, that my usage of *sect* deviates slightly from his. I take the term as a quasi-empirical description of a state of affairs in which one group is in fact "cut off" *(seco/sectum)* from a catholic community or from other groups. For Weber, an elitist rejection of free and open access to the religious community is constitutive for being a "sect." Thus he writes: "['Eine Sekte' ist eine Gemeinschaft] . . . welche ihrem *Sinn und Wesen* nach notwendig auf Universalität verzichten . . . muß . . . weil sie ein aristokratisches Gebilde: ein Verein der religiös voll *Qualifizierten* und nur ihrer sein will" (721).

11. See Alasdair MacIntyre, "Epilogue: 1953, 1968, 1995: Three Perspectives," in *Alasdair MacIntyre's Engagement with Marxism,* ed. Paul Blackledge and Neil Davidson (Leiden: Brill, 2008), 419–21.

12. I note that recently Raz has proposed a "perfectionist" liberalism that is not obviously subject to this particular line of criticism. See Joseph Raz, *The Morality of Freedom* (Oxford: Oxford University Press, 1986).

13. Isaiah Berlin, *Four Essays on Liberty* (Oxford: Oxford University Press, 1969), 131–54.

14. Karl Marx, untitled manuscripts in *Marx-Engels-Werke* (Berlin: Dietz, 1968), supplemental vol. (Erg.) 1 (subsequently cited parenthetically in the text as *MEW,* Erg. 1): 522, 536, 540, etc.

15. Jean-Paul Sartre, "Les communistes et la paix," in *Situations VI: Problèmes du marxisme* (Paris: Gallimard, 1964), 80–384.

16. "Wir finden bei den Alten nie eine Untersuchung, welche Form des Grundeigentums etc. die produktivste, den größten Reichtum schafft? Der Reichtum erscheint nicht als Zweck der Produktion, obgleich sehr wohl Cato untersuchen kann, welche Bestellung des Feldes die erträglichste, oder gar Brutus sein Geld zu den besten Zinsen ausborgen kann. Die Untersuchung ist immer, welche Weise des Eigentums die besten Staatsbürger schafft. Als Selbstzweck erscheint der Reichtum nur bei den wenigen Handelsvölkern—Monopolisten des carrying trade—, die in den Poren der alten Welt leben, wie die Juden in der mittelaltrigen Gesellschaft. . . . So scheint die alte Anschauung, wo der Mensch, in welcher borniertien nationalen, religiösen, politischen Bestimmung auch immer als Zweck der Produktion erscheint, sehr erhaben zu sein gegen die moderne Welt, wo die Produktion als Zweck des Menschen und der Reichtum als Zweck der Produktion erscheint. In fact, aber, wenn die bornierte bürgerliche Form abgestreift wird, was ist der Reichtum anders als die im universellen Austausch erzeugte Universalität der Bedürfnisse, Fähigkeiten, Genüsse, Produktivkräfte etc. der Individuen? Die volle Entwicklung der menschlichen Herrschaft über die Naturkräfte, die der

sogenannten Natur sowohl, wie seiner eigenen Natur? Das absolute Herausarbeiten seiner schöpferischen Anlagen, ohne andre Voraussetzung als die vorhergegangene historische Entwicklung, die diese Totalität der Entwicklung, d.h. der Entwicklung aller menschlichen Kräfte als solcher, nicht gemessen an einem *vorgegebenen* Maßstab, zum Selbstzwecke macht?" Karl Marx, *Grundrisse zur Kritik der politischen Ökonomie* (Berlin: Dietz, 1953), 387. My translation.

17. See Alasdair MacIntyre, *A Short History of Ethics* (London: Routledge, 1967), 177–82.

18. On Marx's theory of needs, see Agnes Heller, *The Theory of Need in Marx* (London: Allison and Busby, 1976), and Ian Fraser, *Hegel and Marx: The Concept of Need* (Edinburgh: University of Edinburgh Press, 1998); see also Lawrence Hamilton, *The Political Philosophy of Needs* (Cambridge: Cambridge University Press, 2003).

19. Note the almost compulsive use of *Gegenstand* and *gegenständlich* in the relevant passage in Marx's untitled manuscripts in *MEW,* Erg. 1:539–42. The model here is the human relation to "objects."

20. The classic expression of this Humboldtian strand is Karl Marx and Friedrich Engels, *Die Deutsche Ideologie,* vol. 3 of *Marx-Engels-Werke* (Berlin: Dietz, 1969), esp. 32–34, 74–75, and 206, and note that Marx was aware of the dangers of "one-sided" or fixated development (238–39).

21. "Die Geschichte der Industrie . . . ist das aufgeschlagene Buch der menschlichen Wesenskräfte."

22. Alasdair MacIntyre, "The *Theses on Feuerbach*: A Road Not Taken," in *Artifacts, Representations, and Social Practice,* ed. Carol C. Gould and Robert S. Cohen (Dordrecht: Kluwer, 1994), 277–90.

23. This is the thesis of Adorno and Horkheimer's *Dialektik der Aufklärung* (Frankfurt: Fischer, 1969), esp. 9–49. See also T. W. Adorno, *Minima Moralia,* § 100 (Frankfurt: Suhrkamp, 1973), 206–8.

24. Εἰ δή τι τέλος ἐστὶ τῶν πρακτῶν ὃ δι' αὐτὸ βουλόμεθα, τἆλλα δὲ διὰ τοῦτο, καὶ μὴ πάντα δι' ἕτερον αἱρούμεθα (πρόεισι γὰρ οὕτω γ' εἰς ἄπειρον, ὥστ' εἶναι κενὴν καὶ ματαίαν τὴν ὄρεξιν), δῆλον ὡς τοῦτ' ἂν εἴη τἀγαθὸν καὶ τὸ ἄριστον. *Nicomachean Ethics* 1.2, my translation.

25. See Martin Heidegger, *Sein und Zeit,* §§ 45–53 (Tübingen: Niemeyer, 1963), 231–67.

26. Obviously the view presented here is incompatible with another often used metaphor, that of life as a "journey" from determinate place A to determinate place B, a metaphor that found its most exquisite development in Dante's *Comedy*. The *Comedy* would repay close study in this context, but here I mention only two aspects that seem to me of importance. First, the lives of all those whom Dante encounters are seen as in some way summed up in some single image: Paolo and Francesca buffeted by the unending wind of desire, the sodomites running an eternal race over a desert, Ulysses in his flame. Can every human life really

be summed up without remainder in such a single image? Is *nothing* lost by this? Second, it is not, it seems to me, a merely aesthetic fact that the "failures" in *Inferno* are so much more interesting than the saints in *Paradiso*.

27. Contra MacIntyre. See MacIntyre, *After Virtue,* esp. ch. 15, 190–209.

28. A further serious problem for any contemporary rehabilitation of Aristotle is the complete absence in his work of any real sense of history as something that matters. He has, to be sure, some trivial remarks about how human inventions have accumulated, some comments about the comparative history of "constitutions," and the odd observation to the effect that human desires develop over time, but none of this amounts to nearly enough to accommodate the modern keen "historischer Sinn" that developed in the nineteenth century, an awareness that the past was, to put it very crudely, "qualitatively" different from the present. His outline history of previous Greek philosophy in book 1 of *Metaphysics* is in itself a sufficient testimonial to his irremediably "presentist" attitude. It has also always seemed paradoxical to me that Christians could try to find a foundation for their beliefs in an Aristotelian framework. After all, it is central to Christianity not merely that a divine revelation took place at some particular time, thus fundamentally changing the moral universe in which people lived, but also that at some specific point in the past God was incarnated. This is most plausibly interpreted as meaning that the very quality of human time changes.

29. John Dewey and Leon Trotsky, *Their Morals and Ours* (New York: Pathfinder Press, 1969), 48. To be sure, if one looks at the context within which Trotsky writes this, one will perhaps have doubts about his understanding of "dialectics." He writes: "From the Marxist point of view the end is justified if it leads to increasing the power of humanity over nature and to the abolition of the power of one person over another. . . . That is permissible, which *really* leads to the liberation of humanity. Since this end can be achieved only through revolution, the liberating morality of the proletariat of necessity is endowed with a revolutionary character. . . . It deduces a rule of conduct from the laws of the development of society, thus primarily from the class struggle, this law of all laws." "Deduction of a rule of conduct" from any *one* "law of all laws" seems contrary to the spirit of dialectic.

30. Ibid., 48.

31. See Hegel, *Phänomenologie des Geistes,* vol. 3 of Moldenhauer and Michel, *Werke in zwanzig Bänden;* also Marx, untitled manuscripts in *MEW,* Erg. 1:568–88.

CHAPTER TEN

Parallel Projects
Alasdair MacIntyre's Virtue Ethics, Thirteenth-Century Pastoral Theology (Leonard Boyle, O.P.), and Thomistic Moral Theology (Servais Pinckaers, O.P.)

JAMES McEVOY

The advocacy of virtue ethics by Alasdair MacIntyre has given this brand of moral philosophy a distinctive place among the moral theories currently taught in departments of philosophy throughout the English-speaking world; indeed it must be acknowledged that his intellectual efforts have given virtue ethics a prominence in present-day discussion such as it has not enjoyed, save within Thomistic and neoscholastic circles, for a very long time. The modest aim of this study is to explore two parallel research paths undertaken by contemporary thinkers, in the hope of throwing some light upon MacIntyre's enterprise, bringing out its originality, and pointing to its wider intellectual relationships. The first of these figures was Leonard Boyle, O.P., the historian of the many treatises on the virtues and vices *(De virtutibus et vitiis)* that circulated after approximately AD 1200, and the second was another Dominican, Servais Pinckaers, the widely published theological interpreter of the moral thought of St. Thomas Aquinas. The present writer had the good fortune to know both men.

Leonard Boyle, O.P.

Life

Leonard Eugene Boyle was born on November 13, 1923, at Ballintra, County Donegal, the son of Owen Boyle and Margaret O'Donnell of Burtonport. Because of his parents' early deaths the child attended school in Counties Westmeath and Cork, being placed under the guardianship of his brother, a *Garda Síochána*. For his secondary schooling he went to the Cistercians at Mount Melleray, County Waterford. Leonard entered the Dominican Order at Cork on September 4, 1943. The following year he was sent to Blackfriars, Oxford, to study theology. There he came under the academic influence of the well-remembered Daniel Angelo Callus, a Maltese Dominican priest whose research concerned principally the thought of Aquinas and his Dominican contemporaries, including members of the English Province who taught at early Oxford.[1] Leonard's first scholarly edition of a Latin text was to be completed under the supervision of Father Callus, as a thesis for the degree of Lector of Theology (S.T.Lr.) within the order; he was awarded the degree in 1951. By that time he had already been ordained (December 1949).

In 1951 the young priest began work at Oxford for a B. Litt. degree, but his research assumed the proportions of a D. Phil. thesis, and he was indeed awarded that degree in 1956. Between 1955 and 1957 he was employed by the National Library of Ireland and the Public Record Office, London, on research work at the Vatican Archives for the Calendar of Papal Registers. He then lectured at the Angelicum and Lateran Universities in Rome, while extending his knowledge of the Vatican Archives.[2] In 1961 he became visiting professor of Latin palaeography at the Pontifical Institute of Medieval Studies (PIMS), Toronto. That initial move to Canada was to determine the shape of the following twenty-five years, for in 1966 he acceded to a full chair at the same institute. He was to reside at Toronto, though making numerous journeys to libraries and visits to conferences, up to the time of his appointment in 1984 as prefect of the Vatican Library. He was the recipient of a long series of distinctions and awards, including many honorary degrees.[3] Leonard Boyle combined academic training and activity in Europe (Oxford, Rome) and North America (principally Toronto) in a way that bridged Old World and New World interests and approaches to scholarship. This intellectual straddling of the two continents recalls the great figure of Étienne Gilson, the Paris-based founder of PIMS. The effort involved in crossing and recrossing the Atlantic, moving from Rome to Toronto and back again, enriched his work as it marked his conversation, so rich in anecdotes and personalities. His early Dominican training in philosophical and theological ideas combined with the overlay of the historian's formation to make him an intellectual historian of exceptional breadth.

Father Leonard died in his sleep on October 25, 1999. With the special permission of the Ministry of Culture in Rome his remains were buried in the crypt of San Clemente, where he had spent much time as a younger man pursuing his hobby of archaeology in the neighborhood of the burial place of St. Cyril, which he had himself helped to rediscover.[4]

Something deserves to be said here concerning the central preoccupation of Father Boyle's scholarly life and the nature of his own most characteristic contribution to historical scholarship.[5]

The Pastoralia of the Later Middle Ages

Many twentieth-century scholars belonging to the Dominican order have pursued research on the early Dominican theologians and philosophers. Father Leonard's path in scholarship was as distinguished as any in that line of scholars that began with Pierre Mandonnet, O.P. (1858–1936), in the early years of the twentieth century. It was, on the other hand, a quite individual path. The truth is that Leonard discovered his own path, or rather that he created it, clearing the growth in front of him as he followed new interests.

Father Leonard was mindful that the order of Dominicans was formed as an order of preachers, not of professors, and that the professors were there only because there were priests to be trained as preachers for their evangelical mission. He pursued medievalist reading in many unreputed byways: treatises on preaching and on the sacrament of confession, classifications of the virtues and vices, and guides for the preparation of conscience. In short, Leonard founded a new discipline within medieval studies, one currently referred to as medieval pastoral theology. At the present time many of the most distinguished researchers concerned with the popular literature of the cure of souls, or *pastoralia,* are Leonard's own former pupils, mostly situated in North America.

I have mentioned the genre of *pastoralia.* In the formation of those almost-forgotten literary forms, which Father Boyle rediscovered, the year 1215 has an importance both symbolical and real. That was the year of the Fourth Lateran Council. The assembled fathers declared that the guidance of souls *(regimen animarum)* was the art of arts. Pastoral care was thenceforth to be regarded as a skill or "art" that could be taught and learned by clerics in the schools. In the years and the generations that followed, a distinctive type of didactic literature emerged that had a generic unity, due to its purpose, but that developed in many directions.[6] It was meant to educate pastors and to prepare them to teach their people by word (in preaching and in administering the sacraments) and by example (in living an exemplary life). This literature of pastoral care drew upon a long tradition of Christian writings reaching back to the Pauline and apostolic letters of the New Testament. By the thirteenth century, however, pastoral texts were being written and copied in some profusion, in the vernacular languages as well as in Latin.[7] Not just bishops and learned monks but every priest charged with the care of souls was expected to learn the techniques of pastoral care. The literature collectively referred to as *pastoralia* introduced new methods and new materials in order to make accessible to every priest some written instruction in the *cura animarum.* Thousands of these texts conveying the basic skills required for pastoral care were composed, in Latin and the vernacular languages, between 1200 and the end of the Middle Ages; up to the present time only a fraction of the surviving material has been edited or received proper study. The pioneering research in this new field of inquiry was that conducted by Father Boyle.[8]

The Genesis of the Summa

We come now to the parallel between Leonard Boyle's work and that of Alasdair MacIntyre. The former's explorations of the abundant pastoral, preaching, penitential, and confessional literature of the later Middle Ages led him to formulate a fresh and original proposition regarding the genesis and shape of the *Summa Theologiae,* that unfinished masterpiece of Aquinas.[9] He came to regard the *Pars Secunda Secundae* as what might be called the genetic core of the entire enterprise. This would have surprised the many who placed the emphasis in the traditional manner upon the *Prima Pars* containing the questions on God, the creation, and anthropology, or on the *Prima Secundae,* with its treatises on happiness, human agency, the passions and virtues, natural law, and so on. Boyle saw in the discussion of the virtues and vices contained in the *Secunda Secundae* the apogee of three generations of aspiration on the part of European moralists, both Dominicans and secular clergymen. That part of the *Summa* is, he suggested, the most complete and systematic product of the efforts expended by numerous scholars since the time of Peter the Chanter (ca. 1200) to encompass in thought the moral life in its most salient features.[10] The *Summa* was dedicated to *incipientes*, to the puzzlement of generations of its readers who wondered just what a youngster just starting theology might be expected to make of that imposing edifice, but Boyle showed that the "beginners" in question were already-ordained priests making the immediate preparation for their professional life as preachers. The dogmatic elements making up much of the *Summa* (roughly, God, the Creation, the Fall, the Redemption, and the sacraments) were intended, Boyle was convinced, to provide a comprehensive framework for the moral discussions of the *Secunda Pars,* which deserved to have as its setting the widest theological and philosophical perspectives available. In this way Thomas planned to right an imbalance he perceived to exist within Dominican professional studies. The formation given within the order favored practical or moral theology, whereas Thomas wanted to place the latter within the setting supplied by what later ages would term dogmatic theology. At the same time he proposed another novelty within the Dominican school, which was the employment of the Aristotelian philosophy of the passions and the virtues within a Christian framework, wherein the theological virtues were united with the cardinal virtues.

Boyle brought out the originality of the *Secunda Pars* by contrasting it with two distinguished Dominican predecessors, the *Summa de Casibus* of Raymund of Penafort and the *Summa de Vitiis et Virtutibus* of William Payraut (Perraldus). Aquinas must have been acutely conscious of these distinguished works by his seniors in the order, even as he was deciding to go his own way; in the prologue to the *Secunda Secundae*, which was to be his own *Summa de Virtutibus et Vitiis,* he remarks: "It is more expeditious by far to take in turn each virtue with its corresponding gift, the vices opposed to it, and the appropriate precepts, than to take each virtue, gift, vice and precept in isolation, for the latter course begets much repetition."[11] As he also says, the course he himself adopts neatly includes all moral matter under the seven great virtues. Boyle detected in these remarks "an oblique apology for abandoning the scheme in Peraldus's *Summa*,"[12] but the claims Aquinas makes are surely closer to being a criticism of the reigning anarchy within the *studia* of the order, as moral studies were pursued either anecdotally, by discussing *casus* (Raymund), or without any organicity, taking the virtues, vices, gifts, and beatitudes in turn, each for itself (William). Thomas was firm in his intent: the best procedure would be to devote a discussion to "each virtue, the gift corresponding to it, and the vices opposed to it." In this way "the whole of moral matter is placed in the context of the virtues; nothing in morals will be overlooked."[13] In the same study Leonard Boyle showed that the *Secunda Secundae* was the most popular part of the entire *Summa*, which was itself the most widely circulated of Thomas's writings. Of approximately six hundred manuscripts examined that witness the text of one part of the *Summa* on its own, the *Secunda Secundae* accounts for 37 percent.[14]

The effect of these novel conclusions was to place the virtue theory of Aquinas in the limelight and to exhibit that part of the *Summa* as the apex of Aquinas's intellectual enterprise in its entirety. This was a bold piece of revisionism conducted by a master of intellectual history, and it was destined to have an impact upon moral theology—an impact that can still be felt thirty years later.

I should explain that while I have dwelt in the foregoing upon Boyle's rediscovery of *pastoralia,* his contributions to related fields of study were scarcely less remarkable. The former accomplishment by itself would not have led to his appointment as prefect of the Vatican Library. The fact is that through pursuing research on a vast quantity of material, little of which was in print, Boyle became an acknowledged expert on medieval handwriting. At the beginning of his researches in the Vatican Library he may have regarded palaeography as simply a tool; but forty years of its use made him one of the leading exponents of the art. His expertise regarding all aspects of medieval book production, from the material side (regarding parchment, paper, quills and ink, and bookbinding), up to the mental exercise involved in explicating abbreviated script and deciding upon the best copy of a work, won him the acclaim of every scholar in the field. This side of his activity was crowned by the publication of his survey of Latin palaeography, a work of his scholarship that he placed at the service of all advanced students of the subject.[15]

The narrative of Boyle's achievements as prefect of the Vatican Apostolic Library cannot be recounted here, even if I were capable of it. Visitors to the library during his tenure of office noted the improved level of service to scholars. He himself led a guided tour every week. He attracted substantial funding to initiate the cataloguing of the huge archives, a work that will go on for many years to come. During these fourteen years he somehow found the time to travel and lecture. He seemed to find it difficult to say no to any request made of him. No less than five volumes of tribute have been published in his honor, though he did not live to see them all appear.[16] It goes without saying that very few scholars indeed are honored on a comparable scale by colleagues and former pupils writing for them in French, German, Italian, and Spanish, as well as English.

Servais-Théodore Pinckaers

Virtue Ethics

The thought of the late Professor Pinckaers is less well known in the English-language world than it should be, for he was for many years one of the most significant and well-published theologians working in the international context of ethics or moral theology. More to the point for our present concerns, his thought meets that of MacIntyre in some respects, notably in their common concern for the theory of virtue.[17]

The following rough categorization of virtue ethics would fit equally the thought of both MacIntyre and Pinckaers without any straining: When it comes to good behavior nothing better than virtue can be discovered; there are no shortcuts to it, nor is there any complete perfection to be had; it is the education of the passions according to reason; virtue is acquired through upbringing/education and personal effort; the virtues, in particular the classical cardinal virtues (prudence, justice, fortitude, and temperance), give rational shape to our various feelings and are conducive to happiness; justice enables us to relate properly to other people and lays the ethical basis for life in society; the human being is inherently sociable, and the human good is realized through virtuous action in full awareness of the common good and hence in community, where the strengths of mind and intellect can best be developed.

Our two thinkers, the philosopher and the theologian, may differ somewhat in emphasis and have different interlocutors, but they have a great deal in common. Pinckaers was in fact thoroughly conversant with the work being done by MacIntyre. It is relevant in the present context to note that the reverse is also true: in the 1980s and 1990s MacIntyre was very conscious of the impact being made by Pinckaers, and the two corresponded with each other, though they never actually met. In fact MacIntyre contributed a preface to the English translations of one of Pinckaers's books.[18]

Life

Père Servais-Théodore Pinckaers died in Fribourg (Switzerland) on April 7, 2008, at the age of eighty-two.[19] Born in the principality of Liège in Belgium in 1925, he entered the Dominican order in 1945 and pursued his studies in theology at the *studium* of La Sarte (Huy), where he obtained the License in Theology (1952). He pursued the study of theology at the Angelicum University (Rome), and upon the completion of his doctorate (which was devoted to the virtue of hope) he returned to La Sarte to teach moral theology. In 1967 the studium was closed and Pinckaers was appointed to the Dominican priory at his native Liège, where he was to engage in pastoral work, including much preaching and retreat giving. He was called in 1973 to fill the French-language chair in fundamental moral theology at the Université de Fribourg, where he lectured until his retirement in 1998. Always a productive researcher, and, one may well say, a prolific writer, he did not slacken his pace during his years as emeritus but remained at work at Fribourg in the university atmosphere. Not long before his death he published a significant work, *Plaidoyer pour la vertu* (2007), and a posthumous book called *Passions et vertu* appeared early in 2009.[20]

Servais Pinckaers did not travel a great deal compared to many academics of his generation, but in the year of his retirement he accepted an invitation to Ireland to deliver a lecture at the Pontifical University Maynooth.[21] He was the author of many books, of which only a few items of central importance for our focus will be mentioned here, a survey of English translations of his oeuvre being already available.[22] A bibliography of his writings and translations of them, complete up to 2004, has appeared.[23] He was also an assiduous exegete of Scripture; two of his books exemplify in a particular way this attainment of his, one on the Passion according to St. Matthew (1997) and the other on the Our Father (1999).[24] His scriptural scholarship is markedly present throughout the corpus of his writings and may be observed to advantage in his New Testament exegesis, Pauline in particular.[25]

Reception of MacIntyre's Trilogy

Hidden away in the published bibliography of Pinckaers is a tiny detail within his oeuvre, but one that, as it turns out, throws light upon this theologian's personal reception of the thought of Alasdair MacIntyre, namely his lengthy review of *After Virtue,* published in the *Revue Thomiste* in 1986.[26] It is worthwhile from our present perspective to open these pages that so conveniently interrelate the two moralists, the theologian on the one hand and the philosopher on the other. The review opens by underlining the value of *After Virtue (AV)* for theologians while acknowledging that it is a piece of strictly philosophical research. The work is notable for the exceptional role accorded in it to historical research, conducted with the philosophical aim of going behind modern perspectives to a forgotten state of ethical thought in its systematic, Aristotelian origins. Following a summary of the contents of *AV,* four principal points of assessment are set out, personal reactions to a book the quality of which is such as "to lift the heart of the moral theologian."

> The first feature is the new and radical value attached in *AV* to the idea of virtue. The latter is drawn right into the middle of contemporary debates, and this in North America, which is at the forefront of technological progress while at the same time being particularly conscious of contemporary ethical problems:
>
> > Virtue, completely devalued by the modern systems and confused with obedience to laws and obligations, arises in this book with new vigor, as a challenge and a hope, amid the confusion and disarray of ethical ideas.

Virtue is presented as the human quality *par excellence*, coming to the aid of humankind in the world of the machine.

Second, the reviewer underlines the strength of MacIntyre's presentation, particularly in its unfolding of "a historical dimension too often neglected by theoreticians of ethics both theological and philosophical." The highlighting of Aristotle's ethical positions in *AV* is just and right; indeed, Pinckaers suggests, it might be accorded a kind of confirmation by means of a parallel study in theology: "For the virtue ethics worked out by St. Thomas [Aquinas] with the help of Aristotle there was substituted in modern times an ethic of obligation constructed on the basis of the Decalogue, understood too narrowly as the codification of the fundamental obligations. Following that, virtue died and became atrophied, in theology just as in philosophy." The debate being initiated by *AV*, the reviewer maintains, may prove to be of decisive importance. The perspectives opened up by the book enable the widening and deepening of the concrete ethical problems being discussed at the time of its publication and lend encouragement to the overcoming of the too-technical and rather casuistical approach that is the dominant one. Only the virtues can make us capable of arriving at an adequate moral judgment upon our actions, while placing the latter within the broad, unifying perspective of a finality capable of embracing the whole of a human life.

Third, the reviewer is convinced that the historical inquiry so central to *AV* can usefully be completed by a theological appraisal of ethical positions taken up already in the Middle Ages. The historical origins of that modern individualism that is the target of *AV* are to be sought in late medieval nominalism, long before the Enlightenment, and the various traits that are picked out in *AV* as characterizing modernity in ethical theory can be detected already in the fourteenth century: voluntarism; the atomization of moral action; the erasure of finality; and concentration on the idea of obligation and the commandments: "It seems to us that the breaking point between virtue ethics and ethics based on obligation is to be sought in the early fourteenth-century confrontation between Ockham and St. Thomas regarding the definition of liberty: liberty of indifference for one, liberty of quality for the other." Thus history can offer its own confirmation, Pinckaers considers, of the systematic reflection conducted in *AV*.

The last of the four "assessment points" concerns the place awarded in *AV* to the moral thought of Aquinas, a place considered by the reviewer to be too much on the margins. He contends that in *AV* the systematic power of Aquinas is regarded as a sort of cramp upon the variety of the virtues. Aquinas, however, is one of the major reference points in the history of moral thinking, as well as being a great interpreter of Aristotle and the Christian fathers. The reproach of being oversystematic, moreover, stands in some contrast to the overall scheme of *AV,* Pinckaers thought. Aquinas's work is surely the masterpiece of virtue ethics, and more even than that, it contains a series of penetrating analyses of all the other elements making up the moral universe in which virtue occupies the highest place. Thomas was able to make a unity of the whole diversity found in the tradition of Greco-Latin moral thinking; there is no reason to fear that his thought would prove to be a hindrance to the diversity one encounters in life.

The final point made by the reviewer concerns the narrative character of ethics. He does not disagree with MacIntyre's position but proposes a nuance concerning "the difference there is between an ordinary narration and history shaped by virtue: the narration recounts history already made, whereas virtue makes history and hence makes up what one might call a constructive word or narration. Thus moral knowledge is of a specific kind, differing from positive historical knowledge and from poetic storytelling: it is dynamic and prescriptive." The review concludes with a warm and admiring tribute to *AV* as a work of power, even revolutionary power—a truly courageous achievement on the part of its author and one that, beginning from a modest hope, could lead to a renaissance of virtue.

Pinckaers was to return to MacIntyre's thought ten years later in an article to which some attention must be devoted at a later stage.[27] Before we turn to that we must illustrate the impact that *AV* continued to make on his published work.

Some quite central, personal, and long-held convictions of Servais Pinckaers himself make their appearance in his review of *AV*. Moral obligation does not have the first or the last word in ethics but must be located in a secondary category when compared to virtue; in short, it is the various virtues that give rise to those obligations on the part of an individual to act justly, to exercise practical wisdom, and so on. The central place accorded in the moral theology of modern times to obligation, and as an inevitable consequence of that to casuistry, derived ultimately from the Ockhamist conception of truest freedom as being the freedom of indifference (aptly illustrated by Buridan's ass, a creature forever poised in indifference between two similar bales of hay). Where obligation, deriving ultimately from the divine lawgiver, is thought to set the fundamental ethical parameters, freedom will all too easily be conceived in binary mode, as the freedom to act or not to act, to obey or not to obey, to A or not-A, in abstraction from any natural inclination toward something apprehended as good or as true, and hence an object of attraction. At its worst and lowest, intellectually speaking, the notion of a liberty of indifference takes the form of the question "Why be moral?" In the obligation scheme, virtue and the virtues can be accorded only a lowly place, as habits for instance; but virtue is not a habit, Pinckaers insisted![28] A Thomistic account of freedom emphasizes its inner relationship to virtue and finality, to the attraction of the good, and to the realization of that happiness in which virtue is not a means to some extrinsic end but the establishment of the individual's finality within actual and continuing moral agency, of the kind that builds up good character.

In a postscript appended to his review Père Pinckaers signals to the reader that the second (1984) edition of *AV* has arrived on his desk, but too late to be reviewed. He notes the addition of a chapter of replies by MacIntyre to his critics. Against criticisms coming from a Kantian direction MacIntyre maintains (the reviewer reports) that the various moral systems all have to be put back into their historical context, and that there are no moral principles of a universal a priori kind; the acceptable ethical system will be the one that emerges as best capable of answering the difficulties raised by its critics. And that is Aristotelian virtue ethics.

Pinckaers himself advances some lines of criticism regarding the positions adopted by MacIntyre:

> There is no moral speculation without a history, nor a history without bringing in moral principles. But the conjunction between speculation and history comes about more profoundly than the author shows, at the level of the very genesis of the thought and its logical outworking that is at play in the systematisation. Furthermore, where ethics is concerned history itself demands, more perhaps than is stated [in *AV*], that certain fundamental (we would say natural and spiritual) principles be uncovered,

which have shaped human history and govern it. In the lack of these principles the historical consideration draws ethics onto the slope of relativism—as a second series of critics has remarked. In a third, brief set [of responses] the author acknowledges the need to discuss, at greater length and better than he has done it [in 1981], the question of the meeting between the religion of the Bible, centered upon the divine law, and the Aristotelian virtue ethics, [a meeting] to which St. Thomas gave a classical answer.

The review concludes with the words, "*After Virtue* réclame donc une suite" (So, *After Virtue* cries out for a follow-up).

That *After Virtue* came to occupy a niche of its own in Pinckaers's awareness of contemporary moral theory is evident from the references to it that dot his writings subsequently to his review of the book. It encouraged him to believe, for instance, that the "virtue-based moral system of St. Thomas" had a future, presaged by *AV* and the discussion to which it gave rise.[29] In 1996, for instance, he was conscious of the "widespread discussion" about virtue, taking place especially in the United States and being led by MacIntyre.[30] By the year 1993 Pinckaers had read the trilogy of MacIntyre and was referring to *Whose Justice? Which Rationality?* (1988) and *Three Versions of Moral Enquiry* (1990). In an essay on conscience (1993) he notes with satisfaction that "in the United States people have progressed in rediscovering the importance of virtue, a philosophical ethic, notably in the Aristotelian tradition. Obviously, I am alluding to the works of Alasdair MacIntyre," but he feels bound to add, "In Europe, we have not come so far."[31]

In his later study of MacIntyre's ethical theory Pinckaers identifies for a largely continental readership the two poles of the moralist's thought: "the critique of the liberal rationalism inherited from the Enlightenment for its failure in ethics and its internal contradictions; and the promotion of a philosophical reflection rooted in a historical tradition and a community."[32] Much of the article serves as an introduction to MacIntyre's oeuvre up to the 1990s. At the time of Pinckaers's writing only the second work of the trilogy *(Whose Justice? Which Rationality?)* had appeared in French translation, so that francophone readers still required this sort of survey that situated MacIntyre's project with reference to its leading rivals, Kantian deontology and utilitarianism. In his account of MacIntyre's development Pinckaers concentrates upon *Three Rival Versions* and its highlighting of Thomistic ethics. He picks out as particularly worthy of note MacIntyre's critique of the contemporary liberal university and his dream of future educational reform. But it must be the concluding reflections that retain our interest here rather than the summary account given by the Dominican moralist of a moral philosophy he clearly admired.

Pinckaers was particularly struck by the capacity shown by MacIntyre to enter "systemically" into a thought, or a historical period of thinking. The entire opposite of a casuist, MacIntyre grasped the systemic dimension of each moral theory, its rootedness in a history or society, or even in a particular university setting. He had described Western thought as a succession of rational systems coexisting as rival traditions. His vigorous and nuanced rational argumentation resulted in penetrating analyses of the rival systems. His dialectical capacity furthermore led him through factual acceptance of contemporary pluralism, and beyond any temptation to resignation before that situation, toward a philosophical confrontation with the fundamental problems underlying the various intellectual divisions. Both the style of moral thinking and the character of the discussion that MacIntyre promoted within the contemporary university reminded Pinckaers of the practice of Aquinas in his own university context: "The scholastic research method practised in the university of the thirteenth century: firstly the 'lectio' of great texts, sources of knowledge and carriers of a rich intellectual tradition; after that the 'disputatio,' meaning by that a dialectical discussion with the contrary views, through the public exercise that was the disputed question; finally, the development of those vast syntheses, the *summae*."[33] At the level of ethical research MacIntyre invited all who would engage with his thought to revise completely the ethical inheritance left by the Encyclopedists and the liberal thinkers, which was still dominant despite its failures and contradictions. Pinckaers reminded his reader that MacIntyre saw in virtue a quality that is first of all acquired by upbringing; it enables one to reach a correct appreciation of the various goods one encounters; it is the condition for just reasoning and for the exercise of prudent rationality in one's judgments; in political society virtue takes principally the form of justice, that will "render to each one what is due," according to a right estimation of the good, where the estimation is arrived at while taking account of the common good.

This idea of virtue presupposes (though without taking for granted) a conception of the human being as sociable or naturally inclined to live in society, including the intellectual and moral levels of social existence. Pinckaers insists that man is not morally undifferentiated;[34] rather, he is moved from within by an aspiration to the good at a more profound level than that which mere self-interest would dictate. A society animated by the virtue of justice is not the artificial creation of some consensus (as social contract theorists of all varieties would have it); its natural, human base is developed in different ways by legislation that regulates civil life as an expression of justice and the other virtues. In this (MacIntyre's) outlook the end of law is the education-in-virtue of the citizens, their progress in the sense of justice, and the development of friendship among them all. The ethics just sketched is the philosophy of virtue and sociability that Thomas Aquinas took over largely from Aristotle, seeing in the Christian dimension of the virtues centered upon charity a kind of higher justice and friendship that surpass all ordinary human expectation.

The serious nature of the questions raised by MacIntyre and their evident contemporary relevance, concluded Pinckaers, merit the attention of the francophone and predominantly theological readership for whom he himself was writing. He was to return on more than one occasion to the desirability, in the case of moral theologians, of a philosophical formation *à la* MacIntyre.

"Casuistry"

Starting early in his theological career Servais Pinckaers set out a far-reaching criticism of the predominant moral theology, which was, he argued vigorously, based more upon obligation and duty than upon virtue. To characterize this tendency he employed the term *casuistry*. His critique of it will lead us toward a deepened appreciation of aspects of his own contribution to moral theology.

The predominant tendency of moral theologians during the modern period (between, roughly, the Renaissance and the twentieth century) was to derive duty or obligation directly from the command of the divine lawgiver and to regard the role of conscience ("practical reasoning") as being that of presenting the law to the moral subject. Morality was thought of as being largely the task of determining in a particular case *(casus)* how the obligation in question (e.g., "Thou shalt not steal," or any other of the Decalogue Commandments) was to be met, according to the dispositions and circumstances of the particular individual concerned. The role attributed to free will was that of choosing between contraries, namely, to follow or not to follow the precept formulated by conscience. Law and obligation were considered to be the most salient connection between the will of the divine legislator and the human will. Freedom was considered a reality only to the extent that choice between alternatives (virtue or sin) was offered, and that choice might in reality go this way or that. On the next occasion, of course, it might well go the way opposite to the choice implemented immediately previously. The moral life was viewed as a multitude of successive acts separated from each other by the initiative of free will. In this scheme virtue was regarded as the (good) habit of obedience to precept, and it enjoyed a role subsidiary to that of the latter. This scheme of things was analyzed and criticized by Servais Pinckaers from the beginning of his career under the heading of "casuistry"; he traced the origins of this dominant framework back to William of Ockham and learnedly followed its development through the centuries in both Catholic and secular culture.[35]

At the risk of reducing his thought to a formula, we might suggest that for most of the moralists of the modern period, in Pinckaers's estimate, the traditional claims that we are free only to do the good and that we are free only while pursuing and doing the good are strictly paradoxical, whereas they belonged to the moral common sense of Platonists, Aristotelians, Augustinians, and Thomists.

The Spirit of the Moralist

The critique of the broad current of what Pinckaers called casuistry might look like a work of demolition, as though Pinckaers were aiming at expunging three or more centuries of moral theology, and moral philosophy also, wiping out in fact the entire modern period. His point of view was, however, nuanced by his intimate knowledge of the history of his subject throughout the twenty centuries of Christianity. He kept replacing his critique in the context of the various periods of history, including the history of philosophy. And he insisted that casuistry in its Catholic form was essentially an attempt to defend ethical and religious values in the presence of a notion of liberty that placed a question mark over everything. These traditional values, present in germ from the earliest period and developed in patristic and medieval times, were tied up with casuistic theories that were meant to defend them but in fact betrayed them. In particular, the notion of liberty of indifference, instead of being accepted by Catholic moralists as a fundamental postulate of the reason, should have been submitted to proper philosophical criticism. But how did Pinckaers regard the critical dimension of his own thought? In his own words:

> It is not a work of demolition that we want to carry out but one of restoration, a bit like the work carried out on ancient Gothic or Romanesque churches with a view to ridding them of additions, themselves of doubtful artistic value, which have accumulated over the later centuries, and to restoring the older style in its purity, truth and vigor. The term *restoration* moreover is subject to a misunderstanding. There can be no question today of returning to the Middle Ages, or of doing neo-Gothic in ethics. It is more a matter of renewing a dialogue with one of the strongest and most authentic forms of theological thinking—a dialogue that is indispensable if we are to find solid foundations on which to build, today, an ethics that would be Christian, theological, and modern all at once.[36]

The moralist should learn not to be dragged along by the towrope of the kind of liberty that claims it has created all moral values when in fact it has itself been the agent of their corruption. If our liberty is to become authentic, liberty itself needs to be set free both from the casuistic idea of law and precept and from the dangerous illusion that is its dialectical opposite; both of these are betrayals. Human freedom, in other words, needs to recognize its own deep orientation toward happiness and its own inherent capacity for just and virtuous action, and moral theory should begin within that matrix.

Beatitude and Friendship: Conjoint Principles

In interpreting Aquinas's theological morality Pinckaers gave first place to happiness; perhaps it would be better for us to speak of "beatitude," since (he insisted) the foundation of Thomistic moral theory is the Beatitudes of the Gospel. Just as Aquinas returned throughout his life to *beatitudo*, always refining the thought that would achieve its final form in the *Summa*, so Servais Pinckaers discussed the theme in numerous contexts and in a wide range of publications.[37] Better perhaps than any other interpreter of Aquinas, he perceived the way in which the building blocks of the moral sections of the *Summa* were fitted together. The Beatitudes, the theological and moral virtues (and the vices), the theory of human action and choice, and the gifts of the Spirit all go into the theory and are fitted together in its architecture: "Thomas puts into our hands all the elements needed to describe Christian happiness in this life. Happiness issues from the exercise of the virtues animated by charity, the 'heart of perfection,' under the inspiration of the gifts which cause us to act with excellence and render us docile to the Holy Spirit. Thus, through the virtues and gifts the most finished spiritual work is achieved, the fulfillment of the Beatitudes. It is like a fruit which has come to full maturity."[38] The relationship of each virtue to one of the gifts, and of that gift to the Beatitude that corresponds to it, is, Pinckaers observed, the structural principle of the *Secunda Secundae*.[39]

Pinckaers became convinced that beatitude and friendship should be regarded as the conjoint bases of Thomistic moral theory.[40] This conviction grew within him over many years, from the level of a hypothesis to that of a theory.[41] Its formulation sets him quite apart from other interpreters of St. Thomas's thought. In the present context we can only indicate briefly the importance, and indeed the originality, of this perspective.

When Thomas employed the idea of *amicitia* to define the principal Christian virtue, charity, he did something that was as audacious as it was original. The ideal of beatitude needed a complement if it was to be purely itself, and not to be dragged down to the level of satisfaction, desire, and self-interest in a way that would inevitably render it totally incompatible with charity, which "does not seek its own interest" (1 Cor. 13:5). The idea of beatitude needs to be intimately related to the ideas of generosity and disinterestedness, or else the Thomistic house will fall. In that case moral theory would be forced to look to law, precept, and obligation as the principles alone capable of countering egoism. But love that is characterized principally by friendship is able to open itself spiritually to the other and to love the other for his or her own sake, that is to say disinterestedly. In loving others for their own sakes and in recognizing them as subjects like oneself and worthy of friendship, one achieves one's own good by entering into a spiritual communion of persons and cocreating a community. Friendship transcends the satisfaction of need or desire, and self-interest generally. It does not oppose, as in a contest, the interest of one to that of the other but is essentially a love for the other for that other's own sake (i.e., as an end), and it takes into itself the good that is that other and enjoys it in an interpersonal communion on the spiritual plane. "Friendship is personal, for it is born of the person, is addressed to a person, and realizes a community of a personal kind," Pinckaers maintained: "No one can be reproached for wanting the generosity and disinterestedness that allow access to friendship."[42] Thus it turns out to have a general moral value: the moral good is what deserves to be loved for itself and that, through the love one grants it, realizes the perfection of the one who loves it: "The good consists, then, in both identity and distinction, that is to say in the community between the perfections of the one who is loved and the one who loves."[43]

Pinckaers and the Catechism of the Catholic Church

The international team charged with composing the postconciliar *Catechism of the Catholic Church* (1992) included Père Pinckaers, who made his contribution to the moral section (which is the third of the four into which the material is divided, the others being on the Creed, the sacraments, and prayer).[44] It is by the nature of the case always difficult to discern with any certitude the contribution made by an individual to an official document of the church. That the moral part of the *Catechism* bears the influence of Pinckaers in both structure and content appears to be beyond doubt. As one observer (Michael Sherwin, O.P., preaching at the Requiem Mass for his predecessor) has put it, "He would not like it to be said that he wrote this section, but we can point out at least that convergences on the levels of structure and of the quotations employed go beyond what chance would allow." It is to one of those remarkable convergences that we wish to draw attention, namely the respective places of virtue and law.

When we turn to the *Catechism*, part 3 ("Life in Christ"), we find, without going into detail, a schema that accords closely with the thought of Pinckaers himself. The first of three sections ("Man's Vocation: Life in the Spirit") discusses beatitude and the Beatitudes, then the themes of freedom, morality, the passions, and conscience, before introducing the virtues. Virtue is defined: "The human virtues are firm attitudes, stable dispositions, habitual perfections of intellect and will that govern our actions, order our passions and guide our conduct according to reason and faith. They make possible ease, self-mastery and joy in leading a morally good life" (§ 1804). Each of the four cardinal virtues (prudence, justice, fortitude, and temperance) is discussed, followed by the three theological virtues (faith, hope, and charity). Next come the gifts of the Holy Spirit (§ 1831, cf. Isaiah 11:1–2) and the fruit(s) of the Spirit (Gal. 5:22–23). When the Decalogue is discussed (§§ 2052–2550), each commandment is located in the context of the New Law and Covenant, and the virtues.

This scheme bears a clear relationship to the moral thought of St. Thomas Aquinas. His central preoccupation lay with discerning the quality of the human action, and the shaping of the best action in the given conditions of the acting subject. The virtues play the principal role in morality by strengthening the natural inclinations toward the good and beatitude. They aim at producing in action the mature fruit of the moral life. The principal virtue is charity, whose inner law is the aspiration to the perfection of love expressed in the evangelical Beatitudes. It is at this point that the gifts of the Holy Spirit come in to complete the virtues; these gifts help one toward acting perfectly, in dependence upon the Spirit of God. Within this framework the commandments are at the service of the virtues. In their negative formulations, in particular, they define the principal preconditions of virtuous action; respecting them provides one with some protection against moral illusions and temptations. The commandments function like signposts marking byways that would lead toward moral perdition. As prohibitions they are sharp moral indicators of failing aspiration or power, due to the waning of freedom. The commandments are an essential part of Christian teaching, but they need to be related to the virtues if they are to yield their true meaning.[45]

The shape that the *Catechism* takes when it gives instruction on the living of the Christian life bears a clear likeness to the moral thinking of Aquinas and owes to him its deepest debt. One might say at the same time that the schema put forward within the *Catechism* is congruent with the moral theology and spirituality of Père Pinckaers, who in his time was perhaps the leading exegete of the *Secunda Pars* of the *Summa*. He himself has commented that the *Catechism* lends firm support to the Decalogue, elucidating the various commandments in terms of their relationship to the virtues.[46]

Ethical and Theological Challenges

It might seem to the student of both these writers that a theologian like Pinckaers, namely one who placed the virtues (theological and cardinal) at the center of moral theology, would have an inherently less demanding task than the philosopher, Alasdair MacIntyre, because of the difference between their intellectual situations: namely the largely Catholic readership of the former and the very wide, and always potentially critical, readership of the latter, working as he has done in a milieu that is without brackets. On the one hand the theologian, especially the Catholic theologian, makes a contribution within a tradition many centuries old by drawing from it elements of faith and belief, historical consciousness, exemplarity and inspiration. For the philosopher on the other hand there is less of what might appear to be a "comfort zone," for his or her work is done in the full gaze of the secular academic world, in which reactions may range from those of fellow travelers to those of sometimes hostile critics. Servais Pinckaers worked in a religious and Catholic milieu all his life. It might be said that in his published oeuvre he took little account of what MacIntyre has termed "rival versions of moral enquiry" and that his own professional situation was relatively sheltered. Clearly he was not pushed, in the way that MacIntyre was, to search within the Aristotelian-Thomistic tradition, of which he himself was a part, for help with the epistemological issues raised by the coexistence of competing and mutually exclusive outlooks, religious and secular.

Pinckaers, however, faced a different challenge: to identify the wellsprings of the tradition within which he worked and to evolve a strategy for the organic articulation of the differing strands composing it. It is for this reason that his major work (as many would judge it to be), *The Sources of Christian Ethics,* was devoted to the identification of the various streams that make up the flowing waters of Catholic moral theology. This hermeneutical task did not come out of nowhere, and it came accompanied by a leitmotif that was inherently sympathetic to it. Pinckaers was seeking to apply the rich cultural and scholarly resources available today to the task of identifying through historical inquiry (one not unlike MacIntyre's own inquiry, as Pinckaers acknowledged) the different elements that should, or even must, find their place within a contemporary

Catholic moral theology having a solid traditional basis and being worked out in deliberate faithfulness to the magisterium of the church.

I would like to conclude this survey of the moral thought of Père Pinckaers with several *pensées* of his regarding virtue, chosen from his book *Plaidoyer pour la vertu* (2007). In it he writes, not specifically as a commentator on Aquinas or an exegete of Scripture, but as a theologian addressing himself to a wide public and using his own voice. His writing would be classified by many today as a form of spirituality, but of course he himself refused to separate moral theology as a science from the theory of human and Christian living often called spirituality.[47] He writes, for example, that "it appears to us indispensable to restore to friendship its value, if an authentic morality of virtue is to be reestablished, one which will surpass the limits of obligations and which will correspond better to the experience of life with the other. It will help at the same time to account for the action of the Holy Spirit in the Christian life through his gifts, his calls, his impulses that place us in relationship to Him, in the mode of liberty."[48] Similarly, he asserts that "virtue is a *habitus* of invention. You might say that there is a certain genius in it, one which is available to everyone, and which fixes upon the action to be constructed. Genius usually relies upon mastery of an expertise; the moral genius presides over the formation of the expertise in being human which is what the virtues teach us"; further, "Suffering accompanies virtue. The latter shapes itself in a constant effort by an oft-repeated victory over laziness, pain and sadness. The learning of virtue includes the experience of suffering which is a multiform experience . . . suffering from being cowardly or intemperate, from having judged wrongly or committed injustice; suffering from being in poor health, physical or moral. Every virtue presupposes a meeting with suffering and reposes upon a struggle to surmount it."[49]

Leonard Boyle and Servais Pinckaers both received their theological formation in studia of the Order of Preachers, the first at Blackfriars, Oxford, and the second at La Sarte. They were taught theology largely on the basis of the Scriptures, church history, and the *Summa Theologiae*. As young students they were accustomed to read the *quaestiones* of the latter and discuss as a group what they had read. This rather timeless approach to theological education admitted them directly into the thought world of Thomas Aquinas and made them aware of his teaching about the virtues, among other aspects of his theology. Boyle's subsequent formation as a historian led him, as we have endeavored to show, to regard the *Pars Secunda Secundae* in a fresh light and to locate its doctrine of the virtues at the very center of Thomas's theological endeavors. This view has proved to be influential during the succeeding decades and down to the present time. It has an evident kinship with the outlook of Alasdair MacIntyre, whose philosophical approach to Aquinas led him to value the holism he identified in his moral thought: "The *Summa* has proved easy enough to domesticate academically in terms other than its own, but to read it in its own terms from within the tradition which Aquinas reconstituted in the course of writing it is the only way to reckon with it in other than mock and distorting encounter."[50] The decades spent by Servais Pinckaers as a professor of moral theology at Fribourg gave him a mastery of his subject and its history broadly comparable to that of MacIntyre in moral philosophy, to the point that their two projects, we have contended, can in significant ways be viewed in parallel, a perspective that throws some light on each of these moralists.

Notes

I wish to thank Julia Hynes for helpful advice, also Hugh O'Neill for useful suggestions and help with the proofs.

1. On Callus's life and writings, see M. F. Montebello, O.P., *Daniel Callus: Historian and Philosopher, 1888–1965* (Malta: Malta University Press, 1994).

2. This eventually bore fruit in the form of a monograph: *A Survey of the Vatican Archives and of Its Medieval Holdings*, Subsidia Mediaevalia 1 (Toronto: PIMS, 1972).

3. Among the latter was the D. Phil. of the Pontifical University, Maynooth (1997). Professor MacIntyre was similarly honored by the Pontifical University (May 19, 2002). A lecture by Father Leonard, "St Thomas Aquinas and the Third Millennium," appears in *Thomas Aquinas: Approaches to Truth. The Aquinas Lectures at Maynooth, 1996–2001*, ed. James McEvoy and Michael Dunne (Dublin: Four Courts, 2002), 38–52.

4. His most widely published work is known to the many pilgrims and tourists who visit the Monastery of San Clemente in Rome, the Irish Dominican

house: *A Short Guide of St Clement's, Rome* (Rome: Collegio San Clemente, 1960) has been bought by generations of visitors to the church and to the unique archaeological site underneath it. It was composed during his early years in Rome; revised in 1989, it has been translated into many languages.

5. A list of Boyle's publications was published with a short biography and tribute by J. Ambrose Raftis, C.S.B., "Leonard E. Boyle, OP (1923–1999)," *Mediaeval Studies* 62 (2000): vii–xxvi.

6. Joseph Goering, a pupil of Boyle, succinctly surveys the "somewhat amorphous" literary genre of pastoral writings in "*Pastoralia:* The Popular Literature of the Care of Souls," in *Medieval Latin: An Introduction and Bibliographical Guide,* ed. F. A. C. Mantello and A. G. Rigg (Washington, DC: Catholic University of America Press, 1996), 670–76 (with selective bibliography).

7. The Latin writings are listed by M. W. Bloomfield, ed., *Incipits of Latin Works on the Virtues and Vices, 1100–1500 AD, Including a Selection of Incipits of Works on the Pater Noster* (Cambridge, MA: Mediaeval Academy of America, 1979).

8. A very readable example of his published research, one article chosen from among many, is "Summae confessorum," in *Les genres littéraires dans les sources théologiques et philosophiques médiévales: Définition, critique et exploitation* (Louvain-La-Neuve: Université catholique de Louvain, 1982), 227–37.

9. Leonard E. Boyle, *The Setting of the Summa Theologiae of Saint Thomas* (Toronto: Pontifical Institute, 1982). This was the fifth Etienne Gilson Lecture at PIMS. It is reprinted with some reworking in *The Ethics of Aquinas,* ed. Stephen J. Pope (Washington, DC: Georgetown University Press, 2002), 1–16.

10. Lombard paid attention to the virtues and shaped much of the subsequent medieval tradition; see Peter Lombard, *The Sentences. Book 3: On the Incarnation of the Word,* trans. Giulio Silano, Mediaeval Studies in Translation 45 (Toronto: PIMS, 2008). See P. W. Rosemann, *Peter Lombard,* Great Medieval Thinkers (Oxford: Oxford University Press, 2004).

11. *ST* IIa IIae, Prologue, quoted in Boyle, "The Setting of the Summa Theologiae of St. Thomas—Revisited," in *The Ethics of Thomas Aquinas,* ed. Stephen J. Pope (Washington, DC: Georgetown University Press, 2002), 10.

12. Ibid., 9.

13. *ST* IIa IIae, Prologue.

14. Boyle, "Setting of the Summa," 11.

15. Leonard E. Boyle, *Mediaeval Latin Palaeography: A Bibliographical Introduction,* Toronto Mediaeval Bibliographies 8 (Toronto: University of Toronto Press, 1984).

16. The first of these was *A Distinct Voice: Medieval Studies in Honor of Leonard E. Boyle, OP,* ed. J. Brown and W. P. Stoneman (Notre Dame: University of Notre Dame Press, 1997).

17. Pinckaers developed his views on virtue through many publications. Perhaps the most succinct (and mature) expression of them is to be found in

Servais Pinckaers, "The Role of Virtue in Moral Theology," in *The Pinckaers Reader: Renewing Thomistic Moral Theology,* ed. John Berkman and Craig S. Titus, trans. Sr. Mary Thomas Noble, O.P., et al. (Washington, DC: Catholic University of America Press, 2005), 288–303, originally published as "Redécouvrir la vertu," *Sapientia* 51 (1996): 151–63.

18. Alasdair MacIntyre, preface to *Morality: The Catholic View,* by Servais Pinckaers (South Bend, IN: St. Augustine's Press, 2001), originally published as *La morale catholique* (Paris: Cerf, 1991).

19. I am indebted to Rev. Prof. Michael Sherwin, O.P., for supplying me with material on the life and publications of his predecessor at the Université de Fribourg (Switzerland), Père Servais Pinckaers, and wish to thank him for his kindness. His eulogy delivered at the funeral of Père Pinckaers (April 10, 2008) has appeared in a recent number of *Nova et Vetera*. He is the director of the Archives Pinckaers at the Albertinum in Fribourg, which contains all of Pinckaers's publications as well as his correspondence and other materials. It is to be hoped that in due course the *Nachlaß* will be published, including the numerous pastoral writings and conferences. For further biographical information on Pinckaers, see Université de Fribourg, Théologie morale fondamentale, Archives Pinckaers, "Biographie," February 14, 2006, www.unifr.ch/tmf/Biographie.

20. Servais Pinckaers, *Plaidoyer pour la vertu* (Paris: Éditions Parole et Silence, 2007), and *Passions et vertu* (Paris: Éditions Parole et Silence, 2009).

21. Servais Pinckaers, "The Desire for Happiness as a Way to God," in *Thomas Aquinas: Approaches to Truth: The Aquinas Lectures at Maynooth, 1996–2001,* ed. James McEvoy and Michael Dunne (Dublin: Four Courts, 2002), 53–65, reprinted with some changes and under a different title ("Beatitude and the Beatitudes in Aquinas's *Summa Theologiae*") in Pinckaers, *Pinckaers Reader,* 115–29. An article by Alasdair MacIntyre is published in the same Dublin 2002 volume: "Truth as a Good: A Reflection on *Fides et Ratio,*" in McEvoy and Dunne, *Thomas Aquinas,* 141–57.

22. Supplied by John Berkman in his introduction to Pinckaers, *Pinckaers Reader,* xi–xxiii.

23. This bibliography can be found in Pinckaers, *Pinckaers Reader,* 397–411.

24. Servais Pinckaers, *Un grand chant d'amour: La passion selon saint Matthieu* (Paris: Parole et Silence, 1997), and *Au coeur de l'Évangile: Le "Notre Père"* (Paris: Parole et Silence, 1999).

25. Servais Pinckaers, *La vie selon l'Esprit: Essai de théologie spirituelle selon saint Paul et saint Thomas d'Aquin* (Luxembourg: Éditions Saint-Paul, 1996).

26. "Recension: *After Virtue: A Study in Moral Theory* (Alasdair MacIntyre)," in *Revue Thomiste* 86 (1986): 137–41. Translations from the French are my own unless otherwise specified.

27. Pinckaers, "Redécouvrir la vertu" (1996).

28. Servais Pinckaers, "La vertu est tout autre chose qu'une habitude," in *Nouvelle Revue Théologique* 82 (April 1960): 387–403; trans. Bernard Gilligan in *Cross Currents* 12 (Winter 1962): 65–81.

29. Servais Pinckaers, "Dominican Moral Theology in the Twentieth Century" [1993], in *Pinckaers Reader*, 85.

30. Pinckaers, "Role of Virtue," 289, 289 n.

31. Servais Pinckaers, "Conscience and Christian Tradition" [1993], in *Pinckaers Reader*, 332 n.

32. Servais Pinckaers, "Alasdair MacIntyre et la morale des vertus," *Nova et Vetera* 71, no. 2 (1996): 77.

33. Ibid., 85.

34. We would be so if the question "Why be moral?" had any sense.

35. The critique in question is a recurrent feature of Pinckaers's writing but is perhaps most explicitly developed in the very influential *The Sources of Christian Ethics,* 3rd ed., trans. Sr. Mary Thomas Noble, O.P. (Edinburgh: T&T Clark, 1995), originally published as *Les sources de la morale chrétienne* (Paris: Éditions du Cerf, 1985); see in particular ch. 14: "Freedom of Indifference: The Origin of Obligational Moral Theory," 327–53.

36. Servais Pinckaers, "Appendice 2," in Thomas d'Aquin, *Somme théologique: Les actes humains, 1a–2ae, qq. 18–21,* new ed., ed. and trans. Servais Pinckaers (Paris: Cerf, 1997), 234–35. Pinckaers of course rejected what he called "the skeletal Aquinas too often taught: the Five Ways and Natural Law."

37. Pinckaers, "Desire for Happiness."

38. Ibid., 61. Like St. Augustine, Pinckaers interrelated the intercessions making up the Pater Noster with the Beatitudes; see Pinckaers, *Au coeur de l'Évangile.*

39. On the practice of the Beatitudes in the light of the virtues and gifts, see ibid., 64–65.

40. In translating *bonheur* as "beatitude" rather than "happiness" we are following the practice of the editors of *The Pinckaers Reader.* "Beatitude" has the value of drawing the attention to Aquinas's understanding of the goal of human life.

41. Its earliest appearance is in Servais Pinckaers, "Der Sinn für die Freundschaftsliebe als Urtatsache der thomistischen Ethik," in *Sein und Ethos: Untersuchungen zur Grundlegung der Ethik,* ed. P. Engelhardt, O.P., Walberberger Studien, Phil. Reihe 1 (Mainz: Grünewald, 1960), 229–35. For its presentation as a theory, see Pinckaers, "Appendice 2."

42. Ibid., 242.

43. Ibid.

44. Servais Pinckaers, *The Catechism of the Catholic Church* (Vatican City: Libreria Editrice Vaticana), 1994.

45. James McEvoy, "The Decalogue in the New Catechism," in *Evangelising for the Third Millennium: The Maynooth Conference on the New Catechism, May 1996,* ed. M. Hogan, S.S.C., and Thomas J. Norris (Dublin: Veritas, 1997), 145–69.

46. Pinckaers, "Role of Virtue," 290.

47. For his views on this subject, see Servais Pinckaers, *La spiritualité du martyre* (Versailles: Éditions St. Paul, 2000).

48. Pinckaers, *Plaidoyer pour la vertu,* 139.

49. Ibid., 100, 259.

50. Alasdair MacIntyre, *Three Rival Versions of Moral Enquiry* (Notre Dame: University of Notre Dame Press, 1990), 135.

CHAPTER ELEVEN

The Perfect Storm
On the Loss of Nature as a Normative Theonomic Principle in Moral Philosophy

STEVEN A. LONG

The title of this essay—"The Perfect Storm"—is perhaps rather an off-putting title for a paper that might be expected to celebrate the positive achievements of Thomistic moral thought in the twentieth century. And in fact the twentieth century saw many positive developments within Thomistic moral theology and philosophy. However, the gravamen of my analysis here is that the confluence of a certain antecedent "problem situation" of Catholic moral reflection with influential currents of thought deriving from the Enlightenment—and found in diverse forms on the continent of Europe and in anglophone thought—conspired in the twentieth century to contradict, obscure, and disrupt the fundamental elements of Thomistic moral thought. This occurred both in the wider intellectual culture and to some degree even within the precincts of Catholic thought among some who think of themselves as broadly Thomistic. While on the one hand the consequent confusions have been deleterious, on the other, the provocation with respect to the actual teaching of St. Thomas Aquinas has midwifed critical and positive responses.

I will first describe the intellectual currents that for a time have threatened to obscure the moral teaching of Aquinas, beginning with the extra-Catholic sources and moving toward the doctrinally intra-Catholic ones. Then in brief conclusion I will acknowledge the manner in which the very omnipresence of these influences has served slowly but surely to elicit from the tradition accounts vindicating the wider horizon of Thomistic moral thought.

The Threefold Speculative Etiology of the Storm

First, as to etiology, three elements may be identified, each of which matriculated to its full volatility during the twentieth century and thence virally interrupted the transmission of Thomistic moral thought so severely as temporarily to seem to threaten the latter's genetic code. These three theoretic elements—the first of secular, and the latter two of intra-Catholic, origination—are (1) transcendental philosophy and analytic logicism; (2) the removal of human freedom from divine providence; and (3) a view of nature and grace that negates the proportionate natural end from which the species is derived. Thomistic moral thought has nevertheless proven far more durable and immune than the marked divagations from the tradition might have led one to suspect. But what precisely are these elements, and how have they contributed to so disruptive an effect?

Transcendental Philosophy and Analytic Logicism

Descending lineally from Enlightenment roots are two related but diverse species of rationalism. On the continent, the influence of Kant reigns supreme in the *transcendental turn to the subject,* articulated not only in those of Kant's school but in subsequent minds of genius such as Husserl and Heidegger and even Catholic savants such as Dietrich von Hildebrand, who fell prey to Kant's misportrayal of natural teleology. The turn to transcendental subjectivity refers principally to Kant's loss of metaphysical realism and negation of normative natural teleology, but also to transcendental phenomenology as prescinding from actual existence or *esse* and so, as John Paul II argued eloquently in his famed *Review of Metaphysics* essay, unfit to found anthropology or ethics. As then Cardinal Karol Wojtyla argued in his essay "Person, Subject, and Community," regarding the abnegation of being by transcendental phenomenology:

This manner of treating consciousness is at the base of the whole so-called "transcendental philosophy." This examines acts of cognition as intentional acts of consciousness directed to transsubjective matter and, therefore, to what is objective or to phenomena. As long as this type of analysis of consciousness possesses the character of a cognitive method, it can and does bear excellent fruit [by providing descriptions of intentional objects]. However, the method should not be considered a philosophy of reality itself. Above all it should not be considered a philosophy of the reality of man or of the human person, since the basis of this method consists in the exclusion *(epoche)* of consciousness from reality or from actually existing being.

This transcendental remotion of thought from being and nature sprouts offshoots found even in Christian thinkers. Dietrich von Hildebrand, for example, concurs with Kant's view of natural teleology in his famous work *Christian Ethics,* in which he argues that the character of the end as good means "nothing more than the fact that this act is suitable for the unfolding of the entelechy of the man" who performs the good act. Hildebrand thus depicts teleology as reducing the nature of the good to the equivalent of something that merely satisfies an urge[1]—a view amazingly congruent with that of Kant from the *Foundations of the Metaphysics of Morals.*

Thus von Hildebrand fails to discern the transcendent aspect of natural finality within teleological ethics as *that for the sake of which* a thing *is* and *acts.* Compare this view of "end"—namely, the view of "end" as "satisfaction of subintelligible *urge*"—with Aquinas's view of teleology, outlined in the *Summa Theologiae* I-II, 2, 5: "Man is ordained to something as his end: since man is not the supreme good. Therefore the last end of man's reason and will cannot be the preservation of man's being." Far from making "end" signify merely the completion and satisfaction of *urge,* Thomistic teleology stresses the transcendent good and the ordering character of the end, while nonetheless insisting that precisely as the good for the sake of which man is, man is *immanently* ordered to God. Indeed, were man *not* ordered to his end, it is unclear what it would mean to assert that this end is the divinely ordained perfection for the sake of which he exists and acts. To suggest that something to which one is not ordered can be one's proper end is rather like suggesting that the natural purpose of the pomegranate is to read Shakespeare. Nonetheless it is undeniable that the rejection of the foundational role of normative unified natural teleology in ethics has constituted a staple of transcendental theorists who variously depict it as utilitarian, crassly egoistic, or reductively naturalistic.

The continental contributions to the momentary eclipse of the classical and Thomistic foundations of moral philosophy and theology may in part be seen in

- a putative fact/value dichotomy divorcing practical reason and the *speculum* which Aquinas held always and necessarily to be required for the very existence of the desire that is presupposed to the operation of practical reason;
- the ensuing and corresponding quasi-Kantian insistence that moral philosophy be purely practical and deontological;
- transcendental negations of the metaphysical and teleological intelligibility of nature;
- denial of any intelligibility of nature superior to positive science;
- the univocal reduction of moral action to intention, treating the integral nature and teleology of moral acts as something merely physical and "natural" in a reductive sense.

By contrast, in England and North America, it is not the transcendental turn to the subject but rather *analytic logicism* that has exerted dislocative influence on the tradition. Logicism is of course most narrowly and specifically defined as the doctrine according to which mathematics reduces wholly to logic; less narrowly, it is the doctrine articulated by A. J. Ayer in his famous comment that "accordingly we may say that philosophy is a department of logic" or by Bertrand Russell in his comment that "philosophy, if what has been said is correct, becomes indistinguishable from logic as that word has now come to be used."[2]

Logicism is of course famous in its relation to Frege's view of existence as merely "the negation of nought" and as a mere "property of a concept." In this respect, until comparatively recently most analytic philosophers have concurred that existence is not a real predicate. Yet Frege's view has crumbled under the realization that his definition of the real applies with equal facility to the merely conceptual. Frege's proposition was that "existence is only the negation of nought"; but the negation of negation—the negation of "nought" or "nothing"—equals something positive *only if we presuppose a real subject*. If one says, "I do not *not* have a nose," this means simply the same as "I have a nose" because I am a real subject. On the other hand, the proposition that "no operatic pink rhinoceruses do not dance" yields not a single operatic pink rhinoceros who actually dances, because there *are* no operatic pink rhinoceroses. In short, because negation of negation can be either real *or* conceptual, it is simply impossible to make negation of negation the operative definition of *actual existence*.

Nonetheless, the denial that existence can be a real predicate was among the analytic strictures conveyed to me in my youth that putatively rendered all of St. Thomas's metaphysics not merely vain but unintelligible, and of course this view renders the metaphysical *framing* of St. Thomas's moral teaching to seem doubly futile: a blind man looking in a dark room for a black cat that isn't there. That so grave an error could be widespread for so long says a very great deal about the insulation of analytic thought from basic accountability in criticism, a phenomenon that persists even at a stage when it is arguable that *analytic* designates only a sociological, and not any unified philosophical, reality.

The point, of course, is not that thinkers formed in the analytic mold necessarily fail to achieve philosophic insight but rather that there is no longer anything specific to analytic formation as such in the philosophic order. Analytic thought no longer canonizes and treats as normative any overarching philosophic teaching, whether in philosophy of logic, philosophy of language, philosophy of nature, or metaphysics. Whereas at one time analytic thought was associated with revolutionary teachings, these have in sequence imploded and been shown either to be false or not to be necessary. For example, thanks to Gödel's theorem, few argue today that mathematics is reducible to logic, and the teaching that this is so certainly does not define analytic philosophic formation. This is also true of the verification principle of early logical positivism, of the early antimetaphysical formulations of Wittgenstein's *Tractatus* as well as the later antimetaphysical *petitio principii* of his later writings; of the Vienna Circle's reduction of knowledge to the conclusions of the positive sciences, and of Gilbert Ryle's rejection of any dualism, whether extreme or Aristotelian; of Strawson's insistence that only descriptive and not revisionary metaphysics is valid (which was impaled upon philosophic theology and the issue of reasoning to the real judgment that God exists); and so on. None of these teachings, including the once widespread insistence of Frege that existence is not a predicate, is essential to analytic philosophy. Analytic thought thus appears to have become a mere partial metaphilosophy, concerned principally with a certain sort of logic and a way of presenting arguments, but innocent of any substantial philosophic method or conclusions. Because mere logic is not a *method* but is required for every cognitive discipline—and because no substantive concurrence in philosophy of logic is essential to the definition of "analytic" philosophy—*analytic* appears to be an *infra*-philosophic designator, pertaining not to philosophy but to the sociology of knowledge.

In any event, the cognate errors, earlier of logical positivism, later of linguistic reductionism, persistently display the same aversion to metaphysical intelligibility and the priority of the speculative within the practical life. And while *analytic* is no longer precisely and accurately a philosophic designator, the residual logicism that is the inheritance of the earlier revolutionary and substantial phase of analytic thought is still extensively influential.

With respect to moral theory, logicism shares with transcendental philosophy the tendency to reduce the object of the moral act to an ideational "proposal" excluding the act itself, its integral matter, and its per se teleological order and effects. Here the similarity between logicism and transcendental philosophy is conspicuous, for each begins with a quasi-Humean denial of necessity and intelligibility in nature and being, and so with the introduction of a dichotomy between nature and the good, between fact and value, that wars against the recognition of normative natural teleology. In the anglophone world this tendency at the margins merges with utilitarian and proportionalist theory, and also with situational ethics, relativism, and nihilism. Yet not only skeptics but also many moral objectivists—affected by transcendental modes of philosophic analysis or by logicism—entertain an evisceration of the object of the moral act whereby it becomes a naked object of intention divorced from nature and natural teleology.

The dual provenance of this view of the object of the moral act, deriving both from transcendental and from analytic considerations, is conspicuous in two very different recent accounts of natural law influential within Catholic life. It has been on recent display in the highly visible arguments of the Swiss moral philosopher Fr. Martin Rhonheimer—arguments from which he has stepped back and that he is no longer pressing, but which have had their effect in the public square, and which reveal the precise flaw of the denaturing of the object of the moral act—that condom use should be deemed licit on the part of spouses seeking to avoid the transmission of the AIDS virus.[3]

Even more strategically visible, the North American "new natural law" scholars John Finnis, Germaine Grisez, and Joseph Boyle—who are not in agreement with Rhonheimer with respect to contraception—have recently described the crushing of the skull of the unborn child in craniotomy as not really harming the child but rather merely "changing the dimensions of the skull."[4] Whether the turn to the subject or analytic logicism be credited, each of these views tends to denude the object of the moral act of its integral nature and teleological order in preference for a unilateral stress on intention. Yet these are arguably mere accidental inflections within the Catholic life proceeding from circumambient transcendental and logicist tendencies. The extreme a priorism of transcendental philosophy—ceding, as Husserl ceded, that the natural world is purely contingent and lacking intelligible necessity, and tending to hold, as Kant held, that *natural end* signifies merely the factive object of empirical urge rather than the normative object of wish—here meets the logicism that, descending from diverse sources, likewise denies to nature any intelligible necessity transcending logic.

Thus one notes in both the transcendental and analytic approaches to moral life a critical distancing from the speculative knowledge of being and natural teleology,[5] conjoined with an overly univocal stress upon *intention*.[6] This coincidence of judgment is all the more marked for the seeming chasm of divergence separating continental rationalism and a priorism from the self-professedly less theoretic and more commonsensical analytic style of thought characteristic of much of the anglophone world. That *both* manage to evacuate the integral nature of human action and to render it in the mode of a mere descriptive proposal articulating intent is a testimony to the distance of each from the proportionate evidences of being, nature, and natural teleology. Each seems to share the view that speculative knowledge as to what *is* is somehow not seminally crucial in the formation of practical reasons for action: as though the desire without which no reasoning is practical, because without it nothing is either sought or avoided, could come to exist apart from the naturally prior intelligible apprehension of something that attracts the will (and before something attracts the will, there is no practical issue in relation to it). For it is only consequent upon the *motio* of the will that practical consideration as such ensues. Practical consideration is concerned with doing and making, which are for the sake of a desired *end;* but if *nothing is known* whereby the will may be attracted, then there is no such inclination of the will toward an end with the consequent generation of concern for doing and making. In other words, the necessary condition for the existence of practical reason is the prior apprehension of speculative reason.

Clearly the intelligible apprehension of the object to which the will is subsequently attracted is by nature *prior* to this rational attraction. While it is accidental to that which is known that *human nature* is such as to be ordained to it, it is not accidental to human nature that it is *such* as to be ordained to the entire hierarchy of ends that naturally defines it, and so it is not accidental to human nature that desire ensues upon knowledge. But the inceptive apprehension is speculative, that is, a knowing that is at the font of, rather than originally generated by, *praxis,* although surely thereafter practical experience augments, enhances, and perfects practical reason as such. The dichotomization of speculative and practical urged commonly by continental and analytic thought is particularly contrary to the realism of Aristotelian and Thomistic moral reflection, in which (1) the primacy of speculative *adequatio* and apprehension as a condition of the practical, (2) the ontological formality of the four causes, in particular of the final cause, and (3) the interpenetration of the object and end of intellect and will all serve to establish the necessary continuity and unity of speculative and practical reason. The common proposal of an absolute dichotomy between speculative and practical reason reflects, not a mode of Thomistic reflection, but rather its negation.[7]

The continental and analytic negations of nature and natural teleology in ethics were in full play by the middle of the twentieth century—in the continental case culturally buttressed by such rejections of *natura* as, for example, are articulated in the existentialisms of Sartre or Camus. Either nature was unintelligible *à outrance,* or its teleological ordering was denied—whether in the name of logicism in general, or of mathematicized models of intelligibility, or of scientism, or of the turn to the subject—and held intrinsically irrelevant to moral life, or considered positively trivial and vulgar. The few scholastically trained moral theologians who have functioned throughout this period will testify chiefly to the astonishing *extent* of the rejection of the analogical intelligibility of nature, being, and normative natural teleology.

One additional strategic point ought to be made regarding transcendental philosophy and logicism as contributing to this deracination of moral philosophy. Owing to their shared antimetaphysical tendencies, and the denial of the unified pertinence of truth for the practical life, each tends, whether explicitly or implicitly, to *subtract* the understanding of moral agency from any wider doctrine of divine providence and from the theocentric character of natural law. One recollects Thomas's formulation (*ST* I, 91, 2) that natural law is "nothing but" the rational participation of the eternal law, and it should be beyond doubt that something's definition is not accidental to it. The active life is ordered to the contemplative life even by nature, and by nature speculative wisdom is superior; the practical life is also ordered in grace toward beatific knowledge of the uncreated triune God: in either case, the last end is not *praxis*.

Yet, whether in behalf of a closed sequence of terrestrial causes and the prestige of positive science, in behalf of the presumed absolute autonomy of the agent, or (in the case of Kant) *both*, the essential and indeed *natural* theonomy of the good life is set aside by both continental and most analytic treatments of practical life. Nature comes to be construed as mere "lower" nature, whose account is in positive science and whose intelligibility has no metaphysical extension. Morality regards a naturally denuded *intention* of the agent, a mere ideational "proposal" or "description," threadbare of any normative teleological *nature,* and occupying a practical stage to which divine government is at best an optional addendum—remote either from the natural desire to see the essence of God as cause of these effects or from the graced ordering to God as Triune Beatitude. That normative teleological order is the impress of the divine wisdom, and that right practical agency and prudence constitute a higher natural participation in the divine government which imitates the divine providence, are as lost to view as is the role of natural contemplation of God and the order of being in a good life. Instead, rather unceremoniously, God exits moral philosophy as a merely heteronomic, extrinsic, and indeed unsubstantiatable and irrelevant posit hardly able to survive even the palest skepticism, much less to constitute either the proportionate natural or ultimate supernatural *end*. This is of course at the far end of the spectrum from the teaching of *Fides et Ratio* § 83, which speaks of "the need for a philosophy of genuinely metaphysical range, capable, that is, of transcending empirical data in order to attain something absolute, ultimate and foundational in its search for truth. *This requirement is implicit in sapiential and analytical knowledge alike; and in particular it is a requirement for knowing the moral good, which has its ultimate foundation in the Supreme Good, God himself* [my italics]."

So much for the identification of the two Enlightenment contributions to the storm—transcendental philosophy and analytic logicism—and their common antimetaphysical and indeed implicit or explicit antitheistic influence upon moral philosophy. A moral philosophy whose speculative metaphysical and natural frame has been lost, and whose practical reflections are alternately logicist, a priorist, existentialist, or purely phenomenological—this was the secular predilection of the second half of the twentieth century, insofar, that is to say, as it was not immersed in the different and equally total materialist secularity and historicist noncognitivism of Marxian ideology.[8]

What can virtue—which is understood properly only as *saturated* by unified teleological order—be taken to mean within such a universe? Prudence *requires* that a correct particular judgment be framed in relation to antecedent knowledge of the hierarchy of ends defining the good life. To say that ends are *not* normatively teleologically commensurate—literally "co-measured"—in relation to the proportionate natural and ultimate supernatural end is to say they have no share in the good life. This being true, there is no particular reason to call them "ends." While human circumstances, inclusive of gifts and weaknesses, are almost indefinitely variable, the natural order of ends defining the good life is fixed—and fixed prior to choice—by the constitution of the real as defining what is per se requisite for human flourishing. It is popular to frame the difference between moral objectivists and noncognitivists as the decisive difference in moral philosophy. But far more crucial is the demarcation line between those who acknowledge, and those who do not, the foundationally normative role of natural teleology prior to choice. For example, *by nature* reason has a central normative role in the good life, and this centrality is not merely a function of individual choice; *by nature* the active life *is ordered* to the contemplative life, and not *merely by choice*. The *order* of inclinations follows the *order* of precepts, which follows the *order* of ends. Failure to see the unified order bestowed upon human nature from creation, while today still virtually a pure postulate of anglophone ethical thought, is neither the beginning nor the end of wisdom.

The Intra-Catholic Contribution to "The Perfect Storm"

However, prior to receiving the full force of these tendencies, Catholic moral thought itself had suffered a certain interior dislocation with respect to its own character. Thus we arrive at a second and intra-Catholic influence that contributed to the supreme challenge posed by the twentieth century to the resources of Thomistic moral thought. This second challenge is perhaps best articulated by contrast with the genealogy of error famously proposed by Fr. Servais Pinckaers, wherein he correctly identifies the distortive role of nominalism deriving from Ockham in impeding our appreciation of the role of the natural desire for happiness, and of virtue, in the Christian moral life.[9] While I concur with Pinckaers regarding Ockham and nominalism, there is a later contributant to the confusion of the tradition that—because of the real factors that underlie it—is arguably even more extensively disruptive in its implications. That factor is (like nominalism) one that decisively rejects the intellectualist account of human freedom, but in this case in the name of an allegedly metaphysically absolute liberty of indifference of the human agent understood as definitive of genuine human autonomy. And, of course, it presupposes that human *freedom* does not have a *nature* but rather is defined purely by its indifference with respect to all prior conditions or requirements for choice.

Whereas in nominalist thought the preference is for voluntarism, the subsequent emergence of a doctrine of absolute libertarian freedom as constituted by a liberty of indifference *even to divine causality and providence* is of even more protean implication for Thomistic thought. This is the view of freedom that Molina (1535–1600) made famous in his formulation in the *Concordia* that *the will is free only when, all requirements being retained, the will could indeed act otherwise.*[10] With respect to "requirements" as terrestrial *objects* of volition, this is true: because the very nature of the will as inclination following the form of reason is such that its object—the universal good or good in general—is irreducible to any finite good, wherefore no finite good can compel the will. But with respect to the divine decrees and the divine causality, which transcend and are presupposed to all finite causes, this teaching is disastrous: for it implies that with respect to the divine decrees the will "can do otherwise" *absolutely speaking*. With one stroke human agency is thus placed outside divine causality, providence, and eternal and natural law. As St. Thomas teaches in *ST* I, 103, 5, *providence extends only so far as power*. Hence if a *creature* of God possesses a *liberty of indifference* with respect to divine causality, this can only render the creature to be *outside the divine power and so outside Providence* and indeed therefore *outside eternal law*—and, in a sense, even outside *being* insofar as being is the proper effect of God.

Molina's proposition—that *the will is free only when, all requirements being retained, the will could indeed act otherwise*—while true of all terrestrial causes, is for the realist an impossible proposition with respect to the hypothetical but immutable divine willing of created effects. For what changes with this hypothetical but immutable divine willing—owing to the divine simplicity—*is not God* but *only the creature itself*. The creature is really related to, and dependent upon, God, but not vice versa. Hence the only difference between God efficaciously willing a created effect, and God *not* efficaciously willing some created effect, is that the efficaciously willed effect actually *exists*. Thus one cannot retain the requirement that God cause the creature freely to act while the creature is not caused freely to act, *because this is a contradiction in terms*. Rather, as St. Thomas teaches, God causes necessary causes necessarily, and contingent causes contingently.[11] Indeed, the free act is comprised within the effect of being, which is the proper effect of God. The divine causality is so perfect that it reaches even to the *mode* of the act it causes as either contingent or necessary.

The insistence upon the Ur-myth of total autonomy vis-à-vis the providential order, and of a liberty that is rooted, not in the modality of intellectual universalism, but in a complete indeterminacy even to God, remains powerfully evocative and is taken up by minds as far from Molina as that of Maurice Merleau-Ponty, whose comments on God and human liberty—that if God is free, the creature cannot be—one recollects from his work *Sens et non-sens*.[12]

Molina's formulation presupposes that because the will is not causally determined by terrestrial causes—with respect to which it is objectively free—therefore the free act does not lie within the providential causality of God. This error may be traced to an erroneous definition of "freedom" itself. For no created being, howsoever noble, can move itself from potency to act.[13] It is true that since the object of the will is the good in general no finite good can compel the will, because no finite good is simply the universal good, that is, good in every respect.[14] Thus the will is always, with respect to its terrestrial objects, *objectively* free. Nonetheless, every motion of the will as such lies within the effect of God's causality, and every creature is such that it depends upon prior motion from God in order to act. And, if this dependence does not obtain, then quite literally there is a creature whose *being* and whose *action* lie outside the scope of the eternal law. A thing can only *act* as it *is: operatio sequitur esse, agere sequitur esse,* the maxims converge on the same point. The actuality of the creature is limited by potency. Were the creature absolutely self-activating it would be a being *a se,* not a creature.[15]

To attribute a created indifference to divine causality is to invent a finite God really related to his effects rather than infinitely perfect and independent; it is to postulate a God who is not the first and transcendent cause of every being, act, and formal perfection but merely one finite cause among many, whose causality is not precisely and in every instance a divine effect. Yet while in respect to *object* every deliberate choice is free because no finite object can compel the will, with respect to the motion of the will from potency to act with regard to its own self-determination in freedom, every free act presupposes a prior motion from God. Yet even at the moment that one is freely moved to choose something, one possesses the power whereby one could—but does not—act differently.

As has been noted, God's providence extends only so far as God's power. Remove the application of the creature's volitional act from the divine power, and one removes forthwith the application of the creature's volitional act from the divine providential government and the eternal law. This *application* is a matter not only of the will's *rational specification* but of its *exercise*. In other words, *if* the creature's application of the natural motion of the will to act *is ineluctably rationally specified,* but this application of the natural motion is not also *in its exercise* subject to divine causality, *then* the action of the creature lies outside the providential governance, and so lies outside the scope of the eternal law. But, to the contrary, no creature can apply itself to act without first having been moved by God, who is more present to the will than is the will to itself. All finite being and operation lie within the zone of the divine effect—being—and so God actually brings it about that this act performed by me is performed by me, and performed in the mode of freedom, by moving me from potency to act with respect to the very act of my own free self-determination. The stress on potency and act preserves this teaching from occasionalism, making clear that it is the human will that performs the act of willing, and so preserving secondary causality.[16]

Hence if the rational will is held to enjoy a liberty of indifference with respect to the divine causality, it is implicitly construed as a being *a se,* and thus an unlimited human autonomy naturally appropriates the sublunary world of natural ethics to itself as though it were its own kingdom. It is difficult to understand how even revelation could make a difference to this implication: Why should a being *a se* stand in need of—or be subject to a desire for—divine revelation, when it itself supposedly is absolutely independent? The very reality upon which the impossibility of God receiving his rule for action from outside is predicated—namely, the divine aseity—is implicitly affirmed of the human will when it is claimed that the motion from *not willing* to *willing* is simply outside the divine causality, rendering the will's action to be *a se.* But if the manifest facts of the human condition conflict too much with the project of treating the finite rational creature as a god, then deflecting these perceptions to revealed religion and putatively keeping moral philosophy free of them is a strategy well known to history: rationalist philosophy compounded with fideist error.

Four hundred years of compromise on a speculative issue of enormous theoretical importance to the contemplation of faith and morals works hardship on theology. It is here that we come to the worst effect of the Molinist teaching. Intra-Catholic meditations on freedom as well as philosophic tendencies rooted in the Enlightenment each carved out a dominion for natural human agency as *absolutely independent* of God. The convergent effect is that of secular and intra-Catholic tendencies of thought, each of which tends toward making the natural realm—and particularly the natural realm of human agency—an utterly separate jurisdiction sealed off from divine providence.

The rejections of the theonomic character of nature and natural order based on absolute freedom and on closed physical causality end by insisting on similar judgments. The advocate of absolute autonomy for the rational creature must deny the subjection of man's will to divine causality and providence—ruling out the "interference" of God with a will supposed either to be purely in act or else to be mysteriously able to move itself from potency to act without first receiving this motion from God. Likewise, the contemporary physicalist or materialist advocate of "causal closure" among physical causes must deny the subjection of any physical agency whatsoever to the higher causality of God lest the closed circle of terrestrial causes be broken. In one case the motive is the preservation of absolute freedom; in the other case, the motive is the preservation of causal closure (and, for some authors, absolute necessity) among exclusively physical causes. One may well note that it seems that for Kant both of these motivations simultaneously hold sway—the categories of phenomenal necessitation just as much as his nakedly natureless a priori posit of human freedom require the denial of any knowable providential government of world and will. But in either case, the effect is the same: the banishing of God from the natural world and especially from the natural world of human agency.

Under such circumstances of the radical misconstruction of nature and natural order, natural law consequently comes to be seen as the drawing of a juridic boundary declaring divine governance of human acts to be *ultra vires*. In this light, the nature/grace distinction gradually comes to be seen as maintaining an artificial and destructive divorce between God and the world, and *a fortiori* between God and the human world. Within such a world, natural law, far from being what it was for St. Thomas—namely, nothing other than the rational participation of the eternal law—becomes instead the demarcation of a realm *outside the governance of the eternal law*. Natural law becomes, as it were, the "stalking horse" of secularism and naturalist reductionism. A more complete inversion of the character of the doctrine of the natural law cannot be imagined—indeed a transvaluation of all values.

A Flawed Intra-Catholic Response

This utter misconstruction and separation of nature and natural order from divine providence and eternal law could not cohere with the requirements of Catholic life in any dimension, for the initial premise of Catholic life is the conviction in the one God who made heaven and earth, everything seen and unseen. It was ineluctable that simple concern for the integrity and wholeness of Catholic life would drive a response to these twin assertions of terrestrial absolutism. But what sort of response might it be? The response to, and rebellion against, the intellectual culture that the compromise with Molinism, and with the Enlightenment ideology of absolute terrestrial independence, introduced was in Henri de Lubac to become the erroneous denial of the proportionate natural end *tout court*.[17] Rather than address the erroneous account of nature which insulates terrestrial causes and human freedom from divine providence, the proposed solution was to be a denial that any properly natural finality could or did exist.

Whereas St. Thomas—in *ST* I, 75, 7 ad 1—clearly distinguishes man and angel not by ultimate supernatural end (which is the same) but by the proximate and natural end from which the species is derived (which is different), de Lubac denied the existence of any "true" natural proximate end for man that is retained even within the context of grace. *Summa Theologiae* I, 75, 7 ad 1 teaches that *even in the regime of grace* man qua man is constituted in his species in relation to the proportionate natural end *rather than*—and *precisely in distinction from*—in relation to the ultimate and supernatural end. That is the teaching of *ST* I, 75, 7 ad 1, and it would be surprising were de Lubac to have agreed with it, believing as he did that man qua man has and can have only one "true" end.[18] De Lubac did advert to imperfect beatitude but shied from any notion that it was properly an *end*, much less an end that could have been man's only fulfillment had God not created man in grace, which later teaching he erroneously supposed to be a novelty of *Suarezian* provenance.[19] Nowhere in *Surnaturel*, in *The Mystery of the Supernatural,* or in *Augustinianism and Modern Theology* does one find de Lubac wrestling with this text—not because he held it to be true but because he could not have conceived how profoundly it characterizes the doctrine of Aquinas.

The foundationless view that nature and natural integrity require separation from divine providence, implying a whole series of antitheistic antinomies with respect to freedom and physical causality, established the remote conditions for eventual rebellion against the very idea of natural end on the grounds that this serves merely as a device keeping man in, and God out, of the equation of human meaning and freedom. But clearly suppression of the natural end runs the risk of converting anthropology, and ethics, into mere fideist projections. And the loss of proportionate natural end—the end from which the human species is derived even within the context of revelation and the call of grace—leads to the treatment of nature as an ontological nullity, the equivalent of a dimensionless point terminating the line of grace. When the proportionate teleology and ontological density of the creature are lost, classical natural law—which is thoroughly theonomic, as it is *nothing other than a rational participation in the eternal law*—is lost. And this unhappy consequence follows upon the false presupposition that the teleological order impressed on nature cannot be the impress of the divine wisdom in creatures unless it includes the supernatural beatific end. Thus it is the flawed but profound response of de Lubac to the desolation of antitheism—denying the proportionate natural end from which the species is derived—that constitutes an intra-Catholic and third causal factor affecting the transmission of the Thomistic tradition of moral analysis.

Yet, as is clear when one meditates the teaching of Aquinas in *ST* I, 12, 1, the natural desire to see God is specified by creatures and created evidence—it reaches to God as "cause of these effects"[20]—whereas the graced desire for supernatural beatitude is specified by the intra-Trinitarian life and love itself. In what sense, if one desired to get to know a man wearing a raincoat, and later discovered that the man was Einstein, could one suppose to oneself that one had initially desired to know Einstein? Materially, but not formally. The same is true of the natural desire to see God vis-à-vis the graced desire for supernatural beatitude. The *ratio* under which the natural desire for God reaches God is infinitely inferior to the graced desire for beatitude. Indeed, to desire God as "cause of these effects" is to desire him under the *ratio* of that which is in no way essential to him, for the creature is not essential to God, who is infinitely perfect and blessed in himself. There is indeed a proportionate natural end, and it is not the same as the ontologically perfect supernatural beatific end, although the latter is by analogy "natural" in the sense that what one may do with the aid of one's friends is in a sense "natural" to one.[21] This actual teaching of Aquinas, however, and the texts articulating it, were either misconstrued by de Lubac (as he misconstrued Thomas's teaching of the possibility of creation *in puris naturalibus*)—in part because of his failure to consult certain other texts—or else simply not considered.[22]

The Effects of the Storm

We are now in a position to appreciate the convergence of these elements that came to full expression in the 1960s and in the quasi-permanent antinomian revolution flowing from this period. The transcendental turn to the subject, analytic logicism, liberty as indifference to divine governance and pure autonomy, and the theological rebellion against the very idea of a proximate natural end as seemingly necessitated by naturalism and the Molinist compromise all tended to obscure the role of normative natural teleology in moral life, the speculative intelligibility of being and nature, and the role of teleology and virtue in the practical life. Of course, clearly if there is no proportionate natural end, there is no proportionate natural teleology. Given the power and depth of this confluent torrent of negation, it is unsurprising that nihilist infatuation with subjection of the *humanum* to technological manipulation should have eventually bubbled to the surface. For it is these worst implications of the evacuation of the ontological density and the teleological order of nature as such that have gradually engendered the requisite corrective inquiries both *ad intra* with respect to Thomistic moral thought and *ad extra* with respect to the contemporaneous condition of the church in a world where abortion, euthanasia, denial of the nature of marriage, and radical departures in bioethics present themselves as "tolerant," "scientific," and even "progressive."

Given the conflation of these factors in the twentieth century, the following questions emerge:

- Is it surprising, under these speculative conditions, that the tradition of natural law reasoning should have been severely challenged and widely rejected?
- Is it surprising that to the degree that theologians and moralists labor within these presuppositions they encounter difficulty in articulating the nature and importance of virtue, the role of the desire for happiness in the good life, and natural teleology as the impress of the divine wisdom?
- Can an adequate theology of the sacrament of penance and reconciliation be made intelligible on the supposition of anthropologies that render "the natural" either a null set or a wholly autonomous human province?
- If a demonstration were in fact needed to show that speculative truths of philosophy of nature and metaphysics not only condition but enter into the substance of moral philosophy, would not the effect of these currents of thought with respect to the mid-twentieth-century paralysis of traditional moral reflection suffice to constitute one?
- Is it surprising that the ecology of proportionate human values—especially with respect to the nature and dignity of man and woman, the

- vocation to marriage, and the nature of the family—should be significantly occluded in public life following a half century of rejection of proportionate natural end, natural law, and natural teleology within ethics?
- Given the loss of natural philosophy and metaphysics, and so of the *praeambula fidei,* is it surprising that theistic discourse itself should come to be considered a purely private preserve with no normative ethical implications for public life?

Precisely owing to the depth and pervasiveness of these influences, Thomistic moral thought in the latter part of the twentieth century began to return to its own native dimensions and resources. Exemplifying such correction one of course finds the teaching of John Paul II in *Veritatis Splendor* and *Fides et Ratio,* each of which vindicates the speculative premises entering into the very constitution of the practical sphere of reflection. The response of Pinckaers to voluntarism and nominalism in the name of virtue and grace in Christian life has been mentioned above and is precisely an answer to the deep disequilibration of moral realism wrought by these erroneous teachings.

One sees the sparks of renewal early, in De Koninck's work on the common good and in his vindication of *scientia;*[23] in Maritain's *The Degrees of Knowledge,* but also his paean to moral and artistic connaturality in *Man and the State* and *Art and Scholasticism;* in Gilson's *The Unity of Philosophical Experience.* Garrigou-Lagrange's early penetrating criticism of Molinism and arguments against de Lubac's *Surnaturel,* while destined for a time to be neglected, pointed to the root difficulties of the twentieth century; these conjoined with his mystical work constitute an important and challenging contribution.[24] Cardinal Wojtyla's engagement with phenomenology while subordinating it to the truths of being, nature, and anthropology and Henry Veatch's vindication of natural teleology are also noteworthy. One thinks likewise of Heinrich Rommen, Yves Simon, and Vernon Bourke—incisive minds with great regard for the role of prudence and virtue, astute awareness of the dangers of ideology, and—especially in Simon's case—keen and wide-ranging speculative intelligence. One thinks also of Fr. Santiago Ramirez, Fr. Marie-Michel Labourdette, and Fr. Jean-Hervé Nicholas—three Thomistic intellects of the highest order, each a systematic and penetrating mind engaging the whole of theology and philosophy. Ramirez offered genuine commentary on the teaching of Aquinas that he also sought to unfold in extensive speculative considerations; Labourdette performed remarkable work in moral theology and undertook salient and profound criticism of *la nouvelle théologie* in irenic rather than merely castigatory mode as editor of *Revue Thomiste;* Nicholas contributed profound works in systematic theology while articulating the classic teachings of the Thomistic school regarding grace.[25]

Ralph McInerny's defense of teleology in his *Ethica Thomistica,* and of the importance of natural knowledge of God in his *Praeambula Fidei,* are arresting and important contributions, as are the many other lapidary philosophic works that have poured from the author's pen when he has not been confecting extremely successful mystery novels.[26]

Alasdair MacIntyre's astute and illuminating exploration of the teleological character of inquiry and of the intelligible practices required by the development and application of tradition, together with his profound engagement with the natural and social dimensions of man's moral life, are conspicuous throughout his work, whose proper assessment will take some time.[27] While critics remain altogether properly arrested by *After Virtue,* the development of MacIntyre's sense of the practical resonances of teleology, and of the relation of practical reason to the larger frame of theological and metaphysical contemplation, will preoccupy careful readers for many years.

The names of authors such as Russell Hittinger, whose crucial work *A Critique of the New Natural Law Theory* drew the entire moral discussion back to Thomistic premises and classical wisdom regarding *natura,* or Fr. Romanus Cessario, O.P., whose variegated testimony to the theologal life and to the sapiential unity of *sacra doctrina,* and to the theological centrality of *habitus* (see his work *The Moral Virtues and Theological Ethics*), are likewise conspicuous in their contribution to the renewal and perfection of Thomistic moral philosophy and theology.[28] The profound and extensive work of Fr. Lawrence Dewan, O.P., particularly with respect to natural law and virtue, constitutes a contribution of incredible depth, rigor, and extension.[29] Even Pope Benedict XVI, whose theological inspiration has perhaps been more Bonaventurean than Thomistic, nonetheless in his Regensburg address powerfully not only adumbrates the role of realist metaphysics and anthropology but with respect to the nature of the voluntary articulates the case for intellectualism—or, at the minimum, for the rejection of voluntarism. These names above, evocative as they are, constitute but a partial and fragmentary listing of what has been a compendious twentieth- and twenty-first-century recovery and recrudescence of classical Thomistic realism.[30]

This quintessentially realist response, open to the whole horizon of speculative and practical engagement with nature and grace, still is unfolding in the face of the various devolutions of modernity and postmodernity and confronts today new technologies affecting medical care that pose with ever greater persistence and power the essential question of the nature of the *humanum* and of the order of ends that define it. The very elements, once hidden, of the denial and negation of *natura* and its theonomic character now work powerfully to educe ever deeper and more principled insight into the natural law and its preconditions in the philosophy of nature, metaphysics, and anthropology, as well as in reflections on the role of connaturality, community, and mentoring in the development and perfection of virtue. Hence it seems inevitable that the strategy of realist moral theology and philosophy will necessarily involve using the very force of the modern and postmodern rejection of nature as the occasion for deepening our rational appreciation of the theonomic character of natural law, its perfection and teleological actuation in virtue, and its further ordering within grace.

Not the least task of *scientia* is in directing us to the major premises— and to the practical articulation in action of the same—that must steer us through the social compromises and failures generated by various denials of right reason. The role of *scientia* in guiding our judgment, precisely amid the social, moral, cultural, and legal complexities to which the abnegation of reason leads, is crucially delicate and profound. The same is true *pari passu* of *virtue,* especially of authentic *prudence,* and its encouragement. The habitudes necessary to practical rectitude and flourishing and their institutional and social tutoring—not to mention the superordinate role of *infused virtue* and *charity*—are crucial precisely in the midst of their derogation by hostility to the idea of a morally normative and teleologically actuated human nature.

The doctrine of natural law occupies a space that modernity and postmodernity have taught themselves to view as void: a speculative doctrine with practical implications; adumbration of a unified order of proportionate ends defining a limited natural felicity while yet susceptible to the supervening and elevating ordering of the *lex nova* in grace; the account of a teleological universe in which social solidarity in virtue aids powerfully in perfecting man's nature; how God knows the world to be. But the extent, creativity, and solidity of the contributions of those named above manifest how far the tradition of Thomistic moral and metaphysical realism surpasses the common thread of modern and postmodern thought, whose relation to the wider universe of discourse is attenuated. If one asks oneself how many of the authors named above are significantly engaged by continental or analytic philosophers today, one sees the magnitude of the problem. This is particularly conspicuous in the analytic world, whose earlier speculative élan has largely transformed to a metaphilosophic and sociological character that institutionally cloaks the need for wider speculative engagement. Yet the resources are not only extant but rich and blossoming, and one can only perform the labor that God directs one to undertake, realizing that its fruit is beyond one's command. Still, if the fruit is proportionate to the character of the work and the extent of the labor, these authors have merited a superabundant harvest, and one brought forth precisely in answer to the drought of moral and metaphysical realism consequent upon the confluence of forces described above.

Thus, by virtue of the intelligent and far-ranging responses elicited by the magnitude of the challenge of the twentieth century, the paradox resounds. After a century surfeited with the systematic renunciation of the speculative and practical propositions that form the coherent whole, not just of moral realism in general, but even of Thomistic thought *tout court,* and after the virtual disappearance of many institutions predictably and holistically ordered to the forwarding of realist moral philosophy, theology, and metaphysics, *nevertheless* the intellectual condition of moral realism is now stronger than it was when the contemporary antinomianism was merely a cloud on the horizon, smaller than a man's hand.

Notes

1. Dietrich von Hildebrand, *Christian Ethics* (New York: David McKay, 1953), 100; note well 95–100, 186–90, in which the depiction of teleology in terms of selfish "urge satisfaction" is fully articulated.
2. A. J. Ayer, *Language, Truth, and Logic* (New York: Dover, 1946), 57; Bertrand Russell, *On Scientific Method in Philosophy* (Oxford: Clarendon Press, 1914), 17.

3. Cf. Fr. Martin Rhonheimer, "The Truth about Condoms," *Tablet*, July 10, 2004. His later cessation of argument for this point—falling decidedly short of any renunciation of the position, but tantamount to awaiting magisterial "clarification" of the brouhaha that his remarks engendered—may be seen in the progress of his contributions to the *National Catholic Bioethics Quarterly* from summer 2007 through summer 2009 in exchanges with several authors, including myself. My article focusing exclusively on the argument and thought of his position in the *Tablet* and not on the entirety of his oeuvre may be seen in "The False Theory Undergirding Condomitic Exceptionalism: A Response to William F. Murphy, Jr. and Rev. Martin Rhonheimer," *National Catholic Bioethics Quarterly* 8, no. 4 (2008): 709–32. See Rhonheimer's response in vol. 9, no. 1 (2009), and my reply in vol. 9, no. 2. What matters here is the high-profile impact of this intervention, whose public effect is in no small part due to the tendency of contemporary thinkers to reduce the object of the moral act to a mental posit void of natural integrity and teleology.

4. Cf. John Finnis, Germain Grisez, and Joseph Boyle, "'Direct' and 'Indirect': A Reply to Critics of Our Action Theory," *Thomist* 65 (2001): 1–44, esp. "The baby's death is a side effect of changing the dimensions of its skull" (32) and the following response to Fr. Stephen Brock's criticisms: "But Brock fails to show the object of the surgeon's chosen act is better described as 'producing the crushed skull of an innocent person' than as 'cranium-narrowing for the purposes of removal from the birth-canal'" (44 n. 38).

5. Of course, "speculative" is not reducible to "theoretical," although the theoretical is speculative. It is a necessary condition for the practical reason that there be desire; and it is a necessary condition of desire that there be a prior apprehension of a truth that must be known as a condition of it subsequently sparking rational desire. The knowledge of this truth—which is prior to rational desire and thus by nature is prior to the activity of practical reason—is speculative, and every practical reasoning presupposes such a *speculum* without which the desire of the end that is formative for practical reason cannot occur. Contrary to the confusions imposed on the text of Aquinas by superficial analytic readings, the basic character of the intellect is for St. Thomas Aquinas speculative, and practical reason is different from speculative reason only in this, that it applies the known truth to operation. Thus the words of *ST* I, 79, 11: "Now, to a thing apprehended by the intellect, it is accidental whether it be directed to operation or not, and according to this the speculative and practical intellects differ. For it is the speculative intellect which directs what it apprehends, not to operation, but solely to the consideration of truth; while the practical intellect is that which directs what it apprehends to operation." Augmenting this, in the ad 2 of the same article, St. Thomas writes: "For the practical intellect knows truth, just as the speculative, but it directs the known truth to operation." *It is accidental whether the apprehended truth be directed to operation or not,* and it is *this accidental difference* that distinguishes the prior purely speculative knowledge from knowledge that is further *directed to operation.* In other

words, its *essential status as knowledge always presupposes speculative adequatio*, on which the conditions of practical agency supervene only *consequent* upon the appetition of the end. Nor does this reduce practical knowledge to the will, because the rational willing of the end is a necessary and not a sufficient condition of practical reason, whose application to operation renders it distinct from purely speculative knowledge.

6. This is somewhat mitigated by individual teleologies with respect to "basic goods" in the new natural law theory, but only "somewhat," as these goods are not teleologically unified; rather, all ethically significant order among ends is considered to be posterior rather than prior to individual choice. The good life thus becomes a mere ad hoc totality of nonordered objects of appetite, lacking any teleologically commensurate parts prior to choice. Nonetheless, the identification of ends makes the new natural law theory a more capacious and somewhat more realistic account than the pure deontology of Kant, with which, however, it has a certain limited resemblance.

7. This is helpfully articulated in Alasdair MacIntyre's profound considerations of the teleology of inquiry and of the implications of the loss of normative teleology for the intellectual life as such, which raises the question of the import of this loss—as Cajetan might have put it—"most formally." Here, as below, I wish to identify a little work of his that I believe is extraordinarily pertinent, his Marquette lecture *First Principles, Final Ends, and Contemporary Philosophical Issues* (Milwaukee: Marquette University Press, 1990).

8. Surely it is not accidental that neither the seminal continental thinkers of the twentieth century nor those of the analytic revolution contributed any real depth or profundity to moral reflection. Where are the moral philosophies of Heidegger or of Husserl? Or of Wittgenstein, Ryle, or Russell? Unsurprisingly, they contribute precisely nothing. Those continental or analytic thinkers who have engaged in moral philosophizing have been, like Anscombe or Marcel, Catholic and realist first, and analytic or continental solely by accident.

9. See, for example, the illustrative analysis in Servais Pinckaers, *The Sources of Christian Ethics*, 3rd ed., trans. Mary Thomas Noble (Washington, DC: Catholic University of America Press, 1995), 251, 252.

10. Cf. Molina's *Concordia*, q. 14, a. 13, disp. II.

11. *ST* I, 22, 4. ad 3: "Et considerandum est quod necessarium et contingens proprie consequuntur ens, inquantum huiusmodi. Unde modus contingentiae et necessitatis cadit sub provisione Dei, qui est universalis provisor totius entis, non autem sub provisione aliquorum particularium provisorum" (We must remember that, properly speaking, *necessary* and *contingent* are consequent upon being as such. Hence the mode both of necessity and of contingency falls under the foresight of God, who provides universally for all being, not under the foresight of causes that provide only for some particular order of things).

12. Maurice Merleau-Ponty, *Sens et non-sens* (Paris: Éditions Nagel, 1948), 356.

13. One recollects *ST* I-II, 109, 1: "Manifestum est autem quod sicut motus omnes corporales reducuntur in motum caelestis corporis sicut in primum movens corporale; ita omnes motus tam corporales quam spirituales reducuntur in primum movens simpliciter, quod est Deus. Et ideo quantumcumque natura aliqua corporalis vel spiritualis ponatur perfecta, non potest in suum actum procedere nisi moveatur a Deo. Quae quidem motio est secundum suae providentiae rationem; non secundum necessitatem naturae, sicut motio corporis caelestis. Non solum autem a Deo est omnis motio sicut a primo movente, sed etiam ab ipso est omnis formalis perfectio sicut a primo actu. Sic igitur actio intellectus et cuiuscumque entis creati dependet a Deo inquantum ad duo: uno modo, inquantum ab ipso habet perfectionem sine formam per quam agit; alio modo, inquantum ab ipso movetur ad agendum." Of course, one must be clear that Molina did not intend to deny that freedom is subject to divine providence, howsoever necessarily this implication flows from his account. But this is, indeed, the effect of denying that the positive perfection of our acts of free choice are caused by God.

14. *SCG* III 70: "Haec autem difficultatem non afferunt si praemissa considerentur. In quolibet enim agente est duo considerare, scilicet rem ipsam quae agit, et virtutem qua agit: sicut ignis calefacit per calorem. Virtus autem inferioris agentis dependet a virtute superioris agentis, inquantum superius agens dat virtutem ipsam inferiori agente per quam agit; vel conservat eam; aut etiam applicat eam ad agendum, sicut artifex applicat instrumentum ad proprium effectum; cui tamen non dat formam per quam agit instrumentum, nec conservat, sed dat ei solum motum. Opportet ergo quod actio inferioris agentis non solum sit ab eo per virtutem proprium, sed per virtutem omnium superiorum agentium; agit enim in virtute omnium. Et sicut agens infimum invenitur immediatum activum; ita virtus primi agentis invenitur immediata ad producendum effectum: nam virtus infimi agentis non habet quod producat hunc effectum ex se, sed ex virtute proximi superioris; et virtus illius hoc habet ex virtute superioris; et sic virtus supremi agentis invenitur ex se productiva effectus, quasi causa immediata; sicut patet in principiis demonstrationum, quorum primum est immediatum. Sicut igitur non est inconveniens quod una actio producatur ex aliquo agente et eius virtute, ita non est inconveniens quod producatur idem effectus ab inferiori agente et Deo: ab utroque immediate, licet alio et alio modo."

15. Cf. *ST* I-II 9, 4 ad 1: "It is essential to the voluntary act that its principle be within the agent: but it is not necessary that this inward principle be the first principle unmoved by another. Wherefore though the voluntary act has an inward proximate principle, nevertheless its first principle is from without. Thus, too, the first principle of the natural movement is from without, that, to wit, which moves nature." Ad 3 concludes: "Thus it needs to be moved by another as first mover." The body of the article affirms that "for everything that is at one time an agent actually, and at another time an agent in potentiality, needs to be moved by a mover. Now it is evident that the will begins to will something, whereas previously it did not will it."

16. Bernard Lonergan, in *Grace and Freedom* (New York: Herder and Herder, 1971), famously holds in ch. 4 of this work that the rational creature's motion from not willing to willing is not a real motion. For example: "To later scholastics this seemed impossible a priori: they held that 'Peter not acting' must be really different from 'Peter acting.' They refused to believe that St. Thomas could disagree with them on this; in fact, St. Thomas disagreed" (69 n. 26). The texts he proceeds to cite, however, suffice only to prove that Thomas thought that motion from potency to act was not essential to *action as such*, because inasmuch as a cause is in act, it is actual. But this is tautological: yes, insofar as the agent is acting, as such, the agent is in act, and it is accidental to being in act *as such* that there has been transition from potency to act: otherwise there could be no Prime Mover and First Cause. Nevertheless, all *created* causes are causes limited by potency; and as St. Thomas himself teaches expressly regarding human willing in *ST* I-II, 9, 4: "For everything that is at one time an agent actually, and at another time an agent in potentiality, needs to be moved by a mover. Now it is evident that the will begins to will something, whereas previously it did not will it. Therefore it must, of necessity, be moved by something to will it. And, indeed, it moves itself, as stated above (art. 3), in so far as through willing the end it reduces itself to the act of willing the means. Now it cannot do this without the aid of counsel: for when a man wills to be healed, he begins to reflect how this can be attained, and through this reflection he comes to the conclusion that he can be healed by a physician: and this he wills. But since he did not always actually will to have health, he must, of necessity, have begun, through something moving him, to will to be healed. And if the will moved itself to will this, it must, of necessity, have done this with the aid of counsel following some previous volition. But this process could not go on to infinity. Wherefore we must, of necessity, suppose that the will advanced to its first movement in virtue of the instigation of some exterior mover, as Aristotle concludes in a chapter of the *Eudemian Ethics*." St. Thomas's replies to the objections in this article clarifies that the will is moved from potency to act with respect to its own act of willing. *Now, clearly, a nonreal motion does not require a real extrinsic mover, only a real motion does.* Lonergan is locked in discourse with precisely the right minds on this issue—Aquinas, John of St. Thomas, Bañez, Del Prado, even Garrigou-Lagrange—and indeed is perhaps the last of the great minds to grapple with these issues in the theology of grace. But the temptation to congruism dies hard. In any case, one must note that on the substance of the matter either Aquinas or Lonergan may be correct, but not both. Either the motion of the created will from not acting to acting is a real motion requiring a real extrinsic divine mover—something held expressly by both Aquinas and Aristotle before him—or else the motion of the created will from not acting to acting is not a real motion and so no real divine mover is implicated. Likewise, Lonergan's claims that *motio prephysicae* is not to be found in Aristotle, and that premotion signifies for Aristotle merely "some relation, disposition, proximity that enables mover to act upon moved"

(71), are contradicted by Aristotle's own insistence upon the reception of divine motion by the separated causes that hence are only hypothetically but not absolutely necessary. Likewise these claims are counterindicated by the very example Lonergan uses of the sun melting the North Pole irrespective of whether the pole moves toward the sun or vice versa. For in order for the sun to melt anything it must generate heat, and the generation of heat by the sun involves multitudes of acts of gaseous combustion whereby what is potentially hot becomes actually hot, and without which no local motion of pole to sun or vice versa will (absent collision!) cause the least change in temperature. *That the agent as such is actual does not mean that such agency in creatures does not require prior activation.* Even in the angels, who are always in act with respect to the object of their knowledge, this is only because *God has infused in them the species that sempiternally activate their knowledge*. Act manifests being, and as all beings that are not pure act are divided by potency and act, their action manifests their composite mode of being.

17. E.g., see Henri de Lubac, *The Mystery of the Supernatural* (New York: Herder and Herder, 1967), ch. 4, especially these words regarding the hypothesis of pure nature, and the existence even *hic et nunc* of an order of ends proportionate to human nature, though nonetheless further ordered in grace: "I do not say that it is false, but I do say that it is insufficient. For it completely fails to show, as people seem to think and as by the logic of the theory it should, that I could have had another, more humble, 'natural' destiny. It only demonstrates—presuming it to be well-founded—that in another universe a being other than myself, with a nature similar to mine, could have been given this humbler destiny. But, I repeat, what has this other being really to do with me? What have I to do with him? *To convince me that I might really have had this humbler destiny—humbler, but note also less onerous—you need only show it to me, even momentarily, as something really imprinted upon me, in my nature as it is. Most people would agree that this is precisely what is, by hypothesis, impossible* [my emphasis]. My destiny is something ontological, and not something I can change as anything else changes its destination" (81). But, to the contrary, the order of ends proportionate to nature is naturally knowable, and it is even to some degree knowable that God would (owing to the divine goodness, and the goodness of his creation) have bestowed merely natural aids to human nature if he had created it outside the order of grace. What cannot be known is the extent of such aids. In this given order we do not eat, or play sports, or read literature, or play music, solely because of the ordering of nature to the beatific vision, an ordering that after all we share with angels who do not share our nature. *We can indeed see the order of proportionate natural ends even in the given multiplex of nature as ordered by and within supernatural grace.* Granted that, because nature is created in grace, man is vain without grace: nonetheless, the reason why grace operates as it does in us is significantly a function of the *prior* ordering of nature (the *ens creatum* of human nature and the order of ends proportionate to it must exist before being further ordered at the instant of creation by the infusion

of sanctifying grace). What de Lubac here claims that "most people" would agree upon seems eminently controvertible, namely that we have no knowledge of the natural order as such merely because it receives the help of grace.

18. Ibid., 261.

19. In "Duplex hominis beatitudo," *Communio* 35 (Winter 2008): 600, de Lubac declares it to be a "novel" doctrine *introduced by Suarez* that there is "a natural beatitude that man would have been able to attain had he been created without being ordered to a supernatural end [sine ordinatione ad finem supernaturalem]." Yet, since St. Thomas in *ST* I, 75, 7 ad 1 and *Quaestiones de Anima* a. 7, ad 10 teaches that the human species is derived from the proximate natural end rather than from supernatural beatitude, and since St. Thomas expressly teaches that man could have been created *in puris naturalibus* (*Quod.* I, 4, 3), and since "man" so created would indeed *persist in species* (this is what it means to say that "man" could be created without grace), it follows that the proportionate natural end whence the species is derived would have been man's sole end. It is odd to call a deductive inference from two sets of St. Thomas's propositions—an inference that Thomas must himself have drawn in order to say that *man* could be created *in puris naturalibus* inasmuch as the species "man" is according to St. Thomas derived from *the natural rather than the supernatural end*—a novelty of Suarezian origination.

20. *ST* I, 12, 1: "Inest enim homini naturale desiderium cognoscendi causam, cum intuetur effectum; et ex hoc admiratio in hominibus consurgit. Si igitur intellectus rationalis creaturae pertingere non possit ad primam causam rerum, remanebit inane desiderium naturae" (For there resides in every man a natural desire to know the cause of any effect which he sees; and thence arises wonder in men. But if the intellect of the rational creature could not reach so far as to the first cause of things, the natural desire would remain void). This is to say that according to St. Thomas the natural desire for God is *elicited* by the knowledge of God's existence and is not to be identified merely with the desire for happiness in general, or with the *voluntas ut natura*, which is for that which proportionately befits the will: but the vision of the infinitely transcendent God is disproportionate to every creature. It is precisely for this reason that Thomas focuses on arguments for the *essential possibility* of the vision of God for man, arguing that as possessed of intellect and will man can be aided and elevated by God to the beatific vision. The proper object of the will as *inclinatio sequens formam intellectam* is the universal good, or the good in general, and this is no more simply *equivalent* to the subsistent universal good than the object of the metaphysician—universal being, *ens commune*—is equivalent to *ipsum esse subsistens per se*.

21. Cf. *ST* I-II, 5, 5 ad 1.

22. Nicholas Healy, in his "Henri de Lubac on Nature and Grace," *Communio* 35 (Winter 2008): 599–612, suggests that de Lubac did consider such texts and that my claim to the contrary in "On the Loss, and the Recovery, of Nature as a Theonomic Principle: Reflections on the Nature/Grace Controversy," *Nova et Vetera* (English ed.) 15, no. 1 (2007), is misguided. For example, he claims that de

Lubac considered *ST* I, 62, 2 "at length" in *The Mystery of the Supernatural*. Yet in that book de Lubac quoted merely one single line from the article in question, and that *precisely not from the first part of the article* that poses the most conspicuous problem for de Lubac's thesis (where St. Thomas *denies* that there can be any inclination or tendency whatsoever for anything above nature without the aid of grace—and *desire* for Thomas is *always* an *inclinatio*). Cf. *The Mystery of the Supernatural*, 113, 113 n. 47. The fact that de Lubac quoted texts from two other articles perhaps misled Healy into supposing that I, 62, 2 was quoted at length. In that article St. Thomas argues that because the natural movement of the will is the principle of all the things that we naturally will, it is impossible for the will to have any inclination whatsoever toward anything above nature unless helped by a supernatural principle. Manifestly since for St. Thomas desire is an inclination, this establishes that it is impossible that there be a *natural* desire for *essentially supernatural beatific vision* on the ground that any inclination whatsoever to what is above nature requires grace. The natural desire to see God—a desire for God as "cause of these effects"—is not simply identical with the graced desire for the Triune God as supernatural beatitude. Nor can what is essentially proper to the *voluntas ut natura*—the will as nature—plausibly be held to consist in the beatific vision, for that vision is proportionate to no finite nature whatsoever, and the will by its nature is ordered to the good in general, universal good: it is not a naturally deific faculty, although it is susceptible to divine aid and elevation whereby it may be made capable of the beatific vision.

ST I, 75, 7 ad 1 and the cognate *Quaestiones de Anima* 7 ad 10 constitute two crucial texts that de Lubac appears never to take up. The passages in *ST* I, 75, 7 ad 1 and *Quaestiones de Anima* 1 ad 10 affirm that man as such receives his *species* in relation to the *proximate natural end* and not—even in the regime of grace—from supernatural beatitude. That man qua man is defined by a purely natural end is not a view with which the thought of de Lubac is associated, and it is difficult to imagine that he would have found agreement with this teaching of Aquinas easy had he known of it. But nowhere in *Surnaturel*, *Augustinianism in Modern Theology*, or *The Mystery of the Supernatural* will one find him grappling with these teachings of which he seemingly was unaware to the extent that he implicitly suggests them to be of *Suarezian* origin. Cf. de Lubac, "Duplex hominis beatitudo," where it is declared to be a "novel" doctrine *introduced by Suarez* that there is "a natural beatitude that man would have been able to attain had he been created without being ordered to a supernatural end [sine ordinatione ad finem supernaturalem]." Since man's species is derived from the natural end, if man had been created *in puris naturalibus* it is true *by definition* that his sole end would thus have been the proportionate natural end. This is not Suarezian; rather, it is the necessary condition for Thomas to say that "man" could have been created outside grace, for whether in this present economy of grace or a different hypothetical order, man as such receives his species from the natural end rather than from the supernatural beatific end: that is the teaching of Aquinas.

Likewise de Lubac failed squarely to confront the reasoning of *De Malo* V, 1 ad 15. Although he indicated knowledge of it in *Surnaturel: Études historiques*, ed. Michael Sales (Paris: Desclée de Brouwer, 1991), 456 ("cette privation n'eut pas revetu le caractere d'une peine," a point that comes singularly from *De Malo* V, 1 ad 15), he did not sufficiently take up its significance in terms of the natural desire, designating the teaching merely as a "paradox" that "poses a problem" and asserting that "this problem is not resolved in explicit terms anywhere in the work of Saint Thomas" and results from a "new philosophical framework" that is "poorly adapted" (mal adapté) to the Christian doctrinal tradition. ("Ce qu'il y a, c'est le paradoxe même de la nature humaine [ou plutôt de l'esprit créé], paradoxe que saint Thomas n'a point inventé, mais dont il a conservé et transmis l'héritage,—quoique dans un cadre philosophique en partie nouveau, qui, lui étant mal adapté, lui donne parfois des allures de contradiction. Disons au moins que la doctrine de cet article, confrontée avec la doctrine thomiste de la béatitude, pose un problème, et que ce problème n'est résolu nulle part en termes exprès dans l'oeuvre de saint Thomas.") De Lubac does not in taking up this passage consider St. Thomas's account of penalty, an account that affects the interpretation of this passage markedly. This omission is itself sufficient to indicate that de Lubac's treatment of this question is inadequate. *De Malo* V, 1 ad 15 teaches that had man been created *in puris naturalibus* and then died, and been bereft of the beatific vision, this lack of the vision would not be a punishment—which could not be true were there a strong and unconditional natural desire for supernatural beatitude (as opposed to a conditional desire to know God under the disproportionate *ratio* of "cause of created effects"). Surely, if man by nature has a strong desire for the supernatural beatific vision, then to be deprived of this vision is the deprivation of a good of nature contrary to the will of the one deprived. This would appear to be not only a punishment but an unjust punishment—yet Thomas says it would *not* constitute a punishment, not only because it would not proceed from fault, but because man as such has no unconditional *natural* desire for supernatural beatitude.

While de Lubac did consider certain pivotal teachings of Aquinas regarding nature and grace—the hypothesis of creation *in puris naturalibus* and the gratuity of creation in grace (although it is difficult to find any reference to *Quod*. I, 4, 3. c)—he did so in a context in which texts essential for their interpretation (for example, those indicated above) were either not considered at all or misread. For example, he cited *Quaestiones disputatae de veritate* XIV, 10, ad 2 in *Duplex hominis beatitudo* (nn. 16 and 17) regarding the doctrine of creation in grace as utterly gratuitous, while not at all engaging that part of the quoted text that states of supernatural beatitude that "the other is the good which is out of all proportion with man's nature because his natural powers are not enough to attain to it either in thought or desire." Natural powers do not attain to God *even in desire:* that is, there is no natural desire for supernatural beatitude without grace. Likewise, the clear teaching of *De Malo*, q. 5, art. 3, resp., denying natural knowledge that the perfect good for which man is created is the supernatural beatific vision, is not sufficiently considered. In any event these texts were treated by de Lubac without sufficient reference to Thomas's own doctrine of the properly natural end.

One cannot complain: de Lubac's genius was for the fathers of the church and for the mystery of the church. But lest one stumble in the darkness cast by his shadow, it is important to correct his error regarding the proportionate natural end. The safeguarding of truth from naturalism that he sought to achieve requires the correct understanding of the limits and dignity of the natural desire for God as distinct from the desire formed in us through supernatural grace: it requires an awareness of natural law, as limited and distinguished from grace, as *theonomic* yet in an inferior mode to that of grace.

23. See Charles De Koninck's classic account of the common good, "On the Primacy of the Common Good: Against the Personalists," *Aquinas Review* 4 (1997): 14–71.

24. One thinks of his works *Reality* (St. Louis, MO: Herder, 1950), *God: His Existence and His Nature,* 2 vols. (St. Louis, MO: Herder, 1955), *Grace* (St. Louis, MO: Herder, 1952), *Beatitude* (St. Louis, MO: Herder, 1956), and *The One God* (St. Louis, MO: Herder, 1959), to say nothing of his profound commentary on the mystical life in *The Three Ages of the Interior Life,* 2 vols. (St. Louis, MO: Herder, 1947).

25. E.g., Santiago Ramirez's four-volume work *De Analogia*; Fr. Marie-Michel Labourdette's "La théologie et ses sources," *Revue Thomiste* 46, no. 2 (1946): 353–71; Fr. Jean-Hervé Nicholas's beautiful evocation of the traditional Thomist account of grace in his little work *The Mystery of God's Grace* (Dubuque, IA: Priory Press, 1960), originally published as *Le mystère de la grâce* (Liège: La pensée catholique, 1951), or, of course, his 1,248-page-long *Synthèse Dogmatique* (Paris: Beauchesne, 1991).

26. Ralph McInerny, *Ethica Thomistica* (Washington, DC: Catholic University of America Press, 1997), and *Praeambula Fidei: Thomism and the God of the Philosophers* (Washington, DC: Catholic University of America Press, 2006). In addition to his own important and extensive speculative contributions, he supervised the translation, editing, and publishing of the collected works of De Koninck in an edition from Notre Dame University Press. He was in the forefront among those who have understood and articulated the crucially central importance of the classical and Thomistic understanding of *natura* for theology and philosophy during the postconciliar epoch, such that North American Thomism without his work and influence is difficult to imagine. All this—and mystery novels too! The presence at one institution of both McInerny and MacIntyre has over the past several years strategically contributed to the University of Notre Dame's Catholic intellectual heritage, secularist institutional *fomes* notwithstanding.

27. One thinks prominently of *After Virtue: A Study in Moral Theory,* 3rd ed. (Notre Dame: University of Notre Dame Press, 2007), *Three Rival Versions of Moral Enquiry: Encyclopedia, Genealogy, and Tradition* (Notre Dame: University

of Notre Dame Press, 1991), and *Dependent Rational Animals: Why Human Beings Need the Virtues* (Peru, IN: Carus, 2001); but his Aquinas lecture—*First Principles, Final Ends, and Contemporary Philosophical Issues* (Milwaukee: Marquette University Press, 1990)—is a gem that will perdure even with these larger works. The realism undergirding the scope of MacIntyre's engagement is bracing and profound, and his principled awareness of natural teleology as the saturative condition for practical life and its relation to the speculative order renders his work ever more richly, articulately, and developmentally expressive of the Aristotelian and Thomistic tradition. As noted above, that two minds such as his and McInerny's should have cohabited the same faculty—and that faculty at the University of Notre Dame, an institution both suffering the effects of the storm described in the text above and possessed of a profound Catholic heritage—is a remarkable datum and indeed grace of this time.

28. Russell Hittinger, *A Critique of the New Natural Law Theory* (Notre Dame: University of Notre Dame Press, 1989); Fr. Romanus Cessario, O.P., *The Moral Virtues and Theological Ethics*, 2nd ed. (Notre Dame: University of Notre Dame Press, 2008). Hittinger's work is the initial and surely the greatest breach in the dam of the project to construe the teaching of Aquinas on terms of peace with Enlightenment and analytic presuppositions. It has encouraged the return to the actual teaching of Aquinas, viewed not through alien continental or analytic lenses, or merely as an artifact of historical exegesis, but as articulating a systematic analysis of incomparable worth. While in particular it is a scandal to those for whom it is an a priori proposition that St. Thomas's work must contain only what can fill the conceptual space occupied by analytic thought, for those able to free themselves so as to interrogate analytic presuppositions from without, it is invaluable. This is a seminal and synecdochic work, summing up much that by analogy also pertains to the Thomistic response to the negation of *natura* within transcendental philosophy. As for Cessario, his influence is of course broadly felt in moral theology, as in his *Introduction to Moral Theology* (Washington, DC: Catholic University of America Press, 2001), but also in theological anthropology—e.g., *The Godly Image* (Petersham, MA: St. Bede's Press, 2002)—and perhaps even more in his splendid *A Short History of Thomism* (Washington, DC: Catholic University of America Press, 2005), which introduces the school of Thomism to a contemporary audience vaguely aware of the artificial vacuum in theology and philosophy and eager to engage the patrimony of St. Thomas Aquinas uncensored by continental and analytic prejudices. This small work, like many masterful small works, manages to point the compass of the inquirer due north into the heart of St. Thomas's doctrine in its perennial pertinence for theological and philosophic contemplation. A small work indeed, but one that adumbrates a great deal with eloquence, limpid clarity, and profundity—but these are among the virtues of this Dominican scholar with which his writing, teaching, and preaching are redolent.

29. One thinks particularly of his book *Wisdom, Law, and Virtue: Essays in Thomistic Ethics* (New York: Fordham University Press, 2008), but his writing

spans the whole of St. Thomas's teaching. Every essay of this author manifests a jeweler's eye for distinctions, and for the profundity of the tradition. Few authors have pressed as deeply into the teaching of Aquinas, especially in the domain of the philosophy and theology of practical reason.

30. Excluded from the list above are many fine savants who for reasons of space simply cannot be named here, including some whose labor has been the vindication of the historical foundations of Thomistic study, admittedly an enterprise that at some hands might threaten to consume its own purpose for being, but in others has been of seraphic aid: but that is for another time. Suffice it to say that many excellent minds have undertaken more limited but nonetheless valuable and profound textual studies, which are ordered to the enrichment of theological and philosophic contemplation unfolding according to its own exigencies and systematic requirements.

CHAPTER TWELVE

Forgiveness at the Limit
Impossible or Possible?

RICHARD KEARNEY

Several contemporary thinkers have responded to the question of the limits of forgiveness. Jankelevitch and Primo Levi have both affirmed the impossibility of forgiving those who do not ask for forgiveness. Arendt talked of the impossibility of forgiving radical evil; and more recently Derrida has written of the impossibility of pure forgiveness *tout court*.

Paul Ricoeur seeks an alternative response to the limit of forgiveness. In an essay entitled "Difficult Forgiveness"—which serves as epilogue to his last major work, *Memory, History, Forgetting* (2004)—he attempts to give due credence to the strong arguments of Derrida, Jankelevitch, and Arendt, while seeking to shift the final emphasis from "impossible" to "difficult." (As he confesses, the key word separating his work from Derrida's is *impossible*.) In what follows I will address this contemporary debate on forgiveness at the limit, with particular reference to the question of pardon as a secret gift.

I

Let me begin with a short account of Derrida's approach to forgiveness before looking to Ricoeur's alternative reading. I believe this crucial debate serves to illustrate the different moral positions adopted by hermeneutics and deconstruction at the turn of the twenty-first century.

Why is pardon impossible for Derrida? We can only forgive the unforgivable, he says, and that is precisely what cannot humanly be forgiven. If someone asks for forgiveness, that person has already atoned and so does not require forgiveness. Only radical evil and hatred, the imprescriptible crime, the irreparable effect, the inexpiable act, are matters for forgiveness. Such forgiveness is therefore, for Derrida, unconditional, undeserved, and ultimately impossible.[1] But if it were possible, it, and it alone, would be true.

How does Derrida come to this conclusion? Pure forgiveness, if it existed, would be beyond repentance, atonement, or any account of the crime. It would include the pardoning of radical evil and would have nothing to do with reconciliation, healing, remorse, or repentance. It would be forgiveness of the "guilty as guilty";[2] and, as such, it would not be applicable to those who had repented or apologized (and were therefore no longer guilty). Conditional forgiveness is not forgiveness, argues Derrida, because it is "corrupted" by calculations of the weight of crime and punishment. Unconditional forgiveness, by contrast, would involve forgiving the unforgivable (*pace* Arendt and Jankelevitch) and is impossible. It has nothing to do with judgment, punishment, or recompense. It is beyond laws, norms, and obligations. Even the Abrahamic account of forgiveness is ultimately compromised, Derrida suggests, in that it introduces the notion of pardon in proportion to repentance and, so doing, limits its own ostensible message of pure gratuity and generosity. True unconditional forgiveness is *madness*, a private and inaccessible event, never a matter of public or political action. It lies beyond the logic of rights or duties.

Unconditional and conditional forgiveness are, Derrida concludes, irreducibly heterogeneous and irreconcilable.[3] Forgiveness calls for a "hyperbolic ethics" beyond ethics. And in this sense Derrida holds out forgiveness as an impossible ideal, even as he admits that in everyday life and history we have to engage in acts of pardon "in a series of conditions of all kinds ('psycho-sociological, political' etc.)."[4] But the problem, as I see it, is that there is no way for Derrida to *transit* or *translate* between the conditional and unconditional. There are no criteria, mediations, or orientations. Pardon is, at best, a leap in the dark, a form of insane guesswork or indiscriminate decision. All we know is that we can forgive only the unforgivable, except perhaps for the unforgiving, namely those who refuse to forgive. And this, of course, places a heavy burden to forgive on the victims of radical evil while affirming that all perpetrators of radical evil be unconditionally forgiven. This seems unjust, to say the least; but we must remember that we are not talking here of what is possible. Maybe pure forgiveness has little to do with real human beings, since it is unrealizable in any case?[5] Who knows?

II

Ricoeur takes Derrida's account on board while moving from the impossible to the possible. From the outset, Ricoeur confesses that his analysis will be formulated in the "optative" mood. It will operate under the sign of a certain "eschatology" of memory.[6] In other words, he lets us know that he is going to discuss the possibility of "difficult" forgiveness in terms of a projection of an act of unbinding—an act that goes beyond the limits of law and prescription, crime and punishment, fault and reparation (limits to be respected and recognized as necessary in the order of politics and justice). But unlike Derrida, who sees such forgiveness as a hyperbolic and impossible ideal, Ricoeur wants to inscribe it under the sign of an "anthropology of capable being": an anthropology grafted onto a philosophy of religion that says, "*You can forgive*" (463).

How does he propose to do this? Let me briefly trace Ricoeur's argument. Just as the voice of evil, fault, and guilt proceeds from the unfathomable depths of human selfhood, the voice of forgiveness is a "voice from above" (467). To the abyss of radical evil responds the vertical height of forgiveness. There is a radical disproportion between this polar dichotomy of depth and height that, Ricoeur concedes, constitutes the "torment" of his analysis. But while he is prepared to agree with Derrida that forgiveness is indeed directed toward the unforgivable (it is without condition, exception, or restriction), he refuses to conclude that it is therefore *impossible*. Suggesting how the seeming impossibility of forgiveness gives way to possibility is the difficult task of his reflection.

First, Ricoeur insists we separate the unforgivable and the imprescriptible, for while the imprescriptible—for example, crimes against humanity, genocide—requires justice to be done, pardon operates at a level of surplus love beyond the limits of justice. "To forgive [genocide] would be to ratify impunity, which would be a grave injustice committed at the expense of the law, and even more so, of the victims" (473). This does not mean of course that forgiveness dispenses with justice, only that it supplements it with a logic of excess and gift beyond the economy of exchange, and outside the circle of accusation and punishment. His solution to this dilemma will ultimately be an unbinding of the agent from the act (or, as Augustine might have put it, of the sinner from the sin). But I shall return to this shortly.

Ricoeur, unlike Derrida, accepts that a certain stage of exchange is part of the odyssey of the "spirit of forgiveness" (478). Ricoeur believes (again *pace* Derrida) that at the level of practice there does exist a correlation between forgiveness requested and forgiveness granted. And he cites the example of certain exceptional public gestures like Chancellor Brandt kneeling in Warsaw or the pope during his visit to Jerusalem. Ricoeur agrees that while only the victims can forgive (no one can do it for them), there is still a possibility of verticality that can supplement, without dispensing with, this limit of forgiveness. This is where Ricoeur rejoins the question of forgiveness as gift (*par-don, ver-geben*). The difficulty with gift as a model of exchange is, Derrida and other critics argue, that it can place the beneficiary under a debt he or she cannot repay. But this is to remain within the economic model of market exchange. And that is precisely what the commandment to love one's enemy contests insofar as it breaks the rule of reciprocity and "requires the extraordinary." Proposing a nonmarket form of gift as love or "extravagance," Ricoeur proposes that "faithful to the gospel rhetoric of hyperbole, according to this commandment the only gift that is justified is the one given to the enemy, from whom, by hypothesis, one expects nothing in return. But precisely, the hypothesis is false: what one expects from love is that it will convert the enemy into a friend according to a vertical event of surplus. And this surplus implies an unfathomable enigma of asymmetry between the height of forgiveness and the abyss of guilt" (482–83). For Ricoeur, forgiveness is difficult indeed—but, again, not impossible!

Ricoeur cites the Truth and Reconciliation Commission in South Africa (1996–99), established by Nelson Mandela and Desmond Tutu, as a model of exchange that seeks to purge a violent past. As a public political process Ricoeur commends it, while recognizing its limits. The purpose of the commission was, in its own words, to "collect testimony, console the injured, indemnify the victims and amnesty those who confessed to committing political crimes" (483). The aim of this process was not in fact pardon as such but reconciliation, in a political sense. And the benefits were clear in therapeutic, moral, and political terms. "In offering a public space for complaints and the recounting of suffering, the commission certainly gave rise to a shared *katharsis*," but the "amnesty granted by the competent committee did not amount to forgiveness on the part of victims" (484). It was a matter of the victims having their memories and stories of suffering told and recognized as true by the perpetrators and the committee. While acknowledging the clear limits of this process of "understanding without revenge" or recompense (the victims were deprived of the satisfaction of any normal sanction of a trial—punishment and judgment of perpetrators), Ricoeur nonetheless celebrates the commission as a "historic opportunity for a public form of the work of memory and mourning in the service of public peace" (485). But Ricoeur goes further, for he dares suggest the possibility of seeing under the figure of such a "public exercise of political reconciliation something like an *incognito* of forgiveness": something that can occur only at the "most secret level of selfhood" and personhood. Pardon is not a universal law to be prescribed or imposed; it is an act of surprising gratuity that may emerge through reconciliation but is by no means necessitated or even implicated by it. In short, the exchange model of reconciliation may be inspired or informed by some secret spirit of forgiveness, though it is by no means its equivalent. Pardon and reconciliation operate at different levels; but they may nonetheless interanimate each other in secret, nonprescriptive ways.

But here again Ricoeur is faced with the vexed question: How does one overcome the ostensible incommensurability between the unconditionality of forgiveness and the conditionality of the request for forgiveness? Again Ricoeur proposes a nonmarket model of exchange of gift and receptivity that nonetheless preserves the polarity of the extremes—of conditional and unconditional. (In asking for pardon one must be open to receiving a negative response from the other: I cannot forgive you). But the ultimate question is: "What force makes one capable of asking, giving or receiving the word of forgiveness?" (486). In short, to what power do we appeal in asking for forgiveness?

Ricoeur looks to the capacities of unbinding (forgiveness) and binding (promising) to suggest a way of mastering the course of time and giving a continuity to the present by giving a future to the past. He borrows here from Hannah Arendt's notion of the continuation and renovation of action (natality) outlined in *The Human Condition* (a response, in part, to Heidegger's preference for Dasein's mortality and rupture). What is crucial for both Ricoeur and Arendt is the notion that forgiving and promising are capacities that depend on human plurality—that is, the idea of persons relating to each other in an intersubjective context. Acknowledging that forgiveness has a religious aura that promising does not, Arendt nonetheless wants to argue that forgiveness, which opposes vengeance, is a *human* power. Even the Gospels, she notes, require that humans forgive each other before they seek forgiveness from God. And this act of unbinding is the token of human freedom, of the ability to find some release from the evils and errors of the past in order to be able to start all over again: what she famously calls the event of natality. Only through a mutual release from what they have done can humans remain free agents (487). But while promising represents the possibility of a political act of will (treaties, accords, pacts between governments and peoples), forgiveness is, concedes Arendt, an act of love that keeps a distance from the political.

Ricoeur agrees with much of this; but he goes further than Arendt in insisting that forgiveness needs to be understood not only as the unbinding of debt but, at the very "heart of selfhood," as the unbinding of the *agent from the act*. But how, we may ask, do we move from the unforgivable fault to the miracle of forgiveness? Ricoeur responds that forgiveness renders the guilty person *able to begin again* by unbinding the person as agent from the act, which, qua act, remains condemned and unforgivable. Here he also goes further than Derrida, who argued that to forgive a person but condemn his act is like pardoning a subject other than the one who committed the act (490): in other words, one would be talking about two different people. But Ricoeur takes a decisive step from impossibility to possibility by appealing to his fundamental notion of *l'homme capable*. This is crucial. The person who committed the crime is *also* an agent *capable* of doing otherwise, that is, of committing good acts (including those, post hoc, of repentance and remorse). Here Ricoeur speaks of the radical uncoupling "at the heart of the very power to act—of agency—namely, between the effectuation and the capacity that it actualizes. This intimate dissociation signifies that the *capacity* of commitment belonging to the moral subject is not exhausted by its various inscriptions in the affairs of the world. This dissociation expresses an act of faith, a *credit* addressed to the resources of self-regeneration" (490).

It is telling that at this pivotal point in his analysis Ricoeur speaks of an "ultimate act of trust," an act based on an "intimate" pairing proposed by the Abrahamic memory of the Religions of the Book—namely the pair "forgiveness" and "repentance." This forms a paradox in that the response to forgiveness is implied in the gift itself, "while the antecedence of the gift is recognized at the very heart of the inaugural gesture of repentance" (491). And he goes further to suggest that if forgiveness is indeed the supreme height—responding to the abyss of fault—it lasts "forever" beyond notions of before and after—and this in contrast to repentance, which occurs in historical time (whether sudden or protracted). So the paradox relates to a circle—namely, the circle between the gift of forgiveness that remains *forever* and what comes to be *in each instance*. Is this not pardon as the entry of eternity into history?

Rather than engaging here in standard theological arguments about grace and nature, divine or human initiative, Ricoeur prefers to remain within the limits of a philosophy of religion grafted onto (1) an anthropology of human persons as "capable beings," (2) a fundamental ontology of being as act and power *(dunamis),* to be traced from Aristotle to Leibniz, Spinoza, and Bergson; and finally (3) a moral philosophy, as in Kant, which recognizes that the "predisposition to good" is more original than the radical propensity to evil *(Religion within the Boundaries of Mere Reason)* (491). Moreover, Ricoeur extends his plea for the primacy of goodness, capacity, and natality—evinced in the circle of forgiveness and repentance—to a hermeneutic analysis of the great myths of creation, previously presented in his *Symbolism of Evil* (1960). There, referring specifically to the Adamic myth, he speaks of the narrative of the Fall as symbolizing something irremediable but in no way inevitable in its consequences.[7] This is a pivotal point for Ricoeur—the excess of capacity over the past. In *Memory, History, Forgetting,* he states that "the gap with respect to creation holds in reserve the possibility of another history inaugurated in each case by the act of repentance and punctuated by all the irruptions of goodness and of innocence over the course of time" (492). Indeed, Ricoeur goes on to add that this "immense project of restoration" can in turn be aided by a philosophical reading of the Jewish and Christian "imagination" of the suffering servant. (The terms *philosophical* and *imagination* are telling.)

Refusing recourse to speculative or transcendental solutions to the paradox of forgiveness and repentance, Ricoeur returns once again to his insistence on a practical philosophy of action uttered in the "optative mood." He endorses, in the final analysis, a discreet eschatology whose ultimate word is happiness. "Under the sign of forgiveness," concludes Ricoeur, "the guilty person is to be considered capable of something other than his offences and his faults. He is held to be restored to his capacity for acting, and action restored to its capacity for continuing. This capacity is signaled in the small acts of consideration in which we recognized the incognito of forgiveness played out on the public stage. And finally, this restored capacity is enlisted by promising as it projects action toward the future. The formula for this liberating word, reduced to the bareness of its utterance, would be: you are better than your actions" (493). In short, the power that enables us to give and receive forgiveness is the phrase: *You are able!* In spite of the ostensible impossibility of forgiveness, you *can* forgive and be forgiven. You can be restored to the world of action and the hope of happiness.

It is significant, I think, that in spite of his insistence on the philosophical nature of his analysis, Ricoeur signs off with the suggestion that under the sign of the ultimate *incognito* of forgiveness can be found an echo of the words of wisdom uttered in the Song of Songs, "Love is as strong as death" (506). The terms *incognito* and *echo* are safety nets here, but one senses that the sacred is not far off.

III

So how does Ricoeur make the final leap from impossible to possible forgiveness? How does he surmount the claim by Derrida, Arendt, and Jankelevitch that forgiveness of radical evil is impossible? Acknowledging that such forgiveness is extremely "difficult" (the title of his essay), Ricoeur ultimately seems to point to a superhuman origin of gift and capacity that belongs to the order of spirit and love, an order that observes a logic of surplus and superabundance. In short, what is impossible to humans—as Derrida rightly notes—is not impossible to God or, by extension, the divine capacity for renovation and rebirth that is the mark of the "gap of creation," the miracle of origin, in each human being. Derrida too admitted that forgiveness is possible only for something or someone beyond the human, but he does not name a tradition of memory, faith, or love to which one might adhere. He leaves the space of the "inhuman" empty, without hermeneutic or practical bridge back to the human. Derrida does not sign off by citing the Song of Songs or giving the last word to love over death. Nor, finally, does he give primacy to the origin of good over evil, restoration over rupture, reconciliation over aporia, happiness over angst. Perhaps it is a similar miracle of love that Derrida privately intends in his call for a messianic "democracy to come"? But he does not say so, and it is impossible to know.

Ricoeur, by contrast, makes his intentions clear even if he acknowledges the huge difficulties involved in moving from the impossible to the possible. First, he openly if gently confesses his adherence to the Jewish and Christian imagination of the suffering servant and the vertical height of forgiveness (it comes "from above"). This is somewhat analogous, I would suggest, to the crucial move in Alcoholics Anonymous where adherents incapable of controlling their lives hand themselves over to "a higher power," who in turn empowers them to do the impossible—unbind themselves as agents from the past acts of addiction, and thereby realize that they are more than their past history and can be restored to a capacity to begin again.

Ricoeur also differs from Derrida, it seems to me, in acknowledging numerous ways in which the leap toward forgiveness can be prepared for, though never guaranteed or demanded as a law or method. One of these ways is the narrative power of exchanging memories and stories with one's enemies, those we cannot forgive.

In conclusion, let me say a few words about the hermeneutic of narrative preforgiveness. In an essay entitled "Reflections on a New Ethos for Europe," Ricoeur outlines an *ethic of narrative hospitality* that may nurture a predisposition but by no means a guarantee of forgiveness. Forgiveness comes from beyond us, as Ricoeur insists, but humans may be more inclined to receive and offer this gift if they learn to love their enemies by exchanging narrative memories with them. This involves "taking responsibility in imagination and in sympathy for the story of the other, through the life narratives which concern the other."[8] In the case of genocide or famine memorials (I am thinking, for example, of the Holocaust and Irish Famine memorials side by side in Battery Park, New York), this takes the form of an exchange between different peoples' histories in such a way that we practice an art of transference and translation that allows us to welcome the story of the other—the memory of the stranger, the victim, the forgotten one.

This practice of narrative hospitality poses a particular problem in the limit case of hereditary hatred. Here, Ricoeur insists, there is no quick therapeutic fix or exoneration but a difficult labor of attending to founding events that are not my own and, at times, to life stories that belong to my long-sworn adversary. As he describes in *Memory, History, Forgetting,* we are faced with the difficult task of learning to "recount otherwise" (477). But the best that such narrative hospitality can achieve is to serve as a "secret alchemy" that may induce a certain "disposition to consideration." Such gestures of narrative imagination and empathy can sometimes lead to an exchange between a request and an offer of forgiveness. But this can never be institutionalized as a political right or duty. And questions of guilt and accountability are not suspended. At best, translating the stories of the other resists the reification of a historical event into a fixed obsession by showing how each event may be told in different ways by narrators other than ourselves. Not that everything becomes relative and arbitrary. On the contrary, acts of trauma and suffering call out for justice, and the best way of achieving this is often to invite empathy with strangers and adversaries by allowing for a plurality of narrative perspectives. The resulting overlap may thus lead to what Gadamer calls a "fusion of horizons" where diverse horizons of consciousness may at last find some common ground—a reciprocal transfer between opposite minds.[9] "The identity of a group, culture, people or nation, is not that of an immutable substance," writes Ricoeur, "nor that of a fixed structure, but that, rather, of a recounted story." A hermeneutic exchange of stories effectively resists an arrogant or rigid conception of cultural identity that prevents us from perceiving the radical implications of narrative hospitality—namely, the possibility of "revising every story which has been handed down and of carving out a place for several stories directed towards the same past."[10] Of course, while this model of narrative hospitality may work in historical conflicts like Northern Ireland, the Balkans, or South Africa, it is not easily applied to limit situations like the Holocaust. For while a plurality of narratives by the victims is desirable (as Primo Levi says, the story must be told again and again so that the Holocaust will never be repeated), a plurality of narratives by the perpetrators—unless explicitly expressing apology, guilt, and remorse—can easily lead to relativism or revisionism. And there are other cases of genocide where a reciprocal exchange of memories is equally difficult. One thinks of the Armenian genocide in Turkey. Might it ever be possible for an open exchange of memories between Turks and Armenians to bring about some kind of reconciliation, preparing eventually for the miraculous "incognito of forgiveness"? Or for a narrative hospitality between Jews and Arabs?

A plurality of narratives should increase, not diminish, respect for the singularity of the events narrated through the various acts of remembering. It might even be said to increase our sense of awareness of such events, especially if it is foreign to us in time, space, or cultural provenance. "*Recounting differently* is not inimical to a certain historical reverence to the extent that the inexhaustible richness of the event is honoured by the diversity of stories which are made of it, and by the competition to which that diversity gives rise."[11] And Ricoeur adds this critical point: "The ability to recount the founding events of our national history in different ways is reinforced by the exchange of cultural memories. This ability to exchange has as a touchstone the will to share symbolically and respectfully in the commemoration of the founding events of other national cultures, as well as those of their ethnic minorities and their minority religious denominations."[12] When it comes to the question of reconciliation and forgiveness, this point applies particularly to events of pain and trauma (as in famine or war memorials). And here again it is a question, not of guaranteeing pardon but, as Ricoeur reminds us in *Memory, History, Forgetting*, of carrying out "an exchange between a request and an offer, in which the unforgivable begins to be chipped away" (477–78). I think the term *chipped away* is critical here. It is a matter of a long working through, not some cheap therapeutic magic.

Narrative hospitality may also prepare for forgiveness insofar as it allows for a retrieval of the betrayed promises of the past, so that we may respond to our "debt to the dead" and endeavor to give them a voice. The goal of narrative retrieval is, therefore, to try to give a future to the past by remembering it in the right way, ethically and poetically. In *Memory, His-*

tory, Forgetting, a crucial aspect of reinterpreting transmitted traditions is the task of discerning past promises that have not been honored. For "the past is not only what is bygone—that which has taken place and can no longer be changed—it also lives in the memory thanks to arrows of futurity which have not been fired or whose trajectory has been interrupted" (8). In other words, the unfulfilled future of the past may well signal the richest part of a tradition—its unactualized *possibilities;* and the emancipation of "this unfulfilled future of the past is the major benefit that we can expect from the crossing of memories and the exchange of narratives" (8). It is especially the founding events of a community—traumatic or dramatic—that need to be reread in this critical manner in order to unlock the potencies and expectancies that the subsequent unfolding of history may have forgotten or travestied. This is why narrative hospitality often involves a recovery of some seminal moment of suffering or hope, of the repressed traumas or impeded promises that are all too often occluded by Official History. "The past is a cemetery of promises which have not been kept," notes Ricoeur. And narrative hospitality can, at best, offer ways of "bringing them back to life like the dry bones in the valley described in the prophecy of Ezekiel" (9). And, for Arendt as for Ricoeur, promising is the other side of forgiving, as it opens history to natality and enables agents to begin again.

One of the ultimate goals of narrative hospitality between enemies is *pardon,* though the goal is of the order not of teleology but of eschatology, not of necessity but of surprise. And here again we encounter the boundary situation of unforgivable guilt and the possibility of "something other" that might make impossible forgiveness possible. If empathy and hospitality toward others are crucial steps in the ethics of remembrance, there is something *more*—something that entails moving beyond narrative imagination to forgiveness. In short, the exchange of memories of suffering demands more than sympathy and duty (though these are essential for any kind of justice). And this something "extra" involves pardon insofar as pardon means "shattering the debt." Here the order of justice and reciprocity can be supplemented, but not replaced, by that of "charity and gift." Such forgiveness demands huge patience, an enduring practice of "working through," mourning, and letting go. But it is not a forgetful forgiveness. Amnesty can never be based on amnesia. It remembers our debt to the dead while at the same time introducing something other, something difficult almost to the point of impossibility, but something all the more important for that reason. One thinks of Brandt kneeling at Warsaw, Havel's apology to the Sudeten Germans, Hume's preparedness to speak with the IRA, Sadat's visit to Jerusalem, Hillesum's refusal to hate her hateful persecutors—all miraculous moments where an ethics of reciprocity is touched and transfigured by a poetics of pardon. The leap made. But I repeat: one does not replace the other—*both* justice *and* pardon are equally important in the act of remembering past trauma. Ricoeur insists on this point. "To the degree that charity exceeds justice we must guard against substituting it for justice. Charity remains a surplus; this surplus of compassion and tenderness is capable of giving the exchange of memories its profound motivation, its daring and its momentum" (11).

When we dare to listen to the stories of enemies or strangers, to other peoples and communities not our own, are we not suddenly all famine sufferers, genocide victims, casualties of war—at least for a special, fleeting moment? A moment, out of time yet also in time, that bears the trace of the incognito of forgiveness?

We return finally to the limit situation of evil that serves as abyssal opposite to the gift of forgiveness. Unforgivable evil is not just something we struggle against. It is also something we undergo. To ignore this passivity of evil suffered is, Ricoeur concludes, to ignore the extent to which evil strikes us as shockingly strange and disempowering. One of the wisest responses to evil is, on this count, to acknowledge its traumatizing effects and work through them *(durcharbeiten)* as best we can. Practical understanding can redirect us toward action only if it has already recognized that some element of estrangement almost always attaches to evil, especially when it concerns illness, horror, catastrophe, or death. No matter how prepared we are to make sense of evil, we are never prepared enough. That is why the "work of mourning" is so important as a way of not allowing the inhuman nature of suffering to result in a complete "loss of self" (what Freud called "melancholia"). For without selfhood no pardon could be possible. Some kind of catharsis is necessary to prevent the slide into fatalism that all too often issues in despairing self-destruction. The critical detachment brought about by cathartic mourning elicits a wisdom that may turn *passive lament* into the possibility of *active complaint*, that is, *protest*.[13] Though protest is, of course, not yet pardon.

Here narrative testimonies, mentioned above, may help the victim to escape the alienation of evil, that is, to move from a position of mute helplessness to a form of self-renewal. Some kind of narrative working through is necessary, it seems, for survivors of evil not to feel crippled by grief or guilt (about the death of others and their own survival) or to succumb to the game of the "expiatory victim" that makes pardon impossible. What the catharsis of the mourning narrative allows is that new actions and responses—including pardon—are still possible *in spite of evil suffered*. It detaches us from the obsessional repetitions and repressions of the past and frees us for a future. For only in unleashing the agent from the act and the victim from the evil—in the miracle of secret pardon—can one escape the disabling cycles of retribution, fate, and destiny: cycles that alienate us from the possibility to forgive by instilling the view that evil is overpoweringly alien—that is, irresistible.

Working through the experience of evil—narratively, practically, cathartically—helps us to take the paralyzing allure out of evil. And in so doing it enables us to remain open to the incognito gift of pardon. Working through is central to an anthropology of capability and an ontology of potency and act in what makes evil *resistible*. In sum, by (a) transforming the alienation and victimization of lament into a moral response of just struggle, and (b) opening the possibility of a spiritual response of forgiveness, we refuse victory to evil, declaring love as strong as death. But while narrative working through, testimony, and catharsis may bring us to the threshold of pardon, they cannot cross it of their own momentum. They can predispose us to the gift of forgiveness but cannot deliver it.

Something "more" is required. Radical evil calls for an answering power of radical good. Against the "never" of evil, which makes pardon impossible, we are asked to embrace what Ricoeur calls the "marvel of a once again" that makes it possible.[14] But the possibility of forgiveness is a "marvel," we noted, precisely because it surpasses the limits of rational calculation and explanation. There is a certain gratuitousness about pardon due to the very fact that the evil it addresses is not part of some dialectical necessity. Pardon is something that makes little sense before we give it but much sense once we do. Before it occurs it seems impossible, unpredictable, incalculable in terms of an economy of exchange. There is no science of forgiveness. And yet this is precisely where hermeneutic sensibility, attentive to the particularity of specific evil events, joins forces with the practice of patient working through—their joint aim being to ensure that past evils might be prevented from recurring. Such prevention calls for pardon as well as protest so that the cycles of repetition and revenge give way to future possibilities of nonevil. This is a good example of Ricoeur's claim that pardon gives a future to the past.

Cathartic narration can, Ricoeur concludes, help to make the impossible task of pardon that bit more possible without ever allowing amnesty to fall into amnesia. The past must be recollected and worked through so that we can identify what it is that we are forgiving. For if pardon is beyond reason, it is never as blind or mad as Derrida suggests. And if it is mobilized by the gratuity of love—which calls for that element of extra—it is never insensitive to the logic of justice. Or to put it in Pascal's terms, pardon has its reasons that reason cannot comprehend. Perhaps only a divinity could forgive indiscriminately. And there may indeed be some crimes that a God alone is able to pardon. Even Christ, as Ricoeur notes, had to ask his father to forgive his crucifiers: "Father, forgive them, for they know not what they do." As man alone he could not do it. Impossible for us, possible for God. Here an ethics of pardon approaches the threshold of a religious hermeneutics.

But, finally, what kind of religious hermeneutics are we talking about? In his essay on evil and in the essay on pardon in *Memory, History, Forgetting,* Ricoeur seems to work within an exclusively Judeo-Christian tradition. But in his last testament, *Vivant jusqu'à la mort,* Ricoeur extends the horizon of "the sacred that makes possible" (God as *Posse,* as he puts it) to all great wisdom traditions, amounting to a call for a radically interconfessional hospitality. Here too there is need for pardon, to forgive the great crimes committed by one religion against another in history. And so in this confessional testimony, which uncharacteristically bridges the divide between the philosophical and the theological, Ricoeur speaks of a "grace" that takes the form of an "intimate transcendence which rips through the veils of confessional religious codes."[15] Some might suggest that Ricoeur is approximating here Derrida's anonymous structure of messianicity, a religion without religion, an Other without face, tradition, or voice. But I think not. For while the advent of such an Other is impossible for Derrida, for Ricoeur it is a sacred marvel that makes the impossible possible in each lived moment that pardon is given or received.

Notes

1. Jacques Derrida, *On Cosmopolitanism and Forgiveness* (London: Routledge, 2001), esp. "On Forgiveness" (in dialogue with Richard Kearney et al.) in *On Cosmopolitanism and Forgiveness*, 52–72. See also Jacques Derrida, "Hospitality, Justice and Responsibility," in *Questioning Ethics: Contemporary Debates in Philosophy,* ed. Mark Dooley and Richard Kearney (London: Routledge, 1999), 65–84. Our discussion of forgiveness here is largely though not exclusively focused on contemporary debates within so-called continental philosophy. A more extensive treatment of the theme would ideally address similar debates within the so-called Anglo-American tradition. For a fine example of the latter, see Charles Griswold, *Forgiveness: A Philosophical Exploration* (Cambridge: Cambridge University Press, 2007). One of MacIntyre's great talents is his ability to draw equally from both schools of thought, along with thinkers like Ricoeur, who is the central figure of our analysis here.

2. Derrida, *On Cosmopolitanism and Forgiveness,* 3.

3. Derrida, "On Forgiveness," 44.

4. Ibid., 49.

5. Derrida, "To Forgive," in *Questioning God,* ed. John Caputo, Mark Dooley, and Michael Scanlon (Bloomington: Indiana University Press, 2001), 21–51. See also the excellent commentary by Marguerite La Caze, *Wonder and Generosity: Their Role in Ethics and Politics* (New York: Columbia University Press, forthcoming), esp. ch. 6.

6. Paul Ricoeur, *Memory, History, Forgetting* (Chicago: Chicago University Press, 2004), 459. Subsequent page citations to this work are given parenthetically in the text.

7. Paul Ricoeur, *The Symbolism of Evil* (Boston: Beacon Press, 1967).

8. Paul Ricoeur, "Reflections on a New Ethos for Europe," in *Paul Ricoeur: The Hermeneutics of Praxis,* ed. Richard Kearney (London: Sage Publications, 1996), 7.

9. Hans-Georg Gadamer, *Truth and Method* (London: Sheed and Ward, 1975).

10. Ricoeur, "Reflections," 7.

11. Ibid., 8.

12. Ibid., 9.

13. Paul Ricoeur, "Memory and Forgetting," in Dooley and Kearney, *Questioning Ethics,* 5–12. See also Paul Ricoeur, "Evil: A Challenge to Philosophy and

Theology," in *Figuring the Sacred: Religion, Narrative and Imagination* (Indianapolis: Fortress Press, 1995), 250–51. See also my analysis of this theme: Richard Kearney, "Evil, Monstrosity and the Sublime," in *Strangers, Gods and Monsters* (London: Routledge, 2003), 83–84.

14. Ricoeur quoted in Richard Kearney, "Evil, Monstrosity," 105–6. See also William Desmond, *Beyond Hegel and Dialectic* (Albany: SUNY Press, 1992), 238–39. And for a comparative and contrasting "Eastern" perspective on the topic of pardon as it relates to a number of contemporary political situations of violence and war, see Joseph S. O'Leary, "Buddhism and Forgiveness," *Japan Mission Journal* 56 (Spring 2002): 37–49.

15. Ricoeur, *Vivant jusqu'à la mort* (Paris: Le Seuil, 2007), 45.

PART III

Thematic Analyses

CHAPTER THIRTEEN

Evolutionary Ethics
A Metaphysical Evaluation

FRAN O'ROURKE

The Origin of Species *introduced a mode of thinking that in the end was bound to transform the logic of knowledge, and hence the treatment of morals, politics and religion.*
—John Dewey

Darwin's theory has no more to do with philosophy than any other hypothesis in natural science.
—Ludwig Wittgenstein

One's only owned by naturel rejection. Charley, you're my darwing. So sing they sequent the assent of man.
—James Joyce

Evolution is the prevailing paradigm for today's understanding of human nature. It is championed by some not only as a biological explanation for the origin and unity of living beings but as a response to all questions of human life and the universe itself, as well as its purpose—or absence thereof. It is rejected by others, who fear that acceptance of the biological theory of evolution entails a naturalistic vision of the world, and of man as a product of nature no different from other animals. Both see in evolutionary theory the equivalent of a metaphysical claim to total explanation. Ethics unsurprisingly has been brought into engagement with evolution, in both dialogue and dispute. Systematic attempts have been made by some theorists to ground morality entirely upon evolutionary principles. Evolution, it is claimed, is the key to all moral questions; ethical norms are laws of evolution: biology is our destiny, morality "a legacy of evolution."[1] Others fear that evolutionary interpretations of human nature must inevitably lead to the obliteration of uniquely human morality. In this essay I will outline one twentieth-century approach to evolutionary ethics and examine some assumptions of evolutionary theory that have a bearing upon the ethical evaluation of man. Although I will not explicitly develop the context in detail, my evaluative comments are largely from an Aristotelian viewpoint. The wider perspective is that of the question of being, which features neither in Aristotle nor in evolutionary theory, but which must finally be confronted to respond ultimately to the ethical question. My wider theme is thus the metaphysical background to the intersection of ethics and evolution.[2]

Evolutionary Ethics of Sociobiology

Among Darwin's disciples who have in recent decades sought to ground ethics upon the biological theory of evolution, the most prominent has been Edward O. Wilson, a renowned Harvard entomologist; other well-known representatives are Michael Ruse and Richard Dawkins.[3] In 1975 Wilson published his monumental work *Sociobiology: The New Synthesis,* which defined sociobiology as "the systematic study of the biological basis of all social behavior."[4] His aim was to lay bare the biological underpinnings of animal behavior and to apply these to man. This was a revolutionary renewal, following upon the Modern Synthesis, which a generation earlier had fortified Darwinism with the insights of molecular genetics. The new discipline of sociobiology sought to integrate the social and human sciences into evolutionary theory. Novelist Tom Wolfe proclaimed: "There's a new Darwin. His name is Edward O. Wilson." Having catalogued in great detail the "social" features of animal behavior, in the final chapter Wilson applied his conclusions to *homo sapiens:* all human behavior, including morality and religion, is based upon genetics. Sociobiology was founded on the conviction that behavior may be explained in terms of basic universal features of human nature laid down by evolution. The implications for moral philosophy are stark, the claim is ambitious: "Scientists and humanists should consider together the possibility that the time has come for ethics to be removed temporarily from the hands of philosophers and biologicized."[5]

By presenting a selection of passages from the authors under consideration I will first outline the claims of evolutionary ethics. One of the attractions of their writing, frequently lacking in mainstream philosophers, is its clarity; Wilson twice won the Pulitzer Prize for General Nonfiction.[6] In the opening paragraphs of *On Human Nature,* written as a popular introduction to sociobiology, he summarizes the essentials of his evolutionary naturalism: "If humankind evolved by Darwinian natural selection, genetic chance and environmental necessity, not God, made the species.... The human mind is a device for survival and reproduction, and reason is just one of its various techniques.... The intellect was not constructed to understand atoms or even to understand itself but to promote the survival of human genes."[7] Michael Ruse expresses the consequence for ethics: "The position of the modern evolutionist is that humans have an awareness of morality—a sense of right and wrong and a feeling of obligation to be thus governed—because such an awareness is of biological worth. Morality is a biological adaptation no less than are hands and feet and teeth.... Morality is just an aid to survival and reproduction, and has no being beyond or without this."[8] In *Sociobiology* Wilson contends that ethical knowledge and motivation have a physiological source: "The hypothalamic-limbic complex of a highly social species, such as man, 'knows,' or more precisely it has been programmed to perform as if it knows, that its underlying genes will be proliferated maximally only if it orchestrates behavioural responses that bring into play an efficient mixture of personal survival, reproduction, and altruism."[9] Science, according to Wilson, has supreme authority in matters of human destiny: "I consider the scientific ethos superior to religion: its repeated triumphs in explaining and controlling the physical world; its self-correcting nature open to all competent to devise and conduct the tests; its readiness to examine all subjects sacred and profane; and now the possibility of explaining traditional religion by the mechanistic models of evolutionary biology. The last achievement will be crucial. If religion, including the dogmatic secular ideologies, can be systematically analyzed and explained as a product of the brain's evolution, its power as an external source of morality will be gone forever."[10] All human activities, including the most lofty, function in the service of genetic evolution: "If the brain evolved by natural selection, even the capacities to select particular esthetic judgments and religious beliefs must have arisen by the same mechanistic process. They are either direct adaptations to past environments in which the ancestral human populations evolved or at most constructions thrown up secondarily by deeper, less visible activities that were once adaptive in this stricter, biological sense."[11]

Physiologically the most important organ, "the brain is a machine of ten billion nerve cells and the mind can somehow be explained as the summed activity of a finite number of chemical and electrical reactions."[12] But, states Wilson: "More to the point, the hypothalamus and limbic systems are engineered to perpetuate DNA."[13] All physiological and cerebral reality and activity are conceived exclusively in the service of purposeless evolution. Ruse states: "Vanity and ignorance alone support the claim that human reason has a privileged status. Because we are the product of a long, directionless, evolutionary process, we are forced to accept that there is something essentially contingent about our most profound claims."[14] Evolution is everything; there is no purpose beyond the evolutionary process: "No species, ours included, possesses a purpose beyond the imperatives created by its genetic history. Species may have vast potential for material and mental progress but they lack any immanent purpose of guidance from agents beyond their immediate environment or even an evolutionary goal toward which their molecular architecture automatically steers them."[15] Briefly for Wilson: "The species lacks any goal external to its own biological nature."[16] Richard Dawkins spells it out: "We are survival machines—robot vehicles blindly programmed to preserve the selfish molecules known as genes.... We, and all other animals, are machines created by our genes."[17] Dawkins claims that the world is void of all purpose whatsoever, and draws the following conclusion: "In a universe of electrons and selfish genes, blind physical forces and genetic replication, some people are going to get hurt, other people are going to get lucky, and you won't find any rhyme or reason in it, nor any justice. The universe that we observe has precisely the properties we should expect if there is, at bottom, no design, no purpose, no evil and no good, nothing but pitiless indifference."[18]

Ultimately and solely important for sociobiology is the perpetuation of genes. They are the units of natural selection and have evolved to manipulate the individuals—"gigantic, lumbering robots"[19]—in which they dwell; the gene, and not the individual, is paramount. If we are nothing more than an aggregate of cells and molecules, what of personal identity and free will? Why be moral? What is it to be moral? The response of Wilson, Ruse, and Dawkins is consistent: the origin, purpose, and content of morality are likewise a function of the genetic imperative: morality is a mechanism inherited from biology to ensure the survival of genetic material into the future. Genes alone are of enduring value and purpose; the individual and the group are too large to be units of natural selection. Dawkins states: "The genes are the immortals . . . genetic entities that come close to deserving the title. We, the individual survival machines in the world, can expect to live a few more decades. But the genes in the world have an expectation of life that must be measured not in decades but in thousands and millions of years. . . . Genes are denizens of geological time: genes are forever."[20] Morality is necessary for the continued success of evolution. Ruse and Wilson assert:

> As evolutionists, we see that no justification of the traditional kind is possible. Morality, or more strictly our belief in morality, is merely an adaptation put in place to further our reproductive ends. Hence the basis of ethics does not lie in God's will or any other part of the framework of the Universe. In an important sense, ethics as we understand it is an illusion fobbed off on us by our genes to get us to cooperate. It is without external grounding. Ethics is produced by evolution but not justified by it, because, like Macbeth's dagger, it serves a powerful purpose without existing in substance.[21]

According to Michael Ruse: "The time has come to take seriously the fact that we humans are modified monkeys, not the favored Creation of a Benevolent God on the Sixth Day. In particular, we must recognize our biological past in trying to understand our interactions with others. We must think again especially about our so-called 'ethical principles.' The question is not whether biology—specifically, our evolution—is connected with ethics, but how."[22]

According to Wilson and Ruse, morality exerts its biological imperative through what are termed "epigenetic rules," laws that have grown accumulatively over evolutionary time. These rules have "proven their adaptive worth in the struggle for existence";[23] they constitute the "hereditary regularities of mental development."[24] The principles governing logical deduction, scientific induction, mathematics, science, religion, and ethics are "rooted in our biology" and are justified by their adaptive value to our proto-human ancestors.[25] The methods of investigation, analysis, inference, judging, and reaching conclusions evolved epigenetically and were inherited by us; they were obeyed by our ancestors because of their selective advantage and survival benefit. Ruse illustrates this, for example, with hypothetical alternative reactions by our ancestors to the threat of tigers: those who reasoned correctly survived, thus validating the reasoning patterns they had obeyed, which were in turn transmitted to their descendants.[26]

Morality is adaptively useful; it is a function of genetic survival, governed by rules of biology. Genes dominate morality and keep cultural evolution under control. Wilson sums up the relationship between nature, nurture, culture, and morality: "Can the cultural evolution of higher ethical values gain a direction and momentum of its own and completely replace genetic evolution? I think not. The genes hold culture on a leash. The leash is very long, but inevitably values will be constrained in accordance with their effects on the human gene pool. The brain is a product of evolution. Human behavior—like the deepest capacities for emotional response which drive and guide it—is the circuitous technique by which human genetic material has been and will be kept intact. Morality has no other demonstrable ultimate function."[27]

I will argue that sociobiology is marked by various deficiencies, methodological and doctrinal. Before I assess the theory from different theoretical points of view, it is worth noting the dearth of references to the historical tradition. In *Sociobiology*, Wilson limits his discussion to the "oddly disjunct conceptualizations" of intuitionism ("the belief that the mind has a direct awareness of true right and wrong") and behaviorism ("moral commitment is entirely learned, with operant conditioning being the dominant mechanism"). Both approaches, he charges, neglect the "genetic evolution of ethics," despite the fact that proponents are obliged to consult and interpret the "emotive centers of their own hypothalamic-limbic system."

In *Consilience* Wilson considers the alternatives of transcendentalism and empiricism. Dawkins confidently dismisses the entire tradition: "There is such a thing as being just plain wrong, and that is what, before 1859, all answers to those questions were."[28] Since the luminaries of the philosophical tradition knew nothing of evolution or the selfish gene, their ethical theories may be dismissed as worthless: philosophers speak in paradigms lost.[29]

Aristotle and Sociobiology

Surprising is the absence in the literature of sociobiology of all reference to Aristotle, founder of biology and author of the first ethical treatises, regarded by Darwin as his greatest master. On the biological level, Aristotle can readily accommodate many aspects of sociobiology. While he did not teach a theory of evolution, he recognizes a scale of perfection within the biological world that, if reconfigured as a temporal progression toward higher perfection, provides elements of an evolutionary theory.[30] Moreover, in the *History of Animals,* an impressive catalogue of zoological fieldwork, Aristotle recognizes affinities between animals and man, especially in the emotions and passions:

> For even the other animals mostly possess traces of the characteristics to do with the soul, such as present differences more obviously in the case of humans. For tameness and wildness, gentleness and roughness, courage and cowardice, fears and boldnesses, temper and mischievousness are present in many of them together with resemblances of intelligent understanding.... For some characters differ by the more-and-less compared with man, as does man compared with a majority of the animals (for certain characters of this kind are present to a greater degree in man, certain others to a greater degree in the other animals), while others differ by analogy.[31]

His remarks on children support the view of sociobiology that human instincts are evident in a primitive form in animals. "This kind of thing is clearest if we look at the age of childhood; for in children, though one can see as it were traces and seeds of the dispositions that they will have later, yet their soul at this period has practically no difference from that of wild animals, so that it is not illogical if some characters are the same in the other animals, while others are very like, and others are analogous."[32] Similarities of instinct between children and animals seem to confirm, within an infinitely shorter time frame than that of evolution, the biological affinity between animals and man.

Aristotle recognized the "social" behavior of certain species, especially that of hymenoptera (ants, bees, wasps), which provides sociobiology with evidence for primitive altruism. He also documented the social behavior of cranes as they emigrated from the Scythian steppes to the source of the Nile. As well as a leader, signalers control the flock with whistle calls; when the flock settles and sleeps, the leader keeps watch and cries an alert in case of danger.[33] More importantly he provides an example of mutual utility, of the kind interpreted by sociobiology as "reciprocal altruism," between the sandpiper and the crocodile: "When crocodiles gape the sandpipers fly in and clean their teeth, and while they themselves are getting their food the crocodile perceives that he is being benefited and does not harm them, but when he wants them to go he moves his neck so as not to crush them in his teeth."[34]

Sociobiology and Philosophical Method

The most patent flaw in the approach of sociobiology to moral philosophy is the gratuitous assertion of E. O. Wilson that morality is no longer a matter for philosophy, that its only hope is to be "biologicized." Theoretically and historically there is no warrant for this verdict. As a sweeping view it ranks with Wilson's wild assertion: "The history of philosophy consists largely of failed models of the brain."[35] Wilson presumes that moral phenomena are no different from biological data and may be analyzed, interpreted, and codified in the same empirical manner. Sociobiology proceeds on the unquestioned assumption that biological evolution is a philosophical panacea. In his popularizing book *On Human Nature*, Wilson declared: "Above all, for our own physical well-being if nothing else, ethical philosophy must not be left in the hands of the merely wise."[36] Peter Singer's reaction is probably typical of philosophers generally: "Most of my colleagues in university departments of philosophy regard Wilson's invasion of their territory as too absurd to merit a considered response."[37] Philip Kitcher has remarked: "Ironically, the very ease with which they come to pronounce on philosophical issues that go beyond their professional expertise tells against their having much influence on our understanding of those issues. Biologists may believe that they have a license to advance views about human freedom and morality without considering what philosophers and other humanists have written about these subjects."[38]

Theodosius Dobzhansky famously remarked that nothing in biology makes sense except in light of evolution. For sociobiology nothing whatsoever has meaning except in light of evolution: biology itself acquires its value from evolution. In turn it is reduced to physics; despite its nomenclature, the naturalist sociobiology of Wilson, Ruse, and Dawkins assumes that the entire realm of nature is a closed system of material causes and effects, without any possible influence from outside. In his ambition to embrace, harmonize, and integrate all scientific approaches into a single synthesis (an approach termed "consilience"), Wilson advances a strongly materialist position: "The central idea of the consilience world view is that all tangible phenomena, from the birth of stars to the workings of social institutions, are based on material processes and are ultimately reducible . . . to the laws of physics."[39] Sociobiology is emphatically and exclusively materialist.[40] As a philosophical doctrine this exceeds the competence of biological science.

One marvels at the confidence with which biologists such as Wilson and Dawkins make grand pronouncements about the ultimate meaning of the biological universe and the purpose of human existence.[41] Science conventionally concerns itself with causes and operations within the observable world.[42] Its methods are empirical, its explanations formulated in theories that appeal to measurable data. Its own validity is a question for philosophy of science. Sociobiology has adopted the ambitious aim of incorporating all knowledge whatsoever under the mantle of consilience, to be measured by the methods of biology. Wilson proclaims: "Science offers the boldest metaphysics of the age. . . . There is a general explanation of [the] origin and nature of the human condition, proceeding from the deep history of genetic evolution to modern culture."[43] Evolution supplies, on this view, the answers to the ultimate questions; it is the key to understand human behavior and the perspective to unify all knowledge. Wilson makes no distinction between the scientific insights of the biological theory of evolution and the philosophical implications of the theory for man's nature and origin.[44]

The theory of evolution is indisputably of immeasurable value in the life sciences, but the wider question of its profound meaning goes beyond science. It becomes itself an *explanandum* within the broader context of philosophical reflection. Because of its object and method, science is obliged to adopt a naturalistic viewpoint: it may not affirm any reality that cannot be measured in terms of space and time. It must follow positivist procedures. When the scientist addresses wider questions, she becomes a philosopher and may not apply the same criteria or means of measurement and investigation. She cannot presume that science has all the answers—or, more importantly, that it asks all the questions. Sociobiology ignores the hierarchy of explanation that reflects irreducible levels of reality; Aristotle was keenly aware of this, as noted by Alasdair MacIntyre: "His is a universe structured in a hierarchical way—that is why the hierarchical structure of the sciences is appropriate for giving a realist account of such a universe—and each level of the hierarchy provides the matter in and through which the forms of the next higher level actualize and perfect themselves. The physical provides the material for biological formation, the biological the material for human formation. Efficient and material causes serve final and formal causes."[45]

The Genetic Fallacy

Since evolution has to do with origins and development, to approach human nature in light of evolution is doubtless of great value. Aristotle affirmed: "He who considers things genetically and originatively will obtain the clearest view of them."[46] For Aristotle, however, γένεσις / *genesis* is more than a temporal beginning; it connotes nature (φύσις) and growth toward a τέλος or goal, so that a complete understanding of a substance refers to all four causes. Evolution, as generally presented, is concerned with material and efficient causes, neglecting the formal and final principles of explanation. In particular evolutionary ethics collapses the final cause into the circumstances of the genesis of qualities and tendencies that constitute the material for moral activity. Explanation in terms of material and efficient causation are incomplete. In the *De Anima*, Aristotle contrasts the respective approaches of the natural philosopher (φυσικός) and the dialectician (διαλεκτικός) in explaining anger. The latter explains it in terms of its purpose, namely the desire for retaliation, whereas the former describes it as a surging of the blood and heat around the heart. "The one is describing the matter, the other the form or formula of the essence."[47] Both accounts are required; each responds at a different level, but the formal account is more meaningful.[48] The naturalist approach to phenomena is a valid but incomplete explanation.[49] On the abandonment of final and formal causes by modern philosophy, Stephen Clark notes that what was first a methodological precaution quickly became an ontological assumption. But as Clark tellingly remarks, "Mathematical formulae have usually been exempt, and beauty keeps breaking in."[50] Evolutionary theorists eagerly formulate development patterns in sophisticated equations.[51]

As well as reducing all aspects of human nature and behavior to the biological and material, the sociobiological account of morality is seriously flawed by the restriction of its value to the conditions from which it arose. Evolutionary ethics is guilty of the "genetic fallacy," as described by Nietzsche in the *Genealogy*: "The cause of the origin of a thing and its eventual utility [die Ursache der Entstehung eines Dings und dessen schliessliche Nützlichkeit], its actual employment and place in a system of purposes [dessen tatsächliche Verwendung und Einordnung in ein System von Zwecken], lie worlds apart; whatever exists, having somehow come into being, is again and again reinterpreted to new ends, taken over, transformed, and redirected by some power superior to it."[52] Sociobiology substitutes causal conditions for moral reasons. The fact that animal behavior developed in certain ways is no reason why we should adopt their history as a moral norm for our present and future actions.

Accusing them of the genetic fallacy, Daniel Dennett rejects the claim of Wilson and Ruse that "morality, or more strictly our belief in morality, is merely an adaptation put in place to further our reproductive ends."[53] Dennett's reply is simple: "Nonsense. Our reproductive ends may have been the ends that kept us in the running till we could develop culture, and they may still play a powerful—sometimes overpowering—role in our thinking, but that does not license any conclusion at all about our current values. It does not follow from the fact that our reproductive ends were the ultimate historical source of our present values, that they are the ultimate (and still principal) beneficiary of our ethical actions."[54] Dennett adds that, once persons are on the scene, they are also potential beneficiaries of biological reproduction: "Hence the truth of an evolutionary explanation would not show that our allegiance to ethical principles or a 'higher code' was an 'illusion.'"[55] Dennett illustrates his point: "It is also true that we grew from fish, but our reasons aren't the reasons of fish just because fish are our ancestors."[56]

There is no doubt but that our biological nature evolved from more basic forms of life. It is equally evident that birds, insects, and animals engage in collective behavior. It is not at all directly evident, however, that the ethical impulse that seems to be innate in most members of the human species has its origin in the collective orientation or "altruistic" behavior of those life forms from which mankind evolved. While it would be consistent with the overall pattern of evolutionary development and progress to conjecture that the social behavior of nonhuman species evolved over time, there is nothing contradictory in the assumption that they might have so behaved from their initial emergence as distinct species. The mother-child bond, for instance, is with few exceptions universal among mammals; did it need to evolve? Reciprocal recognition is instinctive in most species. While we observe some animal kinds acting collectively, many do not: should we expect that they also will eventually evolve social tendencies? *E contrario*, if their survival were thus dependent they should have long since perished.

Personal Morality and Freedom

To accept that we have a genetic propensity to behave morally does not yet explain why we are *obliged* to act morally. Applying Aquinas's comment on the individual nature of knowledge ("Hic homo intelligit"), we may affirm: "Hic homo deliberat et agit." Moral action is a matter of personal motivation, resolve, action, responsibility, and consequence. It requires a sense of personal identity and continued moral commitment over time. The center of moral behavior is the individual person, consciously aware of her- or himself as motivated for individual reasons, and aware of the responsibilities and consequences attending one's actions. A difficulty with evolutionary ethics is its failure to give reasons why we should be moral in the first place; it does not provide any compelling motivation, either positive in terms of reward or negative in terms of sanction. It postulates ethics as a persuasatory strategy inherent in evolutionary progress. I am expected to behave correctly because I thus promote the genetic material of humanity. To what purpose? What is my obligation to posterity—more precisely to the genes for which my descendants are nothing more than carriers? What debt have I to my ancestors, that I should obey the epigenetic rules I have inherited? If I am obligated to human life, the question imposes itself: What is the point of life?

Aristotle's ethics, on the contrary, is immediately appealing because it offers personal reasons and incentives why we should be moral; it is centered upon individual happiness. Rather than ground morality on an impersonal process of species propagation, in which we are insignificant instruments, he recognizes that we are self-conscious individuals with a distinct nature and a rich potentiality to be freely realized. He accepts the tension between elements of personality, hence the need for moral education. It is a matter of immediate self-experience that we deliberate upon conflicting goals and make free and reflective choices. The motivation is happiness; it is pursued naturally and spontaneously, since the good is what the mind recognizes as desirable. With subtle metaphysical insight, Aristotle defines happiness as the perfect activity of our most human powers; its success is virtue. Virtue depends on us, as does also vice.[57] Aristotle's account reflects real-life experience. We are obliged to make moral choices; other animals do not have reason, do not deliberate or choose.[58] They do not have the power to form universal concepts,[59] and they are incapable of action.[60] We are the only animals that can be happy (μὴ μετέχειν τὰ λοιπὰ ζῷα εὐδαιμονίας).[61] The animal's purpose is life (ζῆν), man's is the good life (τὸ εὖ ζῆν). "Animals have no share in well-being or in purposive life."[62]

We may say that for Aristotle, man is essentially ethical. This means both that by nature he tends to act morally and that the norms of ethical behavior are embedded in the kind of being that he is. His nature is the source for the capacity and necessity for ethics, as well as the standard that constitutes moral behavior. Central to Aristotle's ethics is the teleology of human nature, a teleology that is both biological and moral. The distinction of act and potency illumines the distance between man's condition and his goal; it explains the dynamism of action and the weight of obligation. The individual is never all that he can or should be. By nature he is equipped with a definite nature, but one that is never fully determined or complete: that is the task of action and freedom. Morality is the corollary of teleology and a condition for happiness. The individual freely and consciously pursues his natural fulfillment. When early in the *Nicomachean Ethics* Aristotle distinguishes between the various levels of life, beginning with the simple act of plant life, and the sentient life of animals, he refers to the "practical life of the rational part of man" (πρακτική τις τοῦ λόγου ἔχοντος).[63] Human practice flows from reason; man seeks reasons for what he does. He is a reason-seeking animal and acts for reasoned ends.

What, according to Aristotle, is human nature that is the basis of morality? It is evidently complex: most obviously material and biological. At this level, evolutionary theory is enlightening. Man, however, is more than his biology. We behave morally, not because we are programmed to obey an impersonal zoological command, but because as rational agents we recognize that by our actions we choose concretely our individual fulfillment in view of permanent and universal values. As moral agents we discern reasons that justify our actions in accord with demands discerned within our nature, and obligations arising from our relationships. The reduction of moral behavior to an unconscious biological impetus ignores the evidence of immediate experience: our moral deliberation in the face of ineluctable choices, the awareness that we are in control, and our choosing of goals for nonbiological purposes. Life in the concrete is always personal. Each one lives in him- or herself as an individual, not proleptically in one's genes, or vicariously in one's offspring. It is in each case an individual "I" who lives, acts, and shapes a personal world. Evolutionary accounts ignore the irreducible element of subjective experience. It is the difference between the detached aspect of the third person as publicly observed, and the inalienable first-person experience, which is *sui generis* but which each of us knows intimately as inner agent.

Aristotle's agent is individual and free, with a self-contained telos. By contrast, for sociobiology "the organism does not live for itself. Its primary function is not even to reproduce other organisms; it reproduces genes, and it serves as their temporary carrier. . . . The organism is only DNA's way of making more DNA."[64] The individual has no intrinsic purpose; it is an instrument to replicate and perpetuate the genes. This is a unidimensional reductionism that views events entirely in terms of their eventual natural consequences. It places human beings within the confines of biological time, precluding any exploration of a possible nontemporal goal or purpose.

The first victim of such a vision is individual liberty: "The agent itself is created by the interaction of the genes and the environment. It would appear that our freedom is only a self-delusion."[65] The inadequacy of evolutionary ethics is evident in the first-person experience each one has as a free and responsible agent. It is beyond doubt that at crucial times in our lives individuals experience the unshirkable weight of choice and dilemmas, without signposts from an evolutionary past. With individual rationality we transcend our biological and cultural heredity and enter the world of personal freedom: "Men at some time are masters of their fates."[66]

It is difficult to see how evolutionary ethics can avoid the charge of genetic determinism. Ruse writes: "As a function of our biology, our moral ideas are thrust upon us, rather than being things needing or allowing decision at the individual level. This is the claim. Just as we have no choice about having four limbs, so we have no choice about the nature of our moral awareness."[67] It is true that in one sense we have no choice in the matter of morality, a fact emphasized by Kantian deontology, according to which, Ruse notes, "the supreme principle of morality is categorical—it is laid upon us. . . . We are not free to choose what right and wrong are to be."[68] We should clarify: moral imperatives are imposed, not coercively, but as a condition for the happy life, which we can freely reject. Moreover, while morality is imposed—it follows upon our nature—it is not a biological determinant. The analogy of arms and legs leads nowhere: *nec ambulando solvitur*.

Another serious difficulty is sociobiology's derivation of moral norms from inherited social patterns and instincts, the primitive manifestations of which are observed in lower animals. Besides social or communal tendencies, we also observe less desirable instincts such as acquisitiveness and aggression. Should these also be accepted as morally normal? How are we to distinguish between the good and bad instincts that we inherit? Each person is influenced by a variety of physical or biological dispositions that are genetically predetermined. Such predispositions are a necessary starting point for actions: they are the material of moral activity. These may include physical strengths or handicaps, biochemical proclivities (e.g., addictive behavior, mental imbalance). However, these predispositions do not constitute or predetermine the moral character of the agent's actions. When the agent consciously and freely adopts a conscious attitude, becoming "*dominus sui*," actions become responsible and ethical. For Aristotle the free man is one who exists for his own sake and not for another.[69] (Aquinas: "The free man is his own cause": *liber est causa sui*.)[70] Genetics is one among a number of elements affecting an individual's moral life but not the most decisive.[71] What counts is that I take possession of my biological heritage, place it under my control, and shape my moral personality.

I have certain temperamental dispositions resulting from my genetic constitution; I am biologically determined but not entirely so. In the nature *versus* nurture/culture debate, it is often assumed that *natural* means "biological" in the sense of subrational: that is to identify man with his biology. Wilson comments that genes hold culture on a leash.[72] Alasdair MacIntyre conveys the same when he states that "our biological nature certainly places constraints on all cultural possibility." He remarks, however: "Man without culture is a myth. . . . Man who has nothing but a biological nature is a creature of whom we know nothing."[73] Both agree that nature and culture are both essential, but they differ in their understanding of nature. Human nature is for Wilson biological and ultimately physical; for MacIntyre, as for Aristotle, it is something more. While heredity places constraints upon human nature and keeps it on a leash, it does not fasten it in chains.[74]

Our genetic constitution, evolved over millennia, predisposes us to act in certain definite ways. Such propensities are not unique to members of the human species but are shared with our evolutionary cousins, primates and chimpanzees. It cannot be doubted that our biology is fundamentally influenced by our genetic makeup, as it interacts with the environment; there is a historic component in our biochemical constitution. Our biology disposes us to react in certain ways to our natural and human environment, without, however, entirely determining our behavior. We experience ourselves as independent in some measure, in the choices we make and in the life projects upon which we deliberate and execute over long periods of time with an awareness of freedom, commitment, and responsibility. Charles Darwin significantly declared: "A moral being is one who is capable of comparing his past and future actions or motives, and of approving or disapproving of them. We have no reason to suppose that any of the lower animals have this capacity."[75] We can explain man's uniqueness, it may be argued, only by accepting that we may not be entirely identified with our biology. Man's biology enters into his nature as a moral being but does not fully constitute or exhaust it. Man is more than his biology; hence morality cannot in principle be fully explained in terms of biology. Man is moral because of the capacity to chose, to think, and to reason in universal terms. These are not entirely explicable in biological terms.

Ethics and Biology

In *After Virtue*, Alasdair MacIntyre contended that a weak element in Aristotle's theory of virtue was its reliance upon a biological teleology.[76] Hence the dilemma: "If we reject that biology, as we must, is there any way in which that teleology can be preserved?"[77] Needless to say, teleology is indispensable, since virtue is linked to function and finality. "Any adequate teleological account must provide us with some clear and defensible account of the *telos;* and any adequate generally Aristotelian account must supply a teleological account which can replace Aristotle's metaphysical biology."[78] In place of Aristotle's "biologically teleological account" MacIntyre proposed a "socially teleological account" of the virtues.[79] This account happily "does not require the identification of any teleology in nature, and hence it does not require any allegiance to Aristotle's metaphysical biology." MacIntyre suggested that the notion of function as applied to man, upon which the notion of virtue depends, "is far older than Aristotle and it does not initially derive from Aristotle's metaphysical biology. It is rooted in the forms of social life to which the theorists of the classical tradition give expression. For according to that tradition to be a man is to fill a set of roles each of which has its own point and purpose: member of a family, citizen, soldier, philosopher, servant of God. It is only when man is thought of as an individual prior to and apart from all roles that 'man' ceases to be a functional concept."[80] *After Virtue* considered the place of the virtues within social practices, and the lives of individuals within communities. By the time of writing *Dependent Rational Animals* MacIntyre had reversed his position: "Although there is indeed good reason to repudiate important elements in Aristotle's biology, I now judge that I was in error in supposing an ethics independent of biology to be possible."[81]

There is common ground between MacIntyre and sociobiology in the reasons offered for this change of emphasis. First, an account of the moral life and development of biologically constituted beings must take as its starting point "our initial animal condition." Second, an account of that development must involve "comparison between humans and members of other intelligent animal species." MacIntyre emphasized how important it is "to attend to and to understand what human beings have in common with members of other intelligent animal species."[82] While there is little in common between Alasdair MacIntyre and E. O. Wilson, both speak emphatically of "other intelligent animals." While this is only one of many fundamental differences with sociobiologists, it is possibly my only major disagreement with MacIntyre. Other species exhibit behavior suggestive of purposeful activity, but I suggest that it is misleading to interpret this as intelligent. Referring to Aristotle, Aquinas presents the following explanation: "The word *intellectus* implies an innermost knowledge, for *intelligere* is the same as *intus legere* (to read inwardly). This is clear to anyone who considers the difference between intellect and sense, because sensitive knowledge is concerned with external sensible qualities, whereas intellective knowledge penetrates into the very essence of a thing, because 'the object of the intellect is what a thing is' as stated in *De Anima* III 6."[83] While Aquinas's etymological explanation is perhaps questionable, his essential point is valid. It is only by analogy with human behavior that we speak of animal intelligence. Aristotle credits animals with *phronesis* but never with *nous*. Animals display an estimative power *(vis aestimativa)* or "practical intelligence" that seems akin to human reason. If we overstretch the analogy, however, the term becomes equivocal and results in ambiguity. It is important to point out, of course, that while MacIntyre refers to members of some nonhuman species as intelligent, he nowhere ascribes to them rationality of the kind that we possess.

For Aristotle, it is clear that intelligence is a prerequisite for the exercise of moral actions: "The terms 'self-restrained' and 'unrestrained' denote being restrained or not by one's intellect, and thus imply that the intellect is the man himself. Also it is our reasoned acts that are felt to be in the fullest sense our own acts, voluntary acts. It is therefore clear that a man is or is chiefly the dominant part of himself, and that a good man values this part of himself most."[84] Further, "The good man does what he ought, since intelligence always chooses for itself that which is best, and the good man obeys his intelligence."[85]

Given our nature as biological creatures, our morality cannot escape its biological framework. As Aristotle noted, it is the same soul that animates digestion, the passions, sensation, willing, and intellection; these are distinct though related activities. Our morality relies upon our biology but transcends it; while we are integrally biological, our nature may not be reduced to its biology. As Stephen J. Pope remarks: "Morality is 'natural' but it is not 'in the genes,' except in the sense that the capacities that allow for morality are based in our biological make-up. Moral codes are transmitted culturally rather than genetically. The body functions in positive ways to support morality."[86] More important than the role of culture, however, are man's spiritual powers, which are prior to culture and beyond his biology; these alone make freedom and morality possible.

Alasdair MacIntyre agrees with sociobiology when he states that an ethics independent of biology is not possible. There can be no ethics that does not take account of the fact that by nature we are biological beings. Human biology makes material demands upon morality. But while ethics may not ignore man's biological nature, moral norms cannot be drawn from biology: such is the essence of sociobiology. We may prescribe respect for each person's biological integrity, but this obligation follows from a general law of respect for the totality of the person. Because man is a biological entity, moral philosophy pronounces upon biological behavior but requires a distinct foundation.

Man and Fellow Animals

In a February 14, 2009, editorial marking the bicentenary of his birth, the *Irish Times* suggested that Darwin's revolutionary biology robbed man of his central uniqueness and apartness from the rest of life. Evolutionary theory offers a detailed account of the manner in which all living beings are fundamentally related, belonging as they do to the common tree of life. Man resembles not just animals but all living things in his evolutionary origin. The fact that we share 98 percent of our DNA with chimpanzees and 35 percent with daffodils confirms our continuity with all living creatures.⁸⁷ By essence man is an animal—a fact shared with all sentient creatures. It is a gratuitous simplification to suggest, however, that he differs in no way from other animals or that he can be fully explained in biological and physical terms. Man is related to all living things but is distinct and separate; he is not confined within biology or immersed in the material world. Human activity manifests spiritual powers that go beyond the biological. The capacity for universal knowledge, the powers of self-reflection, symbolization, conceptualization, and reasoning attest to this. There are many reasons to infer that human nature is not fully explained through biological evolution. Human activity manifests properties not to be explained as capacities of matter. Spirit, characterized by its ability to transcend spatio-temporal limitations, simply cannot emerge from matter. To be spiritual is to be immaterial; by definition matter cannot be the origin of spirit.

One of the great discoveries of evolution is our shared solidarity with other species in a common ecology. Evolution confirms our continuity with all life forms, especially the origins and characteristics shared with fellow animals. We have much to learn from animal behavior. Descartes evaluated the world in terms of introspection and reductively identified the soul with consciousness; since animals show no evidence of introspection, he emptied them of their interiority and reduced them to the mechanical level. Aristotle by contrast observed the autonomous activity of animals and inferred that they too possess an animating soul. His insights cohere perfectly with the biology of evolution; many contemporary scientists recognize in DNA a more accurate version of Aristotelian εἶδος. Ψυχή is for Aristotle the principle of life, the element that characterizes each living being. Diverse levels of perfection indicate distinct types of soul: most perfect is man, whose rational soul incorporates the vegetative and sensitive powers in a unique principle. Evolution confirms the importance of Aristotle's metaphysical biology. This, however, is ignored by sociobiology, which attributes no importance whatsoever to individuals, animals or men: what count are the genes that pass from one generation to another.

Aristotle's acceptance of an immaterial element in human nature, yet his commitment to the unity of the human composite, posed for his successors the question of the relation between the physical body and an immaterial soul. Many attempts to solve the problem simplify and so avoid the reality—which must truly be described as a mysterious relation, an instance of what Aquinas suitably termed the *admirabilis connexio rerum*. I suggest that philosophers pay too little attention to personal lived experience; it is not easy to frame the concrete and rich intensity of selfhood in categories of the measurable: *individuum est ineffabile.* The experience of which each one is immediately and intensively aware cannot be adequately grasped. This is the first datum to be recognized. Blaise Pascal expresses the paradox of the familiar and the inscrutable status of self-knowledge:

> Who would not think, seeing us compose all things of mind and body, but that this mixture would be quite intelligible to us? Yet it is the very thing we least understand. Man is to himself the most wonderful object in nature; for he cannot conceive what the body is, still less what the mind is, and least of all how a body should be united to a mind. This is the consummation of his difficulties, and yet it is his very being. *Modus quo corporibus adhaerent spiritus comprehendi ab hominibus non potest, et hoc tamen homo est.* (The manner in which the spirit is united to the body can not be understood by man; and yet it is man.)[88]

Pascal rightly declares that we have profound and intimate awareness of human nature. We are aware of the unity of the self as synthesis of body and mind. It may not be clear how this operates; but we do not solve the problem by denying one or another aspect of the given certainty. Man is, Shakespeare notes, "most ignorant of what he's most assured, his glassy essence."[89] E. O. Wilson's approach to the question "Who am I?" reminds one of Pooh-Bah in *The Mikado:* "I am, in point of fact, a particularly haughty and exclusive person, of pre-Adamite ancestral descent. You will understand this when I tell you that I can trace my ancestry back to a protoplasmal primordial atomic globule."

The sociobiology of Edward Wilson and the ethology of Konrad Lorenz study animal behavior to illuminate aspects of human nature, especially social life. This is a valid contribution, to the degree that man resembles other animals: many nonrational tendencies, such as sociability, aggression, lust, fear, and altruism, are studied more easily and objectively at the simpler animal level. The similarities, however, may not be exaggerated or generalized to define the proper essence of man or to deny his uniqueness. Darwin asserted in *The Descent of Man:* "The difference in mind between man and the higher animals, great as it is, certainly is one of degree and not of kind."[90] Teilhard de Chardin was correct, I believe, in arguing the exact opposite. Having described at length the human capacity for reflection, he wrote: "We are separated by a chasm—or a threshold—which it cannot cross. Because we are reflective we are not only different but quite another. It is not merely a matter of change of degree, but of a change of nature, resulting from a change of state."[91] It is axiomatic for sociobiology that there is no essential difference at the metaphysical level between humans and other animals. It is this belief that legitimates the application of conclusions drawn from animal evolution to humans. If there is no difference between us and other biological individuals, it makes sense that the primitive behavior evident in chimpanzees, ants, and so forth may be projected back to the earliest developmental stages of our ancestors. It is crucial that sociobiology should remove all barriers between us and other animals and deny exactly what was asserted by de Chardin. Wilson maintains that two traditionally upheld peculiarities of human nature, language and self-awareness, may no longer be regarded as such. He refers to primatologist David Premack's success at training chimpanzees by means of sign language and plastic symbols to learn up to two hundred words and elementary forms of syntax.[92] Wilson concludes: "Many zoologists now doubt the existence of an unbridgeable linguistic chasm between animals and man." Further: "Another chasm newly bridged is self-awareness."[93] Wilson refers to psychologist Gordon G. Gallup's experiments proving that chimpanzees acquire a sense of self-recognition by observing their reflection in a mirror.

Both of these claims are hasty. It is beyond doubt that chimpanzees have some limited memory and can make certain associations in response to stimuli. They distinguish colors and can separate shapes. But while the chimpanzee responds to the physical shape, it does not have the concept of triangle and will not grasp the theorem of Pythagoras. Dolphins imitate complex acoustic signals in a manner similar to children as they learn to use their speech organs, but they do not engage in concept-based conversation. What is singular to humans is the power of symbolization. We can arbitrarily posit a synnoetic connection between any two events or entities—mental or physical—and assign a meaning to this relationship: it could be mnemonic (wearing my watch on the other wrist reminds me to phone my godson for his birthday) or semantic as in the case of language, which associates thoughts with marks upon a material surface, or with identifiable sound waves. This power of symbolic signification is possible only because the human mind has an unlimited openness to the entirety of reality and can thus create a connection between any two entities. Aristotle expresses this openness in the *De Anima* when he states, "The soul is in a sense all things" (ἡ ψυχὴ τὰ ὄντα πώς ἐστι πάντα).[94] The mind has the ability to intentionally receive any reality in mental form and to intentionally fabricate countless modalities of meaning. The mind, he states, can *become* everything (πάντα γίνεσθαι) and *make* everything (πάντα ποιεῖν).[95]

Wilson concludes from the fact that chimpanzees respond to their reflection in mirrors that they also possess self-knowledge, a power traditionally considered unique to humans. Again we must distinguish. It is clear that, looking at itself in the mirror, the chimp has an inchoate awareness of itself: this is not the self-knowledge enjoyed by humans. The chimpanzee sees itself in the glass darkly, but its knowledge is not transparently self-reflexive: it does not *know that it knows* itself. It cannot contemplate or investigate the act of self-cognition and distinguish in that act between itself as simultaneously subject and object. Certainly it exhibits what *we interpret* as curiosity, but it cannot resolve its puzzlement. It cannot distance itself from the act of knowing in which it is at once subject and object. Harry Frankfurt distinguishes between first- and second-order desires.[96] Only humans can have desires about desires; this is distinctive of what it is to be a person. The same applies to knowledge: only humans have self-reflexive knowledge of themselves as knowing. I can both know and desire my acts of cognition; I can know and desire my acts of volition. St. Augustine perceived an even richer relationship across the diverse powers of the mind: "For I remember that I have memory and understanding, and will; and I understand that I understand, and will, and remember; and I will that I will, and remember, and understand; and I remember together my whole memory, and understanding, and will."[97] Other animals are incapable of such interanimation of mental activities.

Having debunked the unique status of human consciousness and communication, Wilson arrives at an important conclusion, appealing once more to Premack: "If consciousness of self and the ability to communicate ideas with other intelligent beings exist, can other qualities of the human mind be far away? Premack has pondered the implications of transmitting the concept of personal death to chimpanzees, but he is hesitant. 'What if, like man,' he asks, 'the ape dreads death and will deal with this knowledge as bizarrely as we have? . . . The desired objective would be not only to communicate the knowledge of death, but more important, to find a way of making sure that the apes' response would not be that of dread, which, in the human case, has led to the invention of ritual, myth and religion. Until I can suggest concrete steps in teaching the concept of death without fear, I have no intention of imparting the knowledge of mortality to the ape.'"[98] It is difficult to take this passage seriously. We are asked to believe that we could, if we wished, enlighten the ape about its mortal fate but that out of kindness we should refrain from doing so.[99] Some animals suffer anguish from an instinctive anticipation of imminent death; it stretches the imagination, however, to assume that the ape, or any animal, can be reflectively aware of the implications of death and can ponder the alternatives of survival and extinction. This requires the ability to form universal notions, of which animals are incapable. Man alone among animals is conscious of death. Its ineluctable certainty and uncertain significance elicit fear and fascination; it is a *mysterium tremendum et fascinans*.[100] An animal might be trained to enunciate or sign the phrase "To be, or not to be: that is the question" but could never grasp its significance. It could not ask whether in confronting the troubles of life it is nobler to end them freely or to seek fulfillment by creatively transforming them in defiant affirmation.

Interestingly the significance of death for humans is addressed by Wilson in the opening lines of *Sociobiology*, only to be dismissed as irrelevant:

> Camus said that the only serious philosophical question is suicide. That is wrong, even in the strict sense intended. The biologist, who is concerned with questions of physiology and evolutionary history, realizes that self-knowledge is constrained and shaped by the emotional control centers in the hypothalamus and limbic system of the brain. These centers flood our consciousness with all the emotions—hate, love, guilt, fear, and others—that are consulted by ethical philosophers who wish to intuit the standards of good and evil. What, we are then compelled to ask, made the hypothalamus and limbic system? They evolved by natural selection. That simple biological statement must be pursued to explain ethics and ethical philosophers, if not epistemology and epistemologists, at all depths.[101]

Wilson rightly associates the question of suicide with that of the existence of the self but dismisses this as irrelevant, since—from his evolutionist perspective—not the self but the gene is the prime mover. He asserts: "Self-existence, or the suicide that terminates it, is not the central question of philosophy. The hypothalamic-limbic complex automatically denies such logical reduction by countering it with feelings of guilt and altruism. In this one way the philosopher's own emotional control centers are wiser than his solipsist consciousness, 'knowing' that in evolutionary time the individual organism counts for almost nothing. In a Darwinian sense the organism does not live for itself. Its primary function is not even to reproduce other organisms; it reproduces genes, and it serves as their temporary carrier."[102] The suggestion is that, since in the long run only genes matter, the self is unimportant.

Wilson's position is inconsistent: suicide kills the bearer, thwarting the propagation process, but that is a minor point. More importantly, sociobiology is incapable of recognizing the central philosophical question of self-existence. (For understandable philosophico-cultural reasons, neither did Aristotle pose the question, assuming the eternity of the cosmos and perpetuity of all species.) Camus rightly suggests that the fundamental question is whether life is worth living. To ask "Why should I exist?" cannot be detached from the question why anything should exist. It is difficult to see how feelings of guilt or altruism can pronounce one way or another on the question either of self-existence or of existence generally. Guilt and altruism might intervene if, in response to a nihilistic response, one were tempted to choose suicide, although on Wilson's terms, since the self is of no significance, such feelings make little sense.

Wilson's viewpoint recalls Hume's opinion that "the life of a man is of no greater importance to the universe than that of an oyster."[103] From the abstract, impersonal, perspective of universal existence, man is of no consequence; and if the self is merely the instrumental vehicle of the genetic molecule, it is of negligible importance. From the irreducible personal subjective point of view, however, it is distinctly the opposite. In his autobiography Somerset Maugham conveys the contrast: "To myself I am the most important person in the world; though I do not forget that, not even taking into consideration so grand a conception as the Absolute, but from the standpoint of common sense, I am of no consequence whatever. It would have made small difference to the universe if I had never existed."[104]

While my existence is a matter of indifference to the universe on the global impersonal scale, for me it is the most important truth about everything that I am; without that self-experience, the world has no meaning for me. Extrapolating my experience to fellow conscious subjects, without the subjective the world would be devoid of all objective meaning.

Our capacity for universal openness to reality and our ability to return in reflection upon the self allow the question: Why do I exist? As Augustine concretely illustrates, because we are self-consciously aware, each one becomes a question to himself: *Mihi quaestio factus sum*.[105] Each one may ask: What am I? More radically, one cannot escape the more fundamental question: Why am I? This question, significantly, is inseparable from the wider inquiry: Why does anything exist? Why is there something rather than nothing? Kant famously posed three fundamental questions: "What can I know?," "What should I do?," and "What may I hope?"[106] He replied summarily that I can know nature, should do my duty, and may hope for the realization of the highest good. In their deeper contexts these questions are closely related. To respond to the question "What should I do?" by invoking duty, however, does not go far enough. The question "Why be moral?" requires a fuller response, which presumes not only a sure ground for knowledge and a legitimate prospect of hope but more importantly some tacit response to the basic question: Why do I exist? The questions of action and value are inseparable from those of knowledge and existence: What can I hope to know, and why should I be? It must be presumed that the question of knowledge has been answered to some satisfactory degree and that the question of existence is not only legitimate but the most significant and ultimate that I can pose.

In the question of self-existence man questions himself and the totality of the real. One may not a priori equate the world of nature with the totality of the real. One may not determine in advance that reality is just what can be measured scientifically. Richard Dawkins makes this fundamental mistake in his challenge to religion: "A universe with a supernatural presence would be a fundamentally and qualitatively different kind of universe from one without. The difference is, inescapably, a scientific difference. Religions make existence claims, and this means scientific claims."[107] E. O. Wilson affirms: "Every part of existence is considered to be obedient to physical laws requiring no external control."[108] It is interesting to find a similarly reductive position in one of Alasdair Mac-

Intyre's early writings: "The concept of divine existence is of a highly dubious character. Our concept of existence is inexorably linked to our talk about spatio-temporal objects."[109] (It hardly needs pointing out that in later writings MacIntyre espouses a much more fundamental and metaphysical notion of existence.)[110] Philosophers have much to learn from the ontology of William Jefferson Clinton: "It depends on what the meaning of the word 'is' is." The question of being lies outside the range of biology. Lord Martin Rees, president of the Royal Society, begins his book *Our Cosmic Habitat* by asserting: "The preeminent mystery is why anything exists at all. What breathes life into the equations, and actualized them in a real cosmos? Such questions lie beyond science. . . . They are the province of philosophers and theologians."[111]

The final chapter of Wilson's *On Human Nature*, with its encouraging title "Hope," proclaims a future project in which the search for values will "go beyond the utilitarian calculus of genetic fitness."[112] Wilson prophetically announces his aspiration that the true Promethean spirit of science will liberate man by giving him knowledge and dominion over the physical world and will respond to the "deepest needs of human nature, and [be] kept strong by the blind hopes that the journey on which we are now embarked will be farther and better than the one just completed."[113] This is a grand-sounding ambition that promises little. Values are to be measured by the intensity of emotion; the neurophysiology of our responses needs to be deciphered, and their evolutionary history awaits reconstruction.[114] What the deepest needs of human nature are remains unsaid. In his subsequent volume *Consilience* Wilson continues to champion a scientific evolutionist materialism: "Moral reasoning will either remain centered in idioms of theology and philosophy, where it is now, or it will shift toward science-based material analysis."[115] Available evidence "favors a purely material origin of ethics."[116]

In the final analysis, evolutionary ethics is founded upon a biological endless regress in which persons have no ultimacy. Human individuals exist for the exclusive purpose of propagating offspring, whose purpose is likewise simply to propagate. To what purpose? What is the goal of the process in its totality? Aristotle points out that no action is ever complete if its goal is indefinitely deferred. It might be objected that Aristotle is himself guilty of this lacuna, since he also maintains that the highest activity of a living substance is to perpetuate its species. There is, however, for Aristotle a universal final cause, and, having an individual telos, the individual transcends the process of generation. The activity of reproduction is not itself the foundation of morality.

It is arguable that the ultimate ground for moral obligation and universal duty is the status of each member of the human species as an individual consciously aware of his or her freedom within the totality of the real, and the inescapable demand to make one's life personally meaningful, with all the possibilities and limits of our common nature. The recognition of this demand in oneself and in others illumines the moral commands arising from our nature as free and rational beings, conscious of the need to make our way in the world, a task that confronts each and every human being.

Notes

The chapter's epigraphs are from John Dewey, *The Influence of Darwin on Philosophy and Other Essays* (New York: Henry Holt, 1910), 2; Wittgenstein's *Tractatus* 4.1122; and James Joyce, *Finnegans Wake* (London: Penguin, 1992), 252.

1. Michael Ruse and E. O. Wilson, "The Evolution of Ethics," *New Scientist,* October 17, 1985, 52.

2. Stephen Pope remarks: "The most significant level of interchange concerns more fundamental questions about the nature of reality (metaphysics, and especially ontology) and God (theology), rather than practical moral questions." Stephen J. Pope, *Human Evolution and Christian Ethics* (Cambridge: Cambridge University Press, 2007), 5. See p. 6: "The deepest moral disagreements are rooted in competing presuppositions about what is most real, how we can come to understand what is most real, and how this knowledge provides guidance for leading good lives and developing good communities." The dispute, notes Pope, is between moral realism, "which holds that the world is intrinsically morally meaningful[,] and evolutionary ontological naturalism, which denies that it has any meaning other than what we human beings choose to make of it."

3. As presented throughout his various publications, Dawkins's position has not been entirely consistent. In *The Selfish Gene* he stated that if one wants "to build a society in which individuals cooperate generously and unselfishly towards a common good, you can expect little help from biological nature." Rich-

ard Dawkins, *The Selfish Gene* (Oxford: Oxford University Press, 2009), 3. In his later books he appeals to the evidence from biology in defense of altruism.

4. Edward O. Wilson, *Sociobiology: The New Synthesis* (Cambridge, MA: Harvard University Press, 1978), 4, 595. According to Daniel Dennett, Hobbes and Nietzsche were the first sociobiologists. See Daniel Dennett, *Darwin's Dangerous Idea: Evolution and the Meanings of Life* (New York: Simon and Schuster, 1996), 453, 461.

5. Wilson, *Sociobiology*, 562.

6. See Peter Singer, "Ethics and Sociobiology," *Philosophy and Public Affairs* 11 (1982): 44: "Wilson writes as an enthusiast for his subject, occasionally overstepping the bounds of his evidence as enthusiasts often do."

7. Edward O. Wilson, *On Human Nature*, 2nd, rev. ed. (Cambridge, MA: Harvard University Press, 1978), 1–3. William James similarly wrote: "Taking a purely naturalistic view of the matter, it seems reasonable to suppose that, unless consciousness served some useful purpose, it would not have been superadded to life." William James, review of *Grundzüge der physiologischen Psychologie,* by Wilhelm Wundt, *North American Review* 121 (1875): 201.

8. Michael Ruse, *The Darwinian Paradigm* (London: Routledge, 1989), 261–62, 268. The chapter was originally published under the same title, "Evolutionary Theory and Christian Ethics: Are They in Harmony," *Zygon* 29 (1994): 5–24. See also "Evolutionary Ethics: A Phoenix Arisen," *Zygon* 21 (1986): 99: "Our moral sense, our altruistic nature, is an adaptation—a feature helping us in the struggle for existence and reproduction—no less than hands and eyes, teeth and feet. It is a cost-effective way of getting us to cooperate, which avoids both the pitfalls of blind action and the expense of a superbrain of pure rationality." Repr. in *Issues in Evolutionary Ethics,* ed. Paul Thompson (Albany: State University of New York Press, 1995), 230.

9. Wilson, *Sociobiology,* 4. Altruism is defined as "self-destructive behavior performed for the benefit of others" (578).

10. Wilson, *On Human Nature,* 201.

11. Ibid., 2.

12. Ibid., 1.

13. Wilson, *Sociobiology,* 3.

14. Michael Ruse, *Taking Darwin Seriously* (Amherst, NY: Prometheus Books, 1998), 206.

15. Wilson, *On Human Nature,* 2.

16. Ibid., 3.

17. Dawkins, *Selfish Gene,* xxi, 2.

18. Richard Dawkins, "God's Utility Function," *Scientific American,* November 1995, 67. See also Dawkins's *A River Out of Eden* (New York: Basic Books, 1995), 133.

19. Dawkins, *Selfish Gene,* 19.

20. Ibid., 34–35.
21. Ruse and Wilson, "Evolution of Ethics," 51–52.
22. Michael Ruse, "Evolutionary Ethics: A Defence," in *Biology, Ethics, and the Origins of Life*, ed. Holmes Rolston III (Boston: Jones and Bartlett, 1995), 93.
23. Ruse, *Taking Darwin Seriously*, 206.
24. Edward O. Wilson, *Consilience* (London: Little, Brown, 1998), 164.
25. Ruse, *Taking Darwin Seriously*, 155.
26. Ibid., 163.
27. Wilson, *On Human Nature*, 167.
28. Dawkins, *Selfish Gene*, 267. He is referring to a quotation from the zoologist G. G. Simpson, given on p. 1: "The point I want to make now is that all attempts to answer that question before 1859 are worthless and that we will be better off if we ignore them completely."
29. On Dawkins's knowledge of the philosophical tradition, Michael Ruse has remarked: "Frankly, I doubt he has ever read a philosophical work all the way through." Review of Holmes Rolston's *Genes, Genesis, and God*, in *Global Spiral*, Metanexus Institute, www.metanexus.net/magazine/ArticleDetail/tabid/68/id/3000/Default.aspx (accessed February 4, 2010). Peter Singer is equally forthright in his criticism of E. O. Wilson: "Though defending Rawls is not a role that comes easily to me, it has to be said that Wilson's criticisms are a mess." Singer, "Ethics and Sociobiology," 50.
30. See Fran O'Rourke, "Aristotle and the Metaphysics of Evolution," *Review of Metaphysics* 58 (2004): 3–59.
31. Aristotle, *Hist. An.*, VII, 1.588a19–28, trans. D. M. Balme, *History of Animals, Books VII–IX*, Loeb Classical Library (Cambridge, MA: Harvard University Press, 1991).
32. Aristotle, *Hist. An.* VII, 588a32–588b3, trans. Balme.
33. See *Hist An.* VIII, 12, 597a4–5; IX, 10, 614b18–26. Plato had already noted the "political" character of bees, wasps, and ants. See *Phaedo* 82b5–8.
34. *Hist. An.* VIII, 6, 612a21–24, trans. Balme, slightly modified. Herodotus, II, 68, says that this bird, also called "crocodile bird," picks leeches from the crocodile's throat. H. Rackham states: "In reality it picks gnats from the crocodile's open mouth." Aristotle, *Eudemian Ethics*, trans. H. Rackham, Loeb Classical Library (Cambridge, MA: Harvard University Press, 1992), 372 n.
35. Edward O. Wilson, *Naturalist* (New York: Warner, 1995), 224.
36. Wilson, *On Human Nature*, 7.
37. Peter Singer, *The Expanding Circle: Ethics and Sociobiology* (Oxford: Oxford University Press, 1983), xi. Singer remarks: "It is true that the sociobiological approach to ethics often involves undeniable and crude errors. Nevertheless, I believe that the sociobiological approach to ethics does tell us something important about ethics, something we can use to gain a better understanding of ethics than has hitherto been possible" (xi).

38. Philip Kitcher, *Vaulting Ambition* (Cambridge, MA: MIT Press, 1985), 395.

39. Wilson, *Consilience,* 297. Wilson refers to his "deeper agenda that also takes the name of reductionism: to fold the laws and principles of each level of organization into those at more general, hence more fundamental levels. Its strong form is total consilience, which holds that nature is organized by simple universal laws of physics to which all other laws and principles can eventually be reduced. This transcendental world view is the light and way for many scientific materialists. (I admit to being among them)" (59). Wilson paradoxically admits that he might well be wrong: "At least it is surely an oversimplification. At each level of organisation, especially the living cell and above, phenomena exist that require new laws and principles.... Perhaps some of them will remain forever beyond our grasp.... That would not be at all bad. I will confess with pleasure: The challenge and the crackling of thin ice are what give science its metaphysical excitement" (59).

40. Ruse and Wilson, "Evolution of Ethics," 51.

41. As Philip Kitcher notes, their pronouncements are short on specifics: "Ruse and Wilson are surprisingly reticent in expressing substantive moral principles, apparently preferring to discuss general features of human evolution and results about the perception of colors." Kitcher, *Vaulting Ambition,* 447.

42. The American Association for the Advancement of Science, in its "Program of Dialogue between Science and Religion" (1995), declared: "Science is about causes, religion about meaning. Science deals with how things happen in nature, religion with why there is anything rather than nothing. Science answers specific questions about the workings of nature, religion addresses the ultimate ground of nature." Quoted in Dorothy Nelkin, "Less Selfish Than Sacred? Genes and the Religious Impulse in Evolutionary Psychology," in *Alas, Poor Darwin: Arguments against Evolutionary Psychology,* ed. Hilary Rose and Stephen Rose (London: Vintage, 2000), 14.

43. Wilson, *Consilience,* 10–11.

44. For a convincing statement of the need for multiple, layered, complementary explanations in biology, see Steven Rose, *Lifelines: Biology, Freedom, Determinism* (London: Penguin, 1998), 10–13.

45. Alasdair MacIntyre, *Whose Justice? Which Rationality?* (London: Duckworth, 1988), 101.

46. Aristotle, *Politics (Pol.),* I, 2, 1252a24, my translation.

47. Aristotle, *De Anima (De An.),* I, 403b, trans. W. S. Hett, Loeb Classical Library (Cambridge, MA: Harvard University Press, 1986).

48. In the *Phaedo* Socrates likewise offers alternative explanations for his presence in the prison cell: one refers to his muscles and limbs, the other to his respect for the laws and values of the state.

49. When asked if everything could be expressed scientifically, Einstein replied that it could, but that it would make no sense: "It would be a description

without meaning—as if you described a Beethoven symphony as a variation of wave pressure." See Ronald William Clark, *Einstein: The Life and Times* (New York: Wings Books, 1995), 32.

50. Stephen R. L. Clark, *Biology and Christian Ethics* (Cambridge: Cambridge University Press, 2000), 80. See Horace, *Letters* I, 10, 24: *Naturam expelles furca, tamen usque recurret, et mala perrumpet furtim fastidia victrix*: "Drive out nature with a pitchfork, she will hurry back with furtive victory to break your evil scorn."

51. See Wilson, *Naturalist,* 242: "I felt certain that the future principles of evolutionary biology would be written in equations, with the deepest insights expressed by quantitative models."

52. Friedrich Nietzsche, *On the Genealogy of Morals* (New York: Vintage Books, 1967), 77.

53. Ruse and Wilson, "Evolution of Ethics," 51.

54. Dennett, *Darwin's Dangerous Idea,* 470. Dennett claims that Wilson's attempt to biologize ethics is unsuccessful (468).

55. Ibid., 470. Dennett assigns an important role also to memes; I regard the latter as a superfluous and fanciful synonym for popular ideas, which may be readily explained by Aristotelian categories applied to the contents of mind.

56. Ibid., 472.

57. Aristotle, *Nichomachean Ethics (NE)* III, 4, 1113b6: ἐφ' ἡμῖν δὴ καὶ ἡ ἀρετή, ὁμοίως δὲ καὶ ἡ κακία.

58. *De An.* III, 3, 428a25, III, 11, 434a7; *NE* III, 1, 1111b9–11.

59. *De An.* VII, 3, 1147b5.

60. *NE* VI, 2, 1139a20.

61. *NE* X, 8, 1178b24.

62. *Pol.* III, 9, 1280a34: διὰ τὸ μὴ μετέχειν εὐδαιμονίας μηδὲ τοῦ ζῆν κατὰ προαίρεσιν.

63. *NE* I, 7, 1098a4.

64. Wilson, *Sociobiology,* 3.

65. Wilson, *On Human Nature,* 71.

66. *Julius Caesar* 1.2.

67. Ruse, *Taking Darwin Seriously,* 259.

68. Ibid.

69. Aristotle, *Metaphysics* I, 2, 982b26: ἄνθρωπος ἐλεύθερος ὁ αὑτοῦ ἕνεκα καὶ μὴ ἄλλου ὤν.

70. Thomas Aquinas, *Summa Theologiae (ST)* I, 96, 4.

71. Cf. Stephen Pope: "Sociobiologists mistakenly suggest that all people share the same genetic and biological motivations, and that these are dominant over and constitute the underlying causes of all other motivations, however much these seem to be chosen consciously by the agent. Individuals have distinctive genotypes and therefore the genetic factors underlying motivation cannot be identical for all people, yet sociobiologists speak at times as if all human beings

have the same fixed motivational characteristics. A non-reductionistic reading of motivation, on the other hand, holds that the genetic basis of motivation is one among a variety of factors that can influence an individual's particular motivational structure." Pope, *Human Evolution,* 223.

72. Wilson, *On Human Nature,* 167.

73. Alasdair MacIntyre, *After Virtue* (Notre Dame: University of Notre Dame Press, 1981), 150–51.

74. See Anthony O'Hear, *Beyond Evolution: Human Nature and the Limits of Evolutionary Explanation* (Oxford: Clarendon Press, 1997), vii: "We are prisoners neither of our genes nor of the ideas we encounter as we each make our personal and individual way through life."

75. Charles Darwin, *The Descent of Man, and Selection in Relation to Sex* (Princeton: Princeton University Press, 1981), 88–89.

76. I believe that the term *biological teleology* more accurately conveys the meaning of his more frequently used term *metaphysical biology.* See, e.g., MacIntyre, *After Virtue,* 139: "Hence Aristotle's ethics, expounded as he expounds it, presupposes his metaphysical biology." To the best of my knowledge MacIntyre nowhere clarifies what he criticizes as "metaphysical biology"; presumably he had in mind, *inter alia,* Aristotle's views on slavery and women.

77. Ibid., 152.

78. Ibid.

79. Ibid., 183.

80. Ibid., 56.

81. Alasdair MacIntyre, *Dependent Rational Animals* (Chicago: Open Court, 2008), x.

82. Ibid., ix.

83. *ST* II-II, 8, 1: Respondeo dicendum quod nomen intellectus quandam intimam cognitionem importat, dicitur enim intelligere quasi intus legere. Et hoc manifeste patet considerantibus differentiam intellectus et sensus, nam cognitio sensitiva occupatur circa qualitates sensibiles exteriores; cognitio autem intellectiva penetrat usque ad essentiam rei, obiectum enim intellectus est quod quid est, ut dicitur in III de anima.

84. *NE* IX, 8, 1168b34–1169a2: καὶ ἐγκρατὴς δὲ καὶ ἀκρατὴς λέγεται τῷ κρατεῖν τὸν νοῦν ἢ μή, ὡς τούτου ἑκάστου ὄντος· καὶ πεπραγέναι δοκοῦσιν αὐτοὶ καὶ ἑκουσίως τὰ μετὰ λόγου μάλιστα.

85. *NE* IX, 8, 1169a16: ὁ δ'ἐπιεικής, ἃ δεῖ, ταῦτα καὶ πράττει· πᾶς γὰρ νοῦς αἱρεῖται τὸ βέλτιστον ἑαυτῷ, ὁ δ'ἐπιεικὴς πειθαρχεῖ τῷ νῷ.

86. Pope, *Human Evolution,* 256.

87. See Jonathan Marks, "The Human Genome in Evolutionary Context: 98% Chimpanzee and 35% Daffodil," Symposium no. 124: Anthropology in the Age of Genetics, Wenner Gren Foundation, Teresopolis, Brazil, June 11–19, 1999, cited in Hilary Rose and Steven Rose, introduction to H. Rose and Rose, *Alas, Poor Darwin,* 4.

88. *Pensées* 72. The quotation is from St. Augustine, *De Civ. Dei* XXI, 10.

89. *Measure for Measure*, 2.2.

90. Charles Darwin, *The Descent of Man* (London: Penguin, 2004), 151. A little further on in the same paragraph he states: "The moral sense perhaps affords the best and highest distinction between man and the lower animals." See also Singer, *Expanding Circle,* 27–28: "Attempts to draw sharp lines between ourselves and other animals have always failed. We thought we were the only beings capable of language, until we discovered that chimpanzees and gorillas can learn more than a hundred words in sign language, and use them in combinations of their own devising. Scientists are now laboriously discovering what many dog owners have long accepted; we are not the only animals that reason."

91. Teilhard de Chardin, *The Phenomenon of Man* (London: Collins, 1960), 166. De Chardin's lengthy remarks (164–66) are by far the best I have read anywhere on the implications of reflection for the distinction between humans and other animals; unfortunately it is one of the few philosophical insights in his work that I find fully convincing. On the failure to appreciate the uniqueness of human cognition, Keith Ward has commented, "It is rather ironic that it is through the use of those intellectual powers which are so well developed in the human species that thinkers have come to deny any special significance to human life." See Keith Ward, *The Battle for the Soul: The End of Morality in a Secular Society* (London: Hodder and Stoughton, 1985), 57.

92. For a discussion of the reasons why chimpanzees are not capable of language, see O'Hear, *Beyond Evolution,* 38–39.

93. Wilson, *On Human Nature,* 26.

94. *De An.* III, 8, 431b21.

95. *De An.* III, 5, 430a15.

96. Harry G. Frankfurt, "Freedom of the Will and the Concept of a Person," *Journal of Philosophy* 68 (1971): 5–20.

97. Augustine, *De Trinitate* X, 11, 18: "Memini enim me habere memoriam, et intelligentiam, et voluntatem; et intelligo me intelligere, et velle, atque meminisse; et volo me velle, et meminisse, et intelligere, totamque meam memoriam, et intelligentiam, et voluntatem simul memini." This text was taken up later by Alcuin and Anselm.

98. Wilson, *On Human Nature,* 27. The quote is from David Premack, "Language and Intelligence in Ape and Man," *American Scientist* 64 (1976): 681–82.

99. A more realistic approach is offered by Wilson in *Consilience,* 250: "The great apes have the power of self-recognition, but there is no evidence that they can reflect on their own birth and eventual death. Or on the meaning of existence—the complexity of the universe means nothing to them."

100. In "Death," William Butler Yeats contrasts the human anticipation of death with the absence of any such animal experience: "Nor dread nor hope attend / A dying animal; A man awaits his end / Dreading and hoping all."

101. Wilson, *Sociobiology*, 3. Peter Singer comments: "If ethical judgments were nothing but the outflow of our emotional control centers, it would be as inappropriate to criticize ethical judgment as it is to criticize gastronomic preferences. Endorsing capital punishment would be as much an expression of our feelings as taking our tea with lemon, rather than milk." Singer, *Expanding Circle,* 85.

102. Wilson, *Sociobiology,* 3.

103. David Hume, "Of Suicide" [1755], in *David Hume: Selected Essays,* ed. Stephen Copley and Andrew Edgal (Oxford: Oxford University Press, 1993), 319.

104. W. Somerset Maugham, *The Summing Up* (New York: Mentor, 1957), 11.

105. Augustine, *Confessiones* X, 33.

106. Immanuel Kant, *Critique of Pure Reason,* A805/B833.

107. Richard Dawkins, "You Can't Have It Both Ways: Irreconcilable Differences?," *Skeptical Inquirer,* July 1999, 64.

108. Wilson, *On Human Nature,* 192.

109. Alasdair MacIntyre, "The Logical Status of Religious Belief," in *Metaphysical Beliefs: Three Essays,* by Stephen Toulmin, Ronald W. Hepburn, and Alasdair MacIntyre (London: SCM, 1957), 202.

110. See Alasdair MacIntyre, *God, Philosophy, Universities: A Selective History of the Catholic Philosophical Tradition* (Lanham, MD: Rowman and Littlefield, 2009), 40–41, 84–85.

111. Martin Rees, *Our Cosmic Habitat* (Princeton: Princeton University Press, 2001), xi.

112. Wilson, *On Human Nature,* 199.

113. Ibid., 209.

114. Ibid., 199.

115. Wilson, *Consilience,* 267–68.

116. Ibid., 268.

CHAPTER FOURTEEN

The Social Epistemological Normalization of Contestable Narratives
Stories of Just Deserts

OWEN FLANAGAN

Narrative Intelligibility

Consider what it is to share a culture. It is to share schemata which are at one and the same time constitutive of and normative for intelligible action by myself and are also means for my interpretation of the actions of others. My ability to understand what you are doing and my ability to act intelligibly (both to myself and to others) are one and the same ability.

—Alasdair MacIntyre

Alasdair MacIntyre's writings on narrative self-understanding—on "schemata"—and his writings on normativity in the human sciences interpenetrate. Individuals and cultures tell stories that simultaneously express, reveal, and conceal in the "what is normal and expectable," in the "what is not said," and in the "what is not expressible" who and what they are, what they aspire to be, and how they hold themselves and each other interesting and accountable. The human sciences explain how self- and other-comprehension works through narratives and how narratives that render action intelligible are structured, formally and contentfully, in different social ecologies. But the human sciences, especially in their purely descriptive pose, can contribute to concealment, or, what is different, to legitimation of questionable self- and other-understanding, and thus to the practices that such understanding engenders, encourages, and endorses. One way this happens is when allegedly neutral but in fact deeply contestable philosophical or social scientific assumptions are rendered part of common sense and are incorporated into narratives that are normatively expected to apply to lives that are intelligible as good, or decent, or worthy of respect—self-respect and other-respect.

Here I provide a reading of a common contemporary Western, possibly only American, narrative about accomplishment and desert that might seem to be descriptively and normatively spare but in fact is freighted and contestable. Simply stated, the master narrative trope is that hard work and effort pay, that they should pay, and that the direct and indirect payoffs for choosing to be educated and then working conscientiously in a good profession are just desert for rationality, moral seriousness, and conscientious deliberation and choice.

The target narrative expresses an understanding, perhaps even a theory, of luck, work, effort, and desert. The core or master narrative trope is normatively endorsed by (and for) both the victims and the beneficiaries of the narrative and is thought to be based on facts or, if not facts, then minimalist, commonsense assumptions about agency, accomplishment, and desert that in fact are neither factual nor philosophically innocuous. The narrative both reflects and encourages certain practices that pertain to merit, desert, and ownership. How exactly contestable narrative frameworks come to be favored and then become uncontested, taken for granted, seen as truistic, is a complicated question about how social epistemology works to confer its imprimatur on certain ways of conceiving of persons, their projects, and their worth. But this can and does happen, and it can produce moral and political harm. The target narrative of accomplishment and desert is, I claim, such a morally harmful master narrative. Let me explain.

Narratives: Metaphysical and Political

When I speak about myself (or you), especially if I tell part of my story (or yours), I stand on the shoulders of ancestral storytellers who have supplied what are now—but once were contested—commonsense categories and familiar plot lines in service of the interpretation of persons and their lives. These ancestral storytellers were themselves dependent on communities of predecessors who invented and/or stabilized the language we speak, parsed the universe, and introduced word linkages, word spans, that attempt to capture what we now think of as our kind of beings-in-time doing what our kind of beings-in-time do in time.

Many disciplines have a name for the method of taming unruly phenomena by the imposition of a master-narrative or mother-theoretical structure. They speak of scripts, frames, the background, heuristics, ideal types, tropes, themes, ways of world making, Weltanschauung, and even metanarrative, the mother of all narratives, the narrative that ends all narratives by speaking the ultimate truth about us—if there could be such a thing. Each of these grand terms names or gestures at a (possibly, somewhat different) way in which, by means of a general thematic structure, we gain purchase on the patterns that are there or that we impose on the incredible variety of persons and lives.

One important function of self-narration, for both first-person and third-person consumption, is to present oneself as morally decent, possibly as morally good, even virtuous.[1] One feels good about oneself, and social intercourse goes best, when social actors feel morally self-respecting and are perceived by others as morally decent, or better, as truly good. The complexities of modern life suggest that narratives, as opposed to direct observation, and as told by oneself and others who have heard one's story/stories, provide much of the material for assessments of decency. The principle of charity in interpretation teaches that we ought to assume normally that extreme self-deception and social manipulation are not in play and thus that most people speak truthfully when they tell their story (with a hefty dollop of self-serving spin), and thus that our stories are (self-)revealing of our moral personality, our character traits, and their complex situational sensitivities. And even if, or better when, this is not so, narrative gravity pulls for stories that make one seem good, even if one isn't actually so.

Because narratives are designed in part to efficiently play this role of situating us in social space as morally good agents, or as more or less trustworthy, they incorporate all sorts of assumptions about the nature of persons and goodness, some of which are foundational or metaphysical. An assumption is foundational or metaphysical if it articulates, without defense, what is taken to be a settled matter of philosophy—for example, that persons exist; that there are multifarious character traits, many of which subserve moral life and can be used to predict and explain behavior; that some actions are voluntary, some are not; that voluntariness tracks responsibility; and so on. An assumption is foundational or metaphysical in a problematic way, which directly pertains to the target narrative, if it expresses in a taken-for-granted manner a dubious stance about free will—for example, that we are totally self-initiating causes, or that will itself has no prior causes—or if it underestimates fate or luck in life's circumstances. A familiar American narrative of accomplishment and desert serves as an example of a type of narrative that, despite being a commonplace and widely accepted as a way of articulating legitimate grounds for self-esteem and self-respect, in fact makes philosophically questionable assumptions about agency, effort, luck, and desert.[2]

The Target Narrative

The target mother-narrative is familiarly American. It is not itself universal,[3] although it may be universal to make some sort of distinction between acts that merit credit and/or blame and those that don't. The narrative is built broadly around themes such as "Hard work and effort pay." It incorporates subsidiary tropes such as these: "People who work hard deserve to enjoy the fruits of their labor"; "If one chooses to share these fruits that is nice, but it is entirely above and beyond the call of duty"; "Individuals are responsible for their own fates"; "Luck can be mitigated by conscientious planning and hard work"; and "Social safety nets are there for people who would work hard if they could but who, because of bad luck, can't."

The "Hard work and effort pay" master narrative typically exists in a web with some or all of these latter themes embedded in a taken-for-granted way. If one is a conscientious and successful worker, then the elements of the web work conceptually together to warrant positive self-assessment. The master narrative that "hard work and effort pay" is of course intended to be both empirical or descriptive (normally hard work pays) and normative (hard work ought to pay), and thus action-guiding (one ought to work hard).

The narrative metaphysics thesis says that this narrative, as well as many other common narratives (examples follow), incorporates philosophical assumptions. The narrative metaphysics thesis is stronger than the claims that narratives are pinned on socially attractive narrative hooks and that what hooks appeal is culturally variable, both of which are also true.[4] The narrative metaphysics thesis says that at least in some important cases our modes of self-depiction incorporate assumptions that can be called normative or metaphysical in a distinctively philosophical sense—they involve assumptions about agency, free will, luck, fate, responsibility, desert, and the like.

The second point is a sequel to the first. If the socially endorsed story lines about my (or your) self generally, and my (or your) moral self in particular, incorporate a metaphysic of morals, then moral education requires examination, critique, and endorsement or rejection of the metaphysic assumed. Call this the "moral education as metaphysical critique" requirement. Moral education, be it the work of moral self-improvement, moral self-cultivation, or teaching the youth to be better than we elders are, sometimes requires systematic and deliberate attention to our metaphysic of morals.[5] One reason is that the acquisition of morality involves education of the sentiments—for example, building or refining feelings of compassion or the sense of justice as fairness. But to do this, agents need to be taught who—what creatures even—deserve compassion or fair moral consideration, and why they deserve compassion or justice. If one believes, as Cartesians do, that animals do not actually have minds, and thus do not have experiences of pleasure and pain but only simulate them, there will be no reason to extend moral consideration to (other) animals. When there are false assumptions about such matters as sentience, and what oneself or others deserve, the moral educators have an obligation to set things straight. But the moral educators can't do this if they themselves buy into the problematic metaphysic. In this case they will be part of the problem, not the solution.[6]

Let us distinguish two kinds of morally harmful master narratives. The first kind conceals or allows us to overlook a mistake that, if we correct it, will lead us to better be able to abide by the moral principles we already avow. So the moral educator who engages in critique might convince others that their principle of equal consideration of interests requires that the interests of other races, as well as of nonhuman animals, ought, by their own standards, to be taken into account. Making this correction might well require narrative adjustments in the way the space of "persons" or of "rights-bearing creatures" is conceptualized and spoken about. But the required correction is possible. The second kind of morally harmful master narrative is weirder and more puzzling than the first. Here the harm, if there can be said to be harm, comes from the fact that practical life may demand that we apply moral concepts—like responsibility, credit, and blame—when metaphysics can make it seem as if these concepts name nothing real, and thus that it is unfair (in a moral sense) to apply such concepts to ourselves or others. I'll return to this worrisome matter at the end.

For now we can say this much in a clear vein: a major function of master-narrative structures is to situate persons and lives in moral space by depicting types of lives that are deemed decent, good, noble, virtuous, and the like. The patterns of familiar narratives allow us to quickly classify whether individuals are good or not, trustworthy or not, and what sort of karmic outcomes are likely to accrue in their vicinity.

Rags to Riches

Take the "rags to riches" motif, which is closely related to the "hard work and effort pay" motif. In Horatio Alger's *Ragged Dick,* and in most of Alger's other stories, the poor immigrant boy who is morally quite good (but naive) makes it into the bottom rung of middle-class respectability. The character, the shoeshine boy ("bootblack") in this case, doesn't actually get rich in the story. But we are left to think that he will continue going up the ladder of economic success (if he is good, and he is good). In this way, the "rags to riches" master narrative allows inferences that are based upon other common American, Ben Franklin–style tropes, such as, "Virtue and hard work (for men and boys) can overcome any adversity."

It is an interesting question whether a narrative such as "rags to riches" is taken to describe how things normally work out or how they ideally should work (and do sometimes). This matters, since we also have tropes that say such things as "Virtue is its own reward," which could be read as a runner-up promise, a sort a consolation prize in case the material success does not occur. If this is right, then the work "rags to riches" does is less predicting (as it might seem) that effort and work will pay than recommending that one ought to think so, which of course might arouse sensible worries about the opiating properties of such narratives.

Another familiar master-narrative trope that is related to the "rags to riches" and "hard work and effort pay" ones is the "what goes up must go down" trope, which tends to come with a karmic justice subtext—on the way up, fat cats especially, have to do bad stuff, and they will pay. The "robber baron" narrative, for example, enacts the way justice works out and in that way allows the listener to have her vengeful reactive attitudes, some sort of schadenfreude, toward exploiters satisfied. A very different, more recent, and cynical motif is familiar from twentieth-century drama, such as Beckett's *Waiting for Godot*. Postmodernism, with help from existentialism and (scientific) chaos and complexity theory, has given us the story line that "each life is an idiosyncratic absurd performance," which both permits and endorses stories (as "interesting," but perhaps only among a certain social and intellectual class) in which the moral, temporal, interpersonal chaos that is any individual person is a different kind of chaos from every other chaotic person-thingamajig. In this way, each person is a possible object of curiosity for the other members of the community of chaotic conscious beings who know about the person's life or read his story or hear about it. Some absurd beings—Sisyphus, Hamlet perhaps, the compassionate characters in Camus's *La peste,* for example—are admirable amid their absurd, chaotic situation, but that doesn't reduce the absurd and chaotic quality of everything; it just makes it more poignant, and in that way possibly more absurd still. Here there is no pattern (in a life or among lives). But that nonpattern is the pattern. In this case, the narrative structure is overtly philosophical because it is endorsed, as it were, directly by a school of philosophy.

To sum up this section so far: We speak and make sense of ourselves and each other in terms of narratives, which deploy as part of their interpretive arsenal an ontology (there are characters, and they possess traits), as well as metaphysical assumptions about free will, fate, desert, and the conditions of self-worth, which are domesticated in familiar story lines, what I am calling mother-theories or master-narrative structures. These are richly normative and give guidance and direction on how things will go from here and on what is the likely trajectory, both empirically and normatively, of this life or these lives. Master-narrative structures provide interpretive shortcuts, heuristics, ways of indicating where in interpretive space, where in the space of possible story lines, I want you to orient your thought about the person, persons, or type of situation being thought about or talked about.

The Metaphysical Foundations of the Mother-Theory

In light of these points, let us examine what assumptions the dominant American mother-theory about accomplishment and desert makes, and ask whether these assumptions are plausible or not. According to the mother-theory, hard work and conscientious effort are good and ought to be rewarded. If an individual works hard, she deserves (to keep for use) the fruits of her labor. Hard work and conscientious effort are both caused by and signs of virtue, wisdom, and free rational choice. Conversely, people who have not suffered the slings and arrows of outrageous fortune, and who choose to slack off or worse, are responsible for their situation.

This familiar narrative about individual responsibility and desert ramifies into public policy debates. For example, proposals to uncap payroll taxes for the Social Security fund are politically unpopular, and they are unpopular according to every poll, because of dominant views among most Americans about their "right" to keep what they earn. The main rationale for changing the cap that might appeal to American voters would appeal, not to fairness or social solidarity, but to prudence. For example, taxation for welfare makes the poor (or sick or both) less prone to commit crimes and thus to endanger public safety. Without such a purely prudential rationale, taxation for welfare is a form of mandatory charity (which is no charity at all), or even worse, it is state theft.

Regarding desert within a political economy such as ours, a standard view is this: My pretax income and the wealth I already hold are mine. I made what I made, and own what I own, and I deserve to keep it. Any discussion of the right of the state to tax me and/or take some of my stuff starts from my presumptive ownership of my stuff, my money, and my property.[7]

Liam Murphy and Thomas Nagel call this idea "the myth of ownership,"[8] the idea that pretax income and wealth is mine in some "morally meaningful sense." Why is it a myth? Among other reasons, what I make is made possible by a preexisting set of political and economic practices, institutions, and principles. I am indebted to these institutions and practices for what I gross. My gross income and the property I have are not the first link in a link of possessions; they are late links. Why's that? Essentially there would be no secure economy in place, no property, no rights, and so on were it not for the existence of a state constituted to allow such things. So both my gross income and my "preexisting wealth" are outcomes of a complex scheme of distribution and redistribution that antedates my arrival on the planet. It is an utter cosmic coincidence—a matter of luck, good or bad—that I have the gifts (or liabilities) I have, and that I live in a world to which they are suited or not.

The logic of the dominant mother-theory about accomplishment and desert (and its ramifications) can be analyzed in terms of assumptions it makes/assumes/floats on that (we might assume) are so well grounded they don't need mentioning, but that are not so well grounded. Consider these three assumptions that might be taken for granted but ought not to be taken for granted because they are philosophically quite implausible.

1. *A view of agent causation* or libertarian free will that many philosophers think is the dominant folk view, and that Roderick Chisholm endorsed this way: "Each of us when we act, is a prime mover unmoved. In doing what we do, we cause certain things to happen, and nothing—or no one—causes us to cause those events to happen."[9]
2. *A Lockean view of property ownership and desert:* I deserve the income from my labor, and I deserve to keep it. In general, combining #2 with #1 we get: How I do my life, whether I choose good or bad, well or badly, is self-originating (in some deep sense), and thus I deserve credit or blame for what I do, how I live, what I make of things.
3. *Luck Denial.* A denial of the claim that all my general capacities (including—assuming I possess such things—my intelligence, wit, ingenuity, conscientiousness, desire to work hard, social skills, and so on), and all my specific desires and beliefs, are 100 percent contingent on causal antecedents

over which I had no control, and thus that, from the point of view *sub specie aeternitatis,* "luck swallows everything."[10] Nietzsche spoke of *amor fati*—a love of fate. Why? Because despite the eternal and heroic—sweet, dear, and laughable—human attempt to actually do something completely self-originating, it has never happened, nor will it ever happen. It takes a "strong poet" to say this, let alone to embrace the idea. But it may be true.

Luck's Logic

Before proceeding to explain briefly why #1 through #3 are problematic philosophical assumptions, I'll say a bit more about why it is credible to think that #1 through #3, despite being metaphysical, are commonplace assumptions. Candace Clark has explored the deep structure of the logic of American attitudes about work, effort, desert, merit, and luck that show up in our mother-narratives. Here are two key empirical findings:

- *Bimodalism:* Americans tend to have a bimodal rather than a continuum view of desert and luck. "The language Americans use to talk about problems places them *either* in the realm of responsibility *or* inevitability, chance, fate and luck *or* in the realm of intentionality, responsibility and blame."[11] Outcomes of actions are either deserved (if they are results of choice) or not (if they are matters of impersonal luck or fate).
- *Moral Requirements versus Moral Options:* We give ourselves moral permission to ignore feeling compassion/sympathy if the victims of bad luck brought their misfortune on themselves—as in the case of drug addiction, alcoholism, or criminal behavior. "No matter how bad we consider a plight to be, however, if the sufferer, the social actor, has caused it others may not sympathize. A plight is *unlucky* when it is *not* the result of a person's willfulness, malfeasance, negligence, or risk taking, or does not in some way "bring it on him or herself."[12]

These two guiding principles are either equivalent to or conceptually enabled by such theses as #1 through #3 above—to the effect that actions can be divided between those that are caused by my free agency and those that are not—tsunamis, neurological seizures, and the like (as in #1). Furthermore, and for similar reasons, *bimodalism* says that some actions are self-initiated and are not caused by features of the world outside an agent's control (#3), and that it is the products of these agent-initiated or agent-controlled actions for which credit and blame, ownership ("I did it; it is mine"), make sense (as in #2). When persons choose to do what is wrong or inconsiderate or lazy, they deserve to suffer the consequences. If I wish (because I am kind or generous) to help others who cause themselves grief to get back on track, I do what is optional (not required), albeit good.

Narratives of Free Agency

Since the seventeenth century, metaphysicians in the West (one rarely sees the idea of agent causation in China or India) have tried to make sense of the idea of agent causation.[13] No one has been able to do so. The scientific image of persons, independently of the red herring of determinism versus indeterminism (as if indeterminacy in elementary particle physics would secure the respectability of agent causation), assumes—because there is great evidence for the view—that *ex nihilo nihil fit,* that everything that happens has a cause, and that the causes have causes. *Huis clos.* Call this the thesis of the *ubiquity of causation.*[14] The problem this creates for the idea of agent causation is not quite that there is no such thing as a self-initiated or self-controlling action but rather that the state of my self, my will, my desires and preferences are themselves caused. Indeed, the causes of who I am, and what I want, choose, and so on are (always, they must be) antecedent to whatever choice I make.

The ubiquity of causation, once acknowledged as reasonable, not only calls #1 into question from a metaphysical perspective but also is what warrants, if anything does, the rejection of #3—and replacement possibly by the idea that *sub specie aeternitatis,* "luck swallows everything," in Galen Strawson's memorable phrase (the basic idea is old and has been discussed and sometimes endorsed by Stoics, Epicureans, Kant in a famous antinomy, Nietzsche, and many others).

This problem, or these two connected problems of agency, causation, and contingency (#1 and #2), might make it seem as if we are playing with that old disturbing problem of freedom and causation—as indeed we are—and one might claim that the problem is a notorious philosophical black hole and, for that reason, not worth discussing. True. So let's move on to #2—the Lockean view of property and desert. But first note that if the problems of agency, causation, and contingency (#1 and #2) take us into the vicinity of a philosophical black hole, it is not as if our standard self-locating moral narratives, including our target narrative of accomplishment and desert, were remotely neutral on its solution. The standard ways we speak morally involve some amount of conviction that the idea of genuinely self-initiated action makes sense and that there is no need to "love fate" because we are not in its grip, and thus that #1 and #2 are true even if they cannot be justified.

Narratives of Mixing Labor and Desert

A key feature of the dominant narrative of accomplishment and desert assumes that John Locke got things right, more or less, when he gave this argument, which I paraphrase:[15]

1. God gave humans dominion over all of nature.
2. Nature is owned initially equally by all humans.
3. The exception to equal ownership is oneself, one's body: "Every Man has a *Property* in his own *Person.* Thus no Body has any Right to any but himself" (God's plan).
4. God must "Of Necessity" have had a plan for how humans would interact with what is naturally possessed by all, so that his gift of earth's bounty could be enhanced and so that humans could show themselves worthy of God's gift. It would be irrational (which is impossible) for God to have given man "the Earth, and all that is therein . . . for the Support and Comfort of their being" and not (also and at the same time) to have given humans a way to interact morally (without sinning) with this gift.
5. God's plan must be this: Each person in virtue of his natural right to his own body (#3) is given at the same time a right to the products of "the *Labour* of his Body, and the *Work* of his Hands."
6. Thus, whenever a person mixes his *Labor* with what is initially owned by all (#2), he thereby makes it his *property*. "For this *Labour* being the unquestionable Property of the Labourer, no Man but he can have a right to what is once joyned to, at least where there is enough, and as good left in common for others."[16]

The Lockean story about the move from a state where there is no private ownership to one in which there is a just initial acquisition, and then justice in transfer, is widely accepted in America, despite many problems, some obvious—for example, acquisition by theft from the original people, and the phenomenon of the rich getting richer. Indeed, most of the Lockean story (which is not just a history but a justificatory philosophical history), minus much (some or all) of the God talk, is part of common sense and thus is part of our standard narrative of "just deserts." But it is a problem that we contemporary folk take the Lockean theory of property and desert seriously—indeed, take it for granted—without accepting the God talk that actually warrants, justifies, and provides a rationale for each premise in the argument.

The reason this is a problem is that the argument is a philosophical disaster unless the God warrants—or reasons that invoke God's plan—are epistemically credible. But they are not. First, the argument has no foundation if we don't bring in the biblical story of God giving all of nature to humans; and second, if we don't accept the principles of philosophical theology to the effect that there is a God and that he is perfect—that is, that God is the familiar all-knowing, all-loving God of the Abrahamic tradition. Without these assumptions there is no reason to think that there must be "Of Necessity" a divine plan for how we are to make the most of God's gift.

The upshot is that the Lockean view of property and desert may be commonsensical, but this is not because it is based on good arguments. Despite this, there are arguments in favor of doling out property rights in a Lockean manner (#2), and there are interesting arguments for why we should act as if agent causation were true (#1), and why we ought to treat ourselves and others as if we (not the Big Bang) were ultimately responsible for our actions (#3). But these "good" arguments are all practical, pragmatic, and political, not metaphysical.

This matters because, in my experience, people who morally self-locate inside a standard American narrative of accomplishment and desert, and are questioned about the legitimacy of the assignments of credit, merit, ownership, and desert that such narratives permit, commonly appeal to such ideas as #1 through #3 above, in which case they are, or seem to be, claiming metaphysical legitimacy for their practices, when they can't in fact remotely secure the metaphysical grounds that would justify the narratives they tell.

Rival Narratives and Fair(-er) Practices

My conclusions with regard to mother-narratives are clear. The self-locating and self-presenting, other-locating and other-assessing narratives we speak have both descriptive and normative functions. The human sciences are able to explain how narrative self-construction is possible in memory and in language, how it works, and how master narratives serve to mark in a shorthand manner moral merit or demerit, encode moral lessons, instruct on preferred moral trajectories, and/or equip self and other with useful predictive information. Philosophy, along with other critical disciplines, can help us examine what questionable factual, moral, or metaphysical assumptions our narratives make, embed, and enact.

With respect to the specific target narrative of accomplishment and desert, the conclusions are less straightforward. What is clear is that if, or insofar as, that narrative rests on assumptions such as #1 through #3, it is philosophical, indeed metaphysical, and problematically so. The philosophical assumptions it rests on lack epistemic and thus philosophical warrant. If ethics and politics require or should require truth in advertising, then this is a bad result for those who live inside the narrative space that the target narrative dominates. This includes most Americans, even those who question and resist the narrative, for it envelops the social and political space we occupy.

What to do about an untruthful narrative such as the target narrative and how to do it is less clear. It is possible that there just are reasons deep in the biology and psychology of animals like ourselves that require us to live *as if* certain assumptions such as #1 through #3 were true, even when the weight of the philosophical evidence is that they are false. It is possible that the psychology of self-esteem and self-respect, as well as practices that take advantage of our plasticity and responsiveness to social approval and disapproval, rest most naturally on strong convictions about the nature of the self and agency that are unwarranted. This is possible, but nonetheless implausible. Alternative tropes were available in ancient

Greece, where luck was seen as ubiquitous, as well as in Holland and France in the sixteenth century when poor laws were partly rationalized as required because of fate's unsteady hand. And Marxists, Christians, Buddhists, Taoists, and Confucians give strong voice to alternatives to the belief in libertarian individualist views of free will. Arguably, therefore, the target master narrative, rather than being psychologically necessary, is an atypical outcome of serendipitous social-economic-historical convergences. Even if true, it would be naive to think that a narrative will yield its historically gained position because it is shown to be either contingent or, what is different, epistemically unwarranted. Especially in America it can be justification enough for a practice that it works. Nonetheless, if criticism of the taken-for-granted target narrative can be shifted from the claim that it rests on true assumptions to the claim that it serves to motivate effort and hard work, then the practices—welfare, workfare, tax laws, payroll taxes, social security, health care—that the narrative engenders might be more open to adjustments.

The reason is this: if it is said that the target narrative of accomplishment and desert that allegedly works to motivate people to study hard, work conscientiously, and so on is warranted practically rather than metaphysically, then many possible changes in our practices open up. The reason is that the metanarrative will have changed our attitude toward the narrative in this way: we speak this way not because it is metaphysically warranted but because it works to produce some end. The standards for assessing pragmatic success of a way of speaking are different from assessing the truthfulness of that way of speaking. "Santa Claus is coming to town" may get the kids to behave well, but it is false. If the merit of the dominant narrative is shifted so that its defense is understood as practical, not factual (not based on metaphysical axioms), then the subjects of actual fairness, compassion, social solidarity, paternalism, even individualism open up for discussion in new ways.

How the dialectic of disclosing the target narrative to be philosophically ungrounded will evolve is unclear. MacIntyre teaches that "when a standard narrative comes undone, an epistemological crisis ensues."[17] But the target narrative has hardly come undone, so there are at most murmurings, hopes of an epistemological crisis. I have argued that the target narrative should come undone if truth is the standard by which we measure or test its legitimacy. But the narrative is too ingrained in the deepest structure of American capitalism to yield to merely philosophical critique. As problematic as the mother-narrative is, it is thoroughly ingrained in the American psyche. MacIntyre writes, "For it is characteristic of the adherents of rival social interpretations embodied in a complex social practice to deny the reality of rivalry in the interest of the claim that there is an uncontestable underlying structure; social victory at this deep level is the achievement of inducing those who participate in the practice to agree to conceptualizing their activities in such a way that one of the contestable interpretations no longer appears contestable, but simply how things are— 'the facts.'"[18]

As I write, the dominant narrative is seen this way, as resting on the truth. But it does not rest on the truth. Now, MacIntyre also teaches that it is unlikely that a narrative can gain ascendancy and maintain vibrancy and stability for very long if it is radically false, so it must contain a partial truth ("Radically false theories could not so function"). What is the partial truth that the dominant narrative of accomplishment and desert contains? I am not certain. Perhaps it is that hard work and effort do pay. But that truth is made partial by placing the agency of work and effort onto the shoulders of individuals and their wills that can't fairly bear that weight. If there is wisdom in the essay, I owe it to Alasdair MacIntyre, my teacher and friend.

Notes

My first published discussion of the target narrative of accomplishment and desert appeared in "Moral Science, Still Metaphysical after All These Years," in *Moral Personality, Identity and Character: Explorations in Moral Psychology*, ed. Darcia Narvaez and Daniel K. Lapsley (Cambridge: Cambridge University Press, 2009), 52–78.

The MacIntyre work quoted in the epigraph is "Epistemological Crises, Dramatic Narrative, and the Philosophy of Science," in *The Tasks of Philosophy*, vol. 1 of *Selected Essays* (Cambridge: Cambridge University Press, 2007), 4.

1. See the following works by Owen Flanagan: *The Science of the Mind* (Cambridge, MA: MIT Press, 1991); *Varieties of Moral Personality: Ethics and Psychological Realism* (Cambridge, MA: Harvard University Press, 1991); *Consciousness Reconsidered* (Cambridge, MA: MIT Press, 1992); *Self Expressions: Mind, Morals, and the Meaning of Life* (New York: Oxford University Press, 1996); *Dreaming Souls: Sleep, Dreams, and the Evolution of the Conscious Mind* (New

York: Oxford University Press, 2000); *The Problem of the Soul: Two Visions of Mind and How to Reconcile Them* (New York: Basic Books, 2002); *The Really Hard Problem: Meaning in the Material World* (Cambridge, MA: MIT Press, 2007); "Moral Contagion and Logical Persuasion in the Mozi," *Journal of Chinese Philosophy* 35, no. 3 (2008): 473–91; "Moral Science? Still Metaphysical after All These Years," in *Moral Personality, Identity and Character: Explorations in Moral Psychology,* ed. Darcia Narvaez and Daniel K. Lapsley (Cambridge: Cambridge University Press, 2009), 52–78; "The Structures of Meaningful Life Stories," *Argentinian Journal of Philosophy and Psychology* 1, no. 2 (2009): 92–101. See also G. D. Fireman, T. E. McVay, and Owen Flanagan, eds., *Narrative and Consciousness: Literature, Psychology, and the Brain* (New York: Oxford University Press, 2003).

2. Candace Clark, *Misery and Company: Sympathy in Everyday Life* (Chicago: University of Chicago Press, 1997).

3. Frances Gouda, *Poverty and Political Culture: The Rhetoric of Social Welfare in the Netherlands and France, 1815–1854* (Amsterdam: Amsterdam University Press, 1995); Alasdair MacIntyre, *Whose Justice? Which Rationality?* (Notre Dame: University of Notre Dame Press, 1988), and *Three Rival Versions of Moral Enquiry: Encyclopaedia, Genealogy, and Tradition* (Notre Dame: University of Notre Dame Press, 1991).

4. See Flanagan, *Science of the Mind; Varieties of Moral Personality; Consciousness Reconsidered; Self Expressions;* and *Problem of the Soul;* G. D. Fireman et al., *Narrative and Consciousness.*

5. Alasdair MacIntyre, *After Virtue: A Study in Moral Theory* (Notre Dame: University of Notre Dame Press, 1981), and *Whose Justice? Which Rationality?* (Notre Dame: University of Notre Dame Press, 1988); Lawrence Blum, *I'm Not a Racist, but . . . : The Moral Quandary of Race* (Ithaca: Cornell University Press, 2002).

6. MacIntyre, *After Virtue.*

7. See John Rawls, *The Theory of Justice* (Cambridge, MA: Harvard University Press, 1971); Robert Nozick, *Anarchy, State, and Utopia* (New York: Basic Books, 1977).

8. Liam Murphy and Thomas Nagel, *The Myth of Ownership: Taxes and Justice* (Oxford: Oxford University Press, 2002).

9. Roderick Chisholm, *Person and Object* (LaSalle, IL: Open Court, 1976). For a contrary argument as to whether it is indeed the dominant folk view, see E. Nahmias, S. Morris, T. Nadelhoffer, and J. Turner, "Is Incompatibilism Intuitive?," *Philosophy and Phenomenological Research* 73, no. 1 (2006): 28–53.

10. Galen Strawson, "Luck Swallows Everything," *Times Literary Supplement,* July 26, 1998.

11. Clark, *Misery and Company,* 100.

12. Ibid., 84.

13. See Flanagan, "Moral Contagion."

14. See Flanagan, *Problem of the Soul.*
15. See Nozick, *Anarchy, State, and Utopia,* for the secular variant.
16. John Locke, *The Second Treatise of Civil Government,* ch. 5, "On Property," §§ 26 and 27.
17. MacIntyre, "Epistemological Crises."
18. Alasdair MacIntyre, "Social Science Methodology as the Ideology of Bureaucratic Authority" [1988], in *The MacIntyre Reader*, ed. Kevin Knight (Notre Dame: University of Notre Dame Press, 1998), 59.

CHAPTER FIFTEEN

History, Fetishism, and Moral Change

JONATHAN RÉE

One of the most intriguing questions about morality, it seems to me, is what happens when it changes. What happens, for example, when the subordination of women to men, or their exclusion from higher education or the professions, ceases to seem innocuous or natural and starts to be regarded as a grotesque abuse? Or when corporal punishment goes out of style, and homosexuality comes to be tolerated or even respected, or when cruelty to animals arouses indignation rather than indifference, and recklessness with natural resources becomes a badge not of magnificence but of monstrous irresponsibility?

There is of course room for disagreement about such changes of moral opinion. But no one, I think, would maintain that they are devoid of any discussible intellectual content. No one would claim that—like, say, changing fashions in moustaches or skirt lengths—they simply reflect the unaccountable gyrations of taste. There may be zigzags and reverses from time to time, but it seems probable that moral change, over the long term, involves something like a process of learning, or an expansion of horizons, or even—to use a curiously dated word—something you might call progress.

It seems timely, therefore, to turn back to Kant's celebrated treatment of the question "whether the human race is continually improving." Kant was concerned, not with progress in a technical, social, or economic sense, but specifically with what he called the "moral tendency of the human race." He had been heartened by the extent of popular support for the French Revolution in the 1790s, but even without such empirical corroboration he was convinced that the "moral tendency" of humanity was, like human knowledge as a whole, destined by its very nature to carry on improving till there was no room for further improvement: humanity was imbued, he thought, with a transcendental impulse to refine and clarify its moral opinions as time goes by—to hold itself to higher moral standards, or to grow in what might be called moral intelligence.[1]

Kant's faith in moral progress had a powerful attraction for many nineteenth-century thinkers, and its progeny include the positivism of Auguste Comte and various branches of Hegelianism. But their cheerful progressivism is not likely to be promoted with much vigor or conviction any more. If you were to exhibit any signs of moral optimism today you would probably be mocked as the dupe of political boosterism or moral grade inflation, and your friends would try to reeducate you by reciting a catalogue of ferocious wars, futile revolutions, and murderous regimes, topped off with sagacious remarks about the destructiveness and deceitfulness of human nature. The old proverb about pride applies to moral optimism as well, or so you would be told: hope comes before a fall.

But pessimists too can be guilty of narcissistic self-deception and bad faith. If you want to be admired for moral perspicacity, all you need do is cultivate a habit of grumbling indignation and dismay: if you can find vice where all around you see nothing but virtue, or degeneracy where they see improvement, or corruption where they see probity, you can become an acclaimed Person of Principle at no cost to yourself, while everyone else will be made to look like a tiresome Trimmer, an exasperating Pollyanna, or an impermeable Pangloss. "Men are fond of murmuring," as Voltaire once put it (and he knew about such things); "There is a pleasure in complaining," and "We delight in viewing only evil and exaggerating it."[2] As a matter of fact, moral optimism is not as dead as you might think: the idea that there is some kind of logic or rationality behind moral change often floats to the surface of contemporary common sense without occasioning much comment. When people want to protest against horrifying contemporary practices—torture, say, or forced marriage, human trafficking, or racial violence—they are likely to condemn them as "Victorian," "medieval," "primitive," or "antiquated," while expressing astonishment that they should still be countenanced in the twenty-first century. The notion that the epochs of past time can function as terms of moral opprobrium, or that the present date constitutes some kind of moral standard, testifies to a touchingly stubborn faith in something like Kant's a priori doctrine of progress.

On the other hand, optimism is not what it used to be. For Kant and his followers, the development of moral knowledge was, like the growth of geometry or arithmetic, simply the gradual articulation of an intuition that had always been present to the human mind, if only implicitly. But work on the history of mathematics and the natural sciences since Kant's time has suggested a rather different perspective: instead of being seen as the elaboration of truths that have been present all along, merely waiting their turn to be made explicit, the growth of knowledge is more likely to be seen—like evolution in the natural world—as the outcome of opportunistic, adventitious, and unpredictable adaptation in the face of a barrage of external accidents. Is it possible that moral progress—assuming there can be such a thing—will turn out to conform to the same kind of model?

Throughout the twentieth century, moral philosophers have done their best to push the question of moral change off the intellectual agenda. (The honorable but lonely exception is of course Alasdair MacIntyre.)[3] If you look back to *Principia Ethica,* which appeared in 1903, you will find G. E. Moore taking it for granted that ethics is concerned with a single unanalyzable object called "the good"—the "unique object," as he says, which is the only thing we can ever really mean when we talk about "goodness" (or "intrinsic value" or "intrinsic worth").[4] Moore did of course acknowledge the existence of certain "causal truths" that might help us identify the actions most likely to produce the kinds of things that "ought to exist for their own sake," and he realized that our knowledge of such truths was likely to improve over time (viii). But as for morality itself, or our intuitive capacity to recognize goodness, it was as simple, unanalyzable, and immutable as the quality itself. Hence there could be no real progress in morality as such, or at least none apart from correcting what Moore called "the error of confusion" and throwing out any historical flotsam and jetsam that might have made its way into the clear waters of ethical intuition (ix). "Ethical discussion, hitherto," he said, "has perhaps consisted chiefly in reasoning of this totally irrelevant kind" (ix). Genuine ethics did not have a history, in Moore's opinion; only pseudoethics did. Moore's attitude toward "confusion" illustrates the curiously Platonistic character of much twentieth-century moral philosophy—the assumption that genuine knowledge cannot be a creature of historical circumstance, or conversely that any discourse that is indelibly historical cannot really be knowledge. The celebrated "patterns of analysis" in Charles Stevenson's *Ethics and Language* left as little scope for progress in moral perception as Moore's self-evident "ethical premises," and the same indifference to history can be found in R. M. Hare's universal prescriptivism, Sartre's existentialism, Levinas's first philosophy, and Rawls's reflective equilibrium. If historical methods have any lessons for moral philosophy, they were left largely unlearnt in the twentieth century.[5]

This neglect of history was not due to oversight or indifference. If you go back to the main figures of twentieth-century moral philosophy you will be struck by their shared obsession with putting a distance between themselves and the eminent Victorians; and what seems to have bothered them most was the Victorian fascination with history. Moore, for example, was furiously hostile to Jeremy Bentham, John Stuart Mill, and above all Henry Sidgwick. All three of them professed an interest in the question of goodness, but according to Moore they took it into their heads to wander off down historical byways and consequently "confused it with another question." They allowed goodness to cohabit with pleasure, they confounded the "desirable" with the "desired," and they muddled "ends" with "means." Hence they put themselves on a collision course with what Moore called, rather preposterously, his "result"—namely the discovery that "good means good," and not something else, from which it followed that the "untruth" of their doctrines must be "self-evident." Fortunately, Moore could assure us that modern philosophers would avoid such howlers: "We may justly pride ourselves," Moore concluded, "that we have a better chance of answering our question rightly, than Bentham or Mill or Sidgwick or others who have contradicted us."[6]

Henry Sidgwick, who brought out his *Methods of Ethics* in 1874 and saw it through five more editions before his death in 1900, was, from the point of view of twentieth-century moral philosophers, the most eminent of the Victorian moralists. And he was certainly susceptible to the charms of history; indeed, he seemed content to wallow in history without making any effort to achieve a once-and-for-all insight into the ineffable essence of goodness. He confessed that his work amounted to no more than "an examination, at once expository and critical, of the different methods of obtaining reasoned convictions as to what ought to be done which are to be found—either explicit or implicit—in the moral consciousness of mankind generally."[7] The three methods Sidgwick focused on—Psychological Hedonism, Ethical Hedonism, and Intuitionism—were not the only possible forms of moral argument, or the only ones that had played an important part in humanity's past or that might be influential in times to come; but they were, he thought, the most salient in the "moral consciousness" of Europe; and furthermore all three of them were imperfect and subject to change and development.

In the first edition of *Methods,* Sidgwick spoke resignedly of a "fundamental contradiction in our apparent intuitions of what is Reasonable in conduct" (470), concluding that it would never be possible to escape from uncertainty in our attempts to reach "reasoned convictions as to what ought to be done" (v).

> The whole system of our beliefs as to the intrinsic reasonableness of conduct must fall, without a hypothesis unverifiable by experience . . . without a belief . . . that the moral order which we see imperfectly realised in this actual world is yet actually perfect. If we reject this belief . . . the Cosmos of Duty is . . . reduced to a Chaos: and the prolonged effort of the human intellect to frame a perfect ideal of rational conduct is seen to have been foredoomed to inevitable failure. (473)

This was a somber assessment of the effects of applying philosophical intelligence to the phenomena of morality, but Sidgwick, finding himself unable to endorse the "hypothesis" of cosmic perfection, felt obliged to embrace it. He would express himself less melodramatically in later editions of *Methods,* but he never wavered in his conviction that if you are hoping for unassailable certainties in ethics—"conclusions logically inferred from self-evident premises," rather than "propositions . . . which . . . seem to rest on no other grounds than that we have a strong disposition to accept them"—then you are bound to be disappointed.[8] Ethics, for him, was not an immaculate science but a restless and essentially interminable attempt to patch up any failings we may find in received moral standards. In his autobiography, Sidgwick presented his account of ethical deliberation as a product of his own personal history. The education he received up to the age of seventeen had made him feel trapped by the "apparently external and arbitrary pressure of moral rules," and when he went to Trinity College Cambridge in 1855 he felt even more oppressed. He was required to mug up a textbook, *The Elements of Morality,* that had been composed ten years before by William Whewell, who happened to be the master of Sidgwick's college, as well as a conscientious professor of moral philosophy who saw it as his official duty to drill the junior members of the university in the habits of moral uprightness and obedience, as enjoined by the Church of England.[9]

One of the most important events in anyone's philosophical development is their first, giddying experience of intellectual disgust; and in the case of Sidgwick, that energizing rite of passage was supplied by Professor Whewell. The arguments of *Elements of Morality* struck Sidgwick as "hopelessly loose," and its principles as "doubtful and confused," or "dogmatic, unreasoned, incoherent." Though he would eventually soften his criticisms, Sidgwick would never forget the "early aversion" aroused in him by compulsory study of Whewell.[10]

A more positive philosophical awakening occurred when Sidgwick came upon the works of John Stuart Mill, in or around 1860. He was of course overawed by the *System of Logic,* which had come out in 1843; but he must also have been impressed by the furious attack on Whewell that Mill wrote for the *Westminster Review* in 1852.[11] For Mill it had been a poignant confrontation, since he had always acknowledged his debts to Whewell's work on the history and theory of science and had debated very graciously with him after publishing his *Logic.* But he now had a new aim in view: he was worried by what he saw as a relaxation of the sturdy old radicalism of the *Westminster*—of which he himself had once been an inspired and industrious editor—and a new book by Whewell provided him with a perfect pretext for taking the radical fight to the conservative enemy.

The book in question, *The History of Moral Philosophy in England*, was based on a series of lectures originally delivered by Whewell in fulfillment of his obligations as a professor of moral philosophy. Whewell began by suggesting that "an important school of moralists" had been active in Cambridge University ever since its foundation, always resolute for the notion that "moral rectitude consists in eternal and immutable relations recognisable by the reason of man."[12] But he went on to explain that this elevated conception of morality had come under attack when Thomas Hobbes argued that moral goodness was nothing in itself and when various followers of Locke piled in by identifying goodness with some "external object" (ix), such as pleasure, utility, or the greatest happiness of the greatest number, and trying to replace the Platonistic "Morality of Principles" with an Epicurean "Morality of Consequences" (72). Whewell had no doubt where his professorial duty lay: he needed to restore the dignity and high authority of the Platonistic "internal principle" (ix) and to recall the university to its function as a bastion of "solid and substantial truth" (xxvii).

After assuring his readers that he did not have "the slightest wish to speak in disparagement of Dr Whewell's labours," Mill noted that Whewell, as professor of moral philosophy at an established university, suffered the misfortune of being unable to pursue any line of thought except "that which can reconcile itself with orthodoxy."[13] Consequently the tendency of all his efforts, if not the intention, was "to shape the whole of philosophy, physical as well as moral, into a form adapted to serve as a support and a justification for any opinions which happen to be established" (168). Whewell's doctrine of "internal conviction" (171) or "intuition" (172) amounted to a kind of philosophical alchemy, through which the precepts he had absorbed as a child, and the opinions that prevailed among senior members of his university, were to be transmuted into self-evident a priori truths or unquestionable "reasons for themselves" (169).

If Whewell had confined himself, as professors usually do, to providing "bad reasons for common opinions" (169), then, according to Mill, little harm would have been done; but when he used his position to attack Bentham and everyone else who holds that morality needs to be reformed in the light of an "external standard" (179), he was setting an ambush against progressiveness itself, and against "the only methods of philosophizing from which any improvement in ethical opinions can be looked for" (169). Those who prided themselves on an unbending commitment to their own moral convictions—to their inward intuitions of approval or disgust—gave evidence, Mill thought, not of moral rectitude but of mental infirmity.

> This is the mental infirmity which Bentham's philosophy tends especially to correct, and Dr Whewell's to perpetuate. Things which were really believed by all mankind, and for which all were convinced that they had the unequivocal evidence of their senses, have been proved to be false: as that the sun rises and sets. Can immunity from similar error be claimed for the moral feelings? when all experience shows that these feelings are eminently artificial, and the product of culture. . . . The contest between the morality which appeals to an external standard, and that which grounds itself on internal conviction, is the contest of progressive morality against stationary—of reason and argument against the deification of mere opinion and habit. The doctrine that the existing order of things is the natural order, and that, being natural, all innovation upon it is criminal, is as vicious in morals, as it is now at last admitted to be in physics, and in society and government. (179)

Philosophy as Whewell practiced it was, in effect, an attempt to perpetuate and sanctify the empire of unargued prejudice; but he left the subject "so exactly as he found it," Mill said, that his argument could "scarcely be counted as anything more than one of the thousand waves on the dead sea of commonplace" (169).

In another article in the *Westminster,* Mill deployed similar arguments against a work by F. W. Newman (younger brother to J. H. Newman), whom Sidgwick happened to admire for the anguished skepticism of his essays on faith and the soul. But Newman had now published a little book, *Lectures on Political Economy,* in which he took issue with the Christian Socialist project of establishing "Christian villages" based on "common property," arguing that they violated the basic principles of morality and politics, not to mention economics, and that the idea of a communistic sanctuary from private property was no better than "hurtful Quixotism."[14]

Mill had reservations of his own about the communist villages of the Christian Socialists,[15] but he took issue with Newman's argument that they violated the moral duties entailed by "the system of private property."[16]

As well might it be said, if I am a soldier, I am bound to fight against those with whom my government is at war, therefore there ought to be soldiers and war. If there is an established clergy, they are bound to teach the doctrines of their church, therefore there ought to be an established church.... The answer is, that bad as well as good institutions create moral obligations; but to erect these into a moral argument against changing the institutions, is as bad morality as it is bad reasoning.[17]

Sidgwick was thoroughly convinced by Mill's arguments against the validity of any appeal either to customary moral intuitions or to the obligations entailed by actually existing institutions, and in 1867, when he himself was invited to teach moral philosophy at Cambridge, he accepted only on condition that he could include Bentham and Mill among his authorities.[18] Nor did he ever abandon his Millite view of "current civilised morality . . . as merely a stage in a long process of development." "We do not find merely change, when we trace the history of morality; we see progress through wider experience, fuller knowledge, more extended and refined sympathies. Thus reflection shows us in the morality of earlier stages an element of what we now agree to regard as confusion and error. Therefore it seems to me reasonable to suppose that similar defects are likely to lurk in our own current and accepted morality; even if observation and analysis of this morality had not led us—as they have in fact led me—to see such defects in it."[19] But he was careful to explain that the moral progress he hoped for did not involve any notion of "a condition . . . in which the progress is to *terminate* and the 'repose of a mind satisfied' to be won." We could strive to remedy the gross imperfections of existing moral institutions, even if we have no clear idea of what perfection might be, nor even any definite knowledge of quite where our reforms might lead, or what further problems they might create or bring to light. "I hope," Sidgwick said simply, "for progress in ethical conceptions, resulting, as progress in science does, from observation and experiment."[20]

Sidgwick once said he could not understand how human beings could bear to devote themselves to moral philosophy—to "scorn delights and live laborious days," as he put it, in the study of "duty and right and ultimate good"—unless they had some hope of reforming ordinary moral opinions. And as the nineteenth century drew to an end, he allowed himself to speculate about the future of morality, and whether the "truth of the twentieth" might prove to be "more true" than the "truth of the nineteenth century."[21]

He was not very specific about the sorts of truths he had in mind, but readers of *Methods* will recall the suggestion that "current morality is faulty . . . by having too general rigid rules, and not making allowance enough for individual differences." We will probably be a little astonished by his cool interest in replacing the institution of marriage by "Free Love," and we will also be impressed by his dislike of ordinary complacency about "the division of mankind into rich and poor."[22] And if we turn to one of his pioneering essays on sociology, we will find him deploring a habit of overvaluing "the old and eminent virtue of charity," which, he thought, encouraged "indiscriminate almsgiving" of a kind that did more to cheer the giver than to alleviate inequality or help the poor.[23]

Sidgwick died in 1900, at the age of sixty-two, so he was never able to observe the development of morality in the twentieth century; but on the whole he would surely have approved. The practice of judging people as individuals rather than in groups certainly spread, and it became far harder to engage in the casual put-downs of women, the disabled, or members of ethnic minorities that were once part of the currency of "civilised morality." He would also have welcomed the growing acceptance of collective institutional responsibility for social welfare, regulated, organized, and perhaps provided by the state. And he would have been gratified by the processes of globalization, insofar as they have eroded the follies of nationalism and fostered non-national communities, or lines of affiliation that, as he put it, "cut across the boundaries of States."[24]

On the other hand, he would hardly have been impressed by the efforts of twentieth-century moral philosophers. He died before Moore's patricidal career got under way, but he had already taken note of the up-and-coming young man, voicing a premonition that "his *acumen*—which is remarkable in degree—is in excess of his *insight*."[25] If he had lived long enough to read *Principia Ethica,* he would surely have seen it as a throwback to the conservatism of Whewell, and he might well have reached the same conclusion about the entire mainstream of moral philosophy in the twentieth century, with its implicit presupposition that morality is essentially a single self-subsistent thing, with an immaculate, sovereign, and unchanging logic of its own.[26] In short, he would have deplored what you might call the fetishism of morality in twentieth-century moral philosophy.

He could also have found signs of morality fetishism in popular discourse, with its assumption that immorality is the worst kind of evil—perhaps indeed the only kind—and hence that morality should never be compromised by practical considerations of any other kind. Sidgwick, by contrast, belonged to a tradition for which morality was not the supreme judge of human conduct but simply one member of a jury that also included jurisprudence and political economy, possibly sociology, and, above all, "politics," or the discipline that studies "the constitution and action of government."[27] Sidgwick would have been appalled by the phrase *political correctness*—an old Stalinist expression which, in the 1980s, embarked on a second career as a device for embarrassing well-intentioned social activists. He might have pointed out that if political correctness is one of the vices that beset practical reasoning, then "moral correctness" or "ethical correctness" deserved to be condemned as equally vicious. Morality is not enough; and those who find themselves acting not just in their own name but on behalf of some kind of collective entity—a community, a people, a state, or a political movement—may well be obliged to sanction acts of deception, coercion, expropriation, or even violence that would be proscribed by any plausible moral code. Classically, such conflicts between personal virtue and a larger good have been seen as lending a dimension of tragedy and grandeur to political action; and Sidgwick would have been saddened by attempts to short-circuit them and subject them to a peremptory moral veto.

Exactly a hundred years after Mill went for Whewell, Jean-Paul Sartre launched a similar assault on his old friend Albert Camus. His target was Camus's book *L'homme révolté* (*The Rebel*, published in 1951), which offered an analysis of the "prophetic dream of Marx" and argued that it had led to the creation of a "terrorist state."[28] As editor of *Les Temps Modernes*, Sartre assigned the book to Francis Jeanson, who duly denounced Camus as a self-hating liberal humanist who wanted to substitute a lachrymose "red-cross morality" for serious political analysis.[29] Camus wrote a feeble response which appeared alongside Jeanson's hatchetry in August

1952, and Sartre weighed in by accusing Camus of a monstrous form of racism, namely the "racism of moral beauty." Sartre was prepared, up to a point, to acknowledge the horror of the Soviet concentration camps—it was, he said, "a challenge for us all"—but unlike Camus he was not prepared to make common cause with those bourgeois journalists who were seizing on it with glee in order to "give themselves a good conscience." Sartre was horrified by "the ease with which you handle your indignation," as he told Camus. "Is it my fault if these procedures remind me of the criminal court?" he inquired. "Perhaps you should have been appointed as Chief Prosecutor of the Republic of Beautiful Souls." Sartre's belligerence toward his old friend may be unforgivable; but when he talked about the temptation of imagining oneself as "Chief Prosecutor for the Republic of Beautiful Souls" he surely had a point. And Camus, though deeply hurt by the attack, tacitly acknowledged that there was some justice in it. His late book *La chute* is a first-person story of a drifter in an Amsterdam bar who tells us how he has fled in disgust from his former existence as a fashionable Parisian lawyer specializing in the defense of widows, orphans, refugees and anyone else on whom he could sniff the delicious odor of victimhood. He had been offered public honors, but turned them down, he recalls, "with a quiet dignity in which I found my true reward." He began each working day by giving generously to a beggar or two; then he would earn the gratitude of another fragrant victim with a heart-stopping speech in court; and in the evenings he would relax with his elegant literary friends by denouncing "the heartlessness of the ruling class and the hypocrisy of our politicians." Gradually he came to be revolted by his own precious sanctity. ("Just think how many crimes have been committed because the perpetrator could not bear to be in the wrong.") He gave up the glamour of human rights activism in favor of a chastened practice of forgiveness, describing himself as a *juge-pénitent*, a penitent judge, or perhaps a recovering moral fetishist. "I favor every theory that denies human innocence, and every practice based on the presumption of guilt," he says: "I am, dear boy, a disenchanted partisan of slavery." And when he gets to the end he turns to us, his listeners, and enters a gentle plea: "I hope at least," he says, "that you are a little less pleased with yourself than you were."[30]

It was of course leftism that provided the context of this famous quarrel; and it seems to me that leftism, like politics, has been a casualty of the fetishism of morality in the twentieth century. Leftism, as I understand it, is a set of political norms that took shape at the beginning of the nineteenth century as a reaction against liberalism; and—at least till the closing years of the twentieth century, which saw the Left go into a state of decline that may or may not be terminal—the hostility between leftism and liberalism was mutual. The distinctive message of leftism was that radical eighteenth-century progressives like Priestley, Price, and the French and American revolutionaries had underestimated the gravity of the social problems they faced because they thought that once they had gotten rid of slavery, serfdom, aristocracy, and the old monarchical state they need only find equitable ways to share out the national wealth and all manner of things would be well. The leftist response was that the social problem arises not so much from the method of distributing wealth as from the means of producing it and that the transition from feudal to free forms of labor would not be enough to put an end to social injustice. Before long Marx was able to explain why: the surface appearance of the new mode of production did not correspond to its essence, as he put it in *Capital*, and the wage-laborer could be said to suffer from slavery just as much as the feudal worker, though of a more cunning and devious kind. You do not have to be a Marxist to be alarmed at the decline of the Left. Socialism may be off the historical agenda, but that is only one element of the leftist project. Another, no less important, is a critical sense of history. Marxism as a mass movement was in part an attempt to educate the world in the importance of imaginative and wide-ranging comparative history, and it was built on the conviction that if we lose our sense of history we damage our sense of politics too and put our sense of morality in danger. Perhaps it is time for moral philosophy to move on—onwards to the nineteenth century, perhaps.

Notes

1. Immanuel Kant, "Diese moralische Tendenz des Menschengeschlechts." See "A Renewed Attempt to Answer the Question, 'Is the Human Race Constantly Improving?'" [Ob das menschliche Geschlecht im beständigen Fortschreiten zum Besseren sei], published as part of his last major work, *Der Streit der Fakultäten* [*The Conflict of the Faculties,* 1798], trans. H. B. Nisbet, in *Kant: Political Writings*, ed. Hans Reiss (Cambridge: Cambridge University Press, 1991), 182.

2. F. M. A. Voltaire, *The Newtonian Philosophy Compared with That of Leibniz, Translated from the French of M. de Voltaire* (Glasgow: Robert Urie, 1764), 14; there is no exact parallel in ch. 1 of *La métaphysique de Neuton, ou Parallele des sentimens de Neuton et Leibniz* (Amsterdam: Ledet, 1741).

3. See the opening chapters of Alasdair MacIntyre, *A Short History of Ethics* (New York: Macmillan, 1966) and *After Virtue* (London: Duckworth, 1981), also his *Secularization and Moral Change* (Oxford: Oxford University Press, 1967). For detailed discussion of the historicity of knowledge and its implications for morality, see his essays "The Relationship of Philosophy to Its Past," in *Philosophy in History: Essays on the Historiography of Philosophy*, ed. Richard Rorty, Jerome B. Schneewind, and Quentin Skinner (Cambridge: Cambridge University Press, 1984), 31–48, and "Epistemological Crises, Dramatic Narrative, and the Philosophy of Science" [1977] and "Moral Philosophy and Contemporary Social Practice" [1992], in *Selected Essays*, vol. 1 (Cambridge: Cambridge University Press, 2006), 3–23 and 104–22 respectively; see also Jonathan Rée, "The Moral Wilderness," *Prospect Magazine*, December 2008, 77–78.

4. George Edward Moore, *Principia Ethica* (1903; repr., Cambridge: Cambridge University Press, 1965), 17, viii, ix, 224. Subsequent page citations to this work are given parenthetically in the text.

5. William James and John Dewey would count as exceptions if they had not been neglected (or treated as late Victorians) by most moral philosophers of the twentieth century. Stevenson was, it is true, a Deweyan of a sort—he disparaged the idea of ethics as a timeless quest for "a formula" or for "ultimate principles, definitively established," saying that such a project "puts static, otherworldly norms in place of flexible, realistic ones"—but his pragmatism did not make much impression on his followers or his critics. See Charles L. Stevenson, *Ethics and Language* (1944; repr., New Haven: Yale University Press, 1965), 336; see also Moore, *Principia Ethica*, 182.

6. Moore, *Principia Ethica*, 145.

7. Henry Sidgwick, *The Methods of Ethics* (London: Macmillan, 1874), v. Subsequent citations to this work, unless otherwise noted, are to this first edition and are given parenthetically in the text.

8. Henry Sidgwick, *The Methods of Ethics*, 7th ed. (London: Macmillan, 1907), 509.

9. Whewell was elected to a chair of "Moral Theology or Casuistical Divinity" in 1838 but was always determined to act as an ordinary professor of moral philosophy, with responsibility for the edification of the entire academic body; see William Whewell, *Lectures on the History of Moral Philosophy in England* (London: John Parker, 1852), xxviii.

10. See the autobiographical notes printed by E. E. Constance Jones in her preface to Henry Sidgwick, *Methods of Ethics,* 6th ed. (London: Macmillan, 1901), xvii–xxiii; for the impact of Mill's criticisms of Whewell, see J. B. Schneewind,

Sidgwick's Ethics and Victorian Moral Philosophy (Oxford: Oxford University Press, 1977), 131.

11. See Henry Sidgwick, *Philosophy: Its Scope and Relations* (London: Macmillan, 1902), 153: "the work of J. S. Mill, from which, a generation ago, I and many others learnt our 'Logic of the Moral Sciences.'"

12. Whewell, *Lectures on the History,* 49, 85. Subsequent page citations to this work are given parenthetically in the text.

13. [John Stuart Mill], "Whewell on Moral Philosophy," review of *Lectures on the History of Moral Philosophy in England,* and *Elements of Morality, Including Polity,* by William Whewell [1852], in *Collected Works,* ed. J. M. Robson (Toronto: Toronto University Press, 1963–91), 10:167. Subsequent page citations to this work are given parenthetically in the text.

14. Francis William Newman, *Lectures on Political Economy* (London: John Chapman, 1851), 313 ("Christian villages"), 291 ("common property"), 9–11 ("hurtful Quixotism"); for Sidgwick on Newman, see Henry Sidgwick to H. G. Dakyns, June 9, 1862, in Arthur Sidgwick, *Henry Sidgwick: A Memoir* (London: Macmillan, 1906), 81, where he speaks of valuing Newman as an antidote to Comte.

15. Mill himself had refused to enter into discussions with Christian Socialists, partly on the grounds that they clung to "existing opinions & institutions on religious moral & domestic subjects," but also (like Newman) because they rejected well-established "principles of political & social economy." J. S. Mill to an unidentified correspondent, June 9, 1851, in *Collected Works,* 14:70.

16. [John Stuart Mill], review of *Lectures on Political Economy,* by Francis Newman [1851], in *Collected Works,* 5:444–45.

17. Ibid., 456–57.

18. This is the testimony of Alfred Marshall, cited in Schneewind, *Sidgwick's Ethics,* 42. Sidgwick did not however count himself a disciple of Mill; referring to a "crusade . . . against empiricism," Sidgwick said, "I have parted company with Mill I feel for ever" (Henry Sidgwick to Roden Noel, August 1866, in A. Sidgwick, *Henry Sidgwick,* 151), and "Take notice that I have finally parted from Mill and Comte" (Henry Sidgwick to H. G. Dakyns, December 8, 1866, in A. Sidgwick, *Henry Sidgwick,* 157), but the following year he entered into a cordial correspondence with Mill about religious tests.

19. See Henry Sidgwick, *Lectures on the Ethics of T. H. Green, Herbert Spencer and J. Martineau* (London: Macmillan, 1902), 351–52.

20. Henry Sidgwick to Roden Noel, 1872, in A. Sidgwick, *Henry Sidgwick,* 243.

21. H. Sidgwick, *Philosophy,* 199, 182. (The allusion is to Milton's *Lycidas.*)

22. H. Sidgwick, *Methods of Ethics* [7th ed.], 21, 358. Think also of his work on women's education, extension, and charity organization.

23. "Under the influence of the economic forecast . . . of the bad consequences of indiscriminate almsgiving, the old and eminent virtue of charity, in

its narrower signification, has materially changed its practical content for the modern educated man, while retaining its principle and motive unchanged." See Henry Sidgwick, "The Relation of Ethics to Sociology" [1899], in *Miscellaneous Essays and Addresses* (London: Macmillan, 1904), 258.

24. Ibid., 254.

25. Henry Sidgwick to H. G. Dakyns, February 3, 1900, not included in A. Sidgwick, *Henry Sidgwick,* but cited in Schneewind, *Sidgwick's Ethics,* 17.

26. In 1883 he was elected professor of moral philosophy at Cambridge—the very position occupied by Whewell when he first took against him—but he did not stop seeing morality as a historical institution, essentially divided against itself and subject to crisis and dialectical change. "Speaking as a professor of ethics," he once said, "I do not consider myself as holding a brief for the independence of my subject." Sidgwick, "Relation of Ethics," 256.

27. H. Sidgwick, *Philosophy,* 25–26, and *Methods of Ethics* [7th ed.], 15–16.

28. "Un État . . . terroriste," Albert Camus, *L'homme révolté* (Paris: Gallimard, 1951), 221.

29. There is of course such a thing as the fetishism of politics as well as the fetishism of morality.

30. Albert Camus, *La chute* (Paris: Gallimard, 1956). Sartre had moved from communism to anticolonialism when *La chute* came out, and he was able to praise this chastened testament as "the most beautiful" of Camus's books, if also "the least understood."

CHAPTER SIXTEEN

Relativism, Coherence, and the Problems of Philosophy

ELIJAH MILLGRAM

The eventual topic of this paper is the perhaps grandiose question of whether we have any reason to think that philosophical problems can be solved. Philosophy has been around for quite some time, and its record is cause for pessimism: it is not, exactly, that there are *no* established results, but that what results there are, are negative (such-and-such is false, or will not work) or conditional (as Ernest Nagel used to say, "If we had ham, and if we had eggs, then we'd have ham and eggs").[1] I hope in what follows, first of all, to explain the record. My explanation will naturally suggest a way of turning over a new leaf, and I will wrap up the paper by laying out that proposal and critically assessing its prospects.

However, the approach to my topic will have to be roundabout. Along the way, I will detour to consider how the problems of philosophy can be identified and what makes them philosophically interesting. And I will begin at quite some distance from my destination, with the uneven intellectual respectability of relativism among academics.

I

The degree to which the acceptability of relativism varies between academic disciplines is a familiar but still striking fact. In, for instance, literary studies and cultural anthropology—including, importantly, science studies and sociology of knowledge—relativism, among the several competing views of which it is one, has a monopoly on intellectual respectability. In the so-called hard sciences, physics, for example, relativism is an affront and an object of contempt.[2] Philosophy is an interestingly mixed case. Some philosophers are relativists, though most are not. Those philosophers who believe relativism false for the most part still take it seriously, to one or another degree. Sometimes it's regarded as a threat, a dangerous (thus live) doctrine that needs to be refuted, and from them one sometimes hears the phrase "the specter of relativism." And within the professional literature, there is steady discussion of relativism's merits, shortcomings, and consequences.[3]

I need to say what I mean by "relativism" and to do so without flying in the face of Aristotle's advice not to attempt more precision than a subject matter will allow. We are looking for a common denominator that can be examined across disciplines, a cluster of connected, roughly marked-out claims and attitudes. The most important of these is the idea that truth in some domain, or perhaps all truth, is *truth-for*—claims are not true *simpliciter*, but true-for-someone or true-for-something. Truth may be relativized to particular persons, or groups of persons, or societies, or cultures, or social practices (for instance, physics as it is practiced at a particular time), or even interests of one kind or another. By way of illustration, Thomas Laqueur's *Making Sex* conveys what seems to be the outlandish suggestion that, until the eighteenth century, there was only one biological sex, but that thereafter there were two, and this without any biological alteration to effect the transition.[4] Biological facts (or "facts") are being taken to be true, not *tout court*, but *for* the scientific, legal, and popular cultures that accept them; a writer without relativist commitments would put the point rather differently, and simply say that it used to be thought that there was only one biological sex, but that now it is thought (or, perhaps, known) that there are two. Other predicates, covering classes of items not thought to be strictly truth-evaluable, may also be understood as relativized: "good," "beautiful," "appropriately a member of the canon," and so on.

Relativism is signaled by the attitude that many apparently logical conflicts are not in fact that at all. If "right," properly understood, has the force of "right-for-me" when uttered by me, and "right-for-him" when uttered by him, disagreement between the two of us over whether a particular proposed action is right does not show that either of us is *mistaken;* what is wrong-for-me may nonetheless be right-for-him. Disagreement in this case turns out to be practical rather than logical, and to be resolved not by determining who is actually correct, but by practical means: rhetoric, negotiation, or force. If disputes over what belongs in the canon are not, as they might seem on the surface, defenses of conflicting aesthetic judgments, all but one of which must, as a matter of logic, be wrong, then what belongs in the canon is a political question, to be resolved by political means. Where the conflicts are intellectual rather than practical, a natural (although, as it is often pointed out, not logically entailed) concomitant of relativism is polite coexistence. For instance, although among philosophers it is taken for granted that defending an interpretation of a philosophical text involves arguing against competing interpretations, in literary studies this is generally—occasional though notable exceptions notwithstanding—taken to be bad form. Relativism is a posture naturally adopted toward domains characterized by persisting disagreement. Since relativism explains why conflicts cannot be settled by conclusive argument, the move from unresolved disagreement to relativism can be charitably interpreted as an attempt at inference to the best explanation.

Although it is often talked about that way, relativism is not just a fancy name for "Anything goes." Consider a form of relativism that is obviously true: the relativity of meaning to language. There is nothing that "polvo" *just* means, in God's eyes, as it were; rather, it means one thing ("powder") in Spanish, and another ("octopus") in Portuguese. By the same token "polvo" does not mean *just anything* in either language. Unlike "anything goes," a relativism picks out a *basis* (here, the languages) that plays a constitutive role in determining the status of the relativized items. (In this example, the semantics of Spanish make "polvo" mean what it means in Spanish.) Relativism can seem like a very convenient doctrine when it exempts one from arguing with people one does not want to be arguing with, while still allowing one the comforts of being right: right, that is, relative to the basis.

II

Academics are members of guilds that make things with their hands. (If this way of thinking is difficult to adopt, that is probably because the handcrafted objects are often intangible; let me prevail upon you to ignore that difference for the moment.) Rather than thinking of the different academic disciplines as the bureaucratic reflection of a taxonomy of knowledge, and employment by one department of a university rather than another, simply the indication of having learned these bits of knowledge rather than those, look at the different fields as *crafts*, as τέχναι.[5] Outside the university, the practice of apprenticeship to a master craftsman has largely receded and become a curious archaism. But within the university, students are transformed into art historians, philosophers, molecular biologists, and so on through lengthy apprenticeships lasting anywhere from four to fourteen years. More important, for present purposes, than the information they memorize are the skills they acquire: the apprenticeship teaches not only knowing *that* but knowing *how*.[6]

As apprentices, philosophers learn to construct philosophical positions, philosophical arguments, and philosophy papers. They also learn to construct philosophical readings of philosophical texts—a skill not to be confused with the very different skill taught in neighboring departments, that of developing literary readings of literary texts, and of writing papers and books that advance those readings. Theoretical computer scientists learn to build algorithms and proofs, turn their results into talks, and write them up in papers. Laboratory scientists learn to design, assemble, and deploy experimental apparatus. In an age of mass production, these are craftsmen turning out one-of-a-kind items, all of which, even the mediocre samples, take considerable skill to fabricate. Each craft teaches its apprentices to *make* things, and the craftsmen, like carpenters or metalworkers, or, some time back, shoemakers and bridlemakers, have the knowledge—the knowledge-*how*—that comes of training and experience in making things of those kinds.[7]

Alasdair MacIntyre once suggested that emotivism—the view that putative moral judgments are merely the expression of one's feelings—was a response to and representation of the professional practice to which the emotivists had been exposed as students.[8] The related hypothesis I now wish to entertain is that the different academic disciplines' takes on relativism are to a large extent expressions of the craft experiences of the craftsmen in the respective disciplines. If the craftsmen whose skill is constructing readings of literary texts take relativism for granted, and find it incredible that any intelligent person should think otherwise, that is because they know—their *hands* know—that relativism is true of what they do: that several incompatible readings of the same text can all be satisfactory. If theoretical computer scientists almost always find relativism strictly incredible, it is because they know, from working with their hands, that it is not true of what *they* do: a different cultural background, for instance, will not make the algorithm run any faster. The knowledge of experienced craftsmen, however philosophically unsophisticated its articulation, should be taken with utmost seriousness; the bottom line is that, other things not being too unequal, the person in the best position to know how things work is the person who makes them and makes them work.[9] If the craftsmen think that this is the way the things they build work, then, unless you have good reason to think otherwise, your best policy is to believe them. Philosophy, as everyone knows, started off with Socrates debunking the knowledge of craftsmen, and I am willing to tender a belated apology on behalf of the discipline. Socrates was making a mistake; they knew what they were doing, and he did not.

This is not to say that craft knowledge is infallible, and the deliverances of the craftsmen incorrigible. Crafts can be swept by fads, both stylistic and intellectual, and when this happens the craftsman's pronouncements may be merely expressions of the fad, rather than of the practical knowledge stored up in his hands. The craft may be simply unreliable, like astrology, and we may discount the value of craft knowledge for that reason. Like everyone else, craftsmen are subject to cognitive illusions; the history of the Rorschach is a well-known example.[10] The practical self-understanding of the craft's practitioners may be misguided; there is always room for an argument that the craftsmen do not really understand, or are confused about, what they are doing. And—a related point—we need to distinguish between expressions of what we could call the craftsman's operational knowledge and that knowledge itself; taking such knowledge seriously does not always mean taking its expressions at face value.[11] That is, I am not suggesting that we should fetishize craft practitioners' humanly fallible self-understanding. The point is, rather, this: when we find a view (or pattern of views) about relativism that is characteristic of an academic craft, we should look for features of the practice that explain it; and we should be prepared to find—without ruling out other explanations in advance[12]—that those features amount to relativism's being true of that practice.[13]

Relativism is sometimes characterized as the doctrine that nothing is simply true: it is true-for-me, or true-for-you, or true-for-something-else. And an always-ready reply to relativism has been to ask whether *relativism* is true.[14] (Or is it, rather, only true-for-you?) We're now in a position to give the proper answer to that question. Relativism is true, for and of those academic disciplines that take it to be. If, in literary studies, it is generally taken for granted that relativism is true, then it *is* true ... for literary studies. ("True for": when the question of relativism is raised within the field, it is properly answered in the affirmative.) If, among theoretical physicists, relativism seems obviously absurd, we should conclude that relativism is false ... of theoretical physics. ("False of": relativism is not a good characterization of the methods appropriate in physics, and in the sort of inquiry we're conducting, an appropriate account of truth in the field is unlikely to end up casting it as relativized truth.)

But our trust in craft knowledge should not extend beyond the craft experience of the craftsmen. If practitioners of literary studies are relativists about everything, and so also relativists about philosophy, we need not infer from this that relativism is true of philosophy. It is not surprising that craftsmen understand whatever they encounter through the experience of their hands, and that they are likely to generalize the lessons of experience in a way that experience does not warrant. If sociologists of knowledge, studying physics, take it for granted that some form of relativism is true of physics, that suggests very strongly that relativism is true of sociology of knowledge.[15] The objects made by sociologists of knowledge are not results in physics, but papers publishable in their own professional journals; their knowledge-*how* is of the study of physics, not of physics. (There may also be arguments or data—knowledge-*that*—supporting the claim that relativism is true of physics; these would need to be considered on their own merits, and I do not mean to dismiss them ahead of time.)

Is relativism true of this very answer? Is the answer only true-for-us, where "us" registers evaluation from the standpoint of a particular academic craft? Presumably that depends on the discipline, and as this answer is being advanced as a philosophical claim, and because we do not at this point in the argument have a fix on the status of relativism in philosophy, it is premature to say. However, I do want to temper the worry that the suggestion I've just put on the plate isn't really an option. Why isn't the suggestion that relativism being true *for* a discipline typically amounts to it being true *of* a discipline just a fudge?[16]

Philippa Foot has made the helpful point that the easy formal refutations of relativism cannot be right, because there are domains—fashion, for example—of which relativism is clearly true, easy formal refutations notwithstanding.[17] What counts as physical beauty, or snappy dressing, varies with time and location, and depends on what the local standards of beauty and fashion happen to be. Relativism is not true or false—it is true of some domains (like fashion) and false of others. The point is well taken: in thinking about relativism, we need to shift our attention to the substantive features of the subject areas that make the position seem attractive or otherwise.

Recall that I introduced relativism as a loosely characterized cluster of views, a position that it's possible to examine across disciplines. One philosophers' vice—apparently, ever since the very beginning of philosophy!—is that of tightening up the cluster into a position that is just plain incoherent, or implausible, or anyway a view you would need a further reason to advance, over and above the original motivations for relativism. Thus, in the *Theaetetus*, relativism is made out as a position which guarantees that you can't ever be mistaken. (Protagoras is being portrayed as the Jacques Derrida or Paul de Man of ancient Greece.) Refuting *that* is not refuting relativism: relativism is obviously true, as we earlier observed, of the semantics of languages, but many, many people are wrong about what some of the words they use mean, and I'm prepared to be convinced that there are expressions about whose meaning everyone is mistaken. Nothing is gained—not insight, and not clarity—by tightening up the view into an incoherent position and saddling it with extraneous commitments. (So, don't reply to Foot: *that's* not relativism; *real* relativism is about *truth*, not fashion, and the thesis is required to apply exceptionlessly and uniformly.) The construction I am putting on relativism is in my view the best way to make sense of it; there is not a lot of point in insisting that that it is not *real* relativism, if what one is going to insist is real relativism is an unmotivated and incoherent position.

III

The suggestion that disciplinary attitudes toward relativism are often indicators of the truth of relativism for a discipline can be turned into a rubber-and-glue retort in a game of cross-disciplinary name-calling. (As in the playground incantation: "Whatever you say / Is rubber and glue; / It bounces off me, / And sticks to you!") But the point here is not name-calling. The striking fact with which I began, that the academic disciplines have differing takes on relativism, turns out to be a guide to investigating the practices of the various disciplines. I want now to pursue that point as regards philosophy, which, I remarked earlier, is a mixed case. If philosophers are, collectively, of two minds as to the intellectual merits of relativism, the argument so far suggests that we should look to their craft experience for an explanation.[18]

I will in the end claim that—perhaps contrary to one's initial expectations—the conflicting tendencies are to be traced back to a single source. For now, however, notice how surprising it should be that there *are* conflicting tendencies, if only because, at first glance, there are reasons galore in the experience of the practitioner of philosophy for full-fledged relativism. As Hume very nicely put it: "There is nothing which is not the subject of debate, and in which men of learning are not of contrary opinions. The most trivial question escapes not our controversy, and in the most momentous we are not able to give any certain decision. Disputes are multiplied, as if every thing was uncertain; and these disputes are managed with the greatest warmth, as if every thing was certain . . . and no man needs ever despair of gaining proselytes to the most extravagant hypothesis, who has art enough to represent it in any favourable colours."[19]

Disputes in philosophy can seem interminable, and we have seen that a natural explanation of disagreement is relativism: here, that philosophical theses are true or false only relative to something that varies with the disputant. But if the leaning toward relativism seems easy to account for, why don't all, or almost all, philosophers lean all the way? Why isn't relativism the default?

One of the experiences characteristic of philosophizing is realizing that, in order to solve the philosophical problem on which you are working, there is another problem you will have to solve first. Getting clear about the objectivity of value depends, you may decide, on making out an analogy between values and colors; but getting that analogy into a position where it can settle questions of objectivity turns out, you find, to require you to have settled already familiar problems having to do with the nature of counterfactual conditionals and dispositions, as well as puzzles about qualia or "raw feels," supervenience and reductionism, and so on. These problems in turn prove to presuppose solutions to further problems. So how much of philosophy does a single philosophical problem involve?

Here is a way to think about trying to find out. Consider the operation that takes you from a philosophical problem to the philosophical problems at one remove that you would have to have solved in order to be able to solve the initial problem; let us temporarily call this operation Problems Presupposed. (I will in due course take up the respects in which this is a simplified approximation.) Suppose you have some initial set of philosophical problems. Imagine applying Problems Presupposed to the problems in your initial set, and then adding the new philosophical problems you have obtained to that initial set; then applying Problems Presupposed to *this* set, . . . and continuing to repeat this procedure until applying Problems Presupposed generates no new problems to add. The set of philosophical problems you have ended up with is the *closure* of your initial set under the operation Problems Presupposed.[20]

Philosophy and the sciences progress in different directions. The sciences progress by moving *forward*, from one solved problem to the next, building up a stockpile of results that, in favorable circumstances, can be systematized into a general account of the domain of the science. Philosophy, however, progresses by moving *backwards:* not by solving or, at any rate, not by *simply* solving problems, but by uncovering the problems hidden in, or under, or behind the problems one was trying to solve, and by taking them up in turn. This fact is occasionally responsible for startling contrasts. The question "What is the world made of?" is shared by philosophy and physics; both can claim Thales as their founder. Physics has moved forward, establishing facts and advancing theories, and arrived at one of its current answers: space-time and elementary particles, or an assignment of values of fundamental quantities to space-time points, or strings and branes. Philosophy moves backwards: to questions of justification ("How could we know?"), which in turn raise questions of meaning ("What can we refer to?"), and ultimately to answers, when philosophy produces them, that are radically different from those of the natural sciences. One fairly recent philosophers' answer to Thales' question was *sense-data:* a class of (alleged) mental objects, a typical instance of which might be a red patch in one's visual field.[21] Because the natural motion of philosophy is from problems to logically prior problems, the characteristic operation of philosophy is the move from one problem to the further problems that would have to be solved first. By way of emphasizing this,

I will abandon the temporary label PROBLEMS PRESUPPOSED and will refer to this operation as the characteristic operation of philosophy, or, more tersely, *the characteristic operation*.

The procedure I have just described, for determining the closure of a set of philosophical problems under the characteristic operation, may seem to be of no practical interest. It is not as though, for instance, you could use it to survey your philosophical task before actually going ahead with it; only by working your way through some philosophical problem on your agenda will you be able to determine which solutions to further problems it requires. And since you cannot perform the procedure ahead of performing the tasks at hand, it seems to follow that you cannot use the procedure to survey the tasks in advance (perhaps in order to come up with an estimate of the time they will take). However, despite our inability to execute the procedure faster than we can work our way through philosophical problems, we are well placed to say just what the closures under the characteristic operation of given sets of philosophical problems are. That is because the history of philosophy has done our homework for us.

IV

Every so often, philosophy reboots. Frustrated by apparent deadlock in the field, a revolutionary, or a small band of revolutionaries, hits upon a new problem, the solution to which, it is announced, will displace the old and unanswerable questions and either put philosophy in order or do away with it entirely. We are still living off the last of the momentum generated by the logical positivist revolution, whose question "What does it mean?" was supposed to dissolve the problems on the inherited list. And we may now be witnessing an attempt at another such revolution, in what is starting to be called experimental philosophy, a research program launched by the question, "What, as a matter of empirical fact, explains the intuitions of the general population on matters philosophical?" Before positivism, there was (skipping a few steps) Kant, whose question was "What are the limits of reason?" And before Kant, Descartes: "What method will ensure certainty and knowledge?" Eventually, we come back to Socrates and his question, meant to displace the inquiries of the natural philosophers: "What is F?" (where F was usually one or another virtue). Of course, the history of philosophy is no less resistant to schematization than any other kind of history, and I am not suggesting that my description fits neatly. I do, however, think that it is true enough for present purposes.

But in each cycle, it turned out that solving the new problem required having first solved others, and solving these others required having solved still others in turn.[22] In very short order (well under a century, this last time around), the original set of problems was generated from the new problem: closure of the small set of new problems under the characteristic operation had reproduced the original set. I take this to be a deep fact about philosophy: *the set of philosophical problems is the closure of any of its subsets under the characteristic operation.* Consequently, the set of philosophical problems—making up what we can think of as the philosophical problem space—is stable.

That is a bold claim, and while I mean to stick with it, it will bear a certain amount of qualification. First of all, by "any subset," I do not, of course, mean the empty set. I am also willing to allow that there may be exceptions to the "any subset" part of the claim: problems acknowledged to be philosophical that do not generate the entire philosophical problem space in this way because they are too trivial and tangential to the main interests of the field.[23] There is another class of exceptions, problems that are epiphenomena of the philosophical idiom of a given period: artifacts of a way of speaking or of a canonical notation or of a technical apparatus that do not survive its demise. I will return to this latter class of exceptions in a moment.

It might be objected that the reconstruction of the philosophical problem space in a given historical cycle does not simply reproduce the initial set of problems: a new problem, or clutch of problems, has been added to the original list. This objection is mistaken in both its letter and its spirit. A problem used to restart philosophy has normally made prior appearances, albeit typically with much less emphasis. (The Vienna Circle were not the first to ask themselves, How would you tell if such-and-such were true? Or again, John Stuart Mill insistently demanded a psychological explanation for philosophical intuitions.) And because the new, or newly emphasized, problems were in fact necessary for solving the problems on the previous philosophical agenda, whether or not that was realized at the time, then—since the full agenda is not merely the list of problems that one has, but the list completed to include those problems whose solutions are needed for solving the problems that one has—every previous cycle in philosophical history has had the full set of philosophical problems: the ones we have not noticed as well as those we have.

The stability of the problem space explains why the history of philosophy is a part of philosophy proper, and why philosophers so often treat long-dead colleagues as intellectual contemporaries. Because the problems, and the ways they are related to one another, stay fixed, previous attempts at solution can often be adapted to the current debate: witness the recent revival of Kant and of Aristotle in ethics. For the same reason, even when the solutions of the past cannot be adapted to the needs of the present, they provide an illuminating opportunity to rethink our own problems from an alien perspective, and are useful for the sense such exercises give us of the move space we are facing ourselves.

This last claim is bound to provoke the reply that the problems are not, after all, the same. I earlier allowed that there may be philosophical problems that are not generated by the above-described technique, and that do not themselves serve as a basis for generating the full set, because they are peculiar to one or another philosophical idiom or arise only within the context of eventually obsolete technical apparatus. The reply we are considering insists that all philosophical problems belong to this class of alleged exceptions. We have been taught by Kuhn, goes the objection, that the vocabularies, techniques, and—in the bit of jargon that goes with this line—paradigms of different eras are incommensurable. To identify a problem faced by Aristotle with one that preoccupies us is falsely to read our own problems into the past; it is just bad history.[24]

The problem with this reply is that it does not match the practical experience of working philosophers: for instance, the experience of realizing that someone has been here before, marshaled the same considerations, weighed the same trade-offs, and solved that very puzzle in his own elegant, or awkward, or perverse way. Philosophers, even in this most antihistorical of philosophical traditions, turn to history because they know that it works. Moreover, they find that it works best when readings are not anachronistic (where the objection supposes that history will be most useful when it converts the past into the present). The similar-sounding questions asked by philosophers in different periods are not merely homonymous, even though one needs to do a certain amount of squinting to see the problems as the same, because part of being philosophically competent is being able to treat the philosophizing of prior periods as attempting answers to one's present problems. Once again, craft knowledge is not infallible, but it needs to be taken very seriously. There might be an argument that would successfully show the sensibilities of the practitioners to be mistaken on this point; until such an argument is produced, what the reply teaches us about is the craft experience of the practitioners of those disciplines in which the view it expresses is second nature. What historians or sociologists of science believe about incommensurability tells us more about what it is like to do history or sociology of science than it tells us about science, or philosophy, or their respective pasts.

The stability of the problem space also explains why relativism is not the default: why it is not the common sense of professional philosophers. The answers to the problems may shift with one's intuitions, one's priorities and concerns, and who knows what else. But underneath the field lies something very much like a mathematical object, a set with an elegant and peculiar property, that of being the closure under the characteristic operation of philosophy of any of its subsets. It is hard not to wax Platonist about this object, in the way that it is hard for practicing mathematicians not to end up, tacitly or explicitly, Platonists about the objects they study. The philosophical problem space exists in the heaven of the Forms, independent of human will, shifts in perspective, political commitments, and cultural background.[25] It is this sense—arrived at through the experience of one's hands—of the *hardness* of the logical relations between philosophical problems, and so of their independence of the bases of plausible relativisms that, I am suggesting, accounts for the lack of full acceptance, within professional philosophy, of relativism. Truth cannot just be, for example, truth-for-a-given-culture, because one knows, from having hit one's head too many times against the quasi-mathematical object that underlies philosophy, that whether it is true that a particular problem *must* be on the philosophical agenda is not a culture-dependent matter.[26]

I introduced the characteristic operation as a simplified approximation, and the stability of the problem set becomes even more impressive once we consider just what that description suppresses, namely, the way the list of problems for which we immediately need solutions depends on our theoretical choices.[27] Recall the example I took from recent metaethics: in order to work up a secondary-quality account of value, you need to have available treatments of counterfactuals, qualia, and so on. But philosophers learn to navigate around problems they don't know how to deal with. Cornell moral realism is an alternative to secondary-quality approaches; it is an adaptation of Richard Boyd's views in philosophy of science, and so to make it work, one must turn one's attention not to qualia and so on but to issues in philosophy of science, such as convergence and the best explanation for it. On the one hand, what problems I am taken to at one remove can depend on what solution I am trying to work up to my present problem (which is to say that PROBLEMS PRESUPPOSED was not the simple operation we made it out to be); on the other hand, the stability of the problem space of philosophy is established by a historical induction. Evidently the problem space is stable *despite* alternatives at the choice points: it does not matter which theoretical approach to a problem you take; eventually, you are going to end up with same set of problems *anyway*. That is an eye-opening fact; no wonder working philosophers feel the problems they have to work with to be inevitable.

Now that we have an explanation of philosophical resistance to relativism, we need to return to our earlier explanation of its plausibility and consider how it can be squared with the account I have just given. But before doing that, let us pause to pocket some of the profits the enterprise has already generated.

V

What makes a problem a problem of philosophy? How can one show a problem to be philosophically interesting? Here is a passage canvassing answers to the first question, taken from a book picked more or less at random from the shelf:

> Philosophy has no specific object but reworks different forms of knowledge in order to express their ultimate truth.... It examines the great cultural models through which we apprehend the world.... It criticizes the ordinary procedure of other disciplines....
>
> Its task is ... to wonder how a given knowledge is possible, or again to make links between the different sciences, or to think about their foundations or to clarify their language.... Philosophy [is] that which can circulate between different areas of knowledge, notably raising problems inherent in them.[28]

Although taken from a text written in French, and squarely in the French philosophical tradition, these answers, phrased slightly differently, would raise no eyebrows on the analytic side of the water. Here is an American philosopher addressing the same question:

> "Philosophy," as I am using the term, simply designates the attempt to answer questions that are especially fundamental. A question is fundamental if an array of other important questions depends on the answer to it in some important way. . . . Thus, the question, "What is the causal relation?" is philosophical . . . since our understanding of how to construe or regard many important scientific truths depends on our answer to it. . . . So understood, philosophy includes the most fundamental questions of the various special disciplines.[29]

And finally for now, here are remarks on the subject from a thoughtfully written introductory textbook in yet a third tradition:

> Physics, theology, literary criticism and the like all ask and attempt to answer certain questions. Philosophy asks what sort of question the physicist or the theologian asks. Philosophical questions are questions about questions and hence to be called "second-order questions."
>
> Mathematicians spend their lives working out proofs; the philosopher asks: "What is a valid proof in mathematics?" Physicists construct experiments and elaborate theories; the philosopher asks "What is the nature of a good theory and what different types of theory are there?" Theologians produce doctrines and arguments as to the nature of the divine; the philosopher asks, "What is an authentic doctrine and how do you test it?"[30]

The idea of philosophy as metadiscipline (whether Queen or Handmaiden of the Sciences), or as the interdisciplinary discipline, or as the science of leftover problems, or of problems seen to be fundamental, does not tally well with the stability of the problem space. The special sciences change rapidly; to a physicist, the writings of Newton are of only historical interest, and Newton's problems are no longer live issues. If the problems of philosophy were derived from those of the special sciences, we would expect our view of what the philosophical problems are to change along with the sciences. But, as I remarked above, all philosophers, living or dead, are pretty much contemporaries.[31] The problems that Plato saw were philosophical problems are *still* philosophical problems, and our own philosophical problems either were or, we now see, should have been problems for Plato. In fact, as the hands of every successful practitioner of philosophy know, these problems are philosophically interesting regardless of their connections to the special sciences.[32]

If this is right, we need a different way of saying what it is to be a philosophical problem, or (equivalently) what it is for a problem to be philosophically interesting. As it happens, we have one on hand: *A problem is philosophically interesting when it can be generated by applying the characteristic operation to another philosophical problem.* To show that a problem belongs to philosophy, I do not think it is particularly helpful to argue that it is fundamental, or a metaproblem, or that it is interdisciplinary, or that it just does not belong to any other discipline. But you *can* demonstrate that a problem is of philosophical interest by showing that you would have to solve it in order to solve other philosophical problems. Sometimes I am inclined to think that that is the only demonstration you can give; we can name this possibility the *autonomy of philosophy*.

This characteristic of the philosophical problem space does not, of course, distinguish this problem space from others similarly structured.[33] And in saying what makes a problem philosophically interesting I have not in any way spoken to the question of whether philosophically interesting problems are interesting *tout court*, that is, interesting when a prior interest in some problems of philosophy is not already in place.

VI

I have suggested that the practicing philosopher's awareness of the underlying space of philosophical problems accounts for the widespread unwillingness to embrace relativism wholeheartedly. I now want to claim that the structure of the problem space also explains the pull of relativism. A little while ago, I gestured at a Toynbean picture of the rise and fall of philosophical civilizations, each cycle of which regenerates the philosophical problem space from some new choice of initial problems. We have seen why rising philosophical cultures tend to end up resembling each other. But why do they fall? Consider the following explanation of the repeated urge to revolution, to start philosophy over anew, or to do away with it once and for all that terminates one cycle and begins the next.

The characteristic operation of philosophy takes you from an initial problem to another problem that must be solved first; applying the characteristic operation to the latter problem takes you to a further problem that must be solved still earlier, and so you are led, step by step, from your initial problem . . . back to your initial problem, because sooner or later it will turn out that in order to have solved some problem in this series, you have to have solved your initial problem first.[34] The graph corresponding to the problem space contains cycles, and this fact becomes progressively more apparent over the history during which an attempt to restart philosophy is played out.[35] There is no clean starting point; because all one's answers are interdependent, one must give an answer to all the problems of philosophy at once. Philosophical system building is an entirely natural response.[36] It then comes to seem as though there must be different sets of simultaneous answers to all the problems of philosophy and no logically decisive way to choose between them. The alternatives come to seem like options one can move between in roughly the way one can induce visual gestalt switches. One's picture of the philosophical world then seems to depend on something further—preferences, intuitions, or political agendas—to which philosophical truth must be understood as relativized. Eventually, one throws up one's hands and starts over.

If this is right, relativism is both endorsed by one aspect of the philosopher's experience and belied by another. Because it is a good idea to take the practitioner's craft experience seriously, it is tempting simply to split the difference: to conclude that relativism is true of solutions to philosophical problems, but not of the problems themselves. And indeed some such accommodation is implicit in the work of a number of prominent contemporary and recent philosophers. In the face of systematic underdetermination, a quite natural response is to pick one or another set of starting points and use those to attempt to solve the standard menu of philosophical problems. The solutions thus arrived at are treated, more or less implicitly, as true with respect to those starting points. (Philosophers are, after all, quite used to the idea that the conclusions of one's arguments vary with their premises.) The starting points themselves are recommended on pragmatic grounds, as those capable of generating the exhibited solutions.[37]

There are two problems with this kind of attempt at accommodation. First, to take a position on a philosophical problem as an unquestioned starting point, from which one will proceed to solve other philosophical problems, is to reverse the characteristic direction of philosophy; when this happens, the results turn out to be strikingly unphilosophical. The point here is not one of labeling—it is not that we don't want to *call* system building of this kind "philosophy"—but rather that such enterprises find themselves in an awkward position, that of being unable to explain why they have the scope that they do. Such enterprises typically take for granted the set of philosophical problems they are to solve; but those problems, we saw, were generated by the backward motion induced by the characteristic operation of philosophy. If the demand that generates the problem space is legitimate, then it is not possible to adopt, by fiat, starting points one will not look behind. So if one's method of addressing philosophical problems is to adopt, by fiat, starting points one will not look behind, then one will be in no position to explain why it is *those* problems one must solve; and one will, consequently, be in no position to explain why a solution to those problems constitutes a recommendation for those starting points.

The second problem is that the relation, in these cases, between starting point and conclusion is not of a kind that can be successfully construed as underwriting a form of relativism. The relation is that of conclusions to premises, and while the conclusions of an argument do depend on its premises, they are not true relative to the premises. If I believe you are stopping off at the farmstand on the way here (call that belief p), I may infer that you will arrive with enough fresh produce for a dinner (call the conclusion q). My inference to q does depend on my believing p; but q is not thereby true-for-me or true-relative-to-p. That you will turn up with the groceries is just true or false; it is not true relative to my belief and perhaps false relative to someone else's. *Premises* (or, in one philosophical jargon, "intuitions") are not suited to be the basis of a relativism.

Underdetermination is not yet relativism. Relativism requires an appropriate form of dependence, of that which is relativized, on its basis. Where the dependence is not constitutive, as it is not in the case of the conclusion inferentially depending on the premises, there is no room for a relativist understanding of that dependence. Accepting the premise is not what makes the conclusion true, and so the conclusion is not true-relative-to-the-premises.

I said earlier that we must take seriously the craft experience of the practitioners of academic disciplines; but I also allowed that that experience could be misleading. In philosophy, craft experience pulls both toward and away from relativism; if splitting the difference does not work, the pull toward relativism is misleading. The experience of underdetermination is being misinterpreted as the experience of relativism.

VII

Relativism can be a far more comforting state of mind than that of trying to live with underdetermination. Realizing that relativism is true for fashion means giving up the project of discovering what is fashionable from the point of view of the universe, and of coming by a wardrobe that, as it were, participates in or copies the Form of the Fashionable. But there remains the very real task of figuring out what *is* fashionable this season, and of acquiring a wardrobe that is fashionable here and now. Likewise, relativism in philosophy leaves one with the still tangible task of figuring out what is true and right—even if not right and true, plain and simple, but for you, in the circumstances you are in. Accepting underdetermination, on the other hand, means accepting that your problems have no solutions—not even solutions-for-you.[38] And that is a disheartening conclusion to draw: there is no point in working on problems you cannot solve, even if your inability to solve your problems is not going to make them go away.

I want to suggest that this reason for giving up on philosophy is premature. Let me acknowledge that that suggestion may seem at first glance outrageous. We have had some of the brightest people who have ever lived working, for well over two millennia, in what I have argued is a stable problem space. And many of the excuses that might be used for other lagging sciences—lack of empirical data, or of sufficiently fancy gadgetry—are thought to be unavailable to philosophy. If, after all this time, what we have come up with is underdetermination, surely the reason for not giving up cannot be that it is *too early*. But if I am right about the way in which the structure of the philosophical problem space gives rise to (at any rate, apparent) underdetermination, that may nevertheless have been the problem.

Once the relations between the problems of philosophy are understood, the overall problem becomes one of jointly satisfying the constraints induced by those relations—these, recall, being the relations that are (approximately) traced out by repeated applications of the characteristic operation. We can call this problem, that of finding the most coherent joint solution to the problems of philosophy, given those constraints, the *philosophy coherence problem*.[39]

Approaches to the philosophy coherence problem have, until this point, inevitably been ad hoc, since, until very recently, no one has tried to investigate coherence and methods for solving coherence problems in any concrete and useful way. Philosophers have a long history of talking about coherence without being able to say the first thing about what coherence consists in, without having a way of determining when one solution to a problem is more coherent than another, and without having any ideas about how to remedy this particular intellectual shortfall. If the problems of philosophy must be considered jointly, and if, considered jointly, they amount to a coherence problem, then it is not surprising that they have remained unsolved.

The investigation of coherence is still in the very preliminary stages. But we are starting to see new formal and computational analyses of coherence. It is necessary to emphasize that these are crude and in need of further development. But they indicate how content can be given to talk of coherence, how judgments of relative coherence can be assessed, and how techniques for computing coherence can be developed and tested.[40]

Even on the basis of the extremely preliminary work with these techniques to date, two important points can be made. First, I suggested that the awareness of cycles in the philosophical problem space was responsible for the sense that the available constraints fail to determine a unique solution to the problems in that space. If the value you assign A depends on the value you assign B, and vice versa, it can easily seem that there must be more than one way to assign values to A and to B. But experimenting with computational methods of representing joint constraint satisfaction problems shows that inference to be much too fast. It will *sometimes* be true for a specified type of constraint satisfaction problem, and for a given set of cyclical constraints, that there are ties for the best solution; but often there will be unique best solutions. Merely observing the presence of cycles is not enough to give you the conclusion that there is no one right answer.

There is no way to tell if there really are ties, short of generating and ranking the solutions, and so far we do not even have our method for ranking them sorted out—much less all the solutions we need to rank.

Second, if philosophy really does amount to a large coherence problem, it is too early to give up on it, for two reasons. Many constraint satisfaction problems are NP-complete—that is, they belong to a class of problems widely thought to be computationally intractable.[41] NP-complete problems are not normally amenable to solution by brute force methods in *any* reasonable amount of time; if such a problem were at the core of philosophy, over two thousand years of philosophy would not have been nearly long enough. If the philosophy coherence problem is intractable, we will solve it only by developing more sophisticated approaches to it: ways of approximating the solution, or of isolating features of the problem that identify it as a member of a tractable subclass. And because we have only just started to think about how to solve problems of this kind, we have a second reason for holding that until very recently it was simply too early to make any real headway on this problem.

VIII

If the problems of philosophy really do jointly amount to a coherence problem, one might think that their solution was just around the corner. At any rate, the program for solving them might seem quite clear. First, we need to work up a precise specification of the coherence problem; second, we need to develop techniques for computing, or approximately computing, the most coherent solution, given a set of constraints; third, we need to be putting the philosophy coherence problem into a form that will allow these techniques to be applied to it, that is, turning the connections between philosophical problems traced by the characteristic operation into a list of constraints that the correct philosophical view will satisfy.[42] I have been arguing that there is already a good deal of convergence on the constraints; advances in theory of computation can be expected to give us the menu of powerful methods that we need. With the list of constraints, and the right computational methods in hand, the problems of philosophy can be solved in short order—in the manner of Douglas Adams, or anyway the four-color problem, by a computer.[43] The end of philosophy is in sight, and very shortly only the mopping up will be left... just as the logical positivists thought a century ago, and Kant thought a century earlier, ... and so on, back to the beginning of the discipline.

The history suggests that this kind of optimism would be overoptimism, and here is a reason why. For it to be possible to investigate computational solutions to problems of this kind, one needs, first, a list of the constraints one is trying to satisfy. But even if there is overall agreement as to how the problems of philosophy are connected one to another, there is bound to be disagreement on the details: for example, whether one takes two nodes to be linked will depend on what position one has regarding some other node, and there is the question of how relative weights should be assigned to the different constraints. And many constraint satisfaction techniques are quite sensitive to details like these. Second, one will need a precise computational specification of the problem: Exactly which coherence problem are we trying to solve?[44] When we sit down to produce one, and the inputs to it, we will quite certainly find ourselves embroiled in disputes as to what counts as coherence, or what kind of coherence is required to solve *this* problem. Coherence is a label for one of the traditional philosophical problems, and so the problem of which kind of coherence is the right one can be expected to require for its solution other solutions to further problems.[45] And so we will find ourselves facing, once again, all of the problems of philosophy.

Notes

I am grateful to Jon Bendor, Alice Clapman, Steve Downes, Eyjolfur Emilsson, Christoph Fehige, Richard Gale, Don Garrett, Brian Klug, John MacFarlane, Clif McIntosh, Eddy Nahmias, Ram Neta, Carol Poster, Richard Raatzsch, Peri Schwartz-Shea, Bill Talbott, and Mariam Thalos for comments on earlier drafts, and to Michael Bratman, Sarah Buss, Alice Crary, Jenann Ismael, Mark Johnston, Elizabeth Kiss, and Alexander Nehamas for helpful discussion. The paper was improved by comments from audiences at Saint Louis University, the CASBS Meta-Historians Discussion Group, the University of Montana, the University of Utah, Kansas State University, Ohio University, Victoria University of Wellington, the University of New South Wales, Oxford University, the University of Alberta, University College Dublin, and the University of Bologna. Work on this paper was supported by fellowships from the National Endowment for the Humanities and the Center for Advanced Study in the Behavioral Sciences; I am grateful for the financial support provided through the Center by the Andrew W. Mellon Foundation.

1. Reported by Hilary Putnam, "The Meaning of 'Meaning,'" in *Mind, Language and Reality* (Cambridge: Cambridge University Press, 1975), 260.

2. So much so that when Bruno Latour was up for a stint at Princeton's Institute for Advanced Studies, the scientists revolted and the stint disappeared. See David Berreby, ". . . That Damned Elusive Bruno Latour," *Lingua Franca* 4, no. 6 (1994): 24.

3. For a dated but respectable anthology, see Jack Meiland and Michael Krausz, *Relativism: Cognitive and Moral* (Notre Dame: University of Notre Dame Press, 1992), and for a more recent survey volume, Steven Hales, ed., *A Companion to Relativism* (Oxford: Wiley-Blackwell, 2011). The situation is complicated by a further phenomenon: that philosophers who insist that relativism is true often do not allow that opinion to be reflected in their own argumentative practice. Philosophers who not only say that relativism is true but *write* as though it were true can find themselves parting ways with the profession. For example, not long after his *Philosophy and the Mirror of Nature* (Princeton: Princeton University Press, 1979), Richard Rorty moved institutional locations, from a philosophy department to the literature departments where he remained until his death.

4. Thomas Laqueur, *Making Sex* (Cambridge, MA: Harvard University Press, 1990).

5. To be sure, the mapping between crafts and institutional frameworks is not always one-to-one. Some historians are social scientists, and some are humanists, despite being housed in the same departments; and there are many departments in which some variation on this sort of sharing arrangement is to be found. For a history of the way in which such a condominium broke down in German philosophy departments not that long ago, see Martin Kusch, *Psychologism* (London: Routledge, 1995). For some discussion of the craft aspects of the sciences, see Jerome Ravetz, *Scientific Knowledge and Its Social Problems* (New York: Oxford University Press, 1979), esp. 71, 117–18, and ch. 3.

6. For the locus classicus of this distinction, see Gilbert Ryle, *The Concept of Mind* (Chicago: Chicago University Press, 1984), ch. 2. For a comparative study of a few of the guilds, see Tony Becher, *Academic Tribes and Territories* (Milton Keynes: Society for Research into Higher Education/Open University Press, 1989).

7. That said, it is important to register the especially tight entanglement and mutual dependence of knowledge-that and knowledge-how in the academic disciplines. Because what is being produced is (at least in theory) knowledge, and because knowledge is produced largely by deploying other knowledge, a large part of academic knowledge-how depends on having available an appropriate stock of knowledge-that. For example, one proves a theorem using other theo-

rems, and knowing how to assemble a proof is in part a matter of having the necessary theorems at one's fingertips.

The suggestion that philosophy is a craft regularly provokes resistance, on the grounds that crafts have independently specified products, which are consumed by clients who are not themselves the craftsmen (e.g., shoemakers make shoes, which are worn by customers who are not themselves shoemakers); but it is the philosophers who get to decide if what they are doing is any good, and they do not have a product that clients who are not themselves philosophers can assess. My sense is that one of the important motivations for this objection is the idea that crafts are teleologically structured. As Mill puts it: "Every art has one first principle, or general major premise, not borrowed from science; that which enunciates the object aimed at, and affirms it to be a desirable object." John Stuart Mill, *Collected Works* (Toronto/London: University of Toronto Press / Routledge, 1967–89), 8:949.

In fact, however, the standards for just about any healthy craft are set *within* the craft: it is not the users who decide what a good shoe is, but the fashion designers. And this fact is inextricably intertwined with the nonteleological structure of healthy crafts: computer science, for example, may have a defining goal, that of making better computers, and coming to a better understanding of computation, but it is only verbally, and not substantively, an organizing constraint for the craft. The reason it is such an exciting field to be in is that a cutting-edge computer scientist devotes much of his intellectual energy to figuring out what computers, and computation, *will be next*.

8. Alasdair MacIntyre, *After Virtue*, 2nd ed. (Notre Dame: University of Notre Dame Press, 1997), 11–18.

9. This point was brought home to me by Vicki Hearne, *Adam's Task* (New York: Random House, 1987). Her arguments against laboratory animal psychologists turn on the respective objects of two crafts: laboratory psychologists know how to produce experiments that in turn produce publishable results, while animal trainers produce working animals.

10. See Richard Nisbett and Lee Ross, *Human Inference* (Englewood Cliffs, NJ: Prentice-Hall, 1980), 94–97; for a more recent and more popular account, see Robyn Dawes, *House of Cards* (Englewood Cliffs, NJ: Free Press, 1994), 146–54.

11. Suppose, to take a certainly oversimplified view as an illustration, that literary interpretations of texts are there to provide ways of appreciating those texts that enrich the experience of reading them. If they are treated as successes when they do so, then practitioners will learn—as a lesson of professional life—that there is always room for one more reading that makes an encounter with a familiar text surprising and newly enjoyable, and that the new reading need not preclude other readings doing the same job. The practical awareness of these incentives will likely be expressed as a predisposition to relativism about the interpretations of literary texts.

However, notice that literary theory plays a large role in the discipline. If I am right, the function of theory is, in practice, to serve readings that enrich encounters with literary texts. That is, theories are articulated and advanced not because they are true, or because there are good arguments for them, but because they make available new and satisfying (or challenging, or whatever) experiences of literary texts. However, practitioners of the discipline need not be aware of this, and they may look for explanations of their relativism, arrived at as an expression of craft knowledge, to theories they have produced or come by in these ways. (Compare Thomas Mann's closely related remarks on Wagner: "To the artist, new experiences of 'truth' mean new stimuli to play, new expressive possibilites—nothing more. He believes in them . . . only to the degree that is necessary in order to . . . make the deepest possible impression with them." "The Sorrows and Grandeur of Richard Wagner," in *Pro and Contra Wagner*, trans. Allan Blunden [Chicago: University of Chicago Press, 1985], 120.)

12. For instance, that novices enter a discipline because they already find its attitudes toward relativism congenial, and so produce and perpetuate a unanimity that may have little to do with the discipline's underlying features.

Notice that there are disciplines in which relativism is now the dominant view but at some previous time was not (or the other way around). Our argument suggests looking to see if the practice of the discipline has changed in a way that made relativism true of the discipline when it was believed and untrue when it was not. (For this point, and the clarification in the next note, I'm grateful to Jon Bendor.)

13. Bear in mind that disciplines and their practices should not be confused with objects of study. Philosophers and literary critics will give readings of the very same texts, and political science (which is pretty uniformly antirelativist), sociology, and anthropology (which are largely relativist) often study very much the same things. One should not move too quickly from expecting that a discipline's relativism is to be explained by its practice to expecting that it is to be explained by the features of the objects that the discipline investigates.

14. See, e.g., Hilary Putnam, *Reason, Truth and History* (Cambridge: Cambridge University Press, 1981), 119. Such responses go back as far as the *Theaetetus;* for a recent reconstruction of Plato's arguments, see Myles Burnyeat, *The Theaetetus of Plato*, with a translation of Plato's *Theaetetus* by M. J. Levett (Indianapolis: Hackett, 1990).

15. Strongly but, once again, not conclusively. One further alternative explanation is worth mentioning. The experience of the craft practitioner may be that adopting a relativist posture toward the material produces better results, such as more sophisticated and illuminating sociology of knowledge papers, even if relativism is not plausibly true of the material. Compare the practice of clinical psychology, where practitioners accept, for the purposes of therapy, the testimony of their patients. Trying to argue someone out of his conspiracy theory or his memories of trauma is counterproductive; taking the memories or conspiracy theory as a given is more likely to improve the patient's life—or, at any rate, the clinician's

practice. But the patient's beliefs are presumably not true relative to the patient; if they're true, they're simply true, and if false, they are simply false. A rather vivid illustration is the Harvard Medical School psychiatry professor who gained a brief notoriety for extending this practice of accepting a patient's testimony to persons who believed they had been abducted by UFOs. If there are no UFOs, a claim of abduction is not true-relative-to-the-patient's-testimony; it is simply not true, even if accepting the claim makes it more likely that the therapy will have a successful outcome. See John Mack, *Abduction* (New York: Ballantine Books, 1997). However, there may be other factors at work in his case: his claims that the "reality status" of his patients' narratives is not his concern alternate with arguments to the effect, roughly, that so many eyewitnesses can't all be wrong.

16. If you think it's a fudge, you're likely to think the view is inconsistent. Suppose that a physicist agrees that relativism is true of literary studies; isn't relativism thereby true-for-the-physicist; but haven't I claimed that, for the physicist, relativism is false? And anyway, don't relativist claims have to top out, sooner or later, in claims that are to be read as just plain true or false?

Whether or not relativism can go all the way up — whether, eventually, one will just have to insist that one's relativist claims are nonrelatively true — should not be mistaken for an easy question. For an exploration of the possibility that it can, see Robert Nozick, *Invariances* (Cambridge, MA: Harvard University Press, 2001), ch. 1.

17. Philippa Foot, "Moral Relativism," in Meiland and Krausz, *Relativism*, 152–66.

18. Philosophy has not always been an *academic* craft, however — see, e.g., Martha Nussbaum, *The Therapy of Desire* (Princeton: Princeton University Press, 1994), which makes Hellenistic philosophy out to be a sort of institutional ancestor of the Esalen Institute — and many of those now generally accepted as important philosophers (such as Nietzsche and Kierkegaard) were professional outsiders during their own lifetimes.

19. David Hume, *A Treatise of Human Nature*, 2nd ed., ed. L. A. Selby-Bigge and P. H. Nidditch (Oxford: Clarendon Press, 1888/1978), xiv.

20. There is no suggestion here that the closure of the initial set is finite. For purposes of comparison, the closure of the set {2, 3} under multiplication is not a finite set.

21. Many of the philosophers who produced this answer were physics-worshippers and would not have dreamed of denying that the world was made of space-time and elementary particles. This shows that the questions asked by philosophers and by nonphilosophers, even if verbally identical, are in fact very different questions and perhaps bears out to some extent an opinion of the philosophers who produced the just-mentioned answer: the meaning *is* the method of verification.

22. This is a good occasion to ask the reader to bear in mind both that logical and temporal priority relations are different things and that, at the early

stages of these cycles, logical relations tend to be understood as imposing a temporal structure on one's agenda: one problem's presupposing the solution to another gets treated as entailing that the presupposed solution has to be produced earlier. (For a remark that suggests why these tend to be conflated, see Roger Florka, *Descartes's Metaphysical Reasoning* [New York: Routledge, 2001], 19 n. 20.) More on this in note 36.

23. I have had Gettierology suggested to me as an example; for an overview, see Robert Shope, *The Analysis of Knowing* (Princeton: Princeton University Press, 1983), 21–34. However, if the appeal to intuitions typical of Gettier-style arguments raises the question of the status of those intuitions, and if experimental philosophy, like its predecessors, will also generate the entire philosophical problem space, even a debate as esoteric as this one is not an exception to the rule. So although I am willing to allow such exceptions, they are harder to come up with than you might at first glance expect.

24. See, e.g., Rorty, *Philosophy,* 262–63, and compare the related complaint attributed to Dewey by Hilary Putnam, *Ethics without Ontology* (Cambridge, MA: Harvard University Press, 2004), 31, "that philosophies arise out of time-bound reactions to specific problems faced by human beings in given cultural circumstances." The problem is perhaps especially pressing given my earlier use of Hamblin's Dictum in service of the claim that the similar-sounding questions asked by philosophers and by scientists are merely homonymous. C. L. Hamblin, "Questions," *Australasian Journal of Philosophy* 36, no. 3 (1958); the "Dictum" is his "Postulate 2," at 162.

25. Not, of course, independent in one sense: the problems are, inter alia, *about* human will, perspectives, and so on. And thus perhaps not independent in another: if I am right about the stability of the problem space, one way to answer Kant's question "What is Man?" could be: the creature for whom *these* are the philosophical problems. That leaves open the possibility that other creatures have different philosophical problems. (I'm grateful to Gabriele Juvan for discussion here.)

26. Michael Williams, in *Unnatural Doubts* (Princeton: Princeton University Press, 1996), has argued that skepticism (and its mirror image, foundationalism) presupposes "epistemological realism"—that there are (something like) epistemological natural kinds. Surprisingly, in view of the length of his treatment, Williams never gets around to arguing that there *are* no epistemological natural kinds; he evidently takes it to be obvious that there aren't any. But it should not be obvious. If my claim is correct, the problems of philosophy make up something very like an epistemological natural kind. (It is not, of course, one of the kinds directly relevant to the argument Williams constructs.)

27. I'm grateful to Edwin Mares for pressing me on this point.

28. Michèle Le Dœuff, *Hipparchia's Choice*, trans. Trista Selous (Oxford: Blackwell, 1991), 76–78. The last item on the menu is her preferred alternative.

29. Don Garrett, *Cognition and Commitment in Hume's Philosophy* (Oxford: Oxford University Press, 1996), 3–4.

30. Alasdair MacIntyre, *Difficulties in Christian Belief* (New York: Philosophical Library, 1960), 12, 15; see his *God, Philosophy, Universities* (Lanham, MD: Rowman and Littlefield, 2009), 165–66, for a later characterization of philosophy by the same author, this one emphasizing the "fundamental existential questions about the order of things . . . , the asking of which is one of the defining marks of human beings."

31. The notion of philosophy as a metadiscipline also tallies badly with the tendency of philosophy, noted above, to give what sound like answers that compete with those of the special sciences.

32. This is perhaps embarrassing when they are problems in philosophy of science; it is often remarkable how little philosophy of science has to do with science. For a recently familiar example of philosophy of science generated by the characteristic operation, rather than by the dynamics of science, see Ernest Nagel, *The Structure of Science* (Indianapolis: Hackett, 1979).

Especially puzzlingly, even when work in a philosophical subspecialty does seem to be driven by work in one or another scientific discipline, over the course of a few decades technical results *wash out*. An example at the requisite temporal distance might be the impact of Gödel's Theorems on the philosophy of mathematics: once a central preoccupation, they scarcely seem to matter anymore.

The claim I'm now making may have the appearance of a pragmatic contradiction: after all, this very essay is making use of some applied mathematics. Moreover, a very plausible diagnosis of the noticeable drop in quality in so-called core areas of philosophy over the past few decades is that the science is getting stale: mathematical logic was a dramatic intellectual innovation of the early twentieth century; modal logic was an interesting extension of the mid-twentieth century; long after the mathematicians have moved on, the philosophers are still stuck on fifty-to-one-hundred-year-old science. (Logic is often the only science philosophers learn, and you still see, for example, modal logic being recycled into theories of higher-order vagueness.) When you let the science get stale, the ideas go downhill; how can that be compatible with the stability of the philosophical problem space?

My own sense is that the impetus which the sciences impart to philosophizing is very often a matter of a motivating or even inspiring *picture*—what used to be called a *Weltanschauung*—rather than results. As a philosophical culture matures, its claims become more clearly formulated, and they pull free of the picture. But this is only a placeholder for saying what it is to use a motivating picture of this kind.

33. Does it account for the distinctive importance of *figures*—I mean the canon of individual philosophers—to the discipline? Perhaps, if we can understand them as functioning allegorically, that is, as personifications of global joint solutions to the problems of philosophy. I am of several minds as to how far this suggestion can be developed.

34. Just to have an example of how these investigations can come full circle: you might start off by deciding that values are secondary qualities and that in

order to understand values you need a philosophical account of counterfactual conditionals. Proceeding with a possible-worlds account of counterfactual conditionals, you discover you need to explicate the notion of a similarity metric or nearness ordering over the space of possible worlds. But what counts as more similar (or "closer") to what is going to be in large part a matter of what features of a state of affairs are more important than what other features. And making philosophical sense of that sort of importance means—you may end up concluding—first making philosophical sense of values.

35. This is not a coincidence: that the graph representing the problem space contains cycles is entailed by the full set of problems being the closure under the characteristic operation of any of its subsets. The proof is trivial and left as an exercise to the reader.

36. Although not an inevitable one; in the institutional world of analytic philosophy, there are strong professional pressures to specialize, and specialists, even if they are sensitive to the ways in which philosophical problems are connected, don't for the most part build systems. Despite those pressures, we have our share of analytic system builders; recent examples include Robert Brandom, *Making It Explicit* (Cambridge, MA: Harvard University Press, 1994), and David Lewis (see note 37). (I'm grateful to Michael Bratman for pressing me on this point.)

The appearance of systems usually undoes the conflation of logical and temporal priority relations on which I remarked in note 22. At this point, the philosophical problem space comes to resemble a peculiar sort of crossword puzzle, constructed so that every clue suggests two different words of the appropriate length. For each entry, selecting the correct answer requires settling on some other answer; obviously such puzzles are solvable, which they would not be if selecting each word in the puzzle required having, earlier in time, selected another. (Every now and again you get someone who thinks such puzzles *aren't* solvable—but that's to make the mistake of the beginning algebra student who becomes convinced that you can't solve n equations in n unknowns.) Once we reach the stage of system construction, the logical constraints are no longer taken to impose a temporal order on investigative activities, and the exercise comes to be seen as that of finding a solution satisfying all of the constraints at once.

37. For examples of deliberation as to whether to make such a pragmatic recommendation, see David Lewis, "New Work for a Theory of Universals," *Australasian Journal of Philosophy* 61, no. 4 (1983): 343–77, and *On the Plurality of Worlds* (Oxford: Blackwell, 1986), 3–5.

38. Why take underdetermination to amount to no solution rather than a welcome overabundance of them? The question here is whether the enterprise is one of discovery or engineering. Alternative solutions to an engineering problem mean that you have a choice. Alternative solutions to a discovery problem mean that the problem is unsolved. For the present, I am proceeding under the assumption that the problems of philosophy are to be understood as discovery problems.

There is a second complication. The availability of multiple solutions can feel liberating because one thinks that one can then choose the solution one wants, or the solution that will make one's life go best. But the subject matter of philosophy includes ethics and practical reasoning; whether one ought to choose what one most prefers, and what it is for a life to go well, are both philosophical questions. The idea that somehow they are not is a vestige of the early stages of logical positivism; as we have seen, answering these questions would require having also resolved all the other problems of philosophy. If one is willing to use one's answers as a basis for decision without considering their philosophical merits, then one is not seriously in the market for answers to one's philosophical problems in the first place.

39. One further bit of evidence that philosophy constitutes a coherence problem is given by the craft practice, in philosophers' willingness to negotiate *trade-offs* between the components of their theoretical positions: this would make no sense if the philosophical facts were not in some way made so by hanging together properly.

Is the coherence problem new, and have I thereby added a problem to what I claimed was the fixed stock? No: just for instance, Wittgenstein once wrote that "no philosophical problem can be solved until all philosophical problems are solved: which means that as long as they aren't all solved every new difficulty renders all our previous results questionable." Ludwig Wittgenstein, *The Blue and Brown Books* (New York: Harper and Row, 1958), 44.

Now we can give a further reason for the history of philosophy being part of philosophy proper: it allows us to trace out the philosophy coherence problem.

40. See, e.g., Paul Thagard, "Explanatory Coherence," *Behavioral and Brain Sciences* 12 (1989): 435–67, which develops a simple quasi-connectionist computational model of coherence; C. M. Hoadley, Michael Ranney, and Patricia Schank, "WanderECHO: A Connectionist Simulation of Limited Coherence," in *Proceedings of the Sixteenth Annual Conference of the Cognitive Science Society*, ed. A. Ram and K. Eiselt (Hillsdale, NJ: Erlbaum, 1994), 421–26, which attempts to model the role of attention in Thagard-like coherence problems; Paul Thagard and Karsten Verbeurgt, "Coherence as Constraint Satisfaction," *Cognitive Science* 22, no. 1 (1998): 1–24, which proposes a formally specified coherence problem closely resembling MAX CUT.

41. For a somewhat dated, but still useful, introduction to NP-completeness, see Michael Garey and David Johnson, *Computers and Intractability* (New York: W. H. Freeman, 1979). One of the coherence concepts I have already mentioned (note 40, above) has been shown by Verbeurgt to be NP-complete. (The proof is by reduction to MAX CUT.) That coherence problem, however, although very suggestive, differs from the likely shape of the philosophy coherence problem. For one thing, a graph of the latter problem would contain hyperedges. For another, the Thagard/Verbeurgt problem is not directly sensitive to the internal structures of competing theories.

In fact, when we take account of our simplifications in the introduction of the characteristic operation, we can see that the complexity of the constraint satisfaction problem is even greater than our initial rendering of the problem space would have suggested.

42. Notice one constraint on the solution to the philosophical coherence problem: it had better not include the position that coherence is not in fact a legitimate basis for inference. If the philosophical problem space really does have the shape I have been describing, then we have here the entering wedge of a transcendental argument for a coherence theory of philosophical truth.

43. Douglas Adams, *The Hitchhiker's Guide to the Galaxy* (New York: Ballantine, 1997).

44. For an argument to this effect, as well as a warning about a pitfall in devising approximate solutions to hard discovery problems, see Elijah Millgram, "Coherence: The Price of the Ticket," *Journal of Philosophy* 97, no. 2 (2000): 82–93.

45. Just for instance: many invocations of coherence presuppose that it is induced by inferential relations; so an account of what coherence amounts to waits on an account of the inferential relations; but this is the central problem, or one of them, in philosophy of logic. Or again, in philosophy of science, coherence has been supposed to involve *aesthetic* qualities (such as "elegance" or "simplicity"); but what is an aesthetic quality, and why should the aesthetics make a difference to which theory is the right one?

CHAPTER SEVENTEEN

Ethics and the Evil of Being

WILLIAM DESMOND

Nietzsche or St. Benedict

What has been achieved in twentieth-century ethics? The diversity of ethical discussions precludes a simple answer. Currents of thought have come and gone, but the presiding god of modernity still sits on its throne—autonomy. The god may take many forms: Kantian, utilitarian, existentialist; it may tire of its individual form and mutate its self-determination into more social definitions, whether Hegelian, neo-Hegelian, Marxist, neo-Marxist, liberal, neoliberal. It sits there still.

But has not the chorus of postmodern thinkers, led by their Pied Piper, Nietzsche, dethroned that god? It might seem so, for the chorus swells with many songs of otherness, not always quite in tune with the hymns to solitude sung by that lonely Piper. And yet the trickster god Dionysus sits there, there where he seems not to sit, and this Dionysian sovereign, new yet old, springs from the same sacred seed of which autonomy is a tamer, humanistic offspring. Even when the torn postmodern thinkers wring their hands about the fall of the subject and seem again to offer us a vacated throne, there is a power behind the throne, and one cannot but worry that it is still the same old will that wills itself, still busy behind the mask of lacerated autonomy. It is not released freedom. For what is there to be released to, if there is no good beyond the ring of self-determination? One might reply: released to something other. But what other, what kind of other? What if the ring of self-determination coils so curiously and tenaciously around itself as god, as the good, because there is no good, there is no god, and outside the coil or under it the contagion of the evil of being insinuates itself and infects all things?

Iris Murdoch offered an assessment of literary culture and ethical theory about midway through the twentieth century in "Against Dryness" and tried to recuperate some sense of the Platonic good in her more constructive reflections.[1] The evil of being is somewhat more sinister than dryness, though if the dryness is spiritual the parched desert of resulting life may not be very different. Alasdair MacIntyre gives a fine genealogy of ethical modernity in *After Virtue,* where, passing through a mixture of emotivism, utilitarianism, and Kantianism, we are brought to a culmination that as much poses a question as suggests perhaps an "either/or"—"After Virtue: Nietzsche *or* Aristotle, Trotsky *and* St. Benedict."[2] There is something teasing about the exact meaning of the underlined *or,* something perhaps more teasing in the underlined *and.* The stress of the concluding lines is less teasing: "We are waiting not for a Godot, but for another—doubtless—very different St. Benedict" (263). The fire in MacIntyre's belly in *After Virtue* lit many a fire in others, some cooperating, some countering, none allowed the indulgence of continued moral somnolence. Afterwards, the tones of scholarly sobriety are perhaps more to the fore in his work. Here he calls himself an Augustinian Christian, as he did in *Whose Justice? Which Rationality?,*[3] there offering an exotic hybrid of Thomism and Marxism, tantalizing to some, alarming to others, as he did recently at the University College Dublin conference honoring his work. Continuing is the stress on practices, the patterns of their formations, and the importance of their immanent norms. Concern with virtue allows an opening to more premodern ethical philosophies like Aristotelianism and Thomism. But does the god autonomy simply bide its time to renew ever imperiously its demand that these openings again be reformulated in its immanent terms?

This question is not directed to MacIntyre himself, of course, but it does suggest this slight reformulation of his wording: "Either St. Benedict or Nietzsche." There is a choice here that, one senses, still awaits being fully addressed.[4] I think especially of the still hovering shadow of nihilism of which Nietzsche was an impressive diagnostician but a relatively disastrous therapist. It is too much of the old therapy: bleed the patient more, or the dying god. Nietzsche suggested that nihilism was the devaluation of all value, the inversion of the highest values. I would define nihilism rather as the cultural sovereignty of the *counterfeit doubles* of the highest values. These doubles allow us to preach about the highest values, but there is something not quite there in that height, and what has been evacuated has much to do with the god autonomy. The divine above us has been whited out, and there is nothing above us, since autonomy, by being above itself, with nothing above it, has become itself god, its sovereignty now announced, now *incognito,* as it passes over all human things. Nihilism is not the time of the twilight of the idols but the time governed by the hyperactive secretion of new counterfeit doubles of God. Not twilight but the dawning of a virulent era of idols, for nothing flourishes as wildly as do idols in the vacancy following the proclamation that there is no God. Nietzsche's own transvaluation of values might well offer us a new economy of counterfeit doubles.

However one defines nihilism, one could say that in modernity there is a pervasive sense of the *valuelessness of being as such.* We believe ourselves to be the originals of value, but being in itself, as given for itself, is not marked by value. We construct values in a valueless whole. Again Nietzsche can be taken as paradigmatic: "Nature is always worthless— but one has at some time given, donated worth to it, and *we* were those givers and donators! We human beings have first created the world that pertains to human beings!"[5] I want to look at the apotheosis of human autonomy in an ethos where given being as other is still defined in such terms. What is at stake here is not a determinate theory or a particular practice but more a widespread attitude to being, an ontological attunement or dissonance that is not this particular attitude to this determinate circumstance but one that has a floating and more pervasive character, since it bears on an often secret sense of the whole.

This makes our situation more complex than surface appearances indicate. We can be carried by, or be carriers of, such an attitude, which is very hard to pin down, and yet it surfaces in crucial manifestations that suggest something recessed governing the reigning god on the throne. This sense of valuelessness mutates quickly into a sense of being itself as *not being worthy of value*—it is not to be valued for itself, for all value seems derivative from us. We might hedge and say that in itself it is merely neutral or indifferent, but then in this indifference a worry secretly insinuates itself about the evil of being. Evil in this first sense is not this or that evil thing or event; rather, it concerns a foreboding, a kind of mostly repressed horror that, when we disturb it, emits its stench and we are forced into recoil. It works against us and has to be turned over and made to work for us. It is to be deprived not only of its valuelessness but of its potential hostility to us. What is potentially hostile to us cannot but at some point present to us the face of an *enemy*. How do we deal with such possible enmity of being? Our enmity against it? But then we become entangled in the evil from which we think we have extricated ourselves. We conquer evil, and our conquest is itself evil again. Those like Nietzsche who proclaim nihilism as a cleansing renewal in which destruction must precede new creation do not always go deep enough into this more original attunement to being. If there is an evil of being, being is not worthy of affirmation, it is less than worthless. More truly, it is worthy of repudiation. Affirmation of it is not worthy of us, it is evil for us, finally. There is no cleansing and nothing worthy to renew.

How does one think of this evil of being? Can one think of such evil? Can one sustain the thought? This issue is not first one of ethical value as proportioned to human beings. What is at issue is a certain sense of ontological/metaphysical value, and this is the level we have to find. Of course, these two, the humanly ethical and the ontological/metaphysical, cannot be entirely divorced. If there is a sense of the evil of being, or the good, we are addressing the very ethos of being, which itself, so to say, sources human beings, sources them as marked by their own re-sources, enabling them to define values proportionate to themselves. We do not often find the word *ontological* in ethical discussions. Certainly in continental thought we tend to find the two disjoined. The Heideggerian ontologist is dismissive of concern with "values" as mere subjectivistic constructions. The Levinasian ethicist claims the good is beyond ontology and declares ethics itself to be first philosophy. From somewhat different directions, they seem heirs to the dominant divorce of being and the good that is pervasive in modernity. That same divorce has implications for the suggestion of the evil of being, as we shall see. The good without being is as questionable as being without the good.

If this issue calls us to a kind of metaphysical-ontological reflection, one must note the precise sense.[6] It is not a matter of the deduction of some principle or some foundation. Nor is it the construction of some theoretical system, and then its application to practice. It has more to do with a sense of the ethos of being as putatively neutral or not; as hospitable to good, or hostile; as shadowed by evil, or malignant; as perhaps equivocal between good and evil; as perhaps manifesting an asymmetry between good and evil, even in this equivocity, an asymmetry pointing to a certain priority of one over the other. Human beings live in this ethos as reconfigured according to their dominant determination of importances—namely, of what they take to be worthy or worthless. But this reconfiguration is enabled by certain sources of being ethical,[7] often recessed, even while the configuration diversely expresses them. What is at issue then is more like a "step back" into these enabling sources of being ethical—not only in terms of what they express but in terms of what is recessed in them. For what is hidden can be both enabling and disabling. We live ethically out in the front, but the front is enabled or disabled by what does not entirely appear there. An ontological/metaphysical sense of the ethos of being undergrounds the more foreground senses of the valuable for the human being, be this ethical or other (such as aesthetic or religious). If there is something to this, were we to focus solely on the human being and its putative autonomy, we would risk remaining captive to an attunement to being in which it is less the valuelessness of being than the indifference or evil that comes to exercise a secret sway.

On this score, it is interesting to note that in our time the meaning of radical evil receives far more attention than the equally astonishing possibility, rather more astonishing promise, of radical good. I take the following as a small sign: recently Umberto Eco published a book on beauty, and it was a moderate success as a publishing venture; but as a sequel he published a book on the ugly, and it was a signal success in a way the book on beauty was not.[8] Have we fallen under the spell of the avant-garde doctrine that beauty is the false consciousness and consolation of the bourgeoisie? The ugly seems to have more of the bite of the real, whether Lacanian, or perverse or commonsense, who really cares. Beauty is bland. The ugly arouses the thrill of something visceral, charges the beholder with a shot of energy, be it in disgust or in recoil, in dismay or in glee. We cannot remain indifferent. Its immediacy disturbs us, and it seems we take disturbance as an index of the real. Beauty offers a foretaste of peace, but peace is deemed death. I describe, I do not endorse. The end of art is peace.[9] Beauty is peace beyond war and peace.

The fascination with evil is perhaps understandable in a post-Holocaust time, but it also testifies to a certain lopsidedness of the human spirit. It is as if evil, and its shock, were one of the last spaces where something of a kind of excessive transcendence might be felt, albeit in the form of horror. By *transcendence* here I mean something that mocks our powers of self-determination in a taunting or a tantalizing or an assault that seems strangely to loose something self-transcending in us. Disgust or dismay or revulsion are, after all, modes of being beside oneself—in unchosen recoil. We can come to be in love with the thrilling counterfeits of transcendence precipitated by the perverse.

When contemplation of radical good induces the yawn of the advanced intellectual, we are surely in an extraordinary space of the spirit— the spirit of spiritlessness that knows only the blandness of the good. The most natural thing to say, in response, is that it makes no sense to confront the possibility of radical evil without raising, as an equally astonishing perplexity, the possibility of radical good. The lopsidedness has much to do with the evacuation of faith in God, on the one hand, and yet, on the other, the impossibility of avoiding the puss of horror that looks at us, and that we look at, day in day out. Strangely the horror of evil keeps the spirit alive in an age where spiritlessness is advanced as self-advancing cleverness. We must not pay too much heed to those sirens of sophistry, the glickeens of pseudowisdom.

This issue of nihilism bears on the divorce of being and good, a divorce whose effects still remain to be faced. Returning to our adaptation of MacIntyre's "either/or" of Benedict or Nietzsche, there is a pointer for the directions we can face. If Benedict is our choice, we are offered different resources than with Nietzsche—God as the ground of all good, good in an ontological sense, as well as an ethical. Some will demur and find this incredible. Nevertheless, the issue concerns what is ultimately worthy of credit, what is creditworthy in an ultimate sense. What is worthy of faith in the sense of the ultimate fidelity *(fides)*?[10] Worthless being is worthy of no credit, of no fidelity. By definition there is nothing to it that calls forth our ultimate trust. If there is an evil of being, even more so are we to refuse any trust. Not mere recoil from trust but active repudiation of it would seem to be the appropriate response. Life may be nasty, brutish, and short, but why should we lament that it is short? If nasty and brutish, it should be shortened. Why do we do the opposite, and seek to lengthen it, often at exorbitant cost? What in us continues to insist that it is good to be? Why thrill to the evil of being, if the true response should be repudiation? Repudiation in the name of what? Ourselves? Some secret sense of good, or some repressed sense? Why at all this thrill of transcendence to what induces recoil, if to thrill is viscerally to affirm something worthy? Is the evil of being then parasitical on a good it perverts, a good it must affirm even in its denial of it, affirm even in perverting it?

Purposeless Process and "Projects"

Let me step back and set out a few markers to indicate the direction out of which the question comes. In some ways we have to step back centuries, though the question is contemporary. First, we note how modernity can be and is to be described as an epoch in which the value of freedom is sovereign. No other value is quite so accepted without question. All other substantive values are called into question. Freedom seems to remain uncontested: the freedom to be and choose whatever value one wills. This seems like a huge opening for humanity, but in fact our feel for the ethos of being in which this occurs is again all important. This ethos is primarily marked by the already noted valuelessness of being. Of course, we might insist on being as neuter, but further bleeding being of value will not alter the situation. The neuter is not neutral. It too entails an evaluation. This can mask something not valueless at all, something not to be affirmed or to be repudiated.

This valuelessness is concurrent with the objectification of being in modernity. We have wanted to make being intelligible and have tended to define intelligibility in terms of univocal determination, as mathematically precise as possible. In early modern science we witness the rejection of teleology as resistant to such univocal determination. Yet this sense of teleology dominantly defined the sense of the good in preceding epochs. The good is what all things desire, to recall Aristotle. We are marked as not fully possessing the good but as seeking to enjoy it. We are marked by orientation toward the end. However, the end in time is always shrouded in some shadow of equivocality or ambiguity. If we cut out the end from our schema of intelligibility, we seem to cut out just that equivocality. But we also risk reducing what happens to valueless process.

This applies not only to the human being as one more valueless being in the whole but to the whole itself. The whole itself is valueless because it is nothing but purposeless process. Purposeless process is pointless being that just happens between nothing and nothing. As simply happening it is not originally valued as good in its being brought to be, and not ultimately valued as fulfilled in its more complete becoming of itself. Between a valueless beginning and a worthless end, the process of being is nothing but worthless ongoingness. True, such valueless happening is now seemingly available for univocal mind, given that from it have been sheared all equivocal traces of qualitative worth. But if this is a gain it has a sting to it. The more univocally intelligible we make being, the more purposeless it becomes. The more univocal determinability we impose on it, the more its pointlessness strikes home. It strikes home as hitting back at us too: not only is the process as a whole purposeless, but we too ultimately, as participating in this pointless process, are also ultimately without point. It is all for nothing. We too, ultimately, count for nothing.

Of course, we cannot live with no good, and no good to the happening of being. If there is no good to be, to the "to be" as such, nevertheless we are beings who affirm and negate, find something worthy, something worthless. That the valueless objectivity is thought to be relative to us as objectifying it indicates that there is something in all this that cannot be objectified, something contrary to the very ambition to determine univocally the whole. Something in all the univocal determination of the universe other to us cannot be so determined because it is what is doing the determining. We ourselves are in excess of what we objectify—subjects who are determining of ourselves in being determinative of what is other to us. Thus, ethically, this ethos of valuelessness is inseparable from our "projects," the most evident of which is the project of reconfiguring given being as subject to our determination and as serving it. In this reconfiguration of the ethos, if there is no good to be, we make what is good to be. Recall my citation of Nietzsche above: "Nature is always worthless." We become the originals of value. There is nothing original valuable in itself.

Which comes first—the objectification or the subjectification? In fact, since objectification is our "project," in that regard the subject is the spider at the center of the web. *Project* is one of those often used words that begin to receive currency in this context. It is used now without as much self-consciousness as one would desire. Ob-ject, sub-ject, pro-ject: all different modalities of throwing *(jacere)*—throwing or being thrown. Being thrown: we find ourselves just there in the valueless happening. Throwing: we are to be the pro-jecting sub-ject reaching out beyond the given valuelessness, not waiting expectantly for an enigmatic future, but defining it in advance in terms of what we will it to be. In one respect, this is part of the very nature of human anticipation and expectation. But here there are senses of "pro-ject" where we will accept what comes only if it does so on the terms we already define in advance. Developed in a certain manner, this is a recipe for tyranny over time. The ancients were accused of resentment against time, of revenge against time, in their dreaming of eternity. But the modern dominance of "pro-ject" is not any the less a tyranny over time. Instead of a so-called flight to the eternal, there is flight to the "future," flight from the equivocal flightiness of time itself and its resistance to subjection by our measure. This is an immanent revenge against time—revenge against its equivocality as a threat to our autonomy. This too is part of the project of objectification. Nevertheless, in every project, something always exceeds subject, object, and project. Even in the project of univocalization, whether in the mathematization and technological domination of other-being or in our own will to self-determination, there is something disturbingly equivocal that is recessed.[11]

To round off this line of thought: if I am not mistaken, in the valuelessness as such the threatening is also there always—hence our worry about a secret hostility at the heart of things. One thinks of that most modern of projects, Descartes's faith in the power of scientifically generated medicine to prolong life and to delay, perhaps overcome, death. This medical salvation from mortality is the projection that arches over the corrosive fear in time that the end of it all is, in fact, only death. It comes to nothing. We all know of Descartes's foolish anticipation that he would live way beyond the then normal span of life,[12] though now such life expectancy has been democratized just in the way he wanted for himself. He was struck down at fifty-four. (Pascal was right about the drop of water and the thin membrane separating our life and our death, the vapor that is enough to kill us—or too early rising in an inclement clime.) Medical salvation will rescue us from the evil of being as given, in reconstructing being in the light of our projection of the ever extended delay of death, all the way to the science fiction of deathlessness. The shadow of the projection is the foreboding that something dreadful intimately companions us. There is the barely suppressed alarm that, after all, we are as nothing. We are indeed nothing. Dread drives our frantic flight from the metaphysical menace in all this. This might not always be called the evil of being, but if we want to subject time to our measure, as so threatening us, it is not only valueless or a disvalue, it is potentially an enemy and hence evil. Everything other to us easily gets tarred with the same brush. "Projects" are in the business of tarring everything other with the more and more technically perfect brushes we ourselves are busily producing. In outrage we proclaim the rottenness of the apple, but perhaps we are the worm in the apple producing the rottenness. We purr appalled but continue to act the innocent.

Haunted by Heteronomy: Kantian Autonomy

One might object that this is surely refuted by Kant—Kant, the great thinker of autonomy who affirmed the good will as the only unqualified good in this world, indeed outside the world. Surely here we have a profound affirmation of freedom coupled with an affirmation of unconditional worth, namely, of the human being as an end in itself. I think Kant is to be honored for his affirmation of this unconditional value—a value oddly at odds with the hugely reductionist tendencies in modernity in which the human being is homogenized with other things as merely one thing among them. Kant's own adherence to the Newtonian picture of nature shows something of his split mind.

Even granting Kant's affirmation of the human being as an end in itself, the main point still holds. It holds true not least because this affirmation is made in an ontological ethos in which everything other is devoid of being an end in itself—only the human being is such. It is as if in the immense totality of conditions, *mirabile dictu*, a being of unconditional worth emerges. From what this worth emerges we are not told, we cannot be told. From the conditional the unconditional cannot be deduced.

How does a being of unconditional worth come to be in a totality of conditional things, relations, processes, all of which might be said to have relative value, but none of which has unconditional worth in the sense at stake? It is as if in place of the old *deus ex machina* we now have *humanus ex machina*. The one is not any less heterogeneous, not to say miraculous, than the other. The fact remains that all things other to the human being are valueless in the intrinsic sense at issue. This is connected to the relation of Kantian autonomy to heteronomy generally—namely, heteronomy's definition as the opposite of autonomy. The risk is that everything other might potentially be seen as a curb or limitation on autonomy, which, as the word itself implies, is law *(nomos)* for itself *(auto)*, not for another *(heteros)*. Carry this logic in a certain direction and we can well end up with the devaluation of all otherness as such.

It is true that Kant speaks importantly of the kingdom of ends. But there are enigmas attached to that kingdom insofar as King Autonomy sits on the throne here too. For if this kingdom is thought in terms of *self-legislation*, there is no univocal homogeneity that allows unimpeded passage from that self-determining to the ethical relation of the *many as other and together as others*. The many as ethically together is a matter of an *intermediation between* them, not a matter of the *self-mediation* of all, taken either singly or as a communal whole. The logic of intermediation cannot be derived from the logic of self-mediation multiplied. The "inter" has something more to it in excess of all forms of self-mediation, no matter how dialectically complex. Such intermediation, precisely as mediating the "inter," the between, cannot be exhausted by the self-determining logic of autonomous self-legislation. A different understanding of the other and our ethical relation in togetherness with others, beyond the logic of autonomy, must be forthcoming.

There is the fact too that Kant's affirmation of unconditional value is just that—an affirmation. What grounds it, what founds it, is not convincingly explored. The obvious way would be to appeal to an endowing source of goodness more than the self-determining human being. After all, our unconditional worth is not something with which we endow ourselves. We are what we are as moral beings in virtue of it, in virtue of being endowed with it, by it. It constitutes us as the kinds of being we are. But we are not self-constituting on this fundamental level of being intrinsically marked by this worth. I would think this endowed value opens us to the question of ontological value in the sense of a goodness to the "to be" of the human being that is not produced by us but that gives us to be as the kinds of beings we are. Kant does not go this route. If he did, it would bring him differently to God, theologically put. A divine heteronomy of sorts would come back for consideration, a consideration ruled out from the outset by his definition of autonomy in opposition to all heteronomy, God's included.

A Kantian might object that humanity's unconditional value is grounded in human reason and that being thus endowed is sufficient. Such a claim does not touch the meaning of "being endowed" that is here at issue. "Being endowed" suggests possessing a power or resource in virtue of its being given to one by a source other than oneself. Clearly, nature as Newtonian mechanism (for Kant) does not endow the human being with unconditional value, for such a "nature" is a network of conditionalities within which there is no end in itself in the sense at issue. Humanity does not endow itself, for it is the being of humanity to be such an unconditional value by virtue of what it is as a moral being. What other endowing source could there be? If not a source in nature, a trans-natural source then? A noumenal source then? Should one say: a "super-natural" source? If we say this "super-natural" source is human reason, then we return to the implication that the human being as rationally autonomous and self-determining is *"self-endowing."* And this clearly departs from the meaning of "being endowed," as in receipt of determining and self-determining power in a source other than oneself. If we say that the source is not human reason but Reason in a more universal sense, then we move into a space suggesting a sense of cosmic reason, dare one say it, even divine reason. And with this we have breached the terms of autonomous self-determination and opened human reason to "being endowed" by a more ultimate enabling power than itself. That is to say, "being endowed" brings us before a form of heteronomous receiving that finds no place in Kant's fixed dualism between autonomy and heteronomy. There is an analogous difficulty in Kant between the moral law "being given" to one and "giving oneself" the law, a difficulty Kant himself did not adequately face, much less resolve.[13]

Kant, of course, was the heir of a religious legacy, now secularized, in which the absolute worth of the human being is understood in virtue of being absolutely and singularly loved by God. This absolute singularity is in the human being as its ontological endowment. Being endowed means being received, means receiving powers as one's own but from another, powers that in the primal instance are not actively constructed by the one endowed. The one as endowed may be the beneficiary of these powers and construct thenceforth in accord with their enabling potentiation. But if at the outset we silence all reference to the endowing source, the endowment remains but is made radically opaque to itself. Perhaps more extremely, it is radically mutilated, for it is now said to have no root *(radix)* in any ground other than itself. This is as much as to say that the endowment is not an endowment at all. The further step might well be our impulse to shore up our own self-determining claims, issuing in the repudiation of any proper sense of being endowed. The (endowed) human being will now be only what it wills itself to be — not endowed but self-endowing. What it is is nothing but what it endows itself with. In a word, a more radical version of freedom is now tempted to drive ever more into darkness the endowing source that gives it to be.

And then the shadow of a radical equivocity falls over unconditional value. What now counts as valuable for the human being is not given but constructed or to be constructed — and entirely through itself alone. But we cannot do it if the considerations above noted hold true. Were our pathway kept open to the endowing source, the sense of intrinsic value might also widen from the moral human to all of being. This would be, not a univocal extension from one to the other, but a fruitful impulse toward reconsideration of the devaluation of being as other to us. For it too is endowed to be and as such might be thought to carry, to incarnate the traces of worthiness beyond the valuelessness produced by the modern objectification.

Kant struggles with something of this in the *Critique of Judgement*, where he returns to the issue of purposiveness. We cannot get away from this. Nevertheless, for Kant the old caution keeps taking over, and what purposiveness is affirmed is always in the "as if" mode. Finally it lacks ontological bite. Not surprisingly, and finally, the human being is the only value in itself. The starry skies above are still vacant. One wonders how at all this vacancy could cause to surge in the human heart its wonder and awe. Wonder and awe celebrate — it can happen to us involuntarily — what is worthy of praise for itself. "As if" wonder, "as if" awe, "as if" praise — these can be nothing but counterfeit. (I beguile my love with my quasi-lovesong: Dear, my dear, it is indeed "as if" I love you. But darling, do you *really, truly* love me? Yes, dear, it is as if I do indeed love you. Why then, my dear, does your face turn so stony?) The semblance of jubilation can only be but the dissemblance of jubilation. There is something grotesque about it. And oddly we return to something like the picture that terrified thinkers before Kant—the infinite spaces empty of intrinsic value, the human a freak, a monster, and the totality as inhospitable to the intrinsic value that by an absolute difference—almost "as if" miraculously—is said to be in, to be, the human being. What is here grotesque is that this is still a universe in despair—a universe that while perhaps not yet said overtly to be evil, is certainly not good, and ominously once more the shadow of deep foreboding continues to hang over all. (Why Pascal, the surprise is mine, I did not expect to meet you so soon again.)

Endowed Freedom

Suppose one grants that there is no way to ground value on what is other to freedom. If we must do it at all, we must do it in terms of freedom. We might argue that everything other is valuable only relative to a source of evaluation. It does not value itself; it is not valued for itself by itself. But the human being does value itself, is valued for itself by itself. We might say that this is the meaning of its unconditional value, namely, defined by nothing other than itself. So we seem to confirm the stress on freedom as self-determining. Even granting all this (I do not grant it finally in this form), and granting we define freedom as self-determining, we still have to address the nature of this self-determining power. It cannot suffice to consider it as an origin from which we set out vis-à-vis all value while it remains itself immune from question. That this immunity is often (surreptitiously) granted to it settles nothing. The fact remains that the power to be self-determining cannot be completely defined by self-determination. We do not and cannot fully determine ourselves to be self-determining, for even if we were to try to grant or do that, we would always already have to grant the power to be self-determining as somehow elementally given. We determine ourselves to be self-determining—freedom seems to presuppose nothing but itself, and in its very active exercise it makes itself to be what it is—self-determining. But this line of consideration runs aground in presupposing what it sets out to determine and hence less determines itself than offers the pretense of absolute self-determination. It hides from itself the givenness of the peculiar power to be self-determining with which, granted, human being is endowed.

This unavoidability of presupposing its givenness to itself in every venture of self-determining seems to me to be very significant. There is an elemental givenness or endowment that cannot be included in any venture of self-determination but that makes possible all such ventures of self-determination. Something other than self-determination is always already presupposed in every venture of self-determination as enabling self-determination to be (granted to itself as) self-determining. This something other endows the power, and with justice might be called the endowing power. But we are the endowed and the recipients of the endowment; we are not this endowing power. As recipients, we can deny or forget this fact and think of ourselves as the owners of the power—and in due course we can then seek entirely to hide from ourselves that what we claim to own was first received as an endowment. From granting its being free as endowment, we are tempted simply to claim it as our property, as owned by us, and us alone. This is to create a self-circling of self-determination closed on itself—to the forgetfulness of the endowing power as other. Indeed, this may be claimed as the very destiny of freedom. Of course, the very closure of this circle is itself enabled by this endowing power as other to self-determining. We seem to be entirely free from it, but our freedom from it is enabled by it—allowed to be as other to the endowing source. In this way, the illusion of self-contained freedom might be sustained, self-sustained, but it still always is what it is enabled to be by virtue of something other than its own self-determination.

My freedom is mine, and only I can exercise it; it is mine and mine alone. But what is mine is endowed as mine, and hence it is not just mine. I would say the truer response to this doubleness in "mineness" itself would be to grant the endowing power as other—and indeed in the very freedom granted to one, to see it as communicating a certain releasing freedom. The point is not to deny freedom but to understand it as endowed by a releasing source that allows the finite creature to be as other. Understanding this, we understand why the illusion of self-circling freedom also easily comes to be. The allowance makes a way, makes way, and the endowed freedom is tempted to think it is absolutely for itself alone. It closes itself off from what enables and allows it to be free.

Further still, if we grant this endowing source, our starting point above that denies to anything other the character of intrinsic value must also come into question. First, not only an enabling power as other but also a source of valuation other to human self-evaluation must be granted—granted in the very immanence of our self-determination; we do not need here to refer extrinsically to a source of value as other. Immanent freedom itself is enabled to be by such a source. One might think of it as a valuing source, insofar as we grant that immanent freedom is itself received as something worthy for itself and that we ourselves are not the original source of this primal worthiness. This primal worthiness is deemed as such by this endowing source as enabling it to be as for itself and as good for itself. This means crucially that the metaphysical monopoly of our freedom on the determination of value is immanently undercut. We do not have the first or the last word in the deeming of worthiness—of worthiness to be, and worthiness to be as free. Moreover, there is something in excess here, certainly on the boundary between the immanent and the transcendent: the immanent otherness of the endowing source is intimate to freedom itself but is never exhausted by our determination of it. Its intimate otherness is both intimate to our freedom and yet other to it, and both of these at one and the same time. But this other seems to exceed the determination of all finite being given to be, since it endows this being as given and as worthy for itself as being. Once again, the monopoly of human freedom as deeming value is broken open, and indeed opened in a manner that directs us toward the affirmation of ontological value—the worthiness of being as given, worthy to be affirmed because affirmed first as worthy to be.

Second, if we grant this, then we can revisit more fully the possibility that other forms of being than us might also be looked on as endowed with the "to be," their own "to be," and this as affirmed in its own worth, as worthy to be for itself. The simple opposition between us—as source of value, being determining—and other beings as void of value without us, being determined—falls away. The otherness of given finite others, endowed with their "to be" as other, a "to be" affirmed in its own rightness to be, resists the monopolistic tendency of an entirely self-circling self-determination. On the one hand, our freedom is returned to this intimate otherness as enabling it to be and endowing it; on the other hand, things as other are worthy of being deemed worthy for themselves, and not simply in function of our deeming them to be a worthy this or worthy that, purely in function of their relativity to us. A plurivocal sense of other-value opens up in the intimacy of selving and in the outer community of beings as other. True freedom as endowed enablement to be finds itself between these partners. As freedom cannot be just between freedom and itself, so worthiness, whether ontological or ethical, cannot be just between us and ourselves alone.

Haunted by the Evil Genius: Stepping into the Schopenhauerian Shadows

What then again of the evil of being? Suppose one grants that an other source is here opened up. But why not connect this with the evil of being rather than any good worthy to be affirmed? Suppose that Descartes's dismissal of the evil genius turns out to be too callow—perhaps because his notion of the good God is no less callow. His callow God makes the good bland. His defeat of the evil genius does not quite defeat the anxiety of the reversed good. The dread of that genius is the foreboding about evil as the reversed double of good, the reversed double of God. Suppose this genius comes back to haunt modernity at the height of its claims to rational autonomy. Stronger still, suppose the spirit of doubt, masking the spirit of ontological suspicion, enters the heart of philosophy, at the moment that thought thinks itself to be—thinks itself to be able to determine itself securely through the method that projects its coming completion. In the spirit of suspicion—against ontological givenness—negativity enters thought—the spirit that negates and henceforth holds it so that by negation it determines itself. Why not so, if—with a diffident bow to Hegel—negativity is at the heart of the absolute, giving it the energy to be and surpass itself? Suppose, in a more radical qualification, the evil genius enters the intimate soul of God. I myself am inclined to think of this evil genius as the counterfeit double of God, but clearly in the scenario just sketched the evil genius is not that kind of double. The evil genius is God's *own* double. This evil genius is coeval with the good God as its own reversed twin. I call up the shade of Schelling, but I see other shades crowding the background.

My intent here is to return to the point I made at the outset. There is an ontological attunement that reveals itself in ethical terms as much as in psychological, in religious terms as much as in antireligious, in aesthetic terms as well as in economic. Some foreboding of the evil of being deeply dyes the ethos of modern and especially post-Kantian thought. Most obviously one finds it in someone like Schopenhauer. But his thought infiltrates people such as Wagner, Nietzsche, Freud, and many others. Schopenhauer's influence extended to many major artists, such as Tolstoy, Thomas Hardy, George Bernard Shaw, Thomas Mann, Samuel Beckett. That is a large tale, but it is worth briefly noting some post-Kantian developments, for they tell us important lessons about the evil of being.

In Kant himself the ethics of autonomy finds radical evil in its own most intimate heart as an ineradicable disposition. We find in Hegel that evil is logically necessitated for the full self-articulation and self-determination of his absolute or "God." Though Schelling is often seen as entirely other to Hegel, this is not quite true, since Schelling also proposes a ground of evil immanent to divinity itself. This dark matter is invested with a metaphysical stress that is passed over very quickly in the logical self-unfolding of Hegel. Nevertheless, Hegel and Schelling are still blood brothers in the same philosophical family, all differences notwithstanding. Schopenhauer is a surly Schellingian who dispenses entirely with the good God and leaves us nothing but the evil genius in the guise of will, as the dark origin, prior to and beyond determination by the principle of sufficient reason. The evil genius has been allowed into the nest of the absolute, but like a devouring cuckoo it soon dislodges or sends to their death any divine fledglings that might have otherwise matured there. This is so much so that the dove of spirit that mothered this cuckoo is no longer able to identify this alien as anything other than its own. The evil twin of dark will has taken over as number one in the divine house of autonomous thought. Autonomous thought, in turn, loses its sovereignty to this sly power behind the throne.

It is impossible to do justice here to such an important theme, but I find it interesting how it emerges in an ethos of thought dominated by the culture of autonomy. Is it that the old Lutheran sense of original sin in unregenerate man keeps coming back in a variety of mutations, black sheep popping up, like recessed genes, in the family of good will? What do we see? We see the autonomous will running against limits, not only as external boundaries but as internal disabilities of its own willed ability to will itself through itself alone. Think of how it is in the immanence of the will—with father Kant himself—that radical evil appears as a disposition to evil. Goethe excoriated Kant for besmirching the pure cloth of freedom, yet the foul stain of Kant is the truer in reminding us of a disability at the heart of our most ultimate ability. It is in the intimate immanence that the evil reappears again and again.

One thinks of how, in a speculative-theological register, evil in Hegel is assigned logically to the second moment of difference in his Trinitarian divinity. Evil is inseparable from the necessary alienation of the absolute to finite particularity, and the self-assertion of the particular as if it were the whole. But all of this is immanent in the self-becoming of Hegel's "God." The source of evil referred to as immanent in God does not distinguish Schelling from Hegel—not at all, even granting we must not slight their differences. If it is true that not only in the intimacy of our autonomy but in the dark depths of the ultimate itself lies the source of evil, then we cannot speak of the good of being, either divine or created, *tout court*. Divine being as implicated in evil gives rise to evil in finiteness, and in it we participate as much as we do in goodness. Since this goes all the way up and all the way down, one has to talk about a kind of evil of being. There is a respect, then, in which Schopenhauer is the least disingenuous of the lot. He showed his irritation with Spinoza in the latter's manner of dignifying nature with the name of the divine. This is a compliment too far. There is no good God, but let us not speak of devouring nature as if it were God. Big fish eat little fish, but do not ask us to sing *Te Deums* to this monstrous (un)divinity, this cannibalizing whole. Let us not throw flies to spiders for fun and then laugh with glee, as Spinoza is said to have done, when the spider relishes devouring its prey.[14]

Schopenhauer's primordial will is purposeless. It has no final point at all. It is all for nothing. Here is a link with the modern exclusion of ends generally. Recalling an earlier theme, will in itself *is* nothing but *purposeless process*. Instrumental reason and utilitarian desire might have their "projects" that instrumentalize "phenomena," but (reminding us of Heidegger later) they are projections into the void, they come to nothing. Purposelessness is the tale told by an idiocy of being that even the story of scientific rationality cannot avoid. In the evil of being, scientific reason drags with it something idiotic: the whole is pointless, the whole is worthless. This is the "truth" of the will in itself. When later Nietzsche calls the self-circling of the will to power *a monster of energy*, he mimics Schopenhauer, though in a more lyric, even rhapsodic mood, with more of Spinoza's glee than Schopenhauer's dismay.[15] There is no essential difference in the end or origin. This will as insatiable has no end, nothing teleological, but in origin it has more of darkness than of light. It is a dark origin—dark in an ultimate sense, even though (for Schopenhauer) out of it come the Ideas and the principle of sufficient reason.

The root will, the radical will, is prior to Ideas and reason. This means a kind of inverse Platonism. I mean that Ideas are upheld by Schopenhauer, but his essential strategy vis-à-vis the will is not at all analogous to the cave in Plato. There we ascend above ground to try to behold the upper world and the source of light—the sun, the good that, beyond all being, gives life and nurture and intelligibility to all that is. In light of the good there is something to be said of the good of the "to be." Perhaps this is not as radical as in biblical monotheism, where simply to be, as created, is to be good, but certainly there is a good to the "to be." If there is evil, God is not to be impugned in Plato. In Schopenhauer it is as if a kind of regressive movement (transcendental into the dark origins) descends below the lower world, to a second cave within the first cave—to an underground under the underground, and there is no ground to this other underground except the will. This is more like an abyss than a ground—the underground undergrounded by an even more radically abyssal cave of endless night. Out of the bottomless source, like bats from hell, the will rays itself outwardly but for no purpose but to ray itself. What it gives rise to is a world of boundless suffering—the flesh-eating world, where the life of one is the death of the other, the death of one is the life of the other. To be is to be guilty. Hence Schopenhauer's endorsement of the wisdom of the Greek Silenus: better not to be.

The evil of being thus arrives with a highly systematic philosophy to justify what is ultimately unjustifiable, since justice has no ground in being at all, since the evil of being is more primordial than the good, and since what good we know is a function of our instrumentalizing what is given to our desire. Nor have we left the main trail of the tale of modernity: the good is not desired because it is good; the good is good because we desire it; good is a function of desire, of our will; if we do not will it, that is, subject it to a network of relations imposed on it by us, then it is not so much indifferent as essentially alien to us. It is strange but in a manner hostile to our happiness. Since we cannot eliminate that otherness of life itself, the dominant metaphysical mood must be the misery of human existence.

It is of interest that Schopenhauer had no compunction in recommending the traditional doctrine of original sin as more true to this bleak view of things. This is original sin in an atheistic rather than religious register, and announced not quite to save us from evil but to be honest about it. We must grant evil in a fallen world, a world that (in another regard) never fell—for there is no God or higher reality from which it has fallen. Its "to be" is a fallen "to be." In that sense we are dealing with ontological evil, though since this is falling without any fall, it means that the nature of all being is to be evil. While Schopenhauer was a great admirer of Kant, he would not worry at all about the doctrine of radical evil or impugn Kant's credentials, like Goethe, though he also knew Goethe well, through his mother, and, like Hegel, admired him. In fact, he pushes the Kantian radical evil through far more radically: it is not just the disposition of the human, it is the evil of being; it is as much metaphysical as it is ethical. Schopenhauer's primordial will is not just our will—it has an ontological character. It is thus connected to the primordial good or evil of being, and not just of our being and what we will as worthy or worthless. Our existence images the evil whole. Schopenhauer liked to cite Calderón: *El delito mayor del hombre es haber nacido*—Man's greatest offense is to have been born.

We might say that Schopenhauer felt impelled to spill the beans on the dissembling of the evil genius, though no love on his part was lost for that genius. And while he saw a brief redemption in art, and a more lasting redemption in ascetic religion, the fact is that with such a vision of the dark origin it is hard to know how one could attain *any* redemption at all. In any case, redemption is death: better not to be, better the will not be. In art there is the momentary reversal into will-less peace, and the religious reversal is the more radical death of will. But how is any reversal possible if the will as described is the primal dark origin? For then even the reversal of the will is itself in the evil of being—will-lessness is itself will—and all that this entails. It is worse than Luther's bondage of the will,[16] for there is no way out. Release from our will would seem to meet in every direction the will again, and hence it would be no escape from the evil of being, only a new encounter with the universal horror. If there is a way out, as Schopenhauer atheistically still seems to want to insist, one must wonder if the evil genius has truly overcome its good twin, and whether at a certain limit some good "to be" must be granted and we be released into its affirmation. But does not such a release itself entail a different willing, so to say, a willingness beyond will? I would call this an agapeic release.[17] There is an intriguing, brief discussion of eros and agape in *The World as Will and Representation*: "Selfishness is eros, sympathy or compassion is agape."[18] The treatment does not go deep, not deep enough at all. And when we step back and consider the whole, compassion is ultimately a recognition of the suffering of the other as one's own. It is the sympathetic self-recognition of the will in the other, its own other. One might say: pity is the self-pity of the will—self-pity not simply at the level of my will or yours but at the level of the will itself. This is not the release of agapeic willing beyond will.

Loving the Loathsome: Can Nietzsche Will Yes?

One might ask if Nietzsche's search for a "yes" beyond Schopenhauer is connected with such a release. Perhaps, perhaps not. The search is not wrong, but many of the philosophical resources Nietzsche drew on, often out of sight, dip into the same well of ontological and metaphysical presuppositions as Schopenhauer, and hence one wonders if there is any basis to be released from the evil of being. "Nature is always worthless," he has told us, but there is no consolation in attributing to the human being the power to create values, since Nietzsche is no less intent on naturalizing man. And when we then take thought for how it looks in the whole, we cannot evade the conclusion that *homo natura* is also always worthless—in the end, and despite all essays at "yes."

I find an equivocation in Nietzsche, not always given its due, stemming from the fact that, as I hold, he never escaped Schopenhauer entirely. We all know that Nietzsche was early a disciple of Schopenhauer, and this is very evident in the *Birth of Tragedy*, where the dark origin is deeply at work under the metaphysical name of *das Ureine*. Better not to be: the wisdom of Silenus is reiterated by Nietzsche, for this is pivotal to his understanding of tragic wisdom and its transfiguring power. Even the immanence of evil in the divine is intimated—we sense it in the internal suffering of the One that gives rise to the many as a kind of sacred self-alleviation. We know that the "to be" is a kind of primal crime—not a moral guilt but an ontological guilt (we are reminded of Anaximander). This is somehow redeemed in the tragic. The tragic vision allows us to be honest about the dark origin but without being entirely destroyed by it. The Apollonian illusion allows us to contemplate what would destroy us if we were to look too directly at it and risk becoming identified with what would thereby destroy us. The Apollonian is like the shield of Perseus in which we can look at the Gorgon's head; if we looked directly we would be turned to stone. Perseus walks backwards toward Medusa, guided by the reflection in his shield; hence he does not directly look on the Gorgon's face and cannot come under its spell and be turned to stone.

Nietzsche tried to chill the ardor of his earlier aesthetic theodicy, but, having passed through his cooler quasi-positivistic phase, he returned to something not unlike an aesthetic theodicy. This was an *atheistic theodicy* to be sure; nevertheless, it would say "yes" to the whole, despite destruction and suffering, also confronting us with horror in the whole. But would such an atheistic theodicy of immanence not require some hospitality of being to such encompassing affirmation? Nietzsche never provides us with the proper ground of this ontological hospitality. Quite the contrary. Despite the self-authorized official profile, he never really escaped from Schopenhauer's pessimism, and the bitter wisdom of Silenus, companion of Dionysus, again concentrated in words that Nietzsche, like Schopenhauer before him, liked: Best of all, not to be; and second best, to die quickly.[19] Where are the ontological resources in the later Nietzsche that allow us unashamedly to say: "It is good to be"? And is this not just what Nietzsche, in practice, wants to sing: the good of the "to be"? One worries that the song of affirmation of his will to power is a song masking its own metaphysical despair, even as it overtly seeks metaphysical consent beyond despair.[20]

We need the lies of art, he tells us, to save us from the truth—the truth of the dark origin. For the affirmation of life, art is worth more than (this) truth. All of these are well-known claims of Nietzsche. No less well known is Nietzsche's claim to repudiate the pessimism of Schopenhauer, his claim to be his antipodes. Yes, he wanted to affirm what Schopenhauer held we must negate—for to negate the will would be to negate life, and this life must be affirmed—hyperbolically and, as it were, unconditionally. At a certain extremity, there are to be no reservations, it seems. Superficially, this is Nietzsche's yes-saying against Schopenhauer's no-saying and his own earlier no-saying. Superficially: since the dark origin at the bottom of it all is still in play. The hideous Gorgon's head has not lost its power—hence this "yes" must also be to the evil of being, and unreserved. The "yes" to life is the "yes" to the evil, and despite the dark origin.

The basic ontological attunement is not repudiated or transcended. It is "overcome" only in the sense that something "worthy" is affirmed *despite* it. For there is nothing in being itself that is good. One more time, remember: "All nature is worthless"—and we confer value. So what are we affirming? You might say, ourselves. In a moment of what looks like despondency, Zarathustra does say: we always come back to our own selves, what comes back is always ourselves. But surely there is more, surely the "yes" must be to more than self? But if there is something in the otherness worthy to be affirmed, there is a sense of ontological value irreducible to our conferring value on it. For Nietzsche the otherness always still is exposed to the spell of the dark origin. If we must affirm it and affirm it so that we are not destroyed by it, we might try by artistic illusions, by lies—and all this in order to live. Are we looking at Medusa, not only via the shield of Perseus, but with one eye open, one eye shut? But in order to live we have to hold there is something worthy about life that enables us to live and continue to live affirmatively. At bottom there is nothing of this, in being, in truth. But we must affirm "as if" there were. If one were truly to say "yes," in an unreserved sense, a stronger sense of ontological value would have to be granted—not "as if" worth, but the "to be" as good.

I cannot see how Nietzsche could do this, could contemplate it, without an entire transformation of the basic ontological/metaphysical presuppositions that seem to feed into the overt project he offers to us as redeeming the will. It would require an entirely different vision of the world—the world not as worthless but as the enigmatic communication of signs of the good that is not simply the human good or the good proportionate to human morality. There would have to be an other good hyperbolic to us, a good of the deepest significance for our own understanding of moral good. For looking at things thus, we cannot now be the only origins of value. Our origination of value would participate in something more primordial than itself. Ethical value and ontological value would have to be reconsidered—the good of our "to be" and the good of the "to be."

This would entail an entirely different understanding of the ethos of being and its good. It would not be a matter of the subjective versus the objective, not a matter of the subjective reduction or the objective, not a matter of the mastering subject or an overweening (over)humanism, and not a matter of an inhuman desubjectification or abjection of being. It would ask a new, renewed convenience between us and being—between our participation in the good of the "to be" and the good of the "to be" itself. Most of all it would ask a repudiation of the kinds of atheism that have been said to follow the "death of God." It would ask new access to the divine, a new affirmation of God—and not Dionysus, since this god in the Nietzschean image is party to the problem—a God hyperbolic to Dionysus and hyperbolic even to the Dionysian affirmation so ardently sought by Nietzsche. I would say: a God of agape—a love that is not Dionysian but yet a love—love of the good of the "to be" in its intimate singularity as well as enabling communities—an agapeic God of the intimate universal.

Nietzsche's Dionysus is still a god of the immanent whole, and the evil of the particular comes back to haunt even his affirmation of this whole. In a revealing passage, in both despair and celebration that seems to transcend despair, Nietzsche proclaims his Dionysian faith: "the faith that only the particular is loathsome, and that all is redeemed and affirmed in the whole."[21] What kind of affirmation is this, for Nietzsche this "highest of all possible faiths," that finds the particular loathsome? The man of this faith, he says, "does not negate anymore." To call something loathsome is surely to negate again. If the particular is thus loathsome, this must be more a redemption *from* the particular rather than a redemption *of* the particular. This Dionysian faith is said to be incarnated in the likes of Goethe, Nietzsche avers. It is certainly in the family of the Spinozists, and indeed the Hegelians. But the love of the intimate singular in the intimate universal is more than this, the loathsome particular. There is a sense of the erotics of becoming in Nietzsche, but there is no sense of the hyperbolics of the agapeic and the love that is released for the good of the other as other, that releases the finite other in its own being as good for itself.

Look on the loathsome and say "yes." Suspend the alibi of the whole. Look on the repugnant, the deformed, the brutal, the hideous, and say "yes." Look on the loathsome, do not flinch, and say "yes." That we flinch is the twitch that reveals our reserve, our retraction. We are fooling ourselves if we think we can do it alone. Say "yes," and allow the finite whole to be other than a metaphysical alibi—for us. Say "yes," and allow it to be a creation. Say "yes," and allow it to be allowed the mysterious freedom to undo the promise of creation. Say "yes," and allow in freedom the warp of promise that is evil. Could only an agapeic God thus say "yes" without reserve?

Groundless Self-Grounding

I return again to the question of the ground of freedom. In Kant, followed by Hegel, the impulse is toward the will as self-grounding. The question of the endowed character of freedom is not to the fore. What enables freedom is freedom itself. Will is, or mimics, a kind of *causa sui*. Kant's cautiousness always complicates things, sometimes unnecessarily, but the hidden theological reference is not incidental. Those who follow him are not so cautious, though some are more complicated, some less. We do see a notable stress on will as ultimate in modern philosophy. Already in Descartes, will is what makes us most like to God. More extremely in Schelling, will is absolute being. In modern voluntaristic theology, stemming from Scotus, some say, God's will is the absolute *prius*. When we read Descartes's assertion that the eternal truths are themselves products of the divine will, we are put in mind to think the absolute as the ultimate will that simply wills what it will will. It is not like a Platonic demiurge who, in molding the cosmos, looks to pregiven Ideas. It is not, as in Aquinas, where the coincidence of reason and will, of truth and good, of being and good, makes the question take a different shape. Will is not restrained by prior reason. The divine can will truth to be what it is, is not constrained, not indeed constrained in willing otherwise, should it so will.

If will is such an absolute *prius*, oddly we find a structure of thought not entirely different from Schopenhauer's, where the will is prior to the principle of sufficient reason. Will in itself is not marked by sufficient reason. What it wills comes to be as defined by the principle of sufficient reason, but it is not identical with sufficient reason. One might propose that something of the hyperbolic nature of the ultimate or the transcendence of the divine is intended by Scotus or Descartes. This hyperbolic character is not to be reduced to any determinate reason or the principle that determines reasons as sufficient. There is something in excess of these. But can we call this original will good? That is the question. This is the question suggested by Descartes's *malin génie*, a much maligned suggestion itself, but one sees how the metaphysical perplexity goes all the way down. While Descartes's answer in favor of God's trustworthiness and goodness seems unexceptionable, the suspicion of callowness makes it no less remarkable that this goodness comes to be weakened—to the point not only of evaporating but of turning into its opposite, as the philosophy of the unconstrained self-constraining will moves through Kant and German philosophy.

What enables will? What enables it to be? Is there a good to its "to be" that is coincident with its act? Or is all good the result of its original act, such that good is not to be ascribed to its original nature but only to what comes to be from it? But lose the goodness of God as the enabling endower, and let our immanent freedom become free as endowing itself, and we see the consequences in the foreboding of the evil of being. What endows human freedom? Will itself? But what is the ground of will? Kant will say reason. Hegel will also say reason—reason as self-grounding, as absolutely self-determining. There is confidence in reason in their answer, more cautious in one, more unconstrained in the other. Why should we be confident in reason, if more basic than reason is a dark will that might generate reason but in itself is not reason or reasonable? This is the significance of Schopenhauer's thought. The evil genius is not satisfied with being deemed a counterfeit double of God; it wants to be placed more forthrightly on the throne of ultimacy. The evil genius wins its triumph in the loss of confidence in reason as ultimate. There are no ultimate reasons. There might be penultimate reasons, but ultimately it is will as such that is ultimate. It may be true that the evil genius masks its hideous arbitrariness in the surfaces of intelligible structure. But when we realize that the ultimate place goes to this reasonless will, then we must refuse to vest our last confidence in such intelligibilities. Intelligibility now appears to be the mask of absurdity.

Things turn over into their opposites. The root of reason is not reason itself; it is will. The root of reason might be said to be nothing but itself, but what is this root in itself? It is nothing if it does not determine itself—it is nothing until it determines itself—in itself it is nothing—nothing lurks at the root of will. Hence there is a kind of nihilism in the very roots of this philosophy of the will. Only having determined this or that is there any amelioration of this nothing. The nothing makes something to be. If there is some reason to be, whatever is reason in what has come to be has itself no ultimate reason. It is groundless from the point of view of ultimate reasons. The grounds of reason are groundless. And have we not often witnessed the consequences of intelligibility coming to be understood as the mask of absurdity? I already mentioned one of the notable perplexities accompanying advancing rationality in modernity: the more intelligible sense we make of things, the more we seem to be senseless, anomalous accidents in an otherwise absurd universe, indeed even mistakes of the ultimately real. Reason advances more and more into the light that is really only the mask of a more radical darkness. The more sense we make of things, the more senseless we become as things.

One might say: Hegel turns into Schopenhauer—he has done so already in part in the figure of Schelling. Thought thinking itself in one is overtaken by will willing itself in the other. Of course, even Hegel himself speaks of the idea of freedom as just "the free will which wills the free will."[22] In Schelling the groundless will is named as even in the godhead and connected with the source of evil. Push the logic through to its conclusion and we hit something, we hit a kind of nothing that is not logic anymore but absurdity. Even if one of reason's true activities is the *reductio ad absurdum*, what happens here is the reduction raised to a second power, to a hyperbolic power. In the normal *reductio* we see the absurdity by the light of the intelligibility of commonly accepted truth, available to common sense or reason. In this *reductio* even common sense is the mask of absurdity. When it reduces to absurdity, it cannot provide an ultimate touchstone. Every touchstone is another mask of absurdity; there is no ultimate touchstone, and in its own way, the absurd is also absurd. This should make us pause and wonder about the entire direction of this way. Often it is taken to mean that the other side of illusion is not truth but another form of illusion; the other side of falsity is not truth but another face of falsity. The abnormal is the secret of the normal, the sinister is secretly the commanding sister of everything purporting to be consoling.

"All is false," as Nietzsche said loudly. If this is true, it cannot be true, for it too is false; but then if it is false, it is true. We are not far from something like the Cretan Liar paradox universalized—an impossible position. This may be granted, and the "impossible" heaped with hyperboles of praise. The "impossible" might even be called a "god," but is it the evil genius or good? It is impossible to say if the bewitchment caused by the ethos of being as evil continues to cast its spell. It is "possible" to continue speaking intelligibly only if one keeps changing the subject—avoiding each time the uncomfortable truth that the truth of generalized falsity subverts itself, whether as true or as false. If one keeps changing the subject the result is not the logos that runs through all things (as Heraclitus put it), not even the world as flux, but our own articulations as fluxgibberish. The "forms" of the flux, subtended by radical formlessness, are, in turn, the gibberish of the evil genius.

Inheritance and Inversion

One might object that the thinkers mentioned above are mainly from the nineteenth century. Yes, but the nineteenth century posed questions that the twentieth did not answer and I fear sometimes evaded. This is one of the reasons why, at the outset, we need to step back, not only to get some sense of what is recessed in our ethical reconfiguration of the ethos of being, but also to gain some perspective on the more extended shaping of that reconfiguration in modernity. Clearly Nietzsche is still with us as the protean Peter Pan of postmodern pluralism. Schopenhauer is still before us in the twenty-first century. So many of the moves relative to the evil of being have been, so to say, quasi-moves, "*als ob*" moves—it is "as if" we move, but we do not move. So one thinks it is with Nietzsche's move beyond Schopenhauer. Nietzsche enacts "as if" moves and so creates the illusion of movement, even as he denounces Plato for being moved to leave movement behind. That is one of the effects of needing the *"as if" truth* of art to save us from *the truth* of horror.

Because the petrifying gaze of Medusa still stares, of course we must hesitate to move, lest we be turned to stone. But if we continue just to circle around ourselves, are we not also paralyzed, though buffered from that evil eye, and seeming to enjoy our own self-movement? In that respect, we continue to be heirs of Kant, in this sense now of being postmodern Pelagians—even if torn, and in the shadow of intractable evil. Our faith in autonomy may be lacerated, but it is not really released from itself. If outside the self-circling of autonomy the evil eye of Medusa stares, why would one want to be released into that outside?

Is there something like this at work even in what looks like the inversion of Nietzsche? I am thinking of Levinas. The inversion: from glorious selfishness to hyperbolic moral abjection before the other. Are some postmodern admirers of Levinas doing ethical penance for their previous Nietzschean aestheticisms? There are surprising reversals going on here. The Nietzschean aestheticist becomes a Levinasian ethicist—how, it is never explained. Does the leopard change its spots, and this in a *metabasis eis allo genos?* Is this not, with a bow to Schopenhauer, a reversal beyond the principle of sufficient reason? Is it not, dare one say it, a miracle? And what if this ethical penitent or leopard starts to preach about religion? Another miracle? Another *metanoia* beyond reason?

For one is sometimes reminded of Levinas when reflecting on Schopenhauer's dark origin. Again and again Levinas reiterates the horror of the *il y a*. The relentless self-insistence of the *conatus essendi* also reminds us of the evil of being. Levinas does, after all, speak of *la mal de l'être*.[23] Very reminiscent of Schopenhauer: a version of the "It is evil to be" is combined with the evil of the will willing itself. We do come across a *version* of Plato's Good beyond being, but this is not Platonic in any sense that leads to an ontological appreciation of the good of the "to be." Levinas's Good beyond being is bound up with a trauma to the self-insistent ego, a trauma that is ethically saving in the reversal it effects from myself to the other. My question: Is there not *an evil* in such an *ethical good* that sees being as evil? Can we enjoy a Sabbath, much less eat our daily bread with any relish, having tasted of this evil of being? Perhaps there is a Levinasian ethical rupture to Nietzsche's quasi-surpassing of Schopenhauer. But does not its outcome look more like a kind of half-reversal? For we seem to be returned to a quasi-Schopenhauerian space, too close for comfort to its denial of the will, and the self-cancelling affirmation that "it is evil to be." We have not been released agapeically to any unreserved "yes" or "It is good."

The legacy of Kant also lives on in Levinas in his elevation of the moral law. His God is not the God of agapeic generosity. "The categorical imperative reeks of cruelty," Nietzsche attests, not without some warrant.[24] Must we not ask: Does the relation to the other now also reek of cruelty? Some of the Levinasian postmoderns willingly inflict this cruelty on themselves, almost as if in penitential flagellation to expiate their previous glorying in Nietzschean selfishness. Zarathustra's lion has reversed itself and morphed into a shape closer to the weight-bearing, self-whipping camel. The form inverts from self-subliming to self-abjection. And overall the shadow of the heteronymous God seeds secret anxiety lest the good of the "to be" return us there into the now terrifying embrace of the agapeic God.

When the evil eye of ethics itself looks, Medusa-like, on being and petrifies it into the deadening horror of the "evil of being," one is almost ready to extend a laughing forgiveness to the dancing Nietzsche. He recommends to our taste, after all, the *joy* of tragic vision. But in tragedy, as Aristotle told us, we know *both* horror *(phobos)* and pity *(eleos)*. Nietzsche knows much of horror, but touchingly he takes pity on humanity, Nietzsche who otherwise is beyond the shrill in his denunciation of pity. Horror before the evil of being is too much for most, and we must be saved from it, and in tragic art Nietzsche takes pity on us; while he might think of himself and some few great ones as able to look more honestly on the horror, once again, if we are to live, we have to affirm life, horror and all. We must do so with one eye open, one eye shut. The eye of the Dionysian philosopher might be open, but the eye of the Apollonian artist is shut. What evil we see, we do not see; what evil we do not see, we see.

"I am Zarathustra, the Godless: where shall I find my equal? And all those are my equal who give themselves their own will and rid themselves of all submission."[25] Zarathustra's self-promotion pushes the Kantian allergy of autonomy to heteronomy to an atheistic extreme, as well as making a lyrical rhapsody of the Hegelian "free will that wills the free will." He, like they, offers no answer on the good of the "to be." Nietzsche denounces Plato and science and Christianity for nihilism, but I doubt that he escaped nihilism himself when saying "no" to their "no." His "no" was to Schopenhauer's "no," yet it shared with that "no" the ontological/metaphysical mood that underneath it all was not mere valuelessness but a hideous abyss. Life is chaos to all eternity. What then again of the desire to affirm life, all life—Nietzsche's hyperbolic "yes"? This is a "yes" *despite* the hideous abyss, though it might say it is *of* the abyss; it is hence not quite the hyperbolic "yes" in the unreserved sense.

"To give oneself one's own will"—Zarathustra honors this. But to affirm life on the basis of one's own will won't work entirely. For one thing, this risks forgetting the endowed character of one's will, its being given to itself before it gives itself to itself. It especially won't work if the will itself is infected with the same problem to which it claims to be the solution. It won't work if at the heart of the will there is also the same valuelessness. For then the will is only fooling itself in its "yes." Its "yes" is not to what is worthy as other to itself. Nor can its "yes" be honestly to itself as worthy, since now there has seeped into it the suspicion that it too, at its heart of hearts, is also worthless. On these terms, the return of Schopenhauerian pessimism cannot be entirely stayed. It will keep returning, and now and then in even more virulent form, for one's will has tried a variety of escape routes and is now dragged back to prison, back to itself as its own prison. It must either lie down and die or hate itself all the more for being its own dungeon. It cannot free itself, and there seems no other savior for it beyond its own will. Pelagius will give Nietzsche in this mood no comfort. We are left with an inconsolate will in a comfortless keep. Once again, it seems, better not to be.

Stolen Fire: Yes Again, Even the No Is Endowed

And yet the will to affirm life "absurdly" keeps on reasserting itself. This is what Nietzsche also knew. He keeps helping himself to what from the standpoint of his stated philosophical resources he has no right. Like Prometheus, it is stolen fire that allows life to continue to burn, but the nightly gnawing of the liver, the organ of sacred divination, is the price to be paid for cheating the prerogative of Zeus. The gnawing anxiety keeps returning in the night despite the daytime defiance. Daytime defiance in its self-affirming energy is only the masked emptiness of nighttime dread. The crucial thing, of course, is not that we would affirm life. We are affirming life even despite our will. I would say that this is not a grim absurdity at all but, so to say, a benign surd: even despite our will, or the lack of it, the affirmation of life keeps living itself in us. Even when we will counter to life, or think we do, we affirm life. There is no escape here, but it is not a prison. It opens out a porosity to a certain good of the "to be" that is not the product of our own will but that keeps coming over the will again and again, even when the will is not itself willing to affirm what comes over it.

Of course, any will to affirm life is double-edged because life itself is not the absolute good in some purely univocal sense. There is a play of good and evil; there is chiaroscuro. If Nietzsche wants to affirm life unconditionally, unreservedly, this also means affirming this evil too—affirming the monstrous and the hideous, the disgusting, the small, the mean-minded, affirming the unwashed many for whom Nietzsche had contempt—and loving everything that he held made life small—the loathsome majority of the human race, for instance. He recognized this in acknowledging his need to overcome his great nausea at mankind. Once again the character of a "yes" *despite* comes back here. It is not the unreserved "yes" it strives to be. The unreserved "yes" makes sense only if there is something inherently worthy of love—lovable for itself. Can we make sense of this outside an absolute love such as God's? Are we humans ourselves capable of such love? This is a love that does not make any sense purely in terms of ourselves alone.

Surely there is something *hyperbolic* here that cannot be easily traced back to the immanent terms to which Nietzsche himself resorts. Man is a freak even in the will to Nietzschean affirmation. The superman is as much a freakish anomaly as the old God said now to be dead—it is an "above us." It is an "above us" that makes no sense in terms of what is below us: the dark origin, the underground under the underground of the cave. One cannot mount to this "above" purely in terms of digging a second cave beneath the first cave. One cannot get to the surface of the earth that way—unless perchance we are like a Dante led through the inferno by a Virgil to the base of the mountain of purgatory. One cannot look up to something higher, for there is nothing higher in this way of thinking. And one cannot create or "project" that something higher also, given what we are in our lower nature—unless, of course, there is some unacknowledged and unexplained divine spark in us already.

We return to being endowed. Who or what endows us? We did not endow ourselves. If the endowment were not there already, there is no way we would even dream of putting it there. For the dream of putting it there is hyperbolic and presupposes that there is something like it already at work as a ferment or seed or promise. Some intimation of the good of the "to be," our divinely endowed "to be," comes back. If we are to affirm life, we cannot do it without this. Without reference to or relation with the endowing source as other to us, we are given over to groundless affirmation—groundless not in the sense of purely justified as affirming what is good for itself, but in the sense of making no sense, groundless affirmation even to the point where affirmation as such ought not even to be at all. It is not only that its justification becomes otiose but that its very being at all makes no sense. Since it is at work, the conclusion is surely that things must be otherwise and seen otherwise. Otherwise groundless affirmation is hard to keep apart from negation. For then there are no grounds to choose between affirmation and negation, and we end up back in the negations with which we began.

Life stops that because life, no matter what our ideas and theories, is itself affirmation—affirming the good of the "to be." It is so not first as a chosen affirmation but as a lived affirmation. All life is this lived affirmation. And perhaps there is some sense in which Nietzsche was moving in that direction. Even evil is the lived affirmation of life that warps that affirmation in living it. It warps its promise while battening on its promise. But if this is so, then as philosophers we still have to ask—how to make sense of this? Must we not look on the good of the "to be" differently and open again, with St. Benedict rather than Nietzsche, the question of God as the endowing source?

Notes

1. Iris Murdoch, "Against Dryness," in *Existentialists and Mystics: Writings on Philosophy and Literature*, ed. Peter Conradi (London: Chatto and Windus, 1997), 287–95.

2. This is the title of the culminating ch. 18, but the earlier ch. 9 has the title "Nietzsche or Aristotle?" Alasdair MacIntyre, *After Virtue: A Study in Moral Theory,* 2nd ed. (Notre Dame: University of Notre Dame Press, 1984).

3. Alasdair MacIntyre, *Whose Justice? Which Rationality?* (Notre Dame: University of Notre Dame Press, 1988), 10.

4. But see MacIntyre's most recent *God, Philosophy, Universities: A Selective History of the Catholic Philosophical Tradition* (Lanham, MD: Rowman and Littlefield, 2009).

5. Friedrich Nietzsche, *The Gay Science*, § 301: "Die Natur ist immer wertlos: sondern dem hat man einen Wert einmal gegeben, geschenkt, und *wir* waren diese Gebenden und Schenkenden! Wir erst haben die Welt, *die den Menschen etwas angeht*, geschaffen." *Friedrich Nietzsche: Werke in Drei Bänden*, ed. Karl Schlechta (Munich: Carl Hanser, 1959), 2:177. See also: "There are no moral phenomena, there is only a moral interpretation of phenomena" [Es gibt gar keine moralischen Phänomene, sondern nur eine moralische Ausdeutung von Phänomenen] (*Werke*, 2:631), my translation, *Beyond Good and Evil*, § 108. The value of the "to be" is not to be identified with a moral value, of course—or indeed with a "phenomenon." See also Nietzsche's "projection" of his philosopher of the future—the one in whom man is justified, and indeed the rest of existence (*Beyond Good and Evil*, § 21). It is not simply man who is the measure of all things but the philosophers of the future: "commanders and legislators" who say "Thus it shall be!" "They first determine the Whither [Wohin] and the For what [Wozu] of man." (§ 21). Otherwise there is no justification, no worth to the "to be" as such. "We," we philosophers of the future, justify what has no justification in itself.

6. See *Ethical Perspectives* 8, no. 4 (2001), a special issue devoted to the discussion of my book *Ethics and the Between* (Albany: SUNY Press, 2001), and my response, 313–18, to Arnold Burms's "Metaphysical Foundations and Enchanting Coincidences," 307–13, within that issue; also my "Neither Servility nor Sovereignty: Between Metaphysics and Politics," in *Theology and the Political: The New Debate*, ed. Creston Davis, John Milbank, and Slovoj Žižek (Durham: Duke University Press, 2005), 153–82.

7. "Ethical potencies," as I call them in *Ethics and the Between*.

8. *On Beauty* (London: Secker and Warburg, 2004) received demure attention, while *On Ugliness* (New York: Rizzoli, 2007) was a loud success. Kant in the *Critique of Judgement*, trans. Werner S. Pluhar (Indianapolis: Hackett, 1987), § 48, says that *disgust* is the one feeling art should not represent, a prohibition transgressed with gusto by some contemporary art, a transgression relevant to our theme of what revolts us. I wonder sometimes what Kant would make of ironical "gestures" like that of Piero Manzoni, who a few years before his death in 1963 canned ninety samples of his own excrement and called these works "Merda d'Artista." Some were sold to major art institutions, but I believe some of the cans, I should say artworks, have since exploded.

9. Coventry Patmore is the source of the line: "The end of art is peace." In 1912, W. B. Yeats refers to a "delight in art whose end is peace" in "To a Wealthy Man," in *Responsibilities and Other Poems* (1916). See also Seamus Heaney's beautiful poem "The Harvest Bow" in homage to his father.

10. See William Desmond, "The Confidence of Thought: Between Belief and Metaphysics," in *Belief and Metaphysics*, ed. Peter M. Candler and Conor Cunningham (London: SCM, 2007), 11–40.

11. Among other things there is what I call the porosity of being, and our *passio essendi*, each of which is prior to our *conatus essendi*. I would have liked a fuller discussion of these to do justice to the theme, and there is a sense in which the current reflection as a whole is only half of what is required by the evil of being, for that other half would have to offer an archaeology of what is so recessed, and its intimacy with the good of the "to be." This present essay, then, is but one side of a philosophical diptych.

12. See his letter to Christian Huygens, December 4, 1637, penned while he was busy writing *Summary of Medicine*, by means of which he anticipated prolonging his life: "I used to think that death might rob me of thirty or forty years at most, it could not now surprise me unless it threatened my hope of living for more than a hundred years." See Donald Verene, *Philosophy and the Return to Self-Knowledge* (New Haven: Yale University Press, 1997), 27–28.

13. On this, see Desmond, *Ethics and the Between*, 133–42.

14. See Arthur Schopenhauer, *Parerga and Paralipomena*, trans. E. F. J. Payne (Oxford: Oxford University Press, 1974), vol. 1:73.

15. Friedrich Nietzsche, *The Will to Power*, ed. W. Kaufmann, trans. Walter Kaufmann and R. J. Hollingdale (New York: Random House, 1967), 549–50; *Der Wille zur Macht* (Leipzig: Kröner, 1930), 696–97.

16. There is a discussion of original sin and grace in Schopenhauer's *The World as Will and Representation*, trans. E. F. J. Payne (New York: Dover, 1966), vol. 1, § 70, where he sympathetically speaks of Augustine and Luther. Nevertheless, one suspects something mixed up about the discussion, something odd in his atheistic take on "grace."

17. See Desmond, *Ethics and the Between*, passim, but relevantly here, ch. 12 on released freedom and the passion of being, and ch. 16 on the community of agapeic service.

18. Schopenhauer, *World as Will*, 1:375–76.

19. See especially Friedrich Nietzsche, *Die Geburt der Tragödie [The Birth of Tragedy]* (1872), § 3: "Das Allerbeste ist für dich gänzlich unerreichbar: nicht geboren zu sein, nicht zu sein, nichts zu sein. Das Zweitbeste aber ist für dich— bald zu sterben." See William Desmond, *Art, Origins, Otherness: Between Art and Philosophy* (Albany: SUNY Press, 2003), ch. 6, "Eros Frenzied and the Redemption of Art: Nietzsche and the Dionysian Origin"; also ch. 5 on Schopenhauer's dark origin.

20. See David Benatar, *Better Never to Have Been: The Harm of Coming into Existence* (Oxford: Oxford University Press, 2006). A delicious oddity of life: a preacher making a living preaching—against living. A (Schopenhauerian) delight of living: watching a person sawing off the branch on which he is sitting.

A waspish query: Had this author never been, what would have been lost, and we been spared? A book never to have been? And all the better for that?

21. Friedrich Nietzsche, *Twilight of the Idols*, trans. Walter Kaufmann (New York: Vintage Books, 1989), "Skirmishes of an Untimely Man," § 49.

22. G. W. F. Hegel, *Outlines of the Philosophy of Right*, trans. T. M. Knox, rev. S. Houlgate (Oxford: Oxford University Press, 2008), § 27.

23. See E. Levinas, *De l'existence à l'existant* (Paris: Fontaine, 1947), 19; *Existence and Existents*, trans. A. Lingis (The Hague: Nijhof, 1978), 19.

24. Friedrich Nietzsche, *On the Genealogy of Morals and Ecce Homo*, trans. Walter Kaufmann (New York: Vintage Books, 1989), essay 2, § 6.

25. Friedrich Nietzsche, *Thus Spoke Zarathustra: A Book for None and All*, trans. Walter Kaufmann (New York: Penguin, 1978), 3, 5, 3.

CHAPTER EIGHTEEN

The Inescapability of Ethics

GERARD CASEY

As a philosophical theory, as contrasted with a theological view or an assumption of popular science or an emotional intuition about fate, determinism fails because it is unstateable. However far we impinge (for instance for legal or moral purposes) upon the area of free will we cannot philosophically exhibit a situation in which, instead of shifting, it vanishes. The phenomena of rationality and morality are involved in the very attempt to banish them.
—Iris Murdoch, *Metaphysics as a Guide to Morals*

In the *Fawlty Towers* episode "Gourmet Night" we find the hapless hotel owner Basil Fawlty treating his chronically malfunctioning car as if it were yet another person conspiring with the rest of the world to make him fail once again. In what must surely be one of the most achingly funny illustrations of the archetypal love/hate relationship between man and machine, Basil, when the car refuses to start, leaving him stranded with the duck for which his dinner guests are waiting in vain, reacts as follows:

> Come on, *start*, will you? Start, you vicious *bastard!* Come *on!* Oh, my *God!* I'm warning you—if you don't start . . . I'll count to three: One . . . two . . .

three! Right! That's it! I've had enough. *[Jumps out of the car and addresses the vehicle]* You've tried it on just once too often! Right! Well, don't say I haven't warned you! I've laid it on the line to you *time* and *time* again! Right! Well . . . this is it—I'm going to give you a damn good *thrashing! [Disappears from shot, reappearing moments later with a branch of tree with which he proceeds, futilely, to beat the car].*

It's difficult, even when appreciating the fundamental absurdity of Fawlty's action, not to sympathize with him. Who hasn't been frustrated and rendered semiparanoid by sundry misbehaving mechanical devices, persuaded, at least for a moment, that they were out to get us? The humor in the *Fawlty Towers* episode arises, in large part, from our instinctive fellow feeling with Fawlty's hostile reaction to the inert machine and, simultaneously, our realization of the supremely inappropriate nature of that reaction. Emotionally, Basil (and we) regard the malfunctioning mechanical device as malign and evil; rationally, we (perhaps not Basil) understand that it is nothing of the kind.

In a similar way, if bitten by a dog or scratched by a cat, we don't blame the dog for biting or the cat for scratching, at least once we've overcome our momentary annoyance, but we would blame other people if they bit or scratched us, and, unless we're philosophers of a particular persuasion or even when we are philosophers of a particular persuasion "after hours," we believe that our rebuke of the biting or scratching human being is rationally warranted and is not merely an idiosyncratic irritable reaction, as it would be in the case of the cat or dog.

Explanatory Pluralism

To regard the nonhuman animate world or the completely inanimate world as intentional and purposeful and, more often than not, malignant is a deeply rooted, perhaps even atavistic, human tendency to which the writings of anthropologists abundantly attest. We understand from the "inside," as it were, how the human world works, and we have an innate tendency to export this understanding into regions where it has little (the animate world) or no (the inanimate world) purchase. The intellectual history of mankind bears eloquent testimony to the struggle to expel intentional explanations from the nonhuman world to make room for physically causal explanations. More recently, the intellectual history of mankind bears witness to a movement to expel such intentional explanations even from the world of human affairs and to provide physicalist explanations and only such explanations for all phenomena.

We find a discussion of a very early example of anti-intentional explanatory schemes in the *Phaedo*, where Socrates reflects on his early life and remarks how excited he became when he heard of Anaxagoras, who, it was said, claimed that it is the mind that produces order and is the cause of everything. Eagerly, he obtained Anaxagoras's writings, only to be severely disappointed. When it came to the crunch, Anaxagoras made no use of causation by mind; instead, he "adduced causes like air and aether and water and many other absurdities." Socrates remarks that it was as if someone were to claim that "the reason why I am lying here now is that my body is composed of bones and sinews, and that the bones are rigid and separated at the joints, but the sinews are capable of contraction and relaxation, and form an envelope for the bones with the help of the flesh and skin, the latter holding all together, and since the bones move freely in their joints the sinews by relaxing and contracting enable me somehow to bend my limbs, and this is the cause of my sitting here in a bent position."[1] But, as Socrates points out, while such bodily dispositions are obviously necessary conditions of one's posture, they are far from being sufficient conditions. The real *reason* that Socrates is now sitting in prison awaiting execution is not that his bones and sinews are suitably disposed (although they *are* suitably disposed) but rather that he *believes* it to be more honorable to submit to the penalty imposed by his city than to run away and is *acting* accordingly. Socrates does not deny that there can be knowledge of bodily dispositions or that such dispositions are necessary, but he goes on, in a passage that contains a rare example of Plato making a joke, to deny that such knowledge would be such as to render otiose explanations in terms of reasons.

> Or again, if [Anaxagoras] tried to account in the same way for my conversing with you, adducing causes such as sound and air and hearing, and a thousand others, and never troubled to mention the real reasons, which are that since Athens has thought it better to condemn me, therefore I for my part have thought it better to sit here, and more right to stay and submit to

whatever penalty she orders. Because, by dog, I fancy that these sinews and bones would have been in the neighbourhood of Megara or Boeotia long ago—impelled by a conviction of what is best!—if I did not think that it was more right and honourable to submit to whatever penalty my country orders rather than to take to my heels and run away. But to call things like that causes is too absurd. If it were said that without such bones and sinews and all the rest of them I should not be able to do what I think is right, it would be true. But to say that it is because of them that I do what I am doing, and not through choice of what is best—although my actions are controlled by mind—would be a very lax and inaccurate form of expression. Fancy being unable to distinguish between the cause of a thing and the conditions without which it could not be a cause.[2]

It is a necessary condition of Socrates' body being in its prison cell (assuming his not having been carried there by force) that his muscles contracted and his brain cells fired in the appropriate way. Some two and a half thousand years later, Ludwig Wittgenstein essentially addressed the same point raised by Plato in the *Phaedo* when he asked, "What is left over if I subtract the fact that my arm goes up from the fact that I raise my arm?"[3] If my arm is to go from a position of repose to one of being raised, the appropriate physiological events have to take place. Such physiological events are necessary conditions of one's arm's going up, but they are not sufficient, inasmuch as, prescinding from pathological conditions in which one's limbs operate more or less independently of one's desires, in order for one's hand to go up, one must *do* something—one must raise one's arm.[4] This human action is not necessarily the result of long hours of deliberation (though it may be); it may in fact be simple, spontaneous, and unreflective. Nonetheless, it is an action. Contrast that with the situation in which your friend, let us imagine, to embarrass you at an auction, catches your arm and lifts it up high into the air. Here, one's arm is up but one hasn't done anything, as one will subsequently have to explain to the irate auctioneer.[5]

In the matter of explanations, then, we seem to be committed by our practices to an explanatory pluralism. There is a dimension of reality to which physical causal explanations alone are relevant, and these explanations delineate the conditions that are both necessary and sufficient to account for that dimension; and there is a dimension of reality in which such physically causal explanations are, at best, indicative of necessary conditions—the sufficient conditions being given by reference to irreducibly intentional concepts such as beliefs, desires, and actions.

Monistic accounts are inherently intellectually attractive and, other things being equal and with Ockham's razor to hand, are to be preferred to more complex accounts; but while explanations should be as simple as they can be, they should be as complex as they have to be in order not to distort or ignore the data they purport to explain. It is a prejudice simply to assume that there can be one and only one kind of explanation, a point made by Aristotle in his *Nicomachean Ethics*.

> Our discussion will be adequate if it has as much clearness as the subject-matter admits of, for precision is not to be sought for alike in all discussions.... We must be content, then, in speaking of such subjects and with such premisses to indicate the truth roughly and in outline, and in speaking of things which are only for the most part true and with premisses of the same kind to reach conclusions that are no better. In the same spirit, therefore, should each type of statement be *received;* for it is the mark of an educated man to look for precision in each class of things just so far as the nature of the subject admits; it is evidently equally foolish to accept probable reasoning from a mathematician and to demand from a rhetorician scientific proofs.[6]

As already mentioned, it is now generally accepted that it is not appropriate to seek an intentionalistic explanatory monism across the range of explananda—what is not generally considered inappropriate is the corresponding attempt to establish a physicalistic explanatory monism even though such an attempt, if successful, makes the very process of offering and receiving explanations problematic.

Starting from Where We Are—Where Else?

The ineliminable starting point of every inquiry cannot but be the very act of inquiry itself.[7] Furthermore, the conditions of the act of inquiry and whatever follows ineluctably from the act of inquiry cannot, without performative contradiction, be gainsaid. A rejection of the starting points of Aristotle and Descartes involves the rejecter in a performative contradiction.[8] The difference between their respective positions was that while Descartes's *cogito* represents a retreat to subjectivity, from which position escape seems impossible, Aristotle's principle of noncontradiction, involving as it does a commitment to language and communication, is implicitly social. The Cartesian *cogito* leads to the solipsistic self, but the act of inquiry, which is impossible without language, leads not to a single individual but to a whole community of language users. Language is the repository of our common "intentions" and is the property of the entire speech community, not the idiosyncratic plaything of individual speakers. "Human beings are essentially language-using animals, an idea shared by Aristotelianism and hermeneutics."[9] Wittgenstein's "private language argument" has, I believe, definitively established the ineluctably social nature of language. "If you are not certain of any fact, you cannot be certain of the meaning of your words either."[10]

For Wittgenstein, belief, and the expression of belief in propositions, are as much a matter of the natural history of man as is his physical constitution. "As if the giving of grounds did not come to an end sometime. But the end is not an ungrounded presupposition; it is an ungrounded way of *acting*,"[11] and "Giving grounds, however justifying the evidence, comes to an end;—but the end is not certain propositions' striking us immediately as true, i.e. it is not a kind of seeing on our part; it is our *acting*, which lies at the bottom of the language-game."[12] This marriage of language and praxis is central to the thought of the mature Wittgenstein. Our beliefs, our opinions, our certainties are not the epistemic possessions of disembodied spirits but aspects of the activity of essentially embodied creatures. Again, a citation from Wittgenstein, though not originally directed toward this situation, is illuminating. "I want to regard man here as an animal; as a primitive being to which one grants instinct but not ratiocination. As a creature in a primitive state. Any logic good enough for a primitive means of communication needs no apology from us. Language did not emerge from some kind of ratiocination."[13]

As children, we move from functioning originally more or less purely on the stimulus-response level to a situation in which the characteristically human capacity to ask and answer questions begins to emerge. When a child begins to interact verbally with its mother, on the child's side we are dealing first with random noises and then, very quickly, with at most a rudimentary kind of signaling that, considered just as such, is not significantly different in kind from animal communication. On the mother's side, however, the child's actions, movements, sounds, noises, are all interpreted as being the actions of a communicative human being. To use the language of Walker Percy, the distinguished American novelist, physician, and philosopher, the child's initial verbal activity is dyadic, which is to say that it is a purely natural event, yet it is interpreted triadically (intentionally) by those in the child's environment, and the child's speech eventually becomes genuinely triadic.[14]

Wittgenstein writes: "The child, I should like to say, learns to react in such-and-such a way; and in so reacting it doesn't so far know anything. Knowing only begins at a later level."[15] This socially interactive yet pre-semantic (on the child's side) situation is the vital context within which genuine language use will begin, including the characteristically human activity of asking and answering questions. That context of social interaction, however, is not merely a starting point to be left behind as the child matures; it is the continuing environment, the ground that keeps our language rooted to reality, however recondite and sophisticated our knowledge may become.

The Argument Distinguished from Some of Its Near Relations

The argument that I have adumbrated as relevant to the defeat of the deterministic and irrationalist underminers of freedom and rationality needs to be distinguished from several related but distinct arguments. The argument is not a pure logical contradiction. Take two propositions, such as "Dublin is the capital of Ireland" and "Dublin is not the capital of Ireland." Provided all the words in both propositions have the same sense and reference, these propositions are *strictly contradictory:* they do not need to be asserted by anyone. We have here two distinct (albeit related) propositions. It is just a logical truth that a proposition and its contradictory cannot both be true: the truth of one excludes the truth of the other. Even if all rational beings ceased to exist, these two propositions would still be contradictory. Of course, no one would know or care about the contradiction, but that is another matter.

The argument is not a matter of pure self-referential incoherence. A single proposition is *self-referentially incoherent* if it is such that if it is true then it is also false and that if it is false, then it is also true. The classic example of self-referential incoherence is S—"This sentence is false." If S is true, then S is false; if S is false, then S is true. The incoherence of S is purely logical, that is, it is incoherent regardless of who asserts S or, indeed, whether S is in fact asserted by anyone. The "self" in "self-referentially incoherent" refers to the proposition in question and not to any utterer, proposer, articulator, or enunciator of this proposition.

Nor is the argument a matter of behavioral inconsistency or hypocrisy. We have behavioral inconsistency in the situation where A professes to reject actions of type X while engaging in X: for example, when Algernon says he hates country music but spends a significant amount of time listening to it when not required to do so either by coercion or by other extenuating circumstances and spends much of his disposable income on country music CDs and downloads. Changes of mind, of course, must be distinguished from inconsistency. One may be subject to rapid changes of mind and so would be properly described as inconstant; one is inconsistent only if the acceptance and rejection of X occur at the same time and in the same respect.

The Argument

We can draw a reasonably clear distinction between pure contradictory arguments (such as pure logical contradiction and pure self-referential incoherence) and all the other types of self-stultifying arguments. Pure contradictory arguments are what they are independently of any human action or any actual state of affairs. Even in a world in which there were no rational agents, such propositions would still be what they are and have the character that they have. Existential self-refuting arguments, on the other hand, require that some state of affairs must obtain and that some rational agent articulate a claim.

Some philosophical arguments have a unique ability to polarize scholarly opinion. Anselm's argument is one such. From the moment of its first appearance in the eleventh century, this argument has divided philosophers into two camps, the inhabitants of one camp being content to accept that there is something special about the starting point and subject matter of the argument that generates an incontrovertible conclusion, while the inhabitants of the other camp, suspecting that nonlogical rabbits are being pulled out of logical hats, remaining resolutely unpersuaded of its merits. The self-stultifying argument that I have sketched is just such another polarizing intellectual device. Lynne Rudder Baker makes the point, with which it is hard to disagree, that "arguments about the allegedly self-defeating character of anything are, I think, frustrating to people on both sides of the issue. People on each side think that those on the other side miss the point. From my side, it seems that I ask straightforward questions . . . which require answers but receive none."[16]

The argument is based on the notion of existential self-refutation. The proposition "I am not speaking," as spoken aloud by someone, is *existentially self-refuting*. This is not purely self-referentially incoherent; after all, the remark could be made (as here) in writing. Neither is it a pure logical contradiction. If the pronoun were changed to "you" and then I said it while you were silent, it would be true. Its truth or falsity depends upon the action described and whether the agent alleged to be performing this action is or isn't actually performing it.[17]

Getting Serious

Philosophers and the accounts they give must be serious. Being serious doesn't mean that one has to be solemn or portentous—one can be serious and humorous, just as one can be frivolous and pedantic—but a condition of holding a belief, *really* holding that belief, not just notionally adhering to it, is that one's actions should, as far as possible, conform to it. At the very least, if one is serious, there should be no gratuitous contradiction between what one claims to believe and the actions one performs. We might put this in the form of the following maxim, M:

> M: *No theory can be seriously maintained such that, if it were to be true, its maintenance would become impossible, meaningless, contradictory, or self-refuting.*

Apart from the formal constraints on theories of the necessity for consistency and coherence, and the material constraints of explanatory adequacy and coverage, there is also a self-referential constraint on theories, namely, that theories must not render impossible the conditions of their own statement or the conditions of their being maintained. If they do so, they are theoretically self-stultifying. So, to repeat the central point of this paper, unless human beings are fundamentally free in their choices and decisions, it is not possible for statements to be meaningfully asserted: that includes the statement of a radical determinism or a radical irrationalism. The statement of a radical determinism is undermined by its own content's rendering pointless the act of its assertion or by its assertion's rendering meaningless the content of that assertion; likewise for the statement of a radical irrationalism. As the epigraph from Iris Murdoch makes clear, determinism falls foul of the maxim since, of necessity, the very attempt to argue for determinism is itself a free act by the arguer that commends itself to the rational judgment of its intended audience; irrationalism, on the other hand, while not quite as neatly self-destructive as determinism, is nonetheless obviously rationally unsustainable.

In fact, the argument embodied in the maxim can be marshaled against all forms of eliminative materialism or, more generally, all forms of reductive naturalism. Once again, it is hard to disagree with Lynne Rudder Baker when she says that "to deny the common-sense conception of the mental is to abandon all our familiar resources for making sense of any claim, including the denial of the common-sense conception." She continues, "If the thesis denying the common-sense conception is true, then the concepts of rational acceptability, of assertion, of cognitive error, even of truth and falsity are called into question."[18]

Does scientific naturalism, which is currently the dominant and fashionable philosophical orthodoxy, fail to meet the self-referential constraint of the maxim? I believe so. Scientific naturalism derives much of its plausibility from the progressive and inexorable elimination of folk physics by the advances of modern science.[19] From its legitimate application to the physical sciences, the eliminative method is extended to other areas such as psychology, where the theory holds that so-called folk psychology, the complex of interrelated concepts in which we describe and explain our everyday behavior, is similarly eliminable by the development of a scientific psychology. Now, it is clear that there has been, and to some extent still is, a folk physics that purports to explain people's everyday experience of the physical world. Such a folk physics is eliminable. What is not, however, eliminable is people's experience of weight, resistance to movement, and so on. These are facts of human experience that are not subject to scientific dissolution. Similarly, there could indeed be a folk psychology (indeed, the quasi-substantialist notion of the mind characteristic of much modern philosophy is a thesis of just such a refined folk psychology), but however wrong or misguided *particular* beliefs, thoughts, and judgments may be, beliefs, thoughts, and judgments *just as such* are scientifically ineliminable. Unlike the elimination of folk physics in favor of scientific physics, the very attempt to assert the eliminability of our ordinary psychological descriptions and explanations cannot be done without making use of that which is denied. Scientific naturalism is just one *philosophical* theory among others. It originates from within our human experience and so cannot, coherently, *radically* contradict that experience.

Unless we are content to exhibit dissociative identity disorder (multiple personalities), our lives as philosophers cannot be radically divorced from what we do when we are not doing philosophy. In a normal day, we go to work, read and answer our mail, teach our students, work on papers or books, go to meetings, have lunch, make small talk with acquaintances, discuss last night's football game, and so on, all of which actions are shot through with purpose and intentionality. In our nonphilosophical dealings with our families, friends, and colleagues, we treat them as rational moral agents, as people responsible for their actions, sometimes praising them, more often blaming them, but always morally evaluating their actions. We assume, without any difficulty, the reality of the ethical dimension of our lives and the lives of others and the appropriateness of moral judgment. But moral judgments make sense only if human actions are, in some significant way, free. Freedom, in turn, if it is possible at all, is coimplicative with rationality in such a way that only the free can be rational and only the rational can be free.

Some attempt to deny the apparently undeniable. Susan Blackmore holds that "it is possible to live happily and morally without believing in free will."[20] According to her, once we learn to let go of the illusory feeling that we act with free will, "decisions just happen with no sense of anyone making them." She admits that giving up a sense of self is much more difficult, remarking that "I just keep on seeming to exist." In a somewhat similar vein, Nicholas Humphrey believes that "human consciousness is a conjuring trick, designed to fool us into thinking we are in the presence of an inexplicable mystery."[21] He is of the opinion that those, such as Colin McGinn, who think that it is impossible to explain how consciousness can arise from the material operations of the central nervous system are apparently the butts of a practical joke played by natural selection, which has, for its own inscrutable reasons, "succeeded in putting consciousness beyond the reach of rational explanation" and, by so doing, has "undermined the very possibility of showing that this is what it has done."[22] It is interesting to note that while Blackmore denies the reality of the human agent, she is unable to avoid substituting another agent—"this body and its genes and memes and the whole universe"—and that while Humphrey rejects the reality of human consciousness he happily posits (and presumably is conscious of) a quasi-anthropomorphic natural selection that can intend things and be successful. Agency and consciousness, like nature, when expelled through the front door, somehow always manage to sneak back into the house.[23]

At this point, some readers may echo the sentiment of the bystander in *My Fair Lady* who objects to Professor Higgins's choice of Eliza as a subject for linguistic analysis with "Come Sir, I think you've picked a poor example!" Perhaps I have, but when one strips away the veneer of sophistication surrounding reductionist accounts, though the details differ, they all suffer from the same principled problem: it is not possible to reconcile the intentionalistic, purposive, meaningful act of stating the account with the fact that such accounts undermine purpose, meaning, and intention.

Determinism, whether psychological, theological, or metaphysical, undermines freedom and makes morality otiose. Those who preach determinism, if they are to be taken seriously, must be prepared to live by that doctrine. But determinism is practically impossible, and so, I hold, determinism is not a serious philosophical position. Illness, disease, passion, exhaustion may make inroads into the area of our freedom, but they cannot totally eliminate it, or they could do so only at the cost of making us cease to be human. In a similar way, fundamental attacks on human rationality are similarly destructive of morality. If they are to be taken seriously, those who preach irrationalism—whether in the form of deconstructionism, perspectivalism, postmodernism, or polylogism—must live by those doctrines. Irrationalism, though not impossible in quite the same way as determinism, cannot be consistently maintained (although some irrationalists make an impressive effort), and so, I maintain, irrationalism is not a serious philosophical position. There is little point in discussing the respective merits of deontology, say, as against utilitarianism or virtue ethics if at any moment someone can pull the rug out from under the entire discussion by questioning the very possibility of ethics in the first place. We need to demonstrate the nonviability of determinism and irrationalism, and the best way to do this, perhaps the only way, is via the self-stultifying argument.

After the publication of Alasdair MacIntyre's groundbreaking trilogy, normative ethics has reestablished itself in the anglophone world as a respectable philosophical discipline. A glance at the catalogues of the publishers of philosophy books will reveal an astonishing plethora of studies in various aspects of the discipline. Whatever position one takes in the various disputes around the many topics in this area, one presupposition is common to all positions, namely, that ethics, in any of its forms, is possible. But ethics makes no sense and has no point unless human action is capable of moral evaluation; and for human action to be susceptible of moral evaluation it must be free and rational. Any philosophical theory that radically denies freedom or radically undermines rationality ipso facto undermines the very possibility of ethics, but, since ethics is inescapable, determinism and irrationalism are fundamentally incoherent.

Notes

The chapter epigraph is from Iris Murdoch, *Metaphysics as a Guide to Morals* (London: Penguin Books, 1993), 203; emphasis added.

1. Plato, *Phaedo*, 98c–d, trans. Hugh Tredennick (London: Penguin, 1967).
2. Ibid., 98d–99b.
3. Ludwig Wittgenstein, *Philosophical Investigations* (Oxford: Blackwell, 1953), para. 666.
4. Ibid., para. 621.
5. See Andrew Sneddon, *Actions and Responsibility* (Dordrecht: Springer, 2006).
6. Aristotle, *Nicomachean Ethics* 1.3.1094b12–28, trans. W. D. Ross, rev. ed. (Oxford: Oxford University Press, 2009).
7. Some of the ideas in this section first appeared in my "Metaphysics and Certainty: Beyond Justification," in *Proceedings: Metaphysics. Second World Con-*

ference, Rome, July 2–5, 2003, ed. David Murray (Rome: Fondazione Idente di Studi e di Ricerca, 2006).

8. Aristotle, *Metaphysics* 4.4 (1006a12 ff); Descartes, *Meditations.*

9. Hans-Johann Glock, *A Wittgenstein Dictionary* (Oxford: Blackwell, 1996), 294.

10. Ludwig Wittgenstein, *On Certainty* (Oxford: Blackwell, 1969), para. 114.

11. Ibid., para. 110; emphasis added.

12. Ibid., para. 204; emphasis added.

13. Ibid., para. 475.

14. Walker Percy, *The Message in the Bottle* (New York: Picador, 2000), passim.

15. Wittgenstein, *On Certainty,* para. 538.

16. Lynne Rudder Baker, *Saving Belief: A Critique of Physicalism* (Princeton: Princeton University Press, 1987), 137 n.

17. Sometimes you can learn a phrase, such as "Non parlo italiano" or "Ich spreche kein Deutsch," to say in response to someone who attempts to speak to you in Italian or German. This would seem to be existentially self-refuting, but when properly understood it isn't. What it really means is "Please don't expect me to speak Italian or German to you; this is all I have. Help!")

18. Baker, *Saving Belief,* 134.

19. Some of the ideas in this paragraph first appeared in my "Metaphysics, Mathematics and Metaphor," *Analysis and Metaphysics* 7 (2008): 13–22.

20. Susan Blackmore, untitled contribution to *What We Believe but Cannot Prove,* ed. John Brockman (London: Pocket Books, 2006), 41.

21. Nicholas Humphrey, untitled contribution to Brockman, *What We Believe,* 113.

22. Colin McGinn, *The Mysterious Flame: Conscious Minds in a Material World* (New York: Basic Books, 2000), quoted in Nicholas Humphrey's untitled contribution to Brockman, *What We Believe,* 114.

23. "Naturam expelles furca, tamen usque recurret." Horace, *Epistles* I, x, 24.

Epilogue
What Next?

ALASDAIR MacINTYRE

This epilogue is an expression of quite unusual gratitude both for the papers in this volume and for the wide-ranging, yet incisive discussions that earlier versions of them generated at a conference at University College Dublin in March 2009. The range of critical perspectives on various aspects of my work was and is impressive. Were I to live long enough to learn what I need to learn from those criticisms and to revise and develop my work accordingly, I would surely win an unprecedented place in the Guinness Book of Records for longevity. Yet to think in those terms would be to miss the point: my work has become part of a number of remarkable conversations and inquiries that now have a life of their own. The question therefore is: How to carry some of them at least further forward?

What was happily evident in Dublin was that participants in those conversations often include protagonists of standpoints whose adherents have in the past largely ignored each other or felt able to be cursorily dismissive of each other's views. Consider the large lack of conversation for many decades between Marxists and Thomists. There are no papers by Marxists in this volume, but there were insightful Marxist contributors to the discussions in Dublin. And Raymond Geuss's paper, with its thesis that "the story of the twentieth century is the story of the failure of Marxism," makes it clear—perhaps unintentionally—why a dialogue about issues in moral philosophy in which contemporary Marxists were not participating would be a defective and inadequate conversation. So too would be a conversation from which contemporary Thomists were absent. And the contributions that Thomists made to the discussions in Dublin were notable. What then *is* the relevance of Marxist claims to Thomist claims? I begin from Geuss's discussion of Marxism.

Geuss argues that in the twentieth century Marxism "presented the only genuine and potentially viable attempt at reconstituting some notion of objective moral authority." The conception of human development through history that provided Marxists with their grounds for claiming such authority was summarized by Marx in a passage from the *Grundrisse* that Geuss quotes. Marx remarks that in the ancient Greco-Roman world the question about the point and purpose of prosperity "is always which form of prosperity creates the best citizens," whereas in the modern world "production appears as the end of human beings and wealth as the end of production." But, so Marx argues, if we understand the notion of wealth rightly, "what is wealth other than the universality of the needs, abilities, forms of enjoyment, productive powers, etc., generated through universal exchange?" And he goes on here and elsewhere to speak of the development of human creative capabilities becoming an end in itself, an end to be achieved by communism, an end by appeal to which communism is to exhibit its moral superiority.

That is, Marxist claims to political and moral authority, whether advanced in theoretical debate or in debased form in the politics of that murderous parody of Marxism, the Soviet state, presuppose both an account of human nature as directed toward the end of a full development of human powers and a corresponding account of human history in which the movement from the ancient to the modern world is one toward a more adequate understanding of what that end is.

Geuss notes that Marx's thesis raises the question of how his reference to the universality of human needs and the like is to be construed, and Geuss alludes to the distinction drawn by Marxists of the Frankfurt School between "true" and "false" human needs, noting approvingly that they hoped to establish this distinction "without a return to an Aristotelian conception of a substantively fixed human nature that could be used as a criterion." Geuss explains his own approval of this attempt to avoid returning to Aristotle by arguing for a rejection of Aristotle's conception of "a single overarching goal" for human activity, a goal in the light of which our various human actions and projects could be evaluated. Yet Geuss allows that, lacking the standard that such a goal might have provided, the self-proclaimed and self-deceived Marxists of the Soviet bloc and their theoretical allies were condemned to understand the human future in terms of progress in production and consumption, crudely conceived, an understanding that not only failed to differentiate them from the capitalist world—as it now fails to differentiate China from the capitalist world—but also made them vulnerable to the charge that by their own standards their progress was inferior to that of advanced capitalism. (In this respect the Chinese are doing significantly better.)

I take Geuss to be right in his claim that Marxism needed as an underpinning something very like Aristotle's conceptions of the human *telos* and of human flourishing, but I also take his objections to Aristotle to be misconceived. Geuss begins by quoting from *Nicomachean Ethics* I, 1094a18–22, where he interprets Aristotle as saying that the satisfaction of a desire would be empty and pointless if that desire was recurrent, as, he suggests, our desires to satisfy our thirst are. My problem is that I find no hint of this absurd thesis in that passage. What Aristotle argues is that, if every object of choice or desire were chosen or desired only for the sake of something else, then our desires would be empty and pointless—which is surely true. (Note that Aristotle at this point is cautiously edging his way toward no more than a first conditional conclusion about whether human beings have a final end and what it might be.)

Geuss believes that the very notion of such a final end is objectionable, first because it implies that life is "like a race with clear winners and losers," second because to accept it is to ignore the fact that occasional failure can play a positive part in human lives, and third because it presupposes that there is a single narrative of each human life, while, on Geuss's view, no life could be captured by a single narrative, if only because our conceptions of the good that we are pursuing "*change* during our lives." If one were to endorse this critique of Aristotle, one might have to conclude— this may be my inference from Geuss's premises, rather than Geuss's— that because a Marxism that lacked the means to integrate into its theorizing some well-founded Aristotelian conception of a human *telos* would be bound to fail as a form of moral and political theorizing, and because no such conception is well founded, Marxism was for this reason alone bound to fail. But this is of course not my conclusion. For while I agree with Geuss that Marxism both lacks and badly needs something like an Aristotelian conception of the human *telos*, I reject his criticisms of Aristotle.

I am therefore committed to arguing, with Aristotle and with Aquinas, that we do have a conception of what it is to live a human life well rather than badly and to bring such a well-lived life to its completion, but, as I understand that conception, it does not at all entail either that our lives have the character of a competitive race or that both occasional, even recurrent failure and a variety of changes in how we conceive our final good may not be integral to the narratives of our lives. What I cannot do is to argue for these conclusions here. What I can do is to explore to some small extent Aristotle's and more especially Aquinas's conception of what it is to live well, and I approach this task through a consideration of Steven Long's paper, although I owe it to Long to note that his paper is part of a much larger project.[1] A central Thomist thesis is that human actions can be made adequately intelligible as human actions only if we understand them by identifying, first, that which makes this particular action the kind of action that it is; second, whatever immediate end it is to which this action is directed by the agent's intention; and third, that conception of her or his final end which is presupposed by the agent acting as she or he does for this or that immediate end. To identify the action is to answer the question "What are or were you doing in doing that?" To identify the agent's immediate end is to answer the question "What do you or did you take to be the good of doing that?" To identify the conception of her or his final end that is presupposed by that agent acting as she or he does makes it possible for us to ask whether that agent has conceived of her or his final end rightly, that is, whether in fact by acting thus that agent is acting well or badly.

What this Thomistic scheme of thought—and I have of course sketched it much too briefly—enables us to grasp is how we as human agents understand or misunderstand ourselves, as directed or misdirected through our actions and purposes toward our good, and in so doing as living well or badly. But it is of course not in such abstract terms that particular agents in particular times and places understand themselves or that we as observers understand them. It is always in and through the particularities of the social, economic, and cultural relationships of their own time and place that individuals and groups pursue their individual and common goods. And it is in terms of those particularities that they understand themselves and their situation. The range and variety of differences in those relationships are such that it is all too easy for that which human beings have in common, that which makes human agents distinctively human agents, to be obscured. Moreover, the understanding of human agency and well-being that is presupposed by the Thomistic scheme—and the Thomistic claim is that plain persons in their everyday practical lives, insofar as they are clearheaded, understand themselves in those terms—is part of an account of human nature that has metaphysical presuppositions. So in a culture, such as our own, some of whose dominant modes of thought are deeply antimetaphysical, the outcome may be a widespread misunderstanding of agency, of what it is to live well or badly, and of the norms by conformity to which agents are able to live well.

It is just this situation that Steven Long addresses in "The Perfect Storm," one in which the adherents of both continental phenomenology and analytic philosophy, disagreeing on so much else, have agreed in their rejection of the metaphysical underpinnings of the Thomistic view of human nature, while a series of developments within Catholic theology from the late Middle Ages onwards have on very different grounds also put that view in question, sometimes in the name of a theological Thomism that relies on what both Long and I take to be an implausible interpretation of some of Aquinas's key texts. The result has been that—and here I go beyond what Long says—in a period in which at the level of everyday practice the Thomist account of what it is to live well has been treated with skepticism, theoretical inquiry has seemed to provide grounds for applauding that skepticism. One effect has been that in fashionable philosophical circles what Thomists have to say has largely gone unheard, or, if heard, ignored. It is then unsurprising that for a long time discussions of what has rendered Marxism morally and politically inadequate went on in one set of contexts, while discussions of whether the Thomist conceptions of human agency and well-being could be rationally upheld were conducted elsewhere. Further, among both Marxists and their critics it was usually taken for granted that *any* theistic view of human beings had been discredited by the thinkers of the Enlightenment, while among Thomists and their critics it was equally apt to be taken for granted that one could be dismissive of an atheistic Marxism.

What therefore neither party took seriously was the thought that Marx's narrative of how human beings had come to misconceive their own nature, relationships, and powers presupposed not one of the liberal post-Enlightenment conceptions of human nature but something much closer to Aristotle's conception and, that is to say, something uncomfortably close to Aquinas's. Yet, if this is so, dialogue between these very different voices is badly needed, dialogue that acknowledges the need of each to learn from the other and the depth of some of their disagreements. It is a dialogue that would draw upon the significant work already done on Marx's often unrecognized Aristotelian commitments, most notably by Scott Meikle.[2] And it would take seriously Marx's acknowledgment that, when he contrasts the distorted and distorting reification of social relationships characteristic of capitalist economies with forms of society in which "the social relations between individuals in the performance of their labor appear . . . as their own mutual personal relations, and are not disguised," the example of such a society that he cites is that of the European Middle Ages.[3]

Thomists who want their voices to be heard in this dialogue will have something to contribute only insofar as they are Thomistic Aristotelians, understanding Aquinas as an interpreter as well as an endorser of Aristotle. And they will have to learn to speak in idioms other than their own if they are to make the significance of what Aquinas has to say about human ends, powers, and virtues clear to those to whom the standard Thomist vocabulary is alien. Yet of course and happily, when I speak of what needs to be done, I am speaking of an enterprise that has already been undertaken, of a dialogue to some extent already in place. We owe this to, among others, the Dominican philosopher and theologian Herbert McCabe, a Thomist who took Marxism with great seriousness, and Terry Eagleton, a Marxist who takes Thomism with great seriousness. But it is now time for the kind of dialogue that they and others have begun to become more systematic, and this for two reasons.

First, both in philosophy and in everyday life the currently dominant conceptions of human nature and human agency disguise and mislead. They therefore need to be challenged and undermined by a philosophical critique that is able to draw upon both Thomism and Marxism. Second, we need a better characterization than we now have of the predicaments generated by the ethics, politics, and economics of advanced modernity, so that, for example, in our reflections on the role and function of money in our lives we learn to think in terms that are at once economic and moral, terms that enable us to integrate thoughts from Aristotle, Aquinas, and Marx—and also from Simmel, and others—into a single critique.

The difficulties that have to be overcome, if these tasks are to be accomplished, arise from just those aspects of our present situation that make it urgent to undertake them. And some essays in this volume make it clear how complex and various those are. Some arise from the continuing cultural and philosophical influence of emotivism, discussed in one way by James Mahon, in another by Stephen Mulhall. Others take the form that they do because ours is a moral culture that is still trying to reckon with—and characteristically failing to reckon with—Nietzsche, a condition to which both Geuss and Mulhall respond. Still others are versions of problems bequeathed to us by Sidgwick and by his critics, problems illuminated by Jonathan Rée. And finally there is the challenge presented by the kind of naturalism represented by Owen Flanagan.

The difficulties thus posed have both social and philosophical dimensions. What Marxism provides is a sociological starting point for characterizing the social dimensions, for understanding what it is in our social and economic relationships that enables a range of survivals from and revivals of emotivism, Nietzscheanism, utilitarianism, and intuitionism to function as they do. What a Thomistic Aristotelianism provides is a philosophical perspective in terms of which we can distinguish the truths and insights to be found in each of these standpoints from the distorting and misleading doctrines in which those truths and insights have been embedded and then show what is the due place for those truths within the Thomistic Aristotelian view of the nature of things.

If the latter aim is to be accomplished, it will have to be through a series of piecemeal engagements, philosophical controversy by philosophical controversy. But even if Thomistic Aristotelians make significant progress toward this goal, as I believe that they can, two further obstacles will confront them. The first is a matter of the present state of philosophical debate, on which I already remarked in my essay in this volume. In contemporary philosophy, whether continental and phenomenological or analytic, progress in inquiry has not resulted in the settlement of *any* outstanding contested issue. It is not that there is not real and important progress in recent philosophy. Concepts are further clarified, original insights developed, new distinctions drawn. But the subsequent arguments only very occasionally indeed convince any of the protagonists of rival positions. Each party continues to find the objections adduced against their views inconclusive. So it is with disputes between realists and antirealists on a variety of topics, with debates on consciousness, with quarrels over the compatibility or otherwise of conceptions of responsibility and determinism. And we may safely infer that no matter what Thomistic Aristotelians may achieve in developing their philosophical program, their acute and intelligent critics will remain unpersuaded. Does this matter, and if not, why not?

Any worthwhile answer to this question will have to take account of another more radical difficulty, that presented in Elijah Millgram's "Relativism, Coherence, and the Problems of Philosophy." Millgram argues that there are no decisive solutions to the problems of philosophy and that the history of philosophy from period to period is a history of new approaches to and reformulations of what are more or less the same set of problems. So philosophical inquiry can have no terminus, and all proclamations of the approaching end of philosophy are expressions of a deep illusion. Philosophers of a number of different persuasions will, I predict, agree in their rejection of Millgram's interpretation of the history of philosophy. But the moment that they try to show what is wrong with it, that unanimity will disappear. For each of the contending parties will be committed to showing that genuine progress toward and achievement in philosophical problem solving depends upon an endorsement of their own key positions. So we Thomistic Aristotelians will find that engagement with Millgram's theses and arguments returns us to the question of the kind of rational justification that our theses and arguments require. And to this question we already have a sufficient, if complex answer, an answer that begins from—where else?—where we are and what we are.

What we are, if we are Aristotelians, are systematic questioners of a certain kind, questioners who at some point in our past inquiries learned that in asking their central questions Aristotle and some of those who followed him had articulated, although more clearly and reflectively, questions that were already our own, so that, if we were to press those questions further, we had ourselves to become Aristotelians. We then found ourselves committed to the view of human nature and human action advanced by Aristotle, as Aquinas interpreted him, just because that view of human nature and human action was and is presupposed by this activity of questioning, an activity that has as its goal a perfected understanding of ourselves and of others. What justifies us in continuing in this inquiry and in this commitment is that we find ourselves able to provide answers to questions central to that inquiry that satisfy two conditions. They withstand objections from as wide a range of rival standpoints as possible, and they not only throw light on particular issues but enlarge our understanding of what it is to be someone whose nature is to engage in just such inquiry. For it is we ourselves as reflective agents who provide the primary subject matter for our inquiries as philosophers. And it is as such agents and not only as philosophers that we need to understand what it is to reason well or badly in our practical lives.

It is then unsurprising that, as I noticed earlier, there is a set of theses central to Thomism about how agents develop or fail to develop as practical reasoners, about how in their practical reasoning they are apt to misconceive their final end, about how they correct or fail to correct such misconceptions, and about how they therefore direct or misdirect themselves toward that final end. And if one were to spell out in adequate detail what is presupposed by these theses about the nature of human beings as reasoning animals, about the order of things of which they are a part, and about the concepts without which we could not characterize that nature or that order, one would have had to survey every aspect of the Thomistic philosophical scheme. So a great deal turns on the truth or falsity of those theses about human beings as practical reasoners.

One crucial task therefore is to ask what light they throw on the histories of particular agents as they attempt to find answers to the practical questions that their particular social relationships and circumstances pose. How do such agents in fact reason? What are the standards to which they appeal in judging whether they have reasoned and acted well or badly and in deciding how to formulate the questions that they now need to answer? Can we in fact find in their reasoning, choices, and actions application for those concepts that Thomists have identified as structuring reasoning, choice, and action?

If we are to answer such questions, we will have to consider not only how such agents are to be described but also how their social relationships and circumstances are to be characterized. And it is here that Thomists have some important lessons to learn from Marxists, although not only from Marxists, especially concerning the ways in which social relationships and situations are understood or misunderstood as problematic or unproblematic. What would become possible by such a fusion of Thomistic and Marxist modes of thought would be the writing of a kind of biographical history of which up till now there are relatively few examples. What kind of history do I mean?

It is a kind of history in which the focus is on the success or failure as practical reasoners of particular agents who have to find their way through politically and morally difficult situations. Since, on Aquinas's view, rational deliberation requires shared deliberation in the company of others, it is a history, not of individuals as such, but of individuals in their social relationships. And since excellence in practical reasoning has to be learned, and since the key moments in such learning are those moments when agents become able to learn from their failures and misunderstandings, it is a kind of history that acknowledges, as Geuss urges us to acknowledge, both the place that episodes of failure can have in a good life and the changes in our conceptions of our good that mark different stages in our education as practical reasoners. It is thus a history that provides for particular cases answers to the catalogue of Thomistic questions about the nature of action that I rehearsed earlier.

Those of us who have had a standard academic training will not have been well prepared for the writing of that kind of history. The territorial demarcation of the disciplines is such that in general to be a historian precludes being a philosopher and vice versa. Yet the writing of this kind of history requires one to be simultaneously philosopher and historian. Moreover, the work is not in the conventional sense interdisciplinary. It is not a melding together of academic history with academic philosophy but a genre of its own.

Although, as I suggested earlier, there are relatively few examples of writing in this genre, happily those examples that we have include works of great distinction, among them Marx's *Eighteenth Brumaire of Louis Bonaparte*, Jean Richard's life of King Louis IX of France, *Saint Louis*, and Robert Skidelsky's *John Maynard Keynes: 1883–1946*. But even the most distinguished of such works were not written to answer the questions that I have posed, and insofar as they do provide materials for answers to those questions they do so incidentally. Where then should we go for subject matter to write this kind of philosophical history?

Three very different twentieth-century lives come to mind as possible objects of study: those of Vasily Grossman, C. L. R. James, and Denis Faul. Grossman (1905–64), whose early intellectual and moral formation had been that of a successful and conformist novelist of the Stalin era in the 1930s, was transformed by his experiences as a journalist with the Red Army in 1941–45 and in 1960 completed one of the great novels of the century, *Life and Fate*, a novel recognized by the self-serving leadership of the Soviet Communist Party as destructive of their own and the party's self-image. Grossman, unlike them, spoke with a voice of unquestionable moral authority.

C. L. R. James (1901–89) grew up in Trinidad, a child of members of the first generation of Caribbean blacks born free, his father a schoolteacher, his mother a "tireless reader." Add an early and enduring passion for cricket and his disciplined British education at the Queen's College in Port of Spain, from which he learned and against which he rebelled. Add further his discovery of Thackeray. All these James improbably brought with him to his encounter with, adoption of, and then critical and radical revision of the Marxism of the Fourth International, from which he emerged to write history, Shakespearean commentary, political analysis, and works on cricket as game and art that are also political critique. So James too became a unique voice of his age with a peculiar moral authority.

Denis O'Beirne Faul (1932–2006), one of seven children in a Catholic family in Louth, Ireland, had the standard philosophical and theological education of an Irish priest at that time, that is to say, in many respects a Thomist education. In 1957 he became a schoolmaster at St. Patrick's Boys' Academy in Dungannon, County Tyrone, teaching Latin and religion. He and his pupils confronted the gross inequalities of Northern Ireland, where a Protestant Unionist regime exercised political, social, and economic hegemony over the Catholic and Nationalist community. His initial political involvement was in the civil rights movement of 1968. As the violent repression of that movement led to civil war, he became the principal accuser of the Royal Ulster Constabulary and the British Army, scrupulously and truthfully detailing and documenting acts of atrocity and injustice. The response of the British and the Unionists was to label him "an IRA priest" and to spread slander against him.

This label, however, Father Faul had no difficulty in disowning. For when the Provisional IRA too became guilty of atrocity and injustice, he accused them with the same scrupulous truthfulness, while providing aid and comfort for Republican prisoners and their families. And at the end of the conflict, with the negotiation of a necessary and welcome but dishonorable peace, he turned out to have provided the one perspective in which the warring and peacemaking parties of Northern Ireland could have seen themselves as they truly were and are, the perspective afforded by the virtues of truthfulness, justice, generosity, and mercy.

The differences between the Russian Grossman, the Trinidadian James, and the Irish Faul are obvious. What all three, in very different situations of conflicts, did was to situate themselves so that they made the nature of the goods at stake in the conflict clear and so that they exemplified what it was to act and live well or badly in and through those particular situations. Each developed a capacity for practical judgment and reasoning that numerous others with apparently the same educational background and moral formation failed to develop. And to understand their lives would be to understand the concepts that those lives embodied a good deal better. In moral philosophy good examples are always more than examples, just because until we have understood how moral concepts are exemplified in an appropriate range of cases we have not grasped the concepts. There is no way to understand moral concepts adequately independently of their application and exemplification.

One way therefore to carry further some of the discussions at the Dublin conference would be to write the history of such lives, perhaps indeed of these three lives. And this it is my intention to do, as part of a larger project on the nature of and relationship between desire and practical reasoning. But of course there are numerous other ways in which those discussions can and will inform a variety of further projects, something of which we are at once made aware when we turn to those papers in this volume that I have so far left unnoticed.

This postponement has not been the result either of a lack of gratitude on my part or of a want of stimulus to thought in those papers. Four of them, those by Gerard Casey, William Desmond, Richard Kearney, and Fran O'Rourke, redirect our attention to important dimensions of our philosophical and moral situation that it has been too easy to put on one side. Four other papers patiently clarify, correct, and extend aspects of my thought, so that, whatever it is about which I write in the future, I will need on many occasions to remind myself of what they have said. I have therefore the best of reasons for thanking Hans Fink, Kelvin Knight, Arthur Madigan, and James McEvoy—whose death since the conference is a great grief to all his friends—for their generous and insightful treatment of my work. Finally, I have a peculiarly large and continuing indebtedness to Joseph Dunne and John Haldane. Both have evaluated key aspects of my work by artfully placing it in some larger philosophical context, so posing questions to which, on their insightful view, I have not yet given anything like adequate answers.

My gratitude for the conversations in Dublin extends well beyond the authors of the papers published here, but it is impossible for me to name everyone who deserves mention. There were, however, four participants whose presence and whose contributions, formal and informal, gave me unusual pleasure and special reason for gratitude. One is my very good friend and former colleague David Solomon. Another is Cardinal Cahal B. Daly, to whom so many of us in Ireland and elsewhere have owed so much over the years and whose recent death we mourn, as we do also the death of Ernan McMullin, friend and colleague. The fourth is my former student and dear friend John Cleary, time with whom was always well spent, but especially during the conference just before his untimely death. Finally, we all of us owe an inestimable debt to Fran O'Rourke, both as himself the author of a major paper and as tireless and efficient conference organizer, patient and persistent editor, and indeed sine qua non of the whole enterprise.

Notes

1. For this project, see Steven Long, *The Teleological Grammar of the Moral Act* (Naples, FL: Sapientia Press, 2007) and *Natura Pura* (New York: Fordham University Press, 2010).

2. See, for example, *Essentialism in the Thought of Karl Marx* (London: Duckworth, 1985).

3. Karl Marx, *Capital*, vol. 1 (New York: International Publishers, 1967), 77.

Contributors

Gerard Casey is Associate Professor of Philosophy at University College Dublin, Adjunct Professor at the Maryvale Institute (Birmingham, UK), and Adjunct Scholar at the Ludwig von Mises Institute (Alabama). A graduate of University College Cork, he received his MA and PhD from the University of Notre Dame. He has a Bachelor of Laws (LLB) from the University of London and a Master of Laws (LLM) from University College Dublin. He has taught at the University of Notre Dame and the Catholic University of America. He has been a member of University College Dublin's Governing Authority. He serves on the editorial boards of *Geopolitics, History and International Relations, Contemporary Readings in Law and Social Justice,* and *Libertarian Papers* and is a member of the Royal Institute of Philosophy, the Association for Political Theory, the American Philosophical Association, and the Aristotelian Society. His latest book is *Murray Rothbard* (vol. 15 in the series Major Conservative and Libertarian Thinkers; Continuum, 2010).

William Desmond is currently Professor of Philosophy at Katholieke Universiteit Leuven as well as David Cook Visiting Chair in Philosophy at Villanova University. He taught at Loyola in Maryland before going to Leuven, where he was Director of the International Program in Philosophy for thirteen years. He is the author of many books, including the trilogy *Being and the Between* (winner of the Prix Cardinal Mercier and the J. N. Findlay Award for best book in metaphysics, 1995–97; SUNY

Press, 1995), *Ethics and the Between* (SUNY Press, 2001), and *God and the Between* (Blackwell, 2008). Other books include *Is There a Sabbath for Thought? Between Religion and Philosophy* (Fordham University Press, 2005), as well as *Art, Origins, Otherness: Between Art and Philosophy* (SUNY Press, 2003). He has also edited five books and published more than one hundred articles. He is past president of the Hegel Society of America, the Metaphysical Society of America, and the American Catholic Philosophical Association. His most recent books are *The Intimate Strangeness of Being: Metaphysics after Dialectic* (Catholic University of America Press, 2012) and *The William Desmond Reader* (SUNY Press, 2012).

Joseph Dunne is Cregan Professor of Philosophy and Education at Dublin City University, having taught philosophy and philosophy of education for many years at St. Patrick's College Dublin, where he was Head of Human Development. The author of *Back to the Rough Ground: Practical Judgment and the Lure of Technique* (University of Notre Dame Press, 1997), he has also coedited *Questioning Ireland: Debates in Political Philosophy and Public Policy* (IPA, 2000); *Childhood and Its Discontents: The First Seamus Heaney Lectures* (Liffey Press, 2002); and *Education and Practice: Upholding the Integrity of Teaching and Learning* (Blackwell, 2004).

Hans Fink studied at Aarhus University and Balliol College, Oxford, where he received his DPhil in 1974. Since then he has been teaching at Aarhus University and has been Professor and Director of its Centre for Cultural Research. His publications in English include *Social Philosophy* (Methuen, 1981). Together with Alasdair MacIntyre he edited a new American edition of K. E. Løgstrup, *The Ethical Demand* (University of Notre Dame Press, 1997).

Owen Flanagan is James B. Duke Professor of Philosophy at Duke University. He works in the philosophy of mind and moral psychology. He has had the excellent fortune of intersecting with Alasdair MacIntyre first as a graduate student and then as a colleague at Boston University, Wellesley College, and Duke University.

Raymond Geuss was born in December 1946 in Evansville, Indiana. He began full-time university teaching at Heidelberg in 1971 and has taught at Cambridge since 1993. In June 2000 he was naturalized as a citizen of the United Kingdom. He is the author of *The Idea of a Critical Theory* (Cambridge University Press, 1981), *Morality, Culture, and History* (Cambridge University Press, 1999), *History and Illusion in Politics* (Cambridge University Press, 2001), *Public Goods, Private Goods* (Princeton University Press, 2001), *Politik und Glück* (Berliner Wissenschafts-Verlag, 2004), *Outside Ethics* (Princeton University Press, 2005), *Philosophy and Real Politics* (Princeton University Press, 2008), and *Politics and the Imagination* (Princeton University Press, 2010). His *A World Without Why* will appear with Princeton University Press in 2013.

John Haldane is Professor of Philosophy and Director of the Centre for Philosophy and Public Affairs at the University of St. Andrews. His many publications include *Atheism and Theism* (with J. J. C. Smart; Oxford University Press, 1996), *An Intelligent Person's Guide to Religion* (Duckworth, 2003), *Faithful Reason* (Routledge, 2004), and *Seeking Meaning and Making Sense* (Imprint Academic, 2008). He has held the Royden Davis Chair in Humanities at Georgetown University; he has delivered the Gifford Lectures at the University of Aberdeen, and the Joseph Lectures at the Gregorian University in Rome. In 2006 he was appointed by Pope Benedict XVI a Consultor to the Pontifical Council for Culture.

Richard Kearney holds the Charles B. Seelig Chair of Philosophy at Boston College; he was formerly Professor of Philosophy at University College Dublin and Visiting Professor at the University of Paris (Sorbonne) and the University of Nice. He is the author of over twenty books on European philosophy and literature (including two novels and a volume of poetry) and has edited or coedited eighteen more. He is a member of the Royal Irish Academy and was formerly a member of the Arts Council of Ireland, a member of the Higher Education Authority of Ireland, and Chairman of the Irish School of Film at University College Dublin. Recent publications include a trilogy entitled *Philosophy at the Limit*. The three volumes are *On Stories* (Routledge, 2002), *The God Who May Be* (Indiana University Press, 2001), and *Strangers, Gods, and Monsters* (Routledge, 2003). He has also published *Debates in Continental Philosophy* (Fordham University Press, 2004), *The Owl of Minerva* (Ashgate, 2005), *Navigations* (Syracuse University Press, 2007), and *Anatheism* (Columbia

University Press, 2009). He is international director of the Guestbook Project—Hosting the Stranger: Between Hostility and Hospitality.

Kelvin Knight is Reader in Ethics and Politics at London Metropolitan University and Director of CASEP, the Centre for Contemporary Aristotelian Studies in Ethics and Politics. His publications include *Aristotelian Philosophy: Ethics and Politics from Aristotle to MacIntyre* (Polity Press, 2007), *The MacIntyre Reader* (ed., University of Notre Dame Press and Polity Press, 1998), *Revolutionary Aristotelianism: Ethics, Resistance and Utopia* (co-ed., Lucius and Lucius, 2008), and *Virtue and Politics: Alasdair MacIntyre's Revolutionary Aristotelianism* (co-ed., University of Notre Dame Press, 2011). He is currently working on the philosophy of human rights.

Steven A. Long is Professor of Theology at Ave Maria University. He previously has taught at the University of St. Thomas (Minnesota) and at the Catholic University of America. He is the author of *The Teleological Grammar of the Moral Act* (Sapientia Press, 2007), *Natura Pura: On the Recovery of Nature in the Doctrine of Grace* (Fordham University Press, 2010), and *Analogia Entis: On the Analogy of Being, Metaphysics, and the Act of Faith* (University of Notre Dame Press, 2011). With Christopher Thompson he is editor of *Reason and the Rule of Faith: Conversations in the Tradition with John Paul II* (University Press of America, 2011), drawn from the Lilly-funded seminars in the series "Habits of Mind: The Vocation of the Catholic Intellectual." His essays have appeared in *Revue Thomiste,* the *Thomist, Nova et Vetera,* the *National Catholic Bioethics Quarterly, Studies in Christian Ethics,* and other journals.

Alasdair MacIntyre attended Queen Mary College (University of London) and the University of Manchester. He taught at a number of British and American universities, most recently at Duke University and the University of Notre Dame. He is the author of eleven books, including *After Virtue* (University of Notre Dame Press, 1981). He is currently a Research Fellow at the Centre for Contemporary Aristotelian Studies in Ethics and Politics (CASEP) at London Metropolitan University.

Arthur Madigan, S.J., received his PhD from the University of Toronto in 1979 and has since then taught philosophy at Boston College. In February 2011 he was appointed to the Albert J. Fitzgibbons Professorship. He has also served as Edmund F. Miller Visiting Associate Professor of Classics at John Carroll University (1996–97) and Francis C. Wade Professor of Philosophy at Marquette University (1999–2000). He has published translations of Alexander of Aphrodisias's commentaries on books 3 and 4 of Aristotle's *Metaphysics* (Duckworth) and his own commentary on Aristotle's *Metaphysics* 3 (Oxford University Press), as well as numerous articles on ancient philosophy and ethics.

James Edwin Mahon is Associate Professor of Philosophy at Washington and Lee University and Lecturer in the Program in Ethics, Politics, and Economics at Yale University. He has been a Visiting Scholar in the Faculty of Philosophy at the University of Cambridge and a Visiting Fellow in the Department of Philosophy at Princeton University. He is the author of *Motivational Internalism and the Authority of Morality* (VDM Verlag, 2011) as well as articles on Kant's moral philosophy and on lying and deception.

James McEvoy (1943–2010) graduated in philosophy from Queen's University Belfast and in theology from St Patrick's College, Maynooth. In 1974 he received his PhD from the Université Catholique de Louvain *summa cum laude,* and in 1982 was made Maître Agrégé of the Institut supérieur de philosophie. He was awarded the Prix Mercier for his major publication *The Philosophy of Robert Grosseteste* (Clarendon Press, 1982). He held full chairs in Louvain, Maynooth, and Belfast; he was a member of the Royal Irish Academy and a von Humboldt Fellow. During an illustrious academic career he produced a large number of books, chapters, and articles that confirmed his reputation as one of the leading international medievalists of his generation.

Elijah Millgram studied at Harvard. He taught at Princeton and Vanderbilt and is currently E. E. Ericksen Professor of Philosophy at the University of Utah. He is the author of *Practical Induction* (Harvard University Press, 1997), *Ethics Done Right: Practical Reasoning as a Foundation for Moral Theory* (Cambridge University Press, 2005), and *Hard Truths* (Wiley-Blackwell, 2009). His research focuses on the theory of rationality; his historical research interests include Mill, Nietzsche, and Wilde.

Stephen Mulhall is a graduate of Balliol College, Oxford, and the University of Toronto. He has taught at Essex and is currently Fellow and Tutor in Philosophy at New College, Oxford. His research interests include Wittgenstein, Heidegger, the philosophy of religion, philosophy and film, and philosophy and literature. His current project is centered on conceptions of selfhood in the philosophy of Nietzsche and Sartre, as well as in opera, film, and the novel.

Fran O'Rourke is Associate Professor of Philosophy at University College Dublin. He received his MA from University College Galway and studied at the Universities of Vienna, Köln, Louvain, and Leuven, where he received his PhD. He has held Fulbright and Onassis fellowships and in 2003 was Visiting Research Professor at Marquette University. He is primarily interested in the tradition of classical metaphysics and has published widely on Plato, Aristotle, Aquinas, and Heidegger. His book *Pseudo-Dionysius and the Metaphysics of Aquinas* was reissued by University of Notre Dame Press (2005). *Allwisest Stagyrite: Joyce's Quotations from Aristotle* was published by the National Library of Ireland in 2005. He is preparing for publication a collection of essays entitled *Aristotelian Interpretations* and is completing a book on James Joyce, Aristotle, and Aquinas. He has lectured widely both on philosophical influences in James Joyce and on Joyce's use of song; he has performed recitals of Irish songs featured in Joyce's work in the National Concert Hall, Dublin (2004), and the Conservatorio, Trieste (2008).

Jonathan Rée studied at the Universities of Sussex and Oxford and was one of the founders of the magazine *Radical Philosophy*. He taught for many years at Middlesex University but liberated himself from academic life at the turn of the century and is now a freelance author concentrating on history and philosophy. He has contributed to a wide range of journals and newspapers and has extensive experience in broadcasting. His books include *Proletarian Philosophers* (Clarendon Press, 1984), *Philosophical Tales* (Methuen, 1987), *Heidegger* (Routledge, 1999), and *I See a Voice* (Metropolitan Books, 1999).

Index of Names

Adams, Douglas, 412
Adler, Mortimer, 125
Adorno, Theodor, 234, 238, 242
Alger, Horatio, 363
Alinsky, Saul, 138, 144
Ameriks, Karl, 118
Anaxagoras, 462
Anderson, Elizabeth, 45–46, 80, 194, 294
Anderson, John, 21
Anselm, Saint, 467
Aquinas, Saint Thomas, 5, 7–8, 17–20, 22, 25, 30, 33, 48, 65, 74–78, 83, 85, 87–90, 105–7, 111, 114–16, 120, 123–24, 127–33, 137, 139–41, 154, 160, 190, 244, 247–49, 253–61, 263–66, 269, 271–76, 278–79, 281–82, 285–93, 296, 298–303, 334, 338, 343, 355, 424, 448, 474–75, 477–83
Arendt, Hannah, 9, 304–5, 309, 311, 315
Aristotle, 1–2, 4–5, 17, 29, 30, 42, 53, 59, 61, 64, 70, 74–75, 79, 83–103, 105–8, 110–11, 113–16, 120, 123–26, 131, 135–41, 190, 219, 234, 236–38, 252–56, 258–59, 264, 277–78, 296–97, 302, 310, 324, 332, 335–36, 338–40, 342, 345, 347, 349–50, 352, 393, 403, 424, 429, 453, 464–65, 475–77, 480–81
Augustine, Saint, 74–77, 85, 88, 269, 307, 345, 348, 356, 424, 458
Austen, Jane, 87
Austin, J. L., 23, 24
Ayer, Alfred J., 17–19, 22–23, 25, 166, 173–79, 181–83, 187–88, 190, 192, 196–97, 274

Bacon, Francis, 100
Badiou, Alain, 240
Baker, Lynne Rudder, 468–69
Baldwin, Thomas, 194
Bañez, Domingo, 296
Barnes, W. H. F., 183, 196
Barth, Karl, 147–48
Bataille, Georges, 81
Bauer, Bruno, 96
Bauman, Zygmunt, 161
Becher, Tony, 414
Beckett, Samuel, 364, 440
Bell, Clive, 196

494 Index of Names

Benatar, David, 458
Benedict, Saint, 11, 12, 423–24, 428, 456
Benedict XVI, 290
Bentham, Jeremy, 194, 379, 382–83
Bergson, Henri, 310
Berkeley, George, 42
Berlin, Isaiah, 24, 226
Blackburn, Simon, 26–27
Blackmore, Susan, 470–71
Blair, Tony, 236
Bloor, David, 99
Bonaventure, Saint, 290
Borradori, Giovanna, 131, 137
Bourke, Vernon J., 128, 289
Boyd, Richard, 193, 405
Boyle, Joseph, 277
Boyle, Leonard, O.P., 7, 244–50, 265–67
Braithwaite, R. J., 170–72, 183
Brandom, Robert, 83, 94, 97, 100–101, 103, 107–9, 113, 119, 121, 420
Brandt, Willy, 307, 316
Broad, C. D., 172, 183, 199
Brock, Stephen, 293
Brown, Gordon, 228
Buber, Martin, 157
Burms, Arnold, 457
Burns, Elizabeth, 31
Burns, Tom, 31
Burnyeat, Myles, 416

Cajetan, Thomas, 294
Calderón de la Barca, Pedro, 443
Callus, Daniel Angelo, 245
Camus, Albert, 278, 346–47, 364, 386–87
Carmichael, Gerschom, 40
Casey, Gerard, 12, 472–73, 485
Cavell, Stanley, 201–3, 212
Cessario, Romanus, O.P., 8, 290, 302
Chisholm, Roderick, 366, 374
Churchland, Patricia, 50

Churchland, Paul, 50
Cicero, 75
Clark, Candace, 367
Clark, Stephen R. L., 193, 333
Clinton, William Jefferson, 349
Coleridge, Samuel Taylor, 84
Collingwood, Robin George, 128, 181
Comte, Auguste, 390
Conant, James, 212
Conrad, Joseph, 152
Crary, Alice, 205
Critchley, Simon, 161
Croce, Benedetto, 134

Daly, Cahal, 197
D'Andrea, Thomas D., 192
Dante Alighieri, 1, 213, 242
D'Arcy, Martin, 197
Darwin, Charles, 329, 338, 341, 343, 347
Davidson, Donald, 60
Dawes, Robyn, 415
Dawkins, Richard, 324, 326–27, 329, 331, 348, 350–52
de Chardin, Teilhard, 344, 356
De Koninck, Charles, 33, 289
de Lubac, Henri, 8, 286–87, 289, 297–301
de Man, Paul, 398
Del Prado, 296
Dennett, Daniel, 333–34, 351, 354
Derrida, Jacques, 9, 304–7, 311–12, 318, 398
Descartes, René, 342, 362, 401, 431, 439, 448–49, 465
Desmond, Willliam, 11–12, 458–59, 485
Dewan, Lawrence, O.P., 127, 290
Dewey, John, 100, 200, 204, 212, 237, 243, 323, 389
Diamond, Cora, 205
Dickinson, Lowes, 170
Dobzhansky, Theodosius, 331

Drucker, Peter, 138
Duncan-Jones, Austin, 170–74, 183, 196
Dunne, Joseph, 4, 486

Eagleton, Terry, 479
Eco, Umberto, 427
Einstein, Albert, 353
Emerson, Ralph Waldo, 7, 212–15, 217
Emmet, Dorothy, 192
Engels, Friedrich, 20–21, 112

Faul, Denis, 484–85
Fergusson, Adam, 40
Ferrier, James Frederick, 40
Field, G. C., 168, 194, 198
Fink, Hans, 6, 78, 486
Finnis, John, 117, 277
Flanagan, Owen, 10–11, 373, 480
Florka, Roger, 418
Foot, Philippa, 25, 46, 220, 397
Forster, E. M., 152
Fortin, Ernest, 136, 143
Foucault, Michel, 81, 216–17, 239
Frankena, William K., 168, 192, 194
Frankfurt, Harry, 345
Franklin, Benjamin, 87
Fraser, Ian, 242
Frege, Gottlob, 18, 188, 274–75
Freud, Sigmund, 80, 128, 316, 440

Gadamer, Hans-Georg, 60, 85–86, 90, 103, 116, 313
Gaita, Raimond, 4, 62, 71, 73–77
Gallup, Gordon G., 344
Garey, Michael, 421
Garrett, Don, 418
Garrigou-Lagrange, Reginald, 8, 33, 289, 296
Gauguin, Paul, 210–11
Geach, Peter, 23, 26, 27, 197
George, Robert P., 117
Gettier, Edmund, 418

Geuss, Raymond, 7, 474–77, 480, 483
Gibbard, Alan, 27, 198
Gilson, Étienne, 8, 84, 246, 289
Girard, René, 82
Gluckman, Max, 31
Gödel, Kurt, 275, 419
Goethe, Johann Wolfgang von, 84, 441, 443, 447
Goldmann, Lucien, 20, 33
Gouda, Frances, 374
Grisez, Germaine, 279
Griswold, Charles, 319
Groff, Ruth, 118
Grossman, Vasily, 484–85

Habermas, Jürgen, 107–9, 121, 234, 237, 240
Haldane, John, 1, 4, 486
Hale, Bob, 26
Hales, Steven, 414
Hamblin, C. L., 418
Hamilton, Lawrence, 242
Hampshire, Stuart, 24
Hardy, Thomas, 440
Hare, R. M., 22, 152, 179, 191, 199, 379
Havel, Václav, 316
Healy, Nicholas, 298–99
Heaney, Seamus, 2, 457
Hearne, Vicki, 415
Hegel, Georg Wilhelm Friedrich, 83, 94–95, 97–98, 101, 105–7, 109, 115–16, 128, 224, 228, 237–38, 240, 423, 439–41, 443, 447–50
Heidegger, Martin, 53, 84–86, 89–90, 92, 98, 105, 116, 146, 150, 272, 294, 309, 441
Heller, Agnes, 242
Herodotus, 352
Hess, Moses, 96
Hittinger, Russell, 8, 290, 302
Hoadley, C. M., 421
Hobbes, Thomas, 157, 351, 382

Homer, 87, 89
Horace, 354
Horkheimer, Max, 105, 111
Humboldt, Alexander von, 242
Hume, David, 41, 54, 87, 128, 157, 181, 199, 276, 347, 399
Hume, John, 316
Humphrey, Nicholas, 470–71
Husserl, Edmund, 41, 146, 272, 279, 294
Hutcheson, Francis, 40
Huygens, Christian, 458

James, C. L. R., 33, 484–85
James, Henry, 201
James, William, 351, 389
Jankelevitch, Vladimir, 9, 304–5, 311
Jeanson, Francis, 386
John of Salisbury, 109
John of St. Thomas, 296
John Paul II, 130, 272, 289
Johnson, David, 421
Jones, E. E. Constance, 389
Joyce, James, 323
Jünger, Ernst, 81

Kant, Immanuel, 3, 12, 18, 22, 29, 41, 85, 93, 97, 101, 105, 108, 158–59, 191, 202, 209, 211–12, 214, 240, 255–56, 272–74, 277, 279, 285, 294, 337, 348, 368, 376–78, 401, 403, 413, 423, 424, 432–36, 440–41, 443, 448–49, 452–53, 457
Kearney, Richard, 9, 320, 485
Kenny, Anthony, 60
Keynes, John Maynard, 169, 483
Keys, Mary, 117
Kidron, Michael, 33
Kierkegaard, Søren, 147–48, 240, 417
Kirk, Russell, 136–37, 144
Kitcher, Philip, 330, 353
Kline, George L, 134

Knight, Kelvin, 4, 133, 486
Kotarbinski, Tadeusz, 42
Krausz, Michael, 414
Kripke, Saul, 18
Kristjánsson, Kristján, 119
Kuhn, Thomas, 100, 403
Kusch, Martin, 414

La Caze, Marguerite, 319
Labourdette, Marie-Michel, 289–90
Lacan, Jacques, 81, 427
Laqueur, Thomas, 393
Latour, Bruno, 414
Lawrence, D. H., 152
Le Dœuff, Michèle, 405, 418
Leibniz, Gottfried Wilhelm, 42, 310
Lemos, John, 193
Lessing, Gotthold Ephraim, 240
Levi, Primo, 304, 314
Levinas, Emmanuel, 64, 70–71, 75, 78, 147, 379, 452–53
Lewis, David, 18, 20, 420
Lipps, Hans, 146
Locke, John, 366, 369–70, 382
Løgstrup, Knud Ejler, 5–6, 78, 131, 145–61
Lonergan, Bernard, 296–97
Long, Steven A., 8, 477–78
Lorenz, Konrad, 343
Lukacs, Georg, 33, 109
Luther, Martin, 440, 443

MacIntyre, Alasdair, 1–8, 10–11, 37–41, 43–50, 52–55, 57–71, 73–81, 83–90, 92, 97–142, 145–47, 150–52, 154, 158–62, 165–70, 179–82, 187–93, 196, 199, 218, 226–27, 235, 238, 243–44, 247, 251–58, 264, 266, 268, 280, 290, 294, 301–2, 319, 332, 338–41, 349, 355, 358, 372–74, 378, 389, 395, 419, 424, 428, 472

Index of Names

Mack, John, 417
Mackie, J. L., 169, 193, 196
Madigan, Arthur, S.J., 5, 486
Mahon, James, 6, 480
Mandela, Nelson, 307
Mandonnet, Pierre, O.P., 246
Manent, Pierre, 136
Mann, Thomas, 416, 440
Manzoni, Piero, 457
Marcel, Gabriel, 294
Marcuse, Herbert, 97, 104, 116
Maritain, Jacques, 8, 33, 84, 128, 138–39, 144, 291
Marks, Jonathan, 355
Marty, Anton, 195
Marx, Karl, 2, 5–7, 18, 20–21, 33, 83–84, 86, 94–98, 104–9, 112–13, 115–16, 128, 133–34, 140–41, 221–23, 225, 227–35, 237–38, 242, 372, 388, 423–24, 474–80, 482–84
Maugham, Somerset, 347
McCabe, Herbert, 84, 479
McCarthy, Thomas, 118
McDowell, John, 41, 60, 103, 194
McEvoy, James, 7, 486
McInerny, Ralph, 8, 33, 290, 301
McNabb, Vincent, 84–85
Meikle, Scott, 479
Meiland, Jack, 414
Menger, Karl, 174
Merleau-Ponty, Maurice, 282
Messner, Johannes, 139
Mill, John Stuart, 3, 11, 194, 379, 381–84, 386, 390, 402, 415
Miller, Alexander, 198
Millgram, Elijah, 11, 422, 481
Milne, A. J., 197
Molina, Luis de, 281–82, 284–85, 288, 291, 295
Moore, G. E., 22, 167–70, 172–76, 182–84, 187, 190–91, 194, 198, 200, 378–79, 385

Morris, S., 374
Mulhall, Stephen, 7, 11, 480
Murdoch, Iris, 12, 25, 57, 72–73, 424, 460, 469
Murphy, Liam, 366
Murphy, Mark C., 117
Murphy, William F. J., 293
Murray, John Courtney, 139

Nadelhoffer, T., 374
Nagel, Ernest, 392, 419
Nagel, Thomas, 366
Nahmias, E., 374
Needham, Rodney, 20
Neurath, Otto, 174
Newman, Francis William, 383, 390
Newman, John Henry, 141–42, 383
Newton, Isaac, 406, 432, 434
Nicholas, Jean-Hervé, 289–90
Nietzsche, Friedrich, 7, 11–12, 58, 73, 84, 102, 115, 208–9, 211–25, 227, 231–32, 238, 240–41, 333, 351, 367–68, 417, 423–26, 428, 430, 440, 442, 444–47, 451–57, 480
Nisbett, Richard, 415
Novak, Michael, 117
Nowell-Smith, P. H., 168
Nozick, Robert, 374, 417
Nussbaum, Martha, 126–27, 417

Ockham, William of, 253, 255, 259, 281, 464
Ogden, C. K., 170–72, 174, 183–84, 195, 207
O'Hear, Anthony, 355–56
O'Leary, Joseph S., 320
O'Rourke, Fran, 9, 485–86

Pascal, Blaise, 318, 343, 431, 436
Patmore, Coventry, 457
Pecci, Vincenzo Gioacchino (Pope Leo XIII), 84

Percy, Walker, 466
Perraldus (William Payraut), 248–49
Peter the Chanter, 248
Pigden, Charles, 198
Pinckaers, Servais, O.P., 7–8, 132, 244, 250–69, 281, 289
Plato, 17, 20, 79, 105, 206–7, 213, 259, 352, 404, 407, 416, 442, 448, 451–53, 462–63
Plotinus, 42
Pope, Stephen J., 341, 350, 354
Popper, Karl, 17, 166
Premack, David, 344–45
Price, Richard, 388
Prichard, Harold Arthur, 22, 167, 194
Priestly, Joseph, 388
Putnam, Hilary, 416, 418

Quante, Michael, 119
Quine, Willard Van Orman, 18

Rackham, H., 352
Railton, Peter, 193, 198
Ramirez, Santiago, 289–90
Ramsey, Frank P., 170–72, 195
Ranney, Michael, 421
Ravetz, Jerome, 414
Rawls, John, 79, 374, 379
Raymund of Penafort, 248–49
Raz, Joseph, 241
Rée, Jonathan, 11, 391, 480
Rees, Martin, 349
Reid, Thomas, 40, 54
Rhonheimer, Martin, 276, 293
Richards, I. A., 170–72, 174, 183–84, 195–96, 207
Richards, Jean, 483
Ricoeur, Paul, 9, 304, 306–19
Riedel, Manfred, 85
Ritter, Joachim, 85
Rolston, Holmes, 352
Rommen, Heinrich, 139, 291
Rorty, Richard, 89–90, 94, 100–101

Ross, Lee, 415
Ross, W. D., 22, 24, 167
Rousseau, Jean-Jacques, 232
Ruse, Michael, 324–28, 331, 333, 337, 352–53
Russell, Bertrand, 195, 198, 274, 294
Ryle, Gilbert, 188, 275, 294, 414

Sallust, 75
Sartre, Jean-Paul, 19, 22, 25, 152–54, 229, 278, 379, 386–87
Satris, Stephen, 192
Scanlon, Tim, 157
Schank, Patricia, 421
Scheler, Max, 146
Schelling, Friedrich, 440, 448, 450
Schlick, Moritz, 174
Schneewind, J. B., 389
Schopenhauer, Arthur, 12, 81, 439–46, 448–52, 454
Schroeder, Mark, 26
Schueler, G. F., 26
Scotus, Duns, 448–49
Searle, John, 99, 197
Sellars, Wilfrid, 103, 121
Seth Pringle-Pattison, Andrew, 54–55
Shakespeare, William, 343
Shaw, George Bernard, 440
Sherwin, Michael, O.P., 262, 268
Shope, Robert, 418
Sidgwick, Henry, 11, 379–81, 383–86, 389–91
Simon, Yves, 291
Simpson, G. G., 352
Singer, Peter, 330, 351, 357
Skidelsky, Robert, 483
Smith, Adam, 40, 54, 94
Smith, Michael, 197
Socrates, 1, 90, 105, 206, 211–12, 353, 396, 401, 462–63
Sophists, 206
Spinoza, Baruch, 310, 441–42, 447
Stein, Edith, 4, 41, 50, 52–53, 145

Steiner, Franz, 20, 31
Stevenson, Charles L., 7, 166, 170, 179, 182–90, 196, 198–209, 211, 219, 379, 389
Stewart, Dugald, 40
Stocks, J. L., 84
Stout, Jeffrey, 119
Strachey, Lytton, 170
Strauss, Leo, 135–37
Strawson, Galen, 368
Strawson, Peter, 41, 45, 275
Sturgeon, Nicholas, 193
Suarez, Luis, 286, 299

Taparelli d'Azeglio, Luigi, 84
Tarski, Alfred, 18, 166
Taylor, Charles, 4, 62, 72–77, 79–82
Thagard, Paul, 421
Thomas, Alan, 26
Thomson, George, 20
Thomson, James, 18, 166
Tolstoy, Leo, 440
Tomlin, E. W. F., 196–97
Trotsky, Leon, 237–38, 243, 424
Tuomela, Raimo, 99
Turner, J., 374
Tutu, Desmond, 307

Unwin, Nicholas, 26, 193
Urmson, J. O., 182, 195

van Roojen, Mark, 26
Veatch, Henry, 125, 291
Verbeurgt, Karsten, 421
Verene, Donald, 458
Voltaire, 377
von Hildebrand, Dietrich, 272–73
von Nell-Breuning, Oswald, S.J., 139

Wagner, Richard, 416, 440
Waller, Bruce N., 193
Ward, Keith, 356
Weber, Max, 108, 241
Whewell, William, 381–83, 385–86, 389
Whitehead, Alfred North, 42
Williams, Bernard, 7, 208–13
Williams, Michael, 418
Wilson, E. O., 9, 324–31, 333, 338, 340, 343–49, 351, 353
Winch, Peter, 99
Winnicott, Donald, 62
Wisdom, John, 17, 166
Wittgenstein, Ludwig, 41, 46, 98–99, 128, 182, 294, 323, 421, 463, 465–66
Wolfe, Tom, 324
Wolff, Christian, 92–94, 101

Yeats, William Butler, 356, 457